THEGREENGUIDE
Austria

Linke Wienzeile 38 designed by Otto Wagner, Vienna © Brendan Hunter/iStockphoto.com

THE GREEN GUIDE **AUSTRIA**

Editorial Director	Cynthia Ochterbeck
Editor	Sophie Friedman
Contributing Writer	Kristen de Joseph
Production Manager	Natasha George
Cartography	Peter Wrenn
Photo Editor	Yoshimi Kanazawa
Interior Design	Chris Bell
Cover Design	Chris Bell, Christelle Le Déan
Layout	Natasha George

Contact Us

Michelin Travel and Lifestyle North America
One Parkway South
Greenville, SC 29615
USA
travel.lifestyle@us.michelin.com

Michelin Travel Partner
Hannay House
39 Clarendon Road
Watford, Herts WD17 1JA
UK
℘01923 205240
travelpubsales@uk.michelin.com
www.ViaMichelin.com

Special Sales

For information regarding bulk sales,
customized editions and premium sales,
please contact us at:
travel.lifestyle@us.michelin.com

Großglockner Hochalpenstraße, Carinthia
© Austrian National Tourist Office/ Popp Hackner

When and Where to Go

WHEN TO GO

Austria, two-thirds of which is covered by mountains, is justifiably popular for its ski resorts in **winter**, with slopes suitable for everyone from beginners to experts.

There are four principal ski regions; the Arlberg Pass region around Lech and St. Anton lies in the far western corner and is best known for St. Anton, a beguiling place that is typically rustic Alpine in character but also boasts 21C ski (and particularly 21C après-ski) facilities. This area glides seamlessly into the Tirol (Tyrol), Austria's most popular area, made famous when the Winter Olympic Games were held in Innsbruck in 1964 and 1976 and still boasting world-class skiing. The Salzburg region is also developed for winter sports, with major resorts such as the Sportwelt Amadé. Finally, Styria offers a variety of opportunities in the ski resorts of the Dachstein-Tauern and Schladming areas.

In **spring** it is still possible to ski at higher altitudes, with longer days being a welcome bonus. This is also the time to enjoy the country's colourful carnival processions.

Summer is the time when visitors arrive to enjoy Austria's mountain scenery to the fullest and to make the most of a rich cultural scene. Carinthia, with its warm-water lakes, attracts swimmers, water-skiing enthusiasts and anglers. The picturesque lakes of the Salzkammergut are colder, but more romantic.

Mountaineers are drawn to the glaciers of the Ötztal or the Hohe Tauern, as well as the slopes of the Karwendel, the Kaisergebirge, the Dachstein or the Gesäuse. But anyone who is reasonably fit can still get a lot out of these areas by taking funiculars to the lower slopes of the mountains, then following the many marked trails available.

Autumn, with the sun shining and a nip in the air, sheds a particularly beautiful light on the old stone buildings in towns and villages. This is a good season to discover the wealth of Austria's museums. The beautiful wooded valleys of Styria and Carinthia are a delight for walkers.

A journey through the vineyards of the Burgenland or Lower Austria, or along the Danube beneath the Wachau, is also unforgettable at this time of year. Meanwhile, music- and theatre-lovers descend on the capital as Vienna reopens for another glorious season of high culture.

WHERE TO GO

WALKING TOURS

Austria has a well-developed network of marked trails, both down in the valleys and high up in the mountains. If you're enjoying yourself so much that you don't want to come down for the night, then plan to hike hut-to-hut. Mountain huts (hütten) are inns that can be found in the Kaisergebirge, the Karwendel, Stubai Alps, Hohe Tauern and Dachstein ranges, as well as many other areas.

CYCLING TOURS

In view of the country's dramatic topography, its well-developed network of cycle paths is an unexpected treat. The major ones are the Danube Cycle Path, the Salzkammergut Cycle Path and the Tauern Cycle Path from Krimml to Salzburg.

FOOD AND WINE TRAILS

Eastern Austria produces some fine wines and there is a Wine Road to follow in Styria. In the west of Austria there is a Cheese Road in the Bregenzerwald (see p403).

SHORT BREAKS

Innsbruck, Salzburg and Vienna are all great cities for a short break and can be visited around themes such as Music, The Habsburgs or Architecture.

What to See and Do

OUTDOOR FUN
THE GREAT OUTDOORS
National Parks

Austria's magnificent national parks let you appreciate nature at its unspoiled best: rare flora and fauna, magnificent scenery and wonderful trails well off the beaten track. For an overview, see www.nationalparks-austria.at. Also visit www.austria.info/uk and click on the "Lakes and Nature" link on the homepage.

Nationalpark Hohe Tauern (Carinthia, Salzburg province, Tyrol)

The largest nature reserve in the whole of the Alps, this park is still in many parts a wild, primeval landscape. In other areas it has been ingeniously tamed by mountain farmers.

◆ **Sekretariat des Nationalparkrates**, Matrei in Osttirol. ℘04875 5112 0 www.hohetauern.at

◆ **Nationalparkverwaltung Kärnten**, 9843 Großkirchheim. ℘04825 6161

◆ **Nationalparkverwaltung Tirol**, 9971 Matrei in Osttirol. ℘04875 5161 10

◆ **Nationalparkverwaltung Salzburg**, 5730 Mittersill. ℘06562 40849

Nationalpark Neusiedler See-Seewinkel (Burgenland)

The only nature reserve in the steppes of central Europe straddles the border between Austria and Hungary. The visitor information centre offers guided excursions, tours in horse-drawn carts, on horseback or by bicycle. A visit to the park is a must for avid bird watchers.

◆ **Nationalpark Informations-zentrum**, A-7142 Illmitz. ℘02175 3442 www.nationalpark-neusiedlersee-seewinkel.at

Nationalpark Kalkalpen (Upper Austria)

This park in the Pyhrn-Eisenwurzen region extends as far as the High Alps in an ever-changing mosaic of extensive forests, hidden gorges, untouched mountain brooks and bucolic alpine pastures.
Call the tourist office and enquire about their varied programme for walkers of all levels of experience and fitness.

◆ **Nationalparkverwaltung**, A-4591 Molln ℘07584 3651 www.kalkalpen.at

Nationalpark Thayatal (Lower Austria)

This cross-border park is managed in cooperation with the Czech Republic. The Thaya Valley cuts deeply into the ancient rock of the mountains and is renowned for the diversity of its flora and fauna.

◆ **Nationalparkverwaltung**, A-2082 Hardegg ℘02949 7005 0 www.np-thayatal.at

Nationalpark Donau-Auen (Lower Austria)

This park stretches from just east of Vienna to the Slovakian border and is home to a tremendous variety of flora and fauna, earning it the nickname of "Central Europe's rain forest." Its unique features can be discovered on foot or by boat.

◆ **Nationalparkverwaltung**, A-2304 Orth an der Donau, ℘02212 3450 www.donauauen.at

Nationalpark Gesäuse

Rocky cliffs, shaggy meadows, thick forest and the gushing Enns River characterise the country's youngest national park in Styria, central Austria. Its boasts 50 types of wild orchids and serves as the breeding ground for 60 different bird species.

◆ **Bürogemeinschaft Nationalpark**,
A-8911 Admont
☏ 03613 211 60 20
www.nationalpark.co.at

Nationalpark Nockberge (Carinthia)

Confusingly, despite its name, this is not officially recognised by all the authorities as a national park (instead they classify it as a state park). Whatever its status, it is worth a visit. The park lies between the Lieser Valley and the Turracher Höhe range and is characterised by its gently undulating hills of crystalline rock ("Nocken").

◆ **Nationalparkverwaltung**,
A-9565 Ebene Reichenau
☏ 04275 665
www.biosphaerenpark
nockberge.at

Nature Parks

The 48 Austrian nature parks, which are also conservation areas, cluster mostly in eastern Austria, especially Styria, Lower Austria and Burgenland. Further information is available at www.naturparke.at and www.austria. info (choose the "Lakes and Nature" link on the homepage).

BIRD WATCHING

◆ **Burgenland**: Neusiedler See; Seewinkel/Lange Lacke; veterinary care centre for storks and other birdlife at Parndorf (A-7111).
◆ **Carinthia**: Eagle observation point from the castle ruins at Landskron; bird reserve on Grossedlinger Pond (near Wolfsberg); Völkermarkter reservoir.
◆ **Lower Austria**: Danube, Morava and Thaya river wetlands; Thaya Valley near Hardegg.
◆ **Salzburg (province)**: Pinzgau (between the Gastein and Habach valleys); Zeller See (south shore of the lake).
◆ **Styria**: Mur reservoir (southern Styria).

◆ **Upper Austria**: Danube plain in the Linz Valley; Schmiding bird reserve. www.zooschmiding.at.

Further information is available from www.austria.info (type "bird watching" into the search box).

ANGLING

There are no websites or brochures in English devoted to fishing in Austria, however if you visit www. austria.info and type "fishing" into the search bar, you will see that the country offers superb coarse, game and fly fishing holidays.
Specialist UK tour operators include Kings Angling Holidays (www.king sanglingholidays.co.uk).
If your German is good, the following websites may be of use:
www.fischerei.or.at
www.fischwasser.com.

WATERSPORTS AND BOATING

Austria boasts no fewer than 1,000 lakes, including 200 in Carinthia alone. Several of them are so clean that they actually boast water of drinking quality. From mid-May to the end of September there are regular passenger boat or ferry services on some of the larger lakes, such as the Achensee, the Attersee, Lake Constance, the Hallstätter See, the Ossiacher See, the Traunsee, the Wörthersee and the Wolfgangsee. In almost all cases, it is possible to row, sail, surf, water ski or quite simply swim (if the water is warm enough!) in Austria's lakes. Further information on these activities is provided by the tourist offices of the lakeside communities.

Boat trips on the Danube

From early April to the end of October, a number of companies offer boat trips on the Danube. From Vienna you can travel to Budapest and Bratislava in just a few hours:
◆ **DDSG Blue Danube Schiffahrt**
A-1020 Wien, ☏ 015 88 80
www.ddsg-blue-danube.at

- **Donauschiffahrt Ardagger**
  Felleismühle 5, A-3321 Ardagger
  ✆07479 6464
  www.donauschiffahrt-ardagger.at
- **Donauschiffahrt Wurm & Köck**
  Untere Donaulände 1, A-4020 Linz,
  ✆0732 78 36 07
  www.donauschiffahrt.de
- **Brandner Schiffahrt**
  Ufer 15, A-3313 Wallsee. ✆07433
  25 90 21. www.brandner.at

RAFTING & CANOEING

Rafting is permitted from May to
October, but is not allowed in the
Hohe Tauern National Park.
Good rafting rivers include:
- **Carinthia**; the Gail, Gurk, Isel,
  Lieser and Möll
- **Lower Austria**; the Enns,
  Morava, Salza and Thaya
- **Salzburg Province**; the Enns,
  Lammer, Mur, Saalach
  and Salzach
- **Styria**; the Enns and Salza;
- **Tyrol**; the Gerolsbach, Inn, Isel,
  Ötztaler and Tiroler Ache,
  Sanna and Ziller
- **Upper Austria**; the Enns,
  Steyr and Traun

Further information is available from
www.austria.info (type "canoeing"
and "rafting" respectively into the
search bar). Alternatively, German
speakers may wish to contact
the Austrian canoe association:
Österreichischer Kanuverband
*(Gießereistraße 8, A-5280 Braunau,
✆07722 816 00, www.kanuverband.at).*

HANG-GLIDING AND PARAGLIDING

Venues for hang-gliding and
paragliding include:
- **Carinthia** – Bad Kleinkirchheim,
  Katschberg, Seeboden
- **Salzburg** – Dorfgastein, Golling-
  Werfenweng, Mattsee, Salzburg;
- **Styria** – Graz, Gröbming, Ramsau
  am Dachstein
- **Tyrol** – Galtür, Hall, Kössen, Lienz,
  Neustift im Stubaital, Niederau,
  Seefeld

- **Upper Austria** – Hinterstoder,
  Leonstein, Linz, Spital am Pyhrn,
  Weyregg
- **Vorarlberg** – limited to certain
  summits and following prescribed
  routes only

For further details, contact the nearest
tourist office.

GOLF

The popularity of golf in Austria has
steadily increased in recent years
and the country has nearly 200 golf
courses across the nine provinces. For
details, contact the Austrian golfing
association: **Österreichischer Golf-
Verband** *(Marxergasse 25, A-1030
Wien, ✆01 505 3 2 45, www.golf.at).*

CYCLING & MOUNTAIN BIKING

Austria offers more than
10,000km/6,200mi of cycle paths to
sightseers on two wheels. One of the
most popular is the **Donauradweg**, a
cycle path following the Danube from
Passau to Hainburg (305km/190mi).
The Austrian National Tourist Office
publishes a brochure called *Radtouren
in Österreich* with detailed route
descriptions and lodging information
about select long-distance cycle
routes. It can be ordered from
Radtouren in Österreich *(c/o
Oberösterreich Tourismus, Freistädter*

*Cycling along Traunsee
at Altmünster, Salzkammergut*

© Austrian National Tourist Office/ Himsl

Straße 119, A-4041 Linz, ℰ0732 22 10 22), or from the organization's website at www.radtouren.at. Mountain bikers are well taken care of as well in Austria with some 17,000km/10 625mi of well-marked routes throughout the Alpine regions. For further details, contact **Mountain Bike Holidays** (Saalfeldnerstraße 14, A-5751 Maishofen, ℰ06542 804 80 22; www.bike-holidays.com).

British operators include Up and Downhill Holidays (www.upand downhill.com), who offer mountain bike holidays around Ellmau, in the Tyrol, and Mountain Edge (www.mountainedge.co.uk), who lead tours in and around Kitzbühel. For touring at a more leisurely pace, and in possibly less tiring surroundings, check out Bike and Hike Austria (www.bikeandhikeaustria.eu), whose routes in the Salzkammergut region follow various peaceful dedicated cycle paths.

If you are doing it yourself, cycles can be transported by rail for no extra charge, or hired from some 50 Austrian railway stations. Check with the tourist office for details.

HIKING

With a network of about 50,000km/ 31,100mi of waymarked trails, Austria is a hiker's paradise. Ten long-distance trails (Weitwanderwege) make it possible to explore the entire country on foot. Three long-distance European trails also cut across Austria.

For both an overview and articles on walking in Austria, visit www.austria. info/uk and click on the "Walking and Hiking" or "Lakes and Nature" link. British walking-tour operators include Exodus Travels (www.exodustravels. com), who specialise in tours of the Tyrol.

HORSE RIDING

Austria is world renowned for its Lippizaner horses (◉see p203 and p290) and while it is unlikely that you will get an opportunity to lay your hand on one, let alone ride one of

these equine aristocrats in Austria (though it is possible to do so if you cross the border to visit the Slovenia Lipica stud), you may well get the chance to saddle up on another national treasure. The Austrian Haflinger is a lovely breed developed in Austria and northern Italy in the late 1800s: usually friendly, relatively small, always chestnut in colour, with a distinctive gait that is most often described as energetic but smooth. Horse-riding specialists Hidden Trails (www.hiddentrails.com) show riders the best of Alpine and lowland scenery, the former in the Hohe Tauern National Park, the latter in the Innviertel Woodlands, between Salzburg and Passau, on the border of Bavaria, with rides through old forest, lakeside trails and small traditional villages.

WALKING IN THE MOUNTAINS

Austria boasts about 680 mountain peaks above 3,000m/10,000ft and over a thousand carefully managed mountain huts, offering mountain enthusiasts a wide variety of possibilities for walking and climbing routes of every imaginable degree of difficulty.

⊚ For safety reasons, it is essential to plan the route of any mountain excursions very carefully in advance, to ensure that you have the right equipment and to match the route to your level of fitness.

Lightning

In rocky countryside the arrival of lightning is often heralded by an electrostatic charge in the air (and in one's hair). During storms you should not seek shelter on narrow ridges, or under overhanging rocks, just inside the entrance to caves or in clefts in the rock. You should also avoid standing under isolated trees or near metal objects (such as fences). Crampons and ice-axes should not be carried on your person. If possible, you should put at least 15m/49ft between yourself and any outcrop (such as a tree or a rock) and remain in a crouched position with your knees well drawn up to your chest and any exposed areas of skin (such as your hands) not touching any rock. During storms, the car is an excellent refuge, as it acts as a Faraday cage (electrostatic screen).

MOUNTAIN CLIMBING

Mountain guides and climbing schools are to be found in the following areas:
+ **Carinthia**: Ferlach, Gmünd, Großkirchheim, Heiligenblut, Kolbnitz, Kötschach-Mauthen, Spittal an der Drau, Villach
+ **Lower Austria**: Gloggnitz, Puchberg am Schneeberg
+ **Salzburg**: Filzmoos, Kaprun, Maria Alm, Mauterndorf, Neukirchen, Salzburg
+ **Styria**: Bad Aussee, Graz, Ramsau am Dachstein, Schladming;
+ **Tyrol**: Ehrwald, Ellmau, Fulpmes, Galtür, Going, Innsbruck, Kufstein, Landeck, Lanersbach, Mayrhofen, Nauders, Obergurgl, St. Anton, St. Johann, Sölden
+ **Upper Austria**: Ebensee, Gosau am Dachstein, Grünau im Almtal, Gschwandt, Hallstatt, Hinterstoder, Linz, Mondsee, Spital am Pyhrn, Windischgarsten
+ **Vorarlberg**: Bartholomäberg, Brand, Lech, Mittelberg, Vandans

Obtain more information from www. austria.info (type "mountaineering" into the search bar). Serious mountain climbers who speak German should contact the **Verband alpiner Vereine Österreichs** *(Bäckerstraße 16, A-1010 Wien, 01 512 54 88, www.vavoe.at)*, an umbrella organisation for a dozen Alpine hiking organisations, including the Österreichischer Alpenverein (*see Walking in the Mountains*).

WINTER SPORTS

Austria has numerous famous ski areas equipped with excellent infrastructures; useful websites are listed throughout this book, or contact the regional or local tourist offices for more details.

Mountain Safety

The mountains, while spectacular to behold, conceal very real dangers that can catch both inexperienced and experienced hikers unawares. Avalanches, rock-falls, sudden weather changes, heavy mists, unstable terrain, the icy water of mountain streams and lakes, loss of orientation, mistaken judgement of distances – all these represent potentially fatal dangers to mountaineers, skiers and hikers. Mists and storms are difficult to anticipate and can manifest themselves unexpectedly even in high summer. At high altitudes, the snow cover remains into early July, and snow banks often make north-facing slopes impassable.

Remember the cardinal rule: never set off alone or without having communicated your planned route and estimated time of return to a third party who is safely at home.

Year-round skiing is possible at the following resorts:
+ in **Carinthia**, Mölltaler Gletscher
+ in **Salzburg**, Kaprun/Kitzsteinhorn
+ in **Styria**, Ramsau/Dachstein
+ in the **Tyrol**, Hintertux/Tuxer Gletscher, Kaunertal, Stubaier Gletscher, Ötztal/Rettenbach-und Tiefenbachferner, Pitztal/Mittelbergferner

For the most current snow and weather reports, as well as avalanche warnings, visit www.lawine.at or call the Alpine Weather line: 0512 29 16 00. For both an overview and articles on all the latest happenings in Austria in skiing and snowboarding, visit www.austria.info/uk and click on '"Skiing and Winter."
Brief descriptions of the country's principal ski resorts follow.

Bad Gastein/Sportgastein

With 175km/109mi of slopes there's plenty of room for all grades, though the runs here are quite challenging and probably best for intermediates who are happy on red runs. Because of the altitude, snow is usually guaranteed. If not, move up the mountain another 1,600m/5,250ft to Sportgastein.

Innsbruck

Former Winter Olympics host, Innsbruck is a perfect venue for winter sports. Eight major ski areas cover 500km/310mi of trails that provide varied terrain for all levels of skiers and snowboarders. Surrounding the Tyrolean capital are 25 village resorts, connected by a free local ski bus.

Ischgl

Alongside its neighbouring resort of Galtur, Ischgl offers high snow-sure pistes and some of the most challenging intermediate and expert runs in the country. Off piste this traditional Tyrolean village is gaining quite a reputation for its wild après-ski scene, and attracting international stars to its open-air concerts.

Kitzbühel

The famous Hahnenkamm racecourse may be the most challenging on the World Cup circuit, but the great problem with Kitzbühel is its altitude and therefore lack of good snow. The slopes can also be crowded.

Lech and Zürs

Long blue and red runs swoop down into the village, dotted with picturesque mountain huts offering rum-laced hot chocolate and stunning views. This was a favourite of Princess Diana and still draws the jet set. A 10min bus ride away is the even more exclusive Zürs, where the skiing, good as it is, often takes a backseat to simply being seen here – Princess Caroline of Monaco is a regular.

Mayrhofen

Another resort dedicated to more than just the skiing, Mayrhofen hosts the Snowbombing festival each April,

Europe's biggest music festival to be held in the ski season. However, the resort is also family friendly and whether you want to get the kids skiing or enjoy the après-ski, you should have a good time here. The Penken and the Ahorn offer good runs nearby and there is a bus link to the huge Zillertal ski area.

St. Anton

These days St. Anton may be only a village in name, but despite its size and party reputation, the centre still has a traditional Tyrolean feel complete with Hansel-and-Gretel-style wooden chalets. The skiing is excellent, with a huge number of pistes. In fact, together with St. Christoph, it has by far the biggest area in the country, boasting a massive 260km/160mi of slopes. A lift pass in St. Anton gives access to the whole Arlberg area, including Lech, Zürs and Stuben. But the resort is equally famous for its après-ski scene.

Neustift

Neustift is famous as the closest resort to the Stubai Glacier. Around 30 high-speed lifts whisk skiers of all abilities to Austria's largest skiable glacier, which reaches the top (Hochstubai) at 3,250m/10,400ft. This is as high as ski resorts go in Austria, and Neustift boasts the finest year-round skiing conditions you could wish for.

Obertauern

An excellent all-round modern resort with an international reputation, Obertauern is ideal for most intermediate skiers.

Saalbach-Hinterglemm

Saalbach-Hinterglemm is pretty, traditional, boasts dozens of fine traditional Alpine mountain restaurants, a lively nightlife and 180km/112mi of ski slopes. The only real disadvantage here is the lack of reliable snow.

Schladming

This cosy village is perfect for intermediate skiers and famous for its annual night slalom, in January, which attracts tens of thousands of spectators. In 2013 the World Ski Championships were held here for the second time.

Söll

A most popular resort for groups of beginners and less-confident intermediates, Söll is a charming place with lovely scenery, gentle slopes and traditional villages. It is famed for its lively nightlife, which in the 1980s actually gained it some notoriety. Thankfully the nights have calmed down a lot since those days.

Best of the Rest

Other resorts that you may wish to consider are: **Obergurgl/Hochgurgl**, best for its high, snow-sure, easy intermediate slopes; **Sölden**, best for adventurous intermediates, who will want to venture up to the snow-sure runs on the Rettenbach and Tiefenbach glaciers; **Zell am See**, a charming lakeside town with a historic core and extensive cross-country trails.

Cross-Country Skiing

Altenmarket/Zauchensee, Flachau/Flachauwinkl, Radstadt (all Salzburg); Leutasch (Tyrol); and Ramsau am Dachstein (Steiermark) are good places to go if you want to get away from the crowds, as each boasts at least 150km/93mi of cross-country ski runs. Largest of all is Seefeld in Tirol with 170km/105mi.

SPAS

Austria has a wide and growing selection of spa resorts equipped for the most varied and state-of-the-art wellness treatments. In the skiing season, many of these spa resorts (such as Bad Gastein) keep their thermal baths open.
For both an overview and articles on the latest spa openings in Austria, visit www.austria.info/uk and click on "Spa and Wellbeing."

SULPHUR SPRINGS

These springs are used mainly to remedy ailments of the joints, muscles, the nervous system and skin troubles at resorts such as Baden, whose thermal beach draws many Viennese, and in the Salzkammergut, at Bad Ischl and Bad Goisern.

SALT SPRINGS

Waters impregnated with sodium chloride (salt) from natural springs or 'mother-waters' (the residues from the refining of industrial salt) are exploited alongside the salt mines themselves. The salts are used in douches and baths and are good for gynaecological and infantile diseases, and for inhaling, to help clear the bronchial tubes. To this group may be added the bicarbonate-bearing waters, like those of Bad Gleichenberg in Styria, which are also recommended for drinking to treat the stomach, intestines and kidneys.

IODISED SPRINGS

These springs are invaluable for curing metabolic and circulatory disorders, and for vision and glandular troubles. They are particularly well represented by Bad Hall in Upper Austria. In addition to the true mineral springs, some hot springs, such as those at Bad Gastein, also have low-level radioactive properties.
The Austrian National Tourist Office has a list of establishments offering various treatments (spa, thermal baths, Kneipp, etc.). Regional tourist offices can provide specialised lists of spa resorts in their area.

ACTIVITIES FOR KIDS 👥

In this guide, sights of particular interest to children are indicated with a kids symbol (👥). Attractions usually offer discounts for children. Across the Alps, the independently managed Kinderhotels (www.kinderhotels.com) specifically cater for families with young children.

SHOPPING
BUSINESS HOURS

Most shops are open Monday to Friday 9am to 6pm and on Thursday and Friday perhaps until 9pm. In the smaller towns shops may close at 1pm on Saturdays; elsewhere they are open until 5pm. In larger places and tourist towns, many open on Sundays around noon. Smaller, independent shops may close at lunch hour.

LOCAL CRAFTS

For good quality, locally made souvenirs, visit the local **Heimatwerk** (*www.heimatwerk.at*), an official outlet for the work of local artisans.

- **Carinthia** – Kärntner Heimatwerk, Herrengasse 8, A-9020 Klagenfurt. ℘0463 555 75. www.kaerntner heimatwerk.at. Typical regional items: costumes, ceramics, carved wooden boxes, wrought iron (Friesach). Website details shops at Villach, Spittal and Wolfsberg.
- **Salzburg** – Salzburger Heimatwerk, Residenzplatz 9, A-5010 Salzburg. ℘0662 84 41 10. www.sbg.heimatwerk.at. Typical regional items: pewter, china, regional costumes.
- **Styria** – Steirisches Heimatwerk, Sporgasse 23, A-8010 Graz. ℘0316 82 71 06. www.heimatwerk. steiermark.at. Typical regional items: printed linens and jewellery from Bad Aussee; carved wooden masks from Mitterndorf; painted pottery from Gams; *Loden* cloth from Ramsau and Mandling.
- **Tyrol** – Tiroler Heimatwerk, Meraner Straße 2, A-6020 Innsbruck. ℘0512 58 23 20. tiroler.heimatwerk.at. Typical regional items: wooden Christmas mangers; tablecloths and embroidered fabrics; wrought iron; majolica from Schwaz; cut and engraved glassware from Kufstein and Kramsach.
- **Upper Austria** – Oberösterreichisches (Oö) Heimatwerk, Landstraße 31, A-4020 Linz. ℘0732 77 33 77. ooe.heimatwerk.at. Typical regional items: painted glassware; wooden boxes; handwoven linen from Haslach; leatherwork and candles from Braunau; wrought iron and steel engravings from Steyr; china from Gmunden; headdresses and silver jewellery from Bad Ischl. Bad Ischl (♿*see website*) has an Oö Heimatwerk.
- **Vienna** – Österreichische Werkstätten: Kärntner Straße 6. ℘01 512 24 18. www.austrianarts.com. This is not a Heimatwerk outlet. It displays and sells designer jewellery, glass design, handbags and accessories. The store also stages exhibitions of international quality. More traditional crafts of the region include Viennese bronze and enamel *petit point*, Augarten porcelain and embroidered blouses.
- **Vorarlberg** – Vorarlberger Heimatwerk, Montfortstraße 4, A-6900 Bregenz. ℘05574 423 25. www.heimatwerk-vorarlberg. at. Wooden articles, painted glassware, hand weaving; embroidery from Schwarzenberg and Lustenau; candles from Schruns.
- **Burgenland** – There is unfortunately no Heimatwerk representation in Austria's easternmost province, but keep an eye out for china from Stoob, woven baskets from Piringsdorf and Weiden am See, and jade jewellery and serpentine marble from Bernstein.

Gourmet Souvenirs

Look for **Sachertorte** (in Vienna) and **Linzertorte** (in Linz), although you will see them across the country. Salzburg is famous for its **Mozartkugeln**, balls of marzipan covered in nougat and dark chocolate. The confectioner Fürst sells the original handmade Salzburg

Mozartkugeln exclusively in its four Salzburg shops.

MARKETS

In the summer there are many street markets in the charming surroundings of village squares. Local tourist offices will have information on local markets and local or regional newspapers will often publish the dates.

The Naschmarkt near the Karlsplatz in Vienna is the largest street market in Austria and well worth a visit for its hustle and bustle, cafés and food stalls, regardless of whether or not you intend to buy anything.

BOOKS
REFERENCE

The Austrians: A Thousand-Year Odyssey by Gordon Brook-Shepherd

A Brief Survey of Austrian History by Richard Rickett

Contemporary Austria and the Legacy of the Third Reich by Robert Knight

Haydn: Chronicle and Works. Vol II: *Haydn at Eszterháza, 1766–1790* by H C Robbins Landon

Fin-de-Siècle Vienna by Carl E Schorske

Mountain Walking in Austria by Cecil Davies

Music and Musicians in Vienna by Richard Rickett

The Fall of the House of Habsburg by Edward Crankshaw

The Habsburg Monarchy, 1618–1815 by Charles Ingrao

The Habsburg Monarchy c. 1765–1918 by Robin Okey

Vienna: The Image of a Culture in Decline by Edward Crankshaw

LITERATURE

Aichinger, Ilse: *Die größere Hoffnung* Bachmann, Ingeborg: *Malina, Die gestundete Zeit*

Frischmuth, Barbara: *Die Schrift des Freundes*

Bernhard, Thomas: *Das Kalkwerk (The Lime Works), Die Berühmten (The Famous), Holzfällen (Woodcutters), Heldenplatz (Heroes' Square)*

Freud, Sigmund: *Die Traumdeutung (The Interpretation of Dreams),*

Das Unbehagen in der Kultur (Civilization and its Discontents)

Handke, Peter: *Die Angst des Tormanns beim Elfmeter (The Goalie's Anxiety at the Penalty Kick), Die linkshändige Frau (The Left-Handed Woman), Publikumsbeschimpfung (Offending the Audience), Wunschloses Unglück (A Sorrow Beyond Dreams)*

Hofmannsthal, Hugo von: *Jedermann (Everyman), Das Salzburger große Welttheater, Der Rosenkavalier* **(libretto)**, *Chandos-Brief* **(essay)**, *Cristinas Heimreise (Christina's Journey Home), Der Turm (The Tower)*

Jelinek, Elfriede: *Die Liebhaberinnen (Women as Lovers), Die Klavierspielerin (The Piano Teacher).*

Masoch, Leopold von: *Eine galizische Geschichte (A Galician Story), Venus im Pelz (Venus in Furs).*

Rilke, Rainer Maria: *Sonette an Orpheus (Sonnets to Orpheus), Duineser Elegien (Duino Elegies)*

Roth, Joseph: *Radetzkymarsch (Radetzky March), Kapuzinergruft (The Capuchin Crypt)*

Schnitzler, Arthur: *Liebelei (Playing with Love), Reigen (Merry-Go-Round), Leutnant Gustl (None But the Brave), Der Weg ins Freie (The Road into the Open)*

Stifter, Adalbert: *Der Nachsommer (Indian Summer), Bunte Steine (Colourful Stones)*

Zweig, Stefan: *Schachnovelle (Chess Story), Sternstunden der Menschheit (The Tide of Fortune), Ungeduld des Herzens (Beware of Pity)*

FILMS

Café Elektric (1927)

A silent movie starring Marlene Dietrich slumming it with her boyfriend who is not all he seems. Filmed in Vienna.

Der Kleine Straßensänger, (An Orphan Boy of Vienna) (1936)

A touching story of an orphan and a street singer who gets the boy accepted by the Vienna Boys Choir.

The Third Man (1949)
A classic film set in Vienna just after World War II.

Sissi (Forever My Love) (1962)
The romantic hurdles faced by the young Emperor Franz Joseph and his beloved Sissi.

The Sound of Music (1965)
A novice nun transforms the children of widower Baron von Trapp into a singing group while falling in love with him. Filmed in Salzburg.

Amadeus (1984)
The story of Salzburg's most famous son, told in flashback by fellow composer Antonio Salieri.

Some scenes were filmed in Vienna, though most were filmed in the former Czechoslovakia.

Before Sunrise (1995)
Ethan Hawke and Julie Delpy spend one night falling in love in Vienna.

The Counterfeiters (2007)
Tells the story of the counterfeiting operation set up by the Nazis in 1936 and the story of the Jew spared because of his counterfeiting skills.

Knight and Day (2010)
Cameron Diaz plays a young woman tangled up with a disgraced spy (Tom Cruise) trying to clear his name.

Calendar of Events

Below is a selection of Austria's most popular events. Most take place annually, although precise dates may vary.
⏱For details, contact the local or regional tourist offices.
For additional events, see the Addresses section under Graz, Innsbruck, Klagenfurt, Linz, Salzburg, St. Pölten and Vienna.

TRADITIONAL AND FOLK FESTIVALS

JANUARY
1–6 Jan: **Gastein Valley** – *Perchtenlauf:* Carnival procession (every 4 years, next time 2018)

FEBRUARY
Imst – *Buabefasnacht:* Boys' carnival procession (every 4–5 years, next event Feb 2018). www.fasnacht.at

Imst – *Schemenlaufen:* carnival procession (every 3–4 years, next event Feb 2020). www.fasnacht.at

Telfs – *Schleicherlaufen:* Carnival procession (every 5 years, next event 2020). www.schleicherlaufen.at

MAY AND JUNE
1st May weekend: **Zell im Zillertal** – *Gauderfest:* Centuries-old beer festival with folk music and other events. www.gauderfest.at

Whit Monday: **Freistritz an der Gail** (west of Villach) – *Gailtaler Kufenstechen:* A joust using a barrel as target, followed by dancing

Corpus Christi *Fronleichnam* (2nd Thu after Whitsun): **Bischofshofen** – *Prangstangen:* Procession with floral poles

Corpus Christi: **Brixental in Tirol** – Procession on horseback

Corpus Christi: **Gmunden** – Procession

Corpus Christi: **Deutschlandsberg** – Procession and carpet of flowers

Corpus Christi: **Hallstatt, Traunkirchen** – Processions on the lake

June 24: **Zederhaus** – *Prangstangentragen:* Flower-decorated poles up to 8m/26ft long are carried to the church in a procession and left there until Assumption Day (15 Aug)

AUGUST
early Aug: **Krakaudorf** Murau *Oswaldisonntag* (first Sun Aug) – "Samson" processions. www.krakautal.at

SEPTEMBER–DECEMBER

late Sept, early Oct: **Burgenland and Lower Austria** – Wine harvest: processions, wine fountains, fireworks

late Nov–Christmas: **Nationwide** – Advent and Christmas markets

5 Dec: **Bad Mitterndorf** – *Nikolospiel:* street festival in honour of St. Nicholas

27 Dec–15 Jan: **Thaur** (northeast of Innsbruck) – Christmas nativity scenes are on display in people's houses, some of which are open to the public

MUSIC AND ARTS FESTIVALS

JANUARY

1 Jan: **Vienna** – *Neujahrskonzert:* New Year concert by the Vienna Philharmonic.

MARCH–MAY

Graz – *Diagonale:* Austrian film festival (late March). www.diagonale.at

Week before Easter: **Salzburg** – *Osterfestspiele:* Annual Easter Festival with classical music and opera (next event 8-17 Apr 2017). www.osterfestspiele-salzburg.at

Vienna – Spring Festival of classical music. www.konzerthaus.at

Apr–May: **Krems und Wachau** – Danube festival, with a wide range of theatre, dance, music and arts. www.donaufestival.at

May–Jun: **Vienna** – Vienna Festival of performing arts. www.festwochen.at

May–Oct: **Millstatt** – Music Weeks classical music festival. www.musikwochen.com

JUNE–SEPTEMBER

Jun–Jul: **Innsbruck** – Tanzsommer: Summer dance festival. www.tanzsommer.at

Jul: **Klagenfurt** – Musikforum Viktring. www.musikforum.at

Jul–Aug: **Ossiach/Villach** – Carinthian Summer Music Festival. www.carinthischersommer.at

Jul–Aug: **Innsbruck** – Ambras Castle Concerts (Jul). Festival of

International Bruckner Festival, Linz

© Austrian National Tourist Office/ Roebl

Early Music (Aug). www.altemusik.at

mid-Jul–late Aug: **Mörbisch** – Operetta festival (Neusiedler See). www.seefestspiele-moerbisch.at

late Jul–late Aug: **Bregenz** – Lakeside festival. www.bregenzerfestspiele.com

Jul–early Sept: **Wiesen** – Open-air festival of contemporary music. www.wiesen.at

late Jul–late Aug: **Salzburg** – Salzburg Festival. www.salzburgerfestspiele.at

SEPTEMBER–NOVEMBER

early Sept: **Linz** – Festival Ars Electronica. www.aec.at/festival

1st week Sept: **Mondsee** – Mondsee festival of chamber music. Mondsee Schloss. www.musiktage-mondsee.at

Sept–Oct: **Linz** – Intern'l Bruckner Festival. www.brucknerhaus.at

Sept–Oct: **St. Pölten** – Musica Sacra www.festival-musica-sacra.at

Oct: **Graz and its surroundings** – Steirischer Herbst: Styrian autumn arts festival. www.steirischerherbst.at

Oct–Nov: **Eisenstadt** – International Haydn Festival in Schloss Esterházy. www.haydnfestival.at

PASSION PLAYS

late May: **Erl** (northeast of Kufstein) – Every 6 years (next event 2019). www.passionsspeiele.at

May–Oct: **Thiersee** – Every 6 years (next event 2021). www.passionsspiele-thiersee.at

Know Before You Go

USEFUL WEBSITES

www.austria.info
The official website maintained by the Austrian National Tourist Office is an excellent pre-trip planning tool with information about the regions, eating and drinking, accommodations, history, famous people and other topics.

www.austria.org
This general website maintained by the Austrian Press and Information Service of the Austrian Embassy in Washington, DC, includes travel information and a link to Facts & Figures.

www.austria.gv.at.
This Austrian federal government website is a portal to the country's political landscape with links to all ministries. Learn about Austrian current affairs and policy stance on such issues as security, bioethics and data protection.

www.tiscover.com
Another useful holiday planner, this site is dedicated to Austria and has detailed information on all provinces, allowing you to book hotels, packages and cars. It also has a route planner and details about road closures, current traffic, weather reports and other useful data.

www.lawine.at
Go here for up-to-date information about snow conditions, avalanche warnings, and other ski- and snow-related information (in German only).

www.aboutaustria.org
General guide to the country covering many aspects in reasonable detail.

TOURIST OFFICES

The Austrian National Tourist Office (ANTO) offers information on special deals of interest to vacationers in Austria and other information.

AUSTRIAN NATIONAL TOURIST OFFICES

- **Australia and New Zealand**
  1st Floor, 36 Carrington Street, Sydney, NSW 2000
  ℘02 9299 3621.
  www.austria.info/au

- **UK and Republic of Ireland**
  54 Hatton Garden, 4th Floor London EC1N 8HN, UK
  ℘800 400 200 00
  www.austria.info/uk

- **USA and Canada**
  PO Box 1142,
  New York, NY 10108-1142
  ℘USA: 212-944-6880
  ℘Canada: 416-967-3381
  www.austria.info/us

TOURIST OFFICES OF THE AUSTRIAN PROVINCES

- **Burgenland**
  Burgenland-Tourismus,
  Johann Permayer-Straße 13,
  A-7000 Eisenstadt
  ℘026 82 63 38 40
  www.burgenland.info

- **Carinthia**
  Kärnten Werbung,
  Völkermarkter Ring 21-23
  A-9020 Klagenfurt
  ℘0463 30 00
  www.kaernten.at

- **Lower Austria**
  Niederösterreich-Werbung,
  Niederösterreich-Ring 2, Haus C,
  A-3100 St. Pölten
  ℘02742 9000 198000
  www.lower-austria.info

- **Salzburg** *(province)*
  SalzburgerLand
  Tourismus GesmbH
  Wiener Bundesstraße 23
  A-5300 Hallwang
  ✆0662 66 88 0
  www.salzburgerland.com

- **Styria**
  Steirische Tourismus GmbH
  St. Peter Hauptstraße 243,
  A-8042 Graz
  ✆0316 40 030
  www.steiermark.com

- **Tyrol**
  Tirol Info
  Maria-Theresien-Straße 55
  A-6020 Innsbruck
  ✆0512 72 72 0
  www.tirol.at

- **Upper Austria**
  Oberösterreich Tourismus
  Freistädter Straße 119
  A-4041 Linz
  ✆0732 7277 100
  www.oberoesterreich.at

- **Vienna**
  Wiener Tourismusverband
  Albertinaplatz/Maysedergasse
  A-1010 Wien
  ✆01 24 555
  www.wien.info

- **Vorarlberg**
  Vorarlberg Tourismus
  Poststraße 11, Pf. 99
  A-6850 Dornbirn
  ✆05572 37 70 33 0
  www.vorarlberg.travel

LOCAL TOURIST INFORMATION CENTRES

These centres are indicated by the symbol 🄸 on the town plans in this guide. Addresses and telephone numbers are given throughout this guide. Further addresses and details can be obtained from the national or regional tourist offices.

INTERNATIONAL VISITORS
FOREIGN CONSULATES IN AUSTRIA (VIENNA)

- **Australia**
  Mattiellistraße 2–4,
  A-1040 Wien,
  ✆01 506 740
  www.austria.embassy.gov.au

- **Canada**
  Laurenzerberg 2, 3rd Floor,
  A-1010 Wien,
  ✆01 531 38 3000
  www.canadainternational.gc.ca

- **United Kingdom**
  Jauresgasse 12,
  A-1030 Wien,
  ✆01 71 61 30
  www.britishembassy.at

- **USA**
  Boltzmanngasse 16,
  A-19090 Wien,
  ✆01 313 390
  at.usembassy.gov

AUSTRIAN EMBASSIES ABROAD

- **In Australia**
  12 Talbot Street,
  Forrest, Canberra ACT 2603
  ✆02 6295 1533
  www.bmeia.gv.at

- **In Canada**
  445 Wilbrod Street,
  Ottawa, ON K1N 6M7
  ✆613 789 1444
  www.bmeia.gv.at

- **In UK**
  18 Belgrave Mews West,
  London SW1X 8HU
  ✆0207 344 3250
  www.bmeia.gv.at

- **In USA**
  3524 International Court NW,
  Washington, DC 20008
  ✆202-895-6700
  www.austria.org

ENTRY REQUIREMENTS

Passport – Citizens of countries within the EU entering Austria need only a national identity card. Nationals of other countries must be in possession of a valid national **passport**. In case of loss or theft, report to your embassy or consulate and the local police.

Visa – Citizens of Australia, Canada, New Zealand, the USA and Israel need a valid passport but no **visa** for tourist stays up to 3 months. Citizens from most other countries need to apply for a visa at the **Austrian Embassy** in their home country (&see p23). Austria is part of the Schengen Agreement for holders of visas to other Schengen countries.

US citizens should consult the Traveler's Checklist (click "U.S. Passports & International Travel") on the website travel.state.gov. for information on visa requirements, customs regulations, medical care, etc., for international travellers.

CUSTOMS REGULATIONS

When travelling within the EU, travellers may import (duty free) 800 cigarettes or 200 cigars or 1kg/2.2lb tobacco, 10l/2.6 US gal spirits, 90l/23.7 US gal wine (max. 60l/15.8 US gal sparkling wine), 110l/29 US gal beer. **When travelling from non-EU countries,** travellers may import (duty free) 200 cigarettes or 50 cigars or 250g/8.8oz tobacco; 2l/0.5gal wine and 1l/.2 US gal liquor; and additional items up to €300 (€430 for airline travellers) in value per traveller. Contact your country's customs office for duty-free restrictions and other regulations about what you may bring back home. The UK's revenue and customs agency, HMRC, produces a helpful guide downloadable free at *www.hmrc.gov.uk*. The U.S. Customs and Border Protection has online information about what to know before you depart. For details about customs requirements, visit the website for US Customs and Border Protection (www.cbp.gov), then click on "Travel" and look for "U.S. Citizens/ Lawful Permanent Residents."

HEALTH

Citizens of the EU should obtain a European Health Insurance Card (EHIC) from their local health authority, which entitles them to receive low-cost or free emergency health care while in Austria. It does not cover emergency repatriation. You can apply for a card at www.ehic.org.uk or pick up a leaflet at your local post office. Non-EU residents should check that their private health insurance policy covers them for travel abroad, and if necessary take out supplementary medical insurance with specific overseas coverage. All prescription drugs should be clearly labelled, and it is recommended that you carry a copy of the prescription with you.

ACCESSIBILITY

For an overview, visit the national tourist office's website *www.austria. info/uk/service-facts*and see the *Accessible Travel* section.
Regional tourist offices also provide information about travelling in Austria. Some have put together handy guides of which the following are available online: Accessible Tirol *(www.tyrol. com/things-to-do/barrier-free)*, Upper Austria's Barrierefreier Urlaub in Oberösterreich *(www.oberoesterreich. at/aktivitaeten/ganzjaehrig/barrierefrei. html, in German only)* and Accessible Vienna *(www.wien.info/en/travel-info/ accessible-vienna)*.
For **barrier-free farm holidays**, access Urlaub am Bauernhof's *www. farmholidays.com*, which has a list of handicapped accessible packages.
For **rail travel** in Austria, the Österreichische Bundesbahnen (ÖBB) operates a hotline *(℘05 17 17; www. oebb.at)* that offers trip-planning assistance for the mobility-impaired. Many of the sights described in this guide are accessible. Those marked with the ♿ symbol offer at least partial access for wheelchairs. However, it is always best to phone ahead for details.

Getting There and Getting Around

BY PLANE

Airlines providing scheduled flights to Austria include: **Austrian Airlines** *(www.austrian.com)*, **Aer Lingus** *(www.aerlingus.com)*, **British Airways** *(www.ba.com)*, **British Midland** *(www.bmiregional.com)*, **easyJet** *(www.easyjet.com)*, **Eurowings** *(www. eurowings.com)*, **Flybe** *(www.flybe. com)*, **Jet2.com** *(www.jet2.com)*, **Niki** *(www.flyniki.com)* and **Ryanair** *(www. ryanair.com)*.

Although services to Graz, Klagenfurt, Linz, Salzburg and Innsbruck are increasing, most flights land at **Vienna International Airport** (Flughafen Wien-Schwechat), www.viennaairport. com (*see VIENNA*).

From North America the only direct flights are operated by **Austrian Airlines** and **United** *(www.united. com)*. Your options widen if you fly to another major European hub, such as London or Frankfurt, and catch a connecting flight there.

BY TRAIN

Austria is well served by rail from destinations throughout Europe. Coming from the UK, the easiest way is to catch the **Eurostar** *(www. eurostar.com)* from London-St. Pancras International to Brussels then the overnight City Night Line sleeper train to Munich for onward connections next morning to Innsbruck, Salzburg, Graz, Klagenfurt and Vienna. Take a lunchtime Eurostar to Brussels, a high-speed Thalys train to Cologne, then the equally efficient *EuroNight* sleeper train to Linz or Vienna, arriving in time for breakfast. For more details visit www.seat61.com/Austria.htm. A good source for tickets and information is **Rail Europe** *(www.raileurope. com)*. The website maintained by **Österreichische Bundesbahnen** (Austrian rail; *www.oebb.at*) has comprehensive timetable information and other details as well. Also visit www.austria.info/uk/travel-planning for an excellent overview of rail travel in Austria.

Steam engines and tourist trains
Steam engines and tourist trains operate in many regions year round, but predominantly during the summer season. These trains offer a pleasant and relaxing way to discover some of Austria's most beautiful natural regions. Further information is available from Erlebnis Bahn & Schiff Österreich *(www.erlebnis-bahn-schiff.at)*.

BY COACH/BUS

ÖBB Postbus *(www.postbus.at)* operates an extensive network across all of Austria, including some of the more remote areas. Prices are similar to those charged for rail travel.

BY CAR

Austria is linked to its neighbouring countries by fast and well-maintained highways. Coming from the UK, you can be just about anywhere in Austria in about 10 to 12 hours, depending on where you arrive on the Continent. Besides the Eurotunnel linking Folkestone with Coquelles near Calais (France), there is ferry service from Dover to Calais, from Hull and Rosyth (near Edinburgh) to Zeebrugge (Belgium), from Harwich to Hoek van Holland (Netherlands) and from Newcastle to Amsterdam.

Michelin offers a free and handy online route-planning service at www. viamichelin.com, which calculates distance, time and fuel consumption. **Motorail train** services (you load your car and yourself onto a train), operate between Vienna and Villach (372km/231mi), Vienna and Salzburg (317km/197mi), Vienna and Innsbruck (572km/355mi), Vienna and Feldkirch (731km/454mi), Graz and Feldkirch (607km/377mi) Villach and Feldkirch (466km/290mi) and Vienna and Lienz (476km/296mi). An hourly motorail

😊 Road Regulations 😊

- Traffic in Austria drives on the right and the minimum driving age is 18.
- Driving with the lights on at all times is now compulsory, as is the wearing of seat belts at all times, and the carrying of a first-aid kit, an emergency triangle, and a warning vest.
- Children under the age of 12 and less than 1.5m/4ft 11in tall must travel in appropriate and approved booster seats.
- The blood alcohol limit is 0.5ml/g.
- The use of cell (mobile) telephones inside a moving vehicle is only permitted if you have a hands-free set.
- Motorcyclists must wear a helmet.

shuttle also runs through the **Tauern tunnel** (Böckstein-Mallnitz, 8km/5mi). For further details, including fares, contact Österreichische Bundesbahnen (Austrian rail, *www.oebb.at*).

DOCUMENTS

You must carry a valid international driver's licence, and third-party insurance coverage is compulsory. Carrying the International Green Card from insurance companies may be helpful.

Speed Limits

Unless signposted otherwise, speed limits are 130kph/80mph on autobahns/highways, 100kph/62mph on country roads and 50kph/31mph in built-up areas. Private cars towing a load in excess of 750kg/1,650lb must not exceed 100kph/62mph on autobahns/highways, 80kph/50mph on country roads and 50kph/31mph in built-up areas.

BREAKDOWN SERVICE

This service is provided *(charge for non-members)* by two Austrian automobile clubs:

- **ÖAMTC** Österreichischer Automobil-, Motorrad-und Touring Club, Schubertring 1-3, A-1010 Wien, ℘01 711 99 10 200, breakdown number ℘120. www.oeamtc.at.
- **ARBÖ** Auto-, Motor-und Rad-fahrer-bund Österreich, Johann-Böhm-Platz 1, A-1020 Wien. ℘01 891 210, www.arboe.at, breakdown number ℘123.

ROAD TOLLS (MAUTGEBÜHREN)

Tolls are levied on autobahns, dual carriageways and urban highways in Austria. Drivers must buy a toll disc (*vignette*, or "Mautpickerl") and display it behind their windshield. Most hire cars will come with a *vignette* supplied; if not, they are available for 10 days (€8,80), 2 months (€25.70) or longer, and can be bought from Austrian motoring associations, larger petrol stations, post offices, tobacconists and at the border crossing points.

Additional Tolls

The following motorways and touristic roads and are not covered by the *vignette*:

- **Arlberg-Schnellstraße** €9.50
- **Brenner-Autobahn** €9 www.autobrennero.it
- **Dachsteinstraße** €14
- **Felbertauernstraße** €11 *www.*felbertauernstrasse.at
- **Gerlos Alpenstraße** €9 www.gerlosstrasse.at
- **Grossglockner Hochalpenstraße** €35. www.grossglockner.at
- **Karawankentunnel** €7
- **Maltatal-Hochalmstraße** €18.50
- **Nockalmstraße** €17.50 www.nockalmstrasse.at
- **Silvretta Hochalpenstraße** €15
- **Tauernautobahn** €11.50 www.tauerntunnel.de
- **Timmelsjoch Hochalpenstraße** €16. www.timmelsjoch.com

😊 Winter Road Closures 😊

In winter the following passes are either closed (as indicated with a **red star**), or simply not recommended for driving:

Seefelder Sattel★ (Innsbruck–Mittenwald); **Rottenmanner Tauern** (Oberes Murtal–Ennstal); **Aflenzer Seeberg** (Mariazell–Aflenz); **Präbichl** (Ennstal–Leoben); **Bielerhöhe★** (Silvrettastraße and Partenen–Galtür); **Hochtannbergpass** (Reutte–Dornbirn); **Timmelsjoch★** (Ötztal–Italy); **Gerlospass★** (Zell am Ziller–Zell am See); **Hochtor★** (Grossglockner–Hoch-alpenstraße); **Kartitsch-Sattel** (Kötschach-Sillian; **Radstädter Tauernpass** (Radstadt–St. Michael im Lungau), take the A10 instead; **Katschberg** (St. Michael im Lungau–Spittal an der Drau); **Turracher Höhe** (Murtal–Carinthian lakes); **Loibltunnel** (Klagenfurt–Slovenia); **Gaberl-Sattel★** (Oberes Murtal–Graz), not recommended in summer either; **Furkajoch** (Laterns–Damüls); **Grossglockner Hochalpenstraße** (Ferlei-ten–Heiligenblut). **Hahntennjoch** (Boden–Imst). **Sölker Pass** (Gröbming–Murau); **Timmelsjoch** (Obergurgl–St. Leonhard im Passeier Tal.

The following toll roads are closed at the points indicated:
Breitlahner Schlegeis-Stausee at Ginzling/Mayrhofen; **Maltatal Hochalmstraße** at Fallerhütte–Kölnbreinsperre; **Silvretta Hochalpenstraße** at Galtür–Partenen; **Sölden-Rettenbachstraße** at Ötztaler Gletscher; **Timmelsjochstraße** at Gurgl.

- **Villacher Alpenstraße** €16.50 www.villacher-alpenstrasse.at

ROUTE PLANNING
The **Michelin map 730** (scale 1:400,000) covers the entire country and gives details of likely road closures in winter. For online route planning, go to www.viamichelin.com.
The hikers' maps published by *Freytag Berndt* are useful for more detailed exploration.

TRAFFIC REPORTS
Traffic news on all of Austria as well as the main connecting roads to neighbouring countries are broadcast every half hour on the *Ö3* radio station (99.9 FM).

CAR RENTAL
Car-rental firms
- **Avis**: ☎0160 18 70, www.avis.at
- **Europcar**: ☎0810 91 19 11, www.europcar.co.at
- **Hertz**: ☎01 795 32, www.hertz.at
- **Sixt**: ☎0 08 10 977 424 (toll-free), *www.sixt.at*

CARAVANS
Some mountain roads have gradients steeper than 20% (1 in 5), as well as very narrow stretches. Steep gradients are indicated on **Michelin map 730**, which also gives dates of likely road closures in winter. Certain stretches of road, such as the approach roads to the Tauerntunnel, may be unsuitable for caravans because of heavy traffic. The table above indicates the most difficult stretches on the various access routes across the Alps (east to west).

DRIVING IN WINTER
In snowy conditions winter tyres should be fitted, or chains if conditions are particularly severe. The ÖAMTC and ARBÖ have snow-chain rental outlets in every Austrian province.

Where to Stay and Eat

WHERE TO STAY

HOTELS

Hotel and restaurant recommendations are listed throughout the Discovering section of this guide. See the cover flap for price ranges and for a description of the symbols used in the Addresses.

FARM HOLIDAYS

These vacations are popular in the Tyrol in particular, and they can often be combined with some sort of activity (e.g. horse riding). Themed holiday accommodations include organic farms and healthy farm holidays. Details are available from the Austrian National Tourist Office or from the Austrian Farm Holiday Association Urlaub am Bauernhof in Österreich (*www. farmholidays.com*).

CAMPING AND CARAVANING

Autria has about 500 campsites, many of which are open year-round. For lists of campsites, contact the following Austrian associations: Camping- und Caravanningclub Austria (CCA) (*www. campingfuehrer.at; also in English*) and the Österreichischer Campingclub (ÖCC) (*www.campingclub.at*).

YOUTH HOSTELS

Austria has about 70 youth hostels affiliated with Hostelling International. Staying here requires an HI membership card from your home country. Non-members need to buy a *Gästekarte* (guest card) for €3.50 per night from any hostel (though a card is free if you are under 15, costs €15 if you are 16–26, and €25 if you are older than 27, along with a one-time €1.50 membership fee). A family card costs €25. For locations check with the Austrian Youth Hostel Association (Österreichischer Jugendherbergsverband; www.oejhv.or.at).

"SCHLANK & SCHÖN"

Health, beauty treatments, stress management and relaxation are the goals of the "Schlank & Schön" ("Slim and Beautiful") organisation, which lists and spotlights accommodations offering wellness facilities and holidays. Their brochure may be available from the Austrian National Tourist Office or search online (*www. health-and-spa.at*).

MAP OF PLACES TO STAY

The map of places to stay shows the principal Austrian vacation resorts (spas, winter sports and mountain resorts).

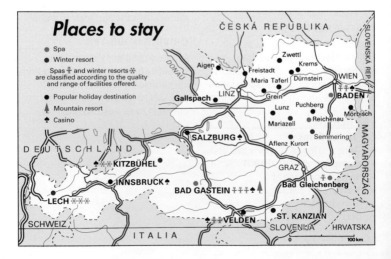

WHERE TO EAT

Specific restaurants in major cities are mentioned in the **Addresses** within the *Discovering* section of this guide. Restaurants tend to be rather formal places with crisp table linen and attentive service. For a more casual atmosphere, head to a Wirtshaus, Gasthof or a Gasthaus, which are traditional inns with a homey, authentic ambience.

In wine regions, the place to go for atmosphere is a Heurige, an earthy wine tavern where food is usually presented buffet style. Austria's famous Kaffeehäuser (cafés) also serve hot meals, while places called Café-Konditorei are best for sampling Austria's delicious cakes and pastries. Celebrated staples here include *Sachertorte*, a chocolate cake filled with apricot jam, and *Linzer Torte*, an almond pastry with red currant jam. Traditional Austrian cuisine is hearty fare, with dishes usually revolving around some cut of meat, potatoes, boiled vegetables and gravy. A full meal consists of three courses, often starting with a clear, flavour-packed soup. The best-known main course is *Wiener Schnitzel*, a thin slice of breaded veal panfried to a crispy, golden tan and served with a slice of lemon. Other classic dishes commonly found on menus are *Zwiebelrostbraten* (roast beef slices doused in fried onion slices); and *Backhendl* (fried breaded chicken).

Austrians truly excel when it comes to desserts. Sweet temptations include *Apfelstrudel* (apple strudel), flaky pastry filled with apples and raisins, sprinkled with powdered sugar, served hot or cold; and *Palatschinken*, a pancake filled with apricot jam or curd cheese.

Wine and beer are the most common beverages of choice. Many Austrians like to finish their meals with a Schnaps, a potent spirit usually flavoured with fruit.

MENU READER

Backhendl	Fried chicken in breadcrumbs
Baunzerl	White bread roll
Buchteln	Sweet dumplings cooked in milk and sugar
Blunzen	Black pudding
Erdäpfel	Potato
Faschiertes	Mince, meat balls
Fisolen	Green beans
Frittaten	Pancakes cut into strips and put in soups
Gansljunges	Dish made out of goose giblets
Geselchtes	Salted or smoked meats
Golatschen	Small, usually square, filled pastry
G'spritzter	Wine mixed with soda water
G'spritzter Obi	Apple juice mixed with soda water
Häuptlsalat	Lettuce
Hasenjunges	Jointed hare
Heuriger	Young wine (less than a year old) or the inn from which you obtain it
Hupfauf	Tirolean dessert
Indian gefüllt	Stuffed baby turkey
Jungfernbraten	Roast loin of pork with caraway seeds
Kaiserfleisch	Cured pork spare ribs
Kaiserschmarren	Dessert made with eggs and raisins

Karfiol	Cauliflower
Kohlsprossen	Brussels sprouts
Kracherl	Fruit-flavoured soft drink
Kren, Apfelkren	Horseradish, horseradish sauce with apples
Kukuruz	Sweetcorn
Marillen	Apricots
Nockerln	Dumplings
Obi	Apple juice
Palatschinken	Thin pancake filled with apricot jam or chocolate sauce
Paradeiser	Tomatoes
Powidl	Plum jam
Quargel	A type of cheese
Ribisel	Blackcurrants
Risibisi	Rice and peas
Schill	Perch
Schlagobers	Whipped cream
Schmankerl	Hot sweet pudding
Schöberl	Little biscuits (similar to croutons), put in soups
Schwämme, Schwammerln	Mushrooms
Seidel Lichtes	Small lager
Steirisches Schöpsernes	Styrian mutton dish
Strudel	Thin pastry roll with various fillings
Tafelspitz	Boiled beef and vegetable stew
Topfen	Type of cream cheese *(Quark)*

Basic Information

BUSINESS HOURS

Most shops are open Monday to Friday 9am to 6pm; on Thursday and Friday some are open until 9pm, and Saturday 9am to 1pm (til 6pm in Vienna and other bigger cities). Shops in tourist areas often remain open longer (Monday to Friday until 9pm, Saturday until 6pm, in some stations and airports daily until 11pm).

COMMUNICATIONS
INTERNET ACCESS

You will easily find cafés with Internet access in all Austrian cities. Many cafés, bars, inns, public spaces and buildings (such as airports or the Rathausplatz in Vienna) offer free Wi-Fi. Accommodations, from upmarket city business hotels to humble two-bedroom guesthouses in the countryside, are beginning to offer Internet access as standard.

MOBILE PHONES

The mobile phone market is highly competitive, with some of the cheapest rates in Europe.
If you intend on using a handset regularly while you are away, the cheapest option is to ensure you have a GSM phone compatible with the Austrian system as well as an Austrian SIM card (Austria, like most countries in the world, uses the 900 and 1800

MHz GSM bands). Austria has excellent phone coverage and unless you are in a very remote area, you should not have a problem with reception.

INTERNATIONAL CALLS

The international dialling code for Austria is 43, so to call from abroad dial +43, then the local code (minus the first zero), then the correspondent's number.

To call abroad from Austria, dial 00, then the appropriate international dialling code (Australia: 61; Canada: 1; Eire: 353; New Zealand: 64; UK: 44; USA: 1), then the local code (minus the first zero, if applicable), then the correspondent's number.

NATIONAL CALLS

There are no standard lengths for telephone numbers in Austria, and some numbers may be as short as three digits. Larger towns have shorter area codes permitting longer subscriber numbers in that area.
Telephone cards (*Telefon-Wertkarte*) for pay phones are on sale at post offices and Tabaktrafiken.

DISCOUNTS AND PASSES

The following cities and regions offer special discount tickets covering a range of leisure and cultural activities, as well as transport: Innsbruck, Carinthia, Linz, Salzburg and Vienna (*see Tourist Information, if applicable, within each entry*).

RAIL PASSES

For EU citizens the **Vorteils** rail card (www.oebb.at) at €99 (under 26 years old €19; seniors €29) is worth considering. For the period of one year it entitles the holder to reductions of 50 percent on standard fares within the ÖBB network and most private lines. For trips outside Austria, the discount is 25 percent. Holders also qualify for cheaper rates in sleeper cars, free bicycle transportation and other benefits.

If you're not an EU citizen and you're planning rail travel within Austria,

the **Eurail Austria Pass** (www.eurail. com) offers unlimited train travel on the entire network of Österreichische Bundesbahnen for 3–8 days within a one-month period. Children age 6–11, as well as children under 6 for whom a seat is required, travel at 50 percent of the adult fare. Prices start at €159 (in second-class carriages) for 3 days. First-class travel starts at €198 for 3 days. The Pass can be purchased only outside Europe at a travel agency and must then be validated by the ÖBB before travel.

For further details on both cards and more discount options, check www.oebb.at.

ELECTRICITY

Voltage in Austria is 220V, 50Hz. The standard European 2-pin plug is used for electrical appliances. An adaptor may be required.

EMERGENCIES

Emergency number 112
Fire 122
Police 133
Ambulance 144
Breakdown service 120 or **123**
Mountain Rescue 140

MAIL/POST

Post offices (where currency can also be changed) are generally open Monday to Friday 8am–noon and 2pm–6pm. Cash desks close at 5pm. A small number of post offices open on Saturday 8am–noon. In major cities, one or two post offices may keep longer hours or even stay open 24hr, including at weekends. Stamps are also sold at *Tabaktrafiken* (tobacconists).

POSTAGE VIA AIR MAIL TO:		
UK	Letter	(20g) 0.65 €
North America	Letter	(20g) 1.40 €
Australia	Letter	(20g) 1.40 €
New Zealand	Letter	(20g) 1.40 €

Letters addressed to a destination in Austria should indicate the international abbreviation 'A' in front of the post code.

MONEY

CURRENCY

There are no restrictions on the amount of currency visitors can take into Austria. Visitors carrying a lot of cash (equal to or exceeding €10,000) are advised to complete a currency declaration form on arrival, because there are restrictions on currency export.

NOTES AND COINS

The **euro** is the only currency accepted as a means of payment in Austria. It is divided into 100 cents, or centimes. Euros come in seven notes (5, 10, 20, 50, 100, 200 and 500 euros) and eight coins (1 and 2 euro coins and 1, 2, 5, 10, 20 and 50 cent coins).

BANKS

Banks are generally open 8am–12:30pm and 1:30pm–3pm on Monday, Tuesday, Wednesday and Friday, and 8am–12:30pm and 1:30pm–5:30pm on Thursday. A passport is necessary as identification when cashing travellers' cheques in banks. Commission charges vary and hotels usually charge more than banks for cashing cheques. One of the most economical ways to access your money in Austria is by using **ATM machines** to get cash directly from your bank account; bank charges vary. Major credit cards such as Visa and MasterCard are generally accepted throughout Austria, although you should always check before making your purchases.

TAX

In Austria a sales tax is added to almost all retail goods, and although it is included in the price the amount will be stated on the bill, e.g. '20% Mwst. inklusive' ('20 percent VAT included'). Tax refunds are available only to visitors from outside the EU for each item that exceeds €75. Ask the shop for a form, and on completion of it at your point of departure (e.g. at the airport), you will then be reimbursed the 20 percent tax, unfortunately *less* a hefty administrative charge that will reduce your reimbursment to nearer 15 percent of the purchase price.

PUBLIC HOLIDAYS

1 January (New Year's Day), **6 January** (Epiphany), **Easter Monday**, **1 May** (Labor Day), **Ascension Day**, **Whit Monday**, **Corpus Christi**, **15 August** (Assumption of the Virgin Mary), **26 October** (Austrian National Holiday), **1 November** (All Saints' Day), **8 December** (Immaculate Conception), **25 and 26 December** (Christmas).

SMOKING

No smoking is allowed in any public places.

TIME

Austria is on Central European Time (GMT +1hr). Clocks move forward one hour on the last Sunday of March and move back the last Sunday of October.

WHEN IT IS NOON IN AUSTRIA, IT IS	
3am	in Los Angeles
6am	in New York
11am	in Dublin
11am	in London
7pm	in Perth
9pm	in Sydney
11pm	in Auckland
In Austria "am" and "pm" are not used but the 24-hour clock is widely applied.	

TIPPING

Tipping is customary in Austria, especially in restaurants, cafés and bars where you should tip about 10 percent. Taxi drivers, hairdressers, hotel housekeeping and other service staff also appreciate a small tip.

CONVERSION TABLES

Weights and Measures

1 kilogram (kg) 6.35 kilograms 0.45 kilograms	2.2 pounds (lb) 14 pounds 16 ounces (oz)	2.2 pounds 1 stone (st) 16 ounces	*To convert kilograms to pounds, multiply by 2.2*
1 metric ton (tn)	1.1 tons	1.1 tons	
1 litre (l) 3.79 litres 4.55 litres	2.11 pints (pt) 1 gallon (gal) 1.20 gallon	1.76 pints 0.83 gallon 1 gallon	*To convert litres to gallons, multiply by 0.26 (US) or 0.22 (UK)*
1 hectare (ha) 1 sq kilometre (km²)	2.47 acres 0.38 sq. miles (sq mi)	2.47 acres 0.38 sq. miles	*To convert hectares to acres, multiply by 2.4*
1 centimetre (cm) 1 metre (m)	0.39 inches (in) 3.28 feet (ft) or 39.37 inches or 1.09 yards (yd)	0.39 inches	*To convert metres to feet, multiply by 3.28; for kilometres to miles, multiply by 0.6*
1 kilometre (km)	0.62 miles (mi)	0.62 miles	

Clothing

Women	☆	▬	⊕
	35	4	2½
	36	5	3½
	37	6	4½
Shoes	38	7	5½
	39	8	6½
	40	9	7½
	41	10	8½
	36	6	8
	38	8	10
Dresses	40	10	12
& suits	42	12	14
	44	14	16
	46	16	18
	36	6	30
	38	8	32
Blouses &	40	10	34
sweaters	42	12	36
	44	14	38
	46	16	40

Men	☆	▬	⊕
	40	7½	7
	41	8½	8
	42	9½	9
Shoes	43	10½	10
	44	11½	11
	45	12½	12
	46	13½	13
	46	36	36
	48	38	38
Suits	50	40	40
	52	42	42
	54	44	44
	56	46	48
	37	14½	14½
	38	15	15
Shirts	39	15½	15½
	40	15¾	15¾
	41	16	16
	42	16½	16½

Sizes often vary depending on the designer. These equivalents are given for guidance only.

Speed

KPH	10	30	50	70	80	90	100	110	120	130
MPH	6	19	31	43	50	56	62	68	75	81

Temperature

Celsius (°C)	0°	5°	10°	15°	20°	25°	30°	40°	60°	80°	100°
Fahrenheit (°F)	32°	41°	50°	59°	68°	77°	86°	104°	140°	176°	212°

To convert Celsius into Fahrenheit, multiply °C by 9, divide by 5, and add 32.
To convert Fahrenheit into Celsius, subtract 32 from °F, multiply by 5, and divide by 9.
NB: Conversion factors on this page are approximate.

Main Staircase,
Kunsthistorisches Museum, Vienna
© Ludovic Maisant/hemis.fr

Austria Today

Austria has a population of 8.7 million people, about a quarter of whom live in Vienna and its hinterland in Lower Austria. Only four other cities have more than 100,000 inhabitants: Graz, Linz, Salzburg and Innsbruck. Austria has a population density of 104 people per sq km, lower than the European average (France: 122sq km/316sq mi, Germany: 234sq km/606sq mi). Almost 98% of Austrians speak German as their first language, and there are six recognised ethnic minorities: Slovenes, Croatians, Hungarians, Czechs, Slovaks and Romani. Around 60% of the population is Roman Catholic; only 3.5% is Protestant, somewhat less than Muslims at 6.8%.

THE ECONOMY

Austria has been a member of the European Union (EU) since January 1995. It has been implementing the Schengen Agreement since 1998 and joined the European Monetary Union in 1999. The euro has been the official currency since January 2002. In 2015, Austria's gross domestic product (GDP) was 340 billion euros; in 2017 GDP is estimated to be 359 billion euros.

AGRICULTURE AND FORESTRY

Although vast areas of mountainous land in Austria are not suitable for cultivation, **agriculture** is an important sector of the Austrian economy, providing for almost 80% of national food requirements. About 8% of the country's workforce are employed in agriculture and forestry. In 2010, there were still 150,170 farm and forestry businesses, although the majority were smaller than 19ha/47 acres.

Forests represent one of Austria's richest natural resources. Consisting mostly of coniferous trees, they cover about 48% of the country's total surface area – a statistic surpassed within Europe only by Sweden and Finland. In 2014, 17 million cu m/600cu ft of timber were felled. Agriculture and forestry represent less than 2% of gross domestic product.

NATURAL RESOURCES AND INDUSTRY

The break-up of the Austro-Hungarian Empire in 1919 cut Austria off from its traditional markets and some of its raw material sources. The situation was exacerbated by the fact that in the 19C Austrian industry had been focused purely on meeting the needs of its own huge empire instead of gearing up to compete in international markets.

These days, however, Austria is ranked the 16th wealthiest country in the world (measured by gross domestic product per capita) and ranks as a highly developed industrial power with a significant services industry sector.

Energy sources

As a mountainous country laced by numerous rivers, Austria is a major producer of **hydroelectric power**. Most of its domestic energy requirements are met by the output from 22 hydroelectric power plants. Those along the Danube alone generate a quarter of the state electricity production.

Oil is a natural resource that has been developed since 1937. It still plays a role in the Austrian economy, with production holding more or less steady at just over 1 million tons per year. Most oil fields cluster northeast of Vienna, in the Vienna Basin, which accounts for 95% of the country's oil production. The single largest field is in Matzen. The remaining 5% come from fields in Upper Austria, near Salzburg. The oil is refined at Schwechat near Vienna, which has a capacity of just below 10 million tons. In addition to domestic oil, it also processes imported crude oil, which travels to Schwechat via the Adria-Wien-Pipeline (AWP). A branch of the huge Transalpine Ölleitung (TAL; Trieste to Ingolstadt in Germany), the pipeline runs from Trieste in Italy to Vienna.

Natural gas from Austria's oilfields is highly prized by the country's industrial concerns. Production hovers

around 2 billion cu m/70 billion cu ft annually. To meet national demand, an additional 6 billion cu m /212 billion cu ft has to be imported each year, mainly from Russia.

MINING AND HEAVY INDUSTRY

Austria is a country with a long tradition in mining and heavy industry. In the Tirol especially, gold, silver and copper were mined intensively up to the 17C. Salt mining and the mining of non-ferrous minerals are still carried out today. In fact, Austria is among the world's most important producers of **magnesite**, a mineral used in fireproofing blast furnaces and smelting ovens; and also in construction work.

Of key importance to **heavy industry** in Austria is production in the metallurgical basin in Styria, home of the well-known Erzberg (Iron Mountain). The biggest opencast mine in Europe, it ships about 6,000 tons of iron ore daily to the blast furnaces of Donawitz, which produce steel sections, and to those of Linz, which produce sheet metal.

SALT MINING

Salt mining is now only of minor importance. Nonetheless, since prehistoric times the precious mineral has played such a key role in the civilization of the eastern Alps that it's hard to overlook the various enterprises still operating in the Salzburg area. The salt waters of numerous spa resorts such as Bad Aussee, Bad Ischl and Hall in Tirol continue to be prized in the treatment of a variety of illnesses. Place names often include the prefix *Salz* or *Hall* – synonymous terms meaning salt or salt works. Touring a salt mine is a memorable experience. Tour guides are often former miners who adhere faithfully to their traditional vocabulary – the greeting *"Glück auf!"* (Hope you come up again!) is still heard. Many also wear their dress uniform and regale you with tales about the underground world.

Melting mountains

Except in the natural springs (*Solequellen*) of Bad Reichenhall in Germany, the mineral deposits in the Salzburg region consist of a mixture, called *Haselgebirge*, of salt, clay and gypsum. The miners begin by making a pit in the bed, which they flood and keep supplied regularly with fresh water. This water dissolves the rock on the spot and so, being saturated with salt (27%), sinks to the bottom of the basin, where it can be pumped, while impurities are left behind.

Modern methods of extraction involve the drilling of boreholes and the dissolving of the deposit by the injection of hot water. The brine (*Sole*) is brought to the surface and pumped into the vats of the salt factories (*Sudhütten*), to be processed into either domestic or industrial salt.

The first pipelines

By the 17C much of the forest around the salt mines had been burnt as fuel in the furnaces. Such burning, coupled with the remoteness of many of the mines, led to attempts by the authorities to relocate the centres of salt production closer to the markets. This effort involved the construction of impressive lengths of pipeline made of timber, lead or cast iron, to bring the brine down from the mountains to the lowlands. The longest of these, **Soleleitungen** ran 79km/49mi from Bad Reichenhall to Rosenheim in Bavaria and was in use from 1810 to 1958. Pumping stations (*Brunnhäuser*) kept up a constant flow of brine. To prevent too sudden a drop, the aqueducts included long mountainside sections, as in the water-conduits *(bisses)* of the Swiss Valais. The footpaths *(Soleleitungswege)* paralleling them made splendid corniche routes. The mine road from Hallstatt to Bad Ischl, for instance, clings dramatically to the mountainside above the lake of Hallstatt.

When the salt had been refined, it was shipped by river – on the Inn below Hall in Tirol and the Lower Traun – or in carts. Many salt roads *(Salzstraßen)* in Austria recall memories of this traffic, so fruitful for the country's economy and the public treasury. One of the best known is the Ellbögener Straße (🔊*see INNSBRUCK: Tour of the Mittelgebirge).*

OTHER MAJOR ECONOMIC ACTIVITIES

Austria's most important and internationally competitive industry sectors are the machine building and steel industries, chemicals and textiles; and engine and automobile parts manufacture, most of it for export. Austria also has international standing in the production of electronic components such as microchips and integrated circuits (it produces components for Airbus and high-speed trains). In general, Austrian industry is strongly export-oriented. About two-thirds of its foreign trade is conducted with fellow European Union countries. The most important customer is Germany, which accounts for one-third of exports.

Food production, especially the luxury food sector, contributes about 3.5% of GDP and principally caters to domestic consumption. The largest proportion of gross domestic product, around 70%, is generated by the services industry.

TOURISM

Austria is a tourist destination par excellence, offering magnificent scenery, major historical monuments, a wide range of leisure opportunities year-round, and an outstanding tourist infrastructure. Tourism is extremely important to the Austrian economy both in terms of job creation and as a source of revenue. In 2015, it generated about **45**.7 billion euros, contributing 13.5% to the GDP. The number of foreign visitors in 2015 was 26.7 million, the majority of whom were German and Dutch. Traditionally, the Tyrol attracts most visitors from home and abroad, followed by Salzburg and Carinthia.

TRADITIONS AND CUSTOMS
RELIGIOUS BELIEFS

Austria is a country steeped in tradition. Old customs are kept very much alive, particularly in rural communities. A deeply rooted religious faith has left its mark on town and countryside alike.

Roofed crosses *(Wiesenkreuze)*, set up at the roadside or in the middle of a field, are thus a common feature of Austria's rural landscape and particularly prevalent in the Tyrol.

A familiar sight in Carinthia is a post *(Bildstock)* with a little roof protecting a faceted pole decorated with paintings of Biblical scenes. Crucifixes are usually displayed inside Austrian homes, in a part of the house called the *Herrgottswinkel* (God's corner). These are especially prevalent in the Tyrol where you'll find them in virtually every house, including guest houses and inns.

Religious figures are also a common subject for the paintings to be found on many an Austrian façade *(Lüftlmalerei)*: St. Florian features particularly prominently in these in his role as protector against fire. Another popular figure is St. George, the dragon slayer. You may also come across churches containing an enormous painting of St. Christopher (such as in Imst). These arose in response to the popular belief that looking at the image of this saint would protect the viewer from a violent death for another day.

The figure of St. John of Nepomuk is often to be found adorning bridges and fountains, of which he is the patron saint (having been martyred by being thrown off a bridge in Prague – 🔊*see p167).*

A CUSTOM FOR ALL SEASONS

🔊*See Calendar of Events.*
The year begins with processions of masked *Perchten* accompanying St.

Nicholas through the villages during the "bitter nights" leading up to Epiphany on 6 January. The costumed figures representing good and evil spirits can be beautiful or ugly – the latter are usually clad with shaggy fur and wearing scary horned masks – and are supposed to banish the cold and dark of winter and bring fertility and blessings for the coming year. The feast of the Epiphany itself brings Christmas celebrations to a close by commemorating the journey of the Three Kings guided by the Star of Bethlehem. Festivities involve children's carol singing and processions (Sternsingen and Dreikönigsritte). In some places, locals parade around sporting giant head-dresses decorated with bells (Glöcklerläufe).

Carnival time, or **Fasching** (Fasnacht in western Austria), is ushered in as early as January in Vienna with the start of the ball season. Elsewhere, Fasching is celebrated with traditional carnival parades, to which a colourful note is added by the masks handed down from generation to generation. Some of the most famous of these parades include those in the Tyrol, at Imst (Imster Schemen) and, every five years, in Telfs (Schleicherlaufen); the Bad Aussee carnival with its original and colourful Trommelweiber and Flinserln; and the Fetzenfasching in Ebensee.

Palm Sunday is marked by the blessing of the "palm branches" – generally willow catkins or box. This is closely followed by May Day celebrations (May 1), complete with maypole (Maibaum), climbing competitions (Maibaumraxeln) and dancing. June sees more processions, which vary according to the particular traditions of the region: carrying 8–10m/25–33ft wooden poles wound around with garlands of fresh flowers in areas of Salzburg (Prangstangen) such as Muhr (29 June) and Zederhaus (24 June); laying down a carpet of flowers (Blumenteppich) in Deutschlandsberg; processions on horseback, as in Brixental in Tyrol, or on water, as in Traunkirchen and Hallstatt. In August, Murau and Krakaudorf in Styria are the scenes of Samsonumzüge – parades involving a giant 5m/16ft

figure of Samson carried by one man. This show of strength was believed in the 17C and 18C to protect the religious procession. In August and September many communities celebrate the consecration of their local church (Kirtag) with a fair. Autumn is the time for the Harvest Festival (Erntedankfest) season. This is also when the livestock is brought down from the mountain pastures to its winter quarters.

The feast of St. Hubert is celebrated on November 3 (church services, parades on horseback, etc.), while St. Leonard (patron saint of livestock) is honoured on November 6. A few days later, on November 11, the feast of St. Martin brightens up the dark winter nights with torchlit processions. The periods of Advent and Christmas make December full of events, from the feast of St. Nicholas (6 December), with the Nikolospiel parade in Bad Mitterndorf, through to the Nativity scenes displayed in public sites and inside people's homes.

TRADITIONAL COSTUMES

Although traditional local costumes are rarely worn as a daily outfit any more, they occasionally make an appearance at religious and local festivals.

The velvet corsages of the women of Bad Ischl, the embroidered silk blouses of those from the Wachau, the colourful, ribbon-laced bodices of the Montafon, the finely pleated costumes of the Bregenzerwald and the lace aprons of the Burgenland are all evidence of a rich tradition of local folklore. Men wear leather or Loden wool breeches (tight at the knee) or shorts (which are less restrictive for the brisk movements of Tyrolean dancing), wide braces with a decorated chest panel, and short, collarless jackets. The shape of the hat indicates the region its wearer comes from.

The traditional **dirndl** (pleated skirt, pastel coloured apron, full white blouse with short puffed sleeves and a buttoned or laced bodice) and the Steirer Anzug ("Alpine dinner jacket," consisting of grey or brown Loden breeches embroidered in green, white socks and a long, flared coat with green embroidery

House built around a square courtyard
in the Mühlviertel (Upper Austria)

Traditional Austrian houses

House in the Bregenzerwald
(Vorarlberg)

Tyrolean country chalet

Rural estate in Lower Austria

M. Guillou/MICHELIN

and gilt buttons) are not that common a sight these days. However, they are the original inspiration behind the so-called "traditional Austrian look," which combines modern styles with traditional decorative features and natural materials such as linen, cotton, felt and heavy, water-resistant sheep's wool (Loden).

RURAL SCENERY

Fences woven from laths were once the most common style delimiting fields in the Salzburg, Tennengau and Pinzgau regions, but they are increasingly rare. Still, it is not unusual to see farmers piling hay at harvest time onto special drying racks made of metal wire or wooden stakes, to keep it off the damp ground while it is drying.

In the Carinthian Alps, grains are grown on the sunny slopes up to a height of 1,500m/4,500ft, but the harvest often has to be gathered early to avoid frost. The sheaves are spread out on wooden dryers with horizontal struts, sometimes covered, so the grain is able to ripen.

URBAN SETTLEMENT

In Styria, Carinthia and the Danubian countryside the most interesting examples of urban development usually sprouted around the main road. When a town was first developed, the old road was widened to form a sort of esplanade, known as the **Anger**.

When all the land on each side of the Anger was built over, the resulting form was known as a **Strassenplatz** (street-square). These street-squares, shaped like spindles or regular oblong rectangles, form the heart of the town, approached by the once fortified gateways.

The square, which is often called Hauptplatz, is usually dotted with fountains and columns, such as the **Pestsäule** (Plague Column) set up to commemorate the victims of a plague.

FOOD AND DRINK

Austrian cooking draws from the culinary traditions of the different peoples who once formed the old Empire: German, Italian, Hungarian, Serb and Czech.

AUSTRIAN COOKING

Soup is served first, followed by the main dish, almost always consisting of meat, fried in breadcrumbs or boiled, accompanied by salad and stewed fruit (such as bilberries: Preiselbeeren). Dumplings (Knödel) made of liver or flour may be served instead of vegetables. Middle Eastern influences can be detected in the liberal use of spices in many Austrian dishes.

Meat

The most famous dish (Wiener Schnitzel) is thin fillet of veal, dusted with egg and breadcrumbs and fried in butter; it's often served with potato salad. Goulash is a highly-flavored stew of Hungarian origin, spiced with red pepper or paprika and garnished with tomatoes, onions and potatoes. In Graz and Styria, duck or chicken, fried in egg and breadcrumbs, is delicious. Game of all kinds is widely available in season.

Dessert

Austrians are famous for the variety of their desserts. The most famous cake, the Sachertorte, invented by Prince Metternich's chef, has a subtle and delicate flavor. It is a large, rich chocolate cake covered with chocolate icing above a thin layer of apricot jam; the original recipe remains a secret (but everyone offers a version of it). Other favourites include a jam tart (Linzertorte), consisting of pastry made with almonds, filled with apricot or raspberry jam and covered with a pastry lattice; a turnover (Strudel) filled with apples, cherries or cream cheese and currants; plum or apricot fritters; and a sweet soufflé (Salzburger Nockerl).

AUSTRIAN WINE

Vineyards cover about 52,500ha/ 129,730 acres in Lower Austria, on the slopes near Vienna, in the Burgenland and in Styria. White wine (66%) is more popular than red, with 37% of Austria's vineyards devoted to the Grüner Veltliner grape. Average annual production is 2.5 million hectoliters/66 million gallons, of which upwards of a third is exported.

White Wines

Well-known Austrian white vintages include Grüner Veltliner, Müller-Thurgau and Welschriesling. Most vintages yield pleasant table wines which are often light and slightly sparkling. New wine, made that year, is drunk in the typical wine taverns called *Heurige* or *Buschenschenken* (&see p182). The district of Wachau in the Danube Valley produces wines with a delicate bouquet (Spitz, Dürnstein, Weissenkirchen, Krems, Langenlois). Grinzing, the most famous of Vienna's suburban wine villages, makes a pleasant sparkling wine.

Red Wines

The red wines, especially the Blauer Portugieser and Blaufränkischer, are of high quality. In Lower Austria, the best-known wines are those from Bad Vöslau, south of Vienna, from Retz (the Retz wine is known as *Spezi* – not to be confused with the popular cola- and orange-mix drink of the same name!), from Haugsdorf and from Matzen, in the Weinviertel. In the Burgenland the wines of Pöttelsdorf, Oggau and particularly Rust, and in Styria those of Leibnitz, have a good reputation.

Wine Regions

Austria is divided into four official wine regions: The Niederösterreich (Lower Austria); Steierland (Styria); Wien (Vienna); and Burgenland (Upper Austria). Niederösterreich alone accounts for 27,128 ha/67,034 acres of Austria's total wine production area, while Wien, the smallest, covers only 612 ha/1,512 acres. The regions are further subdivided into 16 wine-growing areas, of which the Weinviertel, the Neusiedlersee and the Neusiedlersee-Hügelland are the most important.

The best way to get acquainted with Austrian wine is by exploring the country's wine routes. The most famous of these is the Lower Austria Wine Route, an 830km/518mi-long ribbon meandering through the wonderful countryside of the Carnuntum, Weinviertel, Wachau, Thermenregion, Donauland, Kamptal, Traisental and Kremstal growing areas. A section of this route is described in some detail under Östliches Weinviertel (&see p240). Styria has eight wine routes, described under Steirische Weinstraße. (&see STEIRISCHE WEINSTRAßE p284). For details, consult www.austrianwine.com.

History

TIME LINE

The main events since the rise of the Habsburgs are briefly described below.

THE HABSBURGS

1273–1291 Rudolf I, founder of the Habsburg dynasty, is elected by the German princes to succeed the Babenbergs, defeats King Ottokar of Bohemia and divides Austria and Styria between his sons.

1335 Carinthia and Carniola (the area around Ljubljana) are annexed to the Habsburg territory.

1358–65 Reign of **Rudolf IV**. The Tirol is annexed to Austria (1363).

1440–93 Friedrich III, Duke of Styria, inaugurates a policy of political succession and intermarriage that raises the Habsburgs to the highest rank in the west. His son, Maximilian, is the first to benefit from this status.

EXPANSION OF THE HABSBURG EMPIRE

1493–1519 By his marriage to Mary, the daughter of Charles the Bold, **Maximilian I**, Emperor of the Holy Roman Empire, gains possession of the Burgundian states. He marries his son Philip the Fair to Joanna of Castile.

Their son, Charles V, inherits all of their possessions.

1519–56 Reign of **Emperor Charles V**. Vienna is besieged by the Turks (1529).

1556 Abdication of Charles V and partition of the Empire. Charles' brother, Ferdinand I, becomes Emperor and head of the Austrian branch of the House of Habsburg. He founds the Austrian Monarchy and also reigns over Bohemia and Hungary. Charles' son, Philip II, is given Spain, Portugal, Sicily, Naples and northern Italy, the Low Countries and Burgundy.

1618–48 Thirty Years' War begins as a religious conflict and ends as a Europe-wide power struggle.

CONSOLIDATION OF THE AUSTRIAN EMPIRE

1657–1705 Reign of Leopold I. Vienna is again besieged by the Turks (1683). Turks retreat from Hungary, which falls to the Habsburgs (1687).

18C Throughout this century, Austrian policy is overshadowed by three great problems: the Succession to the Empire; the territorial threat from the Turks, the Piedmontese and the French; and the unified administration of very different countries.

1713 In the absence of male heirs, Charles VI sacrifices territorial rights to the great European powers and issues the edict of the Pragmatic Sanction to ensure his daughter's succession. Still, when he dies, Maria Theresia has to fight off its signatories in order to keep her empire: the War of the Austrian Succession (1740–48) is followed by the Seven Years War (1756–63).

1740–90 Reign of **Maria Theresia** (1740–65). With the help of able ministers, she becomes popular for her financial and administrative reforms. Reign of **Joseph II** (1765–90) who, in the authoritarian manner of enlightened despotism, continues the reorganisation begun by his mother.

1781 Abolition of serfdom.

1786 Dissolution of the lay power of 738 monasteries and abbeys under Joseph II.

1792–1835 Reign of **Franz II**. After defeats by Napoleon in Ulm and Austerlitz, Austria signs the **Treaty of Pressburg**. Franz II renounces the title of Holy Roman Emperor and adopts that of **Franz I**, Emperor of Austria. He receives the territory of the archbishops of Salzburg as compensation.

1809 Austrian policy, particularly foreign policy, is directed by Chancellor **Metternich** who seeks revenge against France. Andreas Hofer leads the Tyrolean rebellion against the Franco-Bavarian alliance.

DOWNFALL OF THE MONARCHY

1814–15 **Congress of Vienna** redraws the map of Europe. Austria recovers Lombardy and Venetia, lost in wars with France, and takes a leading position in the Germanic Confederation, of which Metternich is the mastermind.

1848–49 March Revolution in Vienna. Fall of Metternich, Hungarian rebellion is suppressed with the help of Russia.

1848–1916 Reign of **Franz Joseph**.

1866 War between Austria and Prussia. Austria is defeated, gives up on intervening in German politics and looks towards the Balkans.

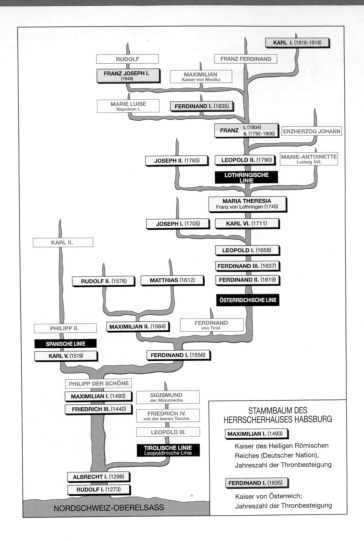

KARL I. (1916-1918)

FRANZ FERDINAND

RUDOLF

FRANZ JOSEPH I. (1848)

MAXIMILIAN
Kaiser von Mexiko

MARIE LUISE
Napoleon I.

FERDINAND I. (1835)

FRANZ I. (1804) II. (1792-1806)

ERZHERZOG JOHANN

JOSEPH II. (1765)

LEOPOLD II. (1790)

MARIE-ANTOINETTE
Ludwig XVI.

LOTHRINGISCHE LINIE

MARIA THERESIA
Franz von Lothringen (1745)

JOSEPH I. (1705)

KARL VI. (1711)

KARL II.

LEOPOLD I. (1658)

FERDINAND III. (1637)

RUDOLF II. (1576)

MATTHIAS (1612)

FERDINAND II. (1619)

ÖSTERREICHISCHE LINIE

PHILIPP II.

MAXIMILIAN II. (1564)

FERDINAND
von Tirol

SPANISCHE LINIE

KARL V. (1519)

FERDINAND I. (1556)

PHILIPP DER SCHÖNE

MAXIMILIAN I. (1493)

SIGISMUND
der Münzreiche

FRIEDRICH III. (1440)

FRIEDRICH IV.
mit der leeren Tasche

LEOPOLD III.

TIROLISCHE LINIE
Leopoldinische Linie

ALBRECHT I. (1298)

RUDOLF I. (1273)

NORDSCHWEIZ-OBERELSASS

STAMMBAUM DES
HERRSCHERHAUSES HABSBURG

MAXIMILIAN I. (1493)

Kaiser des Heiligen Römischen
Reiches (Deutscher Nation),
Jahreszahl der Thronbesteigung

FERDINAND I. (1835)

Kaiser von Österreich;
Jahreszahl der Thronbesteigung

1867 Creation of the dual Austro-Hungarian monarchy, with common foreign, defence and economic policies.

1914 Outbreak of World War I (1914–18), triggered by the assassination of Crown Prince Franz Ferdinand at Sarajevo in Bosnia and Austria's subsequent attack on Serbia.

1916–18 Reign of **Karl I**. Collapse of the Austro-Hungarian monarchy after defeat in the World War I.

THE REPUBLIC

1919 The **Treaty of St. Germain-en-Laye** among the Allies and the new Republic of Austria draws its national border, ceding South Tirol to Italy. Following a plebiscite (1920), southern Carinthia remains in Austria and is not to be ceded to the then Yugoslavia, but a Vorarlberg vote to join Switzerland (82%) is ignored. Women are given the vote.

1920 Federal constitution is passed.

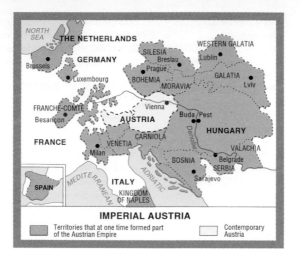

NORTH SEA
THE NETHERLANDS
Brussels
GERMANY
Luxembourg
SILESIA
Breslau
Prague
BOHEMIA
MORAVIA
WESTERN GALATIA
Lublin
GALATIA
Lviv
FRANCHE-COMTE
Besançon
Vienna
AUSTRIA
Buda Pest
HUNGARY
FRANCE
CARNIOLA
Danube
VENETIA
Milan
VALACHIA
Belgrade
SERBIA
BOSNIA
Sarajevo
SPAIN
MEDITERRANEAN
ITALY
KINGDOM OF NAPLES
ADRIATIC

IMPERIAL AUSTRIA

Territories that at one time formed part of the Austrian Empire — Contemporary Austria

1933	Chancellor **Engelbert Dollfuss** inaugurates an authoritarian regime, hostile both to the Social Democrats and to the Nazis.
1934	Social Democratic Party banned. Suppression of Nazi putsch. Assassination of Dollfuss. His successor seeks to avoid war with Germany at all costs.
1938	Hitler annexes Austria to the German Reich. Austrians approve the annexation (**Anschluss**) in a referendum.
1939–45	World War II.
1943	In the Moscow Declaration, the Allies undertake to restore Austria's independence after the war and restore the pre-Anschluss frontiers.
1945	The Russians occupy Vienna on 11 April. On 27 April, a new government forms, led by Karl Renner. Austria and Vienna are divided into four occupied zones.
1949–66	A Grand Coalition government is formed by the "People's Party" (ÖVP) and the Social Democrats (SPÖ).

15 May 1955	Following the **Staatsvertrag** treaty, occupying troops withdraw from Austria.
26 Oct 1955	Austria declares its neutrality.
1956	Austria is accepted into the Council of Europe.
1970–83	Social Democrats form a government under Chancellor Bruno Kreisky, for the first time with an absolute majority in Parliament.
1983–2000	Government is formed again by a Grand Coalition.
1986-1992	Kurt Waldheim becomes Austria's president. Questions over his wartime role in the deportation of Salonica's Jews make him a *persona non grata* in the US. He is not invited to visit any other Western Country.
1989	Death of Zita of Bourbon-Parma, last Empress of Austria in exile since 1919.
Jan 1995	Austria joins the **European Union**.
1998	Austria is admitted to the European Monetary Union.
2000-7	Coalition government formed by the ÖVP and the right-wing Austrian Freedom Party (FPÖ, later BZÖ). EU

briefly imposes sanctions in protest.

2004 Heinz Fischer is sworn in as Austria's new president. Pope John Paul II beatifies the last Habsburg emperor, Karl I.

2007 After the 2006 election, Austria is ruled by a new Grand Coalition headed by Chancellor Dr. Alfred Gusenbauer (SPÖ).

2008 Austria and Switzerland host jointly the European soccer Championship.

Sept 2008 The Grand Coalition fails, leading to a snap election in which the far right parties win big. BZÖ leader and Carinthian governor Jörg Haider dies in a car accident soon after.

2010 British sculptor Anthony Gormley's *Horizon Field* of 100 human figures placed across 150sq km/58sq mi of the Austrian Alps.

2011 Corruption allegations rock the political establishment.

2013 Austria, and other parts of Europe experience the wettest May in 156 years, with rains causing severe flooding in many regions.

2014 Vienna's new Hauptbahnhof (railway station) opens after 7 years of construction at a cost of more than one billion euros.

THE EASTERN MARCH

Celtic tribes had established settlements throughout Austria for about 500 years by the time the Romans arrived in the Danube Valley around 15 BC.

In the 4C, tribal migrations brought on the decline of the Roman Empire, resulting in a political vacuum until the territory fell to Frankish ruler Charlemagne (747–814). He established a province called Ostmark or Ostarrîchi (the forerunner to Österreich). The Magyars conquered the land in 907 but lost it to Otto I, the Great, after the Battle of Lechfeld (955). In 962, Otto was crowned Holy Roman Emperor and in 976, he granted the Ostmark to Leopold von Babenberg.

THE HOUSE OF BABENBERG (976–1246)

The Babenbergs ruled first as margraves, then as dukes from 1156, giving them greater independence from imperial power. They chose as residences Pöchlarn, Melk, Tulln, the Leopoldsberg and finally Vienna and founded the abbeys of Kremsmünster, St. Florian, Melk, Göttweig and Klosterneuburg.

The last of the Babenbergs, Frederick II, was killed in 1246 fighting the Magyars.

BOHEMIAN INTERVENTION (1246–1278)

Frederick died childless, so Ottokar of Bohemia laid claim to the possessions of the Babenbergs, even marrying Frederick's sister. When Ottokar refused to swear allegiance to Rudolf of Habsburg, who had beaten him in the election for king of the Holy Roman Empire, war ensued. Ottokar was killed at Marchfeld and Rudolf granted the duchies of Austria and Styria to his two sons, thereby laying the corner stone of the House of Habsburg rule.

THE IMPERIAL CROWN

Austria Est Imperare Orbi Universo – "Austria shall rule the world" – was the proud motto of the **Habsburg** dynasty (see the Family Tree). And for a while, it looked as though it would be so.

In the 16C, a clever marriage policy vastly enlarged Austria's territory: Maximilian I acquired the Franche-Comté and the Low Countries by marrying Mary of Burgundy, daughter of Charles the Bold. Maximilian's grandson, **Charles V**, ended up as the most powerful sovereign in Europe, being Holy Roman Emperor, King of Spain, possessor of Naples, Sicily and Sardinia and of territories in the two Americas. Upon his abdication in 1556, the Habsburg territory fell to his brother Ferdinand I.

MARIA THERESIA (1740–80)

When Charles VI died without a male heir, the crown went to his daughter Maria Theresia. Intelligent, shrewd and determined, she stood her own against the Prussians in the **War of the Austrian Succession** (1740–48) and the **Seven Years' War** (1756–63), winning the respect from other rulers and the affection of her people. An "enlightened despot," she lived unostentatiously and introduced a number of popular reforms. She and her husband, Holy Roman Emperor Francis I, had 16 children.

THE STRUGGLE WITH FRANCE (1792–1815)

For the 23 years during which France was at war with the rest of Europe, Austria was, together with England, her most determined opponent.

The accession of Napoleon to the Imperial French throne in 1804 dealt a heavy blow to the Habsburg monarchy. Napoleon I opened his reign with the victories of Ulm and Austerlitz (1805), and forced Franz II to sue for peace and renounce the crown of the Holy Roman Empire. In 1809 the defeat of the French on the battlefields of Essling and Aspern and the successful Tyrolean rebellion led by **Andreas Hofer** brought new hope to the Austrians. Eventually, though, the humiliating **Treaty of Vienna** forced Austria to relinquish Carniola, Carinthia, Trieste, Rijeka (or Fiume) and Galicia.

In 1810 Napoleon married Marie-Louise, daughter of the vanquished emperor. Metternich, however, refused to accept defeat and threw all of Austria's forces against Napoleon. In 1814, Austrian troops marched into Paris. The **Congress of Vienna** renewed the power of the Habsburgs.

THE CENTURY OF FRANZ JOSEPH

Franz Joseph's 68-year reign (1848–1916) ranks as a milestone in Austrian history, largely due to the monarch's personality and policies. Although he had to overcome enormous political and personal difficulties (including the suicide of his only son, Rudolf, at Mayerling, and the

Emperor Franz Joseph I

© Austrian National Tourist Office/Trumler

assassination of his wife, Elisabeth), his reign is widely regarded as the zenith of Austria's power and culture.

THE REPUBLIC OF AUSTRIA

Since adopting a federal constitution in 1920, the Republic of Austria has been a Federal State consisting of nine autonomous provinces.

THE AUSTRIAN PROVINCES (BUNDESLÄNDER)

Every five or six years, each province *(Land)* elects a **Provincial Diet** with members ranging from 36 to 56 depending on the province's population. The Diet of Vienna has 100 members. The diet elects the members of the **Provincial Government** *(Landtag)*, which is the administrative organ of the *Land*.

Burgenland

3,962sq km/1,530sq mi – population 291,000 – capital: Eisenstadt
Predominantly agricultural, this German-speaking province on the border of Hungary has been the republic's easternmost province since 1921.
A highlight is the **Neusiedler See** (see p259) on the edge of the Central European steppes.

Carinthia (Kärnten)

9,538sq km/3,683sq mi – population 560,300 – capital: Klagenfurt

This lake-studded southern province has the only considerable national minority in Austria (4% of its residents are of Slovenian descent). In a 1920 referendum, the southern districts voted in favour of staying with Austria rather than become part of Yugoslavia.

Lower Austria (Niederösterreich)

19,186sq km/7,408sq mi – population 1,653,400 – capital: St. Pölten
Considered the country's historical cradle, it is Austria's largest and most prosperous province. It has extensive agriculture, is rich in oil and other natural resources and boasts a thriving industry, mainly concentrated around Vienna.

Upper Austria (Oberösterreich)

11,980sq km/4,625.5sq mi – population 1,453,700 – capital: Linz
This region between the Salzkammergut and Bohemia is highly developed agriculturally and industrially. Tourism is important in the Salzkammergut lakes.

Salzburg

7,156sq km/2,763sq mi – population 545,700 – capital: Salzburg
The former domain of the prince-archbishops of Salzburg became part of Austria in 1805. Its economy was based on salt. The Salzburg Festival, ritzy spas and modern ski resorts lure visitors today.

Styria (Steiermark)

16,401sq km/6,332sq mi – population 1,231,900 – capital: Graz
The "green province" of Austria (half its surface is covered by forest) is one of the oldest industrial regions in Europe, with important timber and steel industries, stock-breeding and mining.

Tyrol

12,640sq km/4,880sq mi – population 739,000 – capital: Innsbruck
The Tyrol generates more tourist euros than any other Austrian province. Although about 35% of its area is given over to agriculture, industry also plays an important role. Southern Tyrol was ceded to Italy in 1919, separating eastern Tyrol from the rest of the province.

Vorarlberg

2,601sq km/1,004sq mi – population 370,400 – capital: Bregenz
The smallest Austrian province has a textile and tourism industry and is a major producer of hydroelectric power.

Vienna (Wien)

415sq km/160sq mi – population 1,714,200
The services and ministries of the Federal Government and of the *Land* of Vienna are headquartered in the capital.

FEDERAL ORGANISATION

The **Federal Assembly** (*Bundestag*) consists of the members of the National Council and of the Federal Council, who share the legislative power.

The **National Council** (*Nationalrat*) has 183 members elected by a nationwide popular vote for four years. The minimum voting age is 18. It is convoked or dissolved by the Federal President. The **Federal Council** (*Bundesrat*) is formed by 61 representatives elected by the provincial diets. Its role is to safeguard the rights of the provinces in the administrative and legislative fields *vis-à-vis* the Federation.

On the federal level, it has the right to propose laws and its approval is necessary for international agreements and treaties. The **Federal President** (*Bundespräsident*) is elected for six years and holds executive power with the Federal Government. The president represents Austria abroad, appoints the chancellor and senior civil servants, and promulgates the laws.

The **Federal Government** (*Bundesregierung*) is made up of a chancellor, a vice-chancellor, ministers and secretaries of state, appointed by the president, advised by the chancellor.

Art and Culture

Over the centuries Austria has been a meeting place for varied cultures. Its artistic achievement has often reflected these external influences, which provided some of its best sources of inspiration. At certain periods, however, a style developed that matched the nation's aspirations, particularly in the 18C under the enlightened rule of the Habsburgs, when Austrian Baroque blossomed so vigorously that previous achievements paled in comparison.

ART AND ARCHITECTURE

The Roman occupation left traces across much of Austria; at Carnuntum (Petronell); in the Danube Valley, downstream from Vienna, which was then called Vindobona; in Enns (Lauriacum), where St. Florian was martyred; in Carinthia, at Teurnia (near Spittal) and Magdalensberg overlooking St. Veit an der Glan; and also in the Tyrol at Aguntum (near Lienz).

ROMANESQUE

From the 12C onwards, church building flourished in Austria as in all Christian Europe. The main centres of the Romanesque style were the Episcopal seats of Salzburg, Passau and Brixen. The style was also promoted by the foundation of many Benedictine, Cistercian and Augustinian convents and monasteries, such as those at Melk, Göttweig, Klosterneuburg, Zwettl, Seckau and Heiligenkreuz. The best preserved buildings from this period are the cathedrals of Gurk and Seckau, but the cloisters at Millstatt and the great door of the Stephansdom in Vienna are all outstanding Romanesque examples.

Mural paintings developed most extensively in the Archbishopric of Salzburg. The interior of Gurk cathedral and the frescoes at Lambach Abbey are especially noteworthy in this context.

GOTHIC

In the 14C and 15C, the Gothic style arrived in Austria. Most Gothic churches are of the **hall church** *(Hallenkirche)* type with nave and aisles of equal height, as in Vienna in the Augustinerkirche, the Minoritenkirche, and the church of Maria am Gestade. The most characteristic Gothic building in Austria is the Stephansdom in Vienna, begun in 1304 by architects who were in touch with their contemporaries in Regensburg and Strasbourg.

Until the 16C there was a preference for sectional vaulting wherein decorative ribs form a pattern of groined or star vaulting in which richness of design contrasts boldly with the bare walls. This **Late Gothic** *(Spätgotik)* style developed into a design of long straight lines – the exact opposite of the ornamental opulence of the Flamboyant Gothic to be seen in France at this period.

Paired naves were the fashion in the Alps, especially in the Tyrol: two naves at Feldkirch, four at Schwaz.

The great Gothic altarpieces, which were a synthesis of architecture, sculpture and painting have, for the most part, sadly suffered extensive damage over the centuries. Two are of exceptional quality: at Kefermarkt, which was restored at the instigation of the writer Adalbert Stifter; and especially at St. Wolfgang, painted and carved in 1481 by a Tyrolean, **Michael Pacher**, the grea-

Ceiling of Gothic church of Schwaz, Tyrol

© Austrian National Tourist Office/Trumler

ABC of Architecture

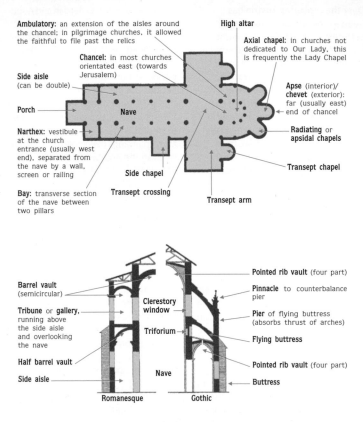

Ambulatory: an extension of the aisles around the chancel; in pilgrimage churches, it allowed the faithful to file past the relics

Chancel: in most churches orientated east (towards Jerusalem)

Side aisle (can be double)

Porch

Nave

Narthex: vestibule at the church entrance (usually west end), separated from the nave by a wall, screen or railing

Side chapel

Transept crossing

Bay: transverse section of the nave between two pillars

High altar

Axial chapel: in churches not dedicated to Our Lady, this is frequently the Lady Chapel

Apse (interior)/ **chevet** (exterior): far (usually east) end of chancel

Radiating or **apsidal chapels**

Transept chapel

Transept arm

Barrel vault (semicircular)

Tribune or **gallery,** running above the side aisle and overlooking the nave

Half barrel vault

Side aisle

Romanesque

Clerestory window

Triforium

Nave

Gothic

Pointed rib vault (four part)

Pinnacle to counterbalance pier

Pier of flying buttress (absorbs thrust of arches)

Flying buttress

Pointed rib vault (four part)

Buttress

Riesentor (west door) of Stephansdom, Vienna (1230-40)

Tympanum: space enclosed by the arch above a door or window, delimited by the archivolt and the extrados

Mandorla: almond-shaped glory around the head or body of a holy figure (such as Christ or Our Lady)

Capital: top of a pillar or column, linking the shaft with the entablature above

Shaft: body of a pillar or column

Architraves: arch mouldings making up the archivolt

Archivolt: ornamental band of mouldings around the outside (extrados) of an arch

Frieze: decorative carved band below the cornice

Pillar: load-bearing element supporting the structure above an opening in the wall

M. Guillou/MICHELIN

Chancel of Wilhering Abbey Church (1734-48)

Altarpiece: shrine-like structure above the altar, usually framing a painting; can also refer to the painting itself

Squinch: section of wall, often decorated, bridging the gap between a square plan structure and a circular or polygonal superstructure

Cornice: structural moulding running round projecting sections of wall, just below ceiling level

Canopy or baldaquin projecting above the pulpit

Chancel organ: small organ in the chancel or by the wall closing it off from the nave; often as a counterpart to the pulpit opposite

High altar: at the far (east) end of the body of the church

Pulpit: elevated platform for the preacher, usually beneath a canopy or sounding board and reached up a flight of steps

Rocaille cartouches: medallion-shaped ornaments with a coat of arms or other motif, framed in elaborate scroll-like ornamentation featuring shell motifs, characteristic of the Rococo

Tabernacle: ornamental box set in the middle of the altar in which the vessels containing the Blessed Sacrament are kept in Roman Catholic churches

M. Guillou/MICHELIN

51

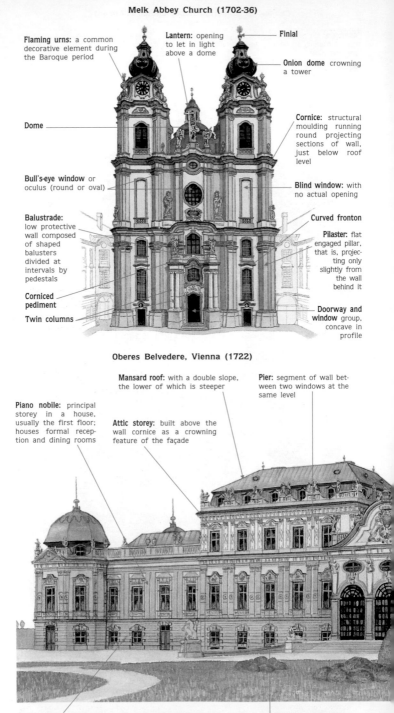

Melk Abbey Church (1702-36)

Flaming urns: a common decorative element during the Baroque period

Lantern: opening to let in light above a dome

Finial

Onion dome crowning a tower

Dome

Cornice: structural moulding running round projecting sections of wall, just below roof level

Bull's-eye window or oculus (round or oval)

Blind window: with no actual opening

Balustrade: low protective wall composed of shaped balusters divided at intervals by pedestals

Curved fronton

Pilaster: flat engaged pillar, that is, projecting only slightly from the wall behind it

Corniced pediment

Twin columns

Doorway and window group, concave in profile

Oberes Belvedere, Vienna (1722)

Mansard roof: with a double slope, the lower of which is steeper

Pier: segment of wall between two windows at the same level

Piano nobile: principal storey in a house, usually the first floor; houses formal reception and dining rooms

Attic storey: built above the wall cornice as a crowning feature of the façade

Socle: lowest storey which offers the possibility of compensating for uneven ground

Axis: row of tall windows along the building's façade

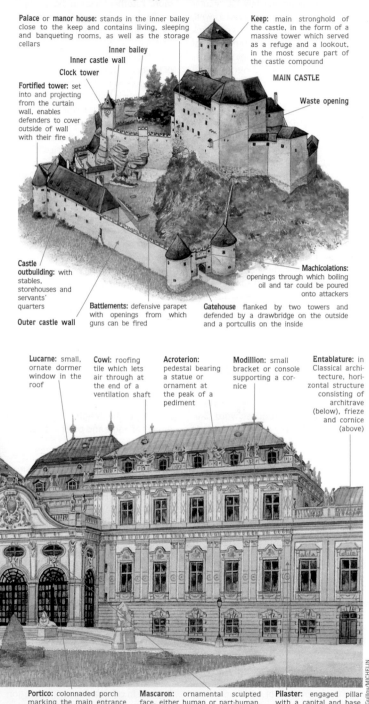

Burg Rappottenstein (12C-16C)

Palace or **manor house:** stands in the inner bailey close to the keep and contains living, sleeping and banqueting rooms, as well as the storage cellars

Inner bailey

Inner castle wall

Clock tower

Fortified tower: set into and projecting from the curtain wall, enables defenders to cover outside of wall with their fire

Keep: main stronghold of the castle, in the form of a massive tower which served as a refuge and a lookout, in the most secure part of the castle compound

MAIN CASTLE

Waste opening

Castle outbuilding: with stables, storehouses and servants' quarters

Outer castle wall

Battlements: defensive parapet with openings from which guns can be fired

Machicolations: openings through which boiling oil and tar could be poured onto attackers

Gatehouse flanked by two towers and defended by a drawbridge on the outside and a portcullis on the inside

Lucarne: small, ornate dormer window in the roof

Cowl: roofing tile which lets air through at the end of a ventilation shaft

Acroterion: pedestal bearing a statue or ornament at the peak of a pediment

Modillion: small bracket or console supporting a cornice

Entablature: in Classical architecture, horizontal structure consisting of architrave (below), frieze and cornice (above)

Portico: colonnaded porch marking the main entrance to a building

Mascaron: ornamental sculpted face, either human or part-human, usually caricatured

Pilaster: engaged pillar with a capital and base

M. Guillou/MICHELIN

test Late Gothic artist. A few 15C secular buildings have been preserved as well, such as the Kornmesserhaus at Bruck an der Mur and the Goldenes Dachl at Innsbruck. The decorative elements adorning their façades, though, herald the Renaissance.

THE RENAISSANCE

Although Austria did not close itself off to new ideas, the Gothic tradition continued to dominate in the 16C. Even the Innsbruck tomb of Emperor Maximilian I (1493–1519), which is regarded as a typical product of the German Renaissance, is still clearly influenced by such famous Gothic tombs as the ones of the dukes of Burgundy in Dijon.

Although comparatively rare, there are some fine examples of the Renaissance in Austria, such as the arcaded courtyards at Schloss Schallaburg near Melk, at Schloss Porcia in Spittal an der Drau and at the Landhaus in Graz. Another major exception is Salzburg, which the prince-archbishops essentially dreamed of making into a second Rome.

BAROQUE (17C–18C)

The revolution in the arts originating in Italy at the end of the 16C derives its name from the Portuguese word *"barroco"* meaning something irregularly shaped (originally used of pearls). The Baroque affected all aspects of the arts – architecture, painting, sculpture – as well as literature and music.

In Austria, the style stimulated the richest artistic period since the Gothic. There are various reasons that this new direction in art found such fertile ground in Austria. In essence a religious art, it accorded perfectly with the mood of mystical rejoicing following the Council of Trent. It enjoyed the favour of the Habsburgs, ardent supporters of the Counter Reformation, and benefited from the euphoria after the defeat of the Turks at the gates of Vienna in 1683. At the time, the entire country was seized by a passion for building – at last the danger that had overshadowed the lives of generations of Austrians was no

more. Another factor in the triumph of the Baroque style was the Austrian love for dramatic effects, elegance, colour and *joie de vivre*.

The churches, monasteries and palaces of the Baroque can be fully understood only in relation to the new liturgical and festive music that emerged ever more strongly after 1600, in which a dominant melodic line supplanted the older and more complex vocal polyphony.

The pomp and circumstance of the new liturgies (in the wake of the Council of Trent, 1545–63) were backed by the rich and powerful sounds of ever more sophisticated church organs.

Austrian Baroque architecture

Austrian Baroque needs to be seen as an essentially home-grown phenomenon, the expression of an authentically Austrian sensibility, and not as an import. With its irregular outlines, abundance of forms and richness of ornament, the Baroque is above all a style of movement. Its dynamism results from colour (the use of both bright and delicate colours, the contrast of black, white and gilt), line (curves and undulations), the exuberant treatment of features, such as pediments, cornices, balustrades and statues, and a delight in unexpected effects of angle and perspective.

The great Baroque abbeys

St. Florian, Melk, Altenburg, Kremsmünster, Göttweig: these great abbeys are manifestations of Austrian Baroque at its peak, surpassing in their magnificence any secular buildings of the period. Often prominently sited, these "monuments of militant Catholicism" (Nikolaus Pevsner) draw together bold terraces, elegant entrance pavilions, inner and outer courtyards and main wings of imposing dimensions into harmonious compositions of unparalleled splendour. The scale and lavishness of ornamentation of these vast structures give rise to a certain duality of feeling: places of worship, they are also temples dedicated to art, to which the Baroque assigned a key role in celebrating divine creation.

Glossary of Architectural Terms

Apse– Semicircular vaulted space terminating the east end of a church

Baldaquin– Altar canopy supported on columns

Barrel vault– Simple, half-cylindrical vault

Bas-relief– Sculpture in which the figures project only slightly from the background

Capital– Molded or carved top of a column supporting the entablature

Cartouche– Ornamental panel with inscription or coat of arms (Baroque)

Chapter-house– Building attached to religious house used for meetings of monks or clergy

Chiaroscuro– Treatment of areas of light and dark in a work of art

Cupola– Small dome

Curtain wall– Stretch of castle wall between two towers

Entablature– Projecting upper part of building supporting the roof

Flamboyant– Final phase of French Gothic style (15C) with flame-like forms

Fresco– Watercolour wall painting on plaster

Grisaille– Monochrome painting in shades of grey

Hall-church– Germanic church in which aisles are of the same height as the nave

Lantern– Windowed turret on top of a dome

Lintel– Horizontal beam over a door or window

Narthex– Rectangular vestibule between the porch and nave of a church

Oriel– Bay window corbelled out from an upper floor level

Ossuary– Place where the bones of the dead are stored

Pendentive– Triangular section of vaulting rising from the angle of two walls to support a dome

Peristyle– Colonnade around a building

Pilaster– Shallow rectangular column projecting from a wall

Predella– Altar platform divided into panels

Putto– Painted or sculpted cherub

Quadripartite vaulting– Vault divided into four quarters or cells

Reredos– Screen to the rear of an altar

Reticulated– Patterned like a net

Rib– Projecting band separating the cells of a vault

Saddleback roof– Roof with a ridge between two gables, suggesting a saddle shape

Sgraffito– Decoration made by scratching through a layer of plaster or glaze to reveal the colour of the surface beneath

Shingle– Wooden tile

Stucco or stuccowork– Decorative plasterwork

Transept– Wing or arm of a church at right angles to the nave

Triptych– Set of three panels or pictures, often folding and used as an altarpiece

Trompe-l'œil– Use of techniques such as perspective, or the combination of sculptures and painted figures, to deceive the viewer into seeing three dimensions where there are only two

Tympanum– Space between the lintel and arch of a doorway

Volute– Spiral scroll on an Ionic capital

Churches

All over Austria stand graceful onion-domed churches, their elegant exteriors concealing the delights awaiting within. It is only once inside the church door that the exuberant Baroque decoration bursts into full and glorious voice, transforming even the most modest of structures. Many such churches actually evolved from Gothic (Rattenberg, Maria-zell) – or even Romanesque (Rein, Stams) – buildings that were remodeled only in the 17C and 18C. A supreme example of Baroque religious architecture in Austria is the unique Dreifaltigkeitskirche (Holy Trinity Church) at Stadl-Paura, every aspect of which symbolises the Trinity.

Secular buildings

Their façades alive with colour and movement, palace and townhouse alike became stage sets for the urban theatre. In the 17C, sumptuous Baroque residences took shape on the edge of towns such as Graz (Schloss Eggenberg), Salzburg (Schloss Hellbrunn) and Vienna (Belvedere).

Great Baroque architects

Numerous famous Italian architects such as Domenico dell'Allio and Carlo Carlone left their mark on Austria's Baroque buildings. But contributing in equal if not greater measure were a number of local masters, many of whom had received their architectural training in Italy or at least undertaken a study tour of the country. Among them was **Johann Bernhard Fischer von Erlach** (1656–1723), who created a monumental, national style based on his own interpretation of foreign (particularly Italian) influences. The Dreifaltigkeitskirche at Salzburg is one of the prototypes of this style. Many of the most beautiful buildings in Vienna bear the stamp of his genius, including the Nationalbibliothek, the Palais Schwarzenberg and the winter palace belonging to Prince Eugene of Savoy. Most of these buildings were completed after his death by his son, Joseph Emmanuel (1693–1742), who also built the indoor riding school (Winterreitschule) in the Hofburg.

Johann Lukas von Hildebrandt (1668–1745) settled in Vienna after a period of study in Italy and worked with Fischer von Erlach. In Vienna he designed the two palaces at the Belvedere, the Peterskirche with its oval cupola, the Piaristenkirche and the Palais Kinsky, and in Salzburg, Schloss Mirabell. His considerable body of work had a significant influence on the artists of his generation.

The Tyrolean architect **Jakob Prandtauer** (1660–1726) had a masterly touch in relating massive structures to their landscape setting. Thus, while his church interiors are conventional, or even somewhat heavy, his staircase at St. Florian and the two pavilions and great bastion at Melk are achievements of a very high order. The abbey at Melk, a jewel of Austrian Baroque, was completed by Prandtauer's son-in-law, **Josef Munggenast** (1680–1741), who later went on to work at Dürnstein, Altenburg and Geras. Prandtauer did not limit his talents to religious architecture, however. He was also responsible for several gorgeous secular buildings, including Schloss Hohenbrunn.

Baroque painting and sculpture

Baroque architecture is unimaginable without its natural complements of painting and sculpture. Together with delicate stuccowork decorations, they breathe joyful life into the spaces created by the architect. Church walls disappear beneath elaborate altarpieces, myriad saints and angels fill the ceilings and an army of statues banishes its Gothic predecessors. Palaces and abbeys are endowed with huge stairways, while cheerfully coloured and stuccoed façades lend a theatrical air to both village street and town square. Great painters and sculptors devoted their talent to the decoration of palaces and churches. Among them were **Johann Michael Rottmayr**, Fischer von Erlach's preferred collaborator and the precursor of a specifically Austrian pictorial style; **Balthasar Permoser**, whose famous marble of the Apotheosis of Prince Eugene graces the Belvedere Museum in Vienna; **Daniel Gran**, who

Schloss Schönbrunn, Vienna

© Maurizio Borgese/hemis.fr

executed the painting of the Natio-nalbibliothek in Vienna; **Paul Troger**, master of Austrian ceiling frescoes; **Martin Johann Schmidt** ("Kremser Schmidt"), whose altarpieces are to be found all over Lower Austria; **Martin Altomonte**, whose airy frescoes and altar paintings grace Wilhering Abbey; and his son **Bartolomeo Altomonte**, who decorated the splendid library at Admont. It is with **Franz Anton Maul-bertsch** (1724-1796) that Austrian Baro-que painting attains its peak along with **Georg Raphael Donner**, who is best known for the fine fountain in the Neuer Markt in Vienna.

ROCOCO

Inspired by the French rocaille, this style reached its highest form of develop-ment in Bavaria. It carries the decorative refinements of the Baroque to their limit, giving them priority over architecture: painting in *trompe-l'œil*, marble, stucco, bronze and wood are used in lavish profusion by artists who allowed their imaginations free rein. The stuccoists combined garlands, medallions, vegeta-tion and shell work. Often two art forms would overlap: a painted figure passes indistinguishably into sculpture, with the head perhaps in *trompe-l'œil* and the body in relief, without the transition bet-ween the two being apparent.

The burning passion of the Baroque gives way to a delight in sophisticated effects, monumentality to delicacy and playfulness. Baldaquins, sham draperies, superimposed galleries, niches overla-den with gilding and painted in pastel shades add to the prevailing impres-sion of being in a theatre rather than a church. The interior of the church at **Wilhering** near Linz is the most accom-plished example of a religious Rococo building, while in the east of the coun-try, Rococo is found again at **Schloss Schönbrunn**.

19C

Neoclassicism

After the excesses of Rococo came the triumph of Neoclassicism, inspired by Greece and Rome, a comparatively austere style characterised by the columns and pediments of Classical antiquity. This tendency, which had little in common with the Austrian and even less with the Viennese cha-racter, was favoured mostly by German rulers, including Ludwig I of Bavaria who transformed Munich. Vienna saw the construction of several buildings of great sobriety like the Technische Hochschule, the Schottenstift and the Münze (Mint). The equestrian statue of Joseph II in the Hofburg by **Franz Anton Zauner** is a typical example of Neoclas-sical sculpture.

Biedermeier (early 19C)

Biedermeier is the name given to the style that dominated the "Vormärz" (Pre-March), the period between the

Congress of Vienna in 1814 and the insurrections of March 1848, the "Year of Revolutions." It is an essentially middle-class style, reflecting the prosperity and settled way of life of this increasingly important section of society that flourished alongside industrialisation and continuing urbanisation.

Comfortable furniture

The cosy interiors inhabited by the rising Vienna bourgeoisie were furnished with simple yet elegant pieces, frequently fashioned in pleasingly light-coloured woods, their design reflecting new ideas of function and comfort. Eventually, though, the discretion and modesty of this utterly unpretentious style fell out of fashion. The Kaiserliches Hofmobiliendepot (national furniture collection) in Vienna has an important collection of Biedermeier furniture and other objects. The term "Biedermeier" comes from a fictional character, Gottlieb Biedermaier, used as the nom-de-plume for writer **Ludwig Eichrodt** and medic **Adolf Kußmaul** who, under this pseudonym, published poems and essays parodying the style and mores of the period.

Biedermeier chair, Kaiserliches Hofmobilienmuseum, Vienna

Realistic painting

Austrian painting, and Viennese painting in particular, developed in a remarkable way during this period.

Georg Ferdinand Waldmüller showed himself to be a master of light and colour in his rendering of landscape, while **Friedrich Gauermann** captured the atmosphere of the age with great accuracy and left many fine drawings of outstanding quality. The art of watercolour was popular during this period. **Rudolf von Alt** was the greatest master in this medium, becoming honorary president of the Vienna Secession at an advanced age.

Historicism (late 19C)

Between 1840 and 1880, on Emperor Franz Joseph's orders, Vienna's encircling fortifications were pulled down and work begun on the great processional way known as the Ringstraße, or "Ring."

The buildings along the new boulevard were designed according to the dictates of **Historicism**, an eclectic movement in fashion at the time and drawing on a great variety of past styles for inspiration: Florentine Renaissance (e.g. Museum für Angewandte Kunst (MAK) by Heinrich von Ferstel, *see p190*), Greek Classical (Parliament by Theophil Hansen, *see p187*), Flemish Gothic (Rathaus by Friedrich Schmidt *see p186*), and French Gothic (Votivkirche, also by Heinrich von Ferstel, *see p186*). Having triumphed in the capital, Historicism went on to leave its mark elsewhere. Towards the end of the 19C, however, opposition to this uncreative and backward-looking style began to grow in Vienna, culminating in open revolt by a number of artists who joined forces to found the famous Vienna Secession movement in 1897.

Late-19C painting and sculpture

Sculpture flourished during this period, not least because of the abundance of public commissions, which included the martial statues of Prince Eugene and Archduke Karl (by **Anton Fernkorn**) in Vienna's Heldenplatz and the moving monument to Andreas Hofer (by Heinrich Natter) on the Bergisel in Innsbruck. The late 19C was a turning point for Austrian painting.

© Austrian National Tourist Office / Wiesenhofer

Secession Building
by Joseph Maria Olbrich Vienna

© E. Suetone/hemis.fr

The great tradition of Realism continued in the work of such landscape painters as **Emil Jakob Schindler**. However, the highly original talent of artists including **Anton Romako** increasingly addressed more serious subject matters, such as decline, decay and death.

JUGENDSTIL (EARLY 20C)

In the final years of the 19C, a new artistic movement known as the Jugendstil swept through all the German-speaking countries, with its epicentre in Munich. It took its name from the widely read magazine *Jugend* (Youth), published between 1896 and 1940, which contained illustrations by artists.

In Vienna, the movement was headed by two exceptionally talented figures, the painter **Gustav Klimt** and the architect **Otto Wagner**. Its influence was felt in the provinces, too, albeit in a more subdued form, and there are good examples of Jugendstil buildings in Wels and Graz. Jugendstil drawing and painting are characterised by flat surfaces, curvilinear forms, and floral decoration. The movement was paralleled by **Art Nouveau** in France, Modern Style in Britain, and Stile Liberty in Italy.

The Secession

On 25 May 1897 a small group of friends, led by Gustav Klimt, founded the **Association of Austrian Artists**, the **Vienna Secession**. The following year, the architect Joseph Maria Olbrich built an exhibition hall – the Secession – in the Karlsplatz. Completed in only six months, this building remains one of the purest expressions of Jugendstil aspirations, even though contemporaries nicknamed it the "Golden Cabbage" because of its dome of gilded laurel leaves. Its façade proclaims the slogan *Der Zeit ihre Kunst – der Kunst ihre Freiheit* (To each age its art, to art its liberty). Olbrich's Secession building was home to numerous exhibitions of contemporary, progressive art, many of them international in scope. It became a focus of opposition to the values represented by Historicism, academic art and the tendency towards pastiche that had characterised artistic life in Vienna during construction of the Ringstraße. For the artists of the Secession, art was above all a matter of personal expression, requiring sincerity and a quest for truth as well as a rejection of prevailing social and aesthetic conventions.

Gustav Klimt (1862–1918)

Painter and interior designer Gustav Klimt was a leading exponent of the Jugendstil, and in many ways the typical Secession artist; his elegant and subtle works are world renowned. Early in his career he put his academic training behind him and abandoned all attempts at naturalism in favour of rich and subtle decorative effects carried out on a two-dimensional surface free of the constraints of perspective. His sinuous line, his original use of colour (especially greens and gold), his stylised

59

© Austrian National Tourist Office/Wiesenhofer

Steinhof church mosaic by Otto Wagner

foliage, his cult of the sensual and the delicacy of his female portraits provoked a revolution in Viennese artistic circles. Symbolism was an additional influence in the work of this major figure, the forerunner of what was later known as **Viennese Expressionism**, represented by painters like Egon Schiele and Oskar Kokoschka.

Otto Wagner (1841–1918)

Wagner was the dominant architectural figure of the Jugendstil period. Born in Biedermeier times and educated in the most classical tradition, he rose to become professor at the Academy of Fine Arts and imperial architectural adviser for the city of Vienna. For more than 20 years his career was one of conventional success; he designed a number of buildings in neo-Renaissance style along the Ring, for example. But in 1899 Wagner broke decisively with his past and joined the Secession. He had already outlined his uncompromisingly contemporary views in his *Modern Architecture* (1895), still a standard reference text. Wagner favoured the use of glass and steel, a rational approach to spatial design and the omission of superfluous ornament. His finest works include the pavilions for the Karlsplatz Stadtbahn station (1894) in Vienna, the Postsparkasse (1906) near the Ring and the Steinhof Church (1907).

Wiener Werkstätten (Vienna Workshops)

The Wiener Werkstätten were founded in 1903 by the banker Fritz Waerndorfer, the architect Josef Hoffmann and the graphic designer **Koloman Moser**, one of the most gifted members of the Secession movement. They were intended to make good art accessible to all and to put both artist and craftsman on a firm professional footing. A wide range of products was made adopting Jugendstil tenets, from household utensils, furniture and wallpaper to fashion garments and jewellery. Though expensive, these products were much in demand among the wealthier strata of society. Beauty of form and the use of high-quality materials were more important than functionality. Financial woes led to the workshops' closure in 1932. Together with Klimt's paintings, the output of the Wiener Werkstätten marks the high point of Austrian Jugendstil and enjoys enduring acclaim.

Josef Hoffmann (1870–1956)

This highly versatile figure was one of Otto Wagner's most talented students. Hoffmann designed not only buildings but also their interiors, including furniture and fittings. He was strongly influenced by the work of Scottish architect and designer Charles Rennie Mackintosh, founder of the Glasgow School of Art Nouveau. Hoffmann co-founded the

Wiener Werkstätten in 1903 and worked closely with them until 1931.

One of the results of this fruitful collaboration is the magnificent **Palais Stoclet** in Brussels. As well as designing material for private clients, Hoffmann also received numerous commissions from the Vienna city council, for whom he produced several housing complexes, including Klosehof. He also designed the interior of the Fledermaus revue theatre (1909).

Adolf Loos (1870–1933)

Educated by the Benedictine monks of Melk, this innovative architect called himself a stonemason, though he was considered by Le Corbusier to be the forerunner of architectural Modernism. An admirer of the sober Classicism of Palladio, Loos made a violent attack on the Historicist architecture of Vienna's Ring in 1898, in the pages of the Secessionist journal *Ver Sacrum*.

He was soon to break with the architects of the Secession, however, accusing them of "gratuitous ornamentalism." Following a period of residence in the US (1893–96), and influenced by the Chicago School, he built a number of villas, housing blocks and cafés in Vienna, adopting the principles of a purely functional architectural style.

In addition, he designed sculpture and furniture. His work reached maturity in his controversial Michaeler Platz building (1910/11), today's **Looshaus**, which attracted bitter criticism because of its total lack of ornament. Loos has gone down in history as one of the high priests of 20C functionalism. His ideas were taken up and developed by architects the world over. He was a particularly strong influence on artists of the International style.

MUSIC

see Vienna, Capital of Music, p188.

MIDDLE AGES

9C Musical culture flourished in the monasteries where Gregorian chant was sung. The earliest examples of written music in Austria are the Lamentations from the abbey at St. Florian and the Codex Millenarius Minor from Kremsmünster.

12C and 13C The Germanic troubadours, known as the **Minnesänger**, celebrated the joys and sorrows of courtly love at the court of the Babenbergs in Vienna as well as at St. Veit an der Glan in Carinthia, drawing their inspiration from the Volkslied (folk song), an authentic expression of popular feeling. The most famous were Reinmar von Hagenau and his pupil, Walther von der Vogelweide, Hermann von Salzburg and Neidhart von Reuenthal.

14C and 15C The burgher-class **Meistersinger** (Mastersingers), organised into guilds, continued the aristocratic *Minnesang* tradition, setting strict rules and testing their skills in competitions.

RENAISSANCE

This era was the age of polyphony, pioneered in Austria by the Tyrolean Oskar von Wolkenstein, who worked at the court at Salzburg. Later it developed throughout the Empire in the work of several musicians belonging to the Franco-Flemish School.

17C

1619 The accession to the Imperial throne of Archduke Ferdinand II marked the beginning of the supremacy of Italian music in Austria, notably in opera and oratorio. His son Ferdinand III and subsequent emperors continued this patronage of classical music, resulting in a long line of Italian masters who directed the music of the Court Chapel, the last of them being none other than Mozart's great rival, **Antonio Salieri** (1750–1825).

GLUCK AND OPERA REFORM

Vienna was the setting for the reform of opera, thanks to the German composer, Gluck.

1714–1787 Christoph Willibald Gluck considered opera as an indivisible work of art, both musical and dramatic; he sought, above all, natural effects, truth, simplicity and a faithful expression of feeling.

1754 Gluck named Kapellmeister of the Opera at the Imperial Court of Maria Theresia.

1774 Two of his operas debut in Paris: *Iphigenia in Aulis* and *Orpheus and Euridice.*

THE VIENNESE CLASSICS

The age of giants: Haydn, Mozart, Beethoven and Schubert. Although only Schubert was born locally, the work of the Big Four in or around Vienna dominated the musical world for almost a century and made the city music's uncontested capital.

1732–1809 Joseph Haydn. A conductor and composer attached to the service of Prince Eszterházy for nearly 30 years, Haydn, the creator of the string quartet, laid down the laws of the classical symphony.

1756–91 Wolfgang Amadeus Mozart. Mozart brought every form of musical expression to perfection, owing to his exceptional fluency in composition and constantly renewed inspiration. His dramatic genius produced great operas of enduring appeal: *The Marriage of Figaro, Don Giovanni, Così fan Tutte* and *The Magic Flute* (see SALZBURG for details of Mozart's life and work).

1770–1827 Ludwig van Beethoven. Heir to Haydn and Mozart, Beethoven had a Romantic conception of music. Much affected by the ideas of the French Revolution, he felt himself to be the bearer of a message for humankind.

1805 First performance of Beethoven's only opera, *Fidelio,* at the Theater an der Wien.

1824 Beethoven's Ninth or Choral Symphony concludes with the *Ode to Joy* (fourth movement) with words by Friedrich Schiller. In 1972 this *Ode to Joy* was adopted as the European anthem.

1797–1828 Franz Schubert. Blessed with a great sensibility, Schubert was an outstanding improviser who rediscovered in the Lieder, the old popular themes of the Middle Ages. His Lieder, of which he wrote more than 600 (more than his symphonies, masses, impromptus and compositions of chamber music) made him the leading lyrical composer of the 19C.

THE VIENNESE WALTZ AND OPERETTA

1820 In Vienna, the **waltz**, a musical genre that had its origins in popular triple-time dance, was triumphant. Adopted first in the inns and then in the theatres on the outskirts of the city, the waltz enjoyed such success that it appeared at the Imperial Court.
Joseph Lanner (1801–43) and **Johann Strauss** (1804–49) helped give the waltz prominence, to the extent that the most popular waltz becomes known worldwide as the Viennese Waltz. The Strauss sons, Joseph and Johann, carried the waltz to

a high degree of technical perfection, taking it further from its origins to make it a symphonic form.

With the performance at the Carltheater in 1858 of Offenbach's *Die Verlobung bei der Laterne*, Vienna's enthusiasm for **operetta** knew no bounds. Encouraged by Offenbach, **Johann Strauss the Younger** (1825–99) enjoyed equal success with his *Fledermaus* and *Zigeunerbaron* (Gipsy Baron). Other great operetta composers were **Franz von Suppé** (1819–95), **Franz Lehár** (1870–1948, *The Merry Widow, The Land of Smiles*), **Ralph Benatzky** (1884–1957, *White Horse Inn*), and **Robert Stolz** (1880–1975, *Spring in the Prater*).

SYMPHONIC RENEWAL

1824–1896 Anton Bruckner ranks among the most significant composers of church music, producing nine great symphonies, numerous mass settings and the *Te Deum*. He spent many years as organist of St. Florian and at Linz Cathedral before his appointment as professor at the Vienna Conservatory.

1833–97 Of German origin but settled in Vienna, **Johannes Brahms** composed a large body of work of a lyrical nature, inestimable in its impact (1868, *A German Requiem*).

1842 Founding of the Vienna Philharmonic Orchestra playing under the guidance of illustrious conductors (Richard Strauss, Wilhelm Furtwängler) chosen by the players themselves.

1860–1903 Hugo Wolf, a tormented spirit who eventually became insane, composed fine Lieder in his lucid periods, based for the most part on the poems of Goethe, Mörike and Eichendorff.

1860–1911 Gustav Mahler, a disciple of Bruckner, was the last of the great Romantic composers. He composed many Lieder as well as nine symphonies. He helped to set in motion the revolutionary changes in music at the turn of the 19th century.

20C

From 1903 the New Viennese School, led by Schönberg, was a major influence in the evolution of modern music, as seen in the work of composers such as Ernst Krenek and Pierre Boulez.

1864–1949 The German composer/ conductor **Richard Strauss** carried on the Classical/ Romantic Austrian tradition, composing symphonic poems and operas. He was one of the founders of the Salzburg Festival.

1874–1951 Arnold Schönberg, whose early works reflect the influence of Wagner and Mahler, revolutionised music by rejecting the tonal system that had prevailed for 300 years. Together with his followers **Anton von Webern** (1883–1945) and **Alban Berg** (1885–1935), Schönberg introduced a new method of atonal composition, based on the concept of series, and known as "dodecaphony," or in its more advanced form, as "serial composition." His change of style did not meet instant approval with the public, however; the première of his first chamber symphony provoked a riot.

Famous Austrians of the 19C and 20C

- Adalbert **STIFTER** (1805–68): Novelist and short story writer *(Indian Summer, 1857)*.
- Gregor Johann **MENDEL** (1822–84): Biologist specializing in heredity.
- Sigmund **FREUD** (1856–1939): Founder of psychoanalysis.
- Arthur **SCHNITZLER** (1862–1931): Writer. His novella, *Leutnant Gustl (1900)*, introduced interior monologue to German literature as a new mode of expression.
- Daniel **SWAROVSKI** (1862–1956): Jeweller and glass-cutter who patented an electric cutting machine that facilitated the production of lead crystal jewellery.
- Rainer Maria **RILKE** (1875–1926): One of the great poets of the 20C.
- Karl **KRAUS** (1874–1936): Journalist, writer *(The Last Days of Mankind, 1974)*.
- Fritz **LANG** (1890–1976): Film producer *(Metropolis*, 1926; *M*, 1931).
- Josef von **STERNBERG** (1894–1969): Film producer, discovered Marlene Dietrich *(The Blue Angel*, 1930).
- Herbert von **KARAJAN** (1908–89): Conductor, founder of the Salzburg Festival (1967).
- Peter **HANDKE** (b. 1942): Producer, novelist and film script-writer with Wim Wenders.
- Dietrich **MATESCHITZ** (b. 1944): Entrepreneur and owner of energy drink Red Bull and the Formula 1 racing team of the same name.
- Elfriede **JELINEK** (b. 1946): Playwright and novelist who won Nobel prize for literature in 2004.
- Niki **LAUDA** (b. 1949): Formula 1 racing driver, three times world champion; founder of the Lauda Air airline company (1979).
- Michael **HANEKE** (b. 1942): acclaimed filmmaker and director of *The Piano Teacher (2001)*, *Funny Games (2007)* and *The White Ribbon (2009)*.

Having pursued his study of atonality in Berlin, Schönberg was exiled from Germany under the Nazis and settled in the US, where he finally adopted US citizenship.

1894–1981 Conductor **Karl Böhm** helped stage two operas composed by his friend Richard Strauss. His fame rests on his seminal interpretations of the works of the German composers.

1908–89 The conductor **Herbert von Karajan** brought classical music to a wide audience by his mastery of audio-visual techniques. He presided over the destinies of the Salzburg Festival and directed the Vienna and the Berlin Philharmonic orchestras.

1947 Salzburg première of the opera *Danton's Death* by **Gottfried von Einem** (b. 1918).

1958 *"Die Reihe"* ensemble founded by **Friedrich Cerha** (b. 1926) and Kurt Schwertsik (b. 1935).

1994 American-born Vienna-resident **Nancy van de Vate**, one of the most heavily recorded living composers of orchestral music, is granted dual citizenship by Austria.

1996 Death of **Gottfried von Einem**, a key figure of Austrian cultural life.

Nature

At the heart of the Alps, Austria covers an area of 84,000sq km/ 32,432.5sq mi, stretching some 580km/360.4mi from Switzerland to Hungary. For a distance of 2,600km/1,615.5mi, it shares a border with Germany, the Czech and Slovak republics, Hungary, Slovenia, Italy, Switzerland and Liechtenstein.

TOPOGRAPHY

The River Danube, which acts as a catchment for virtually all the rivers of Austria, flows west-east 360km/223.7mi across the Danube plateau, a vast upland region abutting the Bohemian mountains to the north and encompassing the mountainous Wachau region. This region is the historical heart of Austria. Two-thirds of the country is covered by the Alpine chain. To the east, Austria runs into the Puszta, or Hungarian plain.

ALPINE COUNTRY

The Austrian Alps are divided from north to south into three chains: the Northern Limestone Alps, the High or Central Alps, and the Southern Limestone Alps, separated from each other by the valleys of the Inn, the Salzach and the Enns rivers in the north, and the Drava (Drau in German) and the Mur rivers in the south.

The Northern Limestone Alps

These mountains overflow into Bavaria and extend, west to east, to the massifs of Rätikon, Lechtal, Karwendel, Kaisergebirge, Steinernes Meer, Tennengebirge, Dachstein, the Alps of Ennstal, Eisenerz, Hochschwab and Schneeberg. The highest point is the Parseierspitze at 3,038m/9,967ft.

Transverse valleys

The Northern Limestone Alps are divided into distinct massifs by transverse valleys, along which the Lech, Ache (the Alz in Bavaria), Saalach and Enns rivers flow towards the Danube plateau. As a result, it's not particularly difficult for drivers to cross or go around these massifs.

Karst plateaux

East of the Ache, the Dachstein, the Hochschwab and the Raxalpe rise sharply to more than 2,000m/6,500ft. Due to the porous nature of the limestone, these mountains are like stony deserts, scored here and there with narrow furrows. Here, the flow of the water is almost entirely subterranean, resulting in the formation of numerous caves, including the famous ones in the Dachstein.

Long river valleys

The Northern Limestone Alps are bounded to the south by a deep cleft, separating them from the High Alps. This cleft is divided into valleys, each with its own river, the Inn, the Salzach and the Enns. This major break in the landscape makes it possible to drive along the chain's entire length.

The High or Central Alps

The High Alps, made mostly of crystalline rock, appear as a succession of ridges topped by glaciers, comprising (west to east): the Ötztal Alps, the Hohe Tauern and the Niedere Tauern. For more than 250km/155mi, the crestline rarely drops below 3,000m/9,842.5ft. The Brenner pass, the medieval route to Venice, links the valleys of the Inn and the Adige. The Grossglockner Hochalpenstraße and the Felbertauern tunnel make it possible to cross the imposing massif of the Hohe Tauern. To the south of the High Alps, the furrows of the Drava, Mur and Mürz rivers form the natural link between Vienna and northern Italy.

The Southern Limestone Alps

The Carnic Alps and the Karawanken are Austrian on their northern slopes only. Under the terms of the St-Germain-en-Laye Peace Treaty in 1919, the southern part of the Tyrol was ceded to Italy and the Julian Alps to what was then Yugoslavia.

ALPINE GLACIERS

About 10,000 years ago, immensely thick Alpine glaciers advanced northward, extending over the Bavarian plateau almost as far as modern Munich.

The glaciers substantially remodeled the relief of the Alpine valleys. They scooped out natural amphitheatres known as cirques (like the one closing off the Brandnertal), scoured valleys into a U-shaped section (like the steep-sided Saalach Valley north of Saalfelden), and created hanging valleys (such as the one above the Achensee). These funnel-shaped basins with their steep cliffs often feature spectacular waterfalls.

Glaciers tended not to follow the existing continuous slope of a valley, but to carve out a series of well-defined steps (as evident in the Karawanken), creating natural sites for modern hydroelectric plants. The reservoirs often lie amid breathtaking mountain scenery, as in the case of the impressive Glockner-Kaprun installation. Carrying along a mass of rocky debris, which when deposited is known as a moraine, the glaciers added an extra, complex layer to the landscape of the pre-alpine plateau. The semi-circular moraines created natural dams behind which water accumulated to form the lakes of the Bavarian plateau and of the northern Salzkammergut.

MOUNTAIN CLIMATES

In contrast to weather in the valleys, the mountain climate varies considerably according to altitude, geography or exposure to sunshine.

Winds

In the late morning warm, expanded air creeps up from the valley and causes cloud formations around the summits. Due to this weather phenomenon, view-points atop the mountains are best visited early to mid-morning. Around 5pm, the cold mountain breezes sweep back down into the valley, creating a sudden plunge in temperature.

The Föhn

This warm fall wind is most strongly felt north of the Alps, in the Alpine valleys of the Rhine, the Inn (especially in the

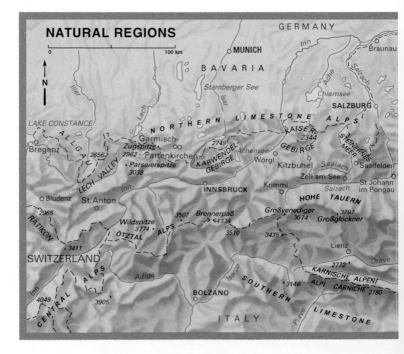

Ötztal) and the Salzach. It is caused by the passage of a deep depression along the north slope of the Alps. Having shed its moisture on the Italian slope of the range, where storms and rain are frequent, the air drawn in by the depression spills over the crestline. Warmed by compression as it loses altitude, it is transformed into a dry, warm wind that creates wonderfully clear skies.

The winds, warm and stripped of their moisture, rapidly melt snow, increasing the likelihood of avalanches, torrential rivers and rapidly spreading wildfires.

The Föhn is often associated with illnesses, ranging from migraines to psychosis; examinations are sometimes suspended in Innsbruck schools and it is said to have been submitted as a mitigating circumstance in criminal trials.

FLORA

In mountain areas the pattern of vegetation is not only influenced by soil type and climate, but also strongly linked to altitude and aspect. Tree species in particular tend to succeed one another in clearly defined vertical stages, though this staging is much modified by human influences as well as by the orientation of the particular slope. South-facing, sunny slopes offer the best growing conditions and have therefore been the most subject to deforestation. North-facing slopes by contrast have tended to keep their trees, which flourish in the prevailing wetter and shadier conditions. This pattern is seen at its best in valleys running east–west.

In most parts of the Alps, farming is practised up to about 1,500m/5,000ft.

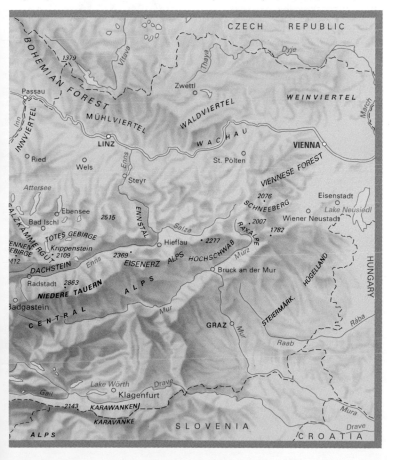

Edelweiss
Leontopodium alpinum
July to September

Stemless Trumpet Gentian
Gentiana acaulis
May to August

Alpine Sea Holly
Eryngium alpinum
July and August

Martagon Lily
Lilium martagon
June to August

Orange Lily
Lilium bulbiferum
June and July

Alpenrose
Rhododendron ferrugineum
July and August

M. Janvier/ MICHELIN

Above this height, a belt of conifer forest gives way to alpine pastures at around 2,200m/7,000ft. Above 3,000m/10,000ft bare rock prevails, only occasionally relieved by mosses and lichens.

TREES

Conifers dominate the Alpine forests: The typical tree of north-facing slopes is the **spruce** (fichte); it has a pointed outline, drooping branches, reddish bark, and sharp needles.

The only European conifer to lose its needles in winter, the **larch** (lärche) is prevalent on south-facing slopes. Its delicate light-green foliage casts a relatively light shade, allowing grass and herbs to grow underneath. The small cones are carried upright on the twigs. The medium-high **Austrian pine** (schwarzkiefer) has a dense crown, dark green foliage and a pale and darkly fissured bark. Its needles grow in pairs. It is undemanding in terms of soil and climate and frequently used in reclamation work in difficult conditions (e.g. on thin limestone soils).

The **arolla** pine (zirbelkiefer) has upward-curving branches that make it look like a candelabrum. It grows right up to the tree line, often twisted into fantastic shapes by the wind. Its bluish-green needles grow in clusters of five. The dense wood of this pine is appreciated by woodcarvers and makers of rustic furniture.

M. Janvier/ MICHELIN

Austrian Pine

ALPINE FLORA

The name "Alpine" is normally used to describe plants growing above the tree line. Because of the short growing season (June to August), they tend to flower early and be resistant to drought (woolly leaf surfaces, thick leaves for water storage).

Flowering plants found in the Austrian Alps include the Alpine rose, gentian, primrose, globe flower, Alpine cyclamen, martagon lily, Alpine aster, carline thistle and various species of snowbell.

Rocky areas host edelweiss, saxifraga, Alpine poppy, and glacier buttercup.

FAUNA

Austria has a rich and varied animal life. The shores of the Neusiedler See are a paradise for some 260 species of birds, including not only waterfowl such as kingfishers, river terns, spoonbills and herons but also tits, warblers and several species of geese. Storks are also regular visitors here. Swans grace the lakes of the Salzkammergut and Upper Austria. The Danube is home to 60 of the 80 species of fish to be found in Austria, including eels, perch, and catfish.

Various kinds of deer, wild boar, badgers and foxes make their home in Austria's forests, while the fields and woodlands are a playground for rabbits and hares.

ALPINE FAUNA

Visitors never fail to succumb to the charms of Austria's cutest Alpine resident, the grey-brown **marmot**. Unfortunately, being of a somewhat shy disposition, it rarely grants ramblers a public audience (see MALTATAL, Nationalpark Nockberge). The **mountain hare** is another cautious creature.

Herds of nimble **chamois** are to be seen principally in the Limestone Alps. **Alpine ibex**, equally agile and also very strong, live above the tree line. Red deer are common throughout Austria. Typical Alpine bird life includes the snow-partridge, the Alpine chough and the capercaillie. On the whole, and especially during the mating season, these birds are more likely to be heard than seen. King of them all, however, is the **golden eagle**, a truly majestic bird with a wingspan of 2m/6.5ft, which, sadly, seldom makes an appearance. There is currently an intensive programme to re-introduce the mighty **bearded vulture**, one of the most iconic raptors of the Alps.

Vineyards around Baden near Vienna, Lower Austria
© Rainer Mirau/Sime/Photononstop

SALZBURG AND THE SALZKAMMERGUT

The UNESCO World Heritage Site of Salzburg is famous for many reasons, not only for its skyline dominated by the Hohensalzburg fortress and the charming lanes that make up the Old Town, but also for its native son Wolfgang Amadeus Mozart and its annual music festivals. It was also the setting for the endearing film *The Sound of Music*. Beyond the city, in the Salzburg region and the nearby Salzkammergut, a magical landscape of mountains, lakes and forests unfolds. Watching over this natural beauty are several spectacular castles, while underground lie caves and the mines that tapped the mineral that gave the region its wealth – and its name, salt.

Highlights

1 **Salzburg** fortress and Old Town, including the **Mozart House** (p85)
2 The **Gosausee**, with spectacular views over the Hoher Dachstein (p100)
3 Graceful **Seeschloss Ort** (p112)
4 **Hallstatt**, one of Austria's most beautifully located villages (p108)
5 The **Dachstein Rieseneishöhle** cave systems (p109)

Salzburg

The city of Salzburg, literally the 'salt town', has its origins as a Roman settlement, Juvavum, founded in 15 BC. However, even before then the area had been populated by Celtic peoples on the sites of earlier Neolithic settlements. Once the Romans left, having bequeathed Christianity to the city, it rose to prominence again in around AD 700 when the monastery of St. Peter was founded. Salzburg was to go on to become the most important ecclesiastical centre in southern Germany.

Ruled by the archbishops from their fortress on the Mönchsberg, the city flourished, and with the coming of the Counter-Reformation, received its now predominantly Baroque appearance. The archbishops gave employment to the young musician and composer Wolfgang Amadeus Mozart, even if he bridled under their rather prescriptive rule and was to make a break from them in Vienna. However, being the birthplace of one of Europe's most illustrious musical figures was to give the city a reputation for music and the arts. This reputation was to bear fruit in the early 20C, when the writer Hugo von Hofmannsthal, composer Richard Strauss, and theatre director Max Reinhardt started the Salzburg Festival, one of the world's most important celebrations of the arts.

Beyond the City

Salzburg itself is overlooked by the Untersberg and other peaks of the Berchtesgaden Alps, many of which rise just over the border in neighbouring Bavaria, Germany. The Province of Salzburg lies to the south and west, generally following the line of the Salzach River, whose valley forms the backbone of the region, and off which extend several beautiful 'spurs'.

Directly south of Salzburg is the town of Hallein, where salt has been extracted from the Dürrnberg since Celtic times. It was from here that the archbishops received much of their income. The mine, which is still working, can be visited and makes an exciting excursion for adults and children alike.

Beyond Hallein, the valley of the Salzach narrows, embracing spectacular gorges, caves and waterfalls, as well as the castle of Hohenwerfen. Here, underground attractions can be seen such as the Eisriesenwelt Caves, which are full of extraordinary ice formations.

To the east stretch the lands of Tauern and Lungau, bordering the region of Steiermark and south of the Dachstein peaks, more properly part of the Salzkammergut. The Tauern and Lungau are full of small villages with splendid churches, among the most remarkable being those at Bischofshofen and Tamsweg. And do not miss the castles at nearby Mauterndorf and Moosham.

Hallstatt by the Hallstätter See

The Salzkammergut

Situated directly east of the city of Salzburg, the Salzkammergut is one of Austria's most beautiful and popular regions. Split between the neighbouring provinces of Salzburg, Oberösterreich (Upper Austria), and Steiermark (Styria), it is hard to locate in administrative terms, but is perhaps best thought of as Austria's lake district. In all there are 76 different lakes dotted across the region, some large, some small, but all of them with their own beauty. They are also, of course, centres for watersports, including swimming, diving and sailing. The lakes are surrounded by mountains, generally lower and greener than those to the west, but many with spectacular rock faces falling straight to the water and offering their own challenges to climbers and walkers.

The name Salzkammergut literally means the 'salt chamber estate' and, like nearby Salzburg, this area is famous for its salt deposits and mines, a number of which can be visited. It was salt that attracted the Celts to the region and one of their most famous settlements, now the site of one of the Salzkammergut's most beautiful and spectacularly located villages, Hallstatt, gave its name to their culture and society. The Hallstatt culture was the predominant Central European culture from the eighth to sixth centuries BC.

In both summer and winter the region is a magnet for tourists, Austrian as well as from elsewhere. But this is not a recent phenomenon; people have been holidaying here since the mid-19C when the resort of Bad Ischl was the premier location, especially when Franz Joseph and Sissi brought the court during the summer to take the waters at the spa.

The southern part of the Salzkammergut is marked by the Dachstein range, high and rugged and with glaciers on the mountains' north face. The glaciers can be seen from the Gosausee, clearly one of the most spectacular and beautiful views in all of the Alps. The Dachstein also contains some of the longest cave systems in Europe and one highlight is undoubtedly a visit to the Dachstein Welterbe.

The largest lake in the region is the Attersee, a favourite spot for sailing. Mountains enclose the south, while at its northern end the countryside is gentle and rolling. The lake is surrounded by lovely villages, as are the Wolfgangsee and Mondsee. The villages of St. Wolfgang and Mondsee are well worth a visit; both have important churches (the latter making an appearance in *The Sound of Music*).

Even more spectacular is the Traunsee. At its northern end lies the popular resort village of Gmunden, while at its southern end, Ebensee is the location of a notorious camp during World War II – and a grim reminder that this part of the world has not always been a tourist's paradise.

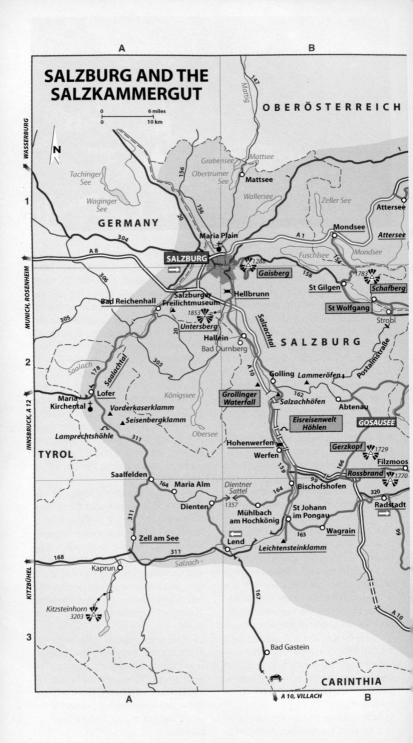

SALZBURG AND THE SALZKAMMERGUT

0 ____ 6 miles
0 ____ 10 km

N

A

B

OBERÖSTERREICH

WASSERBURG

Mattig

Tachinger See

Grabensee

Mattsee

Mattsee

Obertrumer See

Waginger See

156

Wallersee

Zeller See

Attersee

1

GERMANY

Mondsee

Attersee

304

156

20

Maria Plain

A 1

Fuschlsee

Mondsee

MUNICH, ROSENHEIM

A 8

SALZBURG

158

154

Schafberg 1783

306

1288

Gaisberg

St Gilgen

Schafberg

305

Bad Reichenhall

Salzburger Freilichtmuseum

Hellbrunn

St Wolfgang

Strobl

1853

Untersberg

Salzachtal

SALZBURG

20

Hallein
Bad Dürnberg

A 10

Golling

Lammeröfen

Postalmstraße

2

Saalach

178

Saalachtal

Königssee

162

Grollinger Waterfall

Salzachhöfen

Abtenau

305

Maria Kirchental

Lofer

Vorderkaserklamm

Seisenbergklamm

Obersee

Eisreiselwelt Höhlen

GOSAUSEE

Lamprechtshöhle

311

Gerzkopf 1729

Filzmoos

TYROL

Hohenwerfen

Werfen

159

166

Rossbrand 1770

Saalfelden

164

Maria Alm

Dientner Sattel

164

99

Bischofshofen

320

Radstadt

311

Dienten

1357

Mühlbach am Hochkönig

St Johann im Pongau

163

Wagrain

66

INNSBRUCK, A 12

Zell am See

311

Lend

Leichtensteinklamm

168

Kaprun

Salzach

167

KITZBÜHEL

Kitzsteinhorn 3203

3

Bad Gastein

CARINTHIA

A 10, VILLACH

A

B

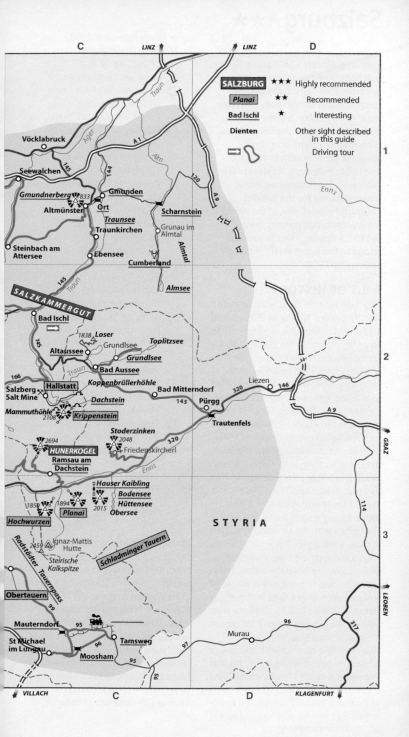

SALZBURG ★★★ Highly recommended
Planai ★★ Recommended
Bad Ischl ★ Interesting
Dienten Other sight described in this guide
Driving tour

Vöcklabruck
Seewalchen
Gmundnerberg △ 833
Altmünster
Steinbach am Attersee
Ebensee
Gmunden
Ort
Traunsee
Traunkirchen
Scharnstein
Grunau im Almtal
Cumberland
Almsee
Enns

SALZKAMMERGUT

Bad Ischl
1838 Loser
Altaussee Grundlsee
Bad Aussee
Hallstatt
Salzberg Salt Mine
Mammuthöhle *2108*
Krippenstein
Dachstein
Toplitzsee
Grundlsee
Koppenbrüllerhöhle Bad Mitterndorf
Pürgg
Liezen
Trautenfels

△ *2694* HUNERKOGEL
Stoderzinken *2048*
Friedenskircherl
Ramsau am Dachstein
Hauser Kaibling
Bodensee
Hüttensee
Übersee
△ *1850 1894*
2015
Hochwurzen *Planai*
Ignaz-Mattis Hütte
△ 2459
Steirische Kalkspitze
Schladminger Tauern

STYRIA

Radstädter Tauernpass
Obertauern
Mauterndorf
95
St Michael im Lungau
Moosham
96
Tamsweg
95
97
Murau
96
317

VILLACH C D KLAGENFURT

75

Salzburg★★★
and the Saalachtal Valley

Salzburg, Mozart's birthplace, is a delight from the moment you spot the massive Hohensalzburg fortress rising above roofs and the meandering Salzach River backed by the mountain of the Untersberg. With their wrought-iron signs, spacious squares with fountains, and noble buildings, its streets are charming. Every summer, music lovers descend for the famous Salzburg Festival, one of the world's most prestigious concert series. In 1997, Salzburg's Old Town was added to the list of World Heritage Sites by UNESCO.

A BIT OF HISTORY

The See of Salzburg was founded shortly before 700 by St. Rupert and was raised in the following century to an archbishopric. In the 13C the bishops were given the title of Princes of the Holy Roman Empire. Their power extended as far as Italy, while their coffers were filled to bulging with revenue from the Salzkammergut salt mines. Three of these rulers showed a taste for building, and in just over half a century converted the little medieval town into a grand residence in the Italian style.

Wolf Dietrich von Raitenau was elected archbishop in 1587. He was a typical representative of the Renaissance: brought up in Rome and closely connected with the Medicis, he longed to make Salzburg the Rome of the North. After a fire destroyed the central cathedral quarter, he hired the Italian architect Scamozzi to build a new house of worship even larger than St. Peter's in Rome. Raitenau had 15 children with Salome Alt, a great beauty for whom he built Schloss Mirabell.

After losing a conflict with the dukes of Bavaria over the salt trade, he was imprisoned in 1612 in Hohensalzburg Castle, where he died after five years of captivity. His only completed building project was his own mausoleum in St. Sebastian cemetery.

▶ **Population:** 152,083.
🛈 **Info:** Mozartplatz 5. ☏0662 88 98 70. www.salzburg.info/en.
▶ **Location:** Salzburg lies on Austria's northern border. Alt. 424m/1,391ft.
🅿 **Parking:** Park & Ride Süd (Alpenstraße), Altstadt-Garage (Mönchsberg), Bahnhof-Garage (Südtiroler Platz), Mirabell-Garage (Mirabellplatz); Airportcenter (Innsbrucker Bundesstraße), Park-garage Auersperg (Auerspergstraße), Parkgarage Linzer Gasse (Glockengasse), Raiffeisen-Garage (Schwarzstraße). Public car parks on Akademiestraße, Basteigasse, Hellbrunn, Mülln, Petersbrunnstraße, Salzburg Airport, Volksgarten.
☺ **Don't Miss:** Hohensalzburg, Residenz, Mozart's Birthplace.
🕐 **Timing:** Allow at least two days for a visit.
👨‍👧 **Kids:** Haus der Natur, Schloss Hellbrunn, Zoo Salzburg, Salzburger Freilichtmuseum.

Markus Sittikus, Raitenau's successor, downscaled the cathedral and entrusted the work to another Italian architect, Santino Solari. The mansion of **Hellbrunn** to the south of Salzburg is another of his architectural legacies. It fell to **Paris Lodron** to complete the work begun by his predecessors, including the cathedral, which was solemnly consecrated in 1628. Lodron also finished the Residence and opened new streets in the town, creating the face of Salzburg for generations to come.

TOURIST INFORMATION

Salzburg Tourist Office
www.salzburg.info/en.
Mozartplatz, *Mozartplatz 5.*
℘*0662 88 98 70.*
Hauptbahnhof *(Main station),*
Bahnhofsvorplatz. ℘*0662 88 98 73 40.*
Salzburg South, *Park & Ride Car*
Park, Alpensiedlung-Süd, Alpenstraße.
℘*0662 88 98 73 60.*
Salzburg Card
This ticket offers free travel on nearly
all public transport in the city, as well
as free entrance to most sights in and
around Salzburg. From May–Oct, the
cost is €26/35/41 for 24/48/72 hours,
respectively. From Nov–Apr, prices
change to €23/31/36; discounts are
available for children. Obtain card
from tourist offices, travel agencies
and hotels. *www.salzburg.info/en.*
Salzburgerland Card
If you're spending most of your time
in Salzburg province and want
to visit the city only for one day, this
discount may be a better alternative.
It is valid for free or discounted
admission to 190 regional attractions
and integrates a *24hr Salzburg Card*.
It is available May–Oct and is valid
either for six days (€59) or 12 days
(€69); discounts available for children.
Obtain card from tourist offices,
hotels, and even some gas stations.
www.salzburgerlandcard.com.
City tours and guided tours
Panorama City Tour (1hr) –
Departures daily at 9.15am, 11am,
noon, 2pm, 4pm, and by request.
Information and reservations
from Salzburg Panorama Tours,
Schrannengasse 2/2. ℘*06 628 83 21 10.*
www.panoramatours.at.
Mozart City Tour (2hr) – Run by
Panorama Tours, departures daily at
9.15am, 11am, noon, 2pm and 3pm.
Kultur Tourismus – Cultural tours,
concentrating on art and architecture
(2hr), departures daily. ℘*0662 83*
48 33. www.kultur-tourismus.com.
Die Nachtwächter (1.5hr) – Tour of
Salzburg by night, departure Apr–Oct

daily 9pm. ℘*0662 63 64 23.*
www.nachtwaechter-salzburg.com.
Salzburg Guides – Local experts who
can be hired by the hour, ℘*06 624 96*
80 11, www.salzburgguides.at.

PUBLIC TRANSPORT

Information and tickets for the city
bus network can be obtained from
the ticket offices of the Salzburg
public transport authorities
(Schrannengasse 4, Lokalbahnhof at the
Hauptbahnhof, Alpenstraße 91; ℘0662
44 80 15 00; www.salzburg-ag.at).
Tickets can also be purchased from
bus drivers, at tobacconists (*Trafiken*)
and from ticket machines at the bus
stop (tickets for a single trip should
be purchased in advance in blocks of
five, before starting on a journey, as
a supplement is charged when they
are bought separately from the bus
driver or a ticket machine). Tickets
must be date-stamped as soon as
you get on the bus.
The Salzburg transport authorities
also offer transferable daily, weekly,
monthly (valid from time of first use)
and family-day-trip **travel cards** for
the city area. The 24hr ticket (valid for
the whole transport network, only
available in blocks of five), with which
you can make as many journeys
as you like, is perhaps the most
convenient. These cards are available
from tobacconists and ticket offices
(daily, weekly and monthly tickets also
from ticket machines).

POST OFFICES

Hauptpostamt (Main post office):
Residenzplatz 9. Open year-round
Mon–Fri 8am–6pm.
Postschalter im Hauptbahnhof
(counter at the main station):
Südtirolerplatz 1. Open year-round
Mon–Fri 8am–8.30pm, Sat 8am–2pm,
Sun 1pm–6pm.

Wolfgang Amadeus Mozart (1756–91)

Mozart statue in Kapuzinerberg

© Tourismus Salzburg GmbH

A child prodigy

Leopold Mozart, a talented composer and violinist in the service of the archbishop of Salzburg, recognised early on the exceptional gifts of his son, Wolfgang, and his older daughter, Nannerl. Young Wolfgang had a remarkable musical memory and sophisticated ear, had started composing by the age of five, and was a keyboard virtuoso by the age of six. He had also started learning the harpsichord at age four. Leopold gave his son a serious musical education and together they undertook a four-year tour of Europe, getting enthusiastic receptions in Munich, Vienna, Frankfurt, Paris, London and The Hague. At Schönbrunn, Empress Maria Theresia herself embraced the talents of young Wolfgang, who remained in Salzburg for three years after the family's return in 1766. In 1772, he was made concertmaster of the court orchestra of the Salzburg prince-archbishop.

First disappointment

Until 1777, Mozart spent long periods in Salzburg. His employer, Archbishop Hieronymus Colloredo, did not approve of his many journeys abroad and relations were consequently strained. After a major quarrel with the prince-archbishop in 1777, Mozart resigned his post and left for Paris, where he came under the influence of opera reformer **Christoph Willibald Gluck**. During the following years he produced much religious music, including the *Coronation Mass*, and symphonic and lyrical pieces such as the opera *Idomeneo*. In 1781, after a further heated altercation with the prince-archbishop, the breach was complete. Mozart left Salzburg for Vienna.

Independence in Vienna

Arriving in Vienna, the 26-year-old Mozart had only a limited means of support. He married Constanze Weber the same year and got initiated into the ideals of Freemasonry. Discovery of Handel's oratorios and of further works by Bach, together with the influence of his friend and mentor, Haydn, contributed to the development of his mature style. The public adulation occasioned by works such as *The Abduction from the Seraglio* of 1781 was not repeated, at least in Vienna, where the public failed to appreciate *The Marriage of Figaro* (1786) and *Don Giovanni* (1787). A sombre period began.

The final years (1788–91)

Mozart's career was to end in poverty and destitution. Though nominated "Composer to the Imperial Chamber" by Joseph II, he never received a commission. His final operas, *Così fan Tutte* (1790) and *La Clemenza di Tito*

(1791) met with a cool reception, barely mitigated by the success of *The Magic Flute* (1791). The composer was to die alone and haunted by the spectre of his own death. On 6 December 1791 the paupers' hearse carried Mozart's corpse to a communal grave in St. Mark's Cemetery in Vienna. His remains have never been identified.

Mozart's musical legacy

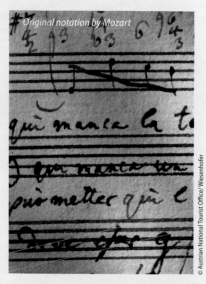

Original notation by Mozart

© Austrian National Tourist Office/Wiesenhofer

Mozart's astonishing output was equalled only by the ease with which he mastered every form of musical expression. His style has a charm that makes him a favourite with a wide public and is appreciated even by the unpractised ear. Pleasant and sparkling motifs ripple beneath a rhythmic counterpoint of sprightly liveliness. But spontaneity and brio need not mean lack of depth. His works are characterised by an exquisitely pure melodic line, sometimes tinged with melancholy. Towards the end of his life, this vague sadness turned into despair, forcefully expressed in the 40th Symphony in G minor, *Don Giovanni*, the 'tragic' quintet in G major (K 516) and the *Requiem* (K 626), composed shortly before Mozart's death (and not completed). Composer Frédéric Chopin (1810–49) was so affected by this great choral work that he requested it be played at his own funeral. These late works reflect Mozart's struggle against poverty and illness.

Salzburg Festival

Guided tour daily (50 min), hours vary: see website for schedule. €7. *Meet outside the Festspielshop.* 0662 80 45 500.
www.salzburgerfestspiele.at/guided-tours.

Many years passed before his native city acknowledged Mozart's outstanding place in musical history. His biography was written in 1828 by Constanze's second husband, Georges Nicolas de Nissen. In 1842 Salzburg put up a statue to Mozart and later founded a musical academy named the **Mozarteum**. Finally, in 1917, the poet Hugo von Hofmannsthal, the composer Richard Strauss, and the producer Max Reinhardt conceived the idea of a Mozart Festival.

The festival was inaugurated in 1920 and is held from late July to the end of August each summer, attracting the cream of the world's musical talent. Performances take place at the great **Festival Hall** (Grosses Festspielhaus), built in 1960 by the architect **Clemens Holzmeister**, the small festival hall (Kleines Festspielhaus), the old Summer Riding School (Felsenreitschule), the **Mozarteum**, and the **Landestheater**. The festival starts with a performance of Hofmannsthal's *Jedermann (Everyman)* on the cathedral forecourt.

FESTUNGSBERG★★

Allow about 2hr to visit the hilltop sights. Ascent on foot (20min) or by **Festungsbahn** *funicular (○open Apr–Jun & Sept–Oct daily 9am–8pm; Jul–Aug daily 9am–10pm; Nov–Mar daily 9am–5pm; closed part of Nov. ☞€6.80 one-way, €8.40 round-trip, or €12, which includes entry to fortress). Access from behind the cathedral, where a street leads up to the funicular station.*

Fortress★★

○Open daily May–Sept 9am–7pm; Jan–Apr and Oct–Dec daily 9.30am–5pm. ☞€12, includes entrance to fortress, museums and audio-guide (€9.20 without funicular). ☎0662 84 24 30 11. www.salzburg-burgen.at.

The former stronghold of the prince-archbishops, the Hohensalzburg stands on a block of Dolomite rock, some 120m/394ft above the Salzach. The castle was begun in 1077 by Archbishop Gebhard, frequently enlarged, and eventually remodeled into a comfortable residence with state rooms by Archbishop Leonhard von Keutschach in the 15C. The archbishops often stayed here until the end of the 15C, reinforcing it considerably by the addition of towers, bastions for cannons and barbicans and the construction of magazines and arms depots.

At the exit from the upper station of the funicular, turn left to the terrace from which stairs and a postern lead into the fortress. Go past the guided tours office and a little way downhill, bearing right along the lists and round the fortified nucleus of the inner castle until you come to a courtyard opposite the south wall of the church.

St. **Georgskirche** is decorated with two beautiful marble reliefs: a group of statuary in red Salzburg marble of Archbishop Leonhard von Keutschach flanked by two priests, and above it a Crucifixion.

The door to the right of the church leads to the terrace of the **Kuenburgbastei**, from which there is a good **view★★** of the Old Town's domes and belfries.

State Rooms and Museums

These rooms and the museums are best explored on a 90min self-guided audio tour, included in the admission fee.

From the Reck watchtower there is a **panorama★**, which is particularly interesting, towards the Tennengebirge and the Salzburg Alps (south).

The state rooms, formerly the archbishops' apartments, were fitted out by Leonhard von Keutschach, and are largely in their original state. Walls are adorned with Gothic woodcarvings, doors are fitted with complicated ironwork, and coffered ceilings have gilded

Old town and Hohensalzburg viewed from Kapuzinerberg

© Tourismus Salzburg GmbH

studs. In the **Goldene Stube** (Gilded Room) is a monumental porcelain stove (1501) decorated with flowers and fruit, Biblical scenes and the coats of arms and portraits of sovereigns of the period.

The **Gerichtssaal** (Hall of Justice) has a coffered ceiling whose beams feature coats of arms of the provinces, dioceses or abbeys under the archbishop's jurisdiction as well as those of the dignitaries of his court.

The admission ticket also includes entry to the Marionette Museum, and the **Rainer-Regimentsmuseum** displaying weapons, uniforms and mementoes of Archduke Rainer's Infantry Regiment, stationed here from 1871 to 1918.

Nonnberg Monastery

Adjacent to the fortress. ○*Open daily 7am–dusk (7pm in summer).*

This Benedictine convent was founded around 700 by St. Rupert, whose niece, St. Erentrud, was its first abbess. It is the oldest convent in the German-speaking world.

The **Stiftskirche**, enclosed by its churchyard, is in Late Gothic style and dates from the end of the 15C. The main doorway was built between 1497 and 1499; it incorporates the older Romanesque tympanum showing the Virgin Mary flanked by John the Baptist and St. Erentrud on one side and by an angel and a kneeling nun on the other. The high altar is adorned by a fine carved and gilded altarpiece. In the central section, a Virgin and Child is attended by St. Rupert and St. Virgil, while the wings depict scenes from The Passion. The vast crypt contains the tomb of St. Erentrud. In the **Johanneskapelle**, the Gothic altarpiece (1498) is attributed to Veit Stoss, with a central section showing the Nativity.

WALKING TOURS

OLD TOWN★★
Domplatz

Three porticos link the buildings around this square, the cathedral and the Residenz, the former ecclesiastical palaces.

In the centre rises a column (1771) dedicated to the Virgin Mary.

Cathedral★

○*Open Mon–Sat 8am–5pm, Sun 1pm–5pm (Mar–Apr, Oct and Dec til 6pm; May–Sep til 7pm).* ℘*0662 80 47 79 50. www.salzburger-dom.at.*

Consecrated in 1628, the monumental Early Baroque dom is largely the work of Italian architect Santino Solari. Its west front, flanked by two towers, is of light-coloured local marble and graced by numerous statues, including those of Sts Rubert, Virgil and Peter and Paul in front of the main door.

The **interior** is impressive both in size and the richness of its decoration. Mozart was baptised in the Romanesque font in 1756. The tombs of the prince-archbishops and a Romanesque Crucifix can be seen in the **crypt**.

Dommuseum

○*Open Wed–Mon 10am–5pm (Jul–Aug daily, Wed til 8pm).* ●€*12.* ℗℘*0662 80 47 18 60. www.kirchen.net/dommuseum.* The cathedral treasure and a fabulous *Kunst- und Wunderkammer*, a gallery of objets d'art, minerals, crafts and precious knickknacks amassed by Archbishop Guidobald von Thun are all presented in a haphazard way as they were in the 17C. Upstairs is religious art from the Middle Ages to the present.

Behind the cathedral, in Kapitelplatz, is the **Kapitelschwemme**, a drinking trough for horses in the form of a monumental fountain. From here, a street leads up to the station of the **Festungs-bahn** (○*see previous page).*

▷ Cross the square and enter the cemetery via a gate to the right of the Festungsbahn.

St Peter's Cemetery★★

Cemetery: ○*Open daily Apr–Sep 6.30am–7pm; Oct–Mar daily 6.30am–6pm.* ●*Free. Catacombs:* ○*Open May–Sept daily 10am–6pm; Oct–Apr daily 10am–5pm.* ●€*2.* ℘*0662 84 45 760. www.stift-stpeter.at.*

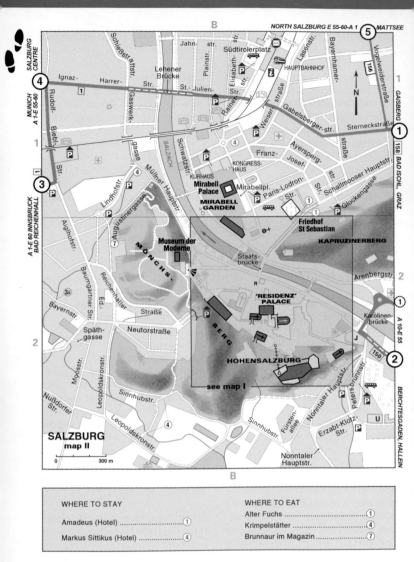

SALZBURG
map II

0   300 m

WHERE TO STAY	
Amadeus (Hotel)	①
Markus Sittikus (Hotel)	④

WHERE TO EAT	
Alter Fuchs	①
Krimpelstätter	④
Brunnauer im Magazin	⑦

The Petersfriedhof abuts the vertical rock wall of the **Mönchsberg** (*see map*), the mountain ridge to the west of the fortress. The rock is hollowed out with early Christian catacombs that can be seen on a short guided tour. The cemetery itself features wrought-iron grilles under Baroque arcades enclosing the chapels where several generations of the patrician families of Salzburg lie. Famous names include Nannerl Mozart, the architect Santino Solari and Michael Haydn. The 15C Margaretenkapelle is a delicate con-struction dating from the Late Gothic period.

▶ Walk through the cemetery to find the entrance to St. Peter's church.

St. Peter's Abbey★★
⊙Open year-round daily 8am–noon, 2.30pm–6.30pm.
The triple-aisled Romanesque basilica was drastically remodelled in the 17C and 18C, but the harmony of the original structure can still be detected amid the Baroque décor.

The best view of the interior is from the gilded **wrought-iron grille★** separating the porch from the nave. An elaborate work of art, it was made in 1768 by Philip Hinterseer. The building's simplicity, heightened in effect by the white walls, emphasises the elegance of Benedikt Zöpf's Rococo decoration, with its fine paintings and pastel shades that enhance the delicate stuccowork. The ceiling of the nave is frescoed with scenes from the life of St. Peter, painted by the Augsburg artist, Johann Weiss. On each of the walls above the great arches, note, among other compositions, an Ascent to Calvary and a Raising of the Cross by Solari. Beneath the upper windows is a set of paintings by Franz X König representing *(right)* the life of St. Benedict and *(left)* the life of St. Rupert. The altarpiece on the high altar and those in the nave have red-marble columns. Most of the altarpiece paintings are the work of Martin Johann Schmidt ("Kremser Schmidt"). Only the south aisle has chapels and also contains the tomb of St. Rupert. In the chapel furthest from the chancel a marble tomb was built by the archbishop for his father, Werner von Raitenau.

▷ Cross the abbey courtyard, turn right into the covered passageway and enter the Franziskanerkirche through the west doorway.

Franciscan Church★
⊙Open daily 6.30am–7.30pm.
The Franziskanerkirche was consecrated in 1223, but has been remodelled several times. It offers a comparison between the Romanesque and Gothic styles.
The plain Romanesque nave, divided from the side aisles by massive pillars whose capitals are adorned with foliage and stylised animals, contrasts with the well-lit chancel from the final Late Gothic 15C. The star vaulting is supported by palm-shaped cylindrical columns. The high altar is the work of Johann Bernhard Fischer von Erlach (1708). The finely modeled statue of the Virgin Mary gracing the Baroque high altar was once part of a

Gothic altarpiece by Michael Pacher in the late 15C.

▷ Exit through the side door and follow Franziskanergasse westward, to the corner of Wiener-Philharmoniker-Gasse and Max Reinhardt Platz.

Museum der Moderne – Rupertinum
Wiener-Philharmoniker-Gasse 9.
⊙Open year-round Tue–Sun 10am–6pm (Wed til 8pm), and Mon during major festivals. ⊙Closed 24, 25 Dec. ⊚€6 Rupertinum, €8 Mönchsberg; combination ticket €12. ⭓. ℘0662 84 22 20.
www.museumdermoderne.at.
The Museum der Moderne now has two spectacular locations. The original one is the **Rupertinum**, a Baroque townhouse on Wiener-Philharmoniker-Gasse built as a seminarya by the archbishops in the 17C (⭓*see also Mönschberg entry*). It contains a fine collection of 20C art covering all major media, including painting, sculpture, graphic works and photography. The collection features works by major artists, including Gustav Klimt and Oskar Kokoschka as well as Austrian Expressionists Herbert Boeckl, Eduard Bäumer and Hans Fronius and such sculptors as Alfred Hrdlicka and Fritz Wotruba.

North of Max-Reinhardt-Platz stands the massive Baroque **Kollegienkirche** (University Church), another work of Johann Bernhard Fischer von Erlach.

▷ Continue west past the Grosses Festspielhaus (Festival Hall).

From Herbert-von-Karajan-Platz (36) there is a tunnel (the Siegmundstor), about 135m/443ft long, which was made in 1767 to go under the Mönchsberg hill. Look back for a fine **view** of the Hohensalzburg Fortress and the Stiftskirche St. Peter.

▷ Continue along Franziskanergasee to Universitätsplatz.

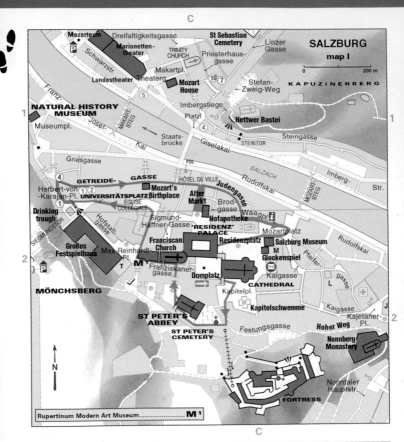

Universitätsplatz★

Kollegienkirche.

Ⓒ*Open year-round daily 9am–6pm.*

This splendid building by Johann Bernard Fischer von Erlach, consecrated in 1707, dominates Universitätsplatz (University Square). The grandiose Baroque church is considered one of the architect's finest constructions. As its name suggests, the church was built for use by the university, which was founded in 1623 by the Benedictines.

On the other side of the square is an array of colourful façades. Below these townhouses (one of which is Mozart's Geburtshaus) are **passageways★** *(Durchhäuser)* and inner courtyards linking the square with Getreidegasse.

▶ Take one of the passages to arrive on Getreidegasse (Ⓒsee below) or go on through Universitätsplatz to reach Herbert-von-Karajan-Platz, where you will find the Pferdeschwemme fountain.

Drinking Trough

This vast horse trough (Pferdeschwemmme), just to the right of the entrance to the Sigmundstor tunnel, was built about 1700 and was exclusively used by the horses in the archbishops' stables. It is adorned with a group of dynamic sculptures, the *Horsebreaker* by Mandl, and murals depicting fiery steeds.

▶ Either retrace your steps to Universitätsplatz and take one of the passageways, or continue on from Herbert-von-Karajan-Platz along Münzgasse and take the first turning on your right in Getreidegasse.

Getreidegasse★★

This is one of the main streets of old Salzburg. Like the rest of the Old Town, which, being crowded between the Mönchsberg and the Salzach, could expand only vertically, it is narrow and lined with five- and six-storey houses. A lively shopping street, Getreidegasse is adorned with many wrought-iron signs that add a picturesque touch, while the houses with their carved window frames lend the street a certain elegance.

Getreidegasse with Christmas decorations

© Tourismus Salzburg GmbH

▶ Walk east down Getreidegasse to a turning on your left, opposite which is a building with a yellow façade.

Mozart's Birthplace

Getreidegasse 9. ◐*Open Jul–Aug daily 9am–8pm; Jan–Jun and Sept–Dec daily 9am–5.30pm. Last entry 30min before*

closing. ⌨*€10, combination ticket with Mozart-Wohnhaus €17.* ☏*0662 84 43 13. www.mozarteum.at.*
The Mozart family lived on the third floor of this building from 1747 to 1773. Wolfgang was born here on 27 January 1756 and composed many of his early works here. In late 2005, the hallowed rooms were turned into a light, sound and design installation by the American set designer and director Robert Wilson. It incorporates instruments played by Mozart, including his harpsichord, his piano and the violin he played as a child, as well as musical manuscripts, letters, portraits, furniture and everyday objects from the times of Mozart.

▶ Continue along Getreidegasse.

Pass the town hall (Rathaus) on the left, and on the right the Alter Markt (Old Market Square), which contains a fountain to St. Florian and a curious **hofapotheke**, a chemist's shop with a lavish Rococo interior.

▶ Cross Alter Markt, pausing at the fountain of St. Florian, patron saint of firemen, and beyond it the hofapotheke, to the narrow street of Judengasse.

Judengasse★

This street (Jews' Alley) cuts through the former Jewish Ghetto. It is narrow and picturesque and like the Getreidegasse, adorned with wrought-iron signs. At no. 4, note a sculptured group in stone representing the Virgin of Maria Plain.

▶ Pass through the Waagplatz to Mozartplatz, then continue to Residenzplatz.

Salzburg Museum: Neue Residenz

Mozartplatz 1. ◐*Open year-round Tue–Sun 9am–5pm.* ☞*Guided tours Thu 6pm.* ⌨*€8.50.* ☏*06 6262 08 08 700. www.salzburgmuseum.at.*
Set in the New Residence palace, this museum, opened in 2007, is dedicated to the history of the city. The first floor

concentrates on famous people who have lived in Salzburg, including the doctor, alchemist and philosopher Paracelsus (1493–1541). On the second floor is a display of archaeological and medieval artefacts as well as the galleries of paintings, costume and religious items that make up the "Salzburg Myth" exhibit that explores the ongoing appeal of the city. Following are galleries for temporary exhibitions.

Residenzplatz

Until the 16C there was a cemetery on this site. Prince-archbishop Wolf Dietrich created the present square, which got its fountain in the 17C. The square is bounded on the south by the cathedral and to the west by the Residenz. On the east, the **Glockenspiel** is a carillon of 35 bells cast in Antwerp at the end of the 17C and set up in Salzburg in 1705.

Residenz★★

The main residence of Salzburg's prince-archbishops was begun during the reign of Wolf Dietrich and completed under his successor, Markus Sittikus. In 1867 Emperor Franz Joseph received Napoleon III here, and the German emperor, Kaiser Wilhelm I, in 1871.

State Rooms

Open Jul–Aug daily 10am–5pm (Wed til 8pm); rest of the year Wed–Mon 10am–5pm. €12, includes self-guided audio tour and gallery. 0662 80 42 26 90. www.salzburg-burgen.at.

The Residenz is entered from Residenzplatz via a marble gate festooned with the coats of arms of various prince-archbishops. A sweeping staircase leads to the Carabinieri Hall. Beyond it are the state rooms, redecorated in the early 18C by Johann Lukas von Hildebrandt and featuring ceiling frescoes by Johann Michael Rottmayr and Martino Altomonte. The young Mozart gave his first court concert at age six in the Conference Hall and later also performed in the Rittersaal (Knight's Hall), which has good acoustics and is still used for concerts today. Gobelin tapestries adorn the opulent **Audienzsaal** (Reception Hall).

Residenzgalerie

Same hours & entry fee as the State Rooms. 0662 84 42 21 09. www.residenzgalerie.at.

The gallery houses a collection of important European paintings from the 16C to the 19C. The exceptional array of 17C Dutch painting includes works by great masters such as Rembrandt, Rubens and Brueghel. The valuable exhibition, which occupies 15 state rooms, is rounded off with a display of 19C masterpieces.

RIGHT BANK OF THE SALZACH★

▶ Climb up to the Kapuzinerkirche via the steep walkway reached from the Linzergasse. From the church, go downhill again for about 50m/55yd, turn left and follow the sign Stadtaussicht-Hettwer Bastei to the viewpoint.

Hettwer Bastei★

The Hettwer Bastei (bastion) on the south side of the Kapuzinerberg offers fine **views★** over Salzburg.

▶ Descend back to Linzergasse and take Dreifaltigkeitsgasse – named after the church by Fischer von Erlach – to Makartplatz, beyond which lies the Schloss Mirabell and Garden.

Mirabell Palace and Garden★

Little is left of the mansion built at the beginning of the 17C by Prince-archbishop Wolf Dietrich as a residence for his mistress, Salome Alt. It was overhauled by Johann Lukas von Hildebrandt in the following century, but suffered severe damage during the 1818 Great Fire that swept the city. The final reconstruction resulted in the rather sober building you see today, which houses parts of the city administration. Of the original building, the **marble staircase★★** with its sculptures by Georg Raphael Donner has survived, as has the Marmorsaal★★ (Hall of Marble), a gilt and coloured stucco extravaganza now used for wedding ceremonies and chamber concerts.

The von Trapp Family

Rodgers and Hammerstein's 1959 Broadway musical *The Sound of Music* (film version starring Julie Andrews from 1965) was based on the true story of the von Trapp family. The young novice, Maria Kutschera (1905–87) became governess to widower Baron Georg von Trapp's seven children and finally married the baron himself. Together they formed a family choir in the mid-1930s, but then fled Nazi-occupied Austria in 1938 and continued their career in the USA.

Salzburg locations used in the film include Nonnberg Monastery, Hohensalzburg Fortress, Mirabell Palace and Gardens, the Felsenreitschule, where the family sing their farewell song in the film, and Schloss Leopoldskron, where the front facing the lake is used as Baron Trapp's house, and in whose music pavilion the love duet takes place.

Particularly more noteworthy is the exquisite **Mirabell Garden** laid out in 1690 by Fischer von Erlach. With an abundance of flowers, statues and sculptures, the garden is a favourite place for relaxing. From a terrace, a fine view over the gardens encompasses the old fortifications and the Hohensalzburg. The old orangery has been restored and encloses a pretty courtyard with bright flowerbeds.

▶ Retrace your steps back to Makartplatz. On the far side is a low building that is the Mozart-Wohnhaus.

Mozart-Wohnhaus (Tanzmeisterhaus)

Makartplatz 8. ○*Open Jul–Aug daily 8.30am–7pm; Jan–Jun and Sept–Dec daily 9am–5.30pm.* ☞*€10, combination ticket with Mozart's Geburtshaus, €17.* ☎*0662 87 31 54. www.mozarteum.at.*
This house, the Mozart family home from 1773 to 1787, was largely destroyed by bombs in 1944 but completely rebuilt in 1994–95. Mozart lived in the house until 1780 and composed a number of his works here.

The self-guided tour with commentary and music takes you through rooms filled with period furniture, old instruments, literature and documentary items on the Mozart family and their contemporary environment. In the **Mozart-Ton- und Filmmuseum**, you can watch and listen to clips from an extensive audio and video archive.

▶ Return to Linzergasse and turn left, heading north to St. Sebastian's Church.

Friedhof St. Sebastian

The original church of St. Sebastian fell victim to the Great Fire of 1818. The cemetery behind the present edifice was conceived by Prince-archbishop Wolf Dietrich, whose grand **mausoleum** dominates the grounds. Its interior is tiled with multi-hued porcelain.
Other famous people buried here include Mozart's wife and father (in the central lane) and in the southwestern corner, the doctor and philospher Paracelsus, who died in Salzburg in 1541.

LEFT BANK OF THE SALZACH

Allow 3hr to walk between and visit the three sights on this tour. Leave from the Natural History Museum at Museumsplatz 5.

👤👤 Natural History Museum★★

Allow at least 2hr. ○*Open year-round daily 9am–5pm.* ☞*€8, children €5.50.* ☎*0662 84 26 53. www.hausdernatur.at.*
The vast and well-presented Haus der Natur has many lively and engaging displays. Particularly interesting sections, especially for children, are those on dinosaurs, the world of outer space with its diorama depicting the first moon landing, human and animal characters in myth and fable, as well as the aquarium and reptile house.

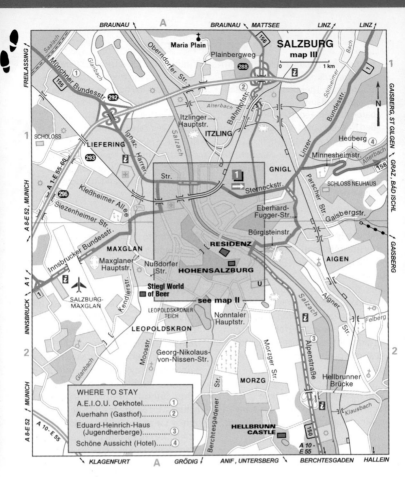

> Not far from the entrance to the museum is the small doorway to the lift on Gstättengasse.

Mönchsberg★★

Lift operates 🕒*Sept–Jun Mon 8am–7pm, Tue–Sun 8am–9pm; Jul–Aug daily 8am–11pm.* 💰*€3.60 round trip.* 📞*0662 88 84 97 50.*

From the Gstättengasse, a lift ascends to a terrace just below the Museum der Moderne, from which there is a fine general **view★★** of the city with modern Salzburg along the right bank of the Salzach and the Old Town between the river and the Hohensalzburg Fortress. To the south are the Tennen- and Hagengebirge, the Untersberg and the Salzburg Alps; eastward rise the Kapuzinerberg and the Gaisberg.

Museum der Moderne – Mönchsberg

🕒*Open Tue, Thu–Sun 10am–6pm, Wed 10am–8pm.* 💰*€12.* 📞*0662 84 22 20.* *www.museumdermoderne.at*

In 1998, the Modern Art Museum expanded into a new, unapologetically modern building atop the **Mönchsberg**, easily reached by the Mönchsberglift (👆*see p88*). The minimalist space frequently hosts temporary exhibitions of cutting-edge contemporary art.

EXCURSIONS
👥 Stiegl's World of Beer

From the centre, take Neutor, Moos- and Nussdorfer Straße. Take the fourth turn on the left. Bräuhausstraße 9. 🕒*Exhibition: open daily 10am–5pm (Jul–Aug til 7pm). Last entry 1hr before* closing. ⊛€11.50, includes beer, or for children a non-alcoholic drink, and souvenir, children €6.50. ℘050 14 920. www.stiegl.at.

This exhibit occupies an old malthouse in one of Salzburg's largest breweries. Themes include ingredients, beer production and advertising. Tours end with a tasting session in the brewing room.

Maria Plain

Plainbergweg 38, Bergheim bei Salzburg. From the central railway station take Elisabethstraße, then Itzlinger Hauptstraße, turn right onto Plainbergweg. ⓒOpen daily 7am–7pm. www.mariaplain.at.

This pilgrimage church was built between 1671–1674 to house a "miraculous" portrait of the Virgin and Child. The Baroque interior contains an altar painting by Francesco de Neve.

♟ Hellbrunn Castle★

ⓒOpen Jul–Aug daily 9am–9pm; May, Jun, Sept daily 9am–5.30pm; Mar–Apr and Oct daily 9am–4.30pm. ⊛€12.50, children €5.50.
Guided tours. ℘0662 82 03 720. www.hellbrunn.at.

This schloss, in the style of an Italian palazzo, began life as the summer residence of Prince-archbishop Markus Sittikus in 1615. A self-guided audio tour of the interior takes in the banquet hall, with its *trompe-l'œil* painting, and the domed Octagon or Music Room. Memorable, especially for children, is a guided walk around the attractive **gardens**, filled with whimsical trick fountains built to entertain the fun-loving prince-archbishop. There is a mechanical theatre with 13 figures that are set in motion by the action of water, as well as amazing shell-encrusted grottoes, and fountains that suddenly start spurting.

♟ Zoo Salzburg

Hellbrunnerstraße 60. ⓒJan–Feb and Nov–Dec daily 9am–4.30pm; Mar daily 9am–5.30pm; Apr–May and Sept–Oct daily 9am–6pm (Jul–Aug til 6.30pm; Aug Fri and Sat til 10.30pm). Last entry half hour before closing. ⊛€10.50,

children €4.50. ℘06 628 20 17 60. www.salzburg-zoo.at.

Salzburg's zoo has large, natural enclosures for most of the animals. Highlights include big cats and Alpine animals.

♟ Salzburger Freilichtmuseum

Hasenweg, Grossgmain. ⓒOpen Jul–Aug daily 9am–6pm; mid-Mar–Jun & Sept–early Oct Tue–Sun 9am–6pm; mid-Oct–Nov Tue–Sun 9am–5pm. ⊛€11, children €5.50. ℘0662 85 00 11. www.freilichtmuseum.com.

Some 60 original buildings from the province, representing six centuries of traditional architecture, have been reassembled in this open-air museum.

Untersberg★

12km/7.4mi. 1hr round-trip drive, plus 15min by cable-car. Leave Salzburg on Alpenstraße towards Berchtesgaden. Just after the major St. Leonhard intersection, bear right and continue to the cable-car station. ⓒRuns year-round daily 9am–4pm. ⊛€23.50 round-trip, children €11.50. ℘06246 72 47 70. www.untersbergbahn.at.

From a height of 1,853m/6,079ft, there is a splendid **panorama** of the Salzburg basin, the Salzburg Alps (Watzmann, Steinernes Meer, Staufen), the Wilder Kaiser and the Dachstein.

🚗 DRIVING TOURS

① GAISBERGSTRAßE★★
13km/8mi.

▷ Leave Salzburg on the B 158 towards St. Gilgen. After about 4km/2.5mi turn right for the scenic drive to Gaisberg.

Park at the end of the road below the Gaisberg summit for a **view★** of Salzburg, the Salzach gap and the Salzburg Alps. A path runs between the guest houses past the transmitting station, taking you to the summit at an altitude of 1,288m/4,226ft. From here, the mountain **panorama★** encompasses Salzkammergut and the Dachstein massif.

② SAALACHTAL VALLEY★
95km/59mi.

The valley of the River Saalach, which breaches the Northern Limestone Alps, forms the quickest link between Salzburg, Zell am See and the Grossglockner. This valley runs north–south between Salzburg and Zell am See. With stops, this tour can easily turn into a day trip.

▶ Leave Salzburg on road no. 1. Shortly past the airport, consider making a 6km/3.7mi detour to Grossgmain and the Salzburg open-air museum. Continue to Bad Reichenhall in Germany.

Bad Reichenhall★
A major producer of table salt, this Bavarian town sits atop some of the richest salt springs in Europe. The salt water spa helps cure respiratory diseases. Although the town is small, it still has its own symphony orchestra, which puts on concerts throughout the year *(www.bad-reichenhaller-philharmonie.de).*

▶ Branch off at Schneizlreuth from the Deutsche Alpenstraße onto the Lofer road.

The road turns away from the Saalach and climbs up to Melleck. The Steinpass marks the Austrian border. The road then returns to the Saalach.

Lofer★
See KAISERGEBIRGE ①.

The section from Lofer to Saalfelden, in a glacial gorge, is strikingly uniform.

Wallfahrtskirche Maria Kirchental
4km/2.5mi south of Lofer. At St. Martin bei Lofer turn right off B 311 onto a narrow toll road (impassable to private vehicles in winter). Open year-round daily 7am–7pm. ℘06588 85 284. www.maria-kirchental.at.
Nicknamed the "Pinzgau Cathedral," this rustic yet graceful late-17C pilgrimage church was designed by the renowned Johann Bernhard Fischer von Erlach. It was redecorated and furnished over the 18C and 19C as the offerings of the pilgrims mounted up.

About 6km/3.7mi beyond Lofer, the road reaches the **Vorderkaser gorge**, the first of a trio of natural attractions. *Combination ticket €9.*

⚲ Vorderkaserklamm
Allow about 45min. Open May–Oct daily 9.30am–5pm. €4.30, children €2.50. ℘06 582 83 52. www.naturgewalten.at.
Shaped by a thundering torrent, this wildly romantic gorge (400m/1,300ft long, 80m/260ft deep and 80cm/31.5in wide in some places) is reached via an easy 2.5km/1.5mi trail through an idyllic recreation area, complete with pools for swimming. From here an initially steep path leads up through the forest to the entrance to the gorge. Footbridges run past waterfalls and under wedged rocks.

⚲ Lamprechtshöhle
8km/5mi beyond Lofer. Dress warmly as the cave is only about 5–7°C/41–45°F. Guided tours (45min) Mon–Fri 8.30am–7pm, Sat–Sun 9am–5pm. €6; children €3. ℘06 582 83 52. www.naturgewalten.at.
One of Europe's most extensive underground cave networks extends some 51km/32mi. Tours cover 700m/765yd of it and end at a viewing platform, from which visitors can peer down into the depths of a giant cavern.

▶ 1km/0.6mi after the Lamprechtshöhle, turn left for the Seisenberg gorge.

Seisenbergklamm
Open May–Oct daily 8.30am–6.30pm. €4.50, children €2.90. ℘06 582 83 52. www.naturgewalten.at.
Steps, footbridges and trails access the Weissbach as it roars through this narrow gorge, about 600m/656yd long and up to 50m/164ft deep. Highlights are the tortured rock formations of the dark **Dunkelklamm**. Beyond here, a

trail climbs through the forest along the Weissbach *(30min)* to Gasthof Lohfeyer, situated in Alpine pastures.

▶ From the town of Weissbach, the road runs through a steep, long canyon and eventually reaches the Saalfelden basin.

Sallfelden 🕭

This market town, with 12 centuries of history, has a historical town centre and varied scenery. In winter, Saalfelden is favoured by cross-country skiers for its 80km/50mi of ski tracks. Towering above the resort are the imposing rock faces of the Steinernes Meer.

▶ 5km/1.8mi SE from Saalfelden is the village of Maria Alm, whose basilica is worth continuing to if you have time. Returning to Sallfelden, follow signs to Zell am See for a drive along the lake.

ADDRESSES

🏨 STAY

🛏 *During Festival, hotel prices are higher.*

🛏 **A.E.I.O.U. OEKOTEL** – *Eugen-Müller-Straße 9.* ℘*0662 43 00 43. www.oekotel.com. 13 rooms.* 🍴. This hotel, located 6km/3.6mi out of town, has simple but decent rooms (bus 4).

🛏 **Jugendherberge Eduard-Heinrich-Haus** – *Eduard-Heinrich-Straße 2.* ℘*0662 62 59 76. http://heinrichhaus.hostel-salzburg.at. 132 beds.* 🍴. This youth hostel is a short distance from the city centre, but is easy to reach by public transport (bus 3).

🛏🍽 **Gasthof Auerhahn** – *Bahnhofstraße 15 (from Salzburg-Itzling, reached via Kaiserschützenstraße).* ℘*0662 45 10 52. www.auerhahn-salzburg.at. 15 rooms.* 🍴. This family-run hotel, a little distance from the centre, has good value, straightforward rooms and excellent service. The restaurant serves good local food.

🛏🍽 **Hotel Schöne Aussicht** – *Heuberg 3 (3km/1.8mi NE of city centre).* ℘*0662 64 06 08. www.salzburgpanorama.at. 28 rooms.* 🍴. Just outside Salzburg, this hotel is set amid pleasant countryside with splendid views over the city.

🛏🍽🍽 **Hotel Amadeus** – *Linzergasse 43–45.* ℘*0662 87 14 01. www.hotel amadeus.at. 26 rooms.* 🍴€16. Situated close to the Old Town, down a small pedestrianised street, the hotel offers traditionally decorated rooms with a distinctly Austrian feel.

🛏🍽🍽 **Hotel Markus Sittikus** – *Markus-Sittikus-Str. 20.* ℘*0662 87 11 21. www.markus-sittikus.at. 39 rooms.* 🍴€14. This classic hotel has neat and clean, traditionally furnished rooms. It sits just behind the Mirabell palace and gardens, a stone's throw from the Old Town.

🛏🍽🍽🍽 **Hotel Blaue Gans** – *Getreidegasse 41–43.* ℘*0662 84 24 91. www.blauegans.at. 40 rooms.* 🍴. Located on Salzburg's main shopping street, this "Art Hotel" features chic and well-designed rooms.

🛏🍽🍽🍽 **Hotel Goldener Hirsch** – *Getreidegasse 37.* ℘*0662 80 840. www. goldenerhirschsalzburg.com. 70 rooms.* 🍴 €33. Possibly Salzburg's finest hotel, set in a 15C building, it exudes understated luxury. Plus two excellent restaurants.

🛏🍽🍽🍽 **Hotel Sacher Salzburg** – *Schwarzstraße 5–7.* ℘*0662 88 977. www.sacher.com. 111 rooms.* 🍴. This classic grand hotel provides a fantastic view over the Old Town.

🛏🍽🍽🍽 **Hotel Stein** – *Giselakai 3–5.* ℘*0662 87 43 460. www.hotelstein.at. 54 rooms.* 🍴. Located across the river from the Old Town, this hotel has large, well-designed rooms with good views. Its Steinterrasse, popular with locals, sits on the top-floor terrace.

🍽 EAT

🛏 **Krimpelstätter** – *Müllner Hauptstraße 31.* ℘*0662 43 22 74. www.krimpelstaetter.at. Tue–Sat 11am–midnight (daily during Festival).* This popular Gasthaus has a lovely *Biergarten*. The local dishes served are excellent.

🛏🍽 **Alter Fuchs** – *Linzergasse 47–49.* ℘*0662 88 20 22. www.alterfuchs.at. Open daily noon–midnight.* Local dishes are straightforward and filling at this simple eating place. The daily menu is a good deal.

🍴🍺 **Zum fidelen Affen** – *Priesterhausgasse 8. ☏0662 87 73 61. www.fideleraffe.at. Mon–Sat, 5pm–midnight.* This traditional tavern offers a good selection of wine and beer, as well as outstanding local fare.

🍴🍺🍽 **Alt Salzburg** – *Bürgerspitalgasse 2. ☏0662 84 14 76. www.restaurant-altsalzburg.at. Mon 6pm–10.30pm, Tue–Sat 11.30am–2pm, 6pm–10.30pm (daily during Festival).* This comfortable, traditional restaurant specialises in classic Austrian dishes.

🍴🍺🍽 **Carpe Diem** – *Getreidegasse 50. ☏0662 84 88 00. www.carpediemfinest fingerfood.com. Daily 8.30am–midnight.* Modern Austrian cooking, with a fair amount of Italian-inspiration, dished up in a chic lounge atmosphere.

🍴🍺🍽 **Stadtkrug** – *Linzergasse 20. ☏0662 87 35 450. www.stadtkrug.at. Wed–Sun 5pm–10.15pm (daily during the Festival). Reservations required.* A good place to find traditional Austrian food. The setting is pleasant and there is a solid wine list.

🍴🍺🍽🍽 **Brunnaur im Magazin**– *Augustinergasse 13. ☏0662 84 15 84 14. www.magazin.co.at. Mon 10am–6pm, Tue–Sat til 8pm. Reservations recommended.* Upmarket fare in one of Salzburg's top foodie destinations with lots of fish and Mediterranean-inspired dishes. Good wines from an extensive list.

CAFES/BARS

Bazar – *Schwarzstraße 3. Mon–Sat 7.30am–7.30pm, Sun 9am–6pm (7.30am–after performances during the Festival).* Stylish café with terrace overlooking the Salzach.

Republiccafé – *Anton-Neumayer Platz 2. Sun–Thu 8.30am–1am, Fri–Sat 8.30am–4am.* This café, bar and club, attached the Republic Theatre, is one of the liveliest places in the Old Town.

m32 – *Mönchsberg 32 (Museum der Moderne Mönchsberg). Tue–Sun 9am–1am (daily during Festival).* This fantastic terrace café has what must be the best view of all over the Old Town.

Steinterasse – *Giselakai 3–5. Daily 7am–midnight.* This stylish and popular terrace overlooking the river and Old Town is an inviting place for a cocktail.

Tomaselli – *Alter Markt 9. Mon–Sat 7am–7pm, Sun 8am–7pm (daily til 9pm during Festival).* This classic coffeehouse makes a good place to sit and watch the world go by.

Die Weisse – *Rupertgasse 10. Mon–Sat 10am–2am.* This rustic inn with its own brewery serves *Weissbier* made on the premises.

SHOPPING

The main shopping areas include the Altstadt (Old Town), the areas around Getreidegasse, the area around the Festspielhäuser, Mozartplatz, Kaigasse, Alter Markt, Linzer Gasse, Marktplatz and Mirabellplatz.

Christmas market

© Hellbrunn/Foto Sulzer/Tourismus Salzburg GmbH

MARKETS

Mirabellplatz: Schrannenmarkt (fresh food, vegetables, flowers), *Thu 5am–1pm.* **Universitätsplatz** and **Wiener-Philharmoniker-Gasse:** Vegetable market, *Mon–Fri 7am–7pm, Sat 6am–3pm.*

SOUVENIRS

Craft goods and traditional costume (Trachten): Salzburger Heimatwerk, *Residenzplatz 9*; souvenir shop in Mozarts Geburtshaus, *Getreidegasse 9*; Mozartkugeln: Café-Konditorei Fürst (inventors of the original recipe), *Brodgasse 13, Sigmund-Haffner-Gasse. Getreidegasse 47* and *Mirabellplatz 5.*

ENTERTAINMENT

Grosses and **Kleines Festspielhaus**, *Hofstallgasse 1*, ✆*0662 80 450. www.salzburgerfestspiele.at.* Opera and concerts.

Landestheater, *Schwarzstraße 22*, ✆*0662 87 15 12 222. www.salzburger-landestheater.at.* Theatre, musicals and dance.

Kleines Theater, *Schallmooser Hauptstraße 50*, ✆*0662 87 21 54. www. kleinestheater.at.* Theatre and cabaret.

Salzburger Marionettentheater, *Schwarzstraße 24*, ✆*0662 87 24 06. www.marionetten.at.* World-famous marionette theatre, shows works by Rossini, Offenbach, Strauss, Tschaikovsky.

ARGEkultur Salzburg, *Ulrike-Gschwandtner-Straße 5*, ✆*0662 84 87 84. www.argekultur.at.* Dance, drama and music.

SZENE-Salzburg, *Anton-Neumayr-Platz 2*, ✆*0662 84 34 48. www.szene-salzburg.net.* Theatre, music and dance.

Rockhouse Salzburg, *Schallmoser Hauptstraße 46*, ✆*0662 88 49 140. www.rockhouse.at.* Jazz, folk, blues, reggae and rock concerts.

CINEMA

Mozartkino, *Kaigasse 33*, ✆*0662 84 22 22. www.mozartkino.at;* **Salzburger Filmkulturzentrum, Das Kino**, *Giselakai 11*, ✆*0662 87 31 00. www.daskino.at.*

© Tourismus Salzburg GmbH

Salzburg Festival, for The Abduction from the Seraglio' at the Large Festival Hall

FESTIVALS

Mozartwoche: *Second half of Jan. www.mozarteum.at.* Solo recitals, chamber, choral and orchestral concerts.

Osterfestspiele: *Sat before Palm Sun–Easter Mon. www.osterfestspiele-salzburg. at.* Easter music festival with opera and concerts.

Salzburger Pfingstfestspiele (specialising in Baroque music): *Sat before Whit weekend until Whit Mon. www.salzburgerfestspiele.at.* Whitsun music festival with opera and concerts.

Salzburger Festspiele: *End Jul–end Aug. www.salzburgerfestspiele.at.* Salzburg Festival with opera, concerts, theatre, literature, poetry readings and Lieder.

SommerSzene: *Jul. www.szene-salzburg. net.* Festival of alternative art, theatre, dance, exhibitions.

Kulturtage: *Late summer.* www. kulturvereinigung.com. Cultural festival with opera and concerts.

Internationaler Salzburger Jazz-Herbst: *Early Nov. www.salzburgerjazz herbst.at.* Autumn jazz festival with jazz, spirituals and Gospel music.

Weihnachtsmärkte (Christmas markets): *every weekend in Advent).* Mirabellplatz and Domplatz and in the castle courtyard of Hohensalzburg.

Salzach Valley★

The Alpine valley of Salzach is an artery of the province of Salzburg, whose hooked shape conforms with the bent course of the gushing Salzach River. Strung out between the Krimml waterfalls and the city of Salzburg is a series of basins called the Pinzgau, the Pongau, the Tennengau and the Flachgau. Until the coming of the railway, each of these isolated sections of the valley tended to lead its own life, quite separate from that of its neighbours.

- ℹ **Info:** www.salzburger land.com.
- ▶ **Location:** The valley extends south of Salzburg in western Austria.
- 🙂 **Don't Miss:** Eisriesenwelt, Gollinger Wasserfall, Salzburger Salzwelten.
- 🕐 **Timing:** This route can be done as a day trip from Salzburg, although if you stop at every sight, you'll probably need 2 days.
- 👨‍👦 **Kids:** Eisriesenwelt, Erlebnisburg Hohenwerfen, Salzwelten Salzburg.

🚗 DRIVING TOURS

1 FROM SALZBURG TO LEND
89km/55mi.

The Salzach Valley, closely hemmed in as far as Lend, opens out north of Schwarzach to form the Pongau basin.

▶ Leave Salzburg on the B 159, heading towards Hallein.

Hallein
The history of this town is inextricably tied to the extraction of salt, or "white gold", found under the mountain of the Dürrnberg. Hallein was at the centre of the region's economy, as well as having been an important cultural hub since at least 600 BC. Surrounded by mountains, and close to Salzburg, it is also a centre for sport and leisure activities.

The lively pedestrianised zone of the **Altstadt★** (Old Town) in the centre of Hallein is most attractive, with romantic small lanes and restored old houses.

On the north side of the parish church are the house and grave of **Franz Xaver Gruber** (1787–1863), composer of the famous Christmas hymn *Stille Nacht, Heilige Nacht* (Silent Night). It is now the site of the **Stille Nacht Museum** (*Gruberplatz 1; ○ open Sep–Jun Fri–Sun 3pm–5pm, Jul–Aug daily; Advent to Epiphany daily noon–6pm; www. stillenachthallein.at*).

The **Keltenmuseum** is set in the offices of the old salt mines (1654) and houses exhibits from the excavation of the Celtic village on the Dürrnberg (*Pflegerplatz 5; ○ daily 9am–5pm; ⊗ €6; ℘ 06245 80 783; www. keltenmuseum.at*). The second floor has three decorated rooms that describe the history of salt extraction.

▶ Return to the B 159 and then turn right towards Bad Dürrnberg.

👨‍👦 Salzwelten Hallein★
Allow 2hr30min. 🙂 *Not suitable for children under 4 years.* 👣 *Guided tours (70min) Apr–Oct daily 9am–5pm; Nov–Mar daily 10am–3pm. ⊗ €21, ticket includes admission to the Kelten Museum and Stille Nacht Museum. ℘ 06132 200 85 11. www.salzwelten.at.* Salt harvested in the Dürrnberg mountain brought wealth to the archbishops of Salzburg; production continued until 1989. Now a small section of the underground warren of tunnels has been developed as a show-mine, where guides lead entertaining tours. The visit ends with a romantic raft trip across the floodlit underground salt lake.

▶ Continue S from Hallein on the B 159 to Golling, taking you across the side of the forested Tennengau.

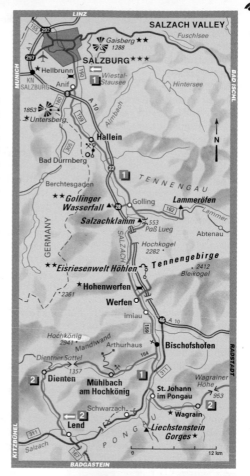

Gollinger Wasserfall★★

30min round trip walk to the foot of the waterfall, 1hr30min to the top;
€2.50.

The Golling Falls tumble down 75m/246ft from the Hoher Göll (2,522m/8,277ft) and can be spectacular depending on the time of year and the amount of water. Park at the Torrener Hof, then follow the road for a short stretch in the direction of Kuchl and pick up the trail to the fall *(follow the red/white markings)* leading through forest. From the bridge and ticket booth, the path climbs gently from the bottom of the cascade.

Lammeröfen

After the entrance to Oberscheffau, 7km/4.3mi beyond the junction, park next to Lammerklause guest house. The walk (1hr round-trip) begins after the bus stop. Open daily May and Oct 9am–5pm; Jun and Sept 9am–6pm; Jul–Aug 9am–7pm. €4.50.
06244 84 42 20.
www.lammerklamm.at.

After about a 20min walk through the relatively wide gorge, the trail reaches the ticket booth. From here, a shorter but more rewarding walk up concrete steps accesses a viewpoint beneath a natural rock vault, where a narrow cleft in the rock lets light into the gorge below.

▶ Return to Golling and continue S again: at the top of the pass is Salzachöfen.

Salzachklamm (Salzachöfen)

This gorge is one of three impressive natural features close to the Lueg Pass (553m/1,800ft), along with the Lammeröfen gorge and Golling water-

Gollinger Wasserfall

© Austrian National Tourist Office/ Mallaun

fall. From the Gasthof Pass-Lueg Höhe, a steep path *(45min round-trip: be careful as it is slippery in rainy weather)* leads to a jumble of rocks forming a natural bridge over the Salzach.

▶ Descend the southern side of the pass and follow the valley of the Salzach S until you come, just before the village of Werfen, to Festung Hohenwerfen.

🔺 Festung Hohenwerfen★

Allow 3hr. 🔺*Interior by guided tour only (1hr). The castle entrance is a 15min uphill walk from the car park.*
🕐*Open Jan–Apr and Oct–Dec daily 9.30am–5pm; May–Sept daily 9am–7pm.* 🔺*Guided tours available.* ✆*€12 or €15.20 with lift, children €6.80 or €8.70. ☎0662 84 24 30 11. www.salzburg-burgen.at.*

The fortress dates back to the 11C, but was extended to its present form in the 16C and 17C by the archbishops of Salzburg, who used it as a military base, residence, hunting lodge and prison. Tours take in the chapel, the torture chamber and the armoury. There is also a museum of falconry and a birds-of-prey trail in the front castle. The birds kept here (long-legged buzzards, white-tailed eagles and red kites) per-

form in **flight displays★** *(daily 11.15am, 3.15pm; mid-Jul–mid-Aug 11.15am, 2.15pm and 4.30pm).*

▶ Continue towards Bischofshofen. At Werfen you can take a turning to the right to see the caves at Eisriesenwelt★★. The B 159 continues to Bischofshofen.

Bischofshofen

The Pongau's largest town has a fine **setting★**, with the Tennengebirge to the north and the Hochkönig to the west. A Celtic settlement stood here and was the centre of a thriving copper mining industry. Salt, another important commodity, was also mined here. Bischofshofen is the fourth and final venue of the world-famous ski-jumping Vierschanzentournee, held on 6 January.

Pfarrkirche

This church is the lowest of three built on a slope and linked by a narrow road, thus forming a typical example of a "family group" of churches. The present building dates to 1450 and was commissioned by the bishop of Chiemsee, who is buried in a marble tomb in the north transept. A copy of the **Rupertuskreuz**, a processional cross, a simple gilded cross encrusted with precious stones, that is

Salzach Valley, with the Hochkönig mountains near Dienten

© Austrian National Tourist Office/Weinhaeupl W.

Austria's oldest religious work of art (c. 700), is on display as well. The original is in the cathedral museum at Salzburg.

▶ Take road no. 311 S to St. Johann im Pongau. Cross the town and take the left-hand turn following signs to Liechtensteinklamm.

Liechtensteinklamm★
Allow 1hr round trip walk. ○*Open May–Sept daily 8am–6pm; Oct daily 9am–4pm.* ⊕€6. ℘06412 60 36. *www.liechtensteinklamm.at.*
This gorge has sheer and overhanging white-streaked rock walls and unusual formations wrought by water that contribute to its charm. At the end of the walkways you'll be rewarded by the sight of a majestic **waterfall★**.

▶ Return back to the turn off for St. Johann and turn left for Lend.

② FROM LEND TO RADSTADT
⊕ *The mountain section between Dienten and Mühlbach has many bends and is often blocked by snow in winter. This 68km/42mi tour can be completed in around 3hr30min in fine weather.*

▶ Leave Lend on the minor road to Dienten and cross the Salzach

The church at **Dienten** soon emerges against the white cliffs of the Hochkönig, impressive in the evening sun. The road reaches its highest point at the Dientener Sattel (1,370m/4,493ft).
Beyond here, there are still several steep sections, including the sharp descent into **Mühlbach**, a centre for mountain walking.

▶ At the road just S of Bischofshofen, retrace your steps on the 311 to St. Johann in Pongau.

St. Johann im Pongau is recognisable by its twin-towered, late-19C neo-Gothic church. Between here and the Enns Valley, the road crosses some lovely countryside.

▶ Instead of turning right for the Liechtensteinklamm, continue straight on to reach Wagrain.

Wagrain★
Situated at 800m/2,625ft, Wagrain has developed into a winter resort and is part of the Ski Alliance that extends between Tennengebirge and Radstädter Tauern. There is a museum devoted to Joseph Mohr, who wrote the text of the hymn *Silent Night*.

Radstadt
⬑*See RADSTADT.*

ADDRESSES

⌂STAY

⊜ **Hinterkellaubauer** – *Kellau 43, 5431 Kuchl.* ℘06244 5050. *www.urlaubambauernhof.at/hinterkellaubauer.* 4 rooms. ⊒. A lovely farm about 2.5km/1.5mi from the village. The décor is rustic and charming and its setting is beautiful.

⊜⊜ **Landgasthof Reitsamerhof** – *Reitsam 22, 5450 Werfen.* ℘06468 53 79. *www.reitsamerhof.at.* 25 rooms. ⊒€10. This hotel has simple, comfortable rooms. The restaurant is decent and in the summer has a lovely terrace.

⊜⊜⊜ **Pension Wagnermigl** – *Marktstraße 61, 5431 Kuchl.* ℘06244 51 39. *www.kuchl.com. Closed Nov–Apr.* 23 rooms. ⊒. This guesthouse is an inviting and comfortable place to stay, with tasteful rooms decorated in a traditional style.

⚹/EAT

⊜⊜ **Kellerbauer** – *Kellerbauerweg 41, Bad Vigaun.* ℘0625 83 474. *www.kellerbauer.at. Closed Mon–Tue.* 5 rooms. ⊒. This restaurant is typical of the region, with good local food and a few international dishes. It has pleasant surroundings and friendly service.

⊜⊜ **Wirtshaus** – *Am Marktplatz 56, Golling.* ℘06244 42 20. *www.doellerer.at Closed Sun–Mon.* 12 rooms. ⊒. Good local food is available at this traditionally decorated Wirtshaus. The proprietors also have a number of rooms for rent.

Eisriesenwelt Caves★★

With more than 40km/24.8mi of subterranean passages, the "world of the ice giants" (Eisriesenwelt Höhlen) is the largest accessible ice-cave system in the world. An 800m/2,625ft-long show cave reveals ice formations shaped into fans, curtains, cathedrals and other fantastical features in icy air, even in summer.

●●TOUR OF THE CAVES

Caves can be seen only by guided tour (1hr15min) Jul–Aug daily 9am–4.45pm; May–Jun and Sept–Oct daily 9am–3.45pm (last tour). ☞€24 (€12 without cable-car). Eisriesenwelt-Linie – Bus leaves from Parkplatz Gries every 25 mins, or from Werfen Bahnhof at 8.18am, 10.18am, 12.18pm and 2.18pm. ✆06468 52 48.

As the average temperature in the caves is around 0°C/32°F in summer, warm clothing is advisable and good 🄗 hiking shoes will serve better when climbing the many steps in the caves. To protect this nature monument, visited by around 2,500 people a day during the opening period, photography is not allowed. Getting to the cave entrance requires a moderate level of fitness, but

🄸 **Info:** ✆06468 52 48. www.eisriesenwelt.at.

▶ **Location:** The entrance to the caves is at 1,641m/5,384ft on the western ciiffs of the Hochkogel about 6km/3.7mi northwest of Werfen.

🄿 **Parking:** There is a car park at about 1,000m/3,281ft elevation on the mountain road.

🕓 **Timing:** Allow at least 3hr for the trip up and through the caves.

you'll be spoiled with terrific views all the way.

From Werfen, the mountain road climbs steeply for 5km/3mi to the 🄿 car park at 1,000m/3,281ft. It can be travelled in your own car, a most difficult drive, or by shuttle bus *(journey time: 5min)* leaving from the Werden train station and from the bottom of the Eisriesenweltstraße near the village. From the car park, it's a 20min walk to the Wimmer Hütte (hut).

At Wimmer Hütte, catch the **cable-car** *(🕓operates Jul–Aug daily 9am–3.20pm; May–Jun and Sept–Oct 9am–3.20pm; ☞€14 round-trip; ✆0664 40 22 481)* to the Dr.-Oedl-Haus mountain inn (1,575m/5,167ft). From the inn, it's another 20min walk to the cave entrance.

●●Guided tour of the caves

About 1hr15min.

By the light of acetylene and magnesium lamps, visitors enter the world of the ice caves, climbing up to the Posselt-Halle gallery (named after the first explorer to discover the caves in 1879).

The Hrymr Hall, with its Hrymr Mountain, and Niflheimr with Frigg's Veil, are both examples of fantastic ice architecture enhanced by clever lighting. At the back of the Ólinn Gallery is a throne-like ice formation called ÁsgarÏr. Another highlight is called the Cathedral.

What's in a name...

The origin of many of the names of the galleries in the Eisriesenwelt subterranean complex is Old Norse mythology, as featured in the Old Icelandic saga "Edda": **Ólinn** is the father of the gods; **Frigg** is his wife and at the same time goddess of fertility; **Hrymr** is an ice giant; **ÁsgarÏr** is the home of the Æsir gods, who are at war with the Vanir; and **Niflheimr** is the world of shadows in the frozen north that existed before this world was created.

Salzkammergut★★★

Salt has given the Salzkammergut region its name and, until recently, exceptional economic importance. For about 4,000 years the "white gold" was the region's main source of prosperity, as is reflected in its towns' proud architecture. Tourism has boomed since the early 20C, thanks to dozens of lakes, legendary mountains, such as the Dachstein and the Totes Gebirge, and long-established spa resorts like Bad Ischl. In 1997, UNESCO honoured the region's exceptional beauty and cultural significance by placing it on its list of World Heritage Sites, together with Hallstatt and the Dachstein.

🚗DRIVING TOURS

THE LAKES★★

1 SALZBURG TO BAD ISCHL
84km/52mi.

▶ Leave Salzburg and take the A 1 autobahn to the Mondsee exit.

Between Salzburg and Mondsee, the autobahn affords views of the Drachen-wand cliffs and the Schafberg spur.

Mondsee
32km/20mi east of Salzburg.
The town of Mondsee lies below the cliffs of the Drachenwand and the Schafberg. It grew around a Benedictine abbey founded in the 9C and dissolved in 1791. It is named after the nearby lake, which is shaped like a crescent moon and whose temperate, clean waters attract scores of watersports enthusiasts in the warmer months.

Basilika Mondsee★
The wedding church from the *Sound of Music* has been a basilica minor since 2005. Swiss-born sculptor **Meinrad Guggenbichler** (1649–1723) spent 44 years in Mondsee, creating seven of the

- **Info:** Götzstraße 12, Bad Ischl. ✆06132 24 00 00. www.salzkammergut.co.at.
- **Location:** The Salzkammergut is east of Salzburg in central Austria.
- **Parking:** Plenty of car parks along the roads beside the lakes.
- **Don't Miss:** St. Gilgen, the Dachstein massif above the Gosausee and the camp and museum at Ebensee.
- **Timing:** This route, over mountain roads, will take you at least a couple of days to complete if you want to explore the area in detail.

13 black-and-gold altars, including the masterful altar of the Holy Sacrament, on the lower left-hand side, with its twisted columns supported by cherubs.

Pfahlbau- und Klostermuseum
Open Jul–Aug Tue–Sun 10am–6pm; May–Jun and Sept Tue–Sun 10am–5pm; Oct Sat–Sun 10am–5pm. €3.50. ✆06 232 22 70. www.museum-mondsee.at.
The Pfahlbaumuseum sheds light on a phase of the Neolithic Era known as the "Mondsee Culture" (about 5,000 years ago) when residents lived above the water in buildings resting on stilts.

Bauern- und Freilichtmuseum
Open May–Jun and Sept Tue–Sun 10am–5pm; Jul–Aug Tue–Sat 10am–6pm. €3.50. ✆06 232 22 70. www.museum-mondsee.at.
Aside from the exhibit, of the traditional farmhouses relocated to this open-air museum, the Rauchhaus (smoke house) is the most interesting. It combines living spaces for humans and animals under a single roof.
The north shore of the Mondsee, which is calm and welcoming at first, becomes a little more severe beyond the Pichl

promontory, where the road climbs over a wooded rise.

Burggrabenklamm

5km/3mi west of Au along the B 152 to the southern tip of the Attersee.
P *Park near the Gasthof Jägerwirt; 30min round trip walk.*

This small but dramatic gorge with an 18m/60ft waterfall is one of the most beautiful in the Salzkammergut. The trail, which is short and often slippery, leads past a statue of St. Mary.

▶ Backtrack on the B 152 to the south shore of the Mondsee.

The pass road connecting Scharfling and St. Gilgen has remarkable **panoramic views**★★ from a car park above St. Gilgen. Beyond the slender onion-domed village bell-tower, the **Wolfgangsee**★★ lake stretches towards the Rinnkogel massif.

St. Gilgen★

Delightful St. Gilgen, at the northwestern tip of the **Wolfgangsee**, is a former outpost of the prince-archbishops of Salzburg and the birthplace of Mozart's mother, Anna-Maria Pertl. His older sister, Nannerl, settled here after marrying the local magistrate. The family legacy is kept alive with a Mozart fountain on Mozartplatz and a small **memorial exhibit** (🕐 *open May–Oct Sat–Sun 10am–noon;* ⊜ €4; ✆ *06227 20 242; www.mozarthaus.info*) in the former law court at Ischlerstraße 15, the very building where Anna was born, and where Nannerl later lived with her family. Another pleasant diversion in town is the **Musikinstrumente Museum**, which displays medieval and exotic instruments from around the world.

The lake, meanwhile, attracts numerous watersports enthusiasts, especially sailors who appreciate its favourable wind conditions. Scheduled boat services stop at numerous sites around the Wolfgangsee, while the nostalgic paddle-steamer *Kaiser Franz Joseph*, which began operating in 1873, offers leisurely lake cruises.

▶ Leave the main road at Strobl to make the detour to St. Wolfgang and then along the direct road to Bad Ischl, avoiding Strobl.

② DACHSTEIN MOUNTAINS

267km/166mi, beginning in Bad Ischl. A couple of days will allow you to make the most of this area.

▶ Take the B 145 south towards Gosaumühle and then Hallstatt.

The Gosausee★★★

The parking place at the end of the road gives access to the banks of the Gosausee. From the lake there is a superb **view**★★ of the limestone **Hoher Dachstein** (2,995m/9,825ft) massif and its small glaciers.

🗨 Don't miss the **walk around the lake**★★★, along a very easy path *(approximately 1hr)*. The route provides constant magnificent views of the peaks of the Gosaukamm, and magical reflections of the surrounding forests and peaks in the lake's waters.

🚶 **Walk to the Gosaulacke**★★ – *From the far end of the lower lake this walk takes an extra 1hr45min. It is highly recommended for energetic walkers.*

The path is quick but rises steadily through bushes and small trees.

On arrival at the **Gosaulacke**★★ (1,154m/3,785ft), set in a wild and wooded landscape, you can make your way to the Holzmeisteralm on the right bank.

St. Gilgen and the Wolfgangsee

© Austrian National Tourist Office/Weinhaeupl W.

Those with more mountain experience can climb to the **Adameck Hut** (2,196m/7,205ft), a classic walk but one that requires a good level of fitness and an early morning departure. *It takes about 3hr to climb up from the higher lake (the path is found just before the Holzmeisteralm). From the Adameck hut, it is about 20min to the Gosau glacier. From the parking place it is either a demanding 8hr day or two easier days with a stay overnight at the hut.*

▶ Return to Gosau and head towards Rußbach over the Gshütt Pass (959m/3,145ft).

Abtenau

This resort in the Lammertal at the foot of the Kogel is a popular departure point for hikes. The drive to St. Wolfgang along the **Postalmstraße★** *(toll payable)* is especially scenic. The Postalm is the largest area of Alpine meadows in Austria, and Europe's second-largest high-lying plateau.

▶ Return E; turn right to Annaberg along the "Salzburg Dolomites" road. Take the road NE out of Eben im Pongau to Filzmoos.

Filzmoos

Towering above the village is the distinctive outline of the **Bischofsmütze** (Bishop's Mitre, *alt. 2,454m/8,051ft*). In summer, Filzmoos is a great base for walks in the surrounding mountains. A climb to the **Gerzkopf★★** summit *(1,729m/5,673ft, 4hr round-trip*

walk from Schattbach) is particularly recommended.

Rossbrand★★

After taking the Papagenobahn cable-car, follow the easy ridge trail west to the summit (2hr round trip).
The great **panorama★★** takes in 150 peaks, mainly of the Dachstein range, the Schladminger Tauern, the Ankogel range, the Hohe Tauern and the Hochkönig.

▶ Carry on towards Ramsau. After 12km/7.4mi, turn left and then take a small toll road to the right up to the foot of the Hunerkogel.

Hunerkogel★★★

Alt. 1,700m/5,576ft. ◷Cable-car operates Easter–early Sep daily 7.50am–5.30pm, mid-Sep–Nov til 5.10pm; Feb–Easter 8.30am–4.50pm. ⊜€36 round-trip. ✆03687 22 04 28 10. www.derdachstein.at. Allow at least 1hr for the round trip.
From the end of the toll road, the Hunerkogel (2,700m/8,858ft) can be seen looming like some impregnable fortress. The ascent of the sheer rock face by the **Dachstein-Südwandbahn** cable-car (also known as the Gletscherbahn Ramsau) is spectacular. The Sky-Walk platform at the top offers breathtaking views of the craggy peaks.

🥾 Ramsau am Dachstein
Alt. 1,150m/3,773ft.
Ramsau is a hiker's delight, even in winter when 70km/43.5mi of groomed

trails make walking easy. The **cross-country skiing ★★★** is excellent here, on more than 150km/93.2mi of tracks. The nearby Dachstein glacier also offers cross-country ski tracks at an altitude of 2,700m/8,858ft.

▷ The road follows the Enns Valley to Trautenfels.

Schloss Trautenfels★★

◔Open mid-Mar–Oct daily 10am–5pm. ≤€9. ℘03682 222 33. www.museum-joanneum.at.
With origins in the 13C, this lovely Baroque country palace has richly decorated rooms, including stuccowork and valuable frescoes by Carpoforo Tencalla. The palace contains the **Universalmuseum Joanneum**, with exhibits on traditional life and natural history in the surrounding region. There is a particularly good collection of local ceramics, and some fine alphorns.

▷ At the Trautenfels crossroads, turn left on road no. 145.

Pürgg★

Art lovers should go up to the blufftop **Johanneskapelle**, a small chapel endowed with **Romanesque frescoes★** depicting the Annunciation, the Birth of Christ, a fabulous fight between cats and mice, the Wise and Foolish Virgins and other scenes.

Bad Mitterndorf ⛷ ⛄

This place is known both as a spa and a winter-sports resort.

▷ Next along the B 145 are Bad Aussee, Grundlsee, Toplitzee and Kammersee.

③ BAD ISCHL TO SALZBURG
267km/166mi

North of Bad Ischl, the Traun corridor, which was one of the great European salt routes, unwinds between the Höllengebirge and Totes Gebirge foothills. Beside the road, a track follows the saltwater conduit *(Soleleitung)*, which since the 17C, has brought the salt waters from Hallstatt to the refinery at Ebensee.

Ebensee

The town of Ebensee, today a centre for the glass and chemical industry, was the location of part of the notorious concentration camp **Mauthausen** *(⌚see p133)* from 1943 to 1945. The underground galleries were originally intended for the relocation of the secret rocket development base at Peenemünde, but ended up being used as an oil refinery and for the production of tank-gear boxes. The working conditions were inhuman and the excavations led to the deaths of many thousands of prisoners, quite a number of them communist and socialist activists from Italy.

▷ Follow the signs to KZ-Gedenkstätte.

KZ-Gedenkstätte

Perhaps bring a coat, as it is a constant 8ºC/46ºF inside the tunnels. The former hospital and crematorium are now a memorial to the victims of the Mauthausen concentration camp. In 1948 Hilda Lepetit from Milan had a monument erected in memory of her husband who died here, the first of many. In 1952 the cemetery outside the camp was moved here to include the victims. Of the concentration camp itself all that really remains is the entrance. However, three minutes on foot from the cemetery *(follow the sign to the **KZ-Gedenkstollen**; ◔open mid-Jun–mid-Sept Tue–Sun 10am–5pm; May–early Jun and mid–end Sept Sat–Sun 10am–5pm; last entry 4.30pm; ≤€4, children €3; ℘06133 56 01; www.memorial-ebensee.at),* it is possible to visit one of the galleries in which the prisoners had to work, with a permanent exhibition on the history of the camp.

The camp was liberated by US troops on 6 May 1945. Of the 27,000 prisoners housed here, more than 8,500 of them died.

Zeitgeschichte Museum★ (Museum of Contemporary History)

Kirchengasse 5 (in the centre of Ebensee near the parish church). ⏱*Open Jan–Oct Tue–Sun 10am–5pm; Nov–Dec Tue–Fri 10am–5pm.* ⌨*€5, children €4; combined ticket with KZ-Gedenkstollen €7.50, children €5.* ☎*06 133 56 01. www.memorial-ebensee.at.*

This exemplary museum documents both European and local history between the years 1918–55. The main divisions of modern Austrian history are explored with fearless honesty (the First Republic, the civil war of 1934, Austrofacism, National Socialism and contemporary Austria's relationship with its Nazi past) through photographs, videos and contemporary documents. Those who are keen on history will particularly appreciate the displays, but it has a wider appeal and provides fascinating insights into the period.

▶ From the spectacular **cliff road★** from Ebensee to Traunkirchen, which runs above the **Traunsee★**, Austria's deepest lake (191m/527ft), one can see the golden peak of the Rötelspitze, and then further north, the Traunstein itself.

Traunkirchen

Perched on a **promontory★**, this town is a popular stop among Salzkammergut explorers who come to appreciate the splendid views over the Traunsee and the rugged mountains. Above the town is perched the Johannesbergkapelle. While here, also visit the **Pfarrkirche** (parish church) surrounded by a terraced graveyard overlooking the lake. It has splendid Baroque furnishings, particularly the **Fisherman's Pulpit★**, made in the form of the Disciples' fishing boat, complete with dripping nets. Since 1632, the town has staged an annual **Corpus Christi festival** on the lake.

Altmünster

Altmünster has a Late Gothic hall-church with sumptuous decoration and a stone high altar dating from 1518.

▶ From Ebensee head back to Altmünster and take the road over the Großalm pass (826m/2,700ft) to Steinbach.

Steinbach am Attersee

The composer **Gustav Mahler** spent his holidays in Steinbach, working in his *Komponierhäuschen* (composing shed). The road skirts the **Attersee★** (also known as Kammersee), the largest lake in the Austrian Alps and popular for fishing and boating. It is bordered to the south by the last cliff-like slopes of the Schafberg. Between Seewalchen and Attersee on the western shore, the road runs through charming sun-drenched hills with orchards. Only the cliffs of the Höllengebirge *(Mountains of Hell)* lend a note of harshness to the scene, coming right down to the lake at the southern end. For good lake views, stop by the Buchberg chapel in **Seewalchen**.

▶ Folow the main road N around the lake to the town of Attersee.

Attersee

This well-known resort has a pilgrimage church, Mariä Himmelfahrt, with fine Baroque furnishings, including works by Meinrad Guggenbichler.

▶ Leave the lake at Attersee and take the A1 autobahn towards Salzburg.

ADDRESSES

🛏STAY AND 🍴EAT

⊜⊜ **1er Beisl im Lexenhof** – *Am Anger 4, 4865 Nußdorf am Attersee.* ☎*07666 80 73. www.lexenhof.at. 14 rooms.* 🛏. This hotel has pleasant and attractive rooms. The restaurant serves seasonal dishes, and there is a beach by the lake.

⊜⊜ **Schloss Mondsee** – *Schlosshof 1a.* ☎*06232 50 01. www.schlossmondsee.at. 55 rooms.* 🛏. This hotel, set in an old abbey, has a restaurant and a Bierkeller, each with good food.

St. Wolfgang★★
and Schafberg

A deluge of visitors is no novelty for St. Wolfgang, sitting on the lake of the same name. Its church, which is a feast of magnificent works of art, has been a place of pilgrimage since the 12C. Today the faithful are joined by music lovers who come to see the original of the "White Horse Inn" and the beautiful landscape and magnificent lake★★ praised in the comic opera of that name *(Im Weißen Rößl)*. The charm of St. Wolfgang is most strongly felt during less busy periods either side of the main summer season and during the winter.

A BIT OF HISTORY

When St. Wolfgang, Bishop of Regensburg, came to reorganise the abbey at Mondsee, he built a chapel on a promontory jutting out into the lake that would bear his name. Soon a small community built up around it. St. Wolfgang was a beloved bishop, and when he was canonised after his death, the chapel became a popular place of pilgrimage. In the 15C it was replaced by a larger church and the marvelous altar by Tyrolean artist Michael Pacher was commissioned by the Abbot of Mondsee.

St. Wolfgang also owes its fame to the Weißes Rössl (White Horse Inn), which inspired the operetta of the same name. The story is about the head waiter who falls in love with the owner of the inn, who herself is attracted to one of her regulars. Ralph Benatzky's musical work drew visitors to the small town already popular with pilgrims of a spiritual persuasion.

SIGHTS
Boat Cruise

In high season a pleasant alternative to driving around the lake to St. Wolfgang is to arrive by **boat** (◷*May–Oct; ℘06138 22 320; www.schafbergbahn.at).* Regular service runs from Strobl and St. Gilgen, calling at Schafberg and the centre of St. Wolfgang.

▶ **Population:** 2,800.

🛈 **Info:** Au 140, A – 5360. ℘06138 80 03. www.stwolfgang.at.

◖ **Location:** St. Wolfgang is in the Salzkammergut, about 48km/30mi east of Salzburg. Alt. 549m/1,801ft.

🅿 **Parking:** Parking is tight in summer. Try the garages at the village entrance and at the Schafberg station, 1km/.06mi beyond the church.

☺ **Don't Miss:** Michael-Pacher Altar.

◷ **Timing:** Budget half a day, more if going up the Schafberg.

Pfarrkirche★★

◷*Open daily 8am–6pm (winter til 4pm). ℘06138 23 21. www.pfarre-sankt-wolfgang.at.*

St. Wolfgang's parish church is the successor to the chapel of a hermitage built, according to legend, by St. Wolfgang, who came to seek solitude on the shores of the lake that would later bear his name. The present late-15C structure on a rocky spur abuts the elegant 16C priory. The outer cloisters, lined with arcades that yield bird's-eye views of the lake, complete the charming ensemble.

Michael-Pacher-Altar★★★

This 12m/39.4ft-high masterpiece (1481) shows rare unity in composition and is considered an outstanding example of Gothic art. The central panel depicts a heavily gilded Coronation of The Virgin, while the complementary paintings illustrate scenes from the life of Mary. Pacher reveals himself to be a master of perspective and detail in this work.

Schwanthaler-Doppelaltar★

This Baroque masterpiece was created by Thomas Schwanthaler in 1675–76, and features more than 100 carved figures full of life and energy. The left panel, executed in black and gold, shows the Holy Family on their pilgrimage to Jerusalem, while the right panel depicts St. Wolfgang.

It is said that Thomas Schwanthaler dissuaded the abbot of Mondsee from replacing Pacher's altarpiece with his own when the church was redecorated in Baroque style, but there is no evidence to corroborate this story.

A third great artist has left his legacy in this church: the Mondsee master **Meinrad Guggenbichler**, to whom the three altars on the north side of the church, including the majestic Rosenkranzaltar, and the pulpit are attributed. His *Man of Sorrows* is particularly heart-rending.

Near the church is the famous **Weißes Rössl** (White Horse Inn, *see below*). The 500-year-old establishment owes its fame to the celebrated eponymous operetta, *Im Weißen Rößl*, written in 1930 by Ralph Benatzky (1884–1957). It was based on the book written in 1896 by Oskar Blumenthal and Gustav Kadelburg, and tells the story of Leopold, the waiter of the inn, and his love for the vivacious landlady, Josepha, who presides over the White Horse on the banks of the Wolfgangsee.

EXCURSION
Schafberg★★
Markt 35, St. Wolfgang. Alt. 1,783m/ 5,830ft. About 4hr round-trip, including 1hr 30min by Schafbergbahn rack railway and 30min walk. ◷*Open May– Oct daily 9.20am–3.30pm (last ascent).* ⊜*€34 round trip, children €17.* ℘*06138 22 320. www.schafbergbahn.at.*

The Schafberg has a rack railway, dating back to 1893, running up to its summit. Some of the journeys are made in historic steam trains (look for nostalgischen Zahnrad Dampflokamotiven on the timetable if you are keen to take one of these).

From the mountain station, make for the hotel on the summit, which is a short distance from the impressive precipice on the north face. From here you can spot numerous lakes, including the Mondsee, Attersee and Wolfgangsee and

A family of artists
The **Schwanthaler family**, from Ried im Innkreis, produced no fewer than 21 artists in a period of 250 years, the majority of whom were sculptors. A 19C descendant, Ludwig Ritter von Schwanthaler, Court Sculptor to King Ludwig I of Bavaria, was responsible for the sculpted figure of Bavaria on the Theresienwiese in Munich.

Mondsee from Schafberg Mountain

© Austrian National Tourist Office/ Weinhaeupl W.

any number of major Alpine peaks and ranges, including the Höllengebirge, the Totes Gebirge and the Dachstein.

ADDRESSES

⍾/EAT

⊜⊜⊜ **Seerestaurant im Weißen Rößl** – *Markt 74. ℘06138 23 06. www. weissesroessl.at. Daily, summer 9am–8pm; winter 10am–6pm.* This hotel tavern was the setting for *The White Horse Inn*, an operetta dear to the Austrian heart. The name also guarantees a steady stream of customers for the owners, although they have not become complacent. Both the terrace and tavern here offer dishes of a good standard.

Bad Ischl ⚓

Bad Ischl is one of Austria's most famous spa towns. For 60 years it was the favourite summer retreat of Emperor Franz Joseph I. In the 1820s it gained fame when his mother, the Archduchess Sophie, came to town for a saline cure to treat her infertility. It wasn't long before she became pregnant with the future emperor; four more children, nicknamed the salt princes, followed. Franz Joseph's presence lured a who's who of European royalty, artists and politicians to Bad Ischl, including composer Franz Lehár, whose house is now a museum. Today the town still bathes in the genteel glow of its 19C heyday, although it is also an attractive, modern health resort and gateway to the five lakes of the Salzkammergut.

▶ **Population:** 13,895.

Info: Auböckplatz 5, A-4820. ✆06132 27 75 70. www.badischl.at.

Location: Bad Ischl lies in the Salzkammergut, about 54km/33.5mi east of Salzburg. Alt 469m/1,539ft.

Parking: Leave your car in the Kaiservila car park.

Don't Miss: Kaiservilla.

Timing: Budget half a day.

👣 TOWN CENTRE

This 30min walk starts at Auböckplatz.
The central square, **Auböckplatz,** is bordered by the Trinkhalle (pump room, 1831) and the parish church. East of here, the main shopping street, **Pfarrgasse,** leads to the Elisabethbrücke across the River Traun. It retains such survivals of 19C spa life as the elegant Zauner Café and pastry shop. Just before the bridge, it merges with the **Esplanade**, a shady riverside walk, where rich *Salzfertiger* (salt refiners) once stored salt for the Treasury before it was sent downstream. In one of their dwellings, the **Seeauer House** (no. 10), with a Rococo façade and triple gables, Franz Joseph got officially engaged to his 15-year-old cousin, Elisabeth of Bavaria ('Sisi') in 1853.
A hotel until 1982, the building now houses the **Stadtmuseum** with exhibits on the salt trade, local folklore and the town's rise to spa resort and imperial summer residence.

👣 VILLA AND PARK★

Departing from the Kaiservilla, this walk will take about 2hr.

Kaiservilla★

🕐*Open Jan–Mar Wed 10am–4pm by 👣guided tour; Apr and Oct daily 10am–4pm; May–Sept daily 9.30am–5pm; Dec Sat–Sun 10am–4pm.* ✎€16.50 (park only €4.60). ✆06132 23 241. www.kaiservilla.at.
The Imperial villa north of the town, on the left bank of the Ischl, was a wedding present from Archduchess Sophie to Franz Josef and Sisi. It was later enlarged to form the shape of an E in honour of Elisabeth. However, it was also used, with the knowledge and apparent approval of Elizabeth, to host the emperor's mistress, the actress and singer Katharina Schratt, whose own villa was nearby. A tour of the private apartments includes the emperor's study, where he signed the fateful declaration of war with Serbia on 28 July 1914. Scores of antlers and various stuffed animals attest to the ruler's passion for hunting the local wildlife. The complex still belongs to his descendents, some of whom are occasionally in residence. The villa is surrounded by a magnificent landscape garden, the **Kaiserpark**.

Marmorschlössl

🕐*Open May–Sept daily 9.30am–5pm; Dec Sat–Sun 10am–4pm; Jan–Mar Wed 10am–4pm; Apr daily 10am–4pm.* ✎€2 (in addition to park admission fee). ✆06132 24 422.

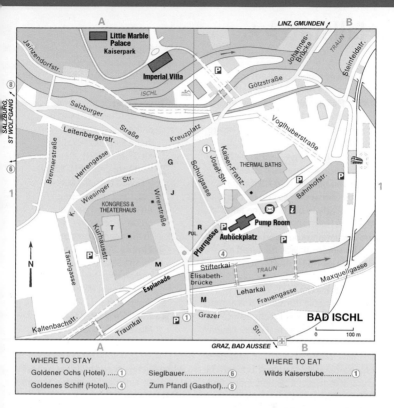

WHERE TO STAY

Goldener Ochs (Hotel) .....①

Goldenes Schiff (Hotel).... ④

Sieglbauer...................⑥

Zum Pfandl (Gasthof)...⑧

WHERE TO EAT

Wilds Kaiserstube.............①

In the park, the small "marble palace" served as Elisabeth's teahouse and favourite retreat. It now houses the **Photomuseum**.

ADDRESSES

🛏STAY

🛏 **Sieglbauer** – *Lindaustraße 56, 4820. ✆0664 73 46 84 84. ferienhof-stadlmann@ hotmail.com. 4 rooms.* ☉. Traditional rooms with a balcony and mountain views are set on a lovely farm outside the town.

🛏🛏 **Gasthof zum Pfandl** – *Steinbruch 1, 4820. 3km/1.8mi to the E on the B158. ✆06132 23 875. www.gasthof-pfandl.at. 16 rooms.* ☉. *Half-board is available.* A small hotel, a short way from the centre but with simple, clean rooms. The restaurant serves regional food.

🛏🛏🛏 **Goldener Ochs** – *Grazer Straße 4, 4820. ✆06132 23 529. www.goldenerochs.at. 48 rooms.* ☉. *Restaurant*🛏🛏🛏. A classic

hotel where the Austrian composer, Franz Lehár – to whom an opera music festival in Bad Ischl is dedicated – used to dine. The rooms are comfortable and clean, and the hotel has an attractive, modern spa in which to indulge.

🛏🛏🛏🛏 **Goldenes Schiff** – *Adalbert-Stifter-Kai 3. ✆06132 24 241. www.goldenes-schiff.at. 55 rooms.* ☉. *Restaurant.* An elegant, design-led hotel in the middle of the town. The minimalist rooms look out onto either the river Traun or attractive backstreets. There is also an excellent restaurant with a lovely terrace.

🍴EAT

🛏🛏 **Wilds Kaiserstube** – *Kaiser-Franz-Josef-Straße 3–5. ✆01632 29415. www. kaiserstube.info. Tue–Sat 11.30am–2.30pm, 5.30pm–10pm.* Undated regional specialities and a separate vegan menu are the specialities of this lovely restaurant. There is a pleasant outdoor area for the summer and a very reasonable daily menu.

Hallstatt★★
and the Krippenstein

Hallstatt crouches beneath the Salzberg in a breathtaking setting on the Hallstätter See★★, a deep and dark green lake backed by the craggy peaks of the Dachstein range. Often deluged by day trippers, it provides the quintessential picture of romantic Austria with streets so steep and narrow that the famous Corpus Christi procession has to take place mostly in boats on the lake. In 1998 the Hallstatt region, including the Dachstein range and central Salzkammergut, was declared a UNESCO World Heritage Site.

A BIT OF HISTORY

The salt mines in the mountains around Hallstatt have been exploited since the Neolithic Era, but the first major heyday came in the Bronze Age around 1200 BC. So many traces of salt mining have been found around Hallstatt that it coined the name of the Hallstatt Period dating from 850 to 500 BC. The most startling evidence is a vast Iron Age cemetery with more than 4,000 graves. The salt mines are still being worked today.

SIGHTS
Pfarrkirche Mariä Himmelfahrt

Overlooking the lake from its perch above the central Marktplatz, Hallstatt's parish church has 12C Romanesque origins but only a squat tower to prove it,

▶ **Population:** 757.

Info: Seestraβe 99, A-4830. ☎06134 82 08. www.hallstatt.net.

Location: Hallstatt on the southwestern shore of the Hallstätter See in the Salzkammergut. Alt 511m/1,677ft.

Parking: Central Hallstatt is closed to traffic May–Oct, daily 10am–5pm. An automated parking guide system directs you to the nearest car park.

Timing: Allow half a day for the Salzbergwerk and another half day for the Museum Hallstatt and the church.

Kids: Salzwelten Hallstatt, Museum Hallstatt.

while the rest of the building is mostly 15C Late Gothic. The three winged **altars★** also date to this period. The most accomplished of these is the one on the right, which shows the Virgin flanked by St. Barbara, patron saint of miners, and St. Catherine, patron saint of woodcutters.

Perhaps more interesting than the church itself is the two-storey Michaelskapelle across the tiny graveyard, which houses the macabre but fascinating **Beinhaus**. This small charnel house contains some 600 skulls, all stacked up

Hallstatt Civilization

Precisely when the Celts came to Hallstat is unclear, but evidence suggests there was an established mining settlement with a powerful ruler here c. 800 BC. However, archaeological finds suggest that mining had been going on since 5000 BC, making the salt mine at Hallstatt the oldest in the world.

Salt was a precious commodity in the Celtic era, and the region was historically very wealthy. Salt was the equivalent of oil today; whoever had reserves of it became impressively rich. Active trade in the commodity south to the Mediterranean and north to the Baltic produced wealth that allowed for the development of a sophisticated culture that became known as the Hallstatt Civilization. It lasted from 800 to 400 BC, and stretched from the northern Alps to southern Germany and from the Champagne-Ardennes to Bohemia.

neatly and painted with flower motifs, the name and other personal details of the person. Shortage of space in the local graveyard meant that 10 years after burial, and once the body had decomposed, it was dug up and the bones stored to make room for the next coffin. New skulls are still added.

👥 Welterbemuseum Hallstatt

🕐*Open Nov–Mar Wed–Sun 11am–3pm; Apr and Oct daily 10am–4pm; May–Sept daily 10am–6pm.* 💶*€9.* 📞*06134 82 80 15. www.museum-hallstatt.at.*

This modern museum, using 3D media and holographic projections to display its exhibits, takes visitors on an educational, high-tech romp through 7,000 years of regional history.

Special emphasis is given to the Hallstatt Period with an impressive selection of archaeological finds, including weapons, tools and human bones. Other sections focus on local geology (of great economic importance), the Celts and Romans, a fire of 1750, coin minting, tourism and many other topics.

👥 Salzwelten Hallstatt

Allow 3hr. 🚶*Guided tours (70min) every half-hour mid-Apr–mid-Sept daily 9.30am–4.30pm; mid–Sept–Oct daily 9.30am–3pm; Nov 9.30am–2.30pm. Be at the valley station at least 30min before last tour begins.* 🌡*Temperature is 8°C/46.4°F inside the mine.* 💶*Salzbergwerk €22, children €11.* 📞*06132 200 2400. www.salzwelten.at.*

Hallstatt's salt mines in the Salzberg above the town are considered the oldest in the world. It was here that a salt-preserved corpse was found in 1734. The tour includes a salt crystal room, an underground salt lake, technical exhibits, displays about mining during the Bronze Age and the Hallstatt Period and other themes. There are wooden slides once used by miners to travel quickly from one level to the next. The mine can be reached on a 45min walk or a short trip on the **Salzbergbahn** funicular (💶*€16, or €30 with tour of the mines).* From the mountain station, it's a 10min walk across the Iron Age graveyard to the mine entrance. Views are great from the **Rudolfsturm**, a tower built to defend the mine.

🥾 HIKES
Ascent of the Krippenstein★★

🕐*Cable-car operates May–Oct daily 8.40am–3 or 3.30pm every 15min.* 💶*€29.30 round-trip.* 📞*050 140. From Hallstatt, 4km/2.5mi in the direction of Obertraun; then bear right 2km/1.2mi beyond the end of the lake.*

The cable-car drops off cave visitors at the **Schönbergalpe** (*alt. 1,345m /4,413ft*) station, before continuing to the upper station. The chapel affords sweeping **views★★** of the Dachstein plateau (*alt. 2,109m/6,919ft*). To get a **view★★** of the lake at Hallstatt, follow the marked path at the beginning of the Krippenstein road to the Pioneers' Cross (*Pionierkreuz, allow an extra 30min*).

Dachstein-Eishöhle★

2hr30min walk from Obertraun or a ride on the Krippensteinbahn cable-car to Schönbergalpe followed by 15min walk. 🧥*Warm clothing advised.* 🚶*Guided tour (1hr) May–Oct daily 9.20am–3.30pm; mid-Jun–mid-Sep daily 9.20am–4pm.* 💶*€30.80 combined ticket with cable-car.* 📞*050 140. www.dachstein-salzkammergut.at.*

The spectacular Giant Ice Cave, whose ice draperies, icicles and other formations are illuminated by coloured lights, can be seen only on a guided tour. It is one of Europe's largest ice caves.

Mammuthöhle

30min there and back on foot from Schönbergalpe station. 1km/0.6mi walk in cave. 🚶*Guided tour (1hr) mid-May–Oct daily 10.30am–2.30pm; mid-Jun–mid-Sep daily 10.15am–3pm.* 💶*€30.80 combined ticket with cable-car.* 📞*050 140. www.dachstein-salzkammergut.at.*

These limestone caves are worth visiting for the sound and light show. The related Koppenbrüllerhöhle cave is 3.5km/2mi from the car park of the Dachstein cable-car.

Bad Aussee ✝

Grundlsee and Altausser See

Bad Aussee is the capital of the Styrian Salzkammergut, a region steeped deeply in tradition. Sitting at the confluence of two upper branches of the Traun, it is surrounded by rugged mountains, including the Dachstein and the Totes Gebirge. The town provides access to two lovely lakes, the Altausseer See and the Grundlsee, and offers an exceptional choice of walks and excursions. Bad Aussee makes both industrial and medical use of the sodium-sulphate waters harvested from the mines of Altaussee.

▶ **Population:** 4,771.

🅸 **Info:** Bahnhofstraße 132, A-8990. ℘03622 54 04 00. www.ausseerland.at.

▶ **Location:** Bad Aussee claims to be at the geographical centre of Austria in the southeastern Salzkammergut.

🅿 **Parking:** Difficult in summer close to the lakes.

✆ **Don't Miss:** A visit to the salt mines at Altaussee.

🕓 **Timing:** Two days are needed to cover all the excursions.

A BIT OF HISTORY
The People's Prince

If Bad Ischl owed its fortune to Emperor Franz Joseph, the great man of Bad Aussee was **Archduke Johann**. His controversial romance with Anna Plochl, daughter of the local postmaster, and their nearly clandestine marriage at Brandhof in 1829 filled the romantic chronicles of the period, confirming the popularity of the "Prince of Styria." Not surprisingly, in Bad Aussee you will find the prince's statue in the municipal gardens (Kurpark), the medallion of the couple on the bridge over the Grundlseer Traun (Erzherzog-Johann-Brücke), and souvenirs of the Plochl family in the former post office (Alte Pferdepost) at Meranplatz 37.

SIGHTS
Chlumeckyplatz

This central square, with a fountain and a plague column, is a pleasant place for a stroll.

The Kammerhof, an impressive Gothic mansion with Renaissance embellishments, was once the office of the salt-mine regulators. Note the marble doorway and window surrounds, the cartouches with cable mouldings, and the coat of arms featuring the Imperial eagle above the main entrance.

It houses the **Kammerhofmuseum** (🕓*May–Jun, mid-Sept–Oct Tue & Sat 3pm–6pm, Sun 10am–12.30pm, Jul–mid-Sept daily 10am–12.30pm and 3pm–6pm;* ⬤€5; ℘03622 53 72 511) with displays on local history and former salt production.

EXCURSIONS
Grundlsee★

5km/3mi to the Grundlsee resort; 10km/6.2mi to the Gössl fork. Leave Bad Aussee by the Grundlseer Straße.

At Seeklause (a landing-stage at the head of the lake) there is a **view★★** over the large Grundlsee, overlooked on the left by the Backenstein promontory. The road skirts its foot after passing through the resort of **Grundlsee**, where you get an open view across to the snow-capped summits of the Totes Gebirge.

Drive along the lake to visit the hamlet of Gössl, where a 20min walk will bring you to the rugged beauty of the **Toplitzsee★**. The views from the lake can be seen only by taking the **motorboat excursion** (🚤*3hr guided tour of 3 lakes May–Oct daily 10.15am, 11.30am, 1.15pm, 2.30pm, 3.45pm and 5pm; www.schifffahrt-grundlsee.at*). Beyond the final isthmus lies the little **Kammersee**, hemmed in by the walls of the Totes Gebirge.

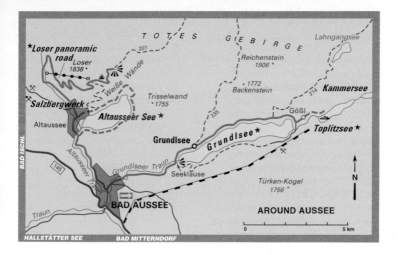

AROUND AUSSEE

Altausseer See★

5km/3mi to the north.

The road ends at the climatic resort of **Altaussee**, where you can walk round the lake *(max 2hr)* or descend into the nearby salt mines (**Salzwelten Altaussee** (🐾🔦*1hr20min guided tour Jun–mid-Sept daily every hour 9am–4pm; mid-Apr–May and mid-Sept–Oct daily 9am, 11am, 1pm and 3pm; Jun–mid-Sept 9am–4pm hourly; Wed 7pm year-round);* 🎫€18; ✆06132 20 02 400; www.salzwelten.at).* On guided tours through the show mine, you can see the chambers where the Nazis stored looted art during World War II, a salt chapel, and an underground lake with a sound and light show.

Loser Panoramastraße★

13km/8mi – about 1hr. Leave Altaussee to the north and follow the Loser Panoramastraße signs: toll point after 3.4km/2mi.

This delightful scenic road climbs to an altitude of 1,600m/5,250ft. From the mountain restaurant (Bergrestaurant) at the car park, there is an extensive view over the Altaussee, the sheer Weiße Wände (White Walls) cliffs that fall into it and in the distance, the snow-covered peaks of the Dachstein range and the Hunerkogel. The car park is the starting point for a number of marked trails.

ADDRESSES

🏨STAY AND 🍽️EAT

🛏️ **Jagdhof** – *Lichtersberg 82, 8992 Altaussee. 4km to the N.* ✆*03622 71 102. www.willkommeninaltaussee.at. 5 rooms and 1 apartment.* 🍴. *Restaurant.* A small, pretty guesthouse with lovely rooms and a restaurant.

🛏️🛏️ **Gasthof Veit** – *Gößl 13, 8993 Grundlsee, at the eastern tip of the lake.* ✆*03622 82 12. www.gasthof-veit.com. 6 rooms.* 🍴, *half board possible. Restaurant.* This small, traditional hotel close to the lake has comfortable rooms. There is a great view of the mountains, and the restaurant serves good, local dishes.

🛏️🛏️🛏️ **Gasthof Blaue Traube** – *Kirchengasse 165.* ✆*03622 52 363. www.blauetraube.at. 13 rooms.* 🍴. *Restaurant.* Simple, comfortable rooms in a charming, quiet hotel. The restaurant serves local and international dishes, and there is a lovely garden.

🛏️🛏️🛏️🛏️ **Die Wasnerin** – *Sommersbergseestraße 19.* ✆*03622 52 108. www.diewasnerin.at.* 🅿️. *90 rooms.* 🍴, *half board included. Restaurant.* This attractive hotel has a splendid view of the mountains. The rooms are well furnished and all have a balcony. There is also a decent restaurant.

Gmunden★

and Vöcklabruck

This popular lakeside summer resort experienced its heyday in the 19C when it became the darling of artists, poets and politicians. These days it is known for its fine ceramics as well as its busy beaches, lake cruises and the Esplanade, an elegant promenade along the northern shore of Lake Traunsee.

▶ **Population:** 13,200.

Info: *Rathausplatz 1, A-4810.* ℘0761 26 43 05. www.gmunden.at.

Location: Gmunden is on the northern shore of Traunsee in the Salzkammergut. Alt 420m/1,378ft.

Parking: There is a car park (*fee*) in Seilergasse.

Don't Miss: A stroll along the Esplanade.

Timing: Allow a day to take the excursions.

HISTORIC CENTRE

The Renaissance **town hall** on Rathausplatz, the main square, has a ceramic glockenspiel that chimes several times daily. North of here, the town's medieval warren of lanes is punctuated by the **Stadtpfarrkirche** with a precious high altar by Thomas Schwanthaler depicting the Adoration of the Magi.

In the former salt administration building east of the town hall, the **Kammerhofmuseum** (*open Wed–Fri 1pm–5pm, Sat–Sun 10am–5pm; €6; ℘07612 79 44 23; www.k-hof.at*) has an exhibit on local history and a selection of the famous local ceramics. Considerably more memorable is the quirky **Klo & So Sanitärmuseum,** part of the same institution, which has a splendidly bizarre collection of toilet bowls, chamber pots, sinks and bidets, including one used by Empress Elisabeth.

SEESCHLOSS ORT★

On a little island accessed by a wooden bridge, this landmark palace (*www.schloss-ort.at*) wraps around a triangular arcaded courtyard with elaborate sgraffito decoration and a Late Gothic exterior staircase. Weddings take place here regularly.

EXCURSIONS
Alm Valley

37km/23mi round trip. Leave Gmunden to the east on B 120.

This Renaissance **Schloss Scharnstein★** castle perches above the Alm River and houses two unusual museums.

Schloss Ort

© Robert Harding/hemis.fr

The 21 rooms of the **Österreichisches Kriminalmuseum** (Austrian Crime Museum; ○open May–mid-OctSat–Sun 10am–5pm; ⊜€6; ℘0664 300 56 77; www.kriminalmuseum.at) traces the fight against crime from the Middle Ages to today. Displays include devices of torture and execution that are not for the faint of heart, let alone children. Fans of contemporary Austrian history will likely enjoy the **Zeitgeschichte Museum Scharnstein** (○by appointment only; ℘0664 300 56 77), which chronicles all 20C milestones, including the Third Reich years.

Gmundnerberg★

9 km/6mi SW. Leave Gmunden in the direction of Bad Ischl. Turn right at **Altmünster** and follow the signs.
This road takes you up to a viewpoint near the Urz'n hotel. By the small church of St. Maria, an orientation board points out the notable peaks and sights. The **view★★** is of the entire Traunsee basin and over the region of the Mühl. On the other side is the Traunkirche, the Traunstein and the Erlakogel.

Vöcklabruck

16km/10mi NW of Gmuden.
With a population of 12,000, Vöcklabruck bestrides the old main road halfway between Salzburg and Linz; its pedigree goes back to the 12C.
Today the place is still a busy market town and educational centre for the surrounding countryside. It also benefits from its proximity to the famous Salzkammergut (↺see SALZKAMMERGUT) tourist area and the nearby Attersee and Traunsee lakes.
As is frequently the case in Austria, the **Stadtplatz** (town square) is simply a widening of the main road. Most buildings are decorated with Baroque façades but are in fact much older, including no. 14, which has an arcaded courtyard much in the style of the Italian Renaissance. The square is bookended by two towers. One of them, the **Unterer Stadtturm** (Lower Tower; ○open Apr–Sept Wed 10am–noon; ⊜€2), features the coats of arms of the various posses-

sions of Burgundy as well as those of the Habsburgs. This is a visual reminder of the marriage of **Emperor Maximilian I**, who owned a house in town, to Mary of Burgundy.

Dörflkirche St. Ägidius

Leave the town via the Unterer Stadtturm and cross the river; the church is just over the bridge on the right.
If the door is closed, ring at the presbytery. ℘0767 27 26 08.
This elegant building is the successor to a much earlier church, first consecrated in 1143. It was built in 1688 by the architect **Carlo Antonio Carlone** and decorated by Giovanni Battista Carlone. Its Baroque splendour was restored in 1980.

Grünau Cumberland Wildpark★

20km/12.5mi E of Gmunden, on the B 120. At Scharnstein, turn right and continue for 7km/4.3mi. ○Open Apr–Oct daily 9am–5pm (visitors must leave by 7pm); Nov–Mar daily 10am–4pm (visitors must leave by 5pm). ⊜€9, children €6. ♿ ℘07616 84 25. www.wildparkgruenau.at.
This 60ha/148-acre animal park is set in a forest, surrounded by mountains. From the walking trails visitors can watch the animals in as near natural conditions as possible. The park is a research centre for the Konrad-Lorenz Institute.

▶ Continue up the valley to Seehaus. The route takes you through the quiet village of Habernau, and then continues S to the Almsee.

Almsee★

34 km/21mi SE of Gmunden, on the B120. At Scharnstein, turn right and continue on for 20km/12.5mi.
The Almsee is another of the Salzkammutgat's lakes. The mountains here form a huge circle, closing off the valley behind the lake.
There are a number of fine, marked footpaths here that guide you through the magnificent scenery.

Radstadt★

The town lies in the Enntal with the Dachstein mountains to the north and the Tauern to the south. It is undoubtedly a very scenic place and is popular in winter due to its proximity to the Obertauern ski area. It was important due to its position on the route along the Enntal and at the northern end of the route that crossed the Tauern mountains. The road over the Radstädter Tauernpass starts in Radstadt and is one of the most scenic passes in Austria.

A BIT OF HISTORY

Radstadt was strategically important because it sat at the crossroads of two major trade routes. The town's wealth was due in part to its position on the trade route with Venice and its licence to stock iron and salt. First mentioned in 1074, it received its town charter in 1289. Realising its strategic significance, the bishops of Salzburg fortified the town in the 13C.

🚗 DRIVING TOUR

FROM RADSTADT TO ST. MICHAEL IM LUNGAU
67km/42mi.

Radstadt★

This pretty town is still enclosed by its tower-studded medieval **town wall** and a partial moat. These walls are of unique symmetrical design, with three towers built between 1527 and 1535 when the bishops of Salzburg decided to strengthen the fortifications in anticipation of an attack by the Turks.

Museum Kapuzinerturm

Schießstatt 3. 🕐*Open Jun–Sept Thu–Fri and Sun 10am–noon, 2.30pm–5pm.* ☜€5 (combi-ticket with Schloss Lerchen, €7). 𝄞06452 74 720. *www.museen-radstadt.at.*
Part of the town walls, this tower, which guards the eastern gateway, houses a

▶ **Population:** 4,940.
🛈 **Info:** *Marktplatz 1.* 𝄞06477 77 72. www.sankt-michael.at.
▶ **Location:** The town lies in the Enn Valley between the Dachstein range and the Tauern Range. Alt. 858m/2,815ft.
☺ **Don't Miss:** Burg Mauterndorf, Schloss Moosham.
🕐 **Timing:** Allow half a day for the town and Gnadenfall and a full day if heading up the Pass.

museum of local life and trades. Particularly notable are the collections of *Krampus* costumes, household items and the architecture of the tower itself.

Museum Schloss Lerchen

Schlossstraße 1. 🕐*Open Thu–Fri 10am–noon, 2.30pm–5pm.* ☜€4 (combi-ticket with Kapuzinerturm, €7). 𝄞06452 74 720. *www.museen-radstadt.at.*
Ten minutes west of the centre, this museum houses displays on the history of Radstadt, farming, crafts and sacred art. Other exhibits focus on the organist Paul Hofhaimer and the local geology. The museum also holds temporary exhibitions and demonstrations.

▶ Take the Radstädter Tauernstraße S towards Obertauern.

Gnadenfall

This lusty cascade of the Taurach leaps off a wooded shelf in two light falls. Hotels crouch between the larches and spruces below the pass at 1,739m/5,705ft. About 800m/875yd short of the pass, a modern (1951) statue of a Roman legionary stands guard over the bridge.

▶ Continue S and the road will take you over the Tauernpass.

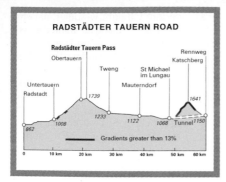

RADSTÄDTER TAUERN ROAD

Radstädter Tauernpass★

23km/14.3mi S on the B 99 Katchberg-Bundesstraße.

In use since Roman times, this pass *(alt. 1,738m/5,702ft)* crosses over into the neighbouring province of Carinthia. It was an important trade route over the Tauern mountains; today it offers wonderful panoramas of the Dachstein range to the north. At the pass is the vast ski area Obertauern.

Obertauern

℘06 456 72 52. www.obertauern.at, www.obertauern.com, www.ski-obertauern.at.

Obertauern *(population 400; alt. 1,739m/5,705ft)* is located about 90km/55.6mi southeast of Salzburg. It lies on a broad terrace on the Radstädter Tauernpass in one of the most beautiful ski areas in the northern Alps. Unlike most Austrian mountain resorts, it did not grow from an existing village, but was developed purely as a winter-sports destination. In summer, hiking is the main lure. Obertauern boasts good, reliable snow levels and 28 ski-lifts, as well as 95km/59mi of pistes, nearly all of them for beginners and intermediate skiers. The resort's fairly modest size is more than made up for by the quality of the facilities, which are among the most modern and comfortable in the country.

Beyond the Radstädter Tauernpass, the road enters a forbidding section, but between Tweng and Mauterndorf pleasant clearings appear on the banks of the calmer Taurach. Soon the roofs

of the Mauterndorf castle peer out from among the trees.

Burg Mauterndorf★

Open May–Jun & Sept–Oct daily 10am–6pm (last entry 4.30pm); Jul–Aug daily 9.30am–6.30pm (last entry 5pm); late Dec–Easter Tue & Thu 11am–7pm (last entry 6pm; Thu guided tour 8pm). €9.50 summer (castle tour and museum), €6 winter (museum is closed in winter). ℘06472 74 26. www.salzburg-burgen.at. Audio-tours available.

Situated on a trade route in use since Roman times, this 13C castle served as a residence for the archbishops of Salzburg who wished to keep a close eye on their possessions in the Lungau region. Today, the ancient walls house family-oriented exhibits taking you on a fun-filled trip back to the late 15C and the castle at the time of Archbishop Leonhard von Keutschach.

Ask about the kids' version of the audio guide. There's also a castle-like playground with a long dragon slide.

A ramble around this castle includes a 90min self-guided audio-tour during which you'll be "eavesdropping" on the

The Archbishop's Turnip

The story goes that **Leonhard von Keutschach** led a lively student life, rarely studying. On a visit to Pinzgau, he was walking in a turnip field with his uncle, Wolf zu Alm, who berated him for neglecting his studies. Piqued by the young man's impertinent reply, the uncle threw a turnip at him saying, "If you don't mend your ways, I will never receive you again!" The turnip changed Leonhard's life; he applied himself to his studies and later became Prince-Archbishop of Salzburg. In gratitude, he included a turnip in his coat of arms.

castle residents as they prepare for a lavish feast back in the 15C. Scores of authentically costumed figures have been arranged in scenes and impart interesting titbits about what daily life was like in those days.

The tour ends in the original Gothic watchman's tower from which you'll enjoy fabulous **views** over the town and countryside. In the south tower, the **Lungauer Landschaftsmuseum** presents an intriguing look at local customs and history.

▶ From Mauterndorf head E on the Turracher-Bundesstraße to Tamsweg.

Tamsweg

50km/31mi south of Radstadt. Marktplatz 4. ℘06474 21 45. www.tamsweg.info/en.
Tamsweg (*population 5,735; alt. 1,024m/ 3,360ft*) is the capital of the remote Lungau region and fosters many old traditions. Most famous among them is the so-called Samsonumzug (Samson Procession), headed by a huge dummy representing Samson and accompanied by two dwarfs. It takes place several days each summer (🕭*see Calendar of Events*).

Marktplatz

Tamsweg's main square is framed by pretty houses, such as the 16C **Rathaus** (town hall) with fanciful corner turrets, and the old **Schloss Kuenburg**, now home to a cultural centre.
Farther along, an old hospice now houses the **Heimatmuseum** (*Kirchengasse 2; ☎open Jun–mid-Sept Wed–Fri 10am–noon, Thu–Fri also 2pm–4pm; |P4; t06474 65 04*), which offers glimpses into the local way of life of yesteryear, including several important Roman artefacts.

St. Leonhardkirche★

Drive south from Tamsweg on the Murau road over the River Mur. Cross the railway and ▣ park at the bottom of the road (right) that climbs up to the church. A footpath further to the right is less steep.
The 15C pilgrimage church of St. Leonard has kept its Early Gothic plan and

design: tall light windows, network vaulting, etc. Its original **stained glass** is among the finest in Austria and includes the famous **gold window** (*Goldfenster*), on the right of the chancel, which consists entirely of yellow and blue glass. Near the high altar, the small altar to St. Leonard features a statuette of the saint held in the branches of a juniper tree. The discovery of the statuette is the basis of the pilgrimage.

▶ From Tamsweg take the Murtal-Bundesstraße towards Unternberg.

Schloss Moosham★

9.5km/6mi SW of Tamsweg. Moosham 12, 5585 Unternberg. ☎Visit by guided tour only Apr–Sept Tue–Sun on the hour 10am–11am and 1pm–4pm (also Mon and noon in Aug); Oct and mid-Dec– Mar Tue–Sun 11am and 2pm. ☞€11, children €6. ℘06476 305. www.schlossmoosham.at.
This medieval castle, first built in the 13C, had belonged to the archbishops of Salzburg since 1285. It was the seat of the administrative tribunal and was the heart of power in the Lungau from 1520 to 1790. In 1886 it became the property of the Wilczek family who extensively restored the castle and brought works of art and furniture from the family collections.
The castle is still privately owned and houses more than 2,000 exhibits (mostly dating from the 16C to the 19C). The lower court★ (*Innenhof*) of the castle is empty and covered in grass, surrounded by wooden galleries, actually reconstructions of the 19C. The tour ends with a visit to the dungeon and court.

▶ Carrying on west from the Schloß will bring you to the Katschberg Bundesstraße, which leads to St. Michael.

St. Michael im Lungau

This attractive resort is flooded with sunshine year round. It is especially busy in winter, when numerous lifts ferry skiers up to the fine slopes.

Schladminger Tauern✳✳✳

This mountain chain stretches 40km/25mi and towers over the broad Ennstal. On the other side of this valley is the **Dachstein massif★★**, with its limestone rocks, steep jagged cliffs and harsh features. The Schladminger Tauern, by contrast, are characterised by long, densely wooded and easily accessible valleys with lakes and rivers. It is precisely these varied landscapes that lend the Ennstal its special appeal.

Since the 1960s, the area has been a popular winter- sports resort. In summer, hikers have access to wide-open, unspoiled areas with spectacular views.

- 🛈 **Info:** Ramsauerstraße 756, Schladming. ℘03687 23 310. www.schladming-dachstein.at.
- ◐ **Location:** In central Austria, about 84km/53mi southeast of Salzburg.
- ⊛ **Don't Miss:** Hunerkogel.
- ◷ **Timing:** Allow a day if taking in one summit.
- 👪 **Kids:** Nature trail around Planai summit.

DACHSTEIN-TAUERN SKI AREA 🎿

Skiers will find 78 lifts, 140km/87mi of downhill ski runs and 350km/217mi of off-piste slopes, but need only a single ski pass for the combined Schladminger Tauern and Dachstein area.

The **downhill ski runs** concentrate mainly on the Schladminger Tauern and consist of five areas: the **Reiteralm** *(alt. 800–1,860m/2,625–6,102ft)* above Pichl; the **Hochwurzen** *(745–1,850m/2,444–6,069ft)* above Rohrmoos; the **Planai** *(745–1,894m/2,444–6,213ft)* above Schladming; **Hauser Kaibling** *(752–2,015m/2,467–6,611ft)* above Haus; and the **Gaisterbergalm** *(680–1,976m/2,231–6,483ft)* above Pruggern. Most are connected and are also served by buses. Fageralm, Stoderzinken and the Dachstein glacier are smaller areas.

Moderately good skiers will be happy here, but less so those who like a bigger challenge. The snow cover is generally good, but the low altitude can sometimes pose problems. Snow-makers are often used on the lower pistes.

For cross-country skiers, the **Schladminger Tauern** provide 60km/37mi of tracks around Rohrmoos, and a further 28km/17mi around Schladming. Dedicated skiers should steer towards **Ramsau am Dachstein** with its internationally renowned **cross-country ski area**.

SCHLADMING 🎿

Alt. 745m/2,444ft. The World Cup downhill races held on the Planai slopes since 1973 have given Schladming plenty of publicity. Après-ski is also provided for, with generous sports facilities. There is an 18-hole golf course at Oberhaus. Schladming's pedestrian zone is a joy to stroll around. Other resorts in the valley include **Rohrmoos**, Pichl, **Haus** (with a pretty Baroque church) and Pruggern. Another alternative is the sunny plateau of **Ramsau**, which is famous for its unspoiled countryside and delightful setting.

VIEWPOINTS
Hunerkogel★★★
Alt. 2,694m/8,836ft. ◖*See DACHSTEIN MOUNTAIN AREA DRIVING TOUR.*

Rossbrand★★
Alt. 1,770m/5,807ft. 28km/17mi west of Schladming. ◖*See DACHSTEIN MOUNTAIN AREA DRIVING TOUR.*

🏔 Planai★★ 🎿
Alt 1,906m/6,253ft. 1hr round-trip from Schladming. Take the cable-car in two stages (sit facing the back for the best view). ◷*Cable-car operates Jun–early Oct daily 9am–5pm; Dec–Apr daily 8.15am–4.15pm.* ⊜€18 round-trip

Dachstein mountains and Schladmin

© Austrian National Tourist Office/Weinhaeupl W.

(summer), €46.50 day pass (winter).
℘03687 22 042. www.planai.at.
Also accessible via a small mountain
(toll) road, 12km/7.4mi.

The view from the mountain station is limited, but if you climb to the summit there is a fine **panorama★★**. Skiers can go via the Burgstallalm piste and also the chairlift of the same name. Hikers can climb the **Krahbergzinken** (alt. 2,134m/7,001ft) in a 2hr30min round trip. Alternatively, take the **nature trail** ▲▴ round the Planai summit in 45min.

Hochwurzen★★

Alt 1,849m/6,066ft. 30min round
trip via cable-car from Rohrmoos.
◑Cable-car operates Dec–mid-Apr
daily 8.45am–4.15pm; mid-Jun–mid-
Oct daily 9am–5pm. ⊚€13.50 round-
trip (summer), €46.50 day pass (winter).
℘03687 22 042.

From here, obtain a **panorama★★** of the Dachstein and a view of Schladming. From the mountain inn terrace you can see the Schladminger Tauern with the Hochgolling and Steirische Kalkspitze summits. The cable-car will take you up to **Hauser Kaibling★** for more stunning views and skiing opportunities.

🔥 HIKING

Schladming and other Ennstal villages are ideal starting points for **walks and hikes★★** in the relatively low-lying surrounding mountain ranges.
A magnificent panorama can be enjoyed from such summits as Höchstein and Hochgolling, but due to the long climb, plan to overnight at the mountain lodge.

🔥 Dreiseen Circuit★

17km/11mi east of Schladming. Allow
4hr to hike the entire circuit. Drive on E
651 towards Liezen then go right onto a
small toll road towards the Bodensee.

An easy trail leads to the **Bodensee★** with its lovely waterfall reached in about 15min. From the far end of the lake, an arduous trail *(1hr)* climbs up to the Hans-Wödl-Hütte mountain lodge *(alt. 1,528m/5,013ft)* on the idyllic **Hüttensee**. A beautiful spruce forest and two waterfalls form the backdrop.
After another 45min the trail reaches the crystal-clear **Obersee** *(alt. 1,672m/5,485ft)*. Return the same way.

ADDRESSES

🏠STAY AND 🍴EAT

⊜⊜ **Hotel Feichter** – *Bahnhofstraße 278, 8970 Schladming. ℘ 03687 22 129. www. hotel-feichter.at. ⌢. Half board possible. Restaurant (lunch Thu–Tue).* A small hotel with simple, clean rooms. The restaurant serves local dishes, plus some international ones.

⊜⊜ **Braunhofer's** – *Teichweg 35, 8971 Rohrmoos-Untertal. 3.5km/2mi S. ℘03687 61 575. www.braunhofer.at. ⌢. Half board possible. Restaurant Mon & Wed–Thu 4pm–9.30pm, Fri–Sun 11am–9.30pm.* Lovely hotel-restaurant with pleasant rooms, some with a balcony. Austrian and international dishes available.

Salzburger Sportwelt❄❄❄

One of five areas forming the Ski Amadé winter-sports region, the Salzburger Sportwelt is crisscrossed by 350km/218mi of pistes served by 100 lifts. Slopes extend between 800m/2,624ft and 2,000m/6,650ft and are especially suitable for beginner and intermediate skiers. The main villages are Flachau, Wagrain, St. Johann-Alpendorf, Radtstadt, Altenmarkt-Zauchensee, Kleinarl, Eben and Filzmoos.

The ski area is located between the Tenner range and the Radstädter Tauern, about 70km/43mi southeast of Salzburg. (🅸 Hauptstraße 159. ℘06457 29 29. www.salzburgersportwelt.at).

Sights

Zauchensee★ – Alt. 1,361m/4,465ft. Zauchensee is the highest resort in the Salzburger Sportwelt and consequently offers the best snow cover. Keen downhill skiers have a beautiful **low-altitude mountain setting★** with ski runs of varying degrees of difficulty. If you are after a village atmosphere and a more extensive range of leisure facilities, visit **Altenmarkt im Pongau.**

Schwarzwand-Seilbahn★★ – Alt. 2,100m/6,890ft. For skiers only. The cable-car leads to the foot of the Schwarzkopf, where a **panorama★★** of the Tennengebirge, the Dachstein and the Radstädter Tauern unfolds.

Rosskopf★★ – Alt. 1,929m/6,329ft. Travel up on the **Flachau cable-car.** ◔Daily Dec–Apr 8.30am–4pm (Feb til 4.15pm); Jul–Aug 9am–noon, 1.30pm–5pm. ☞€17.50 round-trip. ℘06457 22 210. www.flachau.at. At the top of the cable-car ride there is a remarkable **view★** over Modermandl and Faulkogel. Continue by chairlift up to the Rosskopf. Climbing up to the peak takes only a few minutes, and there is a **panorama★★** over Zauchensee and Flachau, the Dachstein, the Radstädter Tauern and the Hohe Tauern.

Mooskopf★★ – Take the Kleinarl chairlift and the Bubble-Shuttleberg chairlift, then walk a few minutes to the summit. ◔Daily Dec–Apr 8.45am–4pm (Feb til 4.15pm). ☞€50 day pass (in high season). ℘06418 27 53 00. www.shuttleberg.com. From the peak a splendid **panorama★★** opens up taking in the Tennengebirge range, the Dachstein, the Ennskraxn massif and other impressive peaks.

Wagrain★ – Alt. 838m/2,749ft. Besides having the area's best lodging and most extensive network of ski-lifts, the town also enjoys a certain fame as the home of Atomic, the largest Austrian ski manufacturer. The snow cover, though, is fairly unreliable.

Koglalm★ – Alt. 1,878m/6,161ft. Enjoy a **panorama★** over Wagrain, Flachau and Kleinarl with the Tennengebirge range, the Dachstein and the Niedere Tauern in the background. Experienced skiers and hikers are able to reach the **Saukarkopf,** where even broader **views★★** open up.

LINZ AND THE DANUBE VALLEY

Oberösterreich, or Upper Austria, as well as including part of the mountains and lakes of Salzkammergut, covers the area either side of the Danube from the German border near Passau to the Enns River in the south. In contrast to the dramatic landscape to the west, the Danube region is less rugged, dotted with thickly forested hills, fortified towns, historic castles and monasteries.

Highlights

A Bit of History

The regional capital, Linz, is the nation's third-largest city and has a history that stretches back beyond Roman times. When you arrive by autobahn or train, Linz may appear at first sight to be a large, industrial city, home to factories such as the Vöstalpine steel works. However, it has a well-preserved old town centre and a lively cultural scene, having benefited from investment in the arts in the run-up to its shared tenure of European Capital of Culture in 2009. Not far from Linz, the abbey of St. Florian is one of the most beautiful Baroque churches in the country. In addition to a splendid art collection, it is closely associated with the composer Anton Bruckner, who was born nearby. To the west of St. Florian are the towns of Wels and Lambach, the former with a historic town centre and the latter with an abbey boasting some fabulous Romanesque frescoes. A further religious site that should not be missed is Kremsmünster, another remodelled Baroque church full of treasures.

The River Enns that joins the Danube River to the south of Linz is the location of Enns and Steyr, towns that have attractive medieval street plans radiating from beautiful central squares lined with historic buildings. Close to Steyr is Christkindl, with its pilgrimage church and from which millions of Christmas cards are sent every year.

The region northeast of the Danube is known as the Mühlviertel. The coun-

Chancel, Abbey Church, Wilhering Monastery

© Martin Siepmann/imageBROKER/age fotostock

120

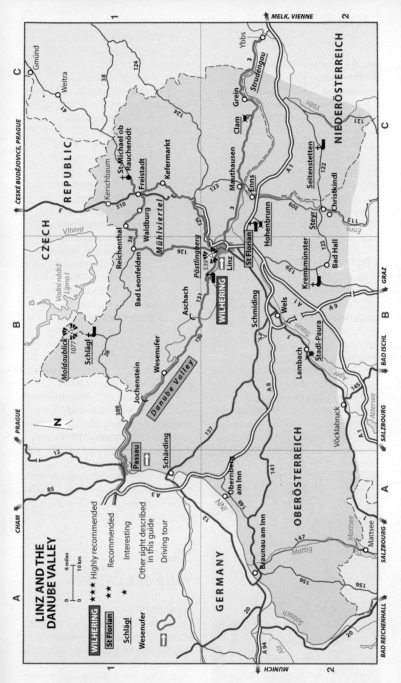

tryside here is wilder, more rugged and covered in thick forest reaching up to the Czech border. Its name derives from the Mühl rivers that flow through the area. Here are more charming small towns, one of the most notable being Freistadt, as well as some of Austria's most important ecclesiastic sights.

Linz★

and Mülhviertel

Linz, the capital of Upper Austria and the country's third-largest city, straddles the Danube at a widening of the river valley. Three bridges link the city with its suburb of Urfahr on the left bank. In fact, Linz owes a good deal of its prosperity to the Danube. Today it is an important industrial centre, whose strong support for culture and the arts won it the (shared) title of European Capital of Culture 2009. Austria's oldest and largest churches are in Linz.

A BIT OF HISTORY

Although settled since around 4000 BC, Linz wasn't really put on the map until the Romans founded a camp called Lentia here in AD 1. In the Middle Ages, the town became a major trading centre and even enjoyed a brief stint as imperial capital under Friedrich III from 1489 to 1493. Protestantism fell on fertile ground here, drawing the astronomer **Johannes Kepler** in its wake, who wrote his best-known work, *Harmonice mundi (The Harmony of the World)*, while in town. Eventually, though the Counter-Reformation struck back

▶ **Population:** 201,595.

Info: Hauptplatz 1, A-4010, ✆0732 70 70 20 09. www.linz.at/tourismus.

▶ **Location:** Linz is in northwestern Austria, not far from Germany. Alt. 266m/873ft.

Ⓟ **Parking:** An automated parking system directs you to the nearest garage *(fee)*, of which there are several in the centre. Free car park by the train station and across the river on Urfahrmarkt.

☺ **Don't Miss:** Lentos Kunstmuseum, Ars Electronica Center, Neuer Dom.

Ⓣ **Timing:** It takes a full day to do Linz justice.

👥 **Kids:** Ars Electronica Center, Grottenbahn.

with a vengeance, and Linz remained a provincial backwater until the Industrial Age arrived in the 19C, bringing factories and railways. Adolf Hitler took a particular liking to the city and locals largely returned the affection. The Nazis built the large steel and ironworks along the Danube that still provide employment to many today. Since the end of World War II, industrial development has accelerated with emphasis on chemicals and other heavy industries.

◀●▶WALKING TOUR

TOUR OF OLD LINZ★

Hauptplatz★

This strikingly large square was laid out in the 13C and has at its centre a Trinity Column *(Dreifaltigkeitssäule)*, erected to commemorate the town's escape from plague, fire and Turkish invasion.

▶ Leave the square along Domgasse.

Dreifaltigkeitssäule, Hauptplatz

© zwawol/iStockphoto.com

TOURIST INFORMATION

TOURIST OFFICE: *Hauptplatz 1.*
Open Mon–Sat 9am–7pm (Oct–Apr til 5pm), Sun and holidays 10am–7pm (Oct–Apr til 5pm). *℘0732 70 70 20 09.*

LINZ CARD: This card entitles you to free admission to seven major museums and galleries, free unlimited use of all LINZ AG public transit lines, and discounts at many more attractions, excursions, cruises, etc. Holders of a 3-day card also get a free round-trip on the **Pöstlingberg mountain railway** and a €5 restaurant voucher. The card is sold at tourist offices. 1-day ticket: €15; 3-day ticket: €25. For full details visit www.linz.at/tourismus.

TRIPS ON THE DANUBE

Boat trip Linz–Passau –
Donauschiffahrt Wurm & Köck, *Untere Donaulände 1, 4020 Linz. ℘0732 78 36 07. www.donauschiffahrt.de.*

CITY TOUR: Linz-City-Express –

tour in a miniature train with commentary (25min) in season (Jul–Aug) 10am–8pm, hourly (if demand is heavy, every 30min). Leaves from the Hauptplatz. €8, children €4. www.geigers.at

PUBLIC TRANSPORT

Individual tickets – Single tickets and day passes *(Tageskarten)* can be obtained from ticket vending machines, while **multiple tickets** *(Mehrfahrtenkarten)* for six journeys and transferable **runabout tickets** *(Netzkarten)*, valid for several days and giving unlimited travel on buses and trams, are available from ticket offices in *Trafiken* (tobacconists').
Information on public transport services is provided by **Linz AG-Kundenzentrum:** *Landstraße 85/1. ℘0732 78 01 70 02. www.linzag.at*

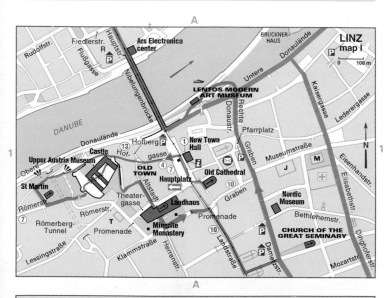

WHERE TO STAY		
Goldener Anker,Gasthof.....④	Mühlviertler Hof ....⑩	La Cave ....⑦
Hotel Wolfinger ....⑦	**WHERE TO EAT**	Stieglbräu ....⑩
	Alte Welt ....①	Zum kleinen Griechen ....⑬

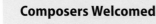

Composers Welcomed

Linz was a staging-post for Mozart in the course of his many tours; in 1782 he wrote his 36th symphony, the "Linz Symphony," here in just four days for a concert he was due to give at the city theatre. Beethoven, too, composed a symphony in Linz, his Eighth, but more than any other composer, the city cherishes the memory of Anton Bruckner, who was cathedral organist here for 12 years. Every year Linz keeps his memory alive through its international festival of classical music, the Brucknerfest.

Alter Dom St. Ignatius (Old Cathedral)

ⓘ *Open year-round daily 7.30am–6.30pm.* 𝄞 *0732 77 08 660.*

This 17C Jesuit church by Pietro Francesco Carolone is the city's most important Baroque house of worship. The simple façade forms a striking contrast to the interior, where stucco, pink marble columns, an elaborately carved pulpit and choir stalls, and a high altar adorned with marble statues make up a highly extravagant décor. Bruckner served as church organist from 1855 to 1868.

▷ Return to the Hauptplatz and take Hofgasse on your left.

Castle

The oldest part of the schloss, which was the residence of Emperor Friedrich III, dates from the end of the 15C.

Schlossmuseum★

ⓘ *Open Tue–Fri 9am–6pm (Thu til 9pm), Sat–Sun and hols 10am–5pm.* ⓘ *Closed 1 Nov, 25, 31 Dec.* ⬤€6.50. & 𝄞 *0732 77 20 52 300. www.landesmuseum.at.*

This museum offers insight into the art and cultural history of Upper Austria. If you have limited time, focus on the collection of paintings from the Gothic period and Austrian landscapes from the 19C and early 20C.

▷ Walk west on Römerstraße.

St. Martin's Church★

First documented in 799, Martinskirche is considered Austria's oldest church. It was built using pieces of debris left over from the 1C Roman camp and combines various Romanesque and Gothic features. A glass door separates you from the interior, which can only be seen during Mass and on guided city tours.

▷ Turn right into the Graben (Moat); continue into the Promenade; turn right to the Landhaus.

Landhaus

This 16C building, now the seat of the provincial government, wraps around an inner courtyard lined on two sides by arcades and anchored by an octagonal fountain. The seven figures on its base represent the planets and recall the years 1612 to 1626 when Johannes Kepler taught at the regional secondary school, then based at the Landhaus.

Minorite Monastery

ⓘ *Open Apr–Oct daily 8am–4pm; Nov–Mar daily 8am–11am.* 𝄞 *0732 77 20 11 364.*

The Gothic Minoritenkirche, founded in the 13C by Franciscans, was remodelled in the Rococo style in the 18C. The altarpiece on the high altar by Bartolomäus Altomonte represents the Annunciation; the altarpieces on the six side altars are the work of Kremser Schmidt.

▷ Go back up the Promenade and turn right on to Landsraße then left onto Harrachstraße.

Church of the Great Seminary★

The 18C Priesterseminarkirche was designed by Johann-Lukas von Hildebrandt with stuccowork by Paolo d'Allio; the Crucifixion painting over the high altar was done by Altomonte.

▷ Take Dametzstraße as far as Bethlehemstraße.

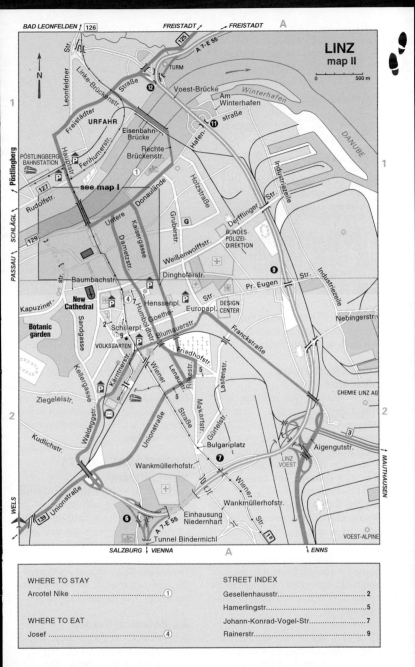

Nordico Museum

🕐 *Open year-roun Tue–Sun 10am–6pm (Thu til 9pm).* 💰€6.50. ♿ 📞0732 70 70 19 12. www.nordico.at.

Despite its name, the Nordico Museum der Stadt Linz is all about the city. It presents changing exhibits about city history and large-scale exhibitions on nature and Linz's cultural history.

◗ Walk along Dametzstraße, Graben then Rechte Donaustraße. At the end

Ars Electronica Center by the Danube

© Austrian National Tourist Office/Viennaslide

of the road turn right onto Untere Donaulände and then immediately left towards the Schiffsstation.

Lentos Modern Art Museum★

🕐Open year-round Tue–Sun 10am–6pm (Thu til 9pm). ≋€8. ✆0732 70 70 36 14. www.lentos.at.

The Lentos Kunstmuseum is a spectacular showcase of modern art that features an international cast of artists, including Gustav Klimt, Lovis Corinth and Max Pechstein as well as post-1945 masters such as Andy Warhol and Keith Haring. Changing exhibitions of equally high calibre supplement the permanent galleries.

Since 2003, the collection has been housed in a bold building★ by the Swiss architects Weber & Hofer. After dark the colour of its façade alternates between blue and red.

◗ Walk along the river towards the small bridge. On your right is the strikingly modern Ars Electronica Center.

♙♙ Ars Electronica Center

🕐Open year-round Tue–Fri 9am–5pm (Thu til 7pm), Sat–Sun and hols 10am–6pm. ≋€8, students with I.D.

€9.50, children under 6 years of age free. ♿ ✆0732 72 720. www.aec.at.

An unapologetically modern building houses this "museum of the future," a high-tech palace devoted to the latest in digital technology and media. Explore virtual worlds in 3D in the Deep Space installation; experiment in the Sound Lab; or view Linz and other cities in the GeoPulse.

ADDITIONAL SIGHTS
New Cathedral

Consecrated in 1924, the neo-Gothic Neuer Dom is the largest church in Austria, able to accommodate 20,000 parishioners. Its spire soars to a lofty 134m/440ft, only 3m/9.8ft shorter than the one of the Stephansdom in Vienna. The stained-glass windows are noteworthy, especially the Linz Window depicting scenes from the town's history.

♙♙ Botanical Garden

Roseggerstraße 20. 🕐Open May–Aug daily 7.30am–7.30pm; Apr and Sept 8am–7pm; Mar and Oct 8am–6pm; Nov–Feb 8am–5pm. 🕐Closed 24–25 & 31 Dec and 1 Jan. ≋€3, children €2. ✆0732 70 70. www.linz.at.

About 10,000 varieties of colourful plants cover the 4ha/10-acre Botanischer Garten; in season it's a delight to

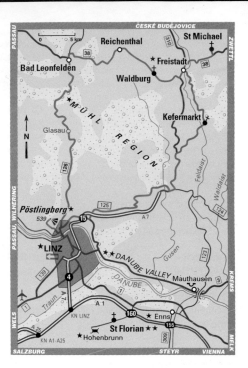

stroll in the rose garden. The grounds also house the largest collection of cacti in Europe. The greenhouses are devoted to orchids and tropical plants.

EXCURSIONS
Pöstlingberg★
4.5km/3mi northwest. Departs from Pöstlingberg station Bergbahnhof.
🕐*year-round Mon–Sat 6am–10pm every 30min (Nov–Mar til 8pm), Sun and hols 7.30am–10pm every 30min.* ✆*€6.10 round-trip.* ✆*0732 34 00 74 06.*
Europe's steepest narrow-gauge mountain railway covers the 2.9km/1.8mi journey to the top of the Pöstlingberg, with its Baroque church, in 16min. From a flower-decked terrace below the church there is an extensive **view★** from nearly 300m/984ft down into the Danube Valley.
Also up here is the **Grottenbahn** 🚶🚶, a dragon-pulled miniature-train chugging through a fairy-tale landscape.

🚗 DRIVING TOUR

MÜHLVIERTEL TOUR★
103km/64mi

The Mühlviertel district derives its name from the small Mühl River, which flows into the Danube above Linz. It is a hilly upland region with wide, forested valleys.

▷ Leave Linz on the road (no. 126) N to Bad Leonfelden.

Leaving Linz, the road enters a verdant gorge and climbs gently, sometimes among rocks, sometimes among orchards. The wild nature of the hills grows more marked near Bad Leonfelden.

Bad Leonfelden
The town square of this spa town is the place to go for mud baths and Kneipp cure hydrotherapy treatments.

▷ Take the B 38 towards Freistadt. After 3km/2mi turn left.

Reichenthal
The village parish church was built in the late 19C. Its most interesting feature is its throne, sculpted by Linz artist Michael Rauscher to depict seven characters that symbolise the Seven Deadly Sins.
About 500m/545yd southwest of the Martplazt is the **Freilichtmuseum Hayrl** (Hayrl Open-air Museum; 🕐 open

Mar–mid-Nov; call for guided tour; €20 per tour for groups of 8 or fewer; 07214 41 80). Set below Waldenfels Castle (private property, no access), and set alongside a stream, this collection of old buildings open to visitors comprises a mill, a furnace, a forge and a sawmill.

Reichenthal is the starting point of the Ten Mills Footpath, which leads across the hills to the Czech border (round-trip from the Marktplatz, 14 km/ 8.5mi, mostly on the flat; allow about 4hr).

▷ Continue towards Freistadt, stopping off at Waldburg to see the three 16C winged altars in the church.

Freistadt★
See FREISTADT.

▷ The B 38 towards Sandl takes you to Oberrauchenödt, where you follow signs to St. Michael ob Rauchenödt.

St. Michael ob Rauchenödt
Perched above the town, this isolated church was built in the 16C in the Gothic style. The choir features a winged altara (c. 1522), with the Archangel Michael flanked by St. Nicolas (left) and St. Stephen (right). The figures represented above the shrine (St. Sebastian, St. Rupert and St. Florian) are attributed to the unknown artist who also carved the saints on the altar at Waldburg.

▷ Return to Freistadt and head S towards Kefermarkt.

Kefermarkt★★
Peaceful Kefermarkt on the Feldaist is surrounded by a restful, hilly landscape marking the transition between the Mühlviertel and the granite plateaux of the Waldviertel.
The Gothic church of **St. Wolfgangskirche★★** (open daily 8am–5pm; 0794 75 91 012; www.kefermarkt.at) contains a remarkable winged **altarpiece★★★** carved of wood by an unknown sculptor. More than 13m/42.6ft high, it is outstanding as much for its size as for the beauty of its proportions and the delicacy of the limewood carvings. The

three expressive figures in the central panel are (left to right as you face them) St. Peter, St. Wolfgang and St. Christopher. The wings of the altar depict religious scenes in low relief.

▷ At the main crossroads in Kefermarkt, turn right towards the railway station; cross the track and the Feldaist. After 7km/4.3mi turn left onto the main road, no. 125, connecting Freistadt and Linz.

ADDRESSES

🛏STAY

🍽 **Göttfried** – Hofgasse 5. 0732 99 70 23. www.goettfried.at. 19 rooms. Situated in the heart of the Old Town, this recently renovated hotel dates from 1670. The chic continental restaurant marries international dishes with local, seasonal products.

🍽 **Mühlviertler Hof** – Graben 26. 0732 77 22 680. www.hotel-muehlviertlerhof.at. 26 rooms. ⌨. The interesting bedrooms in this friendly family-run city-centre hotel are well appointed and exotically themed.

🍽 **Arcotel Nike** – Untere Donaulände 9. 07327 62 60. www.arcotelhotels.com. 174 rooms. ⌨€14. This hotel may seem unexciting, but its rooms are clean and modern; some offer a view of the Danube. It consistently gets good reviews from customers. The restaurant has a pleasant summer terrace.

🍽 **Hotel Wolfinger** – Hauptplatz 19. 0732 773 29 10. www.hotelwolfinger.at. 50 rooms. ⌨. A warm welcome awaits in this centrally located hotel. Antique wooden floors and antique furniture give the rooms an Old-World charm.

🍴EAT

🍽 **Alte Welt** – Hauptplatz 4. 0732 77 00 53. www.altewelt.at. Mon–Fri 11.30am–2.30pm, 5.30pm–midnight. Sat–Sun noon–2.30pm, 5.30pm–midnight. This café and wine cellar enjoys a superb setting in an old arcaded courtyard. The talented chef turns his innovative skills to traditional Austrian cuisine. Youthful and friendly atmosphere.

◒ **Stieglbräu zum Klosterhof** – *Landstr. 30.* ☎*0732 77 33 73. www.klosterhof-linz.at. Daily 9am –midnight.* This is Upper Austria's largest beer garden, seating 1,500 people, with several rustic comfortable rooms off the main garden. The cuisine is traditional Austrian fare, washed down with the finest local beer, of course.

◒◒ **Josef** – *Landstr. 49* ☎*0732 77 31 65. www.josef.eu. Mon–Sat 9am–2am, Sun 9am–2pm.* This is one of the city's most fashionable, buzzing places. It is not only a *Szenebar*, but a *vinotek*, a restaurant serving very good food, a traditional home-brew pub and venue staging live events most nights.

◒◒◒ **Zum kleinen Griechen** – *Hofberg 8 .* ☎*0732 78 24 67. www.zum kleinengriechen.at. Mon–Sat 11.30am–2pm, 6pm–midnight.* Good things come in little packages at this cosy vaulted restaurant, which serves authentic Greek fare and specialises in seafood, steaks, vegetarian dishes and lamb.

BARS

There are numerous bars to be found in a triangle defined by Hofgasse, Hofberg and Altstadt. Try **Kaffee Glockenspiel** *(Hauptplatz 18).* The most typical **brasseries** are **Stieglitz im Klosterhof** *(Landstr. 30)* and **Josef** *(◔see EAT).* They stay open until late and usually offer some form of live entertainment.

CAFÉS

Traximayr – *Promenade 16. www.cafe-traxlmayr.at. Open Mon–Sat 7.30am–10pm, Sun 9am–7pm.* This is the finest "grand Viennese café" in Linz. Come here to read the newspapers and bask on its sunny terrace.

Jindrak – *Herrenstr. 22-24. Open Mon–Sat 8am–6pm. Sun 8.30am–6pm. www.jindrak.at.* Close to the Old Cathedral, this café-pâtisserie is famous for its home-made gâteaux. It's the ideal place to try a slice of Linzer Torte.

K & K Hofbäckerei – *Pfarrgasse 17. www.kuk-hofbaeckerei.at. Mon–Fri 6.30am–6.30pm, Sat 7am–12.30pm.* This small café-pâtisserie is bursting with charm due to its antique storefront and furnishings. Thanks to its wonderful pastries, the place is often full to bursting with happy customers.

ENTERTAINMENT

Landestheater – *Promenade 39.* ☎*0800 21 80 00 . www.landestheater-linz.at.*

Theater Phöenix – *Wiener Str. 25.* ☎*0732 66 65 00. www.theater-phoenix.at.*

Konzerthaus Brucknerhaus – *Untere Donaulände 7.* ☎*0732 76 120. www.brucknerhaus.at.*

Posthof – *Posthofstr. 43.* ☎*0732 78 18 00. www.posthof.at.* Cabaret, theatre, dance, shows and musicals.

Casino Linz – *Rainerstr. 2-4.* ☎*0732 65 44 87. www.casinos.at.*

FESTIVALS

Linz Fest: May/Jun. World music in the Donaupark *(www.linzfest.at).*

Linzer Pflasterspektakel: Late Jul. Music, theatre, dance, cabaret circus acts and much more *(www.pflasterspektakel.at).*

Linzer Kultursommer: Jul and Aug. Various free concerts and theatre events scattered around the city centre.

Festival Ars Electronica: Sept. World-acclaimed festival of art, technology and society *(www.aec.at/festival).*

Internationales Brucknerfest mit Klangwolke: mid-Sept–early Oct. Classical concerts *(www.brucknerhaus.at).*

Advent: Nov–Christmas. Two Christmas markets, various concerts and events, as well as a Christmas crib installed in the castle museum.

SHOPPING

Shops and department stores are concentrated along Landstraße, which is pedestrianised for about 2km/1.2mi from Hauptplatz to Bürgerstraße, and its side streets. There are exclusive boutiques in the arcade on the Landstraße. The Herrenstraße has another pedestrian shopping precinct.

MARKETS

Südbahnhof: Market open Mon–Fri 6am–6pm and Sun 6am–1pm.

Hauptplatz: Farmers' market Fri 9am–2pm.

SOUVENIRS

Crafts: Heimatwerk, *Landstraße 31*; Linzer Torte (local speciality is a jam-filled cake): Café Jindrak (several branches, including *Herrenstraße 22*).

Freistadt★

Freistadt is a former stronghold on the ancient salt route to Bohemia. Its extensive, largely intact, fortifications include a double town wall, towers and gateways. With its pretty main square, web of spidery lanes and picturesque houses, Freistadt makes for an idyllic visit.

▶ **Population:** 7,700.
🛈 **Info:** Waaggasse 6, A-4240. ✆ 07942 75 700. www.freistadt.at.
◐ **Location:** Freistadt is in the lower Mühlviertel, about 30km/18.6mi northeast of Linz. Alt. 560m/1,837ft.
🅿 **Parking:** Parking in the historic centre is short-stay only. Long-stay parking is available in car parks along Linzerstraße.
☺ **Don't Miss:** Hauptplatz.

❧WALKING TOUR

Allow a couple of hours to wander the pretty streets of central Freistadt.

Hauptplatz★
This rectangular main square is framed by beautiful old pastel-painted houses adorned with delicate stucco; many are fronted by porches or arcades. In the centre of the wide square (6,500sq m/7,774sq yd) is a carved fountain dedicated to the Virgin Mary, while on the west side looms the **Rathaus** (town hall) in a pure Italian Renaissance style. Waagstraße, behind the town hall, is lined by exceptionally beautiful buildings, many sporting oriels and sgraffito façades.

◐ At the end of the Hauptplatz is the parish church.

Parish Church (Stadtpfarrkirche)
Just south of the Hauptplatz, the parish church boasts an elegant Baroque tower, a characteristic feature of Freistadt's skyline. The church itself is Gothic. The interior reveals a triple-aisled nave crowned with a ribbed vaulted ceilings. Also note the **organ case**, beautifully adorned with statues.
A few steps south of the Stadtpfarrkiche, the Dechantenhof is another impressive building in Baroque style.

◐ Cross back over the Hauptplatz and walk along Böhmergasse then right along the Schlossgasse.

Castle (Schloss)
North of the Hauptplatz is Freistadt's 14C castle. Its robust tower forms part of the **fortifications★★★**.
Inside, the **Schlossmuseum** examines various aspects and phases of regional history, exhibiting more than 17,000 objects as diverse as old clocks, flags, pharmaceutical instruments, traditional costume, and glass paintings.

Schlägl Monastery★

Located at the edge of the Bohemian Forest, Schlägl was founded by a vassal of the Bishop of Passau. The first foundation, 3km/1.8mi from the current location, built between 1202 and 1204 by the Cistercians from Upper Franconia, failed. The Premonstratensian order of Osterhofen, Lower Bavaria, who settled in 1218, had more success. Unlike so many other abbeys over the centuries, it managed to escape secularisation and in the 19C under Abbot Lebschy Dominik, it even flourished, as evidenced by the numerous works of art it purchased during this period, and the contents of its splendid library.

⚅ **Michelin Map:** 730, N3.
▷ **Location:** The monastery is located in the north of Austria, a short distance from the borders with the Czech Republic and Germany.

VISIT

🕐 *Open by guided tour only May–Oct Tue–Sat 10.30am and 2pm, Sun 11am and 2pm; rest of year on request.* ➾€5. *www.stift-schlaegl.at.*

Abbey Church

The main portal (1654), made from red and white marble, shows the patron saint of the monastery, the Virgin and angels and coats of arms. The narthex *(the lobby area at the far end of the main altar)*, above the nave and aisles, is separated by pillars that have retained their character despite Gothic Baroque stucco. Note the unusual height of the nave, as well as the staircase going to the choir.

The interior★ is typical of the Baroque period. The sculptor Johann Worath, originally from South Tyrol, finished the pulpit in 1647. The 12 Apostles and St. John the Baptist appear in shell-shaped niches.

The high altar depicting the Assumption and the side altars were made between 1721 and 1740. The choir grille was crafted by Hans Walz (1635).

In the west gallery, the great **organ** by Andreas Putz is an outstanding example of its genre, common in Alpine churches in the 17C.

The Early Gothic **cloister** is decorated with inscriptions of abbots and houses an exhibition on the history of the monastery and of the current order.

The tower chapel, only discovered in 1988, dates from the first decade of the 15C and is a rare example of of a Gothic *trompe l'oeil.*

With its octagonal central pillar, the **Romanesque crypt** is the oldest part of the monastery, built around 1250. An arch gives access to the **Gothic crypt**.

The **art gallery** was built in 1898 to host part of the abbey's art collection. The **paintings★** and triptychs of the Late Gothic period are of particular interest. One gallery is lined with portraits of former brothers dating back to 1802.

The abbey library was completed in 1852 in Baroque style, based on the model of St. Florian's library in Linz. It holds some 60,000 books.

The abbey's small **farm** hosts a collection of rural crafts and bygones from the Oberes Mühlviertel region.

EXCURSION
Moldaublick★

17km/10.5mi northeast. Go to Aigen im Mühlkreis and head towards Ulrichsberg; shortly after leaving here the L1558 road leads to the right towards Schöneben and the frontier with the Czech Republic.

This short tour traverses countryside. The 24m/79ft-high Moldaublick lookout tower *(137 steps)* commands a **view** of the Czech Republic and the Vltava (Moldau in German) – the longest river in the Czech Republic – as well as its dam.

Danube Valley, from Passau to Grein★★

The Danube is the longest river in Central Europe (2,826km/1,756mi) and the second-longest on the continent (after the Volga). It flows through or skirts 10 states. Four capital cities have been built on its banks, bearing witness to its importance and beauty.

A BIT OF HISTORY

The Austrian section of the Danube is entirely navigable; it has always been a vital artery for the country's economy. As such, its banks are graced with time-worn fortified castles, gracious Renaissance palaces, and historic churches and abbeys. These buildings tell the long and varied history of the river that composers and writers have praised in word and music. Although its waters may not always be the colour evoked in Strauss's *Blue Danube* (1867), it still meanders through some idyllic scenery.

🚗 DRIVING TOURS

1 FROM PASSAU TO LINZ
86km/53.4mi.

From Passau (in Germany) to Aschach, the route runs along the south bank of the river. From the north bank rise the granite heights of the Mühlviertel.

Passau★★

The well-preserved old town of Passau occupies a tongue of land between the Danube and the Inn, its cobbled streets clustered around the cathedral of St. Stephan. Overlooking the "town of three rivers" (the Danube, Inn and Ilz converge here) from their hilltop perches are the formidable Oberhaus fortress to the north and the Baroque pilgrimage church of Mariahilf to the south. From either vantage point highly photogenic views of the town are obtained.

🛈 **Info:** Lindengasse 9, A-4040. 📞0732 72 77 800. www. oberoesterreich.at/donau. ooe (for Upper Austria section); Schlossgasse 3, A-3620 Spitz an der Donau. 📞02713 30 06 060. www.donau.com (for Lower Austria section).

▶ **Location:** The Danube is Austrian for 360km/223.7mi from Achleiten, near the German border, to Hainburg, near Bratislava.

👁 **Don't Miss:** Wachau with Melk Abbey, Artstetten Castle, Krems und Stein, Vienna.

🕐 **Timing:** Allow five days to travel the length of the Austrian Danube.

▶ Leave Passau by crossing the Inn and heading towards Linz.

The wide and majestic river parallels the road, carving through wooded, rocky slopes. At Obernzell, it spills out into the reservoir of the Jochenstein dam, a magnificent lake. The **Jochenstein power station** generates 850 million kWh annually. From Engelhartszell to Wesenufer the valley narrows. The clifftop road offers some fine views, with various castles occasionally coming into view in the distance. A short distance after **Wesenufer**, a pretty village with flowered balconies, the road leaves the riverbank and climbs through a wooded gorge to the picturesque Aschach Valley. Beyond, it crosses the Danube below another one of five Donau power stations, the **Aschach-Kraftwerk**, one of the largest power stations of its kind in Europe.

▶ Beyond Ottensheim and its dam, the road follows the river to Linz. Stop off at the Wilhering Monastery (👟see below) on the way.

② FROM LINZ TO GREIN
72km/45mi.

Linz★
See LINZ.
Below Linz, the valley opens out into a wide, fertile basin where wheat, sugar beet, and fruit trees flourish. To the north lie the slopes and forested ridges of the Mühlviertel and farther on, the Waldviertel.

◗ Leave Linz to the SE via St. Peterstraße towards Grein.

The road continues through the industrial zone of Linz and crosses the Danube at the Steyregg bridge, beyond which it cuts across a plateau to return to the Danube plain at St. Georgen.

◗ Take the turn towards the camp (Lager) at Mauthausen.

Mauthausen
Mauthausen would be just like any other sleepy, historic riverside town had it not been chosen, in 1938, as the site of a Nazi concentration camp, thanks to the proximity of several quarries.

KZ Mauthausen (Concentration Camp)
Open Mar–Oct daily 9am–5:30pm; Nov–Feb Tue–Sun 9am–3:45pm. Free. 07238 22 690. www.mauthausen-memorial.org.
About 200,000 people were imprisoned at Mauthausen and its 49 subsidiary camps. Over half perished working in the granite quarries, or if they had become too sick or weak, by being executed in horrific fashion. Some of the huts and rooms where the prisoners were kept still exist. Another building is now a museum with photographs and other documentation on the horrors perpetrated in this sinister place.
Outside the camp limits are memorials set up by countries whose people perished here. Below the plateau is the infamous "Todesstiege" (Stairway of Death), leading down to the quarry. Famous survivors of this camp include

Burg Clam
© Zoonar/Eder Hans/age fotostock

Simon Wiesenthal (1908–2005), who dedicated his life to tracking down Nazis and bringing them to justice.

From Mauthausen to Dornach the road crosses a vast cultivated plain that gradually changes to a wooded landscape.

◗ Near Saxen, turn right towards Burg Clam.

Burg Clam★
Guided tour (45min) May–Oct daily 10am–4.30pm (last admission). €9. 07269 72 17. www.burgclam.com.
Dominated by its central tower, the castle rises from its leafy surroundings. The rock on which it stands has been fortified since 1149. The residential part of the castle revolves around the irregular arcaded Renaissance **courtyard★**. Inside, highlights include an unusually complete **pharmacy** from 1603, fine Vienna and Meissen porcelain, and some rare Louis XVI armchairs.

◗ Return to the Danube road.

Below Dornach the road hugs the north bank of the river whose waters are hemmed in by rocky, wooded slopes. The approach to Grein (*see p150*) is particularly pretty. *If you wish to continue to the scenic Strudengau, see p150 for the Grein to Arstetten driving tour.*

Wilhering Monastery★★★

The Cistercian abbey of Wilhering hugs the south bank of the Danube upstream from Linz. Starting out as a Romanesque complex, the building was transformed into one of Austria's most striking examples of the Rococo style in the 18C. The most celebrated architects of the day, including Joseph Mathias Götz, Josef Munggenast and Johann Michael Prunner, hoped to obtain the commission, but unexpectedly the job went to an unknown local craftsman called Johann Haslinger.

Info: Linzer Straße 4, Wilhering. ℘07226 23 11 10. www.stiftwilhering.at.

Location: The abbey is 8km/5mi west of Linz.

Don't Miss: Abbey church.

Timing: Allow an hour.

VISIT
Abbey Courtyard

The Baroque pomp of the abbey's courtyard is toned down by a characteristically Cistercian sense of measure and balance. The church façade, a white and pink confection, is subdivided by piers. The portal is the only visible remnant of the original Romanesque church.

Abbey Church

Open Jul–Aug Tue–Sun 11am–6pm. €2. Guided tours (€2.50) by arrangement.

Wilhering's church is an outstanding example of the Rococo style in European architecture. Indeed, it would be difficult to surpass this joyous profusion of decoration, richness of colour, ingenuity of painting and sculpture, and delicacy of stuccowork.

The **high altar** centres on a painting of the Assumption of the Virgin Mary by **Martin Altomonte**. Altomonte also executed the paintings for the **side chapels**, which were his last compositions. When he learned about the huge programme of **frescoes** planned for the ceilings, he got his nephew Bartolemeo hired for the job.

Bartolomeo Altomonte, although less talented than his uncle, did remarkable work at Wilhering, painting almost two-thirds of the church ceiling. The nave is decorated with an enormous painting of Mary as Queen of Heaven, surrounded by her court of saints and angels. The **stucco** artist **Franz Joseph Holzinger** came with his students from St. Florian to spend three consecutive summers (1739–41) decorating the church. However, their style was considered too academic and all their work was destroyed. The abbot then hired young stuccoworkers trained in southern Germany who had eschewed the overbearing compositions of the Late Baroque and adopted a more delicate style.

The **dome** above the transept crossing enters the realm of *trompe-l'œil* and illusion. An erudite architectural composition, painted by the Italian Francesco Messenta, it opens at the top on a glimpse of sky; the men chained to the earth by their sins are protected by the Virgin Mary from divine wrath.

To the right of the choir stalls, the imposing **pulpit** is decked out in black and white stucco and gold and matches the elegant **choir organ** built in 1746 by Nicolas Rumel of Linz. Anton Bruckner was especially fond of it.

The part of the nave accommodating the **great organ** is itself a monumental work of art consisting of a magnificently worked iron gate and an elegant gallery that directs the gaze upward towards the pipes. Overhead, a clock marks the passing of time and a purple curtain in *trompe-l'œil* hangs from the vault, its folds drawn back reveal the scene.

The **cloisters** are reached through a door *(left)* from the narthex. A pre-Gothic 13C **doorway** leads into the old **chapter-house**; a series of fine 18C paintings depicts episodes in the life of St. Bernard.

Schärding★

This picturesque little town on the Inn River belonged to the royal Bavarian Wittelsbach family almost without interruption from 1248 to 1779 when it was ceded to Austria. There are no major sights here, but the lovely Baroque Old Town with cobbled lanes and remains of the medieval fortifications make Schärding a pleasant stop nevertheless.

A BIT OF HISTORY

First mentioned in documents in 804, Schärding has been an important trading site on the Inn ever since. The Bavarian ducal family, the Wittelsbachs, were an important influence on the town's architecture. Such was the economic importance of Schärding that there was a constant need for fortifications. The Bavarian duke, Ludwig the Bearded, was responsible for the fortifications, little of which remain apart from the castle moat. The town suffered damage during two disastrous fires in 1724 and 1779 and during French occupation in 1809.

OLD TOWN
Stadtplatz

Schärding's old town centres on **Stadtplatz**, the main square divided by a row of buildings called a *Grätzel*.

▶ **Population:** 4,997.

▪ **Info:** Innbruckstraße 29, A – 4780 Schärding. ☎07712 43 000. www.schaerding.at. Stadtpl. 2, A-5280 Braunau. ☎07722 62 644. www.tourismus-braunau.at.

▶ **Location:** Schärding lies on Austria's western edge, right on the border with Germany, about 107km/66.5mi west of Linz. Alt. 318m/1,043ft.

🅿 **Parking:** Look for car parks on Bahnhofstraße and Alfred-Kubin-Straße. There's also a garage on Tummelplatzstraße. In Braunau, look for car parks along Ringstraße.

🕐 **Timing:** Plan on spending a couple of hours in town.

Its most distinctive feature, though, is the **Silberzeile★**, a phalanx of statuesque Baroque houses painted in a rainbow of colours. The name, which translates as "Silver Row," is a reference to the deep-pocketed merchants who had them built back in the 17C.

Schärding and the Inn River

Braunau

© Austrian National Tourist Office/Weinhaeupl W.

Stadtpfarrkirche

Just off the square, the Late Baroque **Stadtpfarrkirche** (parish church), dedicated to St. George, has fine proportions that give the well-lit nave a lofty dignity, emphasised by soaring pillars. The left side altar has a panel by Michael Rottmayr (Christ Appearing to St. Theresa) from about 1690.

Linzertor

The upper square is closed off by the Linzer Tor (Linz Gate), while the **Rathaus** (town hall) marks the beginning of the lower square anchored by the St. Georgs-Brunnen (St. George's Fountain) of 1607.

Wassertor

To get to the Inn River, walk through the **Wassertor** (Water Gate), where high water marks provide evidence of disastrous flooding.

Innlände Promenade

Taking a stroll along the **Innlände** riverside promenade opens up attractive perspectives on the town. River steamers stop here as well.

EXCURSIONS
Obernbeg am Inn

31km/19mi south.

Records of the first market here date back to around 950, and for centuries Obernberg was under the domination of Passau. In 1782, the town became part of Austria.

The town's main square, **Marktplatz**, is a beautiful old space with a Bavarian character. At its heart is a carved stone fountain; around the square are elegant houses with colourful façades, some of which are decorated with stucco. Note in particular the façades of the Wörndle houses: the apothecary and the boatman are works by the Bavarian artist Johann Baptist Modler (1740).

Braunau

Braunau *(population 16,700; alt. 352m/1,155ft)* is situated in the Innviertel, right on the border with Germany about 60km/37mi north of Salzburg and 90km/56mi west of Linz.

It has had a civic charter since 1260; it flourished through the salt trade in the 15C, but only became part of Austria in 1779. A bridge over the Inn connects the town with Simbach in Bavaria, Germany. Although infamous as the birthplace of Adolf Hitler, Braunau is really more noteworthy for its pretty town centre and the numerous Gothic houses that survived the Great Fire of 1874.

Altstadt

The focal feature is the **Stadtplatz**, an elongated square framed by houses from various architectural periods. Also see the **Glockengießerhaus** (*Johann-Fischer-Gasse 18*), built in 1385, retaining its original bell-foundry workshop.

Stadtpfarrkirche St. Stephan

Dominating Braunau's skyline is the landmark steeple of the town's parish church. The Late Gothic church, an ebony-yellow brick building, has three naves and is filled with treasures, most notably the late-15C **Bäcker-altar** (Bakers' Altar), donated by the bakers' guild.

Wels

Edging the Traun River, Wels evolved from a small Celtic settlement into the Roman town of Ovilava, which became an important supply centre and was eventually raised to the status of colony. Today, it is the second-largest town in Lower Austria after Linz and is known for its lovely historic centre.

- ▶ **Population:** 60,400.
- ℹ **Info:** Stadtplatz 44, A-4600. ℘07242 67 72 222. www.wels-info.at.
- ▶ **Location:** Wels is about 35km/22mi southwest of Linz. Alt. 317m/1,040ft.
- 🅿 **Parking:** There are car parks on Kaiser-Josef-Platz, below the Traunpark Hotel and on the Marktplatz. Parking is free at the Messe on non-trade show days.
- 🕐 **Timing:** Taking in all the museums, it's easy to make a day of it in Wels.
- 👥 **Kids:** Zoo Schmiding.

👣 WALKING TOUR

THE OLD TOWN

Allow 2hr to wander the Roman and Medieval streets of Wels.

Starting from Polheimerstraße, pass below the Ledererturm (Gate Tower), built in the 13C and enter **Stadtplatz** (🔆*see below*). The houses in this square, and its immediate environs represent some of the finest examples of Upper Austrian vernacular architecture. In the square, at numbers 62 and 63, note the imposing Baroque façade of a house which, from 1630 right up until the 20C, belonged to the monastery of Krems-münster.

▶ At the eastern end of Stadtplatz, turn right on to Traungasse and left on to Am Zwinger to reach the castle.

Castle

🕐*Open year-round Tue–Fri 10am–5pm, Sat 2pm–5pm, Sun and hols 10am–4pm.* ⊛€4.70. ♿ ℘07242 23 57 350. www.wels.at.

The restored imperial Burg Wels, where Emperor Maximilian I died in 1519, now houses four **museum collections**: the Local History Museum, with a remarkable display of Biedermeier items; the Museum of Agriculture, arranged on the theme of the "farmer's year;" the Austrian Museum of Baking, the only one of its kind; and the Museum of Displaced Persons.

▶ Walk away from the castle down Burggasse.

Parish Church

The Stadpfarrkirche has some fine 14C stained-glass windows in the chancel. To the south looms the Kaiserliche Burg, the imperial castle.

▷ Return to the Stadtplatz.

Stadtplatz★

Wels' historic town centres on the elongated Stadtplatz, the main square with a flower-bedecked fountain and rows of attractive buildings, mostly sporting Baroque façades. The golden **Rathaus** (town hall) is certainly striking, although the star of the square is the **Haus der Salome Alt** at no. 4, named after a mistress of Wolf Dietrich of Raitenau, the prince-archbishop of Salzburg. Distinctive features include the Late Gothic oriel and the Renaissance fresco paintings.

Back towards the Ledererturm is the **Stadtmuseum Wels** (*Minoritenplatz 4, marked R on the map;* ◷ *open Tue–Fri 10am–5pm, Sat 2pm–5pm, Sun 10am–4pm;* ⊛ *€4.70;* ✆ *07242 23 51 346).* Each excavation within the town uncovers yet more evidence of its past, particularly the Roman period. This research has resulted in a particularly rich archaeological collection housed in a former monastery. One section re-creates a mock Roman village where you can peek inside tradesmen's workshops, private living quarters and tombs.

EXCURSIONS

Lambach

Lambach (population 3,380; alt. 349m/1,145ft) is about 15km/9.3mi southwest of Wels or 48km/30mi southwest of Linz.

In the Middle Ages, this small town on the River Traun built its wealth on the salt trade. To this economic function was added the prestige of a Benedictine abbey, founded by Bishop Adalbero in the 11C and still active today.

Stiftskirche★ (Abbey Church)

◷*Open year-round Mon–Fri 9am–noon, 1pm–4pm.* ✆*07245 21 71 03 34. www.stift-lambach.at.*

The abbey church, which contains the tomb of Adalbero, was largely rebuilt in the 17C according to Baroque precepts, although some exquisite Byzantine-influenced **frescoes★★** survive from the Romanesque period. Uncovered and restored in 1967, they are considered among the oldest in Europe.

The scene in the central dome shows the Virgin Mary with the Infant Jesus, flanked to the left by the Three Wise Men bearing gifts and to the right by Jerusalem and Herod interrogating the Wise Men.

Klostergebäude (Abbey Buildings)

Highlights in the main abbey buildings include the Baroque **library** with frescoes by Melchior Seidl and 50,000 precious volumes; the well-proportioned **summer refectory** (now a concert hall), with outstanding stucco decoration by Carlo Antonio Carlone; the former abbey tavern, now a **pharmacy**, which also contains some beauti-

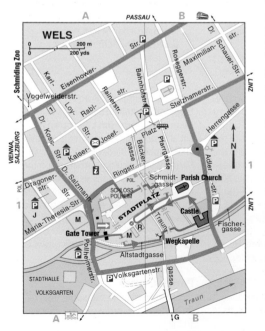

ful stucco-work; and the **ambulatory** by Diego Carlone.

Lambach even has its own theatre, the beautiful 18C Rococo **Kleines Theater★**, the only one of its kind to have survived in Austria.

Pfarr- und Wallfahrtskirche Stadl-Paura★

2km/1.2m. Leave Lambach to the south. Cross the River Traun and turn right after 500m/550yd.

This church is a symmetrical ode to the Trinity. It has a triangular floorplan, three towers, three chancels, three marble portals, three altars, three small organs. and three sacristies. Even the frescoes in the dome and the altar paintings are by a trio of famous artists: Carlo Antonio Carlone, Martino Altomonte and Domenico Parodi.

▲▲ Zoo Schmiding★

Krengelbach. 7km/4.3mi north of Wels.
🕐*Open Mar–Nov daily 9am–6.30pm (last admission 5pm).* ∞€13.50, children €6.50. 📞07249 46 272. *www.zooschmiding.at.*

What used to be merely a bird park has evolved into a modern zoo where animals live in re-created habitats, such as a tropical rain forest (squirrels monkeys, crocodiles, sloths) and the African Savannah (zebras, giraffes). A highlight is the birds of prey aviary.

Kremsmünster★

Kremsmünster is 43km/27mi south of Linz and 25km/15.5mi west of Steyr.
🅿 *In the first courtyard; pay-parking also at Steiner Tor, Kasernenstraße, Ringstraße, plus Park & Ride at the Bahnhof.*

The impressive Benedictine **abbey** of Kremsmünster is a rambling compound in a dramatic bluff-top setting overlooking the Krems Valley. According to legend, it was founded in 777 by Bavarian Duke Tassilo III on the spot where his son was killed by a wild boar in a hunting accident. Nothing remains of the original abbey, which now grandstands in

Baroque splendour, thanks to a large cast of talented architects and artists. From its silhouette rise not only the church's two domed towers but also the bulky "Mathematical Tower," which has an outstanding view of the monastery complex from the sixth floor.

Abbey

🎧*Guided tours of* **abbey and art collection** *(1hr) Apr–Oct daily 10am, 11.30am, 2pm, 3pm and 4pm; Nov–Jan & Mar daily 11am, 2pm and 3.30pm.* ∞€7. 🎧*Guided tours of* **natural science collection** *(1hr30min). Min 4 persons. May–Oct Sat–Sun 10am, noon and 4pm.* ∞€8. *Tickets on sale in the abbey shop in the first courtyard, near the fish pond.* 📞07583 52 75 150. *www.stift-kremsmuenster.net.*

Fischbehälter★

🎧*Free; can be seen without guided tour.*
An unexpected feature in the first abbey courtyard is the five **fish basins** framed by arcades and adorned with water-spouting statues of Samson, David, Neptune, Triton and other mythological creatures. They were designed by Carlo Antonio Carlone around 1690 and enlarged by Josef Prandtauer.

Stiftsgebäude (Abbey Buildings)

The **Kaisersaal** (Emperors' Hall) owes its name to 17C portraits by Martino Altomonte of the Holy Roman Emperors from Rudolf of Habsburg to Charles VI. Ceiling frescoes and stucco mouldings of great delicacy adorn this state hall.

The star exhibit in the abbey treasury is the 8C **Tassilo chalice★★★**, an exquisite work made from gilded copper with silver inlay. It was used in 765 at the duke's wedding and later presented to the abbey's monks.

The abbey **library★** is divided into four rooms that again bear the decorative stamp of Carlone and contain some 160,000 volumes. There's also a smattering of paintings exhibited in several galleries on the second floor.

St. Florian Monastery★★

The abbey of St. Florian, the largest in Upper Austria and an eminent cultural centre, has been run by Augustinian canons since the 11C. The present buildings are in the purest Baroque style, since the monastery was entirely rebuilt between 1686 and 1751 under the direction of Carlo Antonio Carlone and Jakob Prandtauer. The latter was also the architect of Hohenbrunn, the palatial edifice built nearby for one of the abbey's provosts.

VISIT

Visit by guided tour (1hr) only May–mid-Oct daily 11am, 1pm and 3pm. €8.50. www.stift-st-florian.at.

Info: Stiftstraße 1, St. Florian. ℘07224 89 020. www.stift-st-florian.at. Tourist office: ℘07224 56 900. www.oberoesterreich. at/st.florian.

Location: The abbey is 18km/11m southeast of Linz.

Parking: A car park is situated near the entrance to the abbey.

Don't Miss: Artdorfer Galerie.

Timing: Allow two hours.

Exterior

An elegant doorway with two balconies, carved columns and statues leads into the abbey's inner courtyard, which is adorned by a remarkable sculptured fountain, the Adlerbrunnen (Eagle Fountain), and a wrought-iron well-head, dating from 1603.

Bibliothek (Library)

Guided tours start in the library, one of the oldest and most prestigious abbey repositories in the country.

The exquisite allegorical ceiling paintings by Bartolomeo Altomonte represent the union of religion and science. Marquetry in walnut, encrusted with

Library, St. Florian Monastery

© Austrian National Tourist Office/Trumler

The Legend of St. Florian

Florian was head of the Roman administration in Noricum province, who was martyred after converting to Christianity in AD 304. The Roman regime sought to eradicate Christianity, and sent Aquilinus to persecute Christians in the region. When Aquilinus ordered Florian to offer sacrifice to the pagan Roman gods in accordance with Roman religion, he refused, and cheerfully accepted the beatings of the soldiers. After suffering considerable torture and being sentenced to death by fire, he reputedly challenged the Roman soldiers, "I will climb to heaven on the flames." He was therefore thrown into the Enns River with a stone around his neck. The abbey that bears his name was allegedly built near the spot where a local woman first discovered his mangled body. Many miracles were attributed to St. Florian's intercession, including one legendary instance where he is said to have extinguished a fire with a single pitcher of water.

St. Florian is the patron saint of Upper Austria as well as of Poland and of chimney sweeps and firefighters. In addition to his military duties, he was also responsible for organising firefighting brigades. If not depicted as a Roman officer or soldier, he is often portrayed in scenes pouring water over fire, or invoked against fire, floods and drowning. Viennese sculptor Josef Josephu made a celebrated statue of St. Florian that was unveiled in the Am Hof in 1935, shortly before the artist fled the Nazis for New York. After the city's main fire station was bombed in 1945 during World War II, the statue's permanent home became the Fire Brigade Museum. Josephu's bronze was subsequently used as the model for a series of enamelled coins released on 11 September 2002 to raise funds for firefighter charities.

gold, sets off the 150,000 valuable manuscripts and books.

Marmorsaal

Prandtauer designed the magnficent Marble Hall, whose ceiling fresco by Martino and Bartolomeo Altomonte glorifies Prince Eugene of Savoy's victory over the Turks.
It was originally conceived as an imperial dining room but also served as a concert hall.

Kaiserzimmer (Imperial Apartments)

The Imperial apartments are reached via a magnificent grand staircase whose balustrades are adorned with statues, while the walls and ceilings are embellished with stuccowork and frescoes.

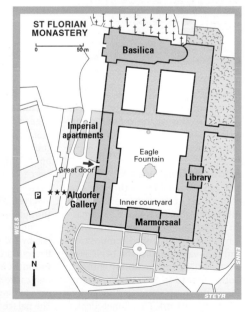

Until 1782 the apartments received such illustrious visitors as Pope Pius VI, emperors and princes.

Anton Bruckner at St. Florian

Anton Bruckner, Austria's greatest 19C composer of church music, was born near St. Florian in 1824. After his father's early death, the boy attended choir school at the abbey, where he was first introduced to religious music. Bruckner trained as a teacher and eventually managed to win an appointment at St. Florian in 1845. To his great joy, he was also appointed abbey organist. It was here that Bruckner decided to devote himself to music. In 1856 he became cathedral organist in Linz, where he composed several masterpieces, including three masses and two of his nine symphonies. Next he went to Vienna to teach at the conservatory. Despite his increasing fame, Bruckner always had a soft spot for St. Florian, and it was there that he wished to be buried beneath the very organ that had been so instrumental to his success as a composer and organist.

Codex, Library, St. Florian Monastery

© Austrian National Tourist Office / Trumler

Basilika

Organ recitals (25min) mid-May–mid-Oct Sun–Mon and Wed–Fri 2.30pm. €4.50.

The Baroque basilica was built under the direction of Carlo Antonio Carlone to replace the old Gothic church. Carlo's brother Bartolomeo was responsible for the stuccowork. The entire ceiling is swathed in frescoes executed by Johann Anton Gumpp and Melchior Steidl from Munich. The great organ was built by Franz Xaver Chrisman (1770–74) and has more than 103 stops and 7,836 pipes. It is now named the **Bruckner Organ** after Anton Bruckner, who worked at the abbey as organist and composer. He's buried in a crypt beneath the organ.

Amid the succession of halls and state rooms note the Faistenberger room, the bedrooms of the emperor and empress, the reception room and the Gobelin room.

Altdorfer Gallery★★★

The most valuable pictures in the abbey's art collection are those by **Albrecht Altdorfer** (1480–1538), a master of the Danube School whose work is noted for its balanced composition and rich, warm colours. The 14 pictures were painted for the abbey church's Gothic altar to St. Sebastian and form the world's most important collection of Altdorfer's work. Four panels depict the martyrdom of St. Sebastian, while the other eight show scenes from The Passion.

EXCURSION
Schloss Hohenbrunn★★

The palace is about 1.5km/1mi west of St. Florian.

Too large for a hunting lodge and too open to the surrounding countryside ever to have made any pretense at defence, Schloss Hohenbrunn is set like a Palladian villa in attractive natural surroundings. It was built in the 18C as a hunting lodge for the abbey of St. Florian by one of Austria's most celebrated Baroque architects, the Tyrolean **Jakob Prandtauer**. Hohenbrunn is in fact the only castle that can definitely be attributed to him.

The palace owes its name (*Hoher Brunnen*, meaning high fountain) to the pumping appliance originally installed in a tower flanking the south façade.

Hunting, and the spoils of hunting, are celebrated wherever you turn at Schloss Hohenbrunn, with art, ornaments, implements and even the stuccowork of the building depicting various triumphant scenes.

Jagdmuseum★★

Quite appropriately, the Schloss now houses this museum (○ open Easter–Oct daily 10am–noon, 1pm–5pm; €3), a thorough and informative exploration of hunting in Upper Austria. Expect plenty of weapons, models, plaster casts of footprints and stuffed animals, but also hunting clothes once worn by Emperor Franz Joseph I and an extraordinary rifle (3.12m/10ft 3in long) belonging to Archduke Karl Salvator.

ADDRESSESS

🏨 STAY AND 🍴 EAT

⊖⊖ **Gasthof Pfistermüller** – Am Bäckerberg 1, 4490 St. Florian bei Linz. ℘07224 42 763. www.pfistermueller.at. ☎. Restaurant Tue–Sat 11am–2pm, 5pm–9pm, Sun 11am–2pm. This small traditional hotel-restaurant offers simple but comfortable and welcoming rooms. The cuisine (⊖⊖) is mainly local with some international specialities. In summer, eat on the sheltered terrace.

⊖⊖⊖ **Zur Kanne** – Marktplatz 7, St. Florian. ℘07224 42 88. www.gasthof-koppler.at. 14 rooms. ☎. Restaurant Tue 5pm–10pm, Wed–Sat 11am– 2pm, 5pm–10pm. First mentioned as a baker's house in 1820, this 17C country guest-house is close to the abbey.

Enns★

Founded as a Roman camp in the 2C AD, Enns is among the oldest towns in Austria. It was here that St. Florian, the patron saint of Upper Austria, suffered martyrdom under Diocletian at the beginning of the 4C. Many of the town's 12C fortifications, including the ramparts, moats, and six watchtowers, have survived.

▶ **Population:** 11,600.
🛈 **Info:** Hauptplatz 19, A-4470. ℘07223 82 777. www.tse-enns.at.
▶ **Location:** Enns is at the confluence of the Danube and the River Enns. Alt. 281m/922ft.
🅿 **Parking:** Look for car parks and garages along or near Stadtgasse.
👁 **Don't Miss:** Pfarrkirche St. Marien.
🕐 **Timing:** Start in the Hauptplatz.

👣 WALKING TOUR

Departing from the Hauptplatz, this 3hr walking tour of the old town will show you the best of Enns.

Hauptplatz

Enns' pretty medieval old core revolves around the Hauptplatz, the central square, punctuated by the landmark **Belfry** (Stadtturm). Soaring 60m/197ft high, the tower is adorned with the Imperial eagle and the Habsburg coat of arms. Climb the 156 steps (○ open May–Oct daily 8am–8pm; Nov–Apr daily 9am–6pm; www.tse-enns.at) to the gallery to enjoy a marvelous **view★**.

Hauptplatz is also surrounded by many attractive Gothic burgher houses with Renaissance arcaded courtyards. The former town hall at No. 19 contains the **Lauriacum Municipal Museum** (○ open Tue–Fri 10am–3pm, Sun 10am–noon, 2pm–4pm; www.museum-lauriacum.at) with Roman-era archaeological exhibits.

Many of the Gothic houses in the **Altstadt** have interior courtyards, which are worth a look (5, 7, 14 and 10 Hauptplatz; 4, 8 and 9 Wiener Straße).

Belfry, Hauptplatz

© Austrian National Tourist Office/Trumler

This is one of the oldest Mendicant Order churches in Austria, built by the Minorites in 1276–77. It's an austere, two-nave church whose ornamentation is limited to beautifully carved keystones; modern 20C glass windows are extraordinarily colourful. Three Gothic arches lead into the **Wallsee Chapel** (Wallseerkapelle), a chapel named for a former local ruling family. A remarkable painting from 1625 depicts the *Lorcher Bishops*, a view of the town featuring local religious dignitaries. Also note the 13C Seated Madonna. Step into the Gothic cloister to enjoy its peaceful ambience.

▶ Take Dr-Renner-Straße to walk along the ramparts to the towers.

▶ Turn out of Hauptplatz into Steingengasse then Ennsberg to catch a glimpse of the ramparts, before going along Wiener Straße.

St. Marien

Open year-round Mon–Sat 7am–7pm (til 5pm Oct–Apr), Sun 8am–7pm (til 5pm Oct–Apr). Guided tours possible as part of a tour of the town. www.tse-enns.at.

Stadtmaur

Erected between 1193 and 1194, the fortified city walls are mostly in excellent condition. In order to finance their construction, the town of Enns received some of the ransom paid by England to Austria for the safe release of Richard the Lionheart, who had been incarcerated at Dürnstein (see p154). The **Frauenteurm** contains a tiny chapel with frescoes dating from between 1320 and 1360.

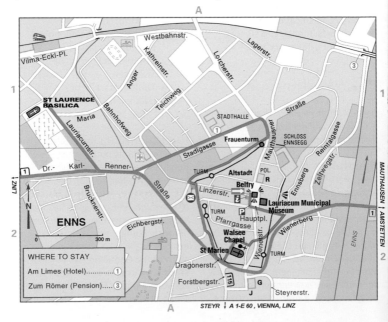

WHERE TO STAY

Am Limes (Hotel) .... ①
Zum Römer (Pension) ...... ③

Join Stadlgasse and walk up it, passing the sports centre and hospital, then turning right onto Lauriacumstraße.

St. Laurence Basilica

Open mid-May–mid-Oct Mon–Fri 9am–11am, 2.30pm–5.30pm. Guided tour (1hr) 4pm. Parts of the church may be visited unaccompanied. €5. 07223 82 237. www.stlaurenz.com.

The Basilika St. Laurenz occupies a site on the edge of the ancient Roman camp. Roman stones were used in the construction of the 13C tower, the oldest extant part of the church, which is attached to a 14C choir. Between the nave and chancel, archaeological excavations have revealed vestiges of walls from earlier buildings on this site: a Gallo-Roman temple (180), the first Christian church (bishop's see, 370) and early Carolingian church buildings (740). Decorative highlights include a Late Gothic tabernacle (1480) and Pietà (1430), as well as Austria's two largest oil paintings from the 18C.

Outside the church is an octagonal ossuary containing a Gothic chapel. The **façade★** depicts an Ecce homo (1690) in which Pontius Pilate is dressed as a Turkish grand vizir.

ADDRESSES

STAY

Hotel am Limes – *Stadlgasse 2b, 4470 Enns. 07223 86 401. www.hotel amlimes.at. 16 rooms.* This charming, small, family-run hotel-restaurant has welcoming rooms with pleasant furnishings. Its restaurant serves local dishes and Italian fare, including homemade pizzas.

Pension Zum Römer – *Mauthausnerstr. 39, 4470 Enns. 07223 84 900. www.zumroemer.at. 21 rooms.* Simple, modern rooms with clean lines are offered by this superior pension just outside the town centre. Don't be put off by its rather clinical exterior. The pleasant breakfast room includes a small terrace.

Steyr★

Steyr had a glorious past and for a while even rivalled Vienna in terms of economic and political importance. It is now Upper Austria's third-largest town (after Linz and Wels) and still an important economic and industrial centre. The picturesque old town, which has preserved its medieval character and charm, clusters at the confluence of the Enns and the Steyr rivers.

▸ **Population:** 38,300.

▪ **Info:** Stadtplatz 27 – A4402. 07252 53 22 90. www.steyr.info.

▸ **Location:** Steyr is about 50km/31mi southeast of Linz. Alt. 310m/1,017ft.

▸ **Don't Miss:** Museum Arbeitswelt.

▸ **Timing:** Allow one day to enjoy the town at a leisurely pace and another for the excursions.

▸ **Kids:** Christkindl.

WALKING TOUR

Depart from the main square; it will take about an hour to see the main sights.

Stadtplatz★

Steyr's elongated main square is lined with fine Late Gothic and Renaissance houses and centred on the 17C **Leo-** **pold's Fountain** (Leopoldibrunnen). Standout buildings include the **Town Hall** (Rathaus) with its Rococo façade surmounted by a tower, and the Gothic **Bummerlhaus** *(no. 32)*, which sports a

Steyr

© Austrian National Tourist Office/Popp Hackner

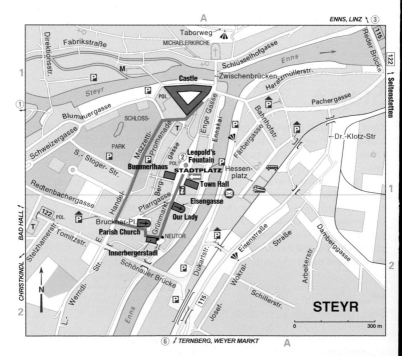

triangular gable and characteristic first-floor overhang. Also duck into the lovely courtyards of the houses at nos. 9, 11 and nos. 36/38.

Church of Our Lady

The former Dominican Marienkirche is decorated in the Baroque style and features an exuberantly gilded high altar, a Virgin and Child (1704) and a Rococo pulpit.

Stadtmuseum Steyr

⊙ Open Apr–Oct Tue–Sun 10am–4pm; Nov–Mar Wed–Sun 10am–4pm; Advent daily 10am–5pm. ⊛ Free. ℘ 07252 57 53 48. www.steyr.info.

A 17C granary known as the **Innerberger Stadl** houses Steyr's charming local history museum, which has a fine collection of Baroque religious figurines as well as a huge Nativity scene carved from olive wood from Bethlehem.

▷ Go past the right-hand side of the Innerbergerstadl, and follow the lane and stairs to the parish church.

Parish Church (Stadtpfarrkirche)

Behind the Innerberger Stadtl, the 15C Gothic Stadtpfarrkirche is the work of Hans Puxbaum, the architect of the Stephansdom in Vienna. Puxbaum also designed the **tabernacle★**, with its delicate tracery, and the baldaquin.

▷ Take Handel-Mazzetti-Promenade to the castle.

Castle (Schloss Lamberg)

The present Baroque castle dates from the 18C. It is now used mostly by the municipal administration, although it's still worth coming here to visit the **Schlossgalerie** with its changing contemporary art exhibits, or to take a stroll around the park.

EXCURSIONS
▲▲ Christkindl

3km/1.8mi west of Steyr.

The village of Christkindl in Upper Austria (the name means Christ Child), with its charming pilgrims' chapel is famous throughout Austria for its early 18C Baroque **Pfarr- und Wallfahrtskirche** (parish church). Pilgrims flock here to see a small "miracle-working" wax figure of Jesus, kept above the globe-shaped tabernacle. In 1720 the altar was adorned with 35 gilded statuettes of angels arranged around the trunk of the "Christ tree" in which the effigy was formerly kept. The gilded Rococo pulpit (1751) is also a magnificent piece of work.

The **Krippenschau** (crib display) in the old working quarters of the presbytery is open to visitors (late Nov–6 Jan).

Highlights include the early 20C mechanical crib, which consists of nearly 300 figures, many of them moveable through a system of cogs and chains. The 1930s Pöttmesser crib features 778 figures and is one of the largest cribs in the world.

Stift Seitenstetten★

19.5km/12mi east of Steyr on the B 122. ☛ Guided tours Easter Monday–Oct daily 10am and 3pm. ⊛ €9.50. ℘ 07477 42 30 00. www.stift-seitenstetten.at.

This Benedictine abbey was founded in 1112 and is still active today, operating a famous grammar school.

The Early Gothic basilica of the **Stiftskirche** (Abbey church) was restored in the Baroque style in the 17C and has rich stucco decoration and frescoes. The high altar is dominated by an Assumption of the Virgin, by Johann Karl Reslfeld of Garsten. Behind the church, the **Ritterkapelle** (Knight's Chapel) is the oldest section of the abbey, dating to the 14C.

Numerous famous artists contributed to the decoration of the abbey buildings. Above the festive **Abteistiege** (abbey staircase) is a ceiling fresco by Bartolomeo Altomonte, while those in the **Marmorsaal** (Marble Hall) and the library are by **Paul Troger**.

Tours also take in the mineral collection displayed in its Rococo cabinets and the abbey's **art collection★**, which includes some fine works by Kremser Schmidt and Paul Troger.

Nibelungengau, Wachau and Waldviertel are three regions that lie within Niederösterreich (Lower Austria) to the north and west of the capital, Vienna. Lower Austria used to be governed from Vienna, but in 1922 was declared a separate region, with the town of St. Pölten becoming the new provincial capital. The town is rather quiet and dominated by modern administrative buildings, but it does have some lovely examples of Baroque architecture and an excellent museum, as well as a lively calendar of events and festivals.

Highlights

A Bit of History

Beyond St. Pölten the region is steeped in myth and history, and is dominated by the valley of the Danube, which in many places is lined with vineyards owing to the mild climate and favourable geology. The **Nibelungengau** is the stretch of the Danube river valley that lies to the west of the huge abbey of Melk, one of Austria's greatest ecclesiastical sites. The abbey is a masterpiece of Baroque architecture, its highpoint being the library, with a collection of almost 100,000 volumes. The region is so called because part of the German medieval epic the *Niebelungenlied*, thought to have been composed somewhere along the Danube, takes place here.

The area of the **Wachau**, the Danube valley and surrounding countryside between Melk and Krems, has been declared a UNESCO World Heritage Site for its historical importance and architectural legacy. Richard I of England was imprisoned in the castle of Dürnstein, now a romantic ruin that is just one of many castles along, or close to, the river: Aggstein, Riegersburg, Heidenreichstein, Hardegg and Schloss Schallaburg. Krems itself is a beautifully preserved old town, with a splendid array of Renaissance buildings. It is also famous for wines from the surrounding vineyards that produce Grüner Veltliner and Riesling. A little farther down river, towards Vienna, lies Tulln, another historic town with a mix of architecture that extends from Roman times to the present. It is famous as the birthplace of Expressionist painter Egon Schiele.

An Undiscovered Corner

To the north of the Danube lies the forested area of the **Waldviertel** (literally the "forest quarter"), often overlooked by visitors, and stretching up to the Czech border. Like the neighbouring Mühlviertel, it feels remote and peaceful; a large part of it is designated a national park. Textile and glass manu-

Thayer Valley National Park

© Austrian National Tourist Office/ Popp

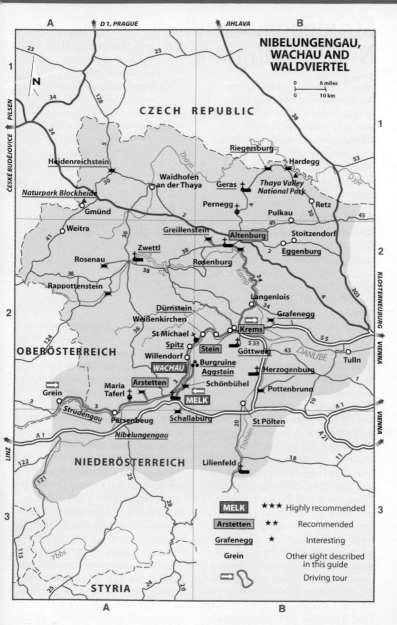

NIBELUNGENGAU, WACHAU AND WALDVIERTEL

A ↑ D 1, PRAGUE ↑ JIHLAVA **B**

0 ___ 6 miles
0 ___ 10 km

CZECH REPUBLIC

Riegersburg
Hardegg
Heidenreichstein
Waidhofen an der Thaya
Geras
Thaya Valley National Park
Retz
Naturpark Blockheide
Pernegg
Pulkau
Gmünd
Weitra
Greillenstein
Altenburg
Stoitzendorf
Zwettl
Eggenburg
Rosenau
Rosenburg
Rappottenstein
Langenlois
Grafenegg
Dürnstein
Weißenkirchen
St Michael
Krems
Spitz
Stein
Willendorf
Göttweig
OBERÖSTERREICH
WACHAU
Burgruine Aggstein
Herzogenburg
Maria Taferl
Arstetten
Schönbühel
Pottenbrunn
Grein
MELK
Strudengau
Persenbeug
Schallaburg
St Pölten
Nibelungengau
NIEDERÖSTERREICH
Lilienfeld
Ybbs
STYRIA

MELK	★★★	Highly recommended
Arstetten	★★	Recommended
Grafenegg	★	Interesting
Grein		Other sight described in this guide
➡		Driving tour

facture have joined forestry and agriculture as the primary industries here. Zwettl, one of the main towns of the Waldviertel, has a magnificent Cistercian abbey.

To the east stretches the Weinviertel, where you can find the walled town of Retz, set in another important wine-producing region. Beneath the town, an extraordinary network of wine cellars composes the largest such network in Austria.

Nearby Eggenburg, like Krems, has some wonderful examples of medieval and Renaissance architecture, as well as exquisite sgraffito decoration (*see boxed text p178*) on the façades of some of its buildings.

Strudengau★ and Nibelungengau★

After leaving the Linz Basin, the Danube winds around beautiful gorges dominated by high wooded cliffs. The Strudengrau and Nibelungengau are two of Austria's most romantic areas. Inextricably linked with the Austrian Imperial family, they also harbour many cultural treasures.

A BIT OF HISTORY
Archduke Franz Ferdinand

Franz Ferdinand, son of Archduke Karl Ludwig and nephew of Emperor Franz Joseph I, was born in 1863 in Graz. With no immediate prospect of succession to the throne, he carved out a successful military career, rising to the rank of admiral. The archduke was also an accomplished horseman, an excellent marksman, a patron of the arts and an avid traveller. With the death of his father in 1896, he became crown prince and heir to the throne.

On Sunday, 28 June 1914, the archduke and his wife were on an official visit to Bosnia, which had recently been annexed by the Empire. The political situation was tense, but nobody had an inkling that a group of young Bosnian anarchists was preparing to assassinate the archduke. As the Austrian motorcade drove through the crowds in Sarajevo, one of the conspirators threw a grenade at the archduke's car. Missing its main target, it exploded underneath the following vehicle, injuring a number of attendants and onlookers. Franz Ferdinand insisted on visiting the wounded attendants in a local hospital, against the advice of local officials, who felt they could not ensure his safety. En route he was attacked again, by another conspirator, Gavrilo Princip, who fired two shots at almost point-blank range, killing both the archduke and his wife. The assassination was to be one of the direct causes for the outbreak of World War I, in which Austria-Hungary was to suffer 1,567,000 dead.

ℹ️ Info: Stadtplatz 5, 4360 Grein. ℘07268 70 55. www.grein.info.

▷ Location: This area lies around 120km/75mi west of Vienna.

🕐 Timing: One day to take the driving tour and visit the sights along it.

🚗 DRIVING TOUR

③ FROM GREIN TO ARTSTETTEN
35km/22mi.

Grein

This charming summer resort town is dominated by the hills of the Mühlviertel. Turreted houses frame the pretty **Stadtplatz** (town square). The parish church's 18C high altar has an altarpiece by Bartolomäus Altomonte.

Grein is justifiably proud of its little **Rokoko-Theater** (🕐*open May–late Oct Mon–Sat 9am–noon and 2pm–6pm, Sun & hols 2pm–4pm; ☞€4.50; •guided tours; ℘07268 70 55; www.grein.info)* in the town hall. Made entirely of wood, it dates back to the end of the 18C and remains in use every summer.

Still owned by the House of Saxe-Coburg-Gotha, **Greinburg Castle** is a four-winged structure wrapped around a romantic fountain-studded Renaissance **courtyard★** with three tiers of arcades. Inside, the **Schifffahrtsmuseum** (🕐*open May–late Oct daily 9am–5pm; ☞€5; ℘07268 70 07 18; www.schlossgreinburg.at)* is a museum of river navigation with models of bridges, landing-stages and locks, as well as works of art evoking life locally on the river.

From Grein to Ybbs, the **Strudengau★**, wedged between high wooded cliffs that are often shrouded in mist, provides a romantic setting. The castle ruins of Burg Struden and Burg Sarmingstein are particularly eye-catching. The river

Grein and the Danube

© Austrian National Tourist Office/ Weinhaeupl W.

embraces willow-covered islands, then expands into a splendid lake formed by the Ybbs-Persenbeug dam.

▷ Head E for 20km/12.5mi on the B3.

Persenbeug

The last Austrian emperor, Karl I, was born in this rocky castle in 1887. The valley surrounding Persenbeug features in the legendary Middle High German epic poem, the *Nibelungenlied (Song of the Nibelungs)*. Here, in the **Nibelungengau**, Gunther and Hagen undertook their ride through the forest and here they gathered their knights to avenge the murder of Siegfried.

In a splendid **site★** on a hillock to the left is the 1660 pilgrimage church of **Maria Taferl**, with its splendid façade and dome by Jakob Prandtauer.

▷ Continue E on the B 3 15km/9mi.

Schloss-Museum Artstetten★★

ⓞ*Open Apr–Oct 9am–5.30pm.*
⊛€8.30. ☎07413 80 06.
www.schloss-artstetten.at.

Artstetten is most famous for being the final residence of Archduke Franz Ferdinand and his family before their assassination in 1914. He and his wife are buried beneath the church. A fortified residence since the 13C, the castle has been repeatedly attacked and rav-

aged by fire. Most of what we see today dates from the 17C and 18C, although the onion-domed silhouette was not added until 1912. In 1823 it became the property of the Imperial family and it still belongs to its descendants today. It is home to the **Erzherzog-Franz-Ferdinand Museum,** which chronicles the life and times of Franz Ferdinand and his family. Displays include personal effects, photos, furniture, weapons and other objects once belonging to the Imperial family and associated with events leading up to the assassination and outbreak of war in 1914.

ADDRESSES

🏨 STAY AND ¶/EAT

⊝⊜ **Privatzimmer Kloibhofer** – *Brucknerstraße 1, 4360 Grein.* ☎07268 378. www.privatzimmer-kloibhofer.at. ✉ 5 rooms. ⌑. This friendly, family-run pension, a 10min walk from the town centre, offers modern, simple rooms, each with a balcony. A hearty continental breakfast is served in the lovely conservatory, which offers fine views.

⊝⊜ **Radlerpension Leeb** – *Hagsdorf 19, 3680 Persenbeug.* ☎and fax 07412 54 718. *www.radler-leeb.at.* 2 rooms, 1 apartment. ⌑. Bright rooms can be found in this pension adjacent to a mountain bike trail. A newly-built bathing lake lies about 1.6km/1mi away.

Wachau★★★

This fertile, verdant region, which stretches 35km/22mi along the Danube between Melk and Krems, is extremely picturesque and boasts ever-changing landscapes. Visitors enjoy its vineyards, onion-domed churches, cliff-top castles, restaurants serving local specialities, charming villages and historic towns. Locally the area is famous for its **Marillen**, or apricot crop. In the summer, the fruit sellers line the roads. Don't miss the opportunity to sample some.

Info: Schlossgasse 3, 3620 Spitz an der Donau. ℘02713 30 06 060. www.donau.com.

Location: Dürnstein, in the heart of the Wachau, lies about 90km/56mi west of Vienna.

Timing: Allow a full day if you want to visit Melk Monastery and Krems und Stein.

Don't Miss: Melk Monastery and Krems und Stein.

🚗 DRIVING TOUR

④ FROM MELK TO KREMS

▷ Take the bridge over the Danube to Melk (see p155); continue along the left bank of the river towards Krems.

Schönbühel

From the main road, **Schloss Schönbühel** can be spotted on the south bank, its rocky promontory setting and onion-domed tower creating a charming picture.

▷ Take the road on the north bank towards Krems.

Burgruine Aggstein

Its exceptional **site★**, some 300m/984ft above the Danube, and its colossal size made this 12C fortress one of Austria's finest strongholds in its heyday. The ruined towers and defensive walls are still an impressive sight today. A steep path (2hr round trip) leads from Aggstein hamlet up to the castle gate. At the top you'll be treated to superb views.

At **Willendorf** a 25,000-year-old limestone statue, known as the **Venus of Willendorf★**, was found in 1906. It is now kept at the Naturhistorisches Museum in Vienna (see VIENNA).

▷ Follow the B 3 N for around 6km/3.7mi.

Burgruine Aggstein with a view of the Danube

© Austrian National Tourist Office/ Homberger

Spitz surrounded by its vineyards

Spitz★

Placid Spitz lies half-hidden behind a curtain of fruit trees below a terraced vineyard. Spitz has fine old townhouses, especially along Schlossgasse, which leads to the 17C castle.

The Gothic **Pfarrkirche** (◷ *open year-round daily 9am–6pm; Oct–Mar daily 8am–5pm; ℘02713 22 31)* has an unusual chancel out of line with the nave.

The organ loft is adorned with statues of Christ and the 12 Apostles (c. 1420). The altarpiece (1799) by Kremser Schmidt over the Baroque altar shows the martyrdom of St. Maurice.

▷ Continue N on the B3 for around 4km/2.5mi. Look out for the fortified **Church of St. Michael** on the north bank of the river.

Weissenkirchen

This wine-growing village has an imposing, Gothic fortified church overlooking a pretty town with cobbled pathways and fine old houses.

The **Wachaumuseum** (◷ *open mid-Apr–Oct Tue–Sun 10am–12.30pm, 1pm–5pm; ⊙€5; ℘02715 22 68; www.weissenkirchen-wachau.at)* is housed in the Teisenhoferhof, a 16C fortified farm with an arcaded courtyard and a richly decorated covered gallery. Inside are works by Wachau painters (from the turn of the 19C).

Weissenkirchen

▷ Continue N along the B 3 following the river as it bends around, for about 8km/5mi.

Dürnstein★

🛈 *Dürnstein 25, A-3601. ℘0271 12 19. www.duernstein.at.*

Dürnstein *(population 870; alt. 209m/686ft),* considered the "pearl" of the Wachau region, lies above a scenic bend of the Danube and boasts beautiful old houses. Girded by ancient walls, it is crowned by the **Bergruine**, the ruined fortress where Richard I (the Lionheart) was held prisoner. Diplomacy was not

Dürnstein

© Austrian National Tourist Office/ Weinhaeupl

the forte of the English king; he had clashed with the Austrian duke, Leopold V, during the conquest of Acre in 1191. Returning from the crusade, via Austria, he was taken prisoner near Vienna and held for several months at Dürnstein. According to legend, he was tracked down by his faithful minstrel, Blondel, who could not rescue his master, since he was transferred to Emperor Heinrich VI, and held prisoner for almost a year at Trifels Castle (Germany) before being freed for an enormous ransom in 1194. The former Augustine canons' monastery **Stift Dürnstein** (◯ *open Apr–Oct daily 9am–6pm, Sun from 10am; ⊛ €3.50; ℘ 02711 227; www. stiftduernstein.at)* was founded in the 15C and got its Baroque look in the 18C courtesy of master architect Josef Munggenast. A splendid gate leads into the courtyard surrounded by old monastic buildings, but the most striking element is the church's landmark blue and white **tower★**.

The church interior is adorned with restrained stuccowork and curved wooden balconies, while the side chapels house paintings by Kremser Schmidt. The trail to the **Burgruine** (*45min round trip walk*) begins at the ramparts east of the town and is worth the climb, not only for its historical echoes, but for the remarkable **view** of Dürnstein and the valley.

▶ Continue on the B 3, then the B 35 to Krems (◉*see p157).*

ADDRESSES

⊠ STAY AND ℣/ EAT

⊜⊜ **Haus Machhörndl** – *Gärtnerweg 4, 3620 Spitz der Donau. ℘0512 900 11 31 58. www.tiscover.at/haus.machhoerndl.* 🖈. *Open Apr–Oct. 3 rooms, 3 apartments.* This riverside house, shared with the owners, has a lovely garden with sunbathing area, views of the Danube and free bikes.

⊜⊜ **Hotel Donauwirt** –*Wachaustraße 47, 3610 Weissenkirchen. ℘02715 22 47. www.donauwirt.at. 12 rooms.* ☐. *Restaurant closed Sun dinner, Tue–Wed.* This modern-traditional house has very pleasant and stylish contemporary bedrooms.The rustic-chic restaurant (⊜⊜⊜) has a smart dining room and a handsome terrace with a view of the Danube River.

⊜⊜ **Jamek** –*Joching 33, 3610 Weissenkirchen. ℘02715 25 96. www.weingaestehaus-jamek.at.* ☐. *Closed 3 weeks Feb. Restaurant closed Sat–Sun.* Simple pleasant rooms, a terrace overlooking the Danube, deck chairs in a lovely garden and a cosy 100-year-old restaurant ensure a pleasant stay in this winery-with-guesthouse.

Melk Monastery★★★

The majestic abbey of Melk, which crowns a rocky bluff overlooking the Danube, is the apogee of Baroque architecture in Austria. Its origins go back to the 10C as the castle of the ruling Babenberg family, but it became a monastery in 1089 when Margrave Leopold II donated the building to the Benedictines. Famous for its scholarship, the abbey has been a spiritual, cultural and intellectual centre for nearly a millennium.

- 🛈 **Info:** Abt-Berthold-Dietmayr-Straße 1. ✆02752 55 50. www.stiftmelk.at.
- ▶ **Location:** Melk is 27km/16.7mi west of St. Pölten in northeastern Austria. Alt. 213m/699ft.
- 🕐 **Timing:** Allow at least half a day for your visit.

THE ABBEY

🕐*Open mid-Mar–Oct daily 9am–4.30pm (til 5.30pm Apr–Oct); Nov–Feb by guided tour only (1hr) 11am and 2pm. Last admission 30min before closing. ♿ ♿€11, €13 with tour. www.stiftmelk.at.*

Exterior

The original abbey was gutted by fire during the Turkish Invasion in 1683. It entirely rebuilt from 1802 onwards by **Jakob Prandtauer** and completed after his death by his pupil **Josef Munggenast**. The outer gateway, giving access to the first courtyard, is framed by statues of the abbey patrons, St. Leopold and St. Coloman, and flanked by two bastions. On the inner gate is the abbey coat of arms. Beyond a vestibule with a ceiling painting of St. Benedict, the **Prälatenhof** (Prelates' Courtyard), is a fine group of buildings adorned with statues of the Prophets.

Kaisergang

Access via the Imperial staircase.
The Emperors' gallery, 196m/643ft in length, provided access to the chambers reserved for important visitors. Some of these rooms now house a **museum**, which presents the abbey's history and its treasures in an engaging and visually appealing fashion using light, sound, video installations and computer animations.

Marmorsaal

The Marble Hall impresses less with its lavishness than with the strength of its design. It is dominated by a series of red-

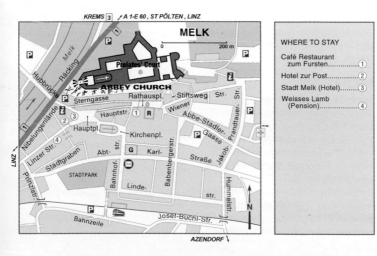

dish pilasters, which incidentally, are not made of marble at all but of coloured stucco. The undisputed highlight here is the ceiling fresco by **Paul Troger**, which centres on the goddess Athena riding a lion-drawn carriage in an allegory of wisdom and enlightenment.

Bibliothek (Library)

A terrace offering sweeping views of the surrounding countryside links Marble Hall with the abbey library, which contains 100,000 books and 1,800 manuscripts. It also has a fine ceiling painting by Paul Troger symbolizing Faith. The gilded wood statues by the doors represent the four faculties.

Stiftskirche★★★

The church interior gives a great impression of lightness, which is due to the sweep of fluted pilasters, a judicious use of colour and the many windows. The decoration is nothing if not lavish, with the dominating brownish-red colour offering the perfect contrast to the liberal use of gold leaf.

A veritable who's who of Baroque master artists contributed to this spectacular church. The ceiling frescoes and most of the side altars show off the exquisite style of **Johann Michael Rottmayr**; some of the altar paintings are the work of Paul Troger. Giuseppe Galli-Bibiena was responsible for the extraordinary high altar dedicated to Sts. Peter and Paul. There are sculptures wherever you look, most of them the work of Lorenzo Mattielli and Peter Widerin. The left side altar in the transept contains the bones of St. Koloman.

EXCURSION
Schloss Schallaburg★

6km/3.7mi south of Melk towards Anzendorf. ⏱*Open mid-Mar–early Nov Mon–Fri 9am–5pm; Sat–Sun 9am–6pm.* ⊕*€11.* ◄*Guided tours available (1hr; minimum 10 people).* ♿ ℘*02754 63 170. www.schallaburg.at.*

The castle has substantial Romanesque remains and a Gothic chapel, but it is the great 16C **Renaissance arcaded courtyard★** with its extraordinary profusion of terra-cotta ornamentation that is striking. Statues, atlases, caryatids, cartouches, floral motifs and ornamental keystones boldly and harmoniously form a masterly composition.

Today, Schallaburg is an **exhibition and cultural centre** for the province of Lower Austria, used every summer for prestigious exhibits. Its website is well worth a look to see what's on.

For children, an adventure playground has been installed in the moat, while gardens inspired by Mannerism contain roses, ornamental trees and apple orchards planted according to typical Renaissance plans.

ADDRESSES

🛏**STAY AND** ℙ/**EAT**

⊜⊜ **Pension Weißes Lamm** – *Linzer Straße 7, 3390 Melk.* ℘*02752 53 243. www. pension-weisses-lamm-melk.at. 15 rooms.* ⊡. This quiet, family-run hotel has simple but pleasantly furnished rooms, all with shower and satellite TV. The Pizzeria Venezia restaurant on-site serves Greek and Mexican dishes.

⊜⊜⊜ **Café Restaurant zum Fürsten** – *Rathausplatz 3, 3390 Melk.* ℘*02752 52 343. www.kaffeehaustradition.at. 7 rooms.* ⊡. Wake up to house-roasted coffee and freshly baked viennoiserie at this typical Viennese café that doubles as a small inn. Located directly on the town hall square, it has a lovely 16C façade.

⊜⊜⊜ **Hotel Stadt Melk** – *Hauptplatz 1, 3390 Melk.* ℘*02752 52 475. www.hotel stadtmelk.at. 13 rooms.* ⊡. This traditional hotel in the town centre, near the river, boasts elegant international-style rooms. The restaurant is split into two parts, one specialising in creative cooking, the other in high-quality regional cuisine. The roof terrace has a splendid view over the Hauptplatz. Staying here can be a little noisy.

⊜⊜⊜⊜ **Hotel zur Post** – *Linzer Straße 1, 3390 Melk.* ℘*02752 523 45. www.post-melk.at. 25 rooms.* ⊡. This hotel, in the shadow of the abbey, features touches of luxury in its guest rooms, restaurant, wine bar and humidor-equipped parlour; it also claims the best ice-cream shop in the city.

Krems und Stein★★

Krems is a delightful wine village snuggled against terraced vineyards on the left bank of the Danube. More than 1,000 years old, it actually consists of three towns in one: Krems, Stein and Und, giving rise to the saying: "Krems und (and) Stein are three towns." It is part of the Wachau region, which was declared a UNESCO World Heritage Site in 2000. Krems was the long-time home of the painter Martin Johann Schmidt (1718–1801), better known as **Kremser Schmidt**, whose work graces many churches and abbeys around the country.

WALKING TOUR

KREMS OLD TOWN
The Old Town has a wealth of picturesque streets and squares that can be explored on this 90min walking tour.

Obere und Untere Landstraße
Historic Krems' main artery, the pedestrian-only Landstraße, is lined with Renaissance and Baroque façades and punctuated by the Steiner Tor, a monumental 15C gateway. Deserving closer inspection is the **Bürgerspitalkirche**, an elegant Gothic chapel whose single rib-vaulted nave exudes a peaceful atmosphere. The high altar is flanked by two superb gilded wooden statues, the work of Matthias Schwanthaler.

▶ Turn N off the Landstraße to reach Pfarrplatz.

Parish Church
The Early Baroque Pfarrkirche, completed in 1630 under the Italian architect Cyprian Biasino, has a sumptuously decorated interior. The nave and chancel vault are adorned with Kremser Schmidt frescoes.

▶ Leave the north of the square via an alley that leads to Piaristengaße.

▶ **Population:** 24,400.
▪ **Info:** Utzstraße 1, A-3500. ℰ02732 82 676. www.krems.gv.at.
◗ **Location:** Krems is at the eastern edge of the Wachau, about 77km/ 42mi west of Vienna. Alt. 221m/725ft.
▣ **Parking:** There is paid parking at Steiner Tor, on Kasernenstraße and on Ringstraße and a free Park & Ride from the Bahnhof (train station).
◉ **Don't Miss:** Piaristenkirche, Weinstadtmuseum, Kunsthalle Krems.
◕ **Timing:** Allow at least a day to take in an excursion as well.
▲♣ **Kids:** Falconry demonstrations at Schloss Rosenberg.

Piaristenkirche★
First run by Jesuits, this church was handed over to the Piarists, an educational order still in charge today, by Maria Theresia in 1776. Dominating the old town, it is a beautiful three-nave Late Gothic hall church with exquisite net vaulting and a bonanza of works by Kremser Schmidt. The most famous among these are the **high altar** painting of the Assumption and the right-side altar showing the founder of the Piarist Order. Notable too are the **choir stalls**, still with stylistic features of the Early Renaissance, although dating from well into the 17C.

▶ From Frauenbergplatz at the eastern end of the Piaristenkirche, walk away from the church and enter Schmelzgasse, which leads to the Weinstadtmuseum.

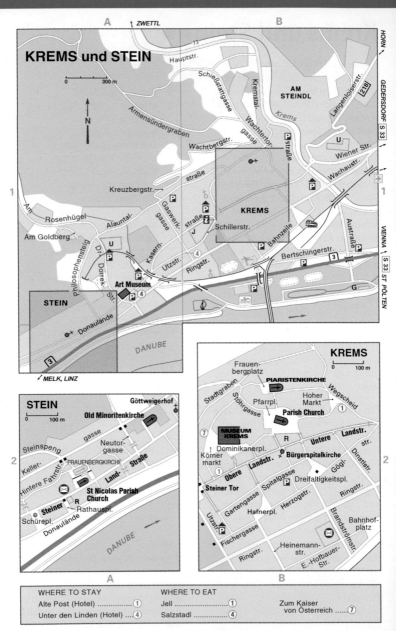

KREMS und STEIN

ZWETTL

KREMS

STEIN

DANUBE

MELK, LINZ

STEIN

Göttweigerhof

Old Minoritenkirche

FRAUENBERGKIRCHE

St Nicolas Parish Church

DANUBE

KREMS

Frauen-bergplatz

PIARISTENKIRCHE

Parish Church

MUSEUM KREMS

Bürgerspitalkirche

Steiner Tor

WHERE TO STAY	WHERE TO EAT	
Alte Post (Hotel) .... ①	Jell .... ①	Zum Kaiser
Unter den Linden (Hotel) ....④	Salzstadl ....④	von Österreich ......⑦

Museum Krems★

⏰ *Open mid-Apr–early Jun Wed–Sun and hols 11am–6pm; mid-Jun–late Oct daily 11am–6pm.* ₰€5. ✆02732 80 15 67. www.museumkrems.at.

This former Dominican monastery provides a delightful setting for the imaginatively presented displays on Krems'

cultural history. Wine takes centre stage, naturally, but there are also some fine works by Kremser Schmidt as well as the famous statuette, **Fanny/Venus of Galgenberg★**. Standing a mere 7.2cm/2.8in tall and made of greenish slate, this little piece is believed to be about 32,000 years old, making it the world's oldest unearthed female figurine. The 700-year-old monastery church impresses with its crisp Gothic architecture, unadulterated by any subsequent Baroque embellishment.

STEIN

About 1km/0.6mi west of the Steiner Tor, Stein is hemmed in by the Danube and terraced vineyards. The main street, **Steiner Landstraße**, which opens out here and there into small squares, is lined with well-preserved, elegant townhouses and arcaded courtyards, reflecting the local wealth.

Approaching Stein from the west, you can't miss the **Art Museum** *(Kunsthalle Krems;* ⏱*closed for renovation until July 2017;* ☎*02732 90 80 10; www.kunsthalle. at)*, a well-respected gallery skilfully converted from an old tobacco factory. The progressively minded shows also spill over into the nearby former **Minoritenkirche**, a three-nave pillared basilica whose 14C frescoes provide an interesting backdrop to the modern art. Further west looms the mighty west tower of **St. Nicholas Parish Church** (Pfarrkirche St. Nikolaus) with its delicate Baroque dome. Inside the church, Kremser Schmidt worked his magic with the ceiling fresco and the altar paintings. The **Frauenbergkirche**, right behind the Pfarrkirche, is now a war memorial.

EXCURSIONS
👥 Motorrad-Museum Krems-Egelsee★

⏱*Open Mar–Oct by appointment only.* ☜*€4.50, children €2.50.* ♿ ☎*02732 41 424. www.motorrad-museum.at.*
Established in 1980, this museum was the first of its kind. It is still Austria's largest motorcycle collection, boasting around 370 motorcycles, mopeds, scooters and every other conceivable motorised two-wheeled vehicle in mint condition from every phase of motorcycling history. It is displayed in an historical factory and is a must-see for motorbike enthusiasts. Look out for the three-seater Böhmerland 600 from 1929, the longest motorcycle that ever went into production.

Imperial staircase, Stift Göttweig

© Austrian National Tourist Office/ Trumler

Stift Göttweig★

6km/3.7mi south of Krems on the road to St. Pölten. ⏱*Open Jun–Sept daily 9am–6pm; midMar–Oct daily 10am–6pm.* ☜*€8.* ☎*02732 85 58 10. www.stiftgoettweig.at.*

The prominent hilltop setting and striking architecture of this Benedictine abbey has garnered it the nickname "Austria's Monte Cassino," from which the order originated. Since 2001, the abbey has been include on UNESCO's list of World Heritage Sites.

Founded in 1083, it was nearly destroyed by fire in 1718, but was restored in Baroque style.

The church **interior★** dazzles with elaborate stuccowork and a number of interesting features, most notably the mighty high altar (1639) and the pulpit, both by Dutch master Hermann Schmidt. Medieval remnants include the Erentrudiskapelle (chapel) and the crypt. In the west wing, the monumental **Imperial staircase★** has a ceiling fresco by **Paul Troger** (1739). Other points of interest include the Imperial State Rooms and the museum, with its changing roster of items from the abbey's treasury.

Schloss Grafenegg★

12km/7.4mi east of Krems. ⏰*Open mid-Apr–late Oct Tue–Sun 10am–5pm.* ⬦€6. ✆*02735 22 05 45.* *www.grafenegg.com.*

Schloss Grafenegg is Austria's significant example of romanticised late-19C Historicist architecture. Surrounded by an English landscape park, the palace keep with its gallery and turrets rises like a miraculous vision above the Tullner Feld plain. The palace is well known for its exhibitions, readings and concerts. The restaurant serves gourmet-level international cuisine, which is best paired with wine from the palace's own estate.

A **castle** has stood on this spot since the Middle Ages, but what you see today is the product of 19C architect Leopold Ernst. It is a vast neo-Gothic pile surrounded by a dry moat and sporting cream–coloured façades festooned with fierce-looking gargoyles. It was severely damaged during 10 years of Soviet occupation after World War II, but has since been extensively restored. The ethereal blue **Schlosskapelle** (palace chapel) is a fine example of neo-Gothic architecture and boasts a Late Gothic winged altar depicting the Coronation of the Virgin Mary. The **Great Salon** and the **Dining Room**, with their attractive wooden panelling and carved ornaments and figures, are additional highlights. In the Great Salon the **coffered ceiling★** is particularly

stunning, as is the stairway decorated with the figure of a knight and busts of the builder and his architect. No less remarkable are the **Yellow Salon** and the adjoining bathroom, study and bedroom, the library and the garden room, whose walls and ceilings are covered in exquisite materials.

🚗 DRIVING TOUR

KAMP VALLEY
36km/22mi.

The lovely little Kamptal is surprisingly beautiful with its many-tiered vineyard terraces where wineries produce quality wines such as Grüner Veltliner. The tour takes in pretty villages, castles, churches and other historic monuments.

▶ Begin at **Langenlois**, the largest wine-producing town in Austria, 11km/7mi NE of Krems und Stein.

Loisium

⏰*Open Apr–Oct daily 10am–7pm (entry on the hour and half hour; last admission 5.30pm), Nov–Mar Wed–Sun.* ⬦€13.50. ✆*02734 32 24 00.* *www.loisium.com.*

Set in a modern aluminium building in the heart of the vineyards, this "World of Wine Adventure" features old wine cellars and galleries enhanced by lighting effects and animation for a behind-the-scenes look at Austria's vineyards back through 900 years of local history. Sample local sparkling wine, *Sekt,* in the wine cellar *(Sektbar).* A shop sells Austrian wines.

▶ Continue to Rosenburg.

Schloss Rosenburg★

⬦*Guided tours (1hr) May–Sept Wed–Sun 10am–5pm; Apr & Oct Fri–Sun only.* ⬦€14. ✆*02982 29 11.* *www.rosenburg.at.*

More than 1,000 years ago, the Babenbergs freed central Austria from the Magyars so that this region could at last be settled. In order to counter the con-

Schloss Grafenegg

© Austrian National Tourist Office/Volker Preusser

stant threat from Bohemia, the nobles built a series of castles in the strategically important Kamptal. Of these, Schloss Rosenburg, built in the first half of the 12C, is one of the most attractive and important. It has been owned by the counts of Hoyos since the 17C.

Pass through the gateway and enter the early 17C courtyard, surrounded on three sides by double galleries and once used for equestrian games. The square **keep** is part of the original castle, but was altered in the Renaissance period by the addition of a balcony.

After standing virtually empty during the 18C, the living rooms and grand public rooms were furnished mainly in the style of the German Renaissance. The **library**, with its remarkable wooden **coffered ceiling★**, is of particular interest, as are the Marble Hall and the palace chapel.

Schloss Rosenburg is a centre for falconry. Kids love the **free flight demonstrations★ ♣♣**, in which hunting falcons, eagles and vultures perform.

◐ Continue towards Altenberg and its monastery, then take the B 38 to reach Röhrenbach.

Schloss Greillenstein★

ⓒ *Open Apr–Oct daily 9.30am–5pm (Jul–Aug til 6pm).* ✿*Guided tours (1hr) 10.30am, 2.30pm.* ⊜*€5, €9 with tour.* ✆*0664 85 76 371. www.greillenstein.at*

This hulking Renaissance castle, with its distinctive single tower, was built in the late 16C as the residence and administrative headquarters of local landowner Hans Georg II of Kufstein. Still owned by the same family, it preserves many original fittings and is also famous for its Baroque sandstone sculptures of dwarves and other fanciful creatures. The Baroque balustrade in front of the castle is adorned with sculptures worthy of a fable: how a raging lion is transformed into the most gentle of beasts, mirroring the triumph of Good over Evil. In the inner courtyard, with its two-tiered arcaded loggia, stand the sandstone dwarves and dragon fountain. From the 16C onwards, Greillenstein had

jurisdiction over 14 local villages. The filing cabinets and pigeon holes containing original period documents are still there, as is the baronial **courtroom★**. Also of note is the **Turkish Room**, which contains souvenirs collected by a family member who served as ambassador to Turkey in 1628/9. During his stay he succeeded in signing a peace treaty that resulted in a ceasefire lasting 25 years. The chapel has delicate net vaulting and an elegant **Renaissance altar★**.

ADDRESSES

🛏 STAY

⊜⊜ **Alte Post** – *Obere Landstraße 32, Krems.* ✆*02732 82 276. www.altepost-krems.at. 23 rooms.* ⊡. *Restaurant open Thu–Mon.* Appointed with works of art, this hotel is a charming and historic place to stay. An arcaded balcony overlooks a cheerful dining courtyard.

⊜⊜ **Hotel Unter den Linden** – *Schillerstraße 5, Krems.* ✆*02732 82 115. www.udl.at. Closed mid-Dec–mid-Feb. 40 rooms.* ⊡ .This large hotel has been run for five generations by the Grech family. Rooms are bright and welcoming. Choose city-, cottage- or country-style.

🍴 EAT

⊜ **Salzstadl** – *Donaulände 32, Stein.* ✆*02732 70 312. www.salzstadl.at. Closed Wed. Sun and hol by reservation.* This cosy inn serves hearty food for lunch and dinner. Entertainment most nights in season. There are two simple but cheerful rooms (⊜).

⊜⊜ **Gasthaus Jell** – *Hoher Markt 8-9, Krems.* ✆*02732 82 345. www.amon-jell.at. Closed Sat-Sun evening and Mon, first 3 weeks of Feb, first 2 weeks Jul.* Eat, drink and laugh is the motto of this cosy little family-run place. It serves excellent regional specials – don't leave without trying the home-cured bacon. In summer the garden terrace is delightful. The inn also has two bedrooms (⊜⊜).

⊜⊜⊜ **Zum Kaiser von Österreich** – *Körnermarkt 9.* ✆*0800 400 171 052. www.kaiser-von-oesterreich.at. Closed Sun, Mon.* Traditional Austrian dishes creatively reinvented, often with Mediterranean influences are served.

Tulln

Tulln grew up on the site of the Roman camp of Comagena founded in 1C AD. Between 1042 and 1113, the town was the residence of the Babenberg dynasty, predecessors of the Habsburgs. Tulln's most famous son is artist Egon Schiele (1890–1918). Today Tulln is known as *Blumenstadt,* "the city of flowers", for its many parks and open spaces.

SIGHTS
Minoritenkirche★

This Baroque building in Minorienplatz, constructed in 1739, was dedicated to St. John of Nepomuk *(see p167)*. Inside, to the left of the high altar, there is a glimpse of the sacristy with a splendid inlaid cabinet dating from the 18C.

Minoritenkloster Museums★

Minoritenplatz 1. Open year-round daily 8am–5pm. 02272 69 00.
Tulln's old monastery has been successfully converted into a museum complex that also houses the tourist office.
The collections of the **Römermuseum** take up most of the space, and include items from Roman to recent times discovered during excavations beneath the monastery.

▶ **Population:** 16,000.

Info: Minoritenplatz 1. 02272 69 00. www.tulln.at.

Location: Tulln is on the Danube, about 40km/25mi west of Vienna. Alt. 180m/591ft.

Parking: Look for parking on the Hauptplatz or in garages in Albrechtsgasse, Frauentorgasse or at the main train station.

Don't Miss: Egon-Schiele-Museum, Karner.

Timing: You can visit all the sights easily in one day.

Kids: The fire engine collection in the Minoritenkloster.

In the attic, the **Austrian Sugar Museum** (Tulln is a major producer), which traces the evolution of sugar production, from primitive sugarcane mills to modern factories. A changing roster of contemporary art exhibits is also housed under the same roof.
Fans of the Austrian painter Friedensreich Hundertwasser should ask

Minoritenkloster and Minoritenkirche

M. Hertlein/MICHELIN

Egon Schiele

Egon Schiele was born in Tulln in 1890. He attended the Academy of Fine Arts in Vienna, and became a protégé of Klimt, who bought some early work and introduced him to potential patrons and models. Working primarily in watercolour, gouache and pencil, Schiele developed a figurative style, producing portraits of friends and acquaintances, many of whom give the impression of being haunted by death with their skeletal expressions.

Often focusing on sex, Schiele did not shy away from depicting the grotesque or pornographic, courting controversy. He and a young lover were driven out of one town by residents shocked by their lifestyle, and in 1912 Schiele was arrested for seducing a girl below the age of consent.

Marriage in 1915 coincided with greater professional success, but Schiele died three years later of Spanish flu.

museum staff for access to the **Hundert-wasser-Schiff** *Regentag*, an old salt freighter moored in the harbour behind the monastery. It contains a small exhibit about the journeys made by the artist.

Egon-Schiele-Museum

Donaulände 28. ◐*Open Apr–Sept Tue–Sun and hols 10am–5pm.* ☞€5.50. 50. ℘02272 64 570. *www.egon-schiele.eu.*

The old local prison now houses an exhibition on the life and work of Tulln-born painter Egon Schiele. On the ground floor are biographical documentation as well as the reproduction of a jail cell in Neulengbach, where he was held for a few days in 1912 for possession of child pornography.

Upstairs is a smattering of originals, including drawings, lithographs, watercolours and a few oil paintings, most of them early works (1905–08).

Admission also includes entry to the room in the main train station where Schiele was born (his father was stationmaster). Let museum staff know if you would like to see it and they will make arrangements.

Römerturm

This fortified tower has survived almost unchanged in shape and height since being built under Roman Emperor Diocletian (AD 284–305).

In the Middle Ages it was used as an arsenal, and from the early 19C as a salt storehouse, which explains why locals also call it the Salzturm (salt tower).

Pfarrkirche St. Stefan

Wiener Straße.

This 12C Romanesque basilica was transformed in the 15C to the Gothic style and then remodeled in the Baroque style in the 18C. Outstanding elements include the Romanesque western portal, which is adorned with busts of the 12 Apostles. The altarpiece dates to 1786 and represents the stoning of St. Stephen.

The highlight is the 13C polygonal **Karnera**, one of the finest **funerary chapels** (ossuaries) in Austria. The **doorway★★** is decorated with palm-leaf capitals and geometric motifs; the domed interior is adorned with Romanesque frescoes that were drastically restored in 1874 in the 19C style.

🚗 DRIVING TOUR

5 DANUBE VALLEY
83km/51mi.

This scenic 2hr trip along the Danube begins in Krems und Stein on the S 5, and continues to Tulln, where you cross the river and turn onto the 14, then onto Klosterneuburg, and finishes in Vienna.

St. Pölten★

Founded by the Romans in AD 1, St. Pölten became the provincial capital of Lower Austria in 1987, when the government moved its offices from Vienna to the Landhausviertel quarter on the Traisen River. Today, the quarter's modern architecture and entertainment venues inject a dose of life into what is otherwise a rather sleepy town. Its heyday dates back two centuries to the Baroque period when many of Austria's greatest artists, including Jakob Prandtauer, Josef and Franz Munggenast, Daniel Gran, Paul Troger and Bartolomeo Altomonte, lived and worked here. Evidence of their creativity is found at every turn, making a stroll around the Old Town a lesson in Baroque.

▶ **Population:** 58,400.

Info: Rathausplatz 1, A-3100. ℘02742 33 30. www.st-poelten.gv.at.

◐ **Location:** St. Pölten is about 65km/41mi west of Vienna. Alt. 271m/889ft.

P **Parking:** Parking garages on Eybnerstraße, Dr.-Karl-Renner-Promenade, Bräuhausgasse, Rossmarkt, Rathausplatz. In the Landhausplatz garage, parking is free weekdays 6pm–5am and all day Sat, Sun and hols.

◉ **Don't Miss:** the Dom, the Landesmuseum, the Klangturm.

◔ **Timing:** Devote at least one full day to St. Pölten.

Kids: The Klangturm, the Landesmuseum.

RATHAUS DISTRICT
Rathausplatz

The main town square is bordered by beautiful patrician houses and punctuated by the massive marble **Trinity Column**, completed in 1782 by Andreas Gruber. It shows St. Hippolytus, St. Florian (recognisable by his attribute of a burning house), St. Sebastian (arrow) and St. Leopold (model of a church). Lording over the square is the pinkish **Rathaus** (town hall), created in the

16C by connecting two existing Gothic houses. In 1727 Josef Munggenast added the Baroque façade. The tower has become the emblem of St. Pölten. To the left of the Rathaus is the 16C **Schuberthaus**, in which the composer stayed in 1821, holding "Schubertiade" musical evenings.

On the square's north side, the **Franziskanerkirche** (1757–79), with its lively

St. Pölten Rathausplatz

© Austrian National Tourist Office/Bartl

TOURIST INFORMATION

Tourismusinformation (*Rathausplatz 1*) – The local **Calendar of Events** for the city and its surroundings comes out monthly between May and October and can be obtained from the tourist office and hotels.

CITY TOURS: The tourist office organises various themed walking tours of varying length. Check for a current schedule.

For self-guided tours (in English), the office has produced the free mobile app "Hearonymus". The tours take in old town and the Landhausviertel and last about 2hr15min.

For an easy introduction to St. Pölten, catch a ride aboard the free **Hauptstadtexpress** (*Thu before Easter–Dec Thu–Sat 10am–5pm hourly, except hols*), a little tourist train stopping at major attractions throughout the city centre.

PUBLIC TRANSPORT

A single-trip ticket costs €2.10 (valid for 1hr and permits a change of vehicle and direction of travel). After 7.30pm (Mon–Fri; from 5.30pm Sat–5am Mon and all day on holidays) a taxi service (Anruf-Sammel-Taxis) operates as a supplementary on-demand service from any bus stop in the city direct to your chosen destination. Call at least 30min in advance ℘*02742 25 35 45.*

POST OFFICES

City centre post office: *Linzer Straße 34. Mon–Fri 8am–6pm:* Main post office: *Bahnhofsplatz 1a. Mon–Fri 7am–7pm, Sat 9am–1pm.*

Rococo façade is noted for its exuberant high altar by Andreas Gruber and the four-sided altar paintings by Kremser Schmidt. To the right of the Rathaus, the 1707 **Prandtauerkirche** is named after its designer, Jakob Prandtauer. The Crucifixion scene on the high altar by Johann Lukas von Hildebrandt is attributed to the Spanish painter José de Ribera (1588–1652).

Stadtmuseum

🕐*Open year-round Wed–Sun 10am–5pm.* 👛€5. ℘*02742 333 26 43. www.stadtmuseum-stpoelten.at.*
The city history museum is part of a cultural centre, housed in the converted Carmelite convent attached to the Prandtauerkirche. Exhibits include Jugendstil works.

Institut der Englischen Fräulein★

From Prandtauerstraße turn left onto Linzer Straße (no. 11).
The most outstanding Baroque façade in St. Pölten belongs to this girls' school that was originally affiliated with an order founded by the English nun, Mary Ward, in 1709 to educate the daughters of the aristocracy. Prandtauer designed the sumptuous pink and white exterior whose black wrought-iron grills make a striking contrast. Four portals, richly decorated with scrolls and busts of angels, divide up the long building, as do several sculpture-filled niches. The small **Institutskirche** (church) is lavishly decorated with frescoes by Paul Troger and Bartolomeo Altomonte.

Riemerplatz

This space is another beautiful Baroque square lined with fine Baroque façades especially the Herbertstein Palace.

CATHEDRAL DISTRICT

Dom Mariä Himmelfahrt★

Enlivened by only an ornate spire and the two figures of St. Hippolytus and St. Augustine, the cathedral's austere façade belies the Baroque splendour that awaits behind its portals. The soft tones of the stucco marble and paintings, the sheen of the liberally applied gilding and the inlaid work combine to create a rich and warm effect.

The conversion to the Baroque style began in 1722 under Jakob Prandtauer and was completed in 1735 under Josef

Munggenast. The 1658 high altar painting by Tobias Pock depicts the Assumption of Mary.

The splendid **choir stalls★** with their elaborately carved wooden decoration and the organ case are by Peter Widerin. The ceiling frescoes and the 10 large **wall-paintings★**, which show scenes from the life of Christ, are the work of Thomas Friedrich Gedon and clearly demonstrate the influence of **Daniel Gran**. Gran himself, along with Bartolomeo Altomonte, painted the frescoes in the side aisles as well as the altarpieces in the side altars.

The **Rosenkranzkapelle** is the only remaining section from the original medieval church. It has cross-ribbed vaulting and pillars with intricately decorated capitals. The entrance to this chapel is via the choir stalls.

Diözesan-Museum★

On the upper floor of the cloister courtyard. ◷*Open May–Oct Tue–Fri 9am–noon and 2pm–5pm, Sat 10am–1pm (Jul–Aug also Sun and hols 10am–1pm).* ☞€4. ℘02742 32 43 31. *www.dz-museum.at.*

This museum houses religious art from the Romanesque period to the present, in particular Gothic altarpieces and sculptures, and works by leading Austrian Baroque artists. The crowning glory is the **Stiftsbibliothek★**, the sumptuous library with sculptures attributed to Peter Widerin, and frescoes by Daniel Gran and Paul Troger depicting the four faculties: theology, philosophy, medicine and law.

Stöhr Haus

This is an important example of a Jugendstil building at no. 41 Kremser Gasse, built in 1899 by Joseph Maria Olbrich, creator of the Vienna Secession building.

GOVERNMENT AND CULTURAL DISTRICT

Since becoming the seat of the Lower Austrian government, St. Pölten has built a new government and cultural district about 500m/547yds southeast of the old town by the Traisen.

The quarter's main commercial artery is the Landhaus Boulevard, which culminates in the elegant new state parliament building. Beyond here are the main cultural institutions, including the Festspielhaus concert hall, designed by Klaus Kada, and the Landesmuseum.

For a birds-eye view of the quarter, head to the 46m/150ft viewing platform of the **Klangturm** (*Sound tower*, ♿◷*open year-round Mon–Sat 8am–6pm, Sun 9am–5pm;* ☞*free;* ℘*02742 90 05 17 121; www.klangturm.at*), designed by Ernst Hoffmann, which is illuminated at night. The tower also doubles as an information centre and houses changing exhibitions of artistic installations experimenting with sound.

Parliament building of Lower Austria

The Bridge Saint

Bohemia-born **St. John of Nepomuk** went to Prague in 1370, rising to become vicar-general to the archbishop. In a dispute between the archbishop and King Wenceslas I, he defended the rights of the Church and especially the sanctity of the Confessional. For this reason, in 1393, the King had him tortured and thrown from the bridge into the Vltava. However, as he hit the water a miraculous ring of stars appeared around him. Hence, statues of this martyr have come to grace many bridges in southern Germany, Bohemia and Austria.

♟♟ Museum Niederösterreich

Open year-round Tue–Sun 9am–5pm. €5.50. ℘02742 90 80 90. www.museumnoe.at.

Housed in a radically modern building by Hans Hollein, the Lower Austrian provincial museum presents exhibits on nature, art and history in an engaging fashion that often makes clever use of interactive technology. The collection is divided into two "houses": the Haus der Natur (Nature House), recently improved and expanded; and the Haus der Geschichte (History House), expected to be unveiled in September 2017, which will present the museum's prized art collection in its historical context. (The museum will remain open with reduced entry fees until its completion.) Special exhibits and child-oriented events add additional dimensions.

EXCURSIONS

Schloss Pottenbrunn

5km/3mi northeast via Wiener Straße and Ratzersdorfer Straße.

This ancient moated castle took on its Renaissance Italianate character – marked by arcaded galleries that are cantilevered around the tower and the main building – in the 16C. A bulbous Baroque dome sits atop the tower.

Stift Herzogenburg★

12km/7.4mi north of St. Pölten on the S33. ● Guided tours (75min) Apr–Oct daily 9.30am, 11am, 1.30pm, 3pm, 4.30pm; Nov–Mar by appointment. €9. ℘02782 83 11 213. www.stift-herzogenburg.at.

The Augustinian canons' monastery was founded in 1112 by Bishop Ulrich of Passau, and given a complete Baroque makeover in the 18C in a collaboration of three of the era's greatest architects: Jakob Prandtauer, Johann Fischer von Erlach and Joseph Munggenast.

Festsaal fresco, Stift Herzogenburg

© Martin Siepmann/age fotostock

Franz Munggenast rebuilt the **church**, which was adorned with frescoes by Bartolomeo Altomonte, who also painted the altarpieces on the side altars. The picture on the high altar is by Daniel Gran. The highlight of the monastic buildings is the **Festsaal★** (festival hall), designed by Fischer von Erlach and crowned by Altomonte's huge allegorical fresco to the glory of the prince-bishops of Passau.

Tours also take in the **library**, which is liberally decorated with pictures, frescoes and *grisailles* (paintings in tones of grey), and a room filled with Late Gothic works by artists belonging to the Danubian School.

Kirchstetten

15km/9.3mi east.

This village was for many years the summer retreat of the Anglo-American poet **W H Auden** (1907–73) and the Austrian poet, Josef Weinheber (1892–1945). Auden is buried here in Kirchstetten's churchyard.

St. John of Nepomuk Monuments★

24km/15mi southeast of St. Pölten.

This ornate group of monuments is devoted to St. John of Nepomuk (*see Infobox above*) and others. What makes it a unusual is that, unlike elsewhere in Catholic Central Europe, the statue of the saint is not actually placed on a bridge, but on the riverbank. In fact there was a bridge here, but it was moved 50m/164ft downstream in the 18C. Carved from sandstone, the group is the work of Christoph Brandl, from Wilhelmsburg.

Another curiosity: the date of the statues (1712) can be calculated by adding the capital letters, which correspond to Roman numerals, engraved on the base. Stand beside the group of monuments and you can enjoy a superb view★ of Lilienfeld's monastery.

Stift Lilienfeld

25km/15.5mi south of St. Pölten.

Open year-round Mon–Sat 9am–noon and 1.30pm–4.30pm, Sun and hols 1.30pm–4.30pm. €3. 02762 52 420. www.stift-lilienfeld.at.

Founded in 1202 by Babenberg Duke Leopold IV as a Cistercian abbey, Stift Lilienfeld is the largest medieval monastery complex in Austria. Upon returning from a Crusade, the duke presented the monastery with a relic of the Holy Cross, which is still a major object of veneration today. Affiliated with Heiligenkreuz near Vienna, the abbey is a superb example of the transitional style bridging Romanesque and Gothic architecture.

Unlike many monasteries in Austria, the **Abbey★** at Lilienfeld is set amidst, rather than on, the hills (*1hr guided tours Mon–Sat 10am and 2pm, Sun and hols 2pm; in winter by appointment; €7*).

The **Stiftskirche** is the largest church in Lower Austria, measuring 82m/269ft long by 21m/69ft wide. The pillared basilica is essentially Romanesque in concept with its cruciform ground plan and round-arched windows, although the Gothic period brought the addition of flying buttresses.

Have a look at the **west doorway★**, then take in the uplifting ambience of the interior with its Gothic vaulting and **Baroque furnishings★** that blend beautifully with the medieval architecture. The predominant tone is the black of the Türnitz marble from which the altars, the pulpit, the choir organ case and the Leopold memorial are made, lavishly lit up by gleaming gold leaf. The painting of the Assumption of the Virgin Mary on the high altar is the work of Daniel Gran (1746).

The ribbed vaulting of the **cloister★** is supported on finely proportioned consoles by clustered pillars of attractively coloured stone. On the north side are remarkable stained-glass windows from the first half of the 14C. The **chapterhouse** is one of the oldest parts of the whole complex, with stone benches lining the room. Over the cellarium, a well-preserved storage cellar, is the impressive two-aisled, lay brothers' **dormitory**, the only one of its kind in Austria to have survived from the Middle Ages.

As is always the case in a monastery, the **library★** is one of the finest rooms. Dating from 1700, it has magnificent stucco decoration and ceiling frescoes as well as richly inlaid bookcases and doors. Also sneak a peek inside the adjoining picture gallery.

ADDRESSES

🛏 STAY

🍽🍽 **Stadthotel Hauser Eck** – *Schulgasse 2. ☎02742 73 336. www. hausereck.at. 28 rooms.* ⌖. Located in the pedestrianised part of town, this Jugendstil building is classed as a historic monument. The interior and rooms are modern and stylish, and there is a good restaurant on the premises.

🍽🍽🍽🍽 **Hotel Metropol** – *Schillerplatz 1. ☎02742 70 70 00. www.hotel-metropol.at. 40 rooms.* ∴ This modern city-centre hotel is used by the business community.

🍴 EAT

🍽 **Gasthof Winkler** – *Mühlweg 64. ☎02742 36 49 44. www.gasthofwinkler.at. Closed Mon.* Menu at this gasthof varies with the seasons. Lovely garden.

🍽🍽 **Zum Gwercher** – *Stattersdorf (SE of city centre), Schiffmannstraße 98. ☎02742 23 110. www.gwercher.at.* Welcoming restaurant with a large garden inside the courtyard. Wide selection of wines and cigars.

🍽🍽🍽🍽 **Galerie** – *Fuhrmannsgasse 1. ☎02742 35 13 05. www.restaurantgalerie.at. Mon–Fri lunch and dinner. Closed Feb, one week in Jan, Easter, first fortnight Aug and all public holidays.* Top-quality restaurant, considered the best in town.

CAFÉS AND BARS

Café Punschkrapferl – *Wiener Straße 193. www.punschkrapferl.at.* More than 80 pastries to choose from plus ice creams and a salad bar.

Café Schubert – *Herrenplatz 1. www.cafeschubert.at.* Renowned for its pastry, this traditional Viennese-style coffeehouse also offers a daily meal sourced from the local market.

Emmi – *Linzer Straße 1. ☎0650 425 06 25. Closed Sun.* This café and roastery serves coffee, pastry and other snacks in an artsy but homey interior.

SHOPPING

The main streets of the pedestrian shopping zone are Kremser Gasse and Wiener Straße. There is a wide variety of shops here, catering to every taste and budget.

ENTERTAINMENT

Landestheater Niederösterreich – *Rathausplatz 11. ☎02742 90 80 600. www. landestheater.net. Season runs Sept–May.* Theatre, musicals, operettas, children's productions.

Bühne im Hof – *Julius-Raab Promenade 37. ☎02742 90 80 50. www.bih.at.* Cabaret, dance, concerts.

Festspielhaus – *Kulturbezirk 2. ☎02742 90 80 80 811. www.festspielhaus.at.* Wide range of entertainment on offer: classical music, folk music, jazz, pop, rock, opera, operettas, musicals, ballet, folk dancing.

CINEMAS

The **Hollywood Megaplex** (*☎02742 28 80; Engelbert-Laimer-Straße 1 on the right of the Traisen; www. megaplex.at*) offers Eight cinema screens, plus various eating and other entertainment options, all under a single roof.

FESTIVALS

Meisterkonzerte: *Mid-Oct–mid-May.* Concerts of classical music in the Stadtsaal and Festspielhaus.

St. Pöltner Festwochen: *Mid-May– late Jun.* Concerts, plays, cabaret.

Film im Dom: *May.* The "Cinema Paradiso" association presents cinema films inside the Domkirche; the event is expected to return to its traditional open-air location on the Domplatz in 2015.

Summer Blues Festival: *Jul.* Blues performances and fine food on the Ratzersdorfer Lake.

Film-Festival: *Jul–Aug.* Films and food from all over the world on the Rathausplatz.

Musica Sacra: *Sept–mid-Oct.* Performances of international church music in the cathedral and the abbey churches of Herzogenburg and Lilienfeld.

More information about dates and other details on all of the above is available from the tourist office at *☎02742 35 33 54*, or online at www.st-poelten.gv.at.

Altenburg Monastery★★

Founded in 1144, this Benedictine abbey was repeatedly attacked in medieval times and in virtual ruin when a handful of monks set out to reconstruct it in 1645. The result is a masterpiece of Baroque, boasting one of the finest abbey libraries in Austria as well as numerous stunning frescoes by the masterful Paul Troger. Much damage was inflicted on the abbey in both World Wars, but restoration has gone far to re-create its original splendour.

- **Info:** ℘02982 34 51. www.stift-altenburg.at.
- **Location:** Stift Altenburg is about 86km/53.4mi northwest of Vienna.
- **Parking:** Parking places are readily available.
- **Don't Miss:** The library, the crypt and the church.
- **Timing:** Allow an hour for the tour, another for the church.

VISIT
Stiftskirche★★★
Originally a Gothic church, the abbey was gently transferred to the Baroque style between 1730 and 1733.
Star features of this well-proportioned edifice are the **ceiling frescoes** by Paul Troger that depict the struggle between Good and Evil. Troger also painted the Assumption above the high altar and several pictures on the side altars. The **stuccowork** was done by the workshop of Franz Joseph Holzinger of St. Florian. The **organ** (1773) is elegantly encased in delicately gilded woodwork.

Stiftsgebäude
Open May–late Oct daily 10am–5pm. Last admission 4pm. ☞€12. www.stift-altenburg.at.
This is one of the most complete and vibrant Baroque abbey building complexes in the country.
The vestibule of the **Library**, with a dome fresco by Johann Jakob Zeiler, is a mere overture to the magnificence of the church-like library, a collaboration of master architects, painters, and sculptors. Paul Troger painted the ceiling frescoes on the theme of Human and Divine Wisdom. It is at Altenburg

Altenburg Monastery

© Christian Handl/imageBROKER/age fotostock

more than anywhere else that one can appreciate the Baroque concept of the library, which keeps 10,000 books, as the temple of the spirit and enlightenment. The vast, luminous space of the **Krypta** (crypt) has no equal among the abbeys of Austria. Its frescoes, painted by several of Troger's pupils, deal lightly with death, mixing the macabre with floral motifs. Painted with exuberant frescoes, the four rooms of the **Sala Terrena** are the epitome of Baroque extravagance while also evoking the charm and humour typical of the style.

Gardens

The gardens have been remodelled and opened to the public. In 2006 came the Garden of Religions, a modern space covering 3ha/7.5-acre, devoted to non-Christian religions, including symbols of Islam, Judaism, Buddhism and Hinduism. In 2009 the Garden of Peace was opened. This quiet and relaxing space takes in a vineyard, an orchard, several sculptures, and a terrace with a beautiful view of the façade of the monastery.

EXCURSIONS
Eggenburg★

Lying between the Waldviertel and the Weinviertel, the town of Eggenburg features some beautiful medieval and Renaissance architecture. It can still boast an historic town centre, a town wall preserved almost in its entirety, and three medieval gate towers: the Holturm, the Wahrsagerturm and the Kanzlerturm.

Eggenburg's main square, the **Hauptplatz**, is lined by charming old houses, including the **Gemaltes Haus,** with a

sgraffito façade sporting images from the Old Testament. Other outstanding features are the **Pranger** (pillory), the Adlerbrunnen (Eagle Fountain), the Mariensäule (Mary Column), and the **Pestsäule** (Trinity Plague column).

♣♣ Krahuletz-Museum★

⊙Open mid-Mar–Dec Mon–Fri 9am–5pm, Sat–Sun and hols 10am–5pm. ⊛€7. ☎02984 34 00. www.krahuletzmuseum.at.

This collection of minerals, fossils and archaeological finds is of international standing. It was assembled by local geology professor Johann Krahuletz in the 19C.

Cleverly presented, and very hands-on, the informative displays include a **landscape model★** showing the transformation from the Eggenburg-on-Sea of 20 million years ago, via the primeval Danube of 11 million years ago, through to the present day. Upstairs, exhibits focus on regional cultural history and include a collection of watches and clocks.

Along a geology-themed walking trail outside, you can search for fossils, such as shells, shark's teeth and snails, in what was once the Eggenburg Sea.

Stoitzendorf

4km/2.5mi east of Eggenburg on B303. Follow the signs for Kellergasse.

Stoitzendorf's **Kellergasse** is an example of the old style of roads to be found in Austrian wine-growing areas just outside the villages. It is lined with small, mostly single-storey Presshäuser, where the grapes are pressed, and where the young wine is also sampled (⊙see infobox, p171). Here in the western

Ausg'steckt Is

Heuriger (wine taverns) are found wherever wine is made in Austria. Heuriger also describes a press house (Presshäuser), as they are the place where grapes are pressed, too. The must is stored in barrels for fermentation in tunnel-like cellars. In any Austrian wine region, whenever you see a pine or fir branch and lantern displayed above the door, this symbol indicates that the Heuriger is open, or ausgesteckt (a peculiarly Austrian term), and the landlord is pouring his wines, to serve alongside such hearty homemade snacks as Blunzn (blood sausage), Geselchtes (smoked pork) and Speck (streaky bacon).

Windmill in Retz

© Austrian National Tourist Office/Lehmann H.

wine-growing area, these buildings are embedded in the soft loam soil.

Pulkau

8km/5mi northwest of Eggenburg.
From the monastery, 26km/16mi on B45.
Pulkau is a large wine-producing township near the Czech border. Its **parish church** has traces of early 14C frescoes, and the **Heilig-Blut-Kirche** has a 16C altarpiece carved and painted by artists of the Danube School.

Österreichisches Motorradmuseum

8km/5mi northwest of Eggenburg.
Take B35 N; bear left on LH42,
turn right onto L1200, which
becomes B45.In Sigmundsherberg.
Kleinmeiseldorferstrasse 8. ⊙*Open*
mid-Mar–mid-Nov Sat–Sun and hols
10am–5pm. ⊛€7. ℘*0664 649 38 55.*
www.motorradmuseum.at.
The Austrian Motorcycle Museum has the largest collection of its kind in the country. Some 300 models illustrate the last 100 years of motorbike history.

Retz

36km/22mi northeast of Altenburg via
the B45, then the B35.
Retz *(population 4,170)*, near the Thaya Valley, is an important wine-growing and farming centre in a hilly region of

the Bohemian Forest. The Old Town still has its medieval ramparts and defensive towers. Its emblem is a windmill, built in 1772 and still operational.
Retz's rectangular **Hauptplatz★** (main square) is anchored by a Holy Trinity Column and surrounded by several architecturally remarkable buildings. Most notable are the crenellated **Verderberhaus** on the north side and the **Sgraffitohaus**, opposite. The latter is a handsome building with a carved doorway and a façade covered with inscribed maxims. Also here is the ochre-coloured **Rathaus** (town hall, with tourist information), which was converted from a Gothic church in the 16C.
Local wines can be sampled on guided tours *(1hr30min)* of the **Retzer Erlebniskeller** *(meet outside the Rathaus; May–Oct daily 10.30am, 2pm, 4pm; Mar–Apr and Nov–Dec daily 2pm; Jan–Feb Sat–Sun and hols 2pm;* ⊛€11; ℘*02942 27 00; www.erlebniskeller.at)*. At 21km/13mi long and 30m/98ft deep, this wine cellar is Austria's largest, once storing the entire region's harvest.

ADDRESSES

⌂STAY

⊖ **Gasthof Goldener Adler/Nordring** –
3591 Fuglau. 3.4km/2mi E of Altenburg.
℘*02989 82 62. www.nordring.at/*
der-gasthof. 13 rooms. This welcoming, traditional roadside inn has been in the Eisenhauer family since 1917. Rooms are nicely decorated.

⌁/EAT

⊖ **Klosterkuchl** – *Altenburg Monastery.*
℘*0273 42 01 68. www.stift-altenburg.at.*
Open May–Nov daily from 10am, other hours vary by season. Regional cuisine in the monastery inn uses local products and organic vegetables grown by the monks, who also supply the wine.

⊖⊖ **Pollak's Retzbacher Hof** – *Bahnstr.*
1, Unterretzbach. 4km/2.5mi from Retz.
℘*02942 20 171. www.retzbacherhof.at.*
Closed Sun evening, Mon, Tue and hols.
The high quality food at this acclaimed family-run restaurant is locally sourced. Dine in the garden in summer.

Zwettl Monastery★

The great Cistercian abbey of Zwettl lies in a bend of the romantic Kamptal Valley in the Waldviertel. It was founded in 1137 by Hadmar I von Künring, whose dynasty ruled over the Waldviertel for centuries. The abbey flourished in the Middle Ages and again after the Counter-Reformation. It even survived Joseph II's reforms and the Nazi period unscathed. Today it is still a vigorous spiritual, cultural and economic hub of the region.

▤ **Info:** Sparkassenplatz 4, 3910 Zwettl. ℘02822 50 31 29. www.zwettl.info.

▷ **Location:** The abbey is about 49km/30mi northwest of Krems and 3km/1.8mi east of the town of Zwettl.

⊛ **Don't Miss:** The cloisters of the abbey church.

♟ **Kids:** An excursion to Rappottenstein Castle.

◷ **Timing:** The monastery is closed in winter.

VISIT
Stiftskirche (Abbey church)★

Visit by guided tour. Church and treasury tours mid-Mar–Oct daily 11am (except Sun), 2pm and 5pm. Library and treasury tours mid-Mar–Oct Sun and hols 11am. ◉€10.50. ℘02822 20 20 250. www.stift-zwettl.at.

The basic structure of the 14C church is Gothic, but the requisite Baroque make-over in the 18C added the elegant **west front★** and slender tower topped with a curving roof and a lantern. The **high altar★** provides the majestic backdrop for a realistic representation of an oak tree, which recalls both the legend of the abbey's foundation (it is said to be built on the spot where an oak grew green leaves in winter) and also the Tree of Salvation. The **choir stalls★** are richly inlaid and bear gilded vases and statues. The **Kreuzgang★** (cloisters), completed in 1240, are a fine example of the transitional style between Romanesque and Gothic. In the hexagonal *lavatorium*, or washing place, small columns have crocketed or plain vase capitals. The **Kapitelsaal** (chapter-house) is the oldest part of the abbey, dating from after 1175. Vaulting ribs radiate from a massive central pillar, dividing the room into four bays.

Library, Zwettl Monastery

© Austrian National Tourist Office/Trumler

EXCUSIONS
Schloss Rosenau

8km/5mi west of Zwettl. ⏰*Open Apr–Oct daily 9am–5pm.* ⚬⚬*€7.* ✆*02822 58 22 10. www.rosenau.at.*
Designed in 1593 in Renaissance style, the castle was rebuilt during the first half of the 18C in Baroque, according to plans by Josef Munggenast. A masonic lodge briefly held its meetings here, until its dissolution under Joseph II in 1785, hence its current (partial) use as the **Austrian Museum of Freemasonry**. The museum offers an excellent overview of the history of this movement. The castle has also been recently refurbished to house a luxury hotel, restaurant and conference facilities.
The parish church, also built within the castle, is a gem, with its ceiling fresco attributed to Paul Troger.

♟ Burg Rappottenstein
12km/7.5mi south of Zwettl.
👣*Guided tours (50min) every hour: Easter, last fortnight Apr and Oct Sat–Sun and hols 11am–4pm (except 1pm); May–Sept Tue–Sun 11am–4pm (except 1pm); Jul–Aug also 10am and 5pm.* ⚬⚬*€9, child €5.* ✆*02828 82 50. www.burg-rappottenstein.at.*

Burg Rappottenstein

Rapoto von Künring completed this castle in 1176 in the style of the fortresses of Hohenstaufen. The oldest part of it is Romanesque, with Gothic and Renaissance works added later. The pentagonal chapel, consecrated in 1379 by the Bishop of Passau, has a ribbed vault. The archives room and the hall are decorated with 16C **frescoes★** of scenes of bourgeois life and the court.
In 1664 the castle was bought by the family Abensperg-Traun, who, remarkably, still own it today.

ADDRESSES

🛏 STAY AND 🍴 EAT

🍽🍽 **Das Dorftreff** – *Rudmanns 83, 3910 Zwettl.* ✆*02822 52 02 14. www.dasdorftreff.at. 3 rooms.* 🚪. This comfy, modernised inn serves authentic regional dishes and has simply furnished bedrooms

🍽🍽🍽 **Alte Remise** – *3924 Schloss Rosenau, between Zwettl and Weitra.* ✆*02822 582 03. www.rosenau.at. Closed Mon all year round and Mon–Tue Nov–Apr. 11 rooms.* 🚪. Set in the parkland of the local castle, this fine old *gasthaus*, built in 1604, has lovely rooms and a large terrace for outdoor dining on local and regional dishes.

🍽🍽🍽 **Hotel Schwarzalm**– *Almweg 1, 3910 Zwettl-Geschwendt. 3.5km/2mi SE via the B 36 direction Ottenschlag, then left after 2km/1.2mi.* ✆*02822 53 17 30. www.schwarzalm.at. 40 rooms.* 🚪. *Restaurant.* An attractive, modern hotel, run on feng-shui principles, blends perfectly with its verdant setting and enjoys countryside views through full-length windows. Full Wellness facilities and fine dining (🍽🍽).

ACTIVITIES

Zwettlbad– *Hammerweg 10, 3910.* ✆*0282 25 21 75. www.zwettlbad.at. Jun–Aug daily 9am–8pm, Sept–May Mon–Wed 3pm–9pm, Thu 2pm–9pm, Fri 2pm–9.30pm, Sat 9am–9pm, Sun and holidays 9am–8pm. €7.60.* Family-friendly lido with different pools and spa facilities make this an ideal place for exercise and relaxation.

© Austrian National Tourist Office/ Simoner

Geras Monastery★

The Premonstratensian abbey of Geras, set in a quiet spot far from the main tourist centres, enjoys considerable renown in Lower Austria. It is surrounded by the Naturpark Geras, a nature reserve where fallow deer, roe deer, wild boar and other animals roam within large enclosures.

🛈 **Info:** Hauptstraße 16, A-2093. ℘02912 70 50. www.geras.gv.at.

▶ **Location:** Geras is in the eastern Waldviertel, not far from the Czech border.

⊙ **Don't Miss:** The Abbey's Marmorsaal (Marble Hall).

🕓 **Timing:** Allow an hour for the Abbey tour.

VISIT
Stift (Abbey)

🕓*Open May–Oct Tue–Sun 10am–5pm ("👣guided tours daily); Mar–Apr and Nov–Dec Tue–Sat 10am–3pm. ⊚€9. ℘02912 34 52 89. www.stiftgeras.at.*
This Premonstratensian monastery was founded in 1153, but was redesigned and enlarged in Baroque style by Joseph Munggenast in the 18C. The highlight of the guided tour is the solemn and refined **Marmorsaal★** (Marble Hall), the former summer refectory, reached via a grand staircase with a statue of Pallas Athene, the Greek goddess of wisdom. The hall's fine **ceiling fresco★** by Paul Troger depicts the miracle of the loaves and fishes. Troger is also responsible for the paintings hanging above the two fireplaces, including the *Wedding Feast at Cana*.

Stiftskirche
The colourful abbey church is Romanesque in origin, but was completely redone in Baroque style after a fire in 1730. It has delicate stuccowork and sensitive frescoes depicting the life of the Virgin painted by Franz Zoller, a pupil of Paul Troger. The main door is decorated with statues of St. Norbert and St. Augustine, two major figures of the Premonstratensian Order.

Naturpark Geras
🕓*Open Palm Sun–Oct Tue–Sun 9am–6pm. ⊚€4. ℘0664 55 26 553. www.naturparkgeras.at.*
Roe and fallow deer as well as boar roam in large enclosures at this nature reserve. Waterfowl and woodland birds visit the open space that surrounds the abbey.

Geras Monastery

© Arco / F. Waldhäusl/age fotostock

EXCURSION
Pernegg
12km/7.4mi southwest of Geras.
Set in peaceful, unspoiled countryside, Kloster Pernegg monastery was founded in 1153 as a Premonstratensian convent, but became affiliated with Geras Abbey following the death of the last nun in 1585. Since 1995 it has been used as a centre for religious seminars and fasting retreats.
Its church blends Late Gothic, Renaissance and Baroque elements and features a modern high altar decorated with a 16C Crucifixion.

Riegersburg Castle★

The unspoiled, peaceful landscape of the northeastern Waldviertel provides a backdrop for the most important Baroque palace in Lower Austria. The former moated castle was bought by Sigmund Friedrich Count Khevenhüller, governor of Lower Austria and converted into a four-winged Baroque palace by the masterful Franz Anton Pilgram. The decoration is rich, but not ostentatious. Still owned by the same family, the building is a fine example of an 18C country seat.

🛈 **Info:** ✆03153 86 70. www.riegersburg.com.
▷ **Location:** The Schloss is in the far north of Austria, close to the Czech border.
👁 **Don't Miss:** Riegersburg Castle Yellow Salon.
👪 **Kids:** Thaya Valley National Park.
🕐 **Timing:** Allow about an hour for each castle.

VISIT
The Exterior

The main façade is punctuated by a central portico with five columns topped by arched windows and flanked by corner pavilions. The tympanum bears the crest of Khevenhüller, surmounted by a statue of Atlas carrying the world. The work of sculptor Joseph Krackerhe, the pediment, which dates from 1733, is adorned with statues of Wisdom, Unity, Justice and the Franchise.

State Rooms

🕐*Open Apr–mid-Sept daily 10am–5pm; Jul–Aug daily 10am–6pm.* 🎟*€11.* ♿. ✆*0664 21 45 855. www.riegersburg-hardegg.com.*

The palace interior is filled with high-quality furnishings. The plain but beautifully proportioned **banqueting hall** (Festsaal) features stuccowork above the door showing Count Johann Joseph Khevenhüller-Metsch, Maria Theresia's Chief Lord Chamberlain, whose diaries are said to have inspired the libretto for Richard Strauss' opera, *Der Rosenkavalier*. The portraits of Maria Theresia and her mother Elisabeth Christine are by court painter Martin van Meytens. The **Baroque room** houses a view of Naples composed of 35 copper engravings dating from 1730 to 1775. The furniture in the Salon includes Queen Anne and Chippendale pieces, as well as furnishings in the Austrian Baroque style and a handsome tabernacle cupboard.

The **tower room**, hung with plate-printed cotton, contains furniture from the 18C. Note the pretty portable

Riegersburg Castle

© Austrian National Tourist Office/ Mayer

desk from England. The **dining room** contains French furniture and houses a famous portrait of Prince Eugene of Savoy by Austrian painter Auerbach.

The **stucco ceiling★** of the **Yellow Salon** depicts an allegory of princely virtue. The room is furnished with Marie-Antoinette chairs and two beautiful Florentine commodes with delicate inlaid work. The **Chinese Salon** also features a magnificent stucco ceiling.

In the north wing is the elegant **Schlosskapelle** (chapel), consecrated in 1755. The altar is integrated into the architectural structure and is surmounted by rich stuccowork. The altarpiece depicts St. Sigismund.

The **Schlossküche** (palace kitchen) on the ground floor, in use until 1955 and still featuring its original appointments, working equipment and large brick oven, is the only remaining manorial kitchen in Austria.

From the café you can access the park with its pond.

EXCURSION
Burg Hardegg

8km/5mi to the east. ⏱*Open Apr–mid-Nov daily 10am–5pm; Jul–Aug daily 10am–6pm.* €7.50. *0664 21 45 855. www.riegersburg-hardegg.com.*

Hardegg on the Thaya River is dominated by its bluff-top castle, whose formidable keep and thick walls create an impression of impregnability. The origins of this strategically important fortress date back to AD 1000, but extensions were added right up to the 14C. After a chequered history, the fortress passed into the hands of the Khevenhüller family in 1730, and at the end of the 19C it was converted into a mausoleum for the Lower Austrian line of this dynasty.

👥 Thaya Valley National Park

9km/5.5mi east of Riegersburg via the B 30. ⏱ *Information centre open mid-Mar–Sept daily 9am–6pm; Oct daily 10am–5pm.* *02949 70 050. www.np-thayatal.at.*

This national park, established in 2000, is located along 25km/15.5mi of the river Thaya. It helps protect the diversity of an entire ecosystem, where some 1,600 different plants have been identified. A hundred species of birds and nearly 1,000 species of butterflies live in this magical setting of meadows, forests and wilderness.

An excellent information centre includes a café-restaurant with a sunny terrace, serving regional dishes. Children love the Nature Adventure World playground here, and all ages enjoy the hands-on multimedia exhibit NaturGeschichten (€4.50, €3 children).

ADDRESSES

🛏 STAY AND 🍴 EAT

🍴 **Weinbauernhof Familie Amtmann** – *Hofberg 60, 8333 Riegersburg.* *03153 75 65. www.amtmann-urlaub.at. 3 rooms, 1 apartment.* ⬚. This modern house set on a farm has magnificent views of the Riegersburg. Rooms are attractive and modern-traditional in style.

🍴 **Malerwinkl Wirtshaus Vinothek und Kunsthotel** – *8361 Hatzendorf 152. 7km/4mi SE of Riegersburg.* *03155 22 53. www.malerwinkl.com. 10 rooms.* ⬚. This charming "art-hotel" has bright, playfully decorated rooms some with balconies, while the restaurant *(closed Mon)* serves excellent Styrian and Italian food.

ACTIVITIES

👥 **Zotter Schokoladen Manufaktur GmbH**– *Bergl 56, Riegersburg.* *03152 55 54. www.zotter.at. May–Oct Mon–Sat 9am–8pm; Nov–Apr Mon–Sat 9am–7pm.* €14.90. Visit the factory of famous chocolate brand Zotter, high-quality manufacturer of entirely organic chocolates, including such flavours as red wine and cheese, walnut and grape.

Gmünd

(Waldviertal)

In 2008 the city of Gmünd celebrated its 2,000th anniversary. As a border town it has known good times – taking advantage of being able to deal with both Austria and (what is now) the Czech Republic – and bad times – losing part of its territory to the former Czechoslovakia after World War I. Today it has much to offer visitors: a charming Old Town, an idyllic location on the banks of the Lainsitz, and Blockheide Park.

VISIT
Stadtplatz

The distintive mid-16C **Old Town Hall** dominates the town's central square. Its windows are framed attractively by sgraffito decoration and its gabled tower, rebuilt in 1988, is an eye-catching landmark.

The **Glas-und Steinmuseum** *(Museum of Glass and Stone; Stadtplatz 34; ℘028 5 252 50 62 45; ⓞopen May–Sept Mon–Fri 10am–noon, except Thu, and 2pm–4.30pm, Sat–Sun and hols 9am–noon; ➔€2)* recalls how the glass industry

> ▶ **Population:** *2,600*.
> ⓖ **Michelin Map:** No 730 Q2 Basse-Autriche.
> ⓘ **Info:** Schremser Straße 6. ℘02852 52 50 61 00. www.gmuend.at.
> ⓞ **Location:** Gmünd is 95km/ 60mi northeast of Linz. Alt. 485m/1,590ft.
> ⓚ **Kids:** An excursion to either Naturpark Blockheide or to see the bald ibises at the Waldrapp Wildlife Refuge.
> ⓞ **Timing:** Allow half a day to see the town, plus whatever is required for its many excursions.

once thrived in Gmünd. Glass-making equipment, crafts, painting and a variety of drinking vessels in different styles (Biedermeier, Hyllit etc) are on display. In 1565 and 1570, the gabled houses at nos. 31 and 33 Stadtplatz, built in Late Gothic style, were given Renaissance façades and covered with **sgraffito**, including decoration portraying mythological scenes.

ⓚ Naturpark Blockheide★

ⓞ*Open May–Sept daily 10am–6pm, Apr & Oct til 5pm.* ➔*Themed guided tours.* ℘0680 50 62 837. www.blockheide.at.

Northeast of town, this lovely nature reserve is distinguished by bizarrely shaped granite blocks with nicknames like *Pilzstein* (mushroom rock) and *Teufelsbett* (devil's bed). A former water reservoir at the park's highest point acts as an information centre with snack stands nearby. The viewing tower offers views as far as the Czech Republic. There is also an open-air display of geology as well as a children's playground.

EXCURSIONS
Weitra

8km/5mi southwest on Route 41.
Home to the oldest brewery in Austria (founded in 1321), this village is dominated by its majestic castle (1590–1606),

The Art of Sgraffito

The name of this technique, popular in northern Italy during the Renaissance, comes from the Italian *graffiare*, meaning to scratch. It was subsequently adopted in the Waldviertel, neighbouring Bohemia, and in Silesia and Saxony. The basic technique is to apply a layer of coloured plaster that is covered with a white mortar of a lesser thickness, onto the rough plaster of the wall to be sgraffitied. It is then incised and scraped before hardening, so as to reveal the underlying layers that have already been finished. Biblical or mythical scenes glorifying the Virtues are frequently chosen as subjects for decorating buildings.

with four wings, an entrance tower and crenellated walls. The castle's theatre, added in the 18C, is still used today by local drama groups. Beautiful mansions, dating from the 16C to the 19C, some decorated with sgraffito *(Rathausplatz 4 and 13)*, border the triangular town hall. Note the *Gratzl* (the name given to a house specially built in the centre of a town square).

Burg Heidenreichstein★

19km/12mi northeast. ☛*Guided tours (50min) mid-Apr–mid Oct Tue–Sun 10am, 11am, 2pm, 3pm, 4pm.* ⊚*€10.* ℘*02862 52 268. www.kinsky-heidenreichstein.at.*

Generally considered the most attractive moated castle in Austria, this burg was built on a hill sometime in the late 12C/early 13C, and remodelled in the 15C and 16C. It has four wings with three circular corner towers.

After belonging to the Princes of Palffy for centuries, it is now the property of Count Kinsky, who lives here all year. The rooms open to visitors are decorated with furniture dating from the Gothic, Renaissance and Baroque periods.

Waidhofen an der Thaya

Waidhofen (population 5,600; alt. 510m/1,673ft) is approx. equidistant (120km/75mi) from Vienna and Linz. 🛈*Hauptplatz 1.* ℘*02842 50 399. www.waidhofen-thaya-stadt.at.*

Waidhofen is situated on the left bank of the River Thaya in bucolic surroundings of farmland and forest. The town grew from a fortified settlement first recorded in 1171. The parish church stands on the highest point, while the town fortress was built on the lowest ground, to the east.

In the **Altstadt** (Old Town), the north promenade with the powder tower and the south promenade with a partially preserved defence tower are all that remain of the original fortifications. There are some interesting old houses along Wiener straße (no. 14, the Heimathaus), Böhmgasse and Pfarrgasse. In the centre of the **Hauptplatz** (town square) stands the **Rathaus**, a fine

Burg Heidenreichstein

© Austrian National Tourist Office / Kneidinger

example of an essentially Gothic town hall, even if it does owe its stepped gables to the Renaissance. The ridge turret was added in 1721. In 1709 the **Dreifaltigkeitssäule** (Holy Trinity Column) was put up to protect the town from plague, fire and war.

The **Pfarrkirche**'s modest, if finely proportioned, exterior offers no hint of its lavish Baroque interior. The vault of the nave is decorated with frescoes and stuccowork by Josef Michael Daysinger and depicts scenes from the life of Mary. The magnificent **high altar** (1721) fills the chancel with its lofty columns.

Also note the beautifully carved **stalls** with a double-headed eagle on the upper part to symbolise the church's function in an Imperial parish, as well as the pulpit and the organ gallery.

🧍‍♂️🧍‍♀️ Waldrapp Wildlife Refuge

Hollenbach 98. ⊙*Open May–Sept Mon–Thu 8.30am–11am and 1.15pm–3.30pm, Fri 8.30am–10.30am, Sat–Sun by appointment.* ☛*Guided tours by prior arrangement.* ⊚*€3, children €1.50.* ℘*06 4 94 93 929. www.waldrapp.at.*

This wildlife refuge is devoted to saving the Waldrapp *(Bald Ibis)*, a species of ibis that was once common in the Waldviertal, from extinction (their numbers are now on the increase, thanks to those efforts). Visitors can see the birds and learn about their life and habitat. An art gallery focuses on the Waldrapp.

VIENNA

The residence of the Imperial court for six centuries, Vienna is indelibly stamped with the seal of the Habsburg dynasty. Even now as capital of the Republic of Austria, Vienna has retained its incomparable grandeur and considerable prestige as one of Europe's most important cultural and artistic centres. For many, the name Vienna evokes the rhythm of the waltz or the shape of the Prater's Giant Wheel. The city's global renown, however, is due above all to its historic buildings, its magnificent art collections, and a musical tradition preserved by the opera and Vienna's famous choirs and orchestras. Excellent museums and elegant shops line its grand avenues. Even politically Vienna plays a pivotal role on the world stage as the permanent headquarters of OPEC (Organization of Petroleum Exporting Countries) since 1965. Several UN organizations, including the International Atomic Energy Agency (IAEA), are also based in the city.

Highlights

1 Experience the Viennese tradition of **coffee and cake** (p195)
2 Explore the opulent rooms of the impressive **Hofburg** palace (p199)
3 Visit **Jugendstil** buildings in Wieden (p212)
4 Take a day trip to the UNESCO World Heritage Site of **Schloss Schönbrunn** (p219)
5 Drive around the **Kahlenberg Heights**, stopping off at the wine village of **Grinzing** (p226)

A Bit of History

From Antiquity to the Habsburgs

Vienna began its existence as a modest Roman camp called Vindobona, founded around 15 BC. It gradually grew into a larger settlement and trading site, but didn't gain capital status until 1155 when Heinrich II Jasomirgott moved his residence to Vienna.

The town flourished economically and culturally in the early 13C under Leopold the Glorious, whose rule saw the construction of a massive fortified wall and the Church of St. Stephen, which became a bishop's seat in 1469.

By the time the last of the Babenbergs died in 1246, Vienna had become, after Cologne, the most important city on German-speaking soil. Its growth from then on was inseparably linked with the fortunes of the Habsburgs, who reigned over Austria from 1273 to 1918.

The Turks

A major impediment to Vienna's development was the persistent threat posed by the Ottoman army, which numbered as high as 300,000 men. The city was besieged twice, first in 1529 and then again in 1683. During the latter siege, the Emperor and the court fled Vienna, leaving its defence in the hands of 24,000 troops who managed to stave off all attacks for nearly two months. In the end, a relief force of 80,000 Austrians, Poles, Bavarians, Swabians and Franconians led by the Emperor's close ally, the Polish King Jan III Sobieski, succeeded in driving back the Turkish army for good. The battle marked a turning point in the power struggle between the central European powers and the Ottoman army, which had been waged for three centuries.

Following this famous victory, the Western sovereigns recognised the preeminence of the Emperor. The Austrian Empire now entered a long period of prosperity, finally allowing Vienna to blossom into a glamourous Imperial capital, marked by the influence of Baroque architecture.

Palaces, mansions and churches sprang up, eventually overflowing the narrow limits of the 17C city walls and leading to the development of new quarters and extensive suburbs.

The Congress of Vienna

Napoleon occupied Vienna twice, in 1805 and again in 1809, but when his empire collapsed in 1814, it fell to the Austrian capital to host the famous

Burgtheater

© Georg Soulek/Burgtheater

international gathering that was to redraw the map of Europe. For a year the Congress of Vienna furnished a pretext for splendid festivities. Receptions and balls were held at the embassies, in the state rooms at the Hofburg, and in the Great Gallery at Schönbrunn Palace. *"Le Congrès ne marche pas, il danse"* (The Congress does not walk, it dances), Prince de Ligne summed it up so poignantly. More than any other city, Vienna could offer choice entertainment to its guests: exquisite art collections, theatre, opera, and classical concerts. Ludwig van Beethoven himself conducted a gala concert, and his opera *Fidelio* was received with enthusiasm. Even after the delegates left, the idyllic Vienna of the Biedermeier (see p58) continued its carefree lifestyle, with people idling their time away in cafés, relaxing over wine in the Vienna Woods or listening to Schubert's dreamy Lieder (songs).

Growth of Vienna

Vienna had to await the reign of **Franz Joseph** (1848–1916) for the large-scale planning and building that made it what it is today. In 1857 the Emperor ordered the removal of the bastions and the formation of a circular boulevard – the **"Ring"** – around the old town. Famous architects and artists contributed to this great project, which is lined by Vienna's most important public buildings as well as by the numerous tenement blocks

characteristic of the city. In 1890, the outer boroughs were incorporated as well and the second ring of fortifications razed, making space for an outer circular road, known as the **"Gürtel"** (belt).

Vienna Between the Wars

On 11 November 1918, in Schönbrunn Palace, the last Habsburg emperor Karl I signed his abdication, bringing an end to the Austro-Hungarian monarchy. In 1920 the First Austrian Republic was declared. The decade that followed was to see huge strides forward in social provision in Vienna, with the building of many public housing projects, the most famous of which is the mile-long Karl-Marx-Hof. The era of "Red Vienna'"with its radical social democratic politics was also a period of, at times, vicious struggle between left and right in Austria, and especially in the capital. The conflict came to a head in 1927 when a protest and strike against the murderous activities of right-wing thugs was brutally suppressed by the police, and many protestors were killed.

With the onset of the 1930s, and with the backing of the Catholic Church, the chancellor Engelbert Dollfuss instigated a single-party-state under Austrofascism in defiance of the Austrian Nazis who favoured union with Germany. In the end the Nazis were to win out when, in 1938, the Anschluss (union) made Austria a province of a wider Germany.

Vienna★★★

VIENNA TODAY

After the end of World War II, Vienna was occupied by France, the Soviet Union, Britain and the US and divided into four zones. It was not until 1955 that the Second Republic was established and the new state treaty signed. The date on which this occurred, 26 October, is now a public holiday. Austria also undertook to be a neutral state, and its position between East and West during the Cold War meant that it played an important part in negotiations between the two power blocs, perhaps most notably when Kennedy and Kruschchov met at Schönbrunn in 1961. Under the leadership of the popular social democratic chancellor Bruno Kreisky, Vienna also became one of the headquarters of the UN as well as that of other important international organisations such as OPEC and the IAEA. Vienna did not neglect its vast cultural heritage: it has continued to promote itself as the world's premier centre for classical music, and to protect its considerable architectural legacy. For these efforts, the old city was made a UNESCO World Heritage Site.

Drinking in Vienna

A convivial atmosphere can be enjoyed in the **Keller**, where snacks and cold meals are downed with a glass of beer or wine. Some establishments (*Gasthäuser, Weinhäuser*) offering good home cooking are known as **Beisel**. Other places for locals to wind down are taverns (*Weinstuben*) and the cheerful wine pubs called **Heuriger**. The latter are located in the wine-growing villages surrounding the city, such as Grinzing. Usually run by the wine-growers, they are recognised by the pine branch fastened above the entrance. In cosy rooms or leafy courtyards, you can sample the new wine (*Heuriger*) along with snacks or a simple meal.

▶ **Population:** 1,750,000.

Info: Albertinaplatz 1, A-1025. ℰ0124 555. www.wien.info. Also in the Vienna Airport arrivals hall.

▶ **Location:** Vienna is in the northwest corner of Austria, not far from the borders with the Czech Republic, Slovakia and Hungary. Alt. 156m/512ft.

P **Parking:** Finding parking is easy thanks to an electronic guide system that directs you to the nearest garage and also shows the number of available spaces. 24hr parking garages in city centre (1. Bezirk, the first district) include: Am Morzinplatz (Franz-Josefs-Kai), Rathauspark (Ring/Stadiongasse), Am Hof, Beethovenplatz 3, Cobdengasse 2. For a complete list, visit www.parkeninwien.at.

Don't Miss: Hofburg, Kulturhistorisches Museum, Stephansdom, Schloss Schönbrunn.

Timing: Allow at least three days for your Vienna stay.

Kids: Zoom Kindermuseum, Prater, Tiergarten, The Irrgarten and Labyrinth, Technisches Museum, Naturhistorisches Museum.

Today Vienna is an intriguing mix of old and new, tradition and innovation. It still has its coffeehouses, the Vienna Philharmonic and *Heurige,* but also exciting modern architecture, a lively student scene, and festivals celebrating the most contemporary works of art and music. Its wealth of museums and galleries, palaces and churches, continue to attract huge numbers of visitors and yet Vienna remains a vibrant, livable city.

GETTING THERE

BY AIR: Vienna International Airport. *(Tourist Office open daily 7am–10pm) SE of city centre. Take S-Bahn Line 7 (to Wien Mitte) or City Airport Train (CAT).*
BY RAIL: Westbahnhof *(7min W of city centre via U-Bahn Line 3).*
Haupbahnhof *(5min S of city centre via U-Bahn Line 1).*
BY CAR: From north: Floridsdorfer Brücke, Donauinsel exit. **From south** (via A2): Zentrum exit. **From west** via A1: Wien/Auhof petrol station.

TOURIST INFORMATION

CITY CENTRE: *Am Albertinaplatz 1, 1. Bezirk, daily 9am–7pm,* ✆*0124 555.*
The tourist office publishes a free monthly cultural calendar of events.
Vienna on the Internet – *www.wien. info* (tourist information) and *www. wien.gv.at/english* (city government).
WIEN-KARTE: Vienna Card *(€13.90/ €21.90/P24.90; www.wienkarte.at)* permits unlimited travel on the city's underground/subway **(U-Bahn)**, bus, tram, and most night buses for 24hr, 48hr or 72hr, starting from first validation. In addition, you qualify for 1-3 consecutive days of discounts at museums, sights and attractions, and for certain purchases and meals. Full details are included in the coupon booklet that comes with the ticket. It is available at many hotels, tourist information offices, ticket agencies and information offices of the Viennese transport authorities, or online.
BUS TOURS: Vienna Sightseeing Tours, *Rainergasse 1, 4. Bezirk,* ✆*01712 46 83. www.viennasightseeing.at.*
Hop-on Hop-off city tour operates every 6-60min (mid-Apr–mid-Nov; frequency varies by bus line) among 50 stops from *9.30am–8pm.* Commentaries in 12 languages (including English and German). Cost of a ticket valid for one day is €25 (children *€13*), available from any hotel in Vienna, or travel agencies in Austria and abroad.
The company also offers coach tours *Apr–Oct daily 9.45am and 2.45pm* with a guided tour of Schloss Schönbrunn. Takes 3hr30min. Tour costs €47 per person (including pick-up from hotel).
THEMED TOURS: Vienna Ring tram – *Daily departures every 30min 10am– 5.30pm.* The Staßenbahn-Modelle departs from Schwedenplatz. Takes about 30min. Tickets from Wiener Linien information office at Karlsplatz U-Bahn station. €9, children €4.
✆*01 7909 121. www.wienerlinien.at.*
Horse-drawn carriage tour – *Fiakers* (horse-drawn carriages) take tourists around the city centre. Stands are located on Albertinaplatz and Atephansplatz, and also by the Burgtheater. However, visitors might want to take into account that there have been serious concerns raised about the welfare of the horses and there are efforts to ban the fiakers. Allow €60–€100.
WALKING TOURS: The city of Vienna organises themed walks around town, such as Musical Capital of the World, Jugendstil, The Viennese Coffeehouse (€16, €14 with Vienna card, €8 children; ✆*01 774 89 01; www.wienguide.at*). Takes 90-120min. Monthly programme available from the tourist office at Albertinaplatz 1, including multilingual tour guides, bike and Segway tours (*www. sightseeing-vienna.at*).
"The Third Man" – Part of this tour takes place underground in the sewers of Vienna, and re-traces the steps of the protagonist in Orson Welles' classic film, *The Third Man*. The interesting tour (about 45min) leaves from opposite the Café Museum in the Girardipark, Karlsplatz. During heavy rain, tours do not take place; only children older than 12 are admitted; sturdy footwear is recommended; tours are in English or German. **Advance**

Post offices

The second and third digits in Viennese **post codes** denote the district (Bezirk) in question, thus 1070 denotes the 7 Bezirk, Vienna. The main post offices have 'SB-Zone' (self-service) and are open 24hr/7, but not staffed around the clock. Telephone enquiries can be directed to the Austrian Post hotline at t0180 010 100.

Hauptpostamt, *Fleischmarkt 19, 1. Bezirk.*
Post am Westbahnhof, *Europaplatz 3, 15. Bezirk.*
Post am Franz-Josef-Bahnhof, *Althahnstraße 10, 9. Bezirk.*

booking and information from *Wien Kanal, Modecenterstraße 14 (Block C), A-1030 Wien, ℘01 4000 30 33, www.drittemanntour.at.* **Vienna Walks & Talks** offers a wide range of lively, themed tours. See *www.viennawalks.at.*

CYCLE TOURS: Cyclists in Vienna have 10,00km/621mi of cycle paths at their disposal. Those arriving by train can hire bicycles from Citybike *(☞see above);* lockers are available in train stations. Other cycle hire outlets can be found on the Donauinsel (from about €5/hour or €25/day with some form of identification such as a passport left as a security).

The **Citybike** network offers bicycles for hire from docking stations across the city. The bikes are free for the first hour, and then cost between €1 and €4 for subsequent hours. Payment can be made by credit card or Tourist Card. *www.citybikewien.at.*

Pedal Power cycle tours through Vienna are offered in various languages *Mar–Oct Fri–Sun 10am and 2.30pm, May–Sept daily*; takes about 3hr; €29; further details from *℘01 729 72 34, www.pedalpower.at.*

Segway Tours are available from the City Segway Rental Store Vienna, *℘01 512 5918, www.segwayrentalvienna.com.*

BOAT TOURS: DSG Blue Danube Schiffahrt GmbH *(Handelskai 265, A-1020 Wien; ℘01 588 80; www.ddsg-blue-danube.at)* offers boat tours on the Danube River *Apr–Nov.*

PUBLIC TRANSPORT

Viennese transport authorities, Wiener Linien, operate services in the central zones of the Vienna city area (all districts) and are linked with the east Austrian transport authority (Verkehrsverbund Ost-Region, VOR). Written enquiries and requests for information by telephone can be addressed to either organization:

Wiener Linien, *Erdbergstraße 202, A-1031 Wien, ℘01 790 90. www.wienerlinien.at.*

Verkehrsverbund Ost-Region, *Europaplatz 2/E 1.15, A-1150 Wien, information hotline ℘0810 22 23 24. www.vor.at.* Tourists are advised to pay a visit in person to one of the **information and ticket offices** in the following U-Bahn stations: Stephansplatz, Karlsplatz, Landstraße/Wien-Mitte, Westbahnhof, Schottentor, Meidling, Hietzing, Florisdorf or Erdberg.

FINDING YOUR WAY AROUND

See the inside back cover for a map of the U-Bahn network. A map of the network is also included on the city map published by the Vienna tourist office and available from most hotels, among other places. These outlets can also supply timetables for Vienna's transport system or the more comprehensive timetable, as well as selling tickets (runabout or magnetic strip tickets), or go online to *www.wienerlinien.at.*

Tickets – Tickets are valid for travel on the underground/subway (U-Bahn), tram, high-speed rail (Schnellbahn) and bus. Single tickets (€2.20, or €2.30 if issued on board a bus or tram) can be validated using ticket machines on the transport in question or in U-Bahn stations. It is cheaper, however, to buy tickets in advance from ticket offices or an authorised tobacconist's (Tabaktrafik). Tickets that are well-suited to the needs of tourists include the **24-** (€7.60), **48-** (€13.30) and **72-** (€16.50) **hour Wien-Karte (Vienna Card)** or the **8-day Klima-Karte (Climate ticket)** (€38.40; this ticket allows the bearer unlimited travel within Vienna city centre limits per strip validated, on the date it was validated). The **Wiener Einkaufskarte** (Viennese shopper's ticket) offers an alternative deal: for €6.10 you can make unlimited trips in the city centre for one day *(Mon–Sat 8am–8pm)*. There is always the option of the Wien-Karte, permitting three days of unlimited travel on Viennese public transport *(see Vienna Card above)*.

Night line – When normal city transport finishes running for the day (after about 12.30am until about 4.30am), 21 night bus lines operate in the city centre every 30min, for which special rates apply (runabout tickets are valid on these night buses; tickets available from ticket machines on the bus or as strip tickets bought in advance). Further details and a map of the night line services are available from indicated Vienna transport authority ticket offices.

INNER-CITY CAR PARKS: Vienna old town and the surrounding districts *(Bezirke 1–9 and 20)* are **fee-paying short-stay (2hr) parking zones**. However, these are only signposted as such at the entrance to each district concerned (no further indication is given in the streets

Tram on the Ringstraße
© C. S. Pereyra/age fotostock

themselves – a paid-up parking ticket is obligatory from the minute you park). In commercial streets, parking regulations may vary, in which case these will be specifically indicated. Pre-paid parking tickets can be bought from most authorised tobacconists (Tabaktrafiken) and banks, stations and from Vienna transport authority (Wiener Linien) ticket offices (€1 per half hour). To validate the ticket, write the year and tick the day, month and time. Visitors who have booked a hotel should phone ahead to confirm where to leave their car.

Numerous underground or multi-storey **car parks** are open daily 24hr. The following underground car parks can be found in the 1 Bezirk district: *Franz-Josefs-Kai (Morzinplatz), Rathauspark (Dr.-Karl-Lueger-Ring), (Kärtner Straße 51), Am Hof, Beethovenplatz 3, Cobdengasse 2.* An overview of car parks in Vienna can be requested from the tourist office (*℘0124 555*) or found online at *www.parkeninwien.at*.

The Ring★★

This circular boulevard surrounds the Innere Stadt (the "inner city", more commonly referred to as the First District). It symbolised the entrance of Vienna into the modern era when the old city walls were torn down during the 19C and the space opened up as a ring road. In the 21C it remains at the centre of life in Vienna. Political and cultural institutions, grand cafés and public parks and gardens all lie along this artery, which brilliantly captures the allure of the capital city.

●•WALKING TOUR

1 TOUR OF THE RING ★

Making a complete tour of the Ring is quite an interesting way to discover the city. It is a pleasant 4km/2.5mi walk, but you can also take the tram or bicycle if you are not feeling like Sigmund Freud, who used to complete a circuit of the Ring every day. **By tram** take line number 2 (from Schwedenplatz to Kärntner Ring-Oper) then the number 1 (from Kärtner Ring-Oper to Schwedendeplatz). Driving is not recommended as the ring is busy and you will have little time to see the sights. The walk below starts at the Börse near Schottentor on the north side of the 1st District. Allow 2hrs 30min.

Börse (Stock Exchange)

Schottenring 16.
The architect Theophil Hansen was responsible for some of the grandest buildings on the Ring (Parliament, Academy of Fine Arts). Along with Carl Tietz, he designed the Stock Exchange in a neo-Renaissance style (1874–77).

Votivkirche (Votive Church)

Two tall spires flank the west door of this neo-Gothic church, completed in 1879. Note the Antwerp Altar in the right-hand chapel beyond the transept and the tomb of Count Salm from 1530, with its **reclining figure★** in the baptistry.

Universität (University)

On the north side of the Rathausplatz, the Italian Renaissance-style university by Heinrich von Ferstel houses the second-oldest German-language university (after Prague).

Beethoven-Gedenkstätte Pasqualatihaus★ (Beethoven House)

Mölker Bastei 8. ●•Guided tours (1hr) Tue–Sun 10am–1pm, 2pm–6pm. ◷Closed 1 Jan, 1 May, 25 Dec. €5. ✆01 535 89 05. www.wienmuseum.at.
Ludwig van Beethoven lived in this house in 1804 and from 1813 to 1815. It is named for the owner, Josef Benedikt Baron Pasqualati. Among other works, Beethoven composed the opera *Fidelio* and *Symphonies 4, 5, 7* and *8* here.

Rathaus (Town Hall)

●•Guided tour (45min) Mon, Wed, Fri 1pm (except when council is in session). ◷Closed holidays. ✆01 525 50.
The neo-Gothic city hall is linked to the Ring by attractive gardens. The tower is topped by the famous *Rathausmann* carrying the city flag. Summer concerts are held in the arcaded courtyard. The reception rooms, council chambers and the huge banqueting hall are all open to the public.

Burgtheater★ (Court Theatre)

●•Guided tour (50min) Burgtheater: Sept–Jun daily 3pm. €7. ✆01 51444 41 40. www.burgtheater.at.
Opened in 1888, this theatre replaced the Hofburgtheater (Court Theater) on the Michaelerplatz, founded in 1741 under Maria Theresia. Gottfried Semper was responsible for the neo-Renaissance façade, while Carl Hasenauer designed the neo-Baroque interior. The Burgtheater has long been considered among the most important German-language theatres, and an engagement here was, and still is, the summit of an acting career. Tours include the **ceiling frescoes★**, painted by Gustav Klimt, his brother Ernst, and Franz Matsch.

Court furniture

Court furniture inspectors were entrusted with transporting furniture, carpets, tapestries and other items to the various royal premises, storing and looking after them. Until the early 19C only the Hofburg was permanently furnished, while the Imperial summer residences and hunting lodges were furnished only when royals were in residence. For coronations and royal weddings (sometimes as far away as Frankfurt or Florence), furniture had to be transported for as many as 1,000 people. Up to 100 wagons would leave in advance of the royal party to outfit the living and function rooms. When Franz II took the reigns (c.1808), the less frequently used palaces and residences were gradually left ready furnished.

Parlament (Parliament)

Guided Tours (55min) Sept–mid-Jul Mon–Thu 11am, 2pm, 3pm and 4pm, Fri also 1pm, Sat also noon; rest of the year Mon–Sat 11am, noon, 1pm, 2pm, 3pm and 4pm. ◓Closed holidays. ⊜€5. www.parlament.gv.at.

The Parliament (1873–83) was built by Theophil Hansen with the façade of an elegant Greek Temple, the classical elements further reinforced by the statue of Athene that stands at the front. The aim of the architect was to pay homage to ancient Athens as the cradle of European democracy.

The richly decorated interior, including the vestibule, hall of columns, ballroom and meeting rooms, has a wealth of statues, stuccoes and paintings.

Volksgarten★

This pleasant, quiet park with its pools, statues and famous rose garden is great for strolling and picnicking. A replica Greek temple, the **Theseus Tempel**, adds an exotic element.

Neue Burg (New Palace)

The Neue Burg was the last wing to be added to the Hofburg, completed just before World War I. It now houses several museums.

Maria-Theresien-Platz

This square's central element is the 1888 monument to Maria Theresia, which is buttressed by equestrian statues of several of her generals. Other figures represent statesmen as well as the composers Gluck, Haydn and Mozart. The two domed buildings facing each other across the square were constructed between 1872 and 1891. They house the Imperial collections in the **Kunsthistorisches Museum★★★** and the **Naturhistorisches Museum★**.

Burggarten (Palace Gardens)

Between the Ring and the Hofburg lie the palace gardens. First laid out in the 19C, they have been open to the public since 1919. At the entrance stands a statue to Goethe, and there are other memorials to Franz Joseph, Franz I (on horseback) and Mozart.

Akademie der bildenden Künste – Gemäldegalerie★★ (Fine Arts Academy)

Enter from Makartgasse. ◓Open Tue–Sun 10am–6pm. ☛Guided tours available. ◓Closed 1 Jan, 24–25 Dec. ⊜€8. ✆01 58816 22 22. www.akademiegalerie.at.

This outstanding collection of paintings is housed in a neo-Renaissance building by Theophil Hansen. It includes the extraordinary *Triptych of the Last Judgement*★★★ by **Hieronymus Bosch** (1460–1516), a terrifying work where monsters and phenomena symbolise the sins and suffering of humankind. Other highlights include: *Lucretia*★★ by Lucas Cranach the Elder, *Boys playing Dice* by Bartolomé Esteban Murillo, a *Self-portrait*★ (c.1615) by Anthony van Dyck and *Portrait of a young Woman*★★ (1632) by Rembrandt. Top works from the 18C collection are the eight *Views of Venice*★ by Francesco Guardi and the famous *Still-life with Flowers and Fruit*★ (1703) by Rachel Ruysch.

Vienna, Capital of Music

Venerable traditions

St. Peter's in Salzburg may have been the cradle of sacred music in the German-speaking world but, by the 12C, Vienna under the Babenbergs had become an important centre of secular music performed by Minnesänger (minstrels or troubadours). Vienna's status as musical capital was further cemented when Maximilian I moved his dazzling court choir here from Innsbruck, which still thrills modern audiences in the **Hofkapelle**.

The great days of Viennese music

The late 18C was dominated by the Classical works of **Joseph Haydn** and **Wolfgang Amadeus Mozart**. The princely palaces became veritable musical workshops, places for great performers and composers to meet. The start of the 19C saw **Ludwig van Beethoven** dominate Vienna's musical life. Around 1825 the musical soirées known as **"Schubertiades"** began, at which Schubert performed Lieder for a circle of friends.

After the revolution of 1848, music societies proliferated, promoting high standards of concert performance and of musical education. The most illustrious of these societies was the "Friends of Music," which counted **Brahms** among its conductors. Brahms enjoyed unparalleled prestige, but **Bruckner**, who had left his native Linz to become court organist, found his sacred masterpieces to be beyond the comprehension of the Viennese public. **Mahler** used his ten years in Vienna as Kapellmeister (conductor of the court orchestra) to undertake the reforms that helped usher in a new musical era.

The force of destiny (1770–1827)

Few other artists were more captivated and inspired by the romantic countryside surrounding Vienna than **Ludwig van Beethoven**. Beethoven arrived in the city at the age of 20 and soon charmed its people with his virtuosity as a pianist. It was in Vienna where he created the works that revolutionised the language of music: the Eroica Symphony, the famous opera *Fidelio*, the Fifth Symphony, and the well-known and monumental Ninth Symphony.

The Second Vienna School

This "school" refers to the works of the Viennese **Arnold Schoenberg** and his students, who ushered in a musical revolution. Schoenberg's 12-tone composition established new relationships between sounds freed from traditional harmonic conventions. Originally self-taught, Schoenberg later studied with the composer Alexander Zemlinsky (1871–1942) and first composed works that still show affinities with the post-Romantic style. But he soon left behind the boundaries of tonality with such works as the Second String Quartet (1908) and the 1912 *Pierrot*

Rock me Amadeus

Two hundred years after Mozart, another Austrian musician won world-wide fame. We're of course talking about Vienna's own Hans Hölzl, better known as the eccentric stage persona, **Falco**. In 1985, he not only won over European audiences with his mega-hit song "Rock me Amadeus," but even hit the top of the American charts, an outstanding feat for a German-language pop song. With his characteristic combination of speech-song and catchy tunes, Falco is the only Austrian pop star to have made it big on the world stage. He was killed in a car accident in the Dominican Republic in 1998 and – unlike his illustrious predecessor – was awarded an "honorary grave" by the City of Vienna in the Zentralfriedhof.

Lunaire, a melodrama in 21 sections for narrator and five instruments, which brought him international recognition. Schoenberg exercised a profound influence on a number of his pupils, most notably Webern and Berg, both Viennese. Webern is best known for his austere miniatures, while Berg's greatest works are arguably his operas *Wozzeck* and *Lulu*.

Johann Strauss the Younger (1888) by Eisenmenger

The triumph of the Viennese Waltz

One byproduct of the Congress of Vienna was the popularization of the Viennese **waltz**. This vigorous and light-hearted dance kept the city on its toes throughout the 19C. Polished, refined, and made a genre in its own right by **Joseph Lanner** and Johann Strauss the Elder, the waltz came to dominate the dance floor under **Johann Strauss the Younger**, whose tributes to the city *(Vienna Blood, Tales from the Vienna Woods)* got an enthusiastic reception.

Viennese Ball Season

During the winter in Vienna, one ball follows close behind another. The famous Emperor's Ball is held on New Year's Eve, reawakening the elegance and splendour of the former Imperial court at the Hofburg. During Carnival time (Fasching), the various associations and professional guilds put on about 300 balls, many in magnificent surroundings (Rathaus, Hofburg, Musikverein). These include the Floral Ball, organised by gardeners and florists, and balls of the Viennese Coffee-Houses and the Vienna Philharmonic Orchestra. Doctors and lawyers each have a ball, and so do hunters and firemen. The most famous is the **Opera Ball**, held in February at the Staatsoper, an exclusive evening (primarily) for the rich and connected, while the most spectacular is the **Life Ball**, a glamourous event with a heavy dose of burlesque that has a serious purpose: to raise funds and awareness for charities dealing with HIV and AIDS.

Painting showing the Ball at the time of Johann Strauss the Younger (1876)

189

Staatsoper★★ (State Opera)

Guided tours (40min) daily, see the board outside the opera house, website or phone for times. ☉*Closed 24 Dec and during rehearsals.* ♿ ☞€7.50. ☏01 514 44 26 06. www.wiener-staatsoper.at.

Begun in 1861 and formally opened in 1869 by Emperor Franz Joseph II with a performance of Mozart's *Don Giovanni*, the opera house was the first of the great public edifices to be completed along the Ring. It has since been helmed by such outstanding directors as Mahler, Strauss, Karl Böhm, von Karajan, Maazel and Abbado. Players in the famous **Vienna Philharmonic** (Wiener Philharmoniker) are recruited from the members of the Staatsoper orchestra.

Tours include the stage and backstage, **interval rooms** and the Gustav Mahler Room decorated with modern tapestries illustrating scenes from Mozart's *Magic Flute*. Décor in the **foyer★** is the work of the painter Moritz von Schwind. The **tea room** and the magnificent **grand staircase★** were among the few sections of the building spared by a 1945 fire.

👥 Haus der Musik★ (House of Music)

Seilerstätte 30. ☉*Open year-round daily 10am–10pm (last entry 9.30pm).* ☞€13, *children* €6. ♿ ☏01 513 48 50. www.hdm.at.

This former palace of the archduke Charles is a museum of music. With its late opening hours it is a good place to spend an evening, especially for visitors with children. The first floor is given over to the history of the Wiener Philharmoniker, where a game allows you to make up your own Viennese waltz. Above is the Haus der Musik itself. Through a number of inventive and interactive displays the museums explores the nature of sound, spatial perception and the history of music in Vienna.

Stadtpark (Municipal Park)

Before you reach MAK you pass beside this attractively landscaped park, laid out in 1862 and famous for its statues of musicians, including Schubert, Bruck-

ner, Lehar and Stolz. Pride of place goes to Vienna's iconic memorial honouring Johann Strauss.

Österreichisches Museum für Angewandte Kunst (MAK)★★

☉*Open Tue 10am–10pm, Wed–Sun 10am–6pm.* ☉*Closed 1 Jan and 25 Dec* ♿☞€9.90 (audio guide €2). ☏01 72 80 00. www.mak.at.

The Austrian museum of applied arts occupies a neo-Renaissance building by Heinrich von Ferstel and has a remarkable – on-going and changing – **display concept★★** where the layout of certain rooms was entrusted to artists: pieces of Baroque, Rococo and Classical furniture were set out by **Donald Judd**, and Barbara Bloom reduced the Historicism and Jugendstil display to Michael Thonet's seminal bentwood chairs.

Highlights include **liturgical vestments★** (c. 1260) from the Benedictine monastery of Göss in Styria; a **tabletop★★** of painted cherrywood from late 15C Swabia; an amazing Biedermeier **cherrywood secretaire★** made in Vienna in 1825; a superb collection of **Oriental carpets and rugs★★**; **drawings★★** prepared by Gustav Klimt for the Palais Stoclet in Brussels; and a selection of items from the **Wiener Werkstätte★★**.

Postsparkasse and Wagner: Werk★

Georg-Coch-Platz 2. Tram lines 1 & 2, Julius-Raab-Platz, U-bahn 3, Stubentor, 1 & 4 Schedenplatz. ☉*Open Mon–Fri 9am–5pm.* ☉*Closed bank holidays, 24-26 Dec.* ☞€8, *main hall free.* ♿ ☏01 599 05 33 825. www.ottowagner.com.

Otto Wagner's seminal building, the postal savings bank was completed in 1912 using the time's modern materials (aluminium, glass bricks) and construction methods. Still a bank today, the building contains a small lobby that recently opened as **Wagner: Werk**, an exhibit about the architect containing photos, documents and other items.

Old Town

Vienna's Old Town, the area that lies within the Ringstraße and also known as the First District, still retains much of its medieval street pattern. A UNESCO World Heritage Site, it contains historic churches, palaces and museums, and is an altogether fascinating area to wander around and explore.

✏📍WALKING TOUR

② **TOUR OF OLD VIENNA ★★**

Between the cathedral and the Danube canal, the heart of Old Vienna evokes a special atmosphere despite reconstruction.

▶ Start from Stephansplatz.

Stephansdom★★★ (St. Stephen's Cathedral)
🕐*Open year-round Mon–Sat 6am–10pm, Sun 7am–10pm.*
✏Guided tour in English (30min) Mon–Sat 10.30am, in German daily 3pm, €5.50. & ✆01 515 52 30 54. www.stephanskirche.at.
Vienna's cathedral is its most dramatic landmark. With a vast roof (exactly twice the height of its walls) of glittering tiles and its mighty south tower (the famous **Steffl**), the edifice exudes a magnificence and significance unparalleled in Austria.

History
A Romanesque basilica consecrated in 1147 originally stood on the site of the present building. It was badly damaged by the great fire of 1258 and today only the west front with the **Riesentor★★** (👁*see Introduction: ABC of Architecture)* and the **Heidentürme** (Towers of the Heathens) remain.
The first Gothic building was begun in 1304, and the Stephansdom was built over the next two centuries. It became a cathedral in 1469. Damaged during the 1683 Turkish siege, it again suffered damage in 1945 when flying sparks from nearby burning houses set fire to the north tower. After the war, it was swiftly restored.

Exterior
The diminutive size of the Stephansplatz, centre of the medieval city, accentuates the immensity of the cathedral, whose **Stephansturm★★★**, one complete steeple or "Steffl," soars to a height of 136.7m/449ft. The north steeple was never completed, but contains the great 21.3t bell known as the **Pummerin** (the largest bell in Austria), which peals only on special occasions and rings in the New Year. The bronze bell was cast in 1711 from 180 Turkish cannons captured in 1683, and hung originally in the south steeple. It was shattered in 1945, and a new Pummerin bell was cast from the remains in 1951.
The crowning glory of Stephansdom is its highly decorative roof. It is covered in 230,000 multicoloured glazed tiles arranged in chevron and diamond patterns. Above the choir on the south side is a mosaic depicting the Habsburg coat of arms with its double-headed eagle. On the north side are the coats of arms of the City of Vienna and the Republic of Austria.
The intricately carved Romanesque west door, called the **Riesentor★** (Giants' Gate), is crowded with statues, including one of Christ in Majesty on the tympanum and others of the Apostles in the recessed arches. Walk around the cathedral in a counter-clockwise direction to the copy of a Gothic lantern of the dead from the old cemetery of St. Stephan (now Stephansplatz) at the southwest corner.

▶ Enter the cathedral through the Giants' Gate (Riesentour).

Interior
Clearly inspired by the traditional Germanic hall church, the long, majestic nave (107m/351ft) is ingeniously linked to the three-aisled chancel. The magnificent carved stone **pulpit★★** dates from c1480 and is a Gothic masterpiece. Its creator has never been identified even

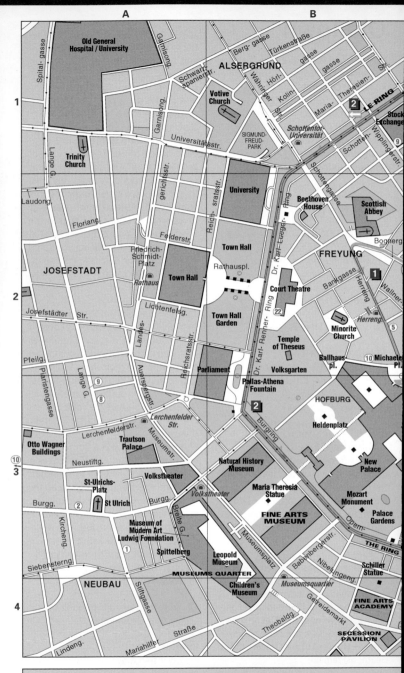

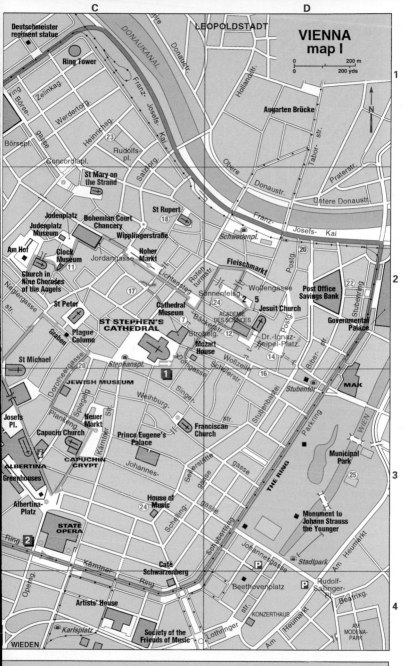

193

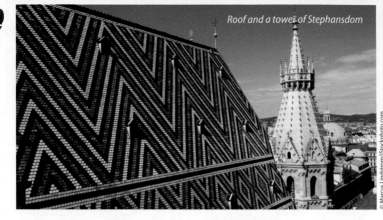

Roof and a tower of Stephansdom

© Marcus Lindstrom/iStockphoto.com

though he portrayed himself, under the ramp, holding his sculptor's tools and looking out of a half-open window (which is why he is known as the *Fenstergucker*). All around are the exceptionally finely carved busts of St. Augustine, St. Ambrose, St. Gregory the Great and St. Jerome.

The left apsidal chapel, known as the Frauenchor (women's choir), contains a painted and gilded altarpiece known as the **Wiener Neustadt altarpiece★**(15C). On the central panel are the Virgin and Child flanked by St. Barbara and St. Catherine. Above is the Coronation of the Virgin Mary. The altarpiece on the high altar in the chancel represents the stoning of St. Stephen.

The right apsidal chapel, the Apostelchor (Apostles' choir), preserves the late 15C **tomb★★** of Emperor Friedrich III, made of red Salzburg marble by Nikolaus Gerhart of Leyden. The artist illustrated the struggle between Good and Evil, by symbolizing the evil spirits as animals trying to enter the tomb to disturb the Emperor, while the good spirits, represented by local personages, prevent them from doing so.

Catacombs
Guided tours (every 15–30min) Mon–Sat 10am–11.30am, 1.30pm–4.30pm, Sun 1.30pm–4.30pm. €5.50. *01 515 52 30 50.*
In the catacombs are urns containing the organs of the emperors of Austria, and chapels established since 1945.

Cathedral Towers
Südturm: open year-round daily 9am–5.30pm. €4.50. *Nordturm (lift to Pummerin great bell): year-round daily 9am–5.30pm.* €5.50.
01 515 52 30 54.
The south tower (Südturm) can be climbed to a height of 73m/240ft by a 343-step tight spiral staircase, while the platform of the north tower (which houses the Pummerin bell) 60m/197ft above ground is reached by lift. In fine weather there are good **views★★** of the city, the Kahlenberg heights and the Danube plain to the east.

Dom- und Diözesanmuseum★ (Cathedral Museum)
Stephansplatz 6. Closed for *renovation until late 2016.* *01 515 52 33 00. www.dommuseum.at.*
This museum in the 14C former Zwettler Hof displays a fine collection of paintings and sculptures alongside the cathedral's most precious treasures.

▷ Behind the cathedral, make your way down Domgasse.

Mozarthaus Vienna★ (Mozart House)
Domgasse 5. Open year-round daily *10am–7pm.* €11. *01 512 17 91. www.mozarthausvienna.at.*
The house where Mozart lived from 1784 to 1787 is now a museum with exhibits about his life and times. Visits start on the third floor, which focuses on his daily

The Coffeehouse

When the Turks fled the city in 1683, they left behind a large quantity of coffee beans, thereby inadvertently launching a great Viennese tradition. Since the 19C the coffeehouse has been an indispensable social part of middle class and intellectual life, a place for people to meet, converse and read the newspapers. The city's classic coffeehouses fill up as the working day ends. Discreetly attired waiters serve the traditional glass of water alongside the coffee, which is available in a bewildering variety *(see below)* and often paired with a piece of cake or pastry. Once the coffee is finished, the waiter collects the cup and brings another glass of water while also keeping the customer supplied with newspapers and magazines. In fact, it is not unusual to linger for hours without repeating the order.

Listed below are some descriptions of the more commonly served types of Viennese coffee, among the 30 or so preparations that are available *(see p230 for a selection of the best places to partake of this Viennese tradition)*:

Großer/kleiner Schwarzer large/small cup of black coffee

Großer/kleiner Brauner large/small cup of black coffee with a dash of milk

Verlängerter Schwarzer/Brauner "Schwarzer"/"Brauner" diluted with water

Einspänner black coffee served in a glass with whipped cream (Schlagobers)

Fiaker black coffee in a glass with a tot of rum

Franziskaner coffee mixed with chocolate chips

Kaffee verkehrt coffee with more milk than coffee

Kaisermelange coffee with egg yolk and brandy

Kapuziner black coffee with a small blob of whipped cream

Konsul mocha diluted with cold water

Mazagran iced coffee with rum

Melange milky coffee (can be served with whipped cream)

Türkischer Kaffee strong coffee prepared in a small copper coffee pot, served hot in tiny cups

Verlängerter mocha diluted with hot water.

Traditionally you don't ask for a cup of coffee (eine Tasse Kaffee) in Vienna – it is "eine Schale Kaffee" (literally, a bowl of coffee). Depending on how much milk or cream you would like, coffee can be ordered "Braun," or even "Gold."

Café Museum, designed by Adolf Loos

© Maurizio Borgese/hemis.fr

life, his sponsors, his passion for gambling and the relationship with the Freemasons. The second floor concentrates on his opera compositions, while on the first is the actual apartment where he lived. The tour ends in a somewhat bizarre marble-clad shrine.

▶ Domgasse and Strobelgasse lead to busy Wollzeile. Take Essiggasse almost opposite, then turn right onto elegant Bäckerstraße.

Jesuitenkirche★ (Jesuit Church)

Dr-Ignaz-Seipel-Platz 1. ⏱Open year-round Mon–Sat 7am–7pm, Sun 8am–7pm. ♿ ☎01 512 52 320. www.jesuitenwien1.at.

Like the Salzburg Cathedral, this church, Baroque style, was inspired by the church of Gesù in Rome. Interesting features include the **pulpit★**, inlaid with mother-of-pearl, and the dome with *trompe-l'œil* painting by Andrea Pozzo, the Jesuit lay brother who was also responsible for the high altar.

▶ Take Sonnenfelsgasse and then Schönlaterngasse.

Schönlaterngasse

One of the most charming streets in the Old Town, the winding "road of the beautiful lantern" takes its name from the 18C iron lantern on the façade of the house at no. 6 (the lantern is a replica; the original is in the Wien Museum). Facing no. 5 is the entrance to the Heiligenkreuzerhof.

▶ Enter the courtyard.

Heiligenkreuzerhof

The courtyard of this 18C mansion, a former dependence of Heiligenkreuz Abbey (*☙see STIFT HEILIGENKREUZ*), is a popular retreat with artists and writers. The chapel of St. Bernhard has an altarpiece by Martin Altomonte.

▶ Take Postgasse to the Fleischmarkt.

Fleischmarkt

The meat market dates back to 1220. At no. 13 is the Griechenkirche zur hl. Dreifaltigkeit (the Greek Church of the Holy Trinity) with its gilded and brick façade. It was first built by Peter Mölln between 1782 and 1787, but was later reconstructed by Theophil Hansen, who gave it the present Byzantine look.

At no. 11, the **Griechenbeisl** ("Greek tavern") is one of the oldest eateries in Vienna; it has welcomed guests such as Johannes Brahms, Mark Twain, Franz Schubert, Richard Wagner and many others. The walls of one of the rooms is covered with the signatures of famous writers.

The small street just to the side of the inn, **Griechengasse★**, is named after the Greek merchants who came to settle in the district in the 18C. The lane still has Gothic remains, including, at no. 9, a 13C tower.

The façade of no. 7 has a Madonna in a niche overlooking a Rococo wrought-iron lantern. In the courtyard is another Gothic tower with Turkish inscriptions on a wood panel, dating from the siege of 1683.

▶ Leaving Fleischmarkt, turn left into Köllnerhofgasse and then right into Lichtensteg. Carry straight on into Hoher Markt.

Hoher Markt

Interesting remains were found here of the Roman camp of Vindobona. In medieval times, the High Market was the heart of the city, and the place where the gallows stood. Today the square is dominated by the 1732 **Virgin Mary's Wedding fountain** (Vermählungsbrunnen) by Joseph Emmanuel Fischer von Erlach. At no. 10 is a Jugendstil **clock★** (1913) by Franz Matsch.

▶ Cross the Hoher Markt and go down Wipplingerstraße.

Wipplingerstraße

Two handsome Baroque buildings grace this street. On the left, the **Altes Rathaus**, Vienna's town hall from the

14C to 19C, features the **fountain of Andromeda**★ (1741) by Raphael Donner in its courtyard.

On the opposite side the old **Böhmische Hofkanzlei** (Bohemian Court Chancery) has an outstanding façade by Johann Bernhard Fischer von Erlach (1708–14).

▷ Skirt the chancellery to arrive at Judenplatz, the heart of Vienna's medieval Jewish ghetto.

Museum Judenplatz

Judenplatz 8. 🕑*Open year-round Sun–Thu 10am–6pm, Fri 10am–5pm.* 🕑*Closed Rosh Hashanah and Yom Kippur.* ✏€10 (includes Jewish Museum Dorotheergasse). ✆01 535 04 31. www.jmw.at.

This museum is dedicated to the Jewish community of Vienna during the Middle Ages. The rooms in the basement have reconstructions of the synagogue and Jewish district around 1400. You can visit the foundations of the first synagogue in Vienna and see some of the artefacts recovered during the excavations.

▷ Go down narrow Parisergasse to Am Hof square.

Uhrenmuseum der Stadt Wien★ (Clock Museum)

Schulhof 2. 🕑*Open year-round Tue–Sun 10am–6pm.* 🕑*Closed 1 Jan, 1 May, 25 Dec.* ✏€7. ✆01 533 22 65. www.wienmuseum.at.

Three floors of displays illustrate how the mechanics and appearance of clocks have changed since the 15C. All types of clocks are represented, from the sundial to the electronic clock, including, of course, the cuckoo clock. Note the amazing **astronomical clock**★ (1769) by David a Sancto Cajetano.

Am Hof

This square, on the site of the Roman military camp, is decorated by a bronze column to the Virgin Mary (Mariensäule, 1667). It was here that Franz II, on 6 August 1806, renounced the Imperial Crown, thus ending the Holy Roman Empire.

▷ From here you can make a detour to admire Freyung square, otherwise take Bognergasse to Graben.

Freyung★

This square, often used to hold seasonal markets, is surrounded by palaces built from the 17C onwards due of its proximity to the Hofburg. At no. 2 is the **Palais Ferstel**, built in 1860 by Heinrich von Ferstel. It has an attractive **passage**★ through to Herrengasse. At no. 4, the **Palais Kinsky**, constructed between 1713 and 1716 by Johann Lukas von Hildebrandt, sports a splendid **Baroque façade**★.

Schotten Stifta (Scottish Abbey)

Freyung 6. 🕑*Open year-round Tue–Fri 11am–5pm, Sat 11am–4.30pm.* ✏€8. ✆01534 98. www.schotten.wien.

At the end of the square are the church and associated buildings of the so-called Scottish monastery. It got its name from the founding monks who were Benedictines from the island of Iona. The church has an old statue of the Virgin (1250), while the abbey buildings contain an art gallery *(entrance through the monastery shop)* with works from the 15C to 19C, including paintings by Rubens and a Gothic Scottish altarpiece (1470) with a view of medieval Vienna.

▷ Take Bognergasse (16) to Graben.

Peterskirche★ (St. Peter's Church)

🕑*Open year-round Mon–Fri 7am–8pm, Sat–Sun 9am–9pm.* ✆01 533 64 33. www.peterskirche.at.

Adorned with lavish frescoes and gilded stuccowork, this church is regarded as the most splendid of Vienna's Baroque churches. It was built from 1702 to 1708 by Johann Lukas von Hildebrandt, among others, to replace a three-aisle Romanesque church, which was itself a replacement of Vienna's earliest place of worship, a 4C building in the camp of Vindobona. The oval cupola above the nave is ornamented with a fresco attributed to Michael Rottmayr (1714) and represents the Assumption. The **interior furnishings**★ are sumptuous down to the last detail. The magnificent high altar is the work of Antonio Galli-Bibiena, and the altar painting was done by Martin Altomonte.

Graben★

The "trench" (Graben) that was dug by the Romans as a defensive ditch is now a lively pedestrianised shopping street. The street has some fine architecture. At no. 10 the Ankerhaus was designed by Otto Wagner in 1894. The Bartolotti Partenfeld palace (1720) at no. 11 was the last Baroque palace built on the street. The small shop Knize at no. 13 was completed by Adolf Loos in 1913 He was also responsible for the public toilets (1905) below street level.

Pestsäule★★
(Plague Column)

The richly decorated Baroque plague column, dominating the elegant Graben, was erected in 1693 to fulfil an oath made by Emperor Leopold I during the disastrous plague epidemic of 1679. He is shown kneeling in prayer.

◖ Go down Dorotheergasse.

Jüdisches Museum der Stadt Wien★ (Jewish Museum)

◷*Open year-round Sun–Fri 10am–6pm.* ◈€*10, includes Museum Judenplatz.* ♿ ✆*01 535 04 31.* *www.jmw.at.*

At 11 Dorotheergasse, the Adelspalais Eskeles (15C) houses the city's **Jewish museum**. It has a permanent collection as well as temporary exhibits on the history of Vienna's and Austria's large Jewish community.

◖ Turn right onto Spiegelgasse to the Donner fountain.

Donnerbrunnen★★

Neuer Markt.

The 1739 fountain by Georg Raphaël Donner has a central statue representing Providence, which is surrounded by cherubs and fish spouting water. The statues orbiting the fountain personify the rivers Traun, Ybbs, Enns and Morava (March). These are bronze copies of the lead originals now displayed in the Belvedere.

Kapuzinergruft★★
(Capucin Crypt)

◷*Open year-round Fri–Wed 10am–6pm, Thu 9am–6pm.* ◈€*5.50.* ♿ ✆*01 512 68 53.*

For more than three centuries, this crypt, built between 1622 and 1632, was the burial place of the imperial family. Twelve emperors, 17 empresses and 100 archdukes are buried here, although their hearts are interred in the Augustinerkirche and their entrails in Stephansdom.

Notable sarcophagi to look out for include that of Joseph Leopold I, designed by Johann Lukas von Hildebrandt; it can be found in the Karlsgruft along with the **sarcophagus of Charles VI★**, which is decorated with badges and an allegory of Austria in mourning, a masterpiece by Balthasar Moll.

Occupying a **double sarcophagus★★**, another exceptional work by Balthasar Moll, are the empress Maria Theresia and her husband Francis of Lorraine. The lead cover is a bier on which an angel gives the call to the Last Judgement. Facing their grave is that of their son, Joseph II. The sarcophagus of the emperor Franz Joseph and that of his wife Elizabeth, assassinated in Geneva in 1898, is another highlight. Their son Prince Rudolf lies in a separate room, while Archduke Franz Ferdinand and his wife are buried elsewhere. The last member of the imperial family to be interred here was the wife of the last emperor Karl I, Zita, who was buried in the crypt on 1 April 1989.

Hofburg★★★

The Imperial palace, the winter residence of the Habsburgs, was progressively enlarged over the centuries, resulting in a hodgepodge of styles. The oldest section, built in the 13C, is the Schweizerhof (Swiss Court), while the Burgkapelle (castle chapel) was erected in the mid-15C. Next came the Amalienburg and the Stallburg in the 16C, followed by the Leopoldinischer Trakt (now the official office of the Federal President) in the 17C. The 18C saw the addition of the Reichskanzleitrakt (Imperial Chancellery), the Spanische Reitschule (Spanish Riding School), and the Nationalbibliothek (National Library). The Neue Burg (New Imperial Palace), completed just before 1914, marked the end of the structural history of the Hofburg.

EXTERIOR
Michaelerplatz★

Designed by JE Fischer von Erlach, this complex was not completed until 1893. The semicircular façade overlooking the square is decorated with two monumental statues–studded fountains. The main arches are closed by bronze gilded grilles. A magnificent gateway, the **Michaelertor★**, flanked by figures

from the Hercules legends, gives access to the octagonal rotunda beneath the famous **Michaelerkuppel★**, one of Vienna's most elegant domes. The square known as In der Burg, anchored by a monument to Emperor Franz II, is reached via this rotunda. From the courtyard, the **Schweizertor★**, a fine Renaissance gateway bearing coats of arms and inscriptions, leads to the **Schweizerhof** and the stairs up to the Hofburgkapelle.

Michaelerkirche★

The core of this church on Michaelerplatz is Romanesque and Gothic (13C), making it one of the oldest in the city. It received its present amalgam of Baroque and Rococo decoration during the 18C. Perhaps the finest art work in the interior is the dramatic altar sculpture *The Fall of Angels*. The church also has an exceptionally fine Baroque organ made in 1714 by Johann David Sieber, and played by Joseph Haydn in 1749.
In front of the church, in the centre of the square, are the remains of Roman houses exposed by excavations.

Josefsplatz★

Arched passageways lead to this square, regarded as Vienna's finest because of its ideal proportions. It owes its name to the impressive equestrian statue of Joseph II, the base of which is adorned with low-relief sculptures in bronze.
On the south side is the early 18C **Österreichische Nationalbibliothek★** (National Library) by Fischer von Erlach.

Heldenplatz★

Heldenplatz overlooks the concave façade of the Neue Burg, built in the Italian Renaissance style between 1881 and 1913. Bounded to the north by the shady Volksgarten, the square boasts two equestrian statues by the sculptor Anton Dominik Fernkorn of Prince Eugene of Savoy and Archduke Karl.
The monumental gateway (1824) on the southwest side is the Äusseres Burgtor, which leads to the Ring; it has served as a war memorial since 1934.

Michaelertor, Michaelerplatz

© N. Blythe/Cephas/Photononstop

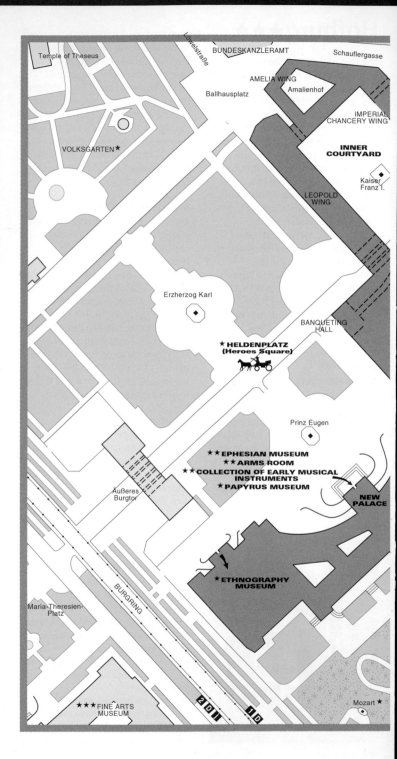

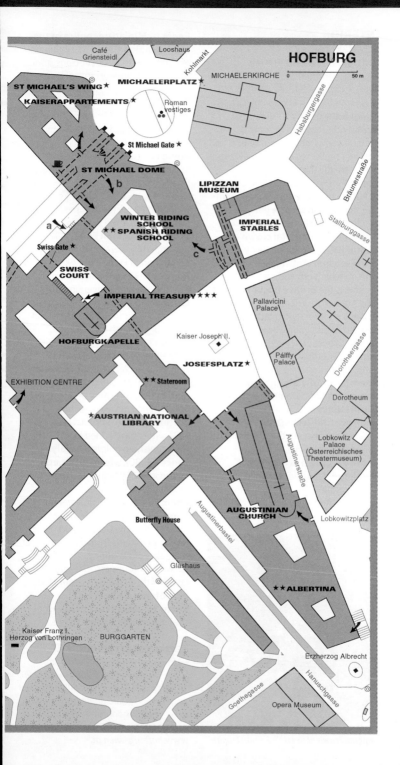

HOFBURG

Café Griensteidl

Looshaus

Kohlmarkt

MICHAELERKIRCHE

0   50 m

MICHAELERPLATZ ★

ST MICHAEL'S WING ★

KAISERAPPARTEMENTS ★

Roman vestiges

St Michael Gate ★

ST MICHAEL DOME

b

a

LIPIZZAN MUSEUM

WINTER RIDING SCHOOL

★★ SPANISH RIDING SCHOOL

IMPERIAL STABLES

c

Swiss Gate ★

SWISS COURT

IMPERIAL TREASURY ★★★

Pallavicini Palace

HOFBURGKAPELLE

Kaiser Joseph II.

Pálffy Palace

JOSEFSPLATZ ★

EXHIBITION CENTRE

★★ Stateroom

★AUSTRIAN NATIONAL LIBRARY

Dorotheum

Lobkowitz Palace (Österreichisches Theatermuseum)

Butterfly House

Augustinerbastei

AUGUSTINIAN CHURCH

Lobkowitzplatz

Glashaus

★★ ALBERTINA

Kaiser Franz I. Herzog von Lothringen

BURGGARTEN

Erzherzog Albrecht

Goethegasse

Opera Museum

Habsburgergasse

Bräunerstraße

Stallburggasse

Dorotheergasse

Augustinerstraße

Hanuschgasse

INTERIOR
Schatzkammer
(Imperial Treasury)★★★

Open year-round Wed–Mon 9am–5.30pm. €12. *01525 240. www.kaiserliche-schatzkammer.at.*

A highlight of any Vienna visit, the treasury displays the insignia of Habsburg power, as well as mementoes and holy relics collected by the family. Listed below are the must-see exhibits:

Room 1 – The regalia of the archdukes of Austria used in ceremonies of homage: the **orb and sceptre** (Prague, 14C) and the ducal mantle (Vienna, 1764).

Room 2 – The **Imperial crown of Rudolf II★**, made in Prague by Jan Vermeyen from Antwerp (early 17C), with matching orb and sceptre. Also notable is the **bronze bust of Rudolf II** by Adriaen de Vries (1607).

Room 3 – Coronation mantle (1830) and ceremonial robes. Insignia of various Orders.

Room 4 – Coronation regalia of Ferdinand I.

Room 5 – **Cradle of the King of Rome★** made of silver gilt. **Portrait of Marie Louise★**.

Room 6 – Christening robes and other effects; keys to the coffins in the Kaisergruft (Imperial crypt).

Room 7 – **Crown of Stephan Bocskay★**. Jewellery, emerald vessel (2,680 carat).

Room 8 – **Agate bowl★** (4C). Narwhal horn measuring 2.43m/8ft.

Imperial crown of the Holy Roman Empire

Kunsthistorisches Museum

Room I – **Miniature replica of the Mariensäule★** (Virgin Mary column), decorated with 3,700 precious stones.

Room II – Reliquary cross of King Ludwig I of Hungary (c. 1370).

Room III – Small ebony temple with an ivory figure of Christ by Christoph Angermair; Florentine crucifix by Giambologna (c. 1590).

Room IV – Reliquary altars from Milan (1660–1680); altar furniture in Dresden china.

Room V – 18C and 19C works of art including 22 bust reliquaries.

Room 9 – **Insignia and crown jewels of the Holy Roman Empire**. The last time they were used was at the coronation of Franz II in 1792.

Room 10 – Ceremonial robes of the Norman kings, including the **Coronation mantle★★** of Roger II of Sicily (Palermo, 1133); ceremonial sword of Friedrich II.

Room 11 – The most outstanding item among the crown jewels of the Holy Roman Empire is the **Imperial crown★★★**, probably made for Otto I (962) in the monastery on the island of Reichenau in Lake Constance, or possibly in Milan. Imperial cross of 1024 with a base added in 1352. An astonishing relic is the **Holy Lance★★** (8C), while the **Imperial sword★** (11C) is attributed to St. Maurice.

Room 12 – Reliquaries, jewel boxes.

Room 13 – Robes and heraldic coats of arms from the Duchy of Burgundy.

Room 14 – Items from the treasure of the dukes of Burgundy.

Room 15 – Items associated with the Order of the Golden Fleece, including the **potence★★** (mid 15C).

Room 16 – **Mass vestments★★** of the Order of the Golden Fleece.

Kaiserappartements★

Open Jul–Aug daily 9am–6pm; Sept–Jun daily 9am–5.30pm. €12.90, includes Sisi Museum and Silberkammer as well as an audio guide (combination tickets with Schönbrunn are also available).* *01 533 75 70. www.hofburg-wien.at.*

Conference Room,
Kaiserappartements

© Schloß Schönbrunn Kultur- und Betriebsges.m.b.H. / Johannes Wagner

The **Imperial apartments** occupy the first floor of the Chancellery wing (Reichskanzleitrakt) and the Amalientrakt and are reached via the Kaiserstiege (Emperor's staircase). Only 20 of about 2,600 rooms in the palace are open to visitors. They are decorated in Rococo style with fanciful stucco ornamentation, luxurious furniture, crystal chandeliers and Aubusson and Flemish tapestry and date from the time of the last royal occupant, Emperor Franz Joseph I and his wife Elisabeth (Sisi). You can see the bedroom, study, audience chamber, bathroom, and Sisi's dressing and exercise room, complete with wall bars and rings.

Admission includes a tour around the **Sisi Museum**, which traces the empress' childhood, life at court and tragic death while also addressing the myth that developed around her, including the numerous films made (very) loosely based on her life.

The **Silberkammer** (Imperial Silver Collection), a magnificent spread of items used by the family until the monarchy's demise in 1918, is also worth a look. Displays include an enormous **vermeil service★** for 140 guests and the famous **Milanese centrepiece★★** of 1838, designed for a table more than 30m/98.4ft long.

There are also several Sèvres services, including the green service of 1776, numerous Empire-style ones from the Vienna Porcelain Factory, and fine sets of crystal glassware.

Hofburgkapelle

🕐*Open Mon–Tue 10am–2pm, Fri 11am–1pm.* 🕐*Closed holidays.* ♿ ✆*01 533 99 27. www.hofmusikkapelle.gv.at.*
Built in the middle of the 15C, the Gothic palace chapel is the oldest part of the present palace. The famous Vienna Boys' Choir sings during Sunday mass as well as during other performances, sometimes accompanied by the Wiener Philharmoniker (🕐*9.15am, arrive by 9am; reservations required; book as far in advance as possible*).

Spanische Hofreitschule★★

Guided tours (1hr): check website for dates and times. ✎*€18. Tickets are available on the same day from the Besucherzentrum (visitor centre) at Michaelerplatz 1 Tue–Sat 9am–4pm, Fri til 7pm if there is a performance. Performances (80min) and training sessions: prices and dates vary; check website. Reserve tickets as early as possible by phone or online.* ✆*01 533 90 31. www.srs.at.*
Feats of dressage dating back to the late 16C are performed in the all-white, indoor **Winter Riding School**, the work of Joseph Fischer von Erlach. The riders wear brown tailcoats, white buckskin breeches, riding boots and cocked hats. The white Lipizzaner stallions (👉*see PACK- UND STUBALPENSTRAßE, Gestüt-Piber),* their tails and manes plaited with gold ribbons, go through their paces with stunning precision, culminating in the school quadrille with a group of

Albertina

horses. Horses perform difficult jumps, steps, and other movements during the **morning training session** (*Morgenarbeit*); although less spectacular, it is easier to get tickets for it (main performances sell out very quickly).

Österreichische Nationalbibliothek★ (Austrian National Library)

Josefsplatz 2. Enter on 1st floor. ⊙*Open year-round Tue–Sun 10am–6pm, Thu 10am–9pm.* ✆€7. ✆01 534 10 39. www.onb.ac.at.

The core collection inside this early 18C building by Joseph Emanuel Fischer von Erlach is formed by the Imperial library, established in the 14C. The **Prunksaal★★** (Great Hall) is a masterpiece of Baroque architecture and decoration with **ceiling frescoes** by **Daniel Gran** in the oval dome and statues by the Strudel brothers. It holds Prince Eugene of Savoy's magnificent library and also hosts special exhibitions.

Augustinerkirche (Augustinian Church)

Built in the 14C within the Hofburg, this Gothic court church hosted the marriages of Maria Theresia and Francis of Lorraine (1736), of Napoleon and Marie Louise (1810) and of Franz Joseph and Elisabeth of Bavaria (1854). In the south aisle is the **tomb★** of Archduchess Maria Christina, Maria Theresia's favourite daughter. This white marble mausoleum is considered a masterpiece of the Italian

sculptor Canova, who worked in Vienna from 1805 to 1809. The **Loretokapelle** *(access via the right side aisle)* holds in its **crypt** 54 urns containing the hearts of the Habsburgs. The Georgskapelle nearby was a meeting place for the knights of the Order of St. George, and later for those of the Order of the Golden Fleece. It contains the cenotaph of Emperor Leopold II.

Albertina★★

⊙*Open year-round Thu–Tue 10am –6pm, Wed 10am–9pm.* ✆€12.90. ♿✆01 534 830. www.albertina.at.

With some 45,000 drawings and watercolours, 35,000 publications and a million prints, the Albertina is considered the world's greatest collection of graphic art, with continually changing exhibitions. Of particular importance is the **Dürer** collection, which contains such famous works as the *Praying Hands* and his *Hare*. Da Vinci, Michelangelo, Picasso are all represented, too. A collection of 20C art is also displayed, with works by the likes of Warhol, Klimt and Schiele.

Österreichisches Theatermuseum

Lobkowitzplatz 2. ⊙*Open year-round Wed–Mon 10am–6pm.* ✆€8. ✆01 525 24 34 60. www.theatermuseum.at.

Just across the square from the Albertina, the Austrian Theatre Museum has an enormous archive and small permanent display but most of the space is given over to temporary exhibitions.

👥 Schmetterlinghaus (Butterfly House)

🕐Open Apr–Oct Mon–Fri 10am–4.45pm, Sat–Sun 10am–6.15pm; Nov–Mar daily 10am–3.45pm. €6.50. ♿ ☎01 533 85 70. www.schmetterlinghaus.at.

Colourful butterflies flutter within a re-created tropical rain forest in the palace garden's Jugendstil glasshouse. Some have even been known to land on the tip of a visitor's nose. The other part of the huge glasshouse is given over to an attractive café, the **Palmenhaus** *(www.palmenhaus.at)*, with seating outside during the summer.

Neue Burg (New Palace)

Heldenplatz. 🕐Open year-round Wed–Sun 10am–6pm. €15. ☎01 525 240. www.khm.at.

The Neue Burg has amassed the following collections:

Hofjagd- und Rüstkammer★★ – This exceptionally rich collection of arms and armour, one of the most important and well-documented in the world, was created in the 15C from the collections of the archdukes Ernst of Styria (1377–1424) and Ferdinand of the Tirol (1527–95). It was then merged in 1806 with the Imperial Court weaponry collection. The filigree work and elaborate decoration on the ceremonial harnesses, helmets and saddles that were made for kings and emperors reflect European history.

Sammlung alter Musikinstrumente★★ – Fittingly for such a musical city this is a great collection of Renaissance, and later, instruments. Of particular historical and artistic interest are a **rebec★**, or early bowed instrument, made from a single piece of wood (an animal's feeding trough) in 15C Venice; a **harpsichord★** (Venice 1559); a **cittern★★** made in Brescia in 1574; a **reed-organ★** from Innsbruck (before 1569). Other highlights include six magnificent, partly gilded, **trumpets★** (Vienna 1741 and 1746), and a **piano★** (Vienna 1867) with ornate inlaid work crafted by **Ludwig Bösendorfer** for the Paris World Exhibition.

Ephesos Museum★★

Archaeological findings from Ephesus in Turkey form the core of this exhibit, augmented by items unearthed at Samothrace on the Aegean. Star items include fragments of the altarpiece of Artemis in the stairway and the 40m/131ft-long marble **Frieze of the Parthian Monument★★** (c.AD 170) in the mezzanine. It depicts the adoption of Marcus Aurelius, battle scenes from the wars with the Parthians, and the consecration and apotheosis of Lucius Verus. On the upper floor are the impressive **Athlete of Ephesus★★** and the **Boy with the Goose★**.

Other Neue Burg Museums

The Neue Burg contains two other museums, one part of the Kunsthistorisches Museum like the other three, the other, the Papyrusmuseum, which is part of the National Library.

Papyrusmuseum★

Entry via the National Library.
🕐Open Oct-Jun Mon-Wed 9am-4pm, Thu noon-7pm, Fri 9am-1pm; Jul-Sept Mon-Fri 9am-1pm. 🕐Closed holidays & 2 Jan, 24 &31 Dec. €4 (combination ticket available with the Prunksaal). ☎01 534 10 425. www.onb.ac.at.

With 180,000 items, the collection of papyri from the National Library is one of the largest in the world. The museum contains about 400 documents (not originals) sorted by subject, such as school, magic, religion.

Welt Museum Wien★

🕐Closed for renovation until late 2017. ♿ ☎01 534 30 50 52. www.weltmuseumwien.at.

The ethnography museum stages temporary exhibitions drawn from its exceptional collections. Notable pieces include examples of Japanese Samurai armour from the 17C and items from Polynesia, some attributed to Captain James Cook. The Early American collection includes an **Aztec feather headdress★★** from Mexico.

Maria Theresien-Platz

and the Museums Quarter

Facing each other across the expanse of this square to the southwest of Heldenplatz are two of Vienna's most important institutions, the Kunsthistoriches (Fine Arts) Museum and the Naturhistorisches (Natural History) Museum. The twin buildings were part of the grand Ringstraße project and took 20 years to build, opening their doors in 1891.

KUNSTHISTORISCHES MUSEUM (FINE ARTS MUSEUM)

○ *Open year-round Tue–Sun 10am–6pm (Thu til 9pm).* €15. ₰ 01525 240. www.khm.at.

The five collections composing Vienna's prestigious **museum of fine arts** are among the largest in the world, displayed over some 4km/2.5mi of galleries. The biggest crowd pleaser is the Gemäldegalerie (Picture Gallery) with its superb collection of paintings.

The other collections are the Ägyptisch-Orientalische Sammlung (Egyptian and Near Eastern Collection), the Antiken-sammlung (Collection of Greek and Roman Antiquities), the Münzkabinett (Coin Cabinet) and the Kunstkammer (Collection of Sculpture and Decorative Arts). *Some of the works mentioned below may be on loan to other institutions or under restoration.*

Egyptian and Near Eastern Collection★★

Mezzanine level, to the right, Galleries I–IX

Gallery I – Coffins, canopic jars, humanmummies; sarcophagus of Nes-schu-tefnut (c. 300 BC); **papyrus bundle columns★** (18th dynasty).

Gallery II – Cult chamber of Ka-ni-nisut (c. 2450 BC).

Gallery III – Ushabti statuettes, ushabti boxes, amulets, wooden stelae.

Gallery IV – Statuettes of divinities: enthroned Isis suckling her child Horus; animal mummies, objects for cult and magic.

Gallery V – Typology of burials from the 1st dynasty to Ptolemaic times; coffins and stelae; papyri: Book of the Dead of Khons-mes.

Gallery VI – Everyday life: clothing, cosmetic implements, jewellery, food, crafts, pottery and stone vessels.

Gallery VIA – Egyptian Writing, Book of the Dead of Khonsu-iu (3C BC); Cuneiform writing; monumental inscriptions, reliefs, bronzes from Yemen (3C BC–AD 2C).

Gallery VII – Statues and reliefs from Old Kingdom, Middle Kingdom, New Kingdom; statue of Khent with her son, painted limestone Statue of Tjanuna.

Gallery VIII – Statues and reliefs from New Kingdom; statue group of Hamemhab and Horus; Late Period and Ptolemaic times; colossal heads of kings

Gallery IX – Reserve head from **Giza★★** (c. 2600 BC), sphinx head of king Sesostris III (c. 1840 BC), statue of **King Thutmosis III★★★** (1504–1452 BC).

Collection of Greek and Roman Antiquities★★

Mezzanine level, to the right, Galleries X–XVIII

Gallery X – Greek sculpture: Doryphoros (Roman copy), *Portrait of Aristotle★* (Roman copy).

Gallery XI – Greek and Roman sculpture: **Amazon sarcophagus★** (4C BC), Grimani reliefs (AD 1C).

Gallery XII – Roman Republic: Senatus Consultum (2C BC), Patera of Aquileia (1C BC).

Gallery XIII – Roman portraits: Roman emperors, Augustus (AD 1C), mummy portraits (AD 2C)

Gallery XIV – Greek pottery: Brygos-Skyphos (5C BC), **Duris Bowl**★(5C BC).

Gallery XV – Roman handicrafts: bronze statuettes, **Head of Zeus**★ (AD 1C).

Gallery XVI – Greek and Roman cameos: Gemma Augustea (AD 1C), Ptolemaic cameo★ (3C BC).

Gallery XVII – Late Antique and Early Medieval period: gold treasure of **Nagyszentmiklós**★ (AD 6–8C).

Gallery XVIII – Early Christian art: portrait of Eutropios (AD 5C), textiles (AD 4–6C).

Cabinet 1 – Cyprus: Bronze Age pottery, figurines, sculpture.

Cabinet 2 – Early Etruscan pottery (Bucchero).

Cabinet 3 – Etruscan: Athena Roccaspromonte (5C BC), Negau helmets (5C BC).

Cabinet 4 – Magna Graecia: pottery, Silver Centaur (2C BC).

Cabinet 5 – Heroon of Trysa.

Cabinet 6 – Roman Austria:treasure from Mauer an der Url (AD 1–3C).

Cabinet 7 – Roman Austria: youth from the **Magdalensberg**★ (16C copy).

Picture Gallery★★★

The following particularly exceptional works are must-sees.

Gallery IX – Michael Coxcie: *Original Sin* and *The Expulsion from the Garden of Eden* (c. 1550); works by Hans Vredeman de Vries and Frans Floris.

Room 14 – Jan van Eyck: *Cardinal Niccolò Albergati*★★ (c. 1435) and *The Goldsmith Jan de Leeuw;* Jean Fouquet: *The Ferrara Court Jester Gonella*★ (c. 1440); Hugo van der Goes: *Diptych with the Fall of Man and Salvation*★★ (c. 1470); Rogier van der Weyden: *Crucifixion Triptych*★ (c. 1440); Hieronymus Bosch: *Christ bearing the Cross.*

Room 15 – **Joos van Cleve: Lucretia**★; Jan Gossaert: *St. Luke painting the Madonna.*

Gallery X – 14 of the total of 45 surviving paintings by **Pieter Bruegel the Elder**. These include: *Christ bearing the Cross*★ (1564), *The Tower of Babel*★★, *Children's Games*★★ (1560), *The Battle between Carnival and Lent*★★ (1559), *Peasant Dance*★ (1568–69) and *Peasant Wedding*★, *Hunters in the Snow*★★★ (1565).

Gallery XI – Jacob Jordaens: *The Bean King's Feast (Twelfth Night)* (c. 1640–45); Frans Snyders: *The Fish Market* (c. 1620–30).

Room 16 – Albrecht Dürer: *Young Venetian Womana* (1505), *The Martyrdom of the Ten Thousand Christians* (1508, with a self portrait of Dürer in the centre of the painting), the *Adoration of the Holy Trinity*★★ (1511) and *Mary with the reclining Child* (1512).

Room 17 – Albrecht Dürer: Portrait of *Emperor Maximilian I*★ (1519); Martin Schongauer: *The Holy Family*★ (c. 1480–90); Lucas Cranach the Elder: *Judith with the Head of Holofernes*★ (c. 1530). Albrecht Altdorfer: *The Birth of Christ*★ (c. 1520–25).

Room 18 – Hans Holbein the Younger: *Jane Seymour*★ (c. 1536–37).

Room 19 – Giuseppe Arcimboldo: *Fire*★ (1566); Georg Flegel: *Dessert with a Bunch of Flowers*★ (1632).

Gallery XII – Anthony van Dyck: *Nicolas Lanier*★★, *Venus in Vulcan's Forge*★.

Room 20 – Peter Paul Rubens: *Young Girl with Fan* (c. 1612–14).

Gallery XIII – *Self-portrait* (c. 1638–40), *Hélène Fourment with Fur Cloak*★★ (c. 1636–38), *St. Ildefonso Altar-piece*★★ (c. 1630–32).

Gallery XIV – *Vincenzo II, Gonzaga* (c. 1604–05), *Medusa's Head* (c. 1617–18).

Room 21 – David Teniers the Younger: *Archduke Leopold Wilhelm in his Picture Gallery in Brussels*★ (c. 1651).

Room 22 – Salomon van Ruysdael: *Landscape with Wooden Fence and Cloudy Sky*

Room 23 – Aert van der Neer: *Riverscape with Boats by Moonlight* (c. 1665–1709).

Room 24 – Thomas Gainsborough: *Suffolk Landscape* (c. 1748); *The Artist's Studio*★★★ (c. 1665–66) by Jan Vermeer.

Gallery XV – Rembrandt: *The Artist's Mother as Hannah the Prophetess* and *The Artist's Son Titus van Rijn reading,* as well as the very interesting pair of paintings *Small Self-portrait*★ (c. 1657) and *Large Self-portrait*★★ (1652).

Gallery I – Titian: *The Gipsy Madonna* (c. 1510), *The Madonna with the Cherries* (c. 1516–17), *Young Woman with a Fur*★ (c. 1535) and *Ecce Homo*★ (1543).

Room 1 – Andrea Mantegna: *St. Sebastian*★★ (c. 1457–59); Giovanni Bellini: *Young Woman at her Toilette* (1515).

Room 2 – Giorgione: *Laura* (1506) and the *Three Philosophers*★★ (c. 1508) Lorenzo Lotto: *Portrait of a Young Boy in front of a White Curtain*★ (c. 1508).

Gallery II – Veronese: *Adoration of the Magi* (c. 1580–88).

Gallery III – Tintoretto: *Lorenzo Soranzo* (1553), *Susanna and the Elders*★★ (c. 1555).

Room 3 – Correggio: *Abduction of Ganymede* (c. 1530).

Room 4 – Perugino: *The Baptism of Christ* (c. 1498–1500); Andrea del Sarto: *The Mourning of Christ* (c. 1519–20); Raphael: the *Madonna in the Meadow*★★ (1505–06).

Room 5 – Bernardino Luini: *Salome with the Head of St. John the Baptist* (c. 1525–30).

Room 7 – Bronzino: *Holy Family with St. Anne and St. John the Baptist* (c. 1540).

Room 10 – Velázquez: *Portraits of the Infanta*★; Murillo: *St. Michael* (c. 1665–68).

Room 11 – Annibale Carracci: *Pietà*★ (c. 1603).

Gallery V – Caravaggio: *David with the Head of Goliath*★ (1606–07) and *Madonna of the Rosary*★ (c. 1606–07).

Gallery VI – Guercino: *Return of the Prodigal Son*★ (c. 1619); Giordano: *Archangel Michael and the Rebellious Angels*★ (c. 1660–65).

Gallery VII – Hyacinthe Rigaud: *Count Ludwig Philipp Wenzel Sinzendorf* (1728); Canaletto: *Vienna from the Belvedere*★ (c. 1758–61).

Kunst Kammer

This section of the museum on the ground floor has re-opened after a major refit, earning plaudits for its stunning

Detail of The Artist's Studio *(c. 1665–66) by Johannes Vermeer*

Kunsthistorisches Museum Vienna

new displays drawn from the exceptionally rich collections. Many of the artefacts are from the Renaissance or Baroque; highlights include the Saliera by Benvenuto Cellini, early German ivories, and bronzes by Giovanni Bologna.

Coin Cabinet

Second floor, to the left. This section of the museum holds a collection of some 700,000 items, making it one of the largest numismatic collections in the world. Besides medals, decorations and insignia, the collection includes Ferdinand II of Tirol's 16C portrait collection.

Kunsthistorisches Museum

Saliera (salt cellar) by Benvenuto Cellini

🧍🧍 NATURHISTORISCHES MUSEUM★ (NATURAL HISTORY MUSEUM)

🕐*Open year-round Wed–Mon 9am–6.30pm (Wed til 9pm).* 🕐*Closed 1 Jan, 25 Dec.* ♿🎫€10, children free. 📞*01521 770. www.nhm-wien.ac.at.*

The collections of this museum are among the finest in the world. Until recently some displays seemed old-fashioned, but now a programme of ongoing modernisation includes a planetarium and a new gallery for dinosaurs. The Prehistory section (*mezzanine level*) includes the famous 25,000-year-old **Venus of Willendorf★**, remarkable finds from the **Hallstatt graves** and a dinosaur room. On the same floor, the **Mineralogy section★★** has such rare and exquisite specimens as a 1m/3.3ft-long piece of quartz crystal from Madagascar, a topaz from Brazil weighing 117kg/258lb and the famous **"bouquet of jewels"★** (1760), a gift from Maria Theresia to her husband, Francis of Lorraine. Upstairs, the Zoology section has the usual array of preserved birds and animals, including such extinct (partly due to having been shot and mounted) species as the moa and the dronte (dodo). There's also an extinct **Stellersche sea cow★** and other animals, including a gharial, a river-dwelling crocodile endemic to India.

MUSEUMS QUARTER

The former Imperial stables are now a cultural complex that ranks among the world's 10 largest. It contains the modern art-focused Leopold Museum; Museum Moderner Kunst; the **Kunsthalle Wien**, a contemporary exhibit space; Architecutre Museum; ZOOM Kindermuseum 🧍🧍; TanzQuartier, a centre for dance; artist studios; media production facilities; and cafés, bars and shops.

Leopold Museum★

🕐*Open year-round Mon, Wed–Sun 10am–6pm, (Thu til 9pm).* 🕐*Closed 24 Dec.* 🎫€13. 🎧*Guided tours available.* 📞*01 525 70. www.leopoldmuseum.org.*

This museum presents a thorough survey of all major names and movements in modern Austrian art, including Viennese Secessionism, Viennese Modernism and Austrian Expressionism. It is based on the private collection assembled by Rudolf and Elisabeth Leopold over five decades. Masterpieces include the world's largest Egon Schiele collection★★ and seminal works by Gustav Klimt, Oskar Kokoschka, Albin Egger-Lienz and Herbert Boeckl. A fine selection of Jugendstil objects by Otto Wagner, Adolf Loos, Josef Hoffmann and others rounds off the presentation.

Museum Moderner Kunst (Museum of Modern Art Ludwig Foundation)

🕐*Open year-round Mon 2pm–7pm, Tue–Sun 10am–7pm (Thu til 9pm).* 🎫€11. 📞*01 525 000. www.mumok.at.*

Known as MUMOK, this museum has the largest collection of modern and

Altar, Maria am Gestade
© Alex Zarubin/Dreamstime.com

Churches of the First District

Franziskanerkirche (Franciscan Church)

This church was transformed into the Baroque style in the 18C. On one of the right-hand altars is a painting of St. Francis by Johann Georg Schmidt, known as **"Wiener Schmidt,"** and an Immaculate Conception of 1722 by Johann Michael Rottmayr. The nearby **Franziskanerplatz** has a Moses fountain (1798) and, like the Ballgasse leading off it to the south, is bordered by picturesque old houses.

Deutschordenskirche

This church was built by the Teutonic Order, a German hospitaller order founded in 1190. The church, a 14C Gothic building remodelled in the Baroque style, contains a beautiful 16C Flemish carved and gilded **altarpiece★** with painted panels. Next to the cobbled inner courtyard is the **Treasure of the Teutonic Order★** (🕐open Tue, Thu, Sat 10am–noon, Wed, Fri 3pm–5pm; 👓€5; 📞01 512 10 65; www.deutscher-orden.at). The wealth accumulated by the order over the centuries is impressive: robes and mementoes of Heads of the Order, such as a **chain of the Order★** (c. 1500), sacred vessels, silverware, arms decorated with gold and precious stones, as well as also clocks, including a **longcase clock★** carried by Hercules (about 1620).

Ruprechtskirche (St. Rupert)

♿🕐Open only for early-music concerts; details at www.alte-musik.co.at.
This church is said to have been founded in 740 by St. Virgil, Bishop of Salzburg, and is the oldest building in Vienna. The nave and the foundations of the tower date from between 1130 and 1170 and the chancel and the doorway from the mid 13C. The church was finally completed in the second half of the 15C. The Romanesque belfry, Austria's oldest surviving stained-glass windows in the apse, and contemporary stained-glass windows by Lydia Roppolt (1953, 1992–93) are all striking features.

Maria am Gestade★ (St. Mary on the Strand)

Salvatorgasse; enter through the south door.
On a terrace above the Danube, this church was built in the 12C and later replaced by a Gothic edifice, of which the general outline still survives. The western façade is decorated with sculptures, and the doorway is covered by a canopy (c. 1410). The seven-sided Gothic tower is surmounted by a delicately pierced **stone cap★**, which is one of the loveliest products of the Viennese Gothic style. Inside, the chancel has interesting stained-glass windows, and statues on the pillars of the nave.

contemporary art in Austria, showcasing a cross-section of international and Austrian 20C art. Works by Jawlensky and Kokoschka represent Expressionism; Fernand Léger, among others, Cubism; Max Ernst and René Magritte Surrealism; Arman Nouveau Réalisme; and Robert Rauschenberg Pop Art.

Examples of international painting of the 1980s and 1990s include works by Georg Baselitz, Jörg Immendorf and Ernesto Tatafiore. "Wiener Aktionismus" (Hermann Nitsch, Günter Brus and Arnulf Rainer).

▲▲ ZOOM Kindermuseum (Children's Museum)

🕐 *See website for schedule.* 🕐 *Closed 1 Jan, 24-26 & 31 Dec.* ⚫€6. ✆ *01 524 79 08. www.kindermuseum.at.*

This children's museum is divided into two sections. Zoom Ozean is a multi-sensory experience designed for kids under six to develop motor skills.

Older youngsters gravitate to the main exhibition, or the lab and studio. All sessions start at set times and reservations are essential.

NEUBAU

Between the Gürtel and the Ring, the district of Neubau stretches either side of Mariahilfer Straße, a long shopping street with most of Vienna's department stores. The workers' blocks and bourgeois townhouses were formerly home to Croatian and Hungarian immigrants, and notable residents include Klimt (who lived at Westbahnstraße 36) and Josef Lanner (waltz composer, born at Mechitaristengasse 5 on 12 April 1801).

Volkstheater

Neustiftgasse 1. U-bahn 2 or 3 Volkstheater.

Built in 1889 by architects Ferdinand Fellner and Hermann Helmer, it offers a varied programme today focusing on avant-garde and contemporary works.

Trautson Palace

Museumstraße 7. �Ⓞ *No public access.*

Initially constructed for Johann Leopold Trautson, the elegant Baroque palace was obtained by Maria Theresia, who had the orangerie converted into stables for her Royal Guard. Though it is no longer open to the public, you can nevertheless enjoy the ornate façade from the street, the central part of which is crowned with Apollo playing a lyre.

Wagnerhaus

Döblergasse 4, Strozzigasse 46. Bus 48A Neubaugasse/Neustiftgasse.

🔊 *Guided tours (30min) by prior arrangement.* ✆ *01 523 22 33.*

Completed in 1912 by Otto Wagner, nos. 2 and 4 of this little street contrast markedly from his other buildings on nearby Linke Wienzelle (🕐 *see below*).

Those on Döblergasse are geometric in design and bear witness to Wagner's creative period during which he embraced the right angle and a certain ornamental austerity. He lived at no. 4, dying here on 11 April 1918.

St. Ulrichs-Platz

U-bahn 2 or 3 Volkstheater. Bus 48A St. Ulrichs-Platz.

The pretty, 18C Baroque square and church offer peace and an opportunity for contemplation a couple of minutes walk north of bustling Mariahilfer Straße. Pass through the gateway in the second (mid-18C) façade to access a tranquil inner courtyard.

Ulrichskirche (St. Ulrich)

🕐 *Open by appointment only;* 🔊 *call to arrange a guided tour.* ⚫€10/hr. ✆ *01 523 12 46. www.stulrich.com.*

The church was built by Josef Reymund between 1721 and 1724 on the site of two 13C chapels. Johann Strauss was baptised and German composer Christoph Willibald Gluck got married here.

Spittelberg★

49 Stiftgasse. U-bahn 2 or 3 Volkstheater, 48A St.-Ulrichs-Platz.

This neighbourhood forms a rectangle contained by Burggasse, Stiftgasse, Siebensterngasse and Kirchberggasse. In the 18C it served as housing for the poor who worked in the city's silk factories, then was adopted by Viennese bohemians. Since the 1970s it has benefited from gentrification, an influx of students from the nearby university, and a popular Christmas market. A pedestrianised zone makes it a pleasant district to wander. On Saturdays (*Apr–Nov*) an arts and crafts market is held around Spittelberggrasse; at no. 8 Stiftgasse, talks and workshops on music and literature are given; and bookshops reside on several cobbled streets.

Free Wi-Fi is available across much of Spittelberg. Look out for "the smallest house in Vienna" at the corner of Burgasse and Breitegasse.

Wieden★★

Beloved by the Viennese, the charming Wiedendistrict is located south of the old town and beyond the Ring. The enormous Karlplatz is a traffic and public transport hub, from which you can explore numerous sites, including the recently renovated Karlskirche and the Secessionsgebäude, an Art Deco masterpiece.

SIGHTS

Karlskirche★★ (St. Charles)

Kreuzherrengasse. ⏱*Open year-round Mon–Sat 9am–6pm, Sun 12pm–7pm.* ⌨*€8 including the lift to the cupola.* ☏*01 504 61 87. www.karlskirche.at.*
This massive domed church, which is dedicated to St. Charles Borromeo, is an 18C work of Johann Bernhard Fischer von Erlach and a harmonious mix of styles and architectural features. It was built following a vow of Emperor Charles VI during the plague of 1713. Admission includes an elevator ride to a **viewing platform** at 32.5m/106.6ft inside the church. From up here you can get a sense of the building's dimensions, inspect Johann Michael Rottmayr's dome frescoes from close up and enjoy sweeping city views. Several centuries' of church treasures can be admired at the new **Museum Borromeo**.

Frescoes inside the dome, Karlskirche

© A. Pöschel/imageBROKER/age fotostock

Wien Museum★ (Vienna Museum)

Karlsplatz 8. ⏱*Open Tue–Sun 10am–6pm.* ⏱*Closed 1 Jan, 1 May, 25 Dec.* ☛*Guided tours available.* ⌨*€10.* ♿ ☏*0150 58 74 70. www.wienmuseum.at.*
The history of Vienna takes centrestage at this museum whose fine array of artifacts includes the **circular plan of Vienna★** (1545) by Augustin Hirschvogel. Other noteworthy displays include excavations from the Roman military camp, medieval stained-glass windows and statues of royalty from the cathedral, booty taken from the Turks after the second siege of Vienna in 1683, porcelain and glassware from Viennese workshops and crafts from the Wiener Werkstätte.
Added to these are the reconstructed interiors of the **Pompeian Room★** (c. 1800) from the Palais Caprara-Geymüller, author Franz Grillparzer's Biedermeier style living room, and Adolf Loos' dining room. Outstanding paintings include Baroque works by Maulbertsch, Rottmayr and Troger and various 19C masterpieces, including *Love★* and *Emilie Flöge* by Gustav Klimt, and *Self-portrait with Splayed fingers★★* and *Blind Mother* by Egon Schiele.

Jugendstil Buildings

Rejecting the academic architecture of the Ring, the architects of the Vienna Secession designed several buildings that put their theories into practice, marking an important stage in the development of modern European architecture (*see p59*).

Wagner-Pavilions★

Karlsplatz.
Otto Wagner's two highly original Viennese Jugendstil pavilions, designed in 1899, face each other north of the Karlskirche. The extraordinary combination of glass, white marble and green-painted metalwork, topped with a corrugated copper roof, was an innovation at the time. One building still serves as an entrance to the U-Bahn and as an exhibition centre, while the other houses a café in the summer months.

Secessionsgebäude★★
(Secession Pavilion)

Friedrichstraße 12. ⊙*Open year-round Tue–Sun 10am–6pm.* ✆€9.50, *includes Beethoven Frieze and current exhibit.*
♿ ☎ *01 587 53 07 11. www.secession.at.*
The Secession building in Vienna has been run as an exhibit hall for contemporary art by the artists' association of the same name since 1898. It is a Jugendstil masterpiece built by **Joseph Maria Olbrich**, a pupil of Wagner.
The undisputed highlight here is the 34m/111ft long **Beethoven Frieze★★**, a monumental 1902 work by **Gustav Klimt** on the theme of the Ninth Symphony.

Wagner Buildings★

Linke Wienzeile 38 & 40.
Otto Wagner's intention when drawing up plans for the riverside boulevard that links Hofburg to Schönbrunn was to make it fit for an emperor. Though the project was never fully realised, along Linke Weinzeile are some apartment buildings with typical Jugendstil features. No. 40 is known as **Majolika Haus** (1898–9) after the painted ceramic flowered tiles used to decorate the façade. They give a rich texture as the colours and decorative elements increase in complexity from the ground floor up to the lions heads on the sixth floor. At no. 38, gold ornamentation has led to the building being called **Miethaus** (Medallion House).

Akademie der bildenden Künste – Gemäldegalerie★★
(Fine Arts Academy)

Schillerplatz 3. ⊙*Open year-round Tue–Sun 10am–6pm.* ⊙*Closed 1 Jan and 24–25 Dec.* ✆€8, *children under 19 yrs. free).* ♿ ☎ *01 588 16 22 22. www.akademiegalerie.at.*
This neo-Renaissance building, built from 1872–76 by Theophil Hansen, has recently undergone a three-year renovation programme that provides a spacious foyer, shop, and new gallery space for contemporary work, while a re-hanging makes the most of Hansen's original rooms. One of the most memo-

Otto Wagner Kirche am Steinhof★★

Baumgartnerhöhe 1 (map p224). Open Sat 3pm–5pm, Sun noon–4pm. ☛*Guided tour (50min) Sat 3pm, Sun 4pm.* ✆€8. ☎*01 910 60 11 007. www.wienkav.at*
Vienna's first modern church was completed by Wagner in 1907 for a mental institution, which it still serves today. Its interior is functional as well as aesthetic. The stoups containing holy water were designed to avoid contamination, the floor slopes towards the altar to create good sight lines for most worshippers, and all parts of the building are easily accessible for maintenance purposes. Such functionality is softened to some extent by the white-gold wall covering. The large **stained-glass windows★** with their typically linear Jugendstil figures are an impressive sight.

rable pieces from this valuable collection is the **Triptych of the Last Judgement★★★** by **Hieronymus Bosch** (1460–1516), in which the fall of man, Jesus judging human souls surrounded by saints, and monstrous demons punishing the wicked are depicted.

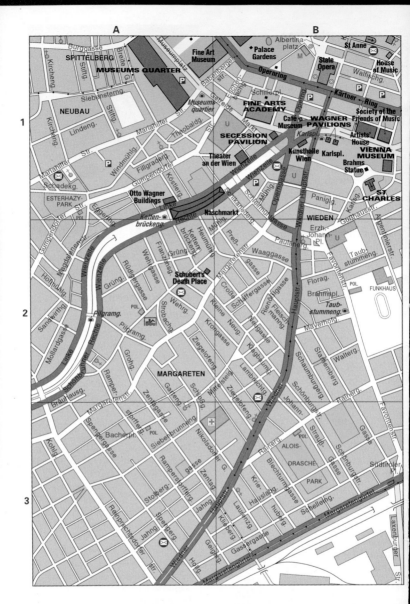

Also on view are:
Lucretia★★ (1532) by Lucas Cranach the Elder; **Young Boys Playing Dice**★ by Bartolomé Esteban Murillo: a **Self Portrait**★ (c. 1615) of a 60-year-old Anton Van Dyck; **Portrait of a Young Woman**★★ (1632) by Rembrandt; and Pieter de Hoogh's **Portrait of**

a Family in a Courtyard in Delft★ (c. 1660). There is a strong showing of 18C painting as well, including the eight **Views of Venice**★ by Francesco Guardi.
Don't leave the gallery without seeing Rachel Ruysch's **Still Life of Flowers and Fruit**★.

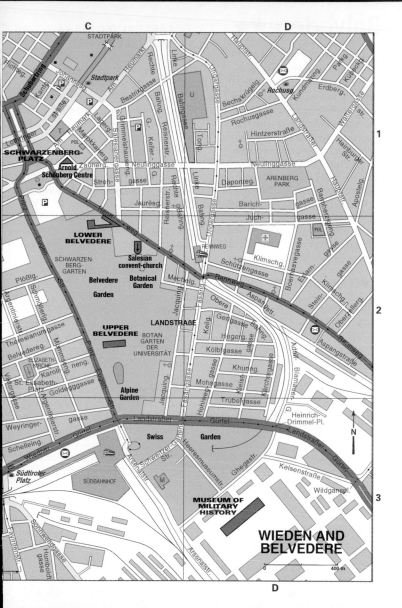

Map: **WIEDEN AND BELVEDERE**

Schubert-Gedenkstätte Sterbezimmer (Schubert's Death Place)

Kettenbrückengasse 6 (2nd floor).
◷ *Open Wed–Thu 10am–1pm and 2pm–6pm.* ◷ *Closed 1 Jan, 1 May, 25 Dec.* ⓔ €5. ☎ 01 581 67 30. *www.wienmuseum.at.*

Franz Schubert stayed in this house, the home of his composer brother Ferdinand from 1 September 1838 until his death on 19 November that year. Here he composed his last work, among them the song "The Shepherd on the Rock." Drafts for new work, his last hand-written letter, personal effects and letters of condolence from family and friends are exhibited in the rooms of this Biedermeier house, which contain furniture and instruments used by the pair.

Belvedere★★

A must-see for all visitors to Vienna, the grand Belvedere palace complex, residence of Austria's greatest military leader Prince Eugene of Savoy, is vast and impressive both inside and out. The two palaces of the Belvedere were built by the architect Lukas von Hildebrandt for Prince Eugene of Savoy (1663–1736) and are seen as major works of Baroque architecture. The Unteres (Lower) Belvedere was built in 1716 as a summer residence, while the Oberes (Upper) Belvedere was completed in 1722 as a place for festivities.

A BIT OF HISTORY

Both Belvedere palaces were used to house collections from the **Österreichische Galerie Belvedere**. Collections of the 19C and 20C were, and still are, in the Oberes Belvedere, while the Museum of Baroque Art and the Museum of Medieval Art occupied the Unteres Belvedere.

Since spring 2008, all the collections have been housed under one roof in the Oberes Belvedere. The **Unteres Belvedere** is now used for temporary exhibits, and the **Prunkstall** houses the Medieval Treasury, a collection of Medieval art previously held in storage and available only to academics and art students.

OBERES BELVEDERE★★ (UPPER BELVEDERE)

⊙Open daily 10am–6pm. ⊛€14.
&. ℘01 795 57 134. www.belvedere.at.
⊙See Introduction: ABC of Architecture.
The palace's main façade faces south and is distinguished by splendid doorways in the central section. The four figures of Atlas to the right of the vestibule, the **Sala Terrena★**, are by Lorenzo Mattielli, while Carlo Carlone was responsible for the frescoes. A grand staircase leads to the vast red **Marmorsaal** (Marble Hall) on the first floor. It was here on 15 May 1955 that the signing of the State Treaty took place, putting an end to the occupation of Austria by the Allied Powers.

Galerie des 19. und 20. Jahrhunderts★★

These galleries show the work of the different schools of the 19C: Classicism, Romanticism, the Biedermeier Era, Historicism and Impressionism. Included are works by French Impressionists Monet, Cezanne, Pissarro, Manet and Renoir as well as van Gogh's The Plain of Auvers. Works of Austrian Impressionists Emil Jacob Schindler, Rudolf Ribarz, Robert Russ deserve your attention, particularly Olga Wisinger-Florian's Blooming Poppy (1895/1900).
Works by Hans Makart (The Five Senses★, Lady at the Spinet★), who dominated the late 19C art scene in Vienna, and Anton Romako (Empress Elisabeth★★, Mathilde

---

Prince Eugene of Savoy (1663–1736)

Eugene of Savoy joined the French army under Louis XIV, but resigned his commission when he was refused the command of a regiment and entered into the service of Leopold I. At the age of 20, he joined the relief army commanded by the Polish King Jan Sobieski, which in 1683 freed Vienna from the Turkish siege. The soldier once spurned by Louis XIV achieved great fame when the Austrian army under his command defeated the Turks in the Battle of Zenta (1697). Prince Eugene, the "saviour of Christendom" at age 25, became Joseph I's confidant and political adviser and senior minister under Charles VI. In 1714, he had the satisfaction of signing the Treaty of Rastatt with Louis XIV. The Prince had two magnificent residences, a town palace in the Himmelpfortgasse (now the Ministry of Finance) and his summer seat, the Belvedere. In 2013 the town palace opened as a museum of Baroque art (Himmelpfortgasse 8; open year-round daily 10am–6pm; €9; ℘01 795 57 134; www.belvedere.at).

Gustav Klimt, The Kiss, *1908/1909 (Oil on canvas 180 x 180 cm)*

© Belvedere, Vienna

Stern★), who suffered under this dominance, are worth seeking out.

Other must-sees are the museum's large collection of Gustav Klimt *(The Kiss★★★, The Bride★★)* and Egon Schiele *(Death and the Maiden★★, Four Trees★★).*

In addition to historical paintings, works by Moritz von Schwind *(Party Game★),* Caspar David Friedrich *(Rocky Landscape in the Elbsandsteingebirge)* and Friedrich von Amerling *(Girl in a Straw Hat★)* are displayed.

The museum has the largest collection of Biedermeier (🕭 *see p57)* works in the world. Ferdinand Georg Waldmüller is the leading representative of this era. His *Corpus Christi Morning* and *The Brushwood Gatherers in the Vienna Woods (1855)* are both good examples of his work.

Die Sammlung Mittelalter★

The works are mostly from the Gothic period from around 1400 until the early 16C. There are rare altar panel paintings and such impressive works as *Christ's*

Crucifixion★ by Conrad Laib (1449); the *Mourning of Christ★* by the Master of the Viennese Schottenaltar (c. 1469); the *Legend of Susanna★* by the Carinthian painter Urban Görtschacher; and several works by the Tirolean painter and sculptor Michael Pacher.

Die Sammlung Barock★

This collection shows the essence of Austrian High Baroque with paintings and sculptures from the late 17C and 18C on display. You can admire the original **Mehlmarkt fountain★★** by **Georg Raphael Donner** (1693–1741), a copy of which stands on the Neuer Markt.

Franz Xaver Messerschmidt's marvelous **character heads★★** group of sculptures are highlight, along with his figures of Maria Theresia and Francis of Lorraine.

The Sacrifice of Iphigenia (c. 1690) and *The Lamentation of Abel* (1692) are two of the many works of **Johann Michael Rottmayr**, known as the Father of Austrian Baroque, that are worth viewing.

Balthasar Permoser's impressive marble sculpture of *The Apotheosis of Prince Eugene*★ has a figure of himself positioned at the feet of the prince. Among the many paintings here, the following are stand-outs: *Christ on the Mount of Olives*★ by Paul Troger (c. 1750), the Classical artist of Baroque painting; *Napoleon on the St. Bernard Pass*★ by Jacques Louis David (1801); and *View of Laxenburg*★ by Johann Christian Brand (1758).

Belvedere Gardens

🕐*Open Apr–Oct daily 6.30am–sunset; Nov–Mar daily 7.30am–sunset.* 🎫*Free.* 📞*01 795 57 134.* *www.bundesgaerten.at.*

The palace is surrounded by some of the grandest and most important Baroque gardens in Europe, laid out in the French style starting in 1697 by Lukas von Hildebrandt, Dominique Girard and Anton Zinner. The upper part represents Olympus, the central part Parnassus and the lower part the domain of the Four Elements. From the highest point there is a wonderful **view**★ over the garden and the city.

UNTERES BELVEDERE★ (LOWER BELVEDERE)

🕐*Open year-round daily 10am–6pm (Wed til 9pm).* 📞*01 795 57 134.* *www.belvedere.at.*

The Lower Belvedere is fronted by a court of honour entered through an impressive gateway bearing the cross of Savoy in its gable. The long building has a well-proportioned façade on the garden side and sumptuous apartments that make an ideal setting for the temporary exhibitions. The former living quarters and staterooms are impressive and works of art in their own right. Attractions include the **Marble Hall**, adorned with frescoes by Martino Altomonte (1659–1745), who also painted the ceiling frescoes in the **Marble Room**★, the state bedroom, **Hall of Grotesques**★, named after the motifs of stuccowork that adorns its walls, and the dazzling **Gold Room**★★ with its mirrors and gilded carved woodwork.

Orangerie

🕐*Open year-round daily 10am–6pm (Wed til 9pm).* 📞*01 795 57 134.*

The orangerie was built by Johann Lukas von Hildebrandt in the first quarter of the 18C to protect exotic tender plants and trees. The interior has been transformed by the architect Susanne Zottl into a home for regularly changing temporary exhibits.

Prunkstall

🕐*Open year-round daily 10am–noon.* 📞*01 795 57 134.*

These ornamental stables, a jewel in the Baroque architectural crown, were built to accommodate the 12 riding horses of Prince Eugene. The building is adorned with stucco and has its own fountain. Horses were once stabled in what is now the **Schatzhaus Mittelalter** (Medieval Treasury). This collection, which opened in 2008, complements the display of Medieval Art in the Oberes Belvedere. Many of the 150 works of art have not been seen in public before; they include panel paintings, sculpture and Gothic triptychs that now give a broader perspective on Medieval art in Austria.

Heeresgeschichtliches Museum★ (Museum of Military History)

🕐*Open year-round daily 9am–5pm.* 🕐*Closed 1 Jan, Easter, 1 May, 1 Nov, 25 & 31 Dec.* 🎫€6. ♿ 📞*01 795 610.* *www.hgm.at.*

The exhaustive and excellent army museum inside a former munitions depot tells the history of Austria through its military exploits. All major conflicts since the Thirty Years' War are covered, including the Turkish threat, the Napoleonic era and World War I. There are special rooms dedicated to Prince Eugene, the heroic general who dealt Turkish troops a decisive defeat; Maria Theresia and her feuds with Prussia; and Archduke Franz Ferdinand's assassination in Sarajevo, featuring the actual car in which he and his wife were shot.

Schloss Schönbrunn★★★

A UNESCO World Heritage Site since 1996, the Imperial Schönbrunn Palace occupies what was once a favoured hunting ground of the Habsburgs. Construction of the family's imposing summer residence, originally based on the plans of Johann Bernhard Fischer von Erlach, began in 1695. The palace got its present form under Maria Theresia and reflects the vision of architect Nicolas Pacassi. The park was laid out by French landscape architect Jean Trehet and later modified by Johann Ferdinand Hetzendorf of Hohenberg, who also contributed the Neptune fountain, Roman ruin, Obelisk and Gloriette.

Tour of the Palace★★★

U-bahn 4, Schönbrunn or Heitzing.
♿🕐*Open Jul–Aug daily 8.30am–6.30pm; Apr–Jun & Sept–Oct daily 8.30am–5.30pm; Nov–Mar daily 8.30am–5pm.* 🎧*€14.20 (Imperial Tour), €17.50 (Grand Tour; both tours include audio-guides).* 📞*0181 11 32 39. www.schoenbrunn.at.*

The main building stretches for 180m/590.5ft in classically restrained Baroque style. The exterior is painted a pleasing colour known as Schönbrunn Yellow; green window frames provide additional accents.

Self-guided audio tours take in either 22 rooms (Imperial Tour) or 40 rooms (Grand Tour) out of a total of 1,440, each of which seems to outdo the other in opulence. Elegant stuccowork, crystal chandeliers, richly ornamented faience stoves, and priceless tapestries and furniture give the apartments an air of exceptional magnificence.

The **apartments of Emperor Franz Joseph and Empress Elisabeth** are followed by three **ceremonial rooms** decorated by the Austrian painter Josef Rosa and two **Chinese chambers★**, one adorned with lacquerwork, the other with porcelain. The **Maria Theresia apartments** are among the most luxurious in the palace. They include the **Blue Salon**, hung with Chinese tapestry, which was the room where negotiations took place that led to Karl I (last of the Habsburgs) abdicating on 11 November 1918.

Other stand-outs are the **Vieux-Lacque Room★**, with black Oriental lacquered panelling framing intricate miniatures; the Napoleon Room, decorated with Flemish tapestry; and the lavish **Millionenzimmer★** with its South American rosewood panelling framing Indo-Persian miniatures painted on paper. The tour culminates in the **Great Gallery★★★**, where the dele-

Great Gallery

©BILDAGENTUR ZOLLES KG/Christian Hofer

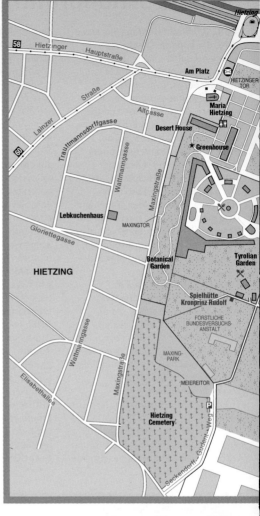

gates to the 1814–15 Congress of Vienna danced and partied.

👥 Schlosspark★★
🕐*Open year-round daily 6am–sunset.*
💶*Free admission.*

The park gardens are a remarkable creation of Baroque art, mixed with an infusion of Rococo and antiquity. Arbors and vast formal beds of flowers serve as backdrops for charming groups of allegorical statues and gracious fountains.

Shaded walks lead to the Neptune's Fountain (Neptunbrunnen), the Roman ruin (Römische Ruine) and the **Zoo★** *(Tiergarten;*
♿🕐*open Apr–Sept daily 9am–6.30pm; Mar, Oct daily 9am–5.30pm; Feb daily 9am–5pm; Nov–Jan daily 9am–4.30pm; 💶€18.50; ☎01 877 92 940; www.zoovienna.at),* the oldest zoological gardens in the world. Originally it was a menagerie founded by Emperor Franz Stephan, who had a deep interest in zoology. Open to the public in 1779, the menagerie eventually evolved into zoological gardens in the 19C.

The first giraffe seen in Europe arrived here in 1828, a gift from the Viceroy of Egypt, and caused quite a stir among Viennese society.

The **Greenhouse★** *(Palmenhaus;* 🕐*open May–Sept daily 9.30am–6pm; Oct–Apr til 5pm; 💶€5; ☎01 877 50 87 406; www.bundesgaerten.at)* is the European continent's largest glass and metal hothouse. It shelters some 4,000 plants from all over the world, from the Himalayas to tropical rain forest vegetation.

The **Labyrinth** 👥 *(Irrgarten; 💶5.50)* will keep the children entertained for hours. The maze was laid out between 1698 and 1740 with a central pavilion from which the maze as a whole could be viewed. Although it fell into disrepair in the 19C, it has been replanted

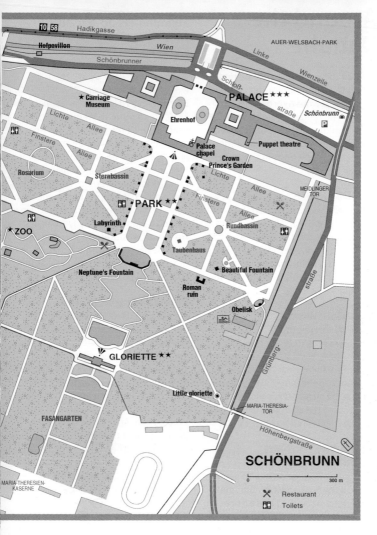

and opened in 1998. The labyrinth was reconstructed according to the original historical design. There are games and mental puzzles to solve along the way.

Gloriette★★

🕐 *Café open daily 9am–sunset.*
📞 *01 879 13 11.*

This elegant colonnaded structure offers fine views of Schönbrunn and west Vienna from its roof terrace. Resembling a triumphal arch, it was built to commemorate Maria Theresia's victory over the Prussians in 1757 during the Seven Years War.

Wagenburg★ (Carriage Museum)

🕐 *Open mid-Mar–Oct daily 9am–5pm.*
💶 *€9.50, children under 19 yrs, free.*
♿ 📞 *01 525 24 4702.*

The **coach house** contains a collection of Imperial coaches dating from the early 18C to the 20C. Note especially the **phaeton of the King of Rome★** and the gilded and ornate **Imperial coach★★** of Emperor Franz Stephan, Maria Theresia's husband, which was pulled by eight white horses.

Around the Danube

The Danube is popular with swimmers during the summer months, while walkers enjoy the riverbank in any season. The following sights are all within striking distance of the river, and will help you to discover some fascinating attractions in less busy parts of the city.

LANDSTRAßE

"The Orient begins at Landstraße," politician and statesman Metternich is said to have claimed in the early 19C, when today's 3. Bezirk, southeast of the city centre, was nothing more than a route east. Among the embassies, consulates and churches are interesting sights.

KunstHausWien★

Untere Weissgerberstraße 13. ⏱*Open year-round daily 10am–6pm.* €*10.* ℘*01712 04 91. www.kunsthauswien.com.* Designed by Hundertwasser, this museum has the world's only permanent exhibit on his work, philosophy and architecture. The other part of the building is used for temporary art exhibits.

Hundertwasserhaus (Hundertwasser House)

Löwengasse/Kegelgasse. o━*No public access. www.hundertwasserhaus.info.* Viennese artist **Friedensreich Hundertwasser** used this 1984 apartment block to create a type of mass housing that marries human needs with the environment. His colourful, eccentric building makes use of arcaded loggias, galleries, statues and other design elements as well as a range of materials (glass, brick, rendering etc). The terraced roof garden is typical of his approach.

ALSERGRUND

The University of Vienna's medicine faculty and the general hospital of the 9. Bezirk have long defined the character of Alsergrund – it's not mere chance that the father of psychoanalysis lived in the vicinity for 50 years.

Sigmund-Freud-Museum★

Berggasse 19. U-bahn 2, Schottentor/ Universität, tram D, Schlickgasse, bus 40A, Berggasse. ⏱*Open year-round daily 10am–6pm.* €*10.* ℘*01 319 15 96. www.freud-museum.at.*
Born in Freiberg in Mähren, Germany in 1856, Freud came to Vienna as a three-year-old with his parents. This apartment, where he lived between 1891 and 1938 before fleeing the Nazi regime for London, has become a place of pilgrimage for students of psychoanalysis. It contains photographs, documents and a short film narrated by Anna Freud, Sigmund's daughter (also a psychoanalyst). His home was opened as a museum in 1971. His consulting room is on the ground floor. An adjacent waiting room contains original furniture.

Palais Liechtenstein★★

Fürstengasse 19. Tram D, Seegasse, bus 40A, Bauernfeldplatz. ⏱━*By guided tour only (in German with English audioguide); advance reservations required.* €*20 (Garden Palace),* €*25 (City Palace,* €*38 (combined ticket).* ℘*01 319 57 670. www.palaisliechtenstein.com.*
In 2004, some 1,600 works of art of Prince Hans-Adam II of Liechtenstein were unveiled to the public after the 18C palace had been closed for 50 years.

Schubert Geburtshaus★ (Schubert's Birthplace)

Nußorfer Straße 54. ⏱*Open Tue–Sun 10am–1pm, 2pm–6pm* ⏱*Closed 1 Jan, 1 May, 25 Dec.* ⏱━*Guided tours available (1hr).* €*5, free first Sun of month.* ℘*01 317 36 01. www.wienmuseum.at.*
Birthplace of Franz Schubert on 31 January 1797, this house is the place where he spent the first four years of his life before the family moved to Säulengasse. There's a small museum about the composer on the first floor.

BETWEEN THE CANAL AND THE DANUBE

👥 Prater★

This immense green space, embraced by two arms of the Danube, was a hunting reserve under Emperor Maximilian II and opened to the public in 1766 under Joseph II. With its cafés, the Prater was very popular in the heyday of the Viennese waltz. Featured in the film *The Third Man*, it won worldwide renown; scenes for the James Bond film *The Living Daylights* were shot here.

The Prater's most popular part is the amusement park called "Wurstelprater," lorded over by the landmark 1897 **Riesenrad★★ (Giant Ferris Wheel)** (*Open Oct–Feb daily 10am–9.45pm, late Jan–Feb & mid-Oct til 7.45pm; May–Aug 9am–11.45pm, Sept til 10:45pm; €9.50; 01 729 54 30; www.wienerriesenrad. com*), which treats you to breathtaking **views★★** of the city.

Johann Strauss Wohnung★ (Johann Strauss House)

Praterstraße 54, 1st floor. U-bahn 1, Nestroyplatz, bus 5A, Praterstraße. Open year-round Tue–Sun 10am–1pm, 2pm–6pm. Closed 1 Jan, 1 May, 25 Dec. €5, free first Sun of month. 01 214 01 21. www.wienmuseum.at.

Johann Strauss' son lived here, the house where *An der schönen blauen Donau* (*Blue Danube*) was composed in 1867.

Augarten Contemporary

Open Wed–Sun noon–5pm (Fri–Sun til 7pm). Free admission. 01 513 98 560. www.tba21.org.

Contemporary art is on view in a beautifully light space in the Augarten.

WEST VIENNA
Haydnhaus★

Haydngasse 19. Open year-round Tue–Sun 10am–1pm, 2pm–6pm. Closed 1 Jan, 1 May, 25 Dec. €5, free first Sun of month. 01 596 13 07. www.wienmuseum.at.

The house where the composer wrote the oratorios *The Creation* (1798) and *The Seasons* (1801) is now a museum. Exhibits illustrate the context of the music and in particular the places that were important in Haydn's life.

Kaiserliches Hofmobilien depot★ (Furniture Museum)

Andreasgasse 7. Open year-round Tue–Sun 10am–6pm. €9.50. 01 524 33 57. www.hofmobiliendepot.at.

The Imperial furniture, carpets and tapestries were stored here when not in use at the royal residences.

The **collection of period furniture** is one of the world's largest. Besides original furniture once used by the Habsburgs, exhibits include the coffin in which Emperor Maximilian of Mexico was shipped back to Europe following his assassination as well as Prince Rudolf's cradle. The **Biedermeier** collection consists of bourgeois period rooms and features bizarre spitoons and early toilets. The Modernist section has amazing furniture by Adolf Loos, Joseph Hoffmann and Otto Wagner.

Technisches Museum (Technical Museum)

Open year-round Mon–Fri 9am–6pm, Sat–Sun 10am–6pm. Closed 1 Jan, 1 May, 1 Nov, 25 & 31 Dec. €12, children free. 01 89 99 80. www.tmw.at.

The museum presents an interactive, comprehensive overview of technology and industry. The history of science, tool manufacturing, mining, heavy industry and energy are among the themes explored.

SOUTH VIENNA
Zentralfriedhof (Central Cemetery)

Open Mar & Oct daily 7am–6pm; Apr–Sept daily 7am–7pm (May–Aug til 8pm), Nov–Feb daily 8am–5pm. 01 534 69 28 405. www.friedhoefewien.at.

Beethoven, Brahms, Gluck, Schubert and Hugo Wolf are all buried in the "Musicians' Corner" (Plot 32A) of this famous cemetery, alongside Johann Strauss the Elder and the Younger, Joseph Lanner, Karl Millöcker, Franz von Suppé. In Plot 32C lie Arnold Schoenberg and Franz Werfel Jürgens, while at 14A Theophil von Hansen and Hans Makart are buried and at 0 Antonio Salieri and Adolf Loos are interred.

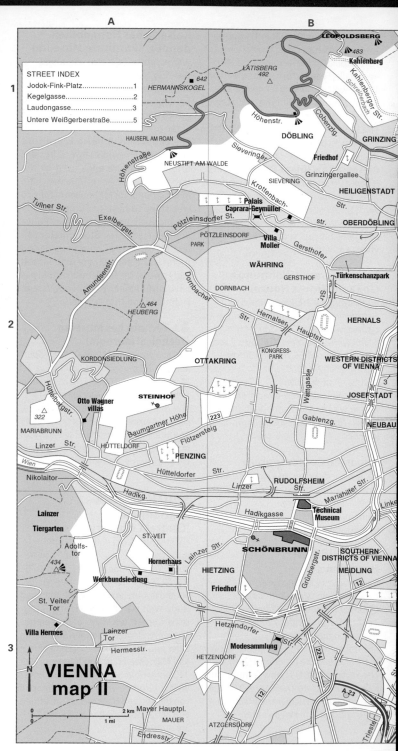

STREET INDEX

VIENNA
map II

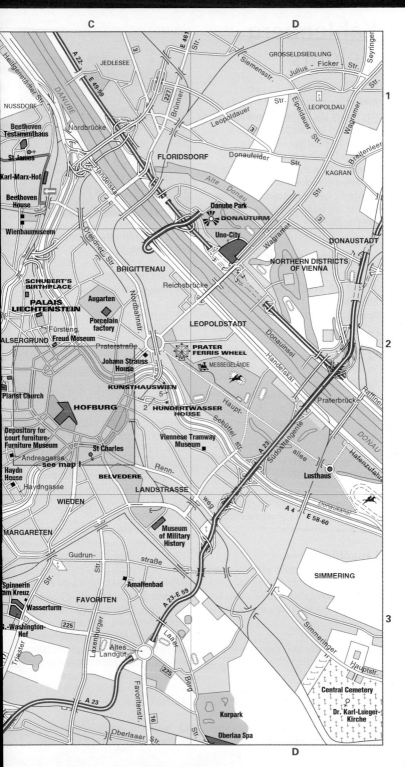

Kahlenberg Heights

Escaping the city centre to the Kahlenberg Heights is a favourite day trip of the Viennese, and few excursions are complete without a visit to a Heuriger to sample young wine, or a stroll through the forested Wienerwald (Vienna Forest) for views over Vienna. The more energetic can follow mountain bike and hiking trails, which begin at the city border.

Vineyards, the Kahlenberg
© Austrian National Tourist Office/ Diejun

🚘 DRIVING TOUR

TOUR OF THE KAHLENBERG HEIGHTS
Round-trip of 33km/21mi (👣 see map p224).

◖ Leave Vienna via Heiligenstädter Straße. At the Klosterneuburg-Kierling railway station turn left into the Stadtplatz and left again. Cross the Kierlingbach creek and go uphill towards the abbey. Park in the Rathausplatz.

Klosterneuburg★
👣 *See KLOSTERNEUBURG*

◖ Follow Leopoldstraße S to the Weidlingbach Valley; cross Weidlinger Straße into Höhenstraße.

Leopoldsberg★★
The most easterly spur of the Wienerwald, Leopoldsberg overlooks the Danube from 423m/1,388ft. Views are best from the Burgplatz opposite the Leopoldskirche.

◖ Go back downhill, then turn left onto Höhenstraße.

Kahlenberg★
There are attractive **views★** over Vienna from the terrace next to the Kahlenberg restaurant (483m/1,584.6ft). In the foreground are the vineyards of Grinzing

and to the right the rolling heights of the Wienerwald.

◖ Continue on Höhenstraße as far as the Häuserl am Roan inn.

🅿 From the car park, enjoy a fine view of Vienna and the Wienerwald.

◖ Return towards the Kahlenberg; turn right into Cobenzlgasse down into Grinzing.

Grinzing★
Grinzing is the best known of Vienna's suburban wine villages. It is a pretty place with a friendly atmosphere best sampled in one of the many taverns, or Heurigen (👣 *see infobox p182*). It can get very busy here in the evenings.

Heiligenstadt
Beethoven devotees flock to Heiligenstadt's central square (Pfarrplatz) to see the little 17C house (no. 2 – now a wine tavern), where the musician lived in 1817. In Probusgasse 6 stands the **Beethoven Wohnung Heiligenstadt** (◷*open daily 10am–1pm, 2pm–6pm;* ◷*closed 1 Jan, 1 May, 25 Dec;* ⊛€5; ℘*01 370 54 08; www. wienmuseum.at*), now a small museum, where the composer wrote his famous letter in 1802 called the *Testament of Heiligenstadt* when in despair over his deafness. The letter, addressed to his brother Carl, was never sent.

◖ Return to Vienna along Hohe Warte and Döblinger Hauptstraße.

ADDRESSES

🛏 STAY

VIENNA OLD TOWN

😊🛏 **Pension City**– *Bauernmarkt 10. U-bahn Stephansplatz.* 📞*01 533 95 21. www.citypension.at. 19 rooms.* 🚗 *€14.50.* Find excellent value for money here, given the good location and carefully decorated rooms of this 19C building.

😊🛏 **Pension Dr. Geissler** – *Postgasse 14. U-bahn Stubentor/Schwedenplatz.* 📞*01 533 28 03. www.hotelpension.at. 23 rooms.* 🚗. One of the cheapest places to stay in the centre of Vienna (if you don't mind sharing a bathroom) is on the eighth floor, with views of the cathedral or an inner courtyard. Less basic rooms cost more.

😊🛏 **Schweizer Pension Solderer** – *Heinrichsgasse 2. U-bahn Schottenring.* 📞*01 533 81 56. www.schweizerpension.com. 11 rooms.* 🚗. Reserve far ahead to stay at this clean, nicely decorated pension next to the Danube canal cycle path.

😊🛏🛏 **Pension Riedl**– *Georg-Coch-Platz 3. U-bahn Stubentor/Schwedenplatz.* 📞*01 512 79 19. www.pensionriedl.at. 10 rooms.* 🚗 *€8.90.* Very friendly welcome at this pension in an Art Nouveau block. Colourful, recently renovated rooms or cheaper, more "retro" decoration for those on a budget are available.

😊🛏🛏 **Pension Neuer Markt**– *Seilergasse 9. U-bahn Stephansplatz.* 📞*01 512 23 16. www.hotelpension.at. 37 rooms.* 🚗. You'll find simple, clean, comfortable rooms behind a grand façade. It's worth requesting a room with a view over Neuer Markt.

😊🛏🛏 **Römischer Kaiser Best Western Premier**– *Annagasse 16. U-bahn Karlsplatz.* 📞*01 51 27 75 10. www.hotel-roemischer-kaiser.at. 24 rooms.* 🚗. This well-appointed Baroque palace from 1684, richly furnished and decorated with chandeliers, stuccowork and gold, has been family run for more than a century.

THE RING AND AROUND

😊🛏 **Hotel-Pension Wild**– *Lange Gasse 10. U-bahn Volkstheater.* 📞*01 406 51 74. www.pension-wild.com. 26 rooms.* 🚗. Opened by the Wild family in 1960, this pension near the Ring has been warmly welcoming guests ever since. Recently refurbished rooms are offered in three categories of to choose from.

😊🛏🛏 **Hotel Rathaus Wine & Design**– *Lange Gasse 13. U-bahn Rathaus.* 📞*01 400 11 22. www.hotel-rathaus-wien.at. 39 rooms.* 🚗 *€18.* Situated in a quiet street in Josefstadt, the hotel has contemporary rooms named after different wines. Friendly welcome and delicious breakfast.

NEUBAU

😊🛏 **Jugendherberge Myrthengasse**– *Myrthengasse 7. U-bahn Thaliastraße/ Volkstheater.* 📞*01 523 63 160. www.oejhv. at/index.php?id=148.* 🚗. Handy for the Museum Quarter, this youth hostel has rooms with 2–6 beds, in a well-equipped 19C block.

😊🛏 **Hostel Ruthensteiner** – *Robert-Hamerling-Gasse 24. U-bahn Westbahnhof.* 📞*01 893 42 02. www.hostelruthensteiner. com.* Having travelled the world together, Walter and Erin opened their friendly, cosmopolitan guesthouse between the Westbahnhoff railway station and Schönbrunn. Choose from dormitories or double rooms with their own bathroom.

😊🛏 **Pension Kraml**– *Brauergasse 5. U-bahn Zieglergasse/Pilgramgasse.* 📞*01 587 85 88. www.pensionkraml.at. 14 rooms.* 🚗. This tastefully decorated, family-run pension sits close to the Mariahilferstraße shopping street.

😊🛏🛏 **Boutiquehotel Stadthalle**– *Hackengasse 20. U-bahn Schweglerstraße.* 📞*01 982 42 72. www.hotelstadthalle.at. 79 rooms.* 🚗. Two options are available at this environmentally friendly place (they have their own wind turbine) near the Westbahnhof: basic pension-style rooms, and a pricer hotel service.

😊🛏🛏 **Altstadt Vienna**– *Kirchengasse 41. U-bahn Volkstheater.* 📞*01 522 66 66. www.altstadt.at. 42 rooms.* 🚗. Home to a former monarch, this Spittelberg building offers comfortable rooms beyond the sumptuous entrance hall; some have been decorated by Italian architect and designer Matteo Thun.

😊🛏🛏 **Schreiners Gastwirtschaft**– *Westbahnstraße 42. U-bahn Burggasse-Stadthalle.* 📞*01 676 475 40 60. www. schreiners.cc. 5 rooms.* 🚗. Rooms at this tavern are spacious, with either balconies or patios overlooking a charming garden. Delicious breakfast included in the rate.

SCHÖNBRUNN AND AROUND

😊🛏🛏 **Hotel Lenas Vienna** – *Graumanngasse 16. U-bahn Lägenfeldgasse.*

🏠*01 40 50 000. www.hotel-reither.com.
50 rooms.* 🛏 *€7.* Family-run hotel promising typically Austrian hospitality, near to Schönbrunn. Rooms have a balcony or a patio.

THE DANUBE AND AROUND

🍽🍽 **Praterstern** – *Mayergasse 6. U-bahn Praterstern.* 🏠*01 214 01 23. www.hotelpraterstern.at. 41 rooms.* 🛏 *€8.* Popular hotel on a quiet road close to the Prater. Unfussy rooms and an inner courtyard, where breakfast is served in summer.

🍽🍽 **Roomz Vienna** – *Paragonstraße 1. U-bahn Gasometer.* 🏠*01 743 17 77. www.roomz-vienna.com. 152 rooms.* 🛏 *€15.* Five U-bahn stops from city centre, this place offers full-service at budget rates. 24hr bar, modern rooms, free sports centre and business facilities.

🍴/EAT

VIENNA OLD TOWN

🍽 **Zwölf Apostelkeller** – *Sonnenfelsgasse 3, 1. Bezirk.* 🏠*(01) 512 67 77. www.zwoelf-apostelkeller.at. Daily 11am–midnight.* Lively place 10m/33ft underground in the medieval catacombs once used by the Viennese for shelter from danger. Traditional dishes and a Heuriger-style buffet. Popular with all ages.

🍽 **Pfudl** – *Bäckerstr. 22, 1. Bezirk.* 🏠*01 512 67 05. www.gasthauspfudl.com. Daily 10am–midnight.* This place ranks among the inns that have become a Viennese institution.

🍽 **Trzesniewski** – *Dorotheergasse 1, 1. Bezirk.* 🏠*01 512 32 91. www.trzesniewski.at. Mon–Fri 8.30am–7.30pm, Sat 9am–5pm, Sun 10am–5pm.* Behind the unpronounceable name is a bistro serving open sandwiches topped with anything from cucumber to bacon to eggs. Eat sitting, standing or as take away.

🍽 **Kanzleramt** – *Schauflergasse 6, 1. Bezirk.* 🏠*01 533 13 09. www.kanzleramt. wien. Mon–Sat 11am–11pm, Sun til 6pm.* Traditional inn next to the Hofburg popular with office workers, civil servants from the surrounding departments and tourists who appreciate the efficient service.

🍽 **Esterházykeller** – *Haarhof 1, 1. Bezirk* 🏠*01 533 34 82. www.esterhazykeller.at. Daily 4pm–11pm. Closed Jul–mid-Sep.* Lively and always busy, this historic Heurige is set in a series of vaulted cellars and serves rustic cuisine. Wine comes from the famous Esterházy estate in Eisenstadt. In good weather tables spill out on to a small patio.

🍽🍽 **Figlmüller** – *Wollzeile 5, 1. Bezirk.* 🏠*01 512 61 77. www.figlmuller.at. Daily 11am–10.30pm.* Local eatery offering the famous Wiener Schnitzel.

🍽🍽 **Oswald & Kalb** – *Bäckerstraße 14, 1. Bezirk.* 🏠*01 512 13 71. Mon–Sat 5pm–midnight.* Classy place popular with the creative set, serving Viennese specialities such as Schnitzel and Tafelspitz, and Mediterranean dishes.

🍽🍽 **Ofenloch** – *Kurrentgasse 8, 1. Bezirk.* 🏠*01 533 88 44. www.restaurant-ofenloch.at. Mon–Sat 11.30am–11pm.* Traditional, seasonal Viennese cuisine served in rustically decorated room or on the terrace on a pedestrianised street.

🍽🍽 **Salzamt** – *Ruprechtsplatz 1, 1. Bezirk.* 🏠*01 533 53 32. www.salzamt-wien.at. Tue–Sun 11.30am–2am, Mon 5pm–2am.* At the heart of Vienna's bar scene in the old Jewish quarter, Salzamat serves Italian and Austrian dishes. Terrace in summer.

THE RING AND AROUND

🍽 **Hansen** – *Wipplinger Straße 34. U-bahn Schottentor.* 🏠*01 532 05 42. www.hansen.co.at. Mon–Fri 9am–11pm, Sat 9am–5pm.* Modern Mediterranean-influenced dishes served in the former stock exchange.

🍽 **Vestibül** – *Universitätsring 2, in the Burgtheater. U-bahn Rathaus.* 🏠*01 532 49 99 10. www.vestibuel.at. Mon–Fri 11am–midnight, Sat 6pm–midnight (closed Sat Jul and Aug).* The Neoclassical Burgtheater is the setting for beautifully presented, light dishes. In summer, you can sit in the garden overlooking the town hall.

🍽🍽🍽 **Steirereck** – *Am Heumarkt 2A, 3. Bezirk.* 🏠*01 713 31 68. www.steirereck.at. Mon–Fri 11.30am–2.30pm, and from 6.30pm.* Located near the Hundertwasserhaus in the Stadtpark. Arguably the best food in Vienna. You can visit its substantial wine cellar.

MUSEUMS QUARTER

🍽 **Café-Restaurant Corbaci** – *Museumsquartier, 7. Bezirk.* 🏠*01 664 736 30 036. www.azw.at. Mon–Sat 11am–midnight, Sun til 11pm.* 🍴 A peaceful corner of the Museum Quarter decorated with tiles. Enjoy a late breakfast, Austrian and Italian dishes, or dining on the terrace in the summer before continuing your sightseeing.

🍽 **Amerlingbeisl**– *Stiftgasse 8, 7. Bezirk. ℘01 526 16 60. www.amerlingbeisl.at. Daily 9am–2am.* Adorable bistro in the Spittelberg home of 19C portrait painter Amerling that serves simple, keenly priced dishes. There's a cultural centre here, too, and a shady terrace for warm weather.

WIEDEN

🍽 **Café Anzengruber** – *Schleifmühl-gasse 19, 4. Bezirk. U-bahn Karlsplatz/ Kettenbrückengasse. ℘01 587 82 97. Mon–Sat 4pm–2am, closed Sun.* Tasty Viennese food in a old inn. A great place to enjoy a *Weißgespritzt* (white wine spritzer).

🍽🍽 **Zum Alten Fassl** – *Ziegelofengasse 37, 5. Bezirk. ℘01 544 42 98. www.zum-alten-fassl.at. Mon–Fri 11.30am–3pm and 5pm–12am, Sat 5pm–12am, Sun and holidays noon–3pm and 5pm–12am.* The area where Wieden meets Margareten is renowned for good restaurants. This traditional inn is no exception, serving all the Viennese classics you'd expect, good quality wines, and offering outdoor dining when the sun is shining.

🍽🍽 **Plachutta** – *Wollzeile 38, 1. Bezirk. U-bahn Studentor. ℘01 512 15 77. www. plachutta.at. Daily 11.30am–midnight.* Restaurant dedicated to the Viennese beef tradition.

BELVEDERE

🍽 **Klein Steiermark im Schweizergarten** – *Heeresmuseumstraße 1. U-bahn Südtiroler Platz. ℘01 799 58 83. www.kleinsteiermark.wien. Daily 11am–11pm.* Styrian specialities in the pretty Schweizer Garten, served in a cosy, wood-panelled room in winter, or on the terrace in summer.

ALSERGRUND

🍽🍽 **Stomach** – *Seegasse 26. U-bahn Roßauer Lände. ℘01 310 20 99. Wed–Sat 4pm–midnight, Sun 10am–10pm.* The place to come for Styrian-style fillet steak, a good wine list and thoughtful vegetarian options. It's worth reserving in advance. Beautiful courtyard for outdoor dining in good weather.

LEOPOLDSTADT

🍽 **Schweizer Haus** – *Prater 116. U-bahn Messe-Prater. ℘01 728 01 520. www.schweizerhaus.at. 15 Mar–Oct daily 11am–11pm.* 🗷. The Swiss House has been an institution since it first started serving the signature grilled ham in 1920.

🍽🍽 **Schöne Perle** – *Große Pfarrgasse 2 (at Leopoldsgasse). U-bahn Taborstraße. ℘01 890 32 04. www.schoene-perle.at. Daily noon–11pm, weekend breakfasts 10am–1pm.* Right near the Augarten, this combination airy bistro and trendy canteen serves Austrian produce and organic juices. All dishes are available to take away.

HEURIGER
(Wine taverns)

GRINZING/HEILIGENSTADT

🍽 **Mayer am Pfarrplatz** – *Pfarrplatz 2. ℘01 370 12 87. www.pfarrplatz.at. Mon–Fri 4pm–midnight, Sat–Sun noon–midnight.* This famous Heuriger is located close to the Beethoven house. It has good traditional food and there is a lovely courtyard.

CAFÉS, BARS AND NIGHTCLUBS

COFFEEHOUSES

The coffeehouse is a Viennese institution, and visitors should therefore make sure that they try out one of the numerous speciality coffees (🕮*see p195*), with perhaps an accompanying slice of cake, in at least one such establishment.

VIENNA OLD TOWN

Diglas – *Wollzeile 10, 1. Bezirk. ℘0151 25 76 50. www.diglas.at. Mon–Sat 8am–10.30pm, Sun 9am–10pm.* Behind the delicate pink façade is a grand café in the elegant Viennese tradition. The small tables in the bay windows are the most sought after. Delicious cakes and a summer terrace.

Frauenhuber – *Himmelpfortgasse 6, 1. Bezirk. ℘01 512 53 53. www.cafe-frauenhuber.at. Mon–Sat 8am–midnight, Sun and holidays 10am–10pm.* This is the oldest café in Vienna (1824). There's a wide choice of dishes, and it makes a great place to linger after a long walk.

Sky Café – *Kärntner Straße 19, 1. Bezirk. ℘01 513 17 12. www.skybox.at. Mon–Fri 10am–2am, Sat 9.30am–2am, Sun 11am–2am.* On the top floor of the Steffl department store, this café-restaurant overlooks the roof of the cathedral, serving light meals during the day and Asian, Mediterranean and Austrian dishes in the evening.

Kleines Café – *Franziskanerplatz 3, 1. Bezirk. Mon–Sat 10am–2am, Sun 1pm–2am.* Owned by actor Hanno Poschi, this intimate café is beloved by students and artists, though most come for the wide selection of beers, wine and spirits than for (an albeit delicious) coffee. Chairs spill out on to Franziskanerplatz opposite a fountain and church.

Gelateria Zanoni & Zanoni – *Lugeck 7. 1. Bezirk. ℘01 512 79 79. www.zanoni.co.at. Daily 7.30am–midnight.* This gelateria is an extremely popular place for Italian ice cream, cakes and snacks.

Eissalon Tuchlauben – *Tuchlauben 15. U-bahn Stephansplatz. ℘01 533 25 53. www.eissalon-tuchlauben.at. Apr–Sept Mon–Sat 10am–11.30pm, Sun 11am–11.30pm; Mar & Oct Mon–Sat 10am–8pm, Sun 11am–8pm.* If the terrace outside Gelateria Zanoni & Zanoni is too busy, head here for your gelato fix.

Bräunerhof – *Stallburggasse 2, 1. Bezirk. ℘01 512 38 93. www.braeunerhof.at. Mon–Fri 8am–9pm, Sat 8am–7pm, Sun 10am–7pm.* Few tourists seek out this classic Viennese café, where the discrete service won't disturb those absorbed in their newspapers and books.

Hawelka – *Dorotheergasse 6, 1. Bezirk. U-bahn Stephansplatz. ℘01 512 82 30. www.hawelka.at. Mon–Sat 8am–1am (Mon–Wed til 12am), Sun 10am–12am.* Specialities here include *Buchteln* (pastry filled with plum jam), served only after 8pm.

Konditorei Oberlaa Stadthaus – *Neuer Markt 16, 1. Bezirk. ℘01 513 29 360. www.oberlaa-wien.at. Daily 8am–8pm.* Renowned for its pastries, this address is a Viennese institution. Enjoy a coffee in the summer garden, which overlooks the Baroque houses of the Neuer Markt. In all, an unforgettable occasion.

Mozart – *Albertinaplatz 2, 1. Bezirk. ℘01 24 10 02 00. www.cafe-mozart.at. Daily 8am–midnight.* Handily located on Albertinaplatz, this cafe makes hot food available all day, together with a wide selection of international newspapers. Good coffee as well.

Sacher – *Philharmonikerstraße 4, 1. Bezirk. U-bahn Karlsplatz. ℘01 51 45 66 61. www.sacher.com. Daily 8am–midnight.* The legendary *Sachertorte* is on sale here, an absolute must-try on the Viennese cake list.

Central – *Herrengasse/Strauchgasse, 1. Bezirk. U-bahn Herrengasse. ℘01 533 37 63 38 24. www.palaisevents.at/cafecentral. Mon–Sat 7.30am–10pm, Sun and holidays 10am–10pm.* Specialities are the Mazagran (iced coffee with rum) and Pharisäer (hot coffee with rum and whipped cream). Piano music from 5pm daily.

Demel – *Kohlmarkt 14, 1. Bezirk. ℘01 535 17 170. www.demel.at. Daily 9am–7pm.* The prices are high, but you get something special for your money at Demel.

Griensteidl – *Michaelerplatz 2, 1. Bezirk. ℘01 535 26 920. www.cafegriensteidl.at. Daily 8am–11.30pm.* This long-established literary café stocks a wide choice of international newspapers. It overlooks the Hofburg on one side and the Looshaus on the other. Seasonal food and all the traditional Viennese coffees are served here.

THE RING AND AROUND

Imperial – *Kärntner Ring 16, 1. Bezirk. U-bahn Karlsplatz. ℘0150 11 04 10. www.imperialvienna.com/en/cafe. Daily 7am–11pm.* Both Sigmund Freud and Anton Bruckner were regular clients at this coffeehouse which opened in 1873.

Landtmann – *Universitätsring 4, 1. Bezirk. U-bahn Schottentor. ℘01 241 00 100. www.landtmann.at. Daily 7.30am–midnight.* Near the Parliament, Rathaus and Burgtheater, this café is a popular meeting place, which also boasts a beautiful summer terrace.

Schwarzenberg – *Kärntner Ring 17. U-bahn Karlsplatz. ℘01 512 89 98. www.cafe-schwarzenberg.at. Mon–Fri 7.30am–midnight, Sat–Sun 8.30am–midnight.* A grand café with a terrace serving *Kaisermelange* and a selection of foreign coffees. Piano music July and August on Wed, Fri and Sat from 5pm–10pm.

Prückel – *Stübenring 24. U-bahn Stubentor. ℘01 512 61 15 12. www.prueckel.at. Daily 8.30am–10pm. Closed 24, 25 and 26 Dec.* Great spot to enjoy a coffee and the newspapers on a 1950s sofa after a visit to MAK. Concerts are held in the evenings of Mon, Wed and Fri.

Österreicher im MAK – *Stübenring 5. U-bahn Stubentor. ℘01 714 01 21. www.oesterreicherimmak.at. Daily 10am–1am.* Regional dishes are the stock in trade at the MAK café-restaurant. And there's a pretty garden as well.

HOFBURG AND KUNSTHISTORISCHES MUSEUM

Palmenhaus – *Burggarten 1. U-bahn Museumsquartier. ℘01 533 10 33. www.palmenhaus.at. Mon–Fri 10am–midnight, Sat 9am–12am, Sun 9am–11pm.* Beneath the huge glass dome of the Burggarten greenhouse, a veritable army of waiters will attend to your every need in this splendid, elegant space. Modern bistro food is served.

Kunsthistorisches Museum Café-restaurant – *Maria-Theresian-Platz. ℘050 876 10 01. www.khm.at. Tue–Sun 10am–6pm (Thu 10pm). Reservations are essential.* Gaze up at the splendid Kunsthistorisches Museum dome while you enjoy lunch or a tea at this popular place.

MUSEUMS QUARTER

HALLE Café-restaurant – *Museumsquartier, 7. Bezirk. ℘01 523 70 01. www.diehalle.at. Daily 10am–2am.* The Kunsthalle café-restaurant attracts many trendy patrons here in the centre of the Museums Quarter. Great for people-watching.

Das Möbel – *Burggasse 10, 7. Bezirk. ℘01 524 94 97. www.dasmoebel.at. Mon–Fri 2pm–midnight, Sat–Sun 10am–midnight.* Unusually, everything is for sale at this café: tables, chairs, lamps – it's like an ever-changing showroom for young Austrian designers.

Bortolotti – *Mariahilfer Straße 22, 7. Bezirk. ℘01 526 19 09. www.bortolotti.at. Mon–Sat 8am–11.30pm Sun 9.30am–11.30pm.* This popular ice cream parlour serves mouth-watering seasonal specials and all the old favourites. Eat in or take away (in a cornet).

WIEDEN

Café Museum – *Operngasse 7, 1. Bezirk. ℘0124 100 620. www.cafemuseum.at. Daily 8am–midnight.* This coffeehouse designed by Adolf Loos in the late 19C is situated near the Secession building.

Kunsthalle-Café – *Karlsplatz/ Treitlstraße 2, 4. Bezirk. ℘01 523 70 01. www.kunsthallewien.at Daily 10am–2am.* Breakfast is served until 4pm to a young, hip crowd at the Kunsthalle. Lounge music inside and a shady wooden terrace outside.

BELVEDERE

Café Schloß Belvedere – *Prinz Eugen Straße 27, Oberes Belvedere. U-bahn Südtiroler Platz. ℘01 798 88 88. Tue–Sun 10am–6pm.* This café at the Upper Belvedere is a good place to recharge your batteries with a creamy cappuccino and slice of cake, or a light meal.

ALSERGRUND

Cafe der Provinz – *Maria-Treu-Gasse 3. U-bahn Rathaus. ℘01 944 22 72.*

www.cafederprovinz.at. Daily 8am–11pm. Crêpes are popular at this little slice of the countryside in Josefstadt. The weekend brunch is deservedly popular.

DONAUSTADT

Café am Donauturm – *Donauturmstraße 4, U-bahn Alte Donau. ℘01 263 35 72. www.donauturm.at. Daily 10am–midnight.* Perched 150m/490ft in the air at the top of the Donauturm, the café on a clear day offers a view that takes in the entire city to the Kaltenberg Heights.

CONFECTIONERY AND PATISSERIE

Altmann und Kühne – *Graben 30, 1. Bezirk. ℘01 533 09 27. www.altmann-kuehne.at.* Enter and you'll see why this fantastically packed confectionery is such an attraction.

BARS

The "**Bermuda triangle**" of the Viennese bar scene is located in the 1. Bezirk around the Ruprechtskirche and Rudolfsplatz (KPR). There is something to cater to every taste here.

Kolar-Beisl, *Kleeblattgasse 5, 1. Bezirk. ℘01 533 52 25. www.kolar-beisl.at. Mon–Sat 11am–1am, Sun 3pm–1am.* A friendly and cosy bar that is good for a quiet drink in the afternoon, or a lively evening after dark.

Krah Krah, *Rabensteig 8, 1. Bezirk. ℘01 533 81 93. www.krah-krah.at. Daily 11am–2am.* Popular local bar offering more than 50 varieties of beer.

Loos-Bar, *Kärntner Durchgang 10, 1. Bezirk. ℘01 512 32 83. www.loosbar. at. Daily noon–4am.* Small, but to be recommended, and not only because it was designed by Adolf Loos.

SHOPPING

Most department stores and specialy boutiques are located in the pedestrian zones in Kärntner Straße, Graben, Kohlmarkt, Naglergasse, Tuchlauben, Stephansplatz, part of Krugerstraße and Franz-Josefs-Kai, Wolfengasse, Seitenstettengasse, Rabensteig, Griechengasse, Ballgasse and Vienna's main shopping street **Mariahilfer Straße**.

SOUVENIRS

Augarten GmbH – *Spiegelgasse 3–4, 1. Bezirk. U-bahn Stephansplatz. ℘01 512 14 94. www.augarten.at. Mon–Sat 10am–6pm.* In Schloss Augarten, 2. Bezirk. Sales outlet for the famous porcelain manufacturer, whose origins date back to 1717.

J. & L. Lobmeyr – *Kärntner Straße 26, 1. Bezirk. U-bahn Stephansplatz.* ✆*01 512 05 08 88. www.lobmeyr.at. Mon–Fri 10am–7pm, Sat 10am–6pm.* A glassware specialist that used to supply the Imperial court, Lobmeyr is famous for its extremely fragile and delicate "Musselinglas."

Julius Meinl – *Am Graben 19. U-bahn Herrengasse.* ✆*01 532 33 34. www. meinlamgraben.at. Mon–Fri 8am–7.30pm, Sat 9am–6pm.* A Baroque building is home to this upscale grocery and *Delikatessen*. There's space to enjoy your purchases on-site, if you can't wait to tuck in.

Lanz Trachten Moden – *Kärntner Straße 10. U-bahn Stephansplatz.* ✆*01 512 24 56. www.lanztrachten.at. Mon–Fri 10am–6.30pm, Sat until 6pm.* Traditional Austrian clothing is the attraction here.

Loden Plankl – *Michaelerplatz 6. U-bahn Herrengasse.* ✆*01 533 80 32. www.loden-plankl.at. Mon–Sat 10am–6pm (Jan & Feb, Jul & Aug until 5pm).* Traditional Austrian clothing from a store that has been trading on Michaelerplatz since 1830.

MAK Design Shop – *Stubenring 5, 1. Bezirk.* ✆*0711 36 228. www.makdesign shop.at. Tue–Sun 10am–6pm (Tue 10pm).* Not just a smart bookshop, the museum store at MAK has hundreds of great gifts as well as books.

Österreichische Werkstätten – *Kärntner Straße 6. U-bahn Stephansplatz.* ✆*01 512 24 18. www.austrianarts.com. Mon–Sat 10am–6.30pm (Sat 6pm).* Austrian arts and handicrafts (jewellery, handbags, accessories, glass design)in the Viennese workshop tradition are for sale here.

Tostmann – *Schottengasse 3a. U-bahn Schottentor.* ✆*01 533 53 31. www.tostmann.at. Mon–Sat 10am–6pm (Sat 5pm).* Traditional Austrian clothing, including the iconic *dirndl*. Pricey, but very good quality merchandise.

FOOD MARKETS

Naschmarkt, *Linke Wienzeile/ Kettenbrückengasse. 4. and 6. Bezirk.* The market's produce stalls make a lively picture, full of local colour, though nowadays the market is increasingly being taken over by bars and eateries. A **flea market** takes place Saturdays (☚*see below)* on Kettenbrückengasse, the extension of Naschmarkt. The food market is divided into the **Naschmarkt** proper (fruit and vegetables) *Mon–Fri 6am–7.30pm, Sat 6am–6pm*, and the

Bauernmarkt (farm produce) *Sat 6am–5pm.*

Biobauernmarkt Freyung – *1. Bezirk. Fri–Sat 9am–6pm.* A small market specialising in local organic produce. A good place to pick up gifts or eat from the stalls.

Schwendermarkt– *Schwendergasse/ Dadlergasse, 15. Bezirk. Mon–Sat 6am–9pm (Sat 5pm).* Opportunities for sampling Austrian food abound here.

FLEA MARKET

Naschmarkt – *Linke Wienzeile. 4. and 6. Bezirk. U-bahn Karlsplatz/ Kettenbrückengasse. Sat 6.30am–6pm.* The flea market is located at the south end of the Naschmarkt. Food stalls sell sushi, kebabs, and Indian snacks, among the bric-a-brac.

Art and antiques markets
Kunst- und Antikmarkt am Donaukanal (art and antiques market on the promenade along the banks of the Danube on the old town side by the *Marienbrücke, 1. Bezirk*): *May–Sept Sat 2pm–8pm, Sun 10am–8pm.*
Am Hof *(1. Bezirk): Mar–mid-Nov Fri and Sat 10am–8pm.*

CHRISTMAS MARKETS
Christkindlmarkt Rathausplatz *mid Nov–Christmas*
Weihnachtsmarkt am Spittelberg *late Nov–Christmas*
Altwiener Christkindlmarkt Freyung *late Nov–Christmas*
Kultur- und Weihnachtsmarkt in front of Schloss Schönbrunn *late Nov–Christmas*
Kunsthandwerksmarkt in front of Karlskirche *late Nov–Christmas*

ENTERTAINMENT
THEATRE
Burgtheater – *Universitätsring 2, 1. Bezirk, A-1010 Wien.* ✆*01 514 44 441 45. www.burgtheater.at.* A European theater offering the entire range of theatrical repertoire. Tickets are sold in advance from the 20th of the month preceding the month in question, for the whole calendar month. Written applications for tickets should be addressed at least 10 days in advance of the date to the Servicecenter Burgtheater *(same address as above)*. Tickets can be ordered by telephone (pay by credit card) daily 10am–9pm from ✆*01 513 15 13* as well as online at *www.culturall.com.* For

performances that are not sold out, tickets can be obtained at 75 percent of their original price beginning 1hr before the performance from the "Abendkasse" (☎01/51 44 44 44 0).

Other theaters linked with the Burgtheater are the **Akademietheater** (Lisztstraße 1, 3. Bezirk, ☎01 514 44 47 40) and the **Kasino** (Schwarzenbergplatz 1, 3. Bezirk, ☎01 514 44 41 40).

English Theatre, Josefsgasse 12, 8. Bezirk. ☎01 402 12 600. www.englishtheatre.at. English-language theatre productions from both Britain and America have been staged here since 1963 (classics, comedies, guest performances by solo artists).

MUSIC VENUES

Staatsoper (Opernring 2. Bezirk; www. wiener-staatsoper.at) and **Volksoper** (Währinger Straße 78, 9. Bezirk; www. volksoper.at) – These two venues are the opera venues of the Austrian capital. Tickets go on sale one month before the performance date. Written applications for tickets must be submitted at least three weeks before the performance to the Bestellbüro, Hanuschgasse 3, A-1010 Wien. Tickets can be ordered by telephone (pay by credit card) ☎01 513 15 13 or online at www.culturall.com. Remainder tickets can be purchased from the Bundestheater ticket offices, Operngasse 2, ☎01 514 44 78 80 or the Volksoper itself (Mon–Fri 8am–6pm, Sat, Sun and hols 9am–noon).

Musikverein – Vienna's association for friends of music (Musikvereinsplatz 1, A-1010 Wien; ☎01 505 86 81; www. musikverein.at) puts on about 500 concerts of classical music per year. Tickets go on sale seven weeks before the concert date, Mon–Fri 9am–8pm, Sat 9am–1pm. For program details, call ☎01 505 13 63 (recorded message) or see the website.

Vienna Boys' Choir (Wiener Sängerknaben) – Concerts by the world-famous Vienna Boys' Choir are extremely popular. The choir performs at its new, purpose-built home MuTH near the Augarten. This state-of-the-art concert hall is one of the finest in the city (Am Augartenspitz 1, 1020 Wien; ☎01 347 8080; www.muth.at). Tickets can be purchased online from the MuTH website.

Sung Masses – In the Burgkapelle at the Hofburg on Sundays and 25 Dec (with the Vienna Boys' Choir and members of the chorus and orchestra of the Vienna State Opera) begin at 9.15am. There is no charge for standing room. Orders must be placed in writing (please do not enclose either cash or cheques) at least 10 weeks in advance to: Hofmusikkapelle, Hofburg, A-1010 Wien, fax 01 533 99 27 75, office@hofburgkapelle.at, or online at www.hofmusikkapelle.gv.at. Collection and payment of pre-ordered tickets is on Fri 11am–1pm and 3pm–5pm or on Sun from 8am–8.30am in the Burgkapelle. Availability permitting, tickets for seats for a particular Sun are sold at the Burgkapelle Tageskasse from 11am–1pm and 3pm–5pm on the immediately preceding Fri, and from 8am–8.30am on the day of the mass.

Wiener Konzerthaus, Lothringerstraße 20, 3. Bezirk. ☎01 24 20 02. www. konzerthaus.at. Orchestra and soloists from all over the world perform here as well as notable local ensembles.

Top-quality **musical productions** are presented by Vereinigte Bühnen Wien GmbH (Linke Wienzeile 6, A-1060 Wien, ☎0158 83 01 10, www.musicalvienna.at), which incorporates two venues.

Ticket reservations – It is always better, and very easy, to book directly through the websites of the individual venues. However, there are numerous offices in the city that can provide a ticket service, though for a premium. If you need assistance, contact Vienna Tourism (www.wien.info) for a list of reputable booking services. One good outlet that covers a wide range of venues and events is **Wien Ticket** (☎01 58885, www. wien-ticket.at). There is also a Wien Ticket stand outside the Staatsoper on Herbert von Karajan-Platz.

OTHER VENUES

Orpheum, Steigenteschgasse 94b, 22. Bezirk. ☎01 481 17 17. www.orpheum.at. Entertainment venue (with adjoining restaurant – ☎01 203 12 54), in which cabaret, music and readings are on offer.

Kulisse, Rosensteingasse 39, 17. Bezirk. ☎01 485 38 70. www.kulisse.at. Musicals, cabaret, children's theatre and its own inn (☎01 481 63 07).

Vindobona, Wallensteinplatz 6, 20. Bezirk. ☎01 512 47 42. www.vindo.at. This is the place to go for cabaret; Sat and Sun are devoted to children's theatre. There is also a restaurant close at hand so that visitors will be well taken care of all evening.

LIVE MUSIC

Jazzland – *Franz-Josefs-Kai 29, 1. Bezirk. ☎01 533 25 75. www.jazzland.at.* International groups appear in this vaulted jazz cellar beneath the Ruprechtskirche. Great atmosphere. Music from 9pm.

Jazzclub Porgy & Bess – *Riemergasse 11, 1. Bezirk. ☎01 503 70 09. www.porgy.at.* Concerts by Austrian and international jazz musicians, live music every day.

Roter Engel – *Rabensteig 5. U-bahn Schwedenplatz. ☎01 535 41 05, Daily 5pm–4am. www.roterengel.at.* Some live music but mostly club nights. The cocktail list seems to go on forever.

NIGHTCLUBS

Passage – *Babenberger Passage, Burgring 3. U-bahn Museums-Quartier. ☎01 961 66 770. www.club-passage.at. Wed–Thu from 10pm, Fri–Sat from 11pm.* This club has a good reputation for Austrian and international DJs. It's located in a disused part of the metro.

Volksgarten – *Burgring 1. U-bahn Volkstheater. ☎01 532 42 41. www.volksgarten.at. Hours vary by event.* 1950s décor and a roof that opens above the dance floor. Reggae, house and R'n'B.

Stadtbahnbögen – Between Volksoper and Thaliastraße stations, numerous bars and clubs are open throughout the week. Try **Chelsea** *(Lerchenfelder Gürtel 29–30, 8. Bezirk; ☎01 407 9309; www.chelsea.co.at)* for blues, hip-hop and rock, **B72** *(Hernalser Gürtel-Bogen 72-73, 8.*

Bezirk; ☎01 409 21 28; www.b72.at) for live music and DJs, or **Rhiz** (U-Bahnbogen 37, 8. Bezirk; t0 1 409 25 05; www.rhiz.org) for electro.

Flex – *Donaukanal/Augartenbrücke 1. U-bahn Schottering. ☎533 75 25. www.flex.at.* Vienna's most famous club has a night to suit all tastes (techno, dub, indie, etc.).

DANUBE RIVERBANK ACTIVITIES

Donauinsel (Neue Donau) – *Linie 1, U-Bahn-Station: Donauinsel.* A total of 42km/26mi of beach, with cycle, surfboard and boat hire outlets, and a rich selection of local bars and restaurants on the "**Copa Cagrana**" (after the Viennese suburb of Kagran, with apologies to Rio) on the river banks attract not only the Viennese – this is a great place to escape the heat of the city and really chill out.

Alte Donau – *Linie 1, U-Bahn-Station: Alte Donau.* The Viennese also come here to enjoy themselves in summer. The old branch of the Danube offers meadows, beaches and numerous bar-restaurants in which you can while away a pleasant evening on the banks of the Danube.

FESTIVALS

Wiener Eistraum – *Jan–Mar.* Ice-skating in front of the Rathaus.
Wiener Festwochen – *May–Jun.* Avant-garde festival of theater, music and art.
Wien Modern – *Late-Oct–Nov.* Festival of contemporary classical music.
SandintheCity – *May–Sept.* Vienna's biggest beach club open 2pm–midnight at Lothringerstraße 22.
Donauinselfest – *Late Jun.* Free open-air concerts that lure thousands of music-lovers to the Donauinsel.
Im-Puls-Tanzfestival – *Jul–Aug.* International dance performances that you can watch, or in which you can take part, in the museum district.
Filmfestival am Rathausplatz – *Jul–Aug.* Free open-air video shows on a giant screen with recordings of classical music, in front of the Vienna Rathaus.
Viennale – *Oct.* International film festival. Details from *www.viennale.at.*
Wiener Ballsaison – *Nov–Ash Wednesday.* Viennese Ball Season, the highlight of which is, of course, the world-renowned Vienna Opera Ball.

Filmfestival am Rathausplatz

© E. Wrba/imageBROKER/age fotostock

TIROLER ZUGSPITZ ARENA
LERMOOS BIBERWIER

Tirol

LERMOOS - BIBERWIER
Bergbahnen
LANGES

BERGBAHNEN LERMOOS/ BIBERWIER 1.000 - 2.100 m   www.bergbahnen-langes.at

VIEW MOUNTAINS - HIKING - BIKING - PARAGLIDING

GRUBIG II LERMOOS

TOBOGGAN RUN - FUNSPORTS - SKI- & WINTER EXPERIENCE

- Mountain lifts in the winter and summer to Grubigstein and Marienberg
- Fantastic views of Zugspitz
- Panoramic trail to cosy mountain huts
- TOP-mountain biking with freeride trails in the best biking region of Austria
- Funsport-mountain roller - Summer toboggan run - paragliding
- Summer operating times from middle of May until the first of November
- 13 ski lifts and 37 km of ski trails
- Exercise area with separate family cabin lifts
- 2,4 km toboggan run
- Winter operating times from first of December until the middle of April
- Easy access from the Garmisch and Füssen/ Reutte motorway

Bergbahnen Langes
Lermoos-Biberwier
Telefon: +43/ (0)5673/ 2323
www.bergbahnen-langes.at

EASTERN AUSTRIA

The area comprising the southern part of Niederösterreich, starting just to the north of Vienna around the abbey of Klosterneuberg, and including much of the Weinviertel, down to Neusiedler See at the southern end of the province of Burgenland, runs along the eastern border of Austria. Vineyards dotted with ecclesiastical monuments characterise much of this region: the Romanesque church of Klosterneuberg is one of the most important in the country, boasting fine Baroque decoration and medieval stained glass.

Highlights

1 A driving tour of Austria's eastern **Wine Country** (p240)

2 Archaeological remains at **Petronell-Caruntum** (p243)

3 The spa resort of **Baden** (p249)

4 The town of **Eisenstadt** and around In the footsteps of Haydn (p256)

5 Outdoor pursuits at the vast lake of **Neusiedler See** (p259)

A Bit of History

East of Klosterneuberg, across the Danube, lies the Weinviertel (the wine quarter), known for its production of excellent wine. The town of Poysdorf is particularly famous for its *Sekt* (sparkling wine). Just to the south of here, along the Slovakian border, is the region known as the Marchfeld. Predominantly agricultural, it has long provided Vienna

with fresh vegetables from its farms and market gardens. A regional speciality is the highly prized *Marchfeldspargel* (white asparagus).

Surrounding Vienna, from the north around Klosterneuberg to the south along the city's western edge, is the Wienerwald (the Vienna Woods). This large area of forest is quite popular with the Viennese for walking and cycling. In between the tracts of woodland are a number of historic towns, among them Mödling and the spa town of Baden, as well as wine villages, of which the most famous is probably Gumpoldsdorf. Beyond the Wienerwald, to the south-west, the hills become higher and turn into the Wieneralpen. These mountains are most easily reached via a spectacular railway up to Semmering.

To the southeast is Burgenland, part of the Pannonian Plain bordering Hungary. Noted for its very hot summers, the region produces some of the finest red wines in Austria. The provincial capital,

Haydnkirche, Eisenstadt

© Austrian National Tourist Office/Volker Preusser

EASTERN AUSTRIA

ČESKÉ BUDĚJOVICE

BRNO   BRNO

CZECH

REPUBLIC

SLOVAK

REPUBLIC

Altenburg

Staatz
Maria Bründl
Poysdorf
Östliches Weinviertel

Asparn
an der Zaya

Weinviertler
Museumdorf

NIEDERÖSTERREICH

Niederösterreichisches
Museum für Volkskultur

LINZ

Krems

Klosterneuburg

Prottes

Marchfeld Schlösser

Niederweiden   Marchegg

VIENNA   Eckartsau   Hof
                                    Bratislava

Purkersdorf   Orth an
der Donau   Hainburg

Böheimkirchen   *Wienerwald*   Kalksburg

Hinterbrühl   Perchtoldsdorf   Petronell-
Carnuntum   Rohrau

Naturpark Sparbach

Heiligenkreuz   Laxenburg   Neusiedl am See

Mayerling   Gumpoldskirchen

Helenental   Baden   Neusiedler
See

Pottenstein   Bad Vöslau   Frauenkirchen

Gutenstein   Berndorf   Eisenstadt

Klostertal   Rust

Puchberg am
Schneeberg   St Margarethen

Kaiserstein   Mörbisch am See

Höllental   Schneeberg   Neunkirchen

Raxalpe   Forchtenstein

Neuberg an
der Mürz   Ste-Rosalie

Semmering   **BURGENLAND   HUNGARY**

Mürzzuschlag

S T Y R I A

LEOBEN, WELS

Graz   Riegersburg

MARIBOR

VIENNA ★★★	Highly recommended
Höllental ★★	Recommended
Semmering ★	Interesting
Neunkirchen	Other sight described in this guide
⇨	Driving tour

Eisenstadt, is not only a pleasant town in its own right, but also the site of the famous schloss where Joseph Haydn spent much of his working life. Just to the east of Eisenstadt is the Neusiedler See. This huge lake, which crosses the Austria-Hungary border, is an important wildlife habitat and centre for sailing.

Klosterneuburg★

In 1113 Babenberg Margrave Leopold III moved the Court from Melk to Klosterneuburg, founding an abbey there the following year. According to legend, it stands in the spot where the Margrave (a medieval hereditary nobleman) found his wife's veil that had blown off many years earlier while the couple was standing on their castle balcony. The abbey, which is still run by Augustinian Canons, remains the town's highlight.

ABBEY (STIFT)

⊙*Open May–mid-Nov daily 9am–6pm; late Nov–Apr daily 10am–5pm.* ⊙*Closed 25, 26 and 31 Dec.* ☛*Guided themed tours.* ⊗€11 per tour. ℘02243 41 10. www.stift-klosterneuburg.at. *Tours in English require advance notice.*

Stiftskirche (Abbey church)

This three-nave Romanesque basilica has origins in the 12C, but has been modified repeatedly, most notably in 1634 when it was given the full Baroque treatment courtesy of the great Giovanni Battista Carlone and Andrea de Retti. The lovely **ceiling frescoes** in the nave were created by Georg Greiner (c. 1689), though the ones by Johann Michael Rottmayr in the chancel depicting the Assumption are considered more accomplished. The high altar by **Matthias Steinl** and the richly gilded **choir stalls** decorated with 24 Habsburg coats of arms are worth seeing, too. The Baroque organ of 1636 is famous for its exquisite sound, and was greatly admired by Anton Bruckner.

Kreuzgang (Cloisters)

The cloisters date from the 13C and 14C and are a fine example of Early Gothic architecture with Burgundian influence. The old pump house contains a seven-armed **bronze candelabrum**, a remarkable 12C Veronese work symbolising the Tree of Jesse.

ℹ **Info:** ℘02243 41 10. www.stift-klosterneuburg.at.
▶ **Location:** Klosterneuburg is about 12km/7.4mi north of Vienna. Alt. 192m/630ft.
👁 **Don't Miss:** The Verdun altarpiece.
🕑 **Timing:** You can easily spend a half- or full day here.

Leopoldkapelle

East of the cloisters, the chapel has ethereal 14C **stained glass★**, although the **Verdun altarpiece★★** is the highlight. This amazing winged altar was fashioned in the 12C by Nicolas of Verdun; it consists of 50 gilded enamel panels, arranged in three rows, depicting famous scenes from the Old and New Testaments.

The chapel also contains the tomb of Leopold III, who was canonised in 1485.

Stiftsbau (Abbey building)★

Emperor Charles VI envisioned an abbey modelled on nothing less than the grand Escorial near Madrid. Construction began in 1730, but only a quarter of the plans were fully realised because of Charles' sudden death in 1740 and a total lack of interest in the project by his daughter, Maria Theresia.

Visitors are greeted by eight giant Atlases by Lorenzo Mattielli in the unfinished **Sala terrena**, the former garden room. There are exhibits about the abbey's history leading to the grand **Chorherrenstiege** (staircase), which is lined by video installations informing visitors about the canons' daily life. In the imperial apartments, the **Gobelin Hall** is adorned with priceless tapestries from Brussels, and the **Marble Hall★**, with its giant oval dome, is decorated with frescoes by Daniel Gran glorifying the Habsburgs.

Stiftsmuseum★

⊙*Same hours as abbey.* ⊗€11. ℘02243 41 10.
The abbey museum is filled with interesting items, most famously a large

Klosterneuburg Monastery

© ElenaSeychelles/iStockphoto.com

painting illustrating the geneaology of the Babenbergs, a statuette of Mercure by Raphael Donner, richly carved ivory decorative objects and four early works by Egon Schiele★ (*see p163*).

ADDITIONAL SIGHT
Baroque Palace★

The palace we see today dates from the reign of Emperor Charles VI (father of Empress Maria Theresia), who initially modelled it on the great Escorial palace in Spain. In contrast to the abbey church (the embodiment of spiritual power), this building was to symbolise the Emperor's temporal power. Donato Felice d'Allio was the principal architect, but the influence of Fischer von Erlach is also apparent. By the time the Emperor died, in October 1740, less than one-eighth of the ambitious project had been carried out. Work resumed in the 19C, but still only a quarter of the initial project was ever finished.

Imperial Apartments

The extraordinary (unfinished) Kaiserstiege (Imperial staircase) provides access to the Kaiserzimmer (apartments), some of which are richly furnished. The exhibition of tapestries is remarkable with the most valuable pieces made in Brussels in the early 18C. The oval-shaped dome of the Marble Hall is decorated with a fresco by Daniel Gran representing the glory of the house of Austria.

Library

Boasting some 200,000 books, 1,250 manuscripts and 850 incunabula, this is the largest private library in Austria.

Nicolas of Verdun

Despite a prolific body of work and extensive travels througout Europe, little is known of Nicolas of Verdun (late 12C-early 13C) other than that he was a goldsmith and enameller from Lorraine. His reputation was founded on a large output of exquisitely wrought shrines, figurines and candlesticks decorated with precious stones. The side panels of the Dreikönigsschrein (Shrine of the Three Kings) in Cologne Cathedral, Germany, are attributed to him, but his name is known to us only from inscriptions on two works: the Mary Shrine in Tournai Cathedral and the enamelled panels in Klosterneuburg, both considered masterpieces of medieval art.

Östliches Weinviertel

Austria's Eastern Wine Country remains off the beaten tourist track. Its remote position in Austria's far northeastern corner means that the countryside has remained unspoiled and filled with natural (and cultural) treasures. Be sure to sample the excellent local wine, best supped in a charming *Kellergasse*, a street of tiny wine cellars.

Info: Kolpingstraße 7 Wiener Straße 1, 2170 Poysdorf. ℘02552 35 15. www.weinviertel.at.

Location: The Weinviertel lies northeast of Vienna, bordering the Czech Republic and Slovakia.

Don't Miss: The view of the stork colony from Schloss Marchegg.

Timing: The Weinviertel makes for a nice day trip from Vienna.

Kids: Weinviertler Museumsdorf, MAMUZ Museumszentrum

➾DRIVING TOURS

PROTTES TO POYSDORF

51km/31mi. ⊙ Watch out for unmarked railway crossings along this drive.

▷ Start in the district capital of Gänserndorf (26km/16mi NE of Vienna; reached via the B 8) and continue to Prottes.

Erdöl-Erdgas-Lehrpfad

Between Gänserndorf and Prottes look-out for numerous pumps in perpetual motion, extracting oil or gas. To learn more about the subject, follow the 4.5km/3mi educational trail through charming countryside, starting at the affiliated **museum** (◷visits by appointment; ℘02282 21 82) in Prottes *(follow red and white markings)*. Along the way you will encounter display panels with background information and original pieces of machinery connected with the extraction of this raw material, including oil detection probes, mobile drilling gear, production derricks, etc.

▷ Drive on via Matzen towards Gross-Schweinbarth.

Niederösterreichisches Museum für Volkskultur

Gross-Schweinbarth, by the B 220; from Prottes keep left towards Gänserndorf. ◷*Open Palm Sun–mid-Nov Fri–Sun 9am–5pm.* ◉€4. ℘0228 923 02.
This museum of traditional regional culture (complete with a wine section) has found the perfect home in an old dairy that once supplied the neighbouring castle.

Displays include traditional costumes, furniture and crockery, as well as a broad range of items dealing with local customs, religious practices and craftwork. The history and role of the dairy farm is also explained. An entire wing is dedicated to amber, explaining the formation, extraction and use of this fossilised resin. There are even specimens enclosing 50-million-year-old insects, conjuring visions of *Jurassic Park*.

Eing'richt

This craft is painstaking: tiny scenes, mainly on religious themes, are patiently crafted – often from very simple materials – and then inserted ("eingerichtet") into bottles. The bottles kept many a farming family occupied on long winter evenings. A small collection of this naive art form is on display in the Niederösterreichisches Museum für Volkskultur in Gross-Schweinbarth.

Take the B 220 towards Pirawarth. At the exit to Gross-Schweinbarth turn right towards Hohenruppersdorf. From there head towards Zistersdorf and then to Niedersulz.

Museumsdorf Niedersulz★

Niedersulz. Open mid-Apr–Oct daily 9.30am–6pm (second half Oct til 5pm). €12. 02534 333. www.museumsdorf.at.

This large open-air museum re-creates an entire Weinviertel village as it might have looked in pre-industrial times. More than 60 buildings, including farmhouses, barns, sheds, chapels and mills, whose existence in their original sites had been threatened, have been reassembled here. The museum site has been planted with flora typical of the region. The layout of houses around a central square, complete with church, inn, presbytery and even a graveyard, creates the impression of walking around a village whose inhabitants are all out working in the fields. The houses contain authentic furnishings or exhibitions on rural life. There's also a "living farm" with domestic and farm animals.

Drive on through Obersulz and Schrick towards Mistelbach. In Lanzendorf turn left and follow the signposts to Schloss Asparn/Zaya – Museum für Urgeschichte.

Asparn an der Zaya

This town, at the foothills of the Leiser Berge, boasts a fine ensemble of historic buildings. These include the **Baroque Minorite convent** from the 18C, which now houses a museum on wine-growing and the local region; the elegant parish church of St. Pancras and St. Francis; and the Renaissance castle.

MAMUZ Museumszentrum

In the castle. Open mid-Mar–late Nov Tue–Sun 10am–5pm. €10, children €3. 02577 84 180. www.mamuz.at.

Exhibits at this museum illustrate the evolution of humankind and human culture to the Middle Ages.

There are reproductions of cave paintings from Altamira, Lascaux and other famous sites, alongside jewellery, ceramics, tools and many other workaday objects.

The museum's archaeological **open-air site★** behind the castle is a particular highlight, with reconstructions of walk-in dwellings from around 25,000 BC to 2C AD.

From Asparn drive on towards Hörersdorf, turn left onto the B 46 to Laa an der Thaya. At the crossroads, carry straight on, signposted to Ruine.

Burgruine Staatz

Park by the Musikerheim and walk along the fortified wall. Guided tours (1hr) May–Oct Sun 3pm. €4. 0664 55 66 398.

The castle ruins can be seen from miles away. From the top, there is a sweeping **view★★** across the Weinviertel and the Carpathian mountains to the northeast.

Continue to Poysdorf.

Shortly before reaching Poysdorf, the road passes the **pilgrimage church of Maria Bründl** in an idyllic, tree-shaded setting. It was completed in 1751 according to plans by Italian architect Donato Felice d'Allio, who was also the mastermind behind the abbey church at Klosterneuburg (*see p238*).

Poysdorf

"Austria's Wine Town", which produces mostly *Sekt*, is a great place for exploring romantic *Kellergassen*. Particularly fine examples of these wine-cellar-lined lanes can be found in Bürsting (*via Singergasse from the tourist office*) and on Berggasse (*below the parish church*). A 1hr circular *Kellergassen* trail leaving from the Stadtmuseum (*follow the beige-white markers*) also takes in some of the delightful vineyards on the edge of town.

From April to October (*daily at 2pm*), wine-growers take turns in opening their premises for public tours and wine-tasting sessions (*www.poysdorf.at*).

TOUR OF MARCHFELD SCHLÖSSER (Marchfeld Castles)

From Vienna to Marchegg. 58km/36mi.

The Marchfeld, a gravel plain to the east of Vienna, is a fertile region and popular hunting ground.

▷ Head E on the B 3 for 24km/15mi.

Orth an der Donau

This newly restored castle dates back to the 12C, but most of the present building, including the four mighty corner towers, date from the 16C. The Baroque annexe was added in the 17C and used as a hunting lodge by the Habsburgs. The castle now houses the Nationalpark Donau-Auen Visitor Centre.

▷ Leave Orth on B 3 towards Wagram. Turn right in Pframa towards Eckartsau.

Eckartsau★

Guided tours (40min) Apr–Oct daily 11am, 2pm and 4pm. €9. ℘02 231 60 00. www.schlosseckartsau.at.
This former hunting castle was remodelled in Baroque style c. 1730 by Joseph Emanuel Fischer von Erlach; Daniel Gran painted the frescoes. It served as the final residence on Austrian soil of the Habsburg family after Karl I's abdication on 11 November 1918. In 1919, the Imperial family left here for exile in Switzerland.

▷ From Eckartsau take the B 3 back towards Kopfstetten to the junction with the B 49. Turn left towards Marchegg, and drive for 2km/1.2mi.

Niederweiden

Johann Bernhard Fischer von Erlach built this Imperial Baroque-style hunting lodge (*◐open mid-Mar–Nov 10am–6pm; €9.5, combination ticket with Schlosshof €19; ℘02285 200 00; www.schlosshof.at*) in 1693. In 1726 it was acquired by Prince Eugene of Savoy before being taken over by Maria Theresia in 1755.

She hired Nicolas Pacassi to make the alterations that give the palace its present form. Beneath the slate mansard roof, the oval **Great Hall★**, painted in Chinese style, hints at the magnificent original decoration.

▷ Leave the B 49 and head towards Schlosshof.

Schlosshof

In 1725 Prince Eugene had the estate of Hof, with its fortified castle (*◐open mid-Mar–Nov daily 10am–6pm; €13; ℘02285 200 00; www.schlosshof.at*) converted by Lukas von Hildebrandt into a huge Baroque palace, while the French gardens were laid out with sculptures and fountains. Maria Theresia acquired Schlosshof together with Niederweiden, added a further storey and furnished it opulently. After 200 years of continuous neglect, Schlosshof has now been restored to its original splendour, boasting fine stuccowork and paintings. The restoration of the **Sala terrena★** deserves particular praise.

▷ Return to B 49 via Groissenbrunn and drive on to Marchegg.

Marchegg

Although rebuilt in the 17C and 18C in the Baroque style, **Schloss Marchegg** (*◐open mid-Mar–Oct daily 10am–4pm; €6; ℘02285 71 00 71; www.schloss.marchegg.at*) has medieval origins. It now houses a a local history museum, the Heimatmuseum, organized around three main themes: society; agriculture and industry; and local history.
View the **stork colony★★** in the water meadows behind the Schloss from the northeast wing's corner room. After a 10,000km/6,200mi flight, the storks arrive in spring after wintering in Africa. The female lays 3-4 eggs (*Apr*), which the stork pair takes turns incubating. The chicks hatch after about a month. By late August they take the long journey back to Africa, staying two years, and returning to Europe in their third year, usually settling where they were born.

Petronell-Carnuntum★

Excavations on the site of Petronell and in the neighbouring community of Bad Deutsch-Altenburg have unearthed remnants of an ancient Roman town from around the 1C AD.

A BIT OF HISTORY
The Capital of Upper Pannonia

Carnuntum was founded as a Roman military winter camp by Emperor Tiberius in 6 AD and became the capital of the Roman province of Upper Pannonia in the 2C AD. In 171 Emperor Marcus Aurelius drove back the local tribes, while also writing part of his *Meditations*. In 308, Emperor Diocletian convened an Imperial Conference in Carnuntum in order to try to hold the Roman Empire together. But for the town the end was near, as first the Goths and then the Huns overran and devastated it around AD 400.

SIGHTS
Römerstadt Carnuntum (Roman City Carnuntum)

Information Centre, Hauptstraße 1A.
Open mid-Mar–mid-Nov daily 9am–5pm. €11. 02163 33 770. www.carnuntum.at.

The archaeological park consists of two main areas: the Zivilstadt (civilian town) in the town of Petronell-Carnuntum and the Militärstadt (military town) in Bad Deutsch-Altenburg. To get oriented and to pick up maps and an audio-guide *(in English, recommended)*, start your visit at the information centre. The ticket is good for all sights and the museum.

Zivilstadt★

The main excavation area is now the **Roman City Quarter**, an open-air museum where you can stroll along actual Roman streets lined with ancient foundations and reconstructed buildings such as the Temple of Diana. A highlight is the **House of Lucius★**, an authentically decorated and furnished home of a textile merchant that provides a rare insight into the lifestyle enjoyed by rich Romans.

Info: Hauptstraße 3. 02163 35 55 10, www.aulandcarnuntum.at.
Location: Petronell-Carnuntum is on the eastern edge of the country, about 40km/26mi east of Vienna. Alt. 330m/1,082ft.
Parking: There's parking at the Freilichtmuseum and at the Museum Carnuntinum.
Don't Miss: The House of Lucius.
Timing: Distances between sights are quite lengthy, so allow at least half a day to see it all.
Kids: Freilichtmuseum Petronell.

About 700m/765yds west of here are the remnants of one of the city's two **amphitheatres**, which had a capacity of 13,000 spectators. Close by, the **Grosse Therme** is one of the largest and fanciest Roman bathing complexes north of the Alps, once decorated with coloured marble and mosaic floors. Now only bits and pieces of floor heating, water canals and the pools survive. South of the open-air museum rises the **Heidentor** (Heathen's Gate), a 4C stone

Roman Amphitheatre, Carnuntum
© Austrian National Tourist Office/Wiesenhofer

arch that once formed part of a much larger monument to Emperor Constantine II. Its curious name dates back to the Middle Ages, when people erroneously thought that it was built by non-Christians, even though Christianity had already taken root among the Romans.

Militärstadt

The only surviving remnant from the military camp is the **Amphitheatre Militärstadt**, where gladiators fought, soldiers paraded and meetings gathered. There's more to see here than at the theatre in Petronell, including cages, tunnels and gateways. A permanent exhibit offers insights into the forms of entertainment enjoyed by Roman society.

Carnuntum★

Badgasse 40–46. ○*Open mid-Mar–mid-Nov daily 9am–5pm.*
℘*02163 33 770.*
The archaeological museum in Bad Deutsch-Altenburg occupies a replica of a beautiful Roman villa. It houses a remarkable collection of ancient artefacts, including exceptional sculpture such as a striking marble statuette of the **Dancing Maenads of Carnuntum★**. The exhibits on the ground floor relate mainly to the **Mithras cult**.

Rundkapelle

Petronell, opposite Information Centre.
This unusual Romanesque round chapel (c. 1200) has a pointed roof and semicircular choir. The façade is simple, with its three-quarter columns and arcades carried on consoles. The **tympanum relief★** over the entrance shows the Baptism of Christ, an indication that the chapel was originally a baptistry.

EXCURSION
Rohrau

4km/2.5mi south of Petronell-Carnuntum.
This 16C Schloss contains the **Graf Harrach'sche Familiensammlung★★** (○*open Easter–Oct Fri–Sun 10am–5pm;* ☞€10; ℘*02164 22 53 16; www.schloss-rohrau.at),* which ranks among the largest and most prestigious private art collections in Austria, with works by 17C and 18C masters from Spain, Naples and Rome, and 16C and 17C masters from Holland and Flanders. Don't miss *The Concert* (16C), a particularly graceful painting, beleived to be by a Dutch artist.

The composer **Joseph Haydn** was born in 1732 in the thatched **Haydn-Geburtshaus** (○*open year-round Tue–Sun 10am–4pm;* ☞€5; ℘*02164 22 68; http://haydngeburtshaus.at)* on the main village road. It now contains an exhibit about the man, his works and his life.

🚗 DRIVING TOUR

⑥ DANUBE VALLEY
84km/52mi.

The route follows the south bank of the river through a wide valley.

▶ From Vienna take the B 9 towards Schwechat.

Wildungsmauer

The small church of St. Nicolas was fortified around 1200. Despite the restorations and additions (transept and porch are 19C), it has retained much of its Romanesque character.

Petronell-Carnuntum

Between Bad Deutsch-Altenburg and Hainburg, you will see the Little Carpathians. These are the foothills of the great chain of the mountains of north central Europe that stretch to the Hungarian plain.

Hainburg

Hainburg had an important strategic role in the Middle Ages on the highway linking Vienna and Bratislava. The town close to the Slovakian border still retains its ring of walls and fortified gateways from the 13C. Above the town are the remains of its 11C castle.

Wienerwald★

The hilly Vienna Woods make up a delightful green lung west of Austria's capital, a region of vine-covered hills and shady woods that offers a welcome escape from the summer heat. The name Wienerwald also conjures up the musical landscapes of Beethoven's *Pastoral Symphony* and of course, that famous Strauss waltz, *Tales from the Vienna Woods*.

Info: Hauptplatz 11. Purkersdorf. ✆02231 621 76. www.wienerwald.info.

Location: Wienerwald is just southwest of Vienna.

Don't Miss: Seegrotte at Hinterbrühl.

Timing: Touring the Wienerwald makes for a leisurely day trip.

Kids: Naturpark Sparbach.

🚗 DRIVING TOUR

WIENERWALD TOUR
115km/71mi.

▶ Leave Vienna on the B 12 and follow the sign Perchtoldsdorf Zentrum.

Perchtoldsdorf

In the centre of the market place stands the fine Pestsäule (Plague Column) of 1713, the work of Johann Bernhard Fischer von Erlach. The **Türkenmuseum** in the Late Gothic town hall keeps alive the memory of the Turkish incursions into Lower Austria. The porch of the parish church of St.

Augustine sports a multi-coloured relief dating from 1449 portraying the **Marientod★** (Death of the Virgin Mary). The interior is dominated by a monumental Baroque high altar adorned with the patron saints of Styria, Carinthia, Upper Austria and Lower Austria.
To the west of the church are the remains of the Herzogsburg, a castle built between the 11C and the 15C.

▶ In Perchtoldsdorf take the B 13 towards Vienna. After 1.3km/0.8mi turn onto the Kaltenleutgebnerstraße which becomes the Hauptstraße. After 11km/6.8mi, turn left for Sulz im Wienerwald. Pass Sittendorf and follow the sign to Naturpark Sparbach.

👥 Naturpark Sparbach

🕐*Open late Mar–Oct daily 9am–6pm.* 👓*€5.* ✆*02237 76 25.* *www.naturpark-sparbach.at.*
Lower Austria's oldest nature reserve has rambling trails and enclosures that house fallow deer, moufflons and other local animals. There is also a children's zoo and lake with a watermill.

▶ Cross the E 60/A 21 autobahn and turn right onto the B 11, direction Gaaden.

Stift Heiligenkreuz★
🕐*See STIFT HEILIGENKREUZ.*

▶ Continue on the B 11, direction Alland. After 4km/2.5mi, turn left for Mayerling.

Mayerling

Mayerling is 36km/22.4mi southwest of Vienna and 6km/3.7mi southwest of Heiligenkreuz.
In 1889 Mayerling was the setting of one of the greatest mysteries in Austrian history: the death of the 30-year-old Crown Prince Rudolf and his lover.
In 1888 **Crown Prince Rudolf**, only son of Emperor Franz Joseph and estranged husband of Stephanie of Belgium, fell in love with the teenage Baroness Maria Vetsera. The Emperor did not approve of such a scandalous affair, and a vociferous argument between the ruler and Rudolf resulted in the latter storming off with his mistress and taking her to the family's hunting lodge at Mayer-

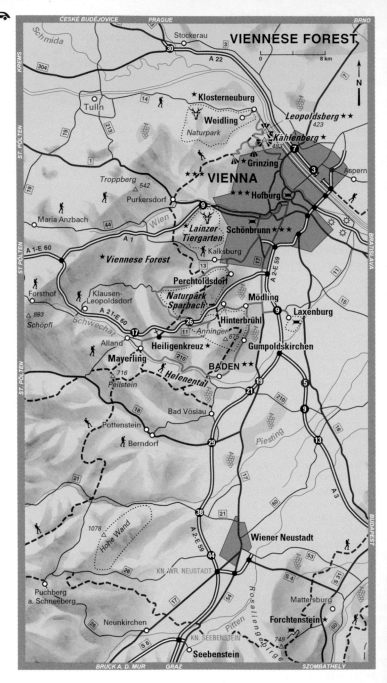

ling. What transpired next has been the source of endless speculation for more than a century. On the morning of 30 January 1889, the lifeless bodies of Maria and Rudolf were found at the lodge, seemingly killed by gunshot in an apparent suicide pact. But why did the fun-loving crown prince kill himself and

Vineyards near Gumpoldskirchen

© Austrian National Tourist Office/ Carniel

his lover? Theories range from clinical depression to an incurable venereal disease to heart failure, a hunting accident, or a politically motivated murder. The mystery remains, making Mayerling a pilgrimage for the curious to this day.

Memorial Chapel rooms
Follow signs Ehemaliges Jagdschloss.
Open Apr–Oct daily 9am–5.30pm;
Nov–Mar Tue & Fri 10.30am–1pm,
Sat–Sun 9am–5pm; €6.70.
02258 22 75.
Grief-stricken by the death of his only son, Emperor Franz Joseph had the hunting lodge demolished and replaced with a Carmelite convent. A neo-Gothic chapel now occupies the site where the bodies were found, and there is a small memorial exhibit with original furniture, photographs and drawings

▶ Turn left onto the B 210, heading towards Baden.

Helenental
The Schwechat winds its way through this valley, which has been featured in traditional songs numerous times. Some 60km/37mi of marked trails make this a good area for getting out and about. Just before Baden, the ruins of the castles of Rauhenstein (12C, *on the left*) and Rauheneck (11C, *on the right*) come into view.

Baden ⚜⚜ *See BADEN.*

▶ To get onto the Weinstraße (Wine Road) to Gumpoldskirchen and Mödling from the centre of Baden, pass under the railway on the Kaiser-Franz-Joseph-Ring and then turn immediately left onto the B 212. Continue under another bridge, turn right at the stop sign and then immediately left for Gumpoldskirchen.

Gumpoldskirchen
This charming place at the foot of the 674m/2,211ft-high Anninger has achieved fame for its superb white wines. A wine trail (*Weinwanderweg*) leads through the vineyards (here called *Rieden*). In town, note the delightful Renaissance town hall in Kirchengasse.

▶ The road meanders through the vineyards, opening up wonderful views towards Mödling and Vienna.

Mödling
This was a favourite haunt of three great composers: Beethoven (*Hauptstraße 79, Achsenaugasse 6*), Schönberg and Webern. The vaulting in the **Pfarrkirche St. Othmar** (1523) is supported by a dozen columns representing the 12 Apostles. The circular 12C charnel house has a frescoed crypt. Mödling also boasts Austria's oldest war memorial in the shape of the Husarentempel, dedicated to the Hussars.

Walking the Vienna Woods

Klosterneuburg - Weidling – North of Vienna. Depart from Klosterneuburg station to reach Weidling via Leopoldsberg hill (alt. 423m/1,388ft, 2hr45min).

Maria Anzbach – Between Vienna and St. Pölten. Circular walk via Kohlreithberg hill (alt. 516m/1,693ft, 2hr).

Böheimkirchen - Pottenbrunn – East of St. Pölten.
From Böheimkirchen station to Pottenbrunn station via the Schildberg (alt. 393m/1,289ft,1hr15min).

Purkersdorf – At the western edge of the Viennese suburbs. Circular walk from Unterpurkersdorf station (2hr).

Kalksburg - Breitenfurt – West of Vienna. From Kalksburg to Breitenfurt via Laabersteigberg (alt. 530m/1,739ft, 4hr 30min).

Klausen-Leopoldsdorf - Alland – Northwest of Mayerling (3hr30min).

Le Schöpfl –West of Mayerling. Circular walk from Forsthof climbing and descending the Schöpfl (alt. 893m/ft, there and back around 2hr).

Mayerling - Bad Vöslau – This is a lovely long-distance walk to Bad Vöslau station (6hr).

Berndorf - Pottenstein – South west of Baden. Berndorf station to Pottenstein station (4hr).

Covering the whole of the Vienna Woods is beyond the scope of this guide. The itineraries of marked trails listed above are, however, among the most enjoyable in the Vienna Woods. Hikers who would like to explore further should buy maps and specialised walking guides from *Freytag & Berndt, Wallnerstraße 3, 1. Bezirk, Vienna,* ℘*01 533 86 85, www.freytagberndt.at.*

▷ Go west on Spitalmühlgasse, which joins Brühlerstraße, following signs for the Seegrotte and E 6/A 21. After the football stadium, turn right onto the Hauptstraße, then right again after the bridge and park.

Hinterbrühl (Seegrotte)

⊙*Boat tours (45min) operate Apr–Oct daily 9am–5pm; Nov–Mar Mon–Fri 9am –3pm, Sat–Sun 9am–3.30pm.*⊛€*10, children €7.* ℘*02236 263 64. www.seegrotte.at.*
The unique **Seegrotte**★ (lake grotto) is the largest underground lake in Europe; small motorboat tours take visitors through this watery labyrinth. The lake was created in 1912, when 20 million litres (4.4 million gallons) of water poured into the lower gallery of this former gypsum mine.

▷ Return to Mödling on the B 11. Pass through the town, and still on the B 11 proceed along the Triester Straße towards Schwechat. The road crosses the E 59/A 2 autobahn. Follow the signs for Laxenburg.

Laxenburg

In 1858 Crown Prince Rudolf was born in the **Blauer Hof**, a former Imperial summer residence, on Schlossplatz. The square is also home to the late 17C **Pfarrkirche** (parish church), with ceiling frescoes after a design by Johann Michael Rottmayr.
Laxenburg's park *(enter from Hofstraße)* was laid out in the English style by Emperor Joseph II. Franz I added a lake with an island topped by the Franzensburg, a faux neo-Gothic castle built by Michael Riedl in the early 19C. Near the park entrance is the **Altes Schloss** where Charles VI signed the Pragmatic Sanction in 1713, enabling his daughter Maria Theresia to ascend the throne.

▷ Return to Vienna on the E 59/A 2 autobahn.

Baden♁♁

Baden is a well equipped, modern spa resort with an historic pedigree. Its heyday was in the early 19C, particularly when Emperor Franz I spent his summers here from 1814 to 1834, attracting such luminaries as Beethoven and Napoleon in his wake. Baden is beautifully located amid vineyards and meadows, and is noted for its charming villas and elegant Biedermeier architecture. It also hosts the well-known Baden Operetta Festival every summer (👁️*see p252*).

A BIT OF HISTORY

It was the Romans who first enjoyed the healing properties of Baden's hot-water springs. The spa's 14 sulfurous springs yield more than 4 million l/880,000gal per day nowadays, reaching a natural temperature of up to 36°C/97°F. The mineral waters are particularly effective in treating rheumatic ailments.

Musicians and composers were particularly fond of this idyllic town: **Mozart** wrote his *Ave Verum* here, **Beethoven** came to Baden hoping to cure his deafness; **Franz Schubert** and great waltz and operetta composers, including **Strauss**, Lanner, Millöcker and Zeller, also visited.

SIGHTS
Kurpark★

The Kurpark sprawls from near the centre of town as far as the Vienna Woods.

▶ **Population:** 25,700.
▪ **Info:** Brusattiplatz 3, A-2500. ✆02252 86 800 600. www.tourismus. baden.at.
▶ **Location:** The town lies on the eastern edge of the Vienna Woods along the Schwechat River, about 25km/15.5mi south of Vienna. Alt. 228m/748ft.
🅿 **Parking:** Parking (👛*fee*) at the Römertherme and at the Parkdeck Zentrum Süd, right by the town's shopping district.
😊 **Don't Miss:** Kurpark and Römertherme.
🕐 **Timing:** Stroll around town, then relax at a thermal bath.
👪 **Kids:** The Thermalstrandbad has a kids' playground and special pools.

At its edge looms the beautifully restored **Casino**, the oldest gambling establishment in Austria and one of the most magnificent. Nearby, the Jugendstil **Sommerarena** (1906), with its movable glass roof, provides a charming backdrop for the operetta festival (👁️*see p252*). Free afternoon concerts take place at the **music pavilion**.

Spa town architecture★ – In the first half of the 19C, numerous thermal establishments were built in Baden in

The Cistercian Order

This reforming Benedictine order took its name from the monastery of Cîteaux in France, founded by Robert of Molesmes in 1098. The order grew rapidly in the 12C under Bernard of Clairvaux, who forbade the levying of tithes and the acquisition of land. He also encouraged precise observance of the Benedictine rules. Cistercian architecture also adheres to strict principles. Churches are simple yet harmonious in their proportions and distinguished by purity of line. There is no bell-tower, only a ridge turret, and no stained glass, only *grisaille* painting. The initial austerity of Cistercian architecture mellowed over the centuries, with the result that pictures and statues are now to be seen in Cistercian churches. The order still remains true to the *charta caritatis*, promulgated in 1115, and has 300 monasteries and convents all over the world.

the Neoclassical style. The **Josefsbad**, a domed, yellow building, now serves as a coffeehouse; the **Frauenbad** *(in Frauengasse)*, with its pillared portico, is an art gallery; the **Franzensbad** is a glassmaking workshop; the **Leopoldsbad** *(on Brusattiplatz)* houses the tourist office.

👥 Spas

Baden's two main public pool complexes are the summer-only **Thermalstrandbad**, an Art Deco outdoor playground with a huge, sandy beach and modern additions, and the top-class indoor **Römertherme** *(www.roemertherme. at)*, the largest fully air-conditioned spa in Europe, with a freely suspended glass roof.

Hauptplatz

Baden's central square is dominated by the impressive, columned **Rathaus** (town hall), constructed in 1815. In front is the ornate Baroque **Dreifaltigkeitssäule** (Trinity Column).

Beethovenhaus

Rathausgasse 10. ⏱*Open Tue–Sun & public holidays 10am–6pm.* ⏱*Closed 1 Jan, 25 Dec.* ⊛€6. ☎*02252 86 80 06 30.*
The great composer wrote part of the *Missa Solemnis* and completed his *Ninth Symphony* while staying here between 1821 and 1823. You can see his bedroom and living room, as well as a small exhibit on his life and work.

Doblhoff Park

The **Rosarium★**, a redolent display of 20,000 roses of 600 different varieties, is the main attraction here. In June, the *Badener Rosentage* (Baden Rose Days) attract flower lovers galore.

EXCURSIONS
Heiligenkreuz Monastery★

Wienerwald, 13km/8mi from Baden. ⏱*Open year-round daily 9am–5.30pm.* 👣*Guided tours (45min) daily 10am, 11am, 2pm, 3pm, 4pm (no 10am tour Sun).* ⊛€9. ☎*02258 87 030. www.stift-heiligenkreuz.org.*
The Cistercian abbey of Heiligenkreuz was founded by the Babenberg Margrave Leopold III as a burial place for his dynasty. A fine example of Romanesque-Gothic architecture with Baroque embellishments, the abbey owes its name to a relic of the Holy Cross donated in the 12C by Duke Leopold V. It is the oldest continuously operating Cistercian abbey in the world and still has around 70 monks. Don't miss the dancing skeletons in the Totenkapelle (Chapel of the Dead).

Stiftskirche★

Behind the austere Romanesque façade lies the nave from the same period and a Gothic chancel from the 13C with fittings dating from the 19C. The other

Heiligenkreuz Monastery

© Austrian National Tourist Office/ Volker Preusser

furnishings are Baroque in style by Giovanni Giuliani. The choir stalls are each decorated with a linden wood relief illustrating scenes from the Life of Christ crowned with busts of saintly bishops, abbots and statesmen.

The Holy Cross reliquary is kept in the 1982 **Kreuzkirche**, a modern side church off to the left of the chancel. The organ here is one of the largest musical instruments in Austria and was built in 1804. Franz Schubert and Anton Bruckner played it, and since Schubert composed a special piece of music for the organ, it is called the **Schubertorgan**.

Cloister

The 13C cloister bridges the Romanesque and the Gothic well, with rounded arches on its north side and pointed Gothic on the opposite side. There are two sculpture groups by Giuliani and a nine-sided fountain room (late 13C) with fine tracery and a Renaissance basin for the ablutions. The grey-black medieval **stained-glass windows** show members of the Babenberg dynasty.

Several chapels sit west of the cloister, including the square **Kapitelsaal** (chapter-house), where the Babenbergs are buried and also depicted in murals. Next door in the **Totenkapelle** (Chapel of the Dead), the monks are laid out before burial. Giuliani was responsible for the decoration, including the rather macabre dancing skeletons: candelabra supported by skeletons in shrouds.

Sacristy

Tours conclude in the sacristy, reached across a small courtyard. The attractively decorated room has an old lavabo recess, and is 18C in style, even with some Rococo touches. The four splendid **sacristy cupboards** with exceptionally fine marquetry were made by lay brothers in the early 19C.

Wiener Neustadt

Wiener Neustadt (population 43,900; alt. 265m/869ft) is about 64km/39.7mi south of Vienna and 33km/20.5mi south of Baden. ⊞ Hauptplatz 1-3. ℘02622 37 33 11. www.smtwn.at.

⊞ *Central pay parking garages are on Ungargasse, and at the beginning of the pedestrianised Herzog-Leopold-Straße. Parking is free from 6pm (Mon–Tue & Wed–Fri) or noon (Thu & Sat) in short-stay spaces only.*

Wiener Neustadt was founded by Duke Leopold V of Babenberg in 1194 as a fortified border post against Hungary. It was allegedly built using part of the ransom paid for Richard the Lionheart. Under Friedrich III, between 1440 and 1493, the town was an Imperial residence. It was here that Maximilian I was born in 1459 and buried in 1519, far from his mammoth mausoleum in Innsbruck. In 1752, Maria Theresia founded a military academy here that is still active today. The historic town centre, now an attractive pedestrian zone, has retained its medieval layout despite suffering heavy damage during World War II.

Burg

Courtyard and church open year-round. ⊜Free admission. ℘0502 012 02 89 04 .
The oldest parts of the castle are 13C, but there have been numerous later modifications. Since 1752, it has been the home of the military academy founded by Maria Theresia.

The main point of interest in the central courtyard is the **Wappenwand** (Heraldic Wall), which is festooned with 107 carved coats of arms from the House of Habsburg. These frame a statue of Friedrich III, the man behind the castle's Gothic **Georgs-kapelle**.

Neuklosterkirche

This Gothic abbey church has some magnificent Baroque altars. Behind the high altar is the beautiful **tomb★** of Eleanor of Portugal, the wife of Friedrich III.

Hauptplatz

The main town square is presided over by the **Rathaus**, with origins in 1488 although converted to the Neoclassical style in 1834. The Virgin Mary Column dates to 1678. The beautiful arcaded houses on the square's north side are from the Gothic period.

Dom

The Late Romanesque cathedral had a Gothic transept and chancel added to it in the 14C, although the furnishings are mostly 18C Baroque. An attractive surviving Romanesque feature is the **Brauttor★**, a doorway decorated with bands of lozenge and zigzag motifs. The 12 larger-than-life-size figures of the Apostles adorning the pillars are by Lorenz Luchsperger. The red marble **pulpit** was created in 1609 by Johann Baptist Zelpi.

In the south tower is the **Turmmuseum** (🕐 *by guided tour only by advance resertation May–Oct Wed–Sun 10.30am & 2.30pm; ✆€2)*. On the way up to the viewing platform are explanatory panels about the role of the former fire watchmen. Pick up keys at the **Stadtmuseum** (*Petersgasse 2a;* 🕐 *open Wed–Sun 10am–4pm, Thu til 8pm; closed holidays;* ✆€6; *02622 373 951; www.stadtmuseum.wrn. at)*, which provides a chronicle of town history.

Seebenstein

17km/10.5mi south on A 2 towards Graz.
🅿 *Park by the local administrative offices. Follow the path to the castle, heading south. After about a 10min walk, take the left fork to the castle.*

Burg Seebenstein

🐾 *Guided tours (50min) Good Friday–late Oct Sat–Sun and holidays 2pm and 3pm.* ✆€5. ✆ *0664 913 47 51. www.seebenstein.at.*

This proud 11C fortress houses a private collection of medieval art, including a fine Madonna by Würzburg sculptor Tilman Riemenschneider (c. 1460–1531).

🅭 Return to the fork and climb a well laid out forest path for about 45min.

Türkensturz

This ruined folly was built in 1825–26 by Prince Johann I of Liechtenstein. Its name harks back to a legendary event during the Turkish invasions of the 16C. It is a wonderful look-out point, offering views of the Raxalpe and Schneeberg range.

ADDRESSES

🛏 STAY

☞ **Ferienwohnungen Rauscher** – *Weikersdorferplatz 10, 2500.* ✆*02252 46 824. www.ferienwohnung-baden.at. Closed Nov–Feb.* This lovely villa with a large, beautiful garden is not far from the town centre.

☞☞ **Amadeus Pension** – *Albrechtsgasse 28, 2500.* ✆*02252 20 91 26. www.amadeus baden.com. 8 rooms.* ⌴. This centrally situated pension offers value for money with its tidy, simply furnished rooms, some of which have prime views of the city's landmarks.

☞☞☞ **Hotel Schloss Weikersdorf** – *Schlossgasse 9-11, 2500.* ✆*02252 48 30 10. www.gerstner-hotels.at. 100 rooms.* ⌴. Situated in a former castle, this hotel retains the atmosphere of its opulent past. Two on-site restaurants offer casual and upmarket Austrian fare.

☞☞☞☞ **Schlosshotel Oth** – *Schlossgasse 23, 2500.* ✆*02252 44 436. www.oth.info. 34 rooms.* ⌴. This pretty traditional house on the edge of Doblhoffpark has beautifully decorated rooms, each with a balcony. There is a flower-filled garden and a very short walk away is a superb public Jugendstil bath.

🍴 EAT

☞☞ **Amterl** – *Hauptplatz 2, 2500.* ✆*02252 45 953. www.amterl.at. Closed Sun dinner.* This updated take on the Austrian heuriger serves classic tavern food with a modern twist.

☞☞ **Urbanus-Schenke** – *Habsburgerstraße 62a, 2500.* ✆*02252 20 95 21. www.urbanusschenke.at.* Typical comfort food served in a cosily traditional Austrian wine tavern.

ACTIVITIES

Römertherme Baden – *Brusattipl. 4.* ✆*02252 45 030. www.roemertherme.at. Daily 10am–10pm. €13.40/3hr or €17/ day.* Spa, Wellness centre, pool and sports facilities.

ENTERTAINMENT

Baden Operetta Festival – *http://operettaheaven.com.* Held each summer.

Schneeberg★

Since the completion of the Semmering railway in the mid 19C, the Schneeberg region has been a popular getaway for outdoor enthusiasts from Vienna. Hiking and touring are popular in summer, while skiers hit the slopes in winter.

🅸 **Info:** Schlossstraße 1, Katzelsdorf. ℘02622 78 960. www.wieneralpen.at.
▶ **Location:** The area is in eastern Austria, some 70km/43.5mi south of Vienna.

🚗 DRIVING TOUR

NEUNKIRCHEN TO SEMMERING★
102km/63mi. ⊗ Beware steep and narrow stretches of road, especially between Hirschwang and Semmering.

Neunkirchen
One of the oldest towns in Lower Austria, Neunkirchen boasts original Renaissance buildings. North of the Hauptplatz with its Trinity Column, the parish church of Mariä Himmelfahrt (mid-12C–16C, Baroque interior) towers above the rooftops. The church was fortified because of the town's frontier setting, and once even had a moat.

▶ In Neunkirchen, turn off the B 17 onto B 26 towards Puchberg.

Puchberg am Schneeberg
This pleasant mountain resort is distinguished by idyllic spa gardens laid out around a lake and a 12C ruined castle. From Puchberg station, the rack railway **Schneebergbahn** makes several trips to Hochschneeberg daily (🕙 *late Apr–Oct, daily 9am–3.30pm; ⊜€36 round-trip; ℘02742 36 09 90 99; www.schneebergbahn.at).* From the mountain station next to a refuge *(with restaurant),* an easy trail leads to the summit in about 90min, with fabulous **views★** along the way. Schneeberg is the highest mountain in Lower Austria.

▶ Leave Puchberg on the B 26 towards Wiener Neustadt, turn left towards Waldegg. In Reichental turn left again towards Gutenstein.

Gutenstein
In the 19C Gutenstein was a popular summer resort, attracting artists such as Lenau, Brahms and Waldmüller.

Wallfahrtskirche Mariahilfberg
3km/1.8mi SW of Gutenstein.
Go left before the church towards Mariahilfberg.
Various Habsburg emperors are among those who have made the pilgrimage to this Baroque church. An altarpiece in the left aisle features a striking depiction of an angel coming to the rescue of a soul burning in Purgatory.

▶ 2km/1.2mi beyond Gutenstein turn left into the Klostertal.

Klostertal★
About 16km/10mi.
This valley is sparsely populated and largely unspoiled. Towards the end, it narrows considerably, already heralding the Höllental.

Höllental★★
About 14km/8.5mi SE of Klostertal.
The Höllental, or Hell Valley, was carved by the River Schwarza between the two limestone massifs of the Schneeberg and the Raxalpe. There is quite a contrast between the delightful Klostertal and the harsher Wildbach Valley.

▶ At Hirschwang, the valley station of the Rax cable-car is to the right of the road.

Raxalpe★
Ascent by Raxseilbahn cable-car in 8min. 🕙Open year-round daily; hours vary: check website; 🕙closed three

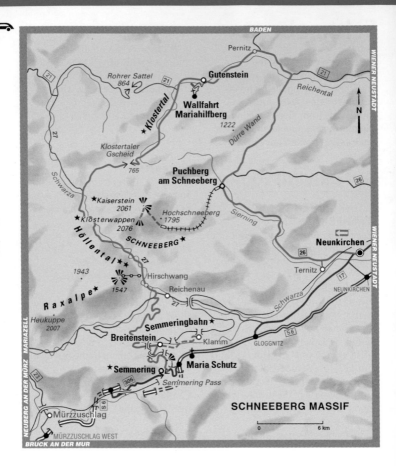

weeks in Nov. 🚋€26 return ℘02666 524 97. www.raxalpe.at.

This steep-sided limestone massif has become a popular climbing centre with several routes departing from the upper station at 1,547m/5,075ft. You can also undertake multi-day tours with overnight stays in mountain huts.

For details, check with the Reichenau tourist office (℘0266 65 28 65). Along the way stunning **views**★ stretch over the Schneeberg, the Höllental and Semmering.

▶ Exiting Hirschwang, turn right for Prein, then left towards Gloggnitz and right towards Semmering.

The winding road leaves the Schwarza Valley and cuts across the picturesque,

rugged Semmering region. Dropping down to Breitensteina, it affords the first glimpses of the superbly engineered viaducts of the **Semmering railway**★ (👁see box p255).

▶ Shortly after the Semmering signpost, turn left towards Haltestelle Wolfsbergkogel. After 200m/220yds turn left again and follow the marked Aussichtswarte Doppelreiterkogel signs. Park and follow the marked trail for about 10min to the look-out point.

The **Doppelreiterkogel look-out point**★★ offers a magnificent view of the Semmering railway, which cuts a particularly fine route at this point, with numerous viaducts and tunnels.

Semmering Railway

Rail links existed between Vienna and Gloggnitz and between Mürzzuschlag and Bruck an der Mur in the mid 1800s, but crossing the Semmering range still required the use of horse-drawn carts. In order to complete the final gap in the southern railway network, Venetian engineer Carlo di Ghega (1802–60) was invited to take over the Semmering railway project.

© Austrian National Tourist Office/ Diejun

Between 1848 and 1854, up to 20,000 workers were busy building the track of Europe's first standard-gauge mountain railway (some 1,000 of them died in accidents or from epidemics during construction). On the 41km/25mi stretch between Gloggnitz and Mürzzuschlag (21km/13mi above ground) the train passes through 15 tunnels, crosses 16 viaducts and more than 100 smaller bridges, overcoming an altitude difference of 480m/1,584 ft. In spite of the tremendous feats of construction – 1.4 million cu m/49 million cu ft of rock alone had to be blasted – the railway blends harmoniously into the beautiful landscape around Semmering. In 1999, UNESCO declared the railway and surrounding countryside a World Heritage Site.

▷ Backtrack and follow the signposts to Hochstraße/Südbahnstraße to get to Semmering.

Semmering★

After the construction of the Semmering railway, this climatic mountain spa and winter-sports centre, built on terraces between 985m/3,231ft and 1,291m/4,235ft, experienced a steep economic boom. The village is dotted with smart villas and hotels, mostly built between 1850 and 1910. Adding to the area's appeal is the exceptionally sunny climate. Information on the Semmering railway is available from the local tourist office (℘2664 200 25).

▷ Take the B 306 towards Mürzzuschlag, then the B 23 for 26km/16mi.

Neuberg an der Mürz★

In 1327 a Cistercian abbey was founded in Neuberg, and the following century, its Gothic cathedral, still an imposing sight today, was completed.
The southeast wing of the monastery sheltered a hunting lodge favoured by Emperor Franz Joseph I, and was used by various members of the Imperial family until the end of the monarchy.

Cathedral★ – Boasting a unique octagonal spire, the cathedral was built in the Gothic style and remodelled in Baroque in the 17C. Near the organ, admire the Western Gothic wall frescoes (1505), representing the Crucifixion.

Coventual buildings – This large complex includes the **Naturmuseum** 👤👤, which features interesting dioramas (⏱ open May–Oct daily 10am–noon, 2pm–4pm; €5.50; ℘0650 21 87 230; www.naturmuseum-neuberg.at). It also contains parts of the former hunting lodge of Emperor Franz Joseph, with original furniture and a collection of 19C paintings.

Don't miss the 14C cloister decorated with beautifully sculpted **figures★**, or the tympanum over the entrance of the dining hall, decorated with a Crucifixion scene dating from 1470.

Beside the picture of the founder, there are 19 Baroque paintings portraying the different abbots of the abbey.

Eisenstadt★

The administrative capital of the Burgenland, Eisenstadt has a mild climate allowing grapes, peaches, apricots and almonds to flourish. It is an important market in the region for wine and has a delightful Old Town. Its main attraction, though, is the legacy of composer Joseph Haydn, who lived here on and off for around 30 years.

A BIT OF HISTORY
Haydn's town

The composer **Joseph Haydn** (1732–1809) was in the employ of Prince Miklós József Esterházy for nearly 30 years, living sometimes at Eisenstadt, sometimes at the Esterháza Palace in Hungary. Haydn had been appointed assistant conductor in 1761; he was promoted to musical director in 1766. With an orchestra and theatre at his disposal, Haydn became famous.

For Haydn's birthplace at Rohrau, see PETRONELL-CARNUNTUM: Excursions.

Court Jews

Medieval statutes forbade Christians to handle interest on loans, which is why, in the 17C and 18C, some Jews came to play a crucial role in financial dealings. The Habsburg rulers appointed Court Jews, who enjoyed freedom of trade. Among them was Samuel Oppenheimer, a banker from Speyer, Germany, who financed Prince Eugen of Savoy's campaigns against the Turks. Another was his son-in-law Samson Wertheimer, who worked for Leopold I, Joseph I and Karl VI. Such privileges remained reserved for a chosen few, and many other members of the Jewish community continued to be oppressed.

▶ **Population:** 14,200.

Info: Hauptstraße 35, ℘02682 673 90. www.eisenstadt-tourismus.at.

◗ **Location:** About 60km/37mi south of Vienna on the south slopes of the Leithagebirge. Alt. 181m/594ft.

P Parking: There are fee-based parking garages at Esterházyplatz, the Rathaus and Hotel Burgenland.

Don't Miss: Schloss Esterházy and its Haydnsaal.

Kids: Burg Forchtenstein.

SIGHTS
Schloss Esterházy★★ (Esterházy Palace)

Open Apr daily 10am–5pm, May–Sept til 6pm, Oct til 5pm; Nov–Mar Fri–Sun & hols 9am–5pm. €11. ℘02682 63 00 47 600. www.esterhazy.at.

Eisenstadt was one of the favourite residences of the Esterházys, the Magyar family who played a significant role in the establishment of Habsburg rule in Hungary. The original 17C Baroque palace, by Italian architect Carlo Martino Carlone, was built on the site of a medieval fortress. A century later it received some Neoclassical touches, courtesy of Charles de Moreau. It now houses local administrative offices, but some rooms can be seen by guided tour.

Esterházy Exhibit & Haydnsaal

The highlight of any palace tour is the **Haydnsaal★**, a magnificent hall resplendent with stucco, *grisailles* of Hungarian kings and frescoes with scenes from Greek mythology. In the 18C the marble floor was replaced with parquet for better acoustics, which you'll get to appreciate during a short concert. It was here that Haydn conducted the Court orchestra most nights. Other rooms recall the importance of the Esterházy family.

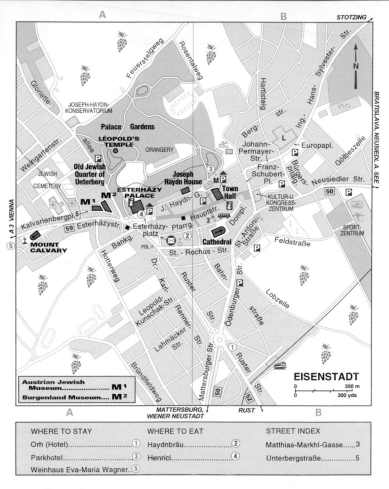

STOTZING

JOSEPH-HAYDN-KONSERVATORIUM

Palace Gardens

LÉOPOLD'S TEMPLE

ORANGERY

Old Jewish Quarter of Unterberg

JEWISH CEMETERY

Joseph Haydn House

ESTERHÁZY PALACE

Town Hall

J. Haydn.-G.

Johann-Permayer-Str.

Franz-Schubert-Pl.

Europapl.

Neusiedler Str.

KULTUR-U.-KONGRESS-ZENTRUM

SPORT-ZENTRUM

Kalvarienbergpl.

Esterházystr.

Esterházy-platz

Pfarrg.

Hauptstr.

Dompl.

St.-Antoni-Straße

Feldstraße

MOUNT CALVARY

Bankg.

POL.

St.-Rochus-Str.

Cathedral

Hotterweg

Dr.-Karl-

Ruster Str.

Bahn-

Odenburger Str.

straße

Lobzeile

Leopold-Kunschak-Str.

Renner Str.

Lahmäcker Str.

Bründlfeldweg

Mattersburger Str.

Ruster Str.

EISENSTADT

0 — 300 m
0 — 300 yds

MATTERSBURG, WIENER NEUSTADT

RUST

| Austrian Jewish Museum | M¹ |
| Burgenland Museum | M² |

WHERE TO STAY		WHERE TO EAT		STREET INDEX	
Orh (Hotel)	①	Haydnbräu	②	Matthias-Markhl-Gasse	3
Parkhotel	③	Henrici	④	Unterbergstraße	5
Weinhaus Eva-Maria Wagner	⑤				

Joseph Haydn House

21 Haydn-Gasse. ○*Open mid-Mar–mid-Nov Tue–Sat 9am–5pm, Sun and hols 10am–5pm (Jun–mid-Nov also Mon).* ⊛€5. ℘*02682 719 60 00. www.haydn-haus.at.*

This modest Baroque house was bought by Haydn in 1776. Inside are period rooms, a piano, an old church organ (on which Beethoven also played), as well as early prints of Haydn compositions.

Kalvarienberg and Haydnkirche★ (Mount Calvary)

○*Open Apr–Oct daily 9am–5pm.* ℘*02682 626 38. www.haydnkirche.at.*

Haydn is buried in the Haydnkirche (also known as Bergkirche), though his skull

was removed at time of death and only reunited with the body in 1954.

The church is located near an artificial hill known as the Kalvarienberg, where 24 **Stations of the Cross★**, made of 260 wooden and 60 stone figures, portray the story of The Passion with a typically Baroque drama and flair.

Town Hall

The 17C Renaissance Rathaus features a highly original façade with three oriel windows, scrolled gables and a round-arched doorway with diamond-cut stonework.

257

The Legend of Rosalia

While Giletus, first lord of Forchtenstein, was away on the battlefield, his wife Rosalia ruled the fortress with an iron fist. Learning of this situation, Giletus decided to describe the incident to her as if he were talking about a stranger, asking her opinion as to appropriate punishment. Rosalia recommended imprisonment in the fortress dungeon; so, condemned by her own words, she ended her days in the dungeon. Her restless spirit, however, returned to haunt the fortress until Giletus had the Rosalienkapelle built to appease it.

Cathedral

The Late-Gothic Domkirche from the 15C and 16C is dedicated to St. Martin, patron saint of the Burgenland. A charming pulpit and the choir, complete with organ, remain of the original Late Baroque interior decoration. Note the relief of the Mount of Olives, dating from before 1500.

Austrian Jewish Museum★

Unterbergstraße 6. ⏲*Open May–Oct Tue–Sun 10am–5pm.* ⏲*Closed late Dec–early Jan.* ᰛ*€4.* ✆*02682 65 145. www.ojm.at.*

When Emperor Leopold I expelled the Jews from Vienna in 1671, many sought refuge in Eisenstadt, where a thriving Jewish community sprang up in the Unterberg district. In a former private home, the Östereichisches Jüdisches Museum has displays on Jewish holidays as well as an impressive synagogue.

Burgenland Museum

Museumsgasse 1-5. ⏲*Open mid-Jan–mid-Nov Tue–Sat 9am–5pm, Sun 10am–5pm (Jun–Nov also Mon); late Nov–mid-Dec Mon–Fri 9am–5pm.* ᰛ*€6.* ✆*02682 719 30 11. www.landesmuseum-burgenland.at.*

This regional museum is devoted to ethnological and cultural history.

EXCURSION
♠⋮ Burg Forchtenstein★

23km/14mi southeast of Wiener Neustadt, via Mattersburg.

☞*Guided tours (1hr15min) on the hour;* ⏲*open Apr–Oct daily 10am–6pm; winter tours Nov–Mar 11am, 1pm, 3pm.* ᰛ*€9.*
✆*02626 812 12. www.esterhazy.at.*

The fortress of Forchtenstein overlooks picturesque scenery from its bluff-top site in the Rosaliengebirge foothills. It is dominated by its massive 50m/164ft keep, which is the oldest surviving part of the original construction.

The fortress was built at the beginning of the 14C by the counts of Mattersdorf. The Esterházy family, owners of Forchtenstein since 1622, added the ring of bastions to stave off Turkish invaders. After the family moved to Schloss Esterházy (⏺*see p256*) in Eisenstadt in the early 18C, Forchtenstein became a treasury, arsenal and archive. It is still owned by the Esterházys.

A tour of the castle takes in one of Europe's largest private family collectionsa, with about 20,000 items. Highlights include the **treasury** (art and precious objects, clocks and automata, silverware, chinoiseries, porcelain); the **picture gallery** (family portraits and battle scenes); and the **arsenal**, holding arms and armour, trophies from the wars against the French and the Prussians, and the "Turkish booty" from the field campaigns of Prince Paul Esterházy (1652–1713). The cistern in the courtyard (142m/465ft deep) was dug by Turkish prisoners of war.

Forchenstein village, which developed around the fortress, has some 2,800 inhabitants, a pilgrimage church (1347) and chapel.

Follow the road uphill from the fortress 4km/2.5mi to reach the **Rosalienkapelle** (1670), a dedicated to Rosalia, curer of plagues, from which there is a **view★** as far as Eisenstadt and the Neusiedler See.

ADDRESSES

🛏 STAY

🍷🍷 **Weinhaus Eva-Maria Wagner** – *Wiener Straße 10-12.* ℘*0676 317 55 90.* *www.weinhaus-evawagner.at.* 🚭. *5 rooms.* This charming small rustic-style winery-hotel has pretty bedrooms, some with a terrace. It is close to the town centre.

🍷🍷🍽 **Parkhotel** – *Joseph-Haydn-Gasse 38.* ℘*02682 75 325. www.parkhotel-eisenstadt.at. 28 rooms.* 🚭. Smart modern international-style hotel, completely renovated in 2006, close to the centre of town. Restaurant on-site.

🍷🍷🍽🍽 **Ohr** – *Ruster Straße 51.* ℘*02682 624 60. www.hotel-ohr.at. 29 rooms.* 🚭. *Closed Mon year-round and Sun eve Oct–Jun.* Modern international-style family-run hotel with individually decorated rooms. Restaurant on the premises.

🍴 EAT

🍷 **Haydnbräu** – *Pfarrgasse 22.* ℘*02682 639 45. www.haydnbraeu.at.* This traditional Brauhaus serves a changing daily menu based on seasonal regional cuisine; five types of beer are brewed on the premises. Its beer garden is located on the town ramparts.

🍷🍷🍽 **Henrici** – *Esterházyplatz 5.* ℘*02682 628 19. www.henrici.at.* This cosy restaurant is located in the grand Classical setting of the former royal stables. The cuisine is Austrian-Italian, cooked with flair, and fine local wines from Burgenland are available. The terrace offers a view of the castle.

Neusiedler See★★

The vast Neusiedler See (*Fertö* in Hungarian) is the westernmost example of a steppe-type lake. A popular weekend getaway for Vienna folk, it is one of the great attractions of the Burgenland. Most of the lake belongs to Austria, but the southern tip lies in the Hungarian Puszta. A paradise for watersports enthusiasts, it is ringed by swimming beaches that have been created from the reed-fringed shore. To preserve this unique habitat with its profusion of plants, rare animals and migratory birds, the region was designated a national park in 1992 and was placed on UNESCO's list of World Heritage Sites in 2001. The lake is also at the centre of an important wine region.

🚗 **DRIVING TOUR**

FROM NEUSIEDL TO MÖRBISCH
49km/30mi.

👫 Neusiedl am See
The place that gives the lake its name has a ruined medieval castle and a 15C

📋 **Info:** Obere Hauptstraße 24, 7100 Neusiedl am See. ℘02167 86 00. www.neusiedlersee.com.

▶ **Location:** The lake is on the eastern edge of the country, about 50km/31mi southeast of Vienna.

🅿 **Parking:** Car parks can be found at several places around the lake.

👁 **Don't Miss:** The town of Rust, famous for its storks' nests.

🕐 **Timing:** This is an easy day trip from Vienna, although the lake is well worth an overnight stay.

👫 **Kids:** Swimming and boating on the lake.

church, but otherwise there's little reason to spend much time here.

▶ Head NW towards Eisenstadt; after Donnerskirchen turn left for Rust.

Between Austria and Hungary

As a result of the Treaty of Saint-Germain-en-Laye (1919), parts of the three western *comitats* (provinces) of Hungary passed to Austria. These form the present province of Burgenland, which clearly shows a certain Magyar influence, for example in its cultural and musical traditions.

House in Apetlon

The Burgenland has retained its ethnic mix of Hungarian, Romany and Sinti minorities, as well as descendants of Croat refugees from the time of the Turkish invasions. These minorities settled in this province – and particularly around the Neusiedler See – since the area had formed part of a buffer zone that had been intentionally depopulated by the Hungarian rulers.

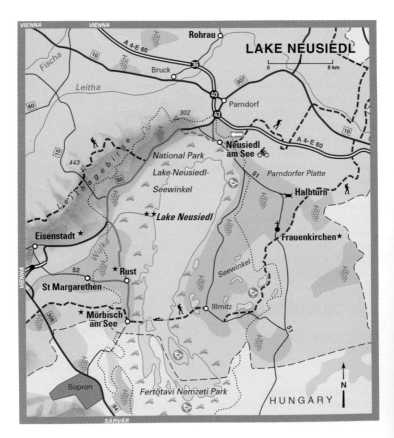

Neusiedler See in winter

© Heinz Hudelist/imageBROKER/age fotostock

Rust★

Rust is famous not only for its storks' nests, to which the birds return faithfully every year, but also for its prosperity as a wine-growing centre. Since 1989, a wine academy has offered seminars and other wine-related events to the public.

The town centre boasts charming Renaissance and Baroque façades, arcaded inner courtyards and a partially preserved fortified town wall. A highlight on the west side of Rathausplatz is the **Fischerkirche**, which has impressive **frescoes★** from the 14C and 15C. Also note the Late Gothic statues on the altar to the Three Magi in the side aisle and the fine organ from 1705. From the village, a causeway through the rushes leads to the **Seebad Rust** (&⊙*open May–mid-Sept daily 9am–7pm;* ⊚€4.50; *℘0268 55 91; www.seebadrust.at),* a small beachside resort area with buildings on piles connected by pontoons.

Mörbisch am See★

With its web of picturesque alleyways, Mörbisch is one of the prettiest places on the Neusiedler See. Almost all the whitewashed houses have stone steps leading up to pillared porches, brightly painted doors and window shutters, corn cobs hanging up to dry, and flowers everywhere.

Leaving the village to the east through the reed beds takes you to a good place for swimming, as well as the floating **Seebühne** stage, where an operetta festival is held in summer (&*see p263).*

▷ Return to Rust, then bear left for St. Margarethen im Burgenland.

St. Margarethen

The village is famous for its Passion play, performed every five years *(next Jun–Aug 2016)* in the old Roman quarry. Several famous buildings in Vienna, such as the

A Capricious Lake

Fringed by enormous reed beds, the Neusiedler See has no permanent outflow, and has only one tributary, the tiny Wulka. The lake's replenishment mostly by rain, snow melt and ground water keeps the water level rather shallow (up to 2m/6.5ft deep), and the water itself saline and warm. The lake has even been known to dry up altogether, although not since the late 19C. Consistent winds blowing from the same direction can drive the water towards one shore, leaving the other shore temporarily dry.

Nightingale

European
Bee-eater

Whinchat

Little Ringed Plover

Lakeside Birdlife

Partridge

Coot

Bar-tailed Godwit

Great Egret

M. Guillou/ MICHELIN

Stephansdom, the Votivkirche, Burgtheater and Parliament, were made from St. Margarethen's sandstone. St. Margarethen is also known for its wine.

EXCURSIONS
Schloss Halbturn
⏱*Open Apr–Oct Tue–Sun 10am–5pm.* €8. ℗*02172 85 94.* *www.schlosshalbturn.com.*

Built in 1701 by Lukas von Hildebrandt, this palace is the most important secular Baroque building in the Burgenland. It served as a hunting lodge for Emperor Charles VI. Ravaged by looting and fire after World War II, the building has now been completely restored to its former glory, with its façade looking very smart in shades of pale blue and cream. In the garden room, which fortunately survived a 1949 fire, **Franz Anton Maulbertsch** was responsible for the remarkable **frescoes★**.

The palace hosts important cultural exhibits from May to September, and also operates a well-respected wine estate *(tastings possible)* and restaurant. Its extensive gardens are perfect for strolls and picnics.

Basilika Frauenkirchen★
⏱*Open May–Sept daily 7am–9pm; Oct–Apr daily 8am–6pm.* ℗*02172 22 24. www.frauenkirchen.net.*

A basilica since 1990, this famous place of **pilgrimage** was commissioned by Prince Paul Esterházy in 1702. It radiates Italian elegance, which is not surprising since its architect was Francesco Martinelli; the stuccowork was done by Pietro Conti and the frescoes by Luca Columba.

The sumptuous altar frames an Early Gothic statue of the Virgin Mary, the main object of veneration. Note the painting of a breast-feeding Madonna in the first side altar in the north aisle and the painted choir stalls.

Nationalpark Neusiedlersee-Seewinkel
⏱*Information centre open Apr–Oct Mon–Fri 8am–5pm, Sat–Sun 10am–5pm; rest of the year Mon–Fri 8am–4pm.* ℗*02175 34 42.* *www.nationalpark-neusiedlersee-seewinkel.at.*

Around the southern half of the east shore lies a national park of reed beds, marshes and small lakes. Seewinkel is a naturalists' paradise, popular with ornithologists for its more than 250 species of birds seen here. **Illmitz**, amid the marshes, makes a good base from which to explore the wetlands.

Stop first at the information centre and enquire about the visitor programme, which includes several excursions *(available in various languages)* to different parts of the national park.

ADDRESSES

🛏STAY

🛏 **Hotel Sifkovits** – *Am Seekanal 8, 7071 Rust.* ℗*02685 20 460. www.sifkovits. at. Open May–mid-Sept. 20 rooms.* 🍽. This small, quiet rustic-modern hotel is quite close to both the Neusiedlersee and to Rust. The lounge occupies a stunning conservatory while bedrooms are comfortable and stylish. Restaurant.

🍴EAT

🍽 **Römerzeche** – *Rathausplatz 11, 7071 Rust.* ℗*02685 332. www.roemerzeche.at. Closed Tue and Dec.* Enjoy a lunch of local cooking in this typical Eastern Austrian wine-tavern, with a fruity white wine from Burgenland.Flower-filled courtyard.

🍽 **Rusterhof** – *Rathausplatz 18, 7071 Rust.* ℗*02685 607 93. Closed Nov–Mar.* This restaurant overlooks the main square and serves fine cuisine inspired by traditional local recipes; try the *pavé* of perch caught in Lake Neusiedl.

ENTERTAINMENT
Mörbisch Seefestspiele Operetta Festival – ℗*02682 662 10. www. seefestspiele-moerbisch.at.* Held each summer *(mid-Jul–mid-Aug)*, the annual open-air operetta festival *(tickets €25–145)* takes place on the floating stage 2km/1.2mi east of Mörbisch.

GRAZ AND STYRIA

The southern Austrian region of Steiermark (Styria) is known as the green heart of the country. The second-largest of the country's provinces, it extends from the Hungarian plains in the east to the high mountains of the Dachstein in the west. Much of Styria comprises green rolling hills from which comes a wide range of agricultural output, including many dairy products, *Kurbiskernöl* (pumpkin seed oil, a local speciality), and some excellent wines that are best explored along what is known as the *Steirische Weinstraße* (Styrian Wine Road). This lush countryside is also the site where the famous Lippizaner horses are reared for the Spanish Riding School in Vienna.

Highlights

A Bit of History

The capital of Styria is Graz, a UNESCO World Heritage Site and one of Austria's most beautiful and culturally lively cities. Located about 200km southwest of Vienna, Graz is dominated by the Schlossberg rock, which is topped by the Uhrturm, a 13C clock tower that has become the city's symbol. Close to Graz, the 17C Schloss Eggenberg is laid out to represent the structure of the Gregorian calendar. Styria is also the location of Austria's most important pilgrimage site, Mariazell. The church here contains what is said to be a miraculous image of the Madonna and still attracts the faithful by the thousands. The church's treasury and art works also make the site a special place to visit.

A Land of Glaciers and Vines

As the terrain changes from high mountains to fields and vineyards, the province reveals many historic small towns and abbeys. Of the latter, St. Paul in Lavantal, Seckau, and especially Stift Admont are some of the most important. Admont has one of the finest Baroque libraries anywhere in Europe. Of the towns, those of the Styrian spa country such as Bad Radkersburg and

Library, Admont Monastery

© Austrian National Tourist Office/ Trumler

GRAZ AND STYRIA

Zwettl

Mariazell	★★	Recommended
Kitzeck	★	Interesting
Leoben		Other sight described in this guide
⇨		Driving tour

0 — 12 miles
0 — 20 km

N

SALZBOURG
A 7
Linz
123
124
310

WELS

OBERÖSTERREICH

DANUBE
Enns
A 1

Steyr
122
309

NIEDERÖSTERREICH

Enns
Ybbs

Lilienfeld

Annaberg

Erlaufsee *Bürgeralpe* 1266
Salzatal Mariazell
Palfau Wildalpen Gusswerk Neuberg an der Mürz
Großreifling Weichselboden
Gstatterboden Hieflau *Leopoldsteiner See* Prescenyklause
Haindl-karbrücke *Aflenz-Kurort*
Frauenberg Eisenerz 1910 *Polster* Thörl
Liezen *Gesäuse* Erzberg Vordernberg Bruck an der Mur
146 *Eisenerzer Alpen*
Admont Monastery Leoben *Bärenschützklamm* Vorau
A 9 Frohnleiten Pöllauberg
STYRIA Pöllau
Seckau Österreichisches Freilichtmuseum *Lurgrotte* Herberstein
St Barbara
Judenburg Gestüt Piber Rein Mariatrost Blumau
Gaberl 1551 Köflach Eggenberg Graz
Murau Pack-und Stubalpenstrasse Gundersdorf Riegersburg
Pack Langegg *Steirisches Thermenland*
Lavant Valley Motorway Bridge Bad Gams ob Frauental *Steirische Weinstraße* Styrassic Park
Friesach Wolfsberg St Andrä Bad Gleichenberg
CARINTHIA Deutschlandsberg Kitzeck Bad Radkersburg
St Veit an der Glan Kleinklein Großklein
St Paul im Lavanttal Ehrenhausen
Leutschach
Klagenfurt Drau Drava MARIBOR

SLOVENIA

Mur
Gurk
Drau

VIENNE
NEUNKIRCHEN
ZALAEGERSZEG
NAGYKANIZSA, M7
VARAŽDIN
ZAGREB
LJUBLJANA
VILLACH
SALZBOURG
WELS

A

B

Bad Gleichenberg are lovely retreats. For history, architecture and culture, places such as Bruck an der Mur, famous for its old ironwork, are well worth exploring,

while Leoben has not only a fascinating local museum but also the Gösser brewery, one of Austria's finest beer-making facilities.

Graz★★

The capital of Styria, Graz is also known as the "Garden City," thanks to its many parks, riverside setting and surrounding rolling hills. In 1999 its extensive and well-preserved historic centre was declared a UNESCO World Heritage Site. Cultural life flourishes with year-round performances and festivals. The nightlife is excellent, too, fuelled in large part by 44,000 students attending six major universities. Austria's second-largest city is also an economic hub that nurtures industries such as brewing, shoe-making and car manufacture.

A BIT OF HISTORY

In 1379 the Habsburgs chose Graz as their residence; it became an Imperial City when Friedrich III, King of Germany and Austria, was crowned Holy Roman Emperor in 1452. The city ramparts were built in the 13C as a defence against the Turkish invasions of Styria and in 1543, under Emperor Ferdinand I, they were strengthened again, with the addition of the Schlossberg. The defence of the city became imperative: a huge arsenal of arms and munitions was built up with raw material coming from Styria's "**Iron Mountain**".

▶ **Population:** 282,500.

Info: Messeplatz 1/ Messeturm, 1st floor, A-8010. ✆0316 80750. www.graztourismus.at.

Location: Graz sits in the valley of the Mur, bounded by the Styrian hills and the last foothills of the Alps in southeastern Austria. Alt 365m/1,194ft.

Parking: Car parks in the town centre tend to be expensive and mainly offer short-term parking. You're better off using Park & Ride: there is one behind the main train station; take bus No 1 or 7 to the centre.

Don't Miss: the Zeughaus, the Mausoleum, the Schlossberg, the Kunsthaus.

Timing: Devote at least two days to Graz.

Kids: the Jagdmuseum.

Following the Habsburg partition of the country in 1564, Graz became the capital of a vast area known as **Inner Austria**, (Styria, Carinthia, Gorizia, Carniola and Istria) as well as the splendid court of

Glockenspielplatz

© Graz Tourismus / Hans Wiesenhofer

TOURIST INFORMATION

Graz Tourism Information:
Herrengasse 16, 8010 Graz. Open daily 10am–6pm (Nov & Jan–Mar 5pm) ✆*0316 807 50. www.graztourismus.at*
Information kiosk at Central Train Station (Hauptbahnhof): *Europaplatz 6, 8020 Graz.* Free brochures and an electronic information system.
CITY TOURS: Guided Tour of Old Town *(90min)*. Meeting point: Graz Tourism office *(Herrengasse 16). Jan–Apr and Nov Sat 2.30pm* in German and English. *May–Oct daily 2.30pm* in English. €10.50.
Handheld audio-visual tour: includes 32 stops, available in English (and other languages). Rent from Tourist Office (ID-card/passport necessary): 2hr €7.50, 4hr €8.50; 8hr €12.50.
Day trips (in English and German) to the Southern Styrian Wine Region and other destinations around Graz are available for groups. Information and bookings from Graz Tourismus *(address above).*

PUBLIC TRANSPORT

Tickets are available from ticket machines, advance booking offices and tobacconists *(Trafiken)*, and from tram and bus drivers. The **Graz 3-day ticket** (€12) offers three days of free travel from the time of validation on all (central) public transport in Graz, including the *Schlossbergbahn* funicular railway and lifts.

It also entitles you to free and reduced admission at selected attractions. Available from the Tourist Office, the Hauptbahnhof and elsewhere. With the **Stundenkarte** you can use any form of public transport in Graz for 1hr (€2.20); with the **10-Zonenkarte** (€19.80) you can make journeys across 10 city zones. A **24-Stundenkarte** (€5) and a **Wochenkarte** (€14.20) also offer travel for 24hr and one week respectively.
Further information on public transport can be obtained from **Mobil Zentral:** *Jakoministr. 1.* ✆*050 678910. www.mobilzentral.at, www.busbahnbim.at.*

BICYCLE HIRE: To explore the city's 75km/47mi of cycle paths, hire a bicycle from the **Graz Bike rental network**, offering more than 190 bikes at 11 locations throughout the city. Prices start at €5/half-day, €10/day. Reserve in-person or online at www.grazbike.at.

INNER CITY PARKING: Parking is permitted in the blue zones for a fee for a certain time *(parking is restricted 9am–8pm on weekdays and til 1pm Sat)*. Parking tickets valid for up to 3hr can be obtained from parking ticket machines. **Park & Ride** lots offer inexpensive or free parking in lots outside the city centre, with easy access to the centre by bus.

Archduke Karl II, which brought many cultural and artistic benefits to the city.

The Reformation

By 1568 three-quarters of the population had embraced Protestantism. In this year a school and seminary were founded *(where the present Paradeishof stands)*, and it was here that the German astronomer **Johannes Kepler** taught between 1594 and 1598.
In 1571 Archduke Karl II called upon the Jesuit religious order to imple-

ment the Counter Reformation. They founded a college *(in the Bürgergasse)* and a school *(the Hofgasse)*. In 1585 the archduke founded **Graz University**, which became the intellectual hub of Inner Austria.
The city's fortunes took a turn for the worse in 1619 when Karl II's son, Archduke Ferdinand II, was elected Holy Roman Emperor. Ferdinand moved the court to Vienna, and Graz, no longer an Imperial residence, lost much of its importance.

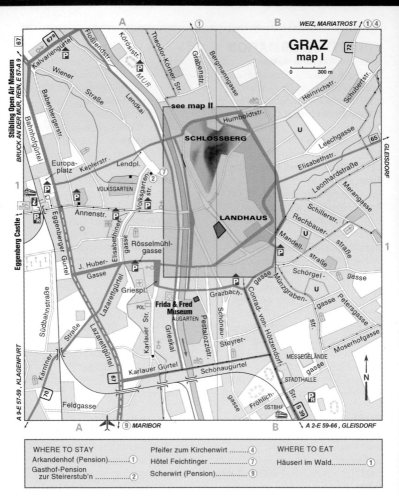

WHERE TO STAY		Pfeifer zum Kirchenwirt ....④	WHERE TO EAT
Arkandenhof (Pension)..........①		Hôtel Feichtinger ....⑦	Häuserl im Wald................①
Gasthof-Pension zur Steirerstub'n ....②		Scherwirt (Pension)...............⑨	

In the 18C, following the reforms of Maria Theresia, the city lost many of its privileges, which is a reason that the city has so few buildings dating from the Late Baroque period.

In the early 19C, the popular Habsburg archduke Johann (1782–1859) settled in Graz, and initiated projects to develop the city's economy and culture. A committed student of the arts, technology, nature and agriculture, he founded model farms, presided over the construction of the Graz-Mürzzuschlag railway (1844) and promoted the development of the Eisenerz area.

In Graz itself, the Technische Hochschule (also known as Erzog Johan University) is proof of his progressive spirit, as is the **Universalmuseum Joanneum**, Austria's oldest museum open to the public, founded in 1811 and the second-largest museum in Austria after the Kunsthistorisches Museum in Vienna. The museum's exhibits are mounted in Schloss Eggenberg (Old Masters), the Kunsthaus (contemporary art), the Volkskundemuseum (crafts and folkore) and other buildings. Natural history is the focus at Raubergasse 10, and around the corner at Neutorgasse 45, the **Kulturhistorische Sammlung** (Cultural History Collection) sheds light on the daily lives of Styrians from the Middle Ages through today. *Combined ticket to all Universalmuseum Joanneum sites: €13 (over 24hr period) or €19 (48hr).*

Landhaus courtyard

© Graz Tourismus / Harry Schiffer

WALKING TOURS

1 OLD TOWN TOUR★★

Hauptplatz★

Right in the heart of Graz, this square is the liveliest of all the city squares. Trams come and go incessantly, disgorging ever more people to join the crowds thronging the market stalls. Behind the brightly painted 17C–19C façades are much older, medieval buildings. The flashiest façade belongs to the arcaded **Haus Luegg,** which is festooned with luxuriant Baroque stuccowork.

The city's oldest pharmacy, at no. 4, dates from 1535, and still has some of its original fittings. The **Erzherzog-Johann-Brunnen** (fountain) of 1878 dominates the square. The fact that the statue of the emperor is relegated to a less important site on the Freiheitsplatz is a tangible reminder of the local people's affection for the enlightened archduke. The four female figures gracing the fountain are allegories of the four main rivers flowing through Styria at the time of the monarchy, though the boundary revisions of 1918 left the province with only two of them (the Mur and the Enns). The southern end of the square is anchored by the neo-Renaissance **Rathaus** (town hall). Standing outside, you get a great view of the Schlossberg

with the familiar outline of the Uhrturm (clock tower).

The Landhaus is reached via the broad and busy **Herrengasse**, with its elegant shops and offices. The **Gemaltes Haus** (painted house, no. 3) was the residence of the archdukes until the construction of the castle in 1450. The murals on historic (notably Roman) themes date from 1742, when they replaced the original decoration by Pietro de Pomis, architect of the mausoleum.

Landhaus★★

Herrengasse 16. Free entry to courtyard daily 5:30am–8pm. Guided tours available with Graz Guides, ℘0316 58 67 20. www.grazguides.at.

The former seat of the Styrian Diet, the Landhaus is a remarkable Renaissance palace built between 1557 and 1565 by Domenico dell'Allio, the military architect who had just completed the total reconstruction of the Schlossberg fortress for Emperor Ferdinand I. Today the Landhaus still serves as the meeting place for the Landtag, the Styrian provincial parliament.

The main façade, with its round-arched windows above an elegant doorway, prepares you for the splendour of the inner courtyard with its three storeys of arcades, flower-bedecked balconies, staircase wells and loggias. The stairway gracing the chapel in the northwest corner of the courtyard is the work of another Italian, Bartolomeo di Bosio. The well-head has a fine bronze dais with amoretti and female figures. In summer, the courtyard forms an enchanting backdrop for various performances.

▶ Exit the courtyard back onto Herrengasse.

Zeughaus (Arsenal)★★★

⏱*Open Apr–Oct Tues–Sun 10am–5pm; Nov–Mar by guided tour (1hr; additional ⊚€2.50) only 11am–2pm (tours depart at 11am, 1pm and 2pm). ⊚€9. ☏0316 80 17 98 10. www.museum-joanneum.at.*

Built in 1642, the Zeughaus was one of many arsenals in the world, but today it is the only one to have been preserved in its original state and with its contents intact. To enter the arsenal is to leave behind the bustle of the Herrengasse and to be transported back four centuries. You almost expect cavalrymen and foot soldiers to appear, fresh from being mustered in the Landhaus courtyard to be kitted out for battle.

Displayed on four floors are more than 32,000 arms of all imaginable kinds, many of a very high standard of craftsmanship. There are pistols, muskets, arquebuses and other firearms; heavy armour, breastplates and harnesses for use in battle or jousting, plus helmets,

pikes, swords: the collection is truly mindboggling.

Head to the top floor for a grand view of the Landhaus courtyard, the city's red rooftops and the Schlossberg with clock tower.

Stadtpfarrkirche zum Heiligen Blut (Precious Blood of Jesus)

The original Gothic church building was remodelled in the Baroque style, then re-Gothicised in the late 19C. Its Baroque **bell-tower★**, the city's finest, was built entirely out of wood in 1780–81 by the architect Josef Stengg and the master carpenter Franz Windisch. It is topped by a three-barred cross, a reminder of its consecration by the Pope.

Inside, on the altar in the south aisle, is an Assumption of the Virgin, attributed to Tintoretto. The stained glass of the chancel, the work of the Salzburg artist Albert Birkle in 1953, has an unusual feature: in the left-hand window, the fourth panel from the bottom on the right shows Hitler and Mussolini observing the flagellation of Christ. Birkle's work had been deemed "degenerate" by the Nazis.

Organ concerts are held in the church on a regular basis.

▶ Enter Altstadtpassage at no. 7 Herrengasse.

Armour in Zeughaus

© Graz Tourismus / Harry Schiffer

Mausoleum

©Graztourismus/Harry Schiffer

Walking through Altstadtpassage, the first courtyard has arcaded and vaulted galleries dating from 1648. A little farther are several courtyards of which one is reminiscent of the Landhaus.

The passageway spills out onto the **Mehlplatz**, flanked by two grand residences with Baroque stucco façades. Go right onto **Glockenspielplatz** (Carillon Square), where, at each carillon performance *(daily at 11am, 3pm and 6pm)*, the costumed figures of a man and a woman emerge and twirl in the pediment of an imposing house with a bell-turret.

▷ Leave Glockenspielplatz via the narrow passageway called Abraham-a-Santa-Clara-Gasse, then turn left for a view of no. 1 Burgergasse, the palazzo-like building that once served as a boardinghouse for aristocratic pupils of the Jesuits. To the right, a stairway leads to the mausoleum.

Mausoleum★★

🕐*Open daily 10.30am–12.30pm and 1.30pm–4pm (Jan–Apr Tue & Fri only).*
🕐*Closed public hols.* 🎟6€.
📞*0316 82 16 83.*

It was Emperor Ferdinand II who commissioned Italian architect **Pietro de Pomis** to build the Imperial mausoleum. Pomis started work in 1614, but the structure was not completed until 1636 by fellow Italian Pietro Valnegro. Inside, the exuberant stucco work and

some of the frescoes were designed by Johann Bernhard Fischer von Erlach. A particularly fine oval dome surmounts the funerary crypt containing the red-marble sarcophagus of Karl II and Maria of Bavaria, the emperor's parents. Only Maria lies inside; the emperor was buried at Seckau Abbey. The tomb of Emperor Ferdinand II lies to the right of the altar.

Domkirche (Cathedral)★

Next to the mausoleum, the vast and luminous Domkirche was designated a cathedral in 1786, having previously served as Imperial court church. It was commissioned by Emperor Friedrich III, whose coat of arms adorns the main entrance, and completed in 1464. Frescoes (1485) on the southwest corner of the entrance show the troubles visited on Graz in the 1480s (Turkish attack, plague and locusts).

The **interior** is a harmonious mix of Gothic reticulated vaulting and Baroque decoration. Of the original décor, two frescoes of St. Christopher (late 15C) have survived. They recall an old belief that one would not die on a day when one had looked at the saint's image.

Near the chancel entrance are two magnificent **reliquary chests★★★**. Brought here by the Jesuits, they were once the marriage chests of Paula di Gonzaga, Duchess of Mantua. Made of ebony and decorated with reliefs in bone and

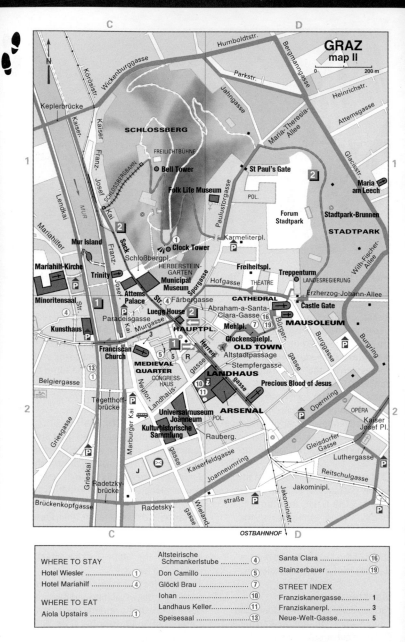

GRAZ
map II

0   200 m

ivory, they date from around 1470 and are in the style of Mantegna. Their subject matter goes back to the *Triumphs* of Petrarch, moral and allegorical poems dealing with the stages of life from the standpoint of a calm acceptance of death. The organ with its 5,354 pipes dates from 1978.

▶ Leave the cathedral by the north entrance. Cross the street by the **Burgtor** (Castle Gate) and go through the impressive stone gateway commanding the first courtyard of the 15C castle.

The erstwhile residence of Friedrich III, the **castle** (burg), heavily rebuilt, now houses the offices of the provincial government (Landes regierung). At the end of the first courtyard, below an archway, is the amazing **Treppenturm★★** (Staircase Tower), an unusual double-spiral stairway. The tower was added in 1499 by his son, Maximilian I, and is a notable technical achievement both in terms of design and the stonemason's craft.

▶ Backtrack to Hofgasse and head west to Freiheitsplatz.

Freiheitsplatz

In the centre of the square stands the statue of Franz II, the last Holy Roman Emperor and elder brother of Archduke Johann. The large red building with a Neoclassical pediment closing the square is the city residence of the abbots of St. Lambrecht.

Follow Hofgasse to the old **Hofbäckerei** (Imperial Bakery) with its fine shop front (on your left just before Sporgasse). Turning right into the Sporgasse, have a look at the **Palais Saurau** at no. 25 with its rusticated Baroque doorway and arcaded doorway; the significance of the Turk brandishing a sword on the gable is a mystery, even to the locals. The Renaissance **Zur Goldenen Pastete** (no. 28) is another picturesque building.

Follow bustling **Sporgasse** as it winds back to the Hauptplatz. At no. 22 is the former Deutschordenshaus (House of the Teutonic Knights); it has an arcaded courtyard in Gothic style. The narrow façade of no. 3 is an interesting example of Jugendstil (Art Nouveau).

▶ Cross the Hauptplatz and continue straight ahead on Murgasse. Cross the Hauptücke bridge.

Kunsthaus Graz★

Open year-round Tue–Sun 10am–5pm. Closed 24 & 25 Dec. €9. Guided tours in English Sat 2pm (€2.50). 0316 80 17 92 00. www.kunsthausgraz.at.

Sprawling on the western bank of the Mur River, the avant-garde Kunsthaus is unmissable among the traditional historic buildings around it. The building's unusual, bulbous shape is colourfully described as a blue alien heart with multiple aortas sprouting from its roof. Opened in 2003 as part of the city's year as Capital of European Culture, the building was designed by British architects Colin Fournier and Peter Cook. The bold landmark contains a wealth of contemporary artworks from the 1960s to the present.

▶ As you leave the Kunsthaus, go left and walk along the river.

Kunsthaus Graz

© Landesmuseum Joanneum/Zepp-Cam

Murinsel (Mur Island)

Like the Kunsthaus, built in 2003 to be an iconic city landmark, this seashell-shaped glass-and-steel island in the middle of the Mur River was designed by New York artist Vito Acconci. It measures 50m/164ft in length and 20m/65ft in width; two footbridges connect it with both banks of the Mur. It holds an outdoor amphitheatre, a café and playground.

② CITY PARKS TOUR★

Allow 4hr to take this walk, which leaves the city centre to explore the hill overlooking Graz and the museums that line the route. Start from the Hauptplatz.

Sackstraße

This street was once a cul-de-sac *(sack)*, which was opened by a tower gateway in the 14C. That site is now occupied by the Palais Attems (no. 17). The artery was lengthened on two occasions in the course of extending the city walls. Because of its proximity to the river, it became an artisans' district, lined with the shops and studios of various tradesmen: millers, tanners, parchment-makers and many others. After 1650, the oldest part of the street became known as "Herrensack"(Gentlemen's cul-de-sac") after the aristocratic mansions that are still here today.

The Krebsenkeller at no. 12 has a **Renaissance courtyard★** whose double windows and arcaded loggias create an Italian feel. The **Palais Herberstein** (no. 16) boasts a monumental staircase as evidence of its past splendour.

At no. 18, the **Palais Khuenburg** was the birthplace of Archduke Franz Ferdinand (*see ARTSTETTEN*), the heir to the throne who was assassinated in 1914. Today it houses the **Stadtmuseum** (Municipal Museum) (&. ⓒopen Mon & Wed–Sun 10am–5pm; ☞€5; ✆0316 872 76 00; www.stadtmuseum-graz.at).

Palais Attems (Attems Palace)★★

Opposite the Stadtmuseum, this pile is without doubt the finest of the city's Baroque palaces. With their profuse decoration of pilasters, mouldings and curvilinear window pediments, Its intricate **façades★★** warrant closer inspection. The palace was built between 1702 and 1716 for Count Attems on a site previously occupied by six townhouses.

Dreifaltigkeitskirche (Holy Trinity Church)

Built in 1704, the church of the Trinity seems to be watching over its neighbour, the Palais Attems. The view from the church door shows the Schlossbergplatz from which 260 steep steps climb up to the Schlossberg itself.

▷ Return to Schlossbergplatz opposite the church.

Schlossberg★

By funicular (Schlossbergbahn) from the northern end of the Sackstraße. ⓒ*Operates every 15min Mon–Thu 9am–midnight, Fri–Sat 9am–2am, Sun 9am–11pm.* ☞€2.20. ✆0316 88 73 391. www.schlossbergbahn.at.
By glass elevator (Schlossberg lift) next to the steps ⓒ*operates daily 8am–12.30am.* ☞€1.40. Or you can walk, via the steps leading up from the Schlossbergplatz.

Rising 123m/403.5ft above the city, this impregnable hilltop bristled with redoubts and fortifications right up to the Napoleonic Wars. Even in 1809, when Graz was occupied by French troops, the fortress withstood all assaults. Much to the chagrin of the townsfolk, one of the provisions of the Treaty of Schönbrunn in 1809 called for the demolition of the Schlossberg. The town's citizens paid a handsome ransom to spare the **Uhrturm** (clock tower) and the **Glockenturm** (bell-tower), whose 5-ton bell Liesl is the biggest in town. The area was later turned into a park; today it is still a popular place for strolling and picnicking.

The Schlossberg is honeycombed by tunnels used as bomb shelters during World War II. A section of them is now used as the **Dom im Berg** (www.domimberg.at), an unusual performance and exhibition space right inside the mountain. The entrance is near the steps leading up the Schlossberg.

A wide, chestnut-tree-lined avenue leads down to the clock tower rising from a colourful flower bed. The dial is unusual; for a long time it had only a single hand showing the hours. The smaller, minute hand was added later. Go down the steps leading to the Herberstein gardens. From the terrace there are fine **views★★** over the city and the Mur Valley.

◖ Climb back up to the clock tower and then go down the first path on the right, which leads back into town to the Karmeliterplatz.

The Trinity Column was erected in the square in 1680 in thanksgiving for relief from the plague.

◖ Go up the Paulustorgasse.

Steirisches Volkskundemuseum (Folk Life Museum)

○*Open late Mar–Dec Wed–Sun 2pm–6pm.* ✆€7. ✆*0316 80 17 98 10 . www.volkskundemuseum-graz.at.*
This revamped museum, devoted to Styrian folk art and traditions, forms part of the Universalmuseum Joanneum; it has been housed since 1913 in a former Capuchin monastery.
The exhibit is divided into three major themes: *Wohnen* (living), *Kleiden* (clothing), and *Glauben* (Faith). Highlights include the Trachtenraum, a large room with 42 life-size figures showcasing the wealth of folkloric garments through the ages, and the Rauchstube, a smoke room typically found in old farmhouses.

Paulustor

Together with the Burgtor, this gateway is all that remains of the city walls. Built towards the end of the 16C, it displays the coats of arms, in marble, of Ferdinand II of Austria and of Maria Anna of Bavaria.

Stadtpark

This English-style park follows the line of the old walls to the east and southeast of the historic city centre. At its centre is the **Forum Stadtpark**, a meeting place of avant-garde artists since the 1960s. Outside this building, the **Stadtpark-Brunnen** is a fountain in a luxuriant setting of fine old trees, shrubs and flowerbeds. Also located in the park, the recently renovated **Künstlerhaus** is a contemporary art exhibition space that features internationally active Styrian artists.

◖ To return to Hauptplatz, go S through the Stadtpark to the Burgtor, take Hofgasse W, then Sporgasse S.

MEDIEVAL QUARTER★

Towards the end of the Middle Ages, a cattle market was held between the river and the ramparts, where the Franziskanerplatz and the Neutorgasse are now. The strange name (*Kälbernes Viertel* meaning Calf Town), still used by locals for the area around the Franciscan church, recalls these times. In 1620 the area was brought within the ramparts when the city's defences were being strengthened.
The quarter has kept much of its charm, and a stroll through its narrow **lanes★** is most enjoyable, particularly the pretty Neue-Welt-Gasse and the Franziskanergasse, both piled high with the wares of produce vendors.

Franziskanerkirche

Traders set up their stalls against the walls of this church, which was re-roofed after World War II and given modern glass. It was here in 1240 that the Minorites installed their convent, which passed into the ownership of a closed Franciscan order in the 16C. The oldest part of the church, the Jakobskapelle, dates back to 1330.

Mariahilf-Kirche★

One of the finest of the city's churches, with elegant twin towers and an impeccably proportioned Baroque façade, this church was the province's most popu-

Schloss Eggenberg

lar place of pilgrimage after Mariazell. It was begun in 1607 by Pietro de Pomis, architect of the Mausoleum and Schloss Eggenberg, who was buried here in 1633. The Late Baroque towers of 1742–44 are by Josef Hueber. Renaissance in structure, the interior of the nave gives an overall impression of harmony and repose. The door on the left of the façade leads to the cloisters, beyond which is a another courtyard with a small building in the style of the Renaissance, albeit designed as late as the end of the 17C.

Its first floor is given over entirely to the **Minoritensaal**, one of the city's concert halls. The building also houses the **Diözesanmuseum** (Diocesan Museum), with changing exhibits in addition to several centuries' worth of religious treasures from throughout Styria.

♣♦ Kindermuseum Frida & Fred

Friedrichgasse 34. ◷*Open Mon, Wed, Thu 9am–5pm, Fri 9am–7pm, Sat–Sun and hols 10am–5pm.* ✆*€5 per exhibit.* ℘*0316 872 77 00. www.fridaundfred.at.* This children's museum, which opened in 2003, has a simple guiding principle: the children can do what they want.

New themed exhibits are mounted each year, but are always aimed at 3–12 year olds, and provide workshops, games, hands-on activities and discovery areas. Children choose their activities. Adult helpers are present, but intervene only if asked (or are required).

Leechkirche (Maria am Leech)

Built between 1275 and 1293, the university church of Maria am Leech is the oldest religious building in Graz. The Early Gothic, multi-layered **west front★** is crowned by a Virgin and Child on the tympanum, a work in Late Romanesque angular style. The **stained glass★**, which dates from 1330 and depicts various saints and the story of Christ's Passion, is of particular interest.

EXCURSIONS
SCHLOSS EGGENBERG★★

3.5km/2.2mi west of Graz. 2nd floor. ☞*State apartments open by guided tour (45min) only Apr–Oct Tue–Sun and hols 10am, 11am, noon, 2pm, 3pm, 4pm.* ✆*€11.50. Castle park* ◷*open daily 8am–7pm (winter 5pm)* ✆*€2.* ℘*0316 80 17 95 32.* *www.welterbe-eggenberg.at.* This delightful Baroque palace is the largest and most culturally significant in Styria. Set in the middle of a lovely green park and gardens, the stately residence reveals the turbulent fortunes of the House of Eggenberg, once one of Styria's most powerful family dynasties. The property also features several collections of the Universalmuseum Joanneum.

The first construction on the property, which had been acquired by the Eggenbergs around 1460, was a medieval castle. In 1625, desiring a residence befitting his status as the newly appointed governor of Inner Austria, Hans Ulrich von Eggenberg engaged Italian architect **Pietro de Pomis** to transform the medieval dwelling into a splendid palace. De Pomis' design incorporated an elaborately detailed allegory of the universe, teeming with images and symbols of the cosmos and the four elements. The four towers stand for the four cardinal points of the compass; there are 365 windows, one for every day of the year; and in the suite of 24 state rooms (one for each hour of the day), 52 windows represent the weeks of the year.

The palace is surrounded by a lovely park that's perfect for a leisurely stroll. From the landscaped grounds, home to free-ranging deer and peacock, enter the impressive galleried courtyard.

Prunkräume★★★ (State Apartments)

The palace jewel is unquestionably the **Planetensaal★★★** (Planet Hall), a huge banqueting hall festooned with elaborate frescoes of the planets, the signs of the Zodiac and the four elements painted by the Styrian artist Hans Adam Weissenkirchner. The hall leads off to the 24 equally lavish staterooms, decorated in a hodgepodge of themes ranging from Classical mythology to Oriental fables and Biblical scenes. Three rooms have Chinese and Japanese décor, styles very much in vogue at the time.

Museums

🕐*Open late Mar–Oct Wed–Sun 10am–5pm; Nov–Dec by guided tour only. ▣€9, extra €2.50 for winter tours.*

Planetensaal
© Universalmuseum Joanneum

Alte Galerie

The spectacular Old Gallery presents a permanent collection of paintings and sculptures from the 13C to the Baroque in 22 rooms, presented by theme rather than in chronological order. Highlights worth seeking out include a stained-glass *Admont Madonna* (1320), a *Martyrdom of St. Thomas à Becket* by Michael Pacher from 1470–80, and a large Mariazell altarpiece from 1518–22. There are also important works by Jan Brueghel the Elder, Pieter Brueghel the Younger, Lucas Cranach the Elder, and German Baroque artists such as Johann Michael Rottmayr, Josef Stammel and Paul Troger.

Archäologiemuseum

This museum, opened in 2009 and based on archaeological finds from the Stone Age to the early Middle Ages, includes the world-famous 2,700-year-old bronze **Strettweg Votive Chariot★★** from the Hallstatt Period, discovered in a burial mound near Judenburg in Styria. The chariot is surrounded by soldiers and hunters on horseback foot; the sculptor has captured them performing the swirling movements of a ritual dance.

Münzkabinett

This priceless coin collection had its origin in the private collection of Archduke Johann and is the second largest of its kind in Austria. It includes 17C coins stamped with the profile of Hans Ulrich von Eggenberg himself.

Planetengarten

Just like the main palace, the design of the Planet Garden is a romantic allegory of the universe. Along the northern edge of the palace grounds, it poetically reflects the seven then-known planets through plants, trees and flowers.

♟♟ Österreichisches Freilichtmuseum (Austrian Open-Air Museum)★★

Stübing. 15km/9mi northwest on the road to Bruck an der Mur. ⏱Open *mid-Mar–Oct daily 9am–5pm.* ⊘€10. ♿ 𝓟 *03 124 53 700.* *www.freilichtmuseum.at.*

Framed by forest, meadows and fields in a little side valley of the Mur, this open-air museum features 100 original farmhouses from throughout Austria, grouped by province – from Burgenland in the east to Vorarlberg in the far west. All the buildings are authentically furnished and provide a nostalgic glimpse into the way of life and working methods of yesteryear.

The museum also puts on temporary exhibits on rural life and traditional culture, while craftspeople give daily demonstrations of their work. ✋Wear comfortable shoes as the complex sprawls over 2km/1.2mi.

Stift Rein★

15km/9.3mi northwest.

Founded in 1129, Rein is the oldest Cistercian abbey in Austria. Its buildings, dominated by the elegant Baroque tower, stand out against a background of wooded hills. Devastated by the Turks, the abbey was fortified in the 15C, then remodelled in the Baroque style in the 18C.

Stiftskirche★★

🗣Visit by guided tour only mid-Mar–Dec 10.30am and 1.30pm; reservations required. ⊘€8. 𝓟03124 51 62 110. www.stift-rein.at.

Johann Georg Stengg, a master builder from Graz, presided over the transformation of the old Romanesque abbey church, which now has the rank of minor papal basilica. A curvilenear façade leads to the light-flooded interior, designed by Josef Adam Molck.

The abbey's library has a collection of precious calendars, including the oldest German one from 1373, and a calendar table used by Johannes Kepler in 1607.

Österreichisches Freilichtmuseum

© Austrian National Tourist Office/ Poettler (Museum-Stuebing)

Wallfahrtskirche Mariatrost

7km/4.3mi east via Road 72.
This glorious pilgrimage church (c. 1714), dedicated to the Virgin Mary, is strikingly sited in a leafy suburban setting and easily identifiable by its twin towers.

Frohnleiten

30km/18.5mi north of Graz.
Situated halfway between Bruck an der Mur, to the north, and Graz, to the south, this market town is set among the rolling hills by the Mur River, and is the starting point for many **hiking trails**. As you enter the town from the south, the bridge offers a glorious **view★** of the Old Town. Notice the 14C Schloss Rabenstein, where popular temporary exhibits are held regularly.
Frohnleiten's central square boasts beautiful house façades. The steeple of the Church of St. Catherine (1786) is the bell tower of the Church of the Assumption; that church, located farther north, was rebuilt after a fire in 1763.

▲▲ Lurgrotte★

There are two entrances to this complex, which is open by ☞ guided tour (1hr) only. Peggau entrance: (9.5km/6mi southeast of Frohnleiten) ⏲*open Apr–Oct 10am–3pm, on the hour.* ✆*€7.* ☎*03 127 25 80. www.lurgrotte.com. Semriach entrance: (18km/11mi southeast of Frohnleiten)* ⏲*open mid-Apr–Oct 11am, 2pm and 3.30pm.* ✆*€7.50.* ☎*03 127 83 19. www.lurgrotte.at.* ☺*Dress warmly as the cave temperature is around 10°C/50°F year round.*
The walk beside the underground river, formed over eons from melt-water, leads deep into the cave, past several bizarre formations, including the Prince stalactite, which weighs 3t and is almost 4m/13ft long.
The cave extends about 5km/3mi underground between Peggau and Semriach, and up until 1975, when the "flood of the century" washed away the paths in the middle of the cave it was possible to walk all the way from one locale to the other. Ever since then, guided tours have taken place separately from

Lurgrotte

© Austrian National Tourist Office/Ponizka

the two entrances to the cave. If you leave Peggau (where a small Museum of Caves and a playground help you forget any waiting time), you walk for about 1km/0.6 into the caves, along the underground Schmelzbach stream passing all kinds of unworldy shapes. The most impressive of these is the Prince, a stalactite dating about a million years, measuring 3.7m, and weighing around 3tonnes.

Bärenschützklamm

41km/25mi north of Graz and 12km/7.5mi north of Frohnleiten. Leave Mixnitz and follow the signs. Hike of 4–5 hrs round-trip (including the walk to the entrance from the parking area), with a change in elevation of some 750m. ⏲*Accessible May–Oct.* ✆*€3.50.* ☎*03867 80 44 11. www.baerenschuetzklamm.at.*
Hikers navigate the gorge by crisscrossing bridges and climbing wooden ladders past 24 waterfalls. After about 1.3km/0.8mi, the trail rises steeply by around 350m/1,150ft.
After crossing the gorge, hike for another 20min to the Guter Hirte refuge hut, where you can rest before retracing your steps.

Schloss Herberstein

SCHLOSS HERBERSTEIN★

57km/29mi northeast of Graz.
🕐*Open mid-Mar–early Nov Thu–Sun 10am–4pm (May–Sept daily 9am–5pm).*
🔎*Guided tour of palace (1hr) on the hour, noon–3pm.* ⊘*€15, includes palace, animal park, gardens and museums.* 🖉*03176 88 250. www.herberstein.co.at.*

The fortress of Herberstein perches on a rocky spur, surrounded on three sides by the course of the Feistritz River, in the middle of a rugged gorge. Modified numerous times during its 700-year existence, it boasts Gothic, Renaissance and Baroque elements. The counts of Herberstein have occupied the castle without interruption since 1290.

Tours take in some of the oldest parts of the building, including a kitchen in use since the 16C, providing glimpses into daily life at the palace in the 19C. The magnificent **Florence Courtyard** is an arcaded enclosure that looks as though it belongs to an Italian palazzo rather than a fortress of northern Europe.

▲▲ Tierwelt Herberstein

🕐*Open May–Sept daily 9am–5pm; Oct & Apr, 10am–4pm; Nov–mid-Mar 10am–3.30pm.* 🖉*03176 80 777. www.tierwelt-herberstein.at.*

This modern interpretation of a cage-free animal park has a history dating back to the 17C. It is home to animals from five continents, including bison, timberwolves, kangaroos and lions. The latter are in a special enclosure that allows them to "hunt" for their dinner. For young visitors, there's also the Tikiba petting zoo and a huge playground.

Historical Gardens

🕐*Open mid-Mar–Apr daily 10am–4.30pm, May–Sept daily 9am–6.30pm, Oct–Nov daily 10am–5pm.*

These gardens were restored in 1997 following old designs and a picture dating from 1681. In the centre stands the rose pavilion with a Fountain of Youth. The beds are geometrically arranged to symbolise different times of the day and human temperaments. The "multimedia space" in the Siegmund Garden forms a bridge between old and new.

Museums

Herberstein is home to the **Gironcoli-Museum** (🕐*open mid-Mar–early Nov daily 10am–5pm; €15*), devoted to the avant-garde sculptures of Bruno Gironcoli, one of Austria's most important contemporary artists. The museum is housed in a converted 16C barn with a modernist annexe.

Another building, the Kunsthaus, houses Gironcoli's impressive collection of African masks, as well as changing exhibits by contemporary artists.

ADDRESSES

🛌 STAY

Pension Arkadenhof – *Tobelbaderstraße 6, 8141 Unterpremstätten. 14km/8.5mi S. ℰ03136 525 23 15. www. pension-arkadenhof.at. 10 rooms. ⊑.* This 100-year old family-run guesthouse is set in beautiful gardens. Bedrooms are simple and pretty.

Pension Scherwirt – *Stattegger Straße 135, 8045 Graz-Andritz. 7km/4mi N. ℰ0316 69 11 69. www.scherwirt.at. 10 rooms. ⊑.*This cosy, family-run pension offers lovely traditional-modern rooms, a small swimming pool and a sauna. Internet access is included.

Gasthof-Pension zur Steirerstub'n – *Lendplatz 8. ℰ0316 71 68 55. www.pension-graz.at. 27 rooms. ⊑.* A 5min walk from the Old Town, this charming pension boasts a fine view of the Schloßberg. Bedrooms are simple but stylish with satellite TV. The restaurant serves well-prepared regional dishes.

Hotel Feichtinger – *Lendplatz 1a. ℰ0316 72 41 00. www.hotel-feichtinger.at. 41 rooms. ⊑.* Smart modern, if rather bland, hotel in the centre. Rooms are well equipped, including free Internet access. Some rooms have a view of the Schlossberg. Organic breakfasts are a hallmark.

Hotel Mariahilf – *Mariahilfer Straße 9. ℰ0316 71 31 63. www.hotel mariahilf.at. 45 rooms. ⊑.* Next to the Kunsthaus, this traditional hotel offers simple rooms with spacious bathrooms, satellite TV and internet access. Some family suites and weekend specials.

Hotel Wiesler – *Grieskai 4-8. ℰ0316 70 660. www.hotelwiesler.com. ℙ ⊑€16. 101 rooms.* Pricey, luxury accommodations and Art Nouveau décor. Breakfast in the Grand café with its beautiful Jugendstil mosaics. Most of the rooms have a view of the Old Town.

MURTAL

Frohnleiternerhof – *Hauptplatz 14, Frohnleiten, near the Open-Air Museum.*

ℰ03126 41 500. www.frohnleitnerhof.at. 40 rooms. ⊑. Comfortable modern hostelry in the town centre. Modern furnishings and many amenities, plus views of the Mur.

NEAR HERBERSTEIN SCHLOSS

Hotel im Schloß Stubenberg – *Stubenberg am See (3km/1.8mi N of Herberstein, towards Pöllau). ℰ03176 88 64. www.schloss-stubenberg.at. Closed mid-Dec, Jan, Feb. 6 rooms, 3 suites. (⊖⊖🍴🍴). ⊑.* Set in a 16C castle, the hotel functions as lodging, a spa and a performance space. Simple but stylish bedrooms are arranged around a courtyard. Some have views of the lake and countryside. The castle tavern (⊖) serves wines and dishes from Styria.

GRAZ-MARIATROST

Pfeifer Kirchenwirt – *Kirchplatz 9. 6km/3.5mi NE of the town centre in the direction of Weiz, 20min by tram. ℰ0316 391 11 20. www. kirchenwirtgraz.com . ℙ. 30 rooms. ⊑.* In the shadow of the famed pilgrimage church, this is a peaceful, comfortable (if dated) hotel with large, well-equipped rooms. In the lovely garden, eat under the trees. Internet access is included.

🍴 EAT

AUSTRIAN/STYRIAN SPECIALITIES

Glöckl Brau – *Glockenspielplatz 2–3. ℰ0316 81 47 81. www.gloecklbraeu.at.* This lively, traditional Wirtshaus restaurant in the heart of town is as popular with locals as it is with visitors. For dinner try the Styrian specials: *Backhendl Salat* (chicken salad) or *Kürbiskernschnitzel* (breaded veal cutlet with pumpkin seed). Good beer list.

Altsteirische Schmankerlstube– *Sackstraße 10. ℰ0316 83 32 11. www.schmankerlstube.at.* Styrian specialities are served in a cosy vaulted rustic dining room or on a simple but pleasant terrace.

Landhaus Keller – *Schmiedgasse 9. ℰ0316 83 02 76. www.landhauskeller.at. Closed Sun and public hols.* One of Graz's oldest restaurants, with a wine cellar containing some 30, 000 bottles, Landhaus Keller is renowned for its beef specialities. In good weather, opt for the Renaissance courtyard.

Stainzerbauer – *Bürgergasse 4. ℰ0316 82 11 06. www.stainzerbauer.at.*

This beautiful, traditional restaurant located in a historic townhouse is run by one of the city's foremost restaurateurs. Lovely Renaissance-era courtyard for summer dining. Excellent wine list.

INTERNATIONAL CUISINE

⊜ **Don Camillo** – *Franziskanerplatz 11.* *℘0316 84 54 96. www.doncamillo.at.* For a bit of Italy in Austria, head to Don Camillo for inexpensive and tasty pastas and appetising pizzas, especially at lunchtime.

⊜⊜⊜ **Speisesaal/ Senf und Söhne** – *Hotel Wiesler, Grieskai 4. ℘0316 70 660. www.hotelwiesler.com.* The buzzing eateries at this Philippe Starck-designed hotel are a real bargain. Enjoy Austrian and international grilled favourites, from bacon and baked beans to T-bone steaks, at reasonable prices in possibly the city's trendiest setting.

⊜⊜ **Häuserl im Wald**– *Roseggerweg 105. From the town centre, head in the direction of Weiz, and take Mariatroster Straße to the right; after 4.5km/2.8mi you will see signs. ℘0316 39 11 65. www.legenstein-hiw.at. Closed Mon.* This restaurant in this rustic country guesthouse in a lovely setting serves mostly international cuisine. The adjacent forest park with domesticated animals keeps little ones happy.

⊜⊜⊜ **Aiola Upstairs** – *Schlossberg 2. ℘0316 81 87 97. http://upstairs.aiola.at.* There's a great view of Graz from the swanky terrace of this modern restaurant, halfway up the Schlossberg. The carefully executed dishes include pastas and Italian cuisine, as well as Styrian specialities.

⊜⊜⊜ **Santa Clara** – *Abraham–a-Santa-Clara-Gasse 1, entrance Bürgergasse 6. ℘0316 81 18 22. Closed Sun lunchtime and two weeks in Feb.* Creative, Mediterranean-influenced dishes are served at this romantic, well-reviewed establishment. It is run by a Francophile couple who determine the daily menu by what's available at the market.

CAFÉS AND BARS

Promenade (*Erzherzog-Johann-Allee 1*); **Operncafé** (*Opernring 22*); **Hofbäckerei Edegger-Tax** (*Hofgasse 6*).

NIGHTLIFE

The centre of Graz nightlife (known among the university set as the Bermuda triangle) is the area bordered by the Färberplatz, Glockenspielplatz and Herrengasse. Here there are hostelries and wine bars to suit every taste. The youth scene is in the University quarter (*Leonhardtstraße, Zinzendorfgasse and Schillerplatz*).

Speciality beers, many of them house-brewed, are the stock-in-trade at **Bierbaron** (*Heinrichstraße 56) and* **Eschenlaube** (*Glacisstraße 63*). **Café Stockwerk** (*Jakominiplatz 18*) offers live jazz music.

Other good bars in Graz include the **Ernst Fuchs Bar** in the Hotel Erzherzog Johann (*Sackstraße 3–5*), the **Café Mitte** (*Freiheitsplatz 2*), the **Cohibar** (*Leonhardtstrasse 3*) and the **M1** (*Färberplatz 1*). There is live music at the **Orange** (*Elisabethstrasse 30*). The **Hemingway American Bar** (*Abraham-a-Santa-Clara-Gasse 2*) is a buzzing cocktail bar, complete with live jazz.

SHOPPING

Herrengasse is considered the prime shopping street in Graz; shopfronts sport well-known labels in apparel, housewares, footwear, wine and gourmet items. You'll also find numerous shops in the pedestrian precincts, such as **Sporgasse/Murgasse**, the streets around the **Hauptplatz** and **Schmiedgasse/Stubenberggasse/ Hans-Sachs-Gasse**.

MARKETS

Kaiser-Josef-Platz (farm produce), *Mon–Sat 6am–1pm.*

Lendplatz (farm produce), *Mon–Sat 6am–1pm.*

SOUVENIRS

Craft goods and traditional costume (*Trachten*): **Steirisches Heimatwerk**, *Sporgasse 23*; **Trachten Schlössl**, *Hauptplatz 3.*

Schlossbergkugeln (Schlossberg balls, local speciality chocolates): **Linzbichler Süsswaren**, *Franziskanerplatz 16.*

Styrian wine: **Delikatessen Frankowitsch**, *Stempfergasse 2.*

ENTERTAINMENT

OPERA AND THEATRES

The **Bühnen Graz** (*℘0316 80 00, www.buehnen-graz.com*) association includes four performing organizations:

the **Opernhaus** at Kaiser-Josef-Platz 10, the **Schauspielhaus** (spoken theatre, 12 premieres every season) on Freiheitsplatz,

La Strada

© Graz Tourismus / Harry Schiffer

Next Liberty (children's and young people's theatre) at Kaiser-Josef-Platz 10, and the **Orpheum** (venue for rock, pop, jazz and cabaret) at Orpheumgasse 8.

T.i.P. (Theater im Palais) *Leonhardstraße 15.* ☎ *0316 38 90.* Hosts musical and spoken theatre by students from Graz University of Music and the Performing Arts.

TheatermëRZ – *Steinfeldgasse 20.* ☎ *0316 72 01 72.* This artists' and authors' theatre has logged numerous international tours. Its programme focuses on the work of author, director and theatre manager, Willi Bernhart: Plays, song programmes, children's and young people's theatre.

P.P.C. – *Neubaugasse 6.* ☎ *0316 81 41 41 33.* Independent cultural centre which hosts all kinds of theatre as well as concerts of rock pop and world music.

Casino Graz – *Landhausgasse 10.* ☎ *0316 83 25 78 112.* Austria's second-largest casino.

CINEMAS

Large multiple-screen cinema complexes offering international films are to be found at **UCI Kinowelt Annenhof** (*Annenstraße 29;* ☎ *0316 72 77; www.uci-kinowelt.at*) and **Cineplexx** (*Alte Poststraße 470,* ☎ *0316 29 09*).

FOR FILMS OTHER THAN CURRENT MAINSTREAM, TRY:
Filmzentrum im Rechbauerkino (*Rechbauerstraße 6;* ☎ *0316 83 05 08*),

KIZ Royalkino (*Conrad von Hötzendorfstrasse 10;* ☎ *0316 82 11 86*) and **Schubertkino** (*Mehlplatz 2,* ☎ *0316 82 90 81*).

FESTIVALS

Diagonale: *Apr.* Festival of Austrian film. *http://en.diagonale.at.*

Generalihof Jazz concerts: *summer.* Open-air performances, free of charge, courtesy of the Graz jazz scene. *www.gamsbartjazz.at.*

Styriarte: *Jun-Jul.* Classical music festival. *http://styriarte.com/en.*

Jazz-Sommer: *Jul–Aug.* Jazz concerts in the Schloßbergbühne Kasematten. *www.grazjazz.at.*

AIMS: *mid-Jul–mid-Aug.* Festival of classical music by the great composers played by students from the **A**merican **I**nstitute of **M**usical **S**tudies. *http://aimsgraz.com.*

La Strada: *end Jul–early Aug.* International festival of puppet and street theatre in the old city. *www.lastrada.at/en.*

Styrian Autumn: *Sept–Oct.* International avant-garde festival of contemporary music, theater, art exhibitions and readings of literary works. *www.steirischerherbst.at.*

Mountainfilm Graz: *Nov.* International film competition, with the Grand Prix Graz awarded in five different categories. *www.mountainfilm.com.*

Steirische Weinstraße★

The Styrian vineyard trail is a delightful journey into traditional Austria; a tranquil, timeless world in the midst of outstandingly beautiful countryside. The region is dotted with *Buschenschenken* (wine taverns), where people meet over a glass of wine and listen to accordion music. It is particularly lovely in autumn when the vineyards are cloaked in a kaleidoscope of brilliant colours. The vast majority (70 percent) of wine produced in Styria is white, with versatile *Welschriesling*, fruity *Weissburgunder* (Pinot blanc) and sprightly *Müller-Thurgau* the dominant varieties. *Zweigelt* is the most important red wine, but *Schilcher*, a rosé, is better known.

- **Info:** Hauptplatz 36 - 8530 Deutschlandsberg. ℘03462 43 152. www. sued-west-steiermark.at.
- **Location:** The wine routes detailed below are all southwest of Graz in southeastern Austria.
- **Timing:** The three tours can be done in a day, but if stopping often to taste or visit sights, then allow three days - one for each tour.
- Austrian laws are very strict about drinking and driving.

🚗DRIVING TOURS

1 SCHILCHER TOUR
91km/56mi.

▶ Leave Graz SW on the B 70. Take the autobahn as far as Steinberg and then follow signs to Stainz.

The south-facing vines grown in the Schilcher hills, which back onto the Koralpe range, are often so steep that harvesting by machine is impossible.

Schilcher

Schilcher is a pink-hued wine produced solely in the Austrian region of Western Styria, made from the *Blauer Wildbacher* grape. Records show that this late-ripening, acidic grape (a distinction is made between the late blue and sloe varieties of *Wildbacher*), with its characteristic flavour and pretty "onion-skin" colour, has been cultivated in west Styria since 1580, though it has only been officially known as Schilcher since 1976.

On leaving the autobahn, the road immediately begins to climb, providing charming **views★★** of the Graz plain, the undulating hills northwest of the town and the Schöckl *(alt. 1,445m/4,741ft)* with its flat summit.

Gundersdorf
As you enter this typical wine-growing village, keep an eye out for the strange wooden stake topped with a bladed propeller. This is a *Klapotetz*, the Styrian version of a scarecrow, spinning and clacking to prevent the birds eating the grapes as they start ripening. If you visit a local vintner, ask to taste the local speciality, *Schilcher* wine (🗧see Box).

▶ Turn right after Gundersdorf, then left towards Langegg and Greisdorf.

Langegg
This village is filled with numerous traditional *heurigen or* wine taverns, housed in simple wood-roofed summer cottages or on terraces attached to wine-growers' houses. For a traditional treat, sample a glass along with slices of **Verackertbrot**, black bread with chopped, spiced bacon, or perhaps with a **Brettljause**, a selection of cold meats served on a wooden platter.

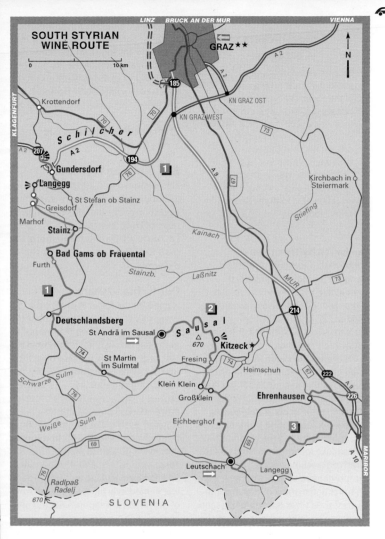

SOUTH STYRIAN
WINE ROUTE

At Langegg there is a delightful **view★★** of the Mur Valley, the Schöckl and the vine-clad hills of Sausal.

▶ Turn left at Marhof and follow the signs to Stainz.

Stainz

Lying in the valley and watched over by its ancient Schloss (palace), the town of Stainz bears traces of its 16C and 17C economic prosperity as a centre of the wine trade. It still boasts a number of old houses with smart façades, particularly in the main square.

The **Schloss** was built in 1229 as an Augustinian abbey, was secularised in 1740 and became the residence of Archduke Johann in 1840.

Of the original Baroque abbey **church** (◷*open daily 7.30am–6pm; winter til 5pm; ✆03 463 22 37*) only the two west towers survive while the rest was rebuilt in 1686 in a subdued Baroque style. Only the vault has been decorated, with painted medallions in a stucco composition. At the centre of the elevated high altar (1695) is a work by Hans Adam Weissenkircher.

Grape-pickers' Cottages

Grape-pickers (*Weinzierle*) traditionally had no property of their own, but lived in small cottages on the estates owned by their employers. The typical west Styrian grape-picker's cottage, called a *Winzerei*, consisted of two rooms, a kitchen, and a front veranda with an attached garden. A separate wooden hut would be used to store coal and animal fodder.

Landwirtschaftsmuseum★

Schlossplatz 1, entrance on the right along the passageway off the first courtyard. ○Open Apr–Oct Tue–Sun 10am–5pm. ○Closed Nov–Mar. €9. ℘03 463 27 7216.
www.museum-joanneum.at.

Set within the palace, this department of the Universalmuseum Joanneum presents objects, documents and photographs relating to agricultural and craft traditions of Styria. Note in particular the collection of the Imperial and Royal Agricultural Society, dating from the mid-19C, and collected on the specific advice of Archduke Johann; from hand tools to threshing machines. Also on display is a comprehensive collection of everyday ceramics and rustic furniture. Note the oil press used to produce pumpkin seed oil (Kernöl),a culinary specialty of the South Styrian region.

Don't miss the pair of complete original *Stüben* panels dating from 1568 and 1596, and a *Seitenstübel*, a small side room with a painted ceiling (1796).

♣♣ Jagdmuseum ★★ (Hunting Museum)

○*Same hours and details as above.*
This state-of-the-art museum (also a section of the Universalmuseum Joanneum), opened at the Schloss in 2006 and is one of the finest collections of art and objects gathered to interpret hunting in an historical, natural and even ethical context.

Baroque trophies, historical weapons, paintings and objets d'art trace the evolution of hunting from the Stone Age to the royal courts of the 17C and 18C. Another part of the exhibit looks at the effects of tourism, sports, transportation and industrial production on the earth.

○ Continue on the same road 5.5km/3.5mi SW.

Bad Gams ob Frauental

This village is well known in Styria for its traditional pottery; there is a potter's workshop on the outskirts of the nearby town of Furth.

En route to Deutschlandsberg the road descends into a plain encircled by forests.

Deutschlandsberg

Named for the fortified castle of Landsberg, this town lies at the foot of the Koralpe near the Slovene border. The prefix *deutsch* was not added until the 19C, and then only because of its location in German-speaking territory. It is famous throughout Styria for its lively Corpus Christi celebrations featuring flower-decked processional altars.

Housed within the formidable Burg Deutschlandsberg, the **Archeo Norico** museum (○open mid-Mar–Oct Tue–Sun 10am–6pm; €9; ℘03 462 5602; www.archeonorico.at) illustrates worship and war in medieval times via a small trove of art objects, weapons and fine metalwork.

North of the town stands the castle of Wildbach, where Schubert is believed to have composed his famous *Trout Quintet*. Only the 12C keep is original; the rest of the castle has been reconstructed. Trails through the vineyards start from the car park.

○ Rejoin the road from Stainz; go S toward St. Andrä-Leibnitz via St. Martin to reach St. Andrä. Turn left onto the valley road that joins with the Sausal Vineyard Trail.

2 SAUSAL TOUR
27km/16.7mi.

St. Andrä is the point of entry to the Sausal hills, which rise to 670m/2,198ft and produce mostly **Rheinriesling**, an elegant crisp white with an excellent bouquet.

▷ Take the road west towards Kitzeck.

Kitzeck★
Set on a ridge at 564m/1,850ft, this is the highest wine-growing village in Europe. It provides **panoramas★★** over a sea of hills. The **Wine Museum** (open *Apr–Oct Mon–Sun 10am–noon, 2pm–5pm, Sat–Sun 10am–noon, 2am–5pm; rest of the year Mon–Fri 9am–noon only;* €3; ℘03 456 35 00), housed in an old farmhouse on a wine-growing estate, contains articles and tools, including a reconstructed device for smoke curing, an old press and a wagon for transporting barrels.

▷ Drive towards Fresing, then continue to Klein-Klein.

Celtic tombs dating from the 6C–4C BC have been discovered in the forest near **Grossklein**. The finds are kept in Schloss Eggenberg (see p276).

▷ In Grossklein turn left towards Heimschuch, then right to Eichberghof.

The road meanders through wild and hilly country, where small south-facing vineyards alternate with fields of maize and patches of woods.

▷ Continue to Leutschach.

3 SOUTH STYRIAN TOUR
22km/13mi.

On either side of the road near **Leutschach,** fields ae planted not with wine but with hops growing on tall poles.

▷ In Leutschach turn left before the church and follow the green road sign

Vineyards, South Styria

© Austrian National Tourist Office/ Himsl

to the Südsteirische Weinstraße (South Styrian Wine Route).

This is the southernmost wine-growing area in Austria; the route hugs the border with Slovenia. This region is also known as the **Styrian Tuscany** because of its sunny climate and resemblance to Italy's Tuscan countryside.
A forest of conifers gives way to rows of vines that cover the gentle hills of Welschriesling and Samling country.

Ehrenhausen
This village was chosen by a branch of the Eggenberg family as the site of a castle and a mausoleum. The **Pfarrkirche** on the main square has a fine bell-tower with a particularly elaborate roof. The church was remodelled in the Baroque style in 1752.
The **Mausoleum★** shelters the tomb of Ruprecht of Eggenberg, who distinguished himself in the struggle against the Turks in the 16C. He is buried in the crypt alongisde his successor, Wolfgang von Eggenberg. Completed in 1640, the building was decorated by students of Johann Fischer von Erlach. The interior is especially striking for the elaborate stuccowork decorating the central dome.
The ruined **castle** retains an elegant courtyard and three tiers of arcading.

▷ Take the autobahn back to Graz.

St. Paul im Lavanttal★

The Benedictine abbey of St. Paul, half-hidden in the trees and slightly above the Lavant Valley, was founded in 1091. It boasts one of Austria's finest Romanesque churches and a well-respected collection of art treasures.

VISIT
Stiftskirche (Abbey church)
The church, which was begun in 1180, follows a cruciform layout culminating in three half-rounded apses. After a fire in the 14C, Gothic vaulting was added and decorated with frescoes by masters Friedrich and Michael Pacher. The south doorway features an image of the Adoration of the Magi, and the west door one of Christ in Majesty.

Stiftsgebäude (Abbey buildings)
The west wing houses the **St. Paul Art Collection ★★**, nicknamed the "Treasure of Carinthia". One of the finest private art collections in Europe, the assemblage includes paintings by Rubens, Rembrandt and Van Dyck; drawings by Dürer, Rembrandt, Holbein and Troger; sculptures; some 20,000 medals and coins; masterpieces of silverware, porcelain and wood; Romanesque church vestments; the 11C Imperial Cross of

Info: ℘04 357 20 19 22. www.stift-stpaul.at. &. Open May–Oct Wed–Sat 10am–4pm, Sun 11am–5pm. ⊜€9.50.

Location: The abbey is in the far south of Austria, near the border with Slovenia, about 85km/53mi east of Klagenfurt. Alt. 400m/1,312ft.

Don't Miss: the Treasure House of Carinthia.

Timing: Plan on spending about two hours here.

Rudolph of Swabia (also called the Adelaide Cross); plus a cabinet of curiosities. No less impressive, the library holds some 180,000 volumes, 4,000 manuscripts, the oldest book in Austria (dating from the 5C) and a printed book from Gutenberg's workshop (mid-15C).

ADDRESSES

⌂STAY AND ⋔/EAT

⊜⊜ **Gasthof Johannesmesner** – *Johannesberg 2. ℘04 357 23 00. www.johannesmesner.at. 6 rooms.* This family-run farmhouse offers simple, cosy guestrooms in a rural setting amid rolling hills and meadows on the outskirts of St. Paul. The dining room makes good use of home-grown products, including delectable cured meats, breads and ciders.

⊜⊜ **Gasthof Poppmeier** – *Hauptstr. 4. ℘04 357 20 87. www.poppmeier.co.at. Closed Mon, Sun evening, first week in Jan and one week early Feb.* This inn dates from 1510 and has been in the same family for several generations. Its restaurant is divided into two rooms, one modern, the other rustic and vaulted. There is also a lovely garden where you can enjoy one of their five draft beers or 40 kinds of wines by the glass, including local varieties. The kitchen draws on local ingredients and serves Carinthian specialities.

© Martin Siepmann/imageBROKER/age fotostock

Door of the vestry, Stiftskirche

Pack-und Stubalpenstraße★

These Alpine roads cut across the gentle, wooded heights of the Pannonian Pre-Alps between the valleys of the River Mur and River Lavant and the Graz basin. Known as the Koralpe, the Packalpe, the Stubalpe and the Gleinalpe, these mountains form a barrier less by their height, which barely exceeds 2,000m/6,562ft, than by their remoteness. The inter-regional road from Graz to Klagenfurt passes over the Packsattel, whereas the old road from Graz to Judenburg via Köflach crosses the Stubalpe, cutting off the wide bend of the River Mur.

- 🛈 **Info:** An der Quelle 3, Köflach. ℘03144 72 77 70. www.lipizzanerheimat.com.
- ▶ **Location:** These roads cut through southern Austria, just west of Graz.
- ☺ **Don't Miss:** A drive across the Lavant Valley Autobahnbrücke.
- 👪 **Kids:** Lipizzaner stud farm, Gestüt Piber.

🚗 DRIVING TOURS

① PACKSATTEL TOUR★
59km/37mi. Begin at Wolfsberg.

Wolfsberg
The historic upper town is set at the foot of its castle and wraps around the Hoher Platz, a square adorned with a column to the Virgin Mary and flanked by fine Biedermeier houses.
Wolfsberg Schloss (🕐 *open during exhibitions only;* ℘*04 352 23 650; www. schloss-wolfsberg.at*) is of medieval origin, but was largely rebuilt in the 16C and acquired in 1846 by Count Hugo I Henckel von Donnersmarck. In 1853 the Count remodelled it in the English Tudor style for his wife Laura (whose mausoleum – sadly she died only four years later in 1857 – lies on the opposite side of the mountain).
 Although the interior of the castle has not been preserved in its original state, its luxuriously appointed rooms, and in particular the oval **Stucco Room★** enchants visitors. The castle now operates as a site for special events.

▶ Leave Wolfsberg on the B 70 in the direction of Graz.

After leaving behind the northern outskirts of the town, the road enters the wooded Lavanttal valley. From the heights of the Twimberg, you can see the Lavant Valley motorway bridge. To get a better view, divert off the B 70 onto the B 78 and pull in at the special parking viewpoint, 500m/545yd after Twimberg.

Autobahnbrücke★
(Lavant Valley Motorway Bridge)
At 1,079m/3,500ft long and 165m/541ft high, this bridge is taller than the Stephansdom in Vienna. It is among the 10 longest bridges and is the second-highest bridge in Austria.

▶ Return to the B70 and continue.

Pack
Close to the **Packer Stausee** (an artificial lake with boating and swimming facilities), this little community enjoys a peaceful **panorama★** of the wooded foothills of the Pannonian Pre-Alps and the Graz plain.
In gentle pastoral surroundings the road reaches the **Packsattel** pass (*alt. 1,166m/3,825ft*), also known as the Packhöhe or the Vier Tore (Four Gates), before dropping into thick woods.
A series of hairpin bends below the Preitenegg ridge lends a little variety to the descent. The route leads past the sombre Schloss Waldenstein, then continues along the ravine of the Waldensteiner Bach to join the Lavant Valley at Twimberg.

Lipizzaner horses in Piber meadow

© Martin Siepmann/imageBROKER/age fotostock

Köflach

This pretty town lies near the summer pastures of the famed white **Lipizzaner stallions**. In early September, during the Lipizzaner Almabtrieb,the horses are driven down from the Alpine pastures to their winter quarters at Piber.

◯ 2km/1.2mi NE of Köflach.

♣♣ Lipizzanergestüt Piber★

Guided tours (1hr) Apr–Oct every hour except noon 10am–4pm. ⊕€13, *children €8.50.* ♿ *℘03 144 33 23. www.srs.at.*

The **Lipizzaner stallions** are bred at this stud farm and sent to the Spanische Reitschule in Vienna. Visitors can stroll the stables or pastures for close-up views of the noble horses, which are born bay or black and only acquire their white coats after four years of age.

◯ Continue 2km/1mi SW to Bärnbach.

Pfarrkirche St. Barbara★

The Church of St. Barbara (1948–57), and the adjoining buildings were remodelled in the late 1980s by Friedensreich Hundertwasser.

② STUBALPE TOUR★

43km/27mi. From Köflach take the B 77 to Judenberg.

Judenburg

Judenburg is the oldest trade centre in Styria. A Jewish community was established here as early as 1103 but driven out in 1496 by order of Emperor Maximilian I. Old buildings and courtyards from the historic town centre cluster around the 75m/82ft-high rocky outcrop known as the **Neue Burg**. For a panorama, climb up to its viewing gallery at 41m/45ft. For another view of the town, take the glass lift up the **Stadtturm** (Town Tower); the **Planetarium** at the top presents shows (◯*see website for show times; ℘04 3572 44088; www.stadtturm.at).*

Altstadt – Around the main square, note the courtyard with its Gothic arches at Hauptplatz 5; the former fortress at Herrengasse 11, now the District Courthouse, with its arcaded Renaissance-style courtyard; and the former Jesuit College *(Kaserngasse 22).* Cross the interior courtyard and follow the steps leading to the School of Music, where there is a Baroque staircase (1660).

At the end of Kaserngasse, at Martiniplatz 4, is the Prankherhaus, which was once part of the old medieval castle. Inside, a wing of an arcaded courtyard has been preserved. On the other side of the wall stands the Church of St. Mary Magdalene (Magdalenenkirche), a twin-nave Gothic hall church dating from 1350. Frescoes from the 14C and 15C survive on the exterior (St. Christopher) and interior. The stained-glass window paintings date from about 1400.

North of Judenburg, in Spielberg, is the Formula 1 circuit, the Red Bull Ring.

◯ From Weisskirchen, take the winding road to the crest of the ridge.

The main Stubalpe ridge is crossed at the **Gaberl Pass** *(alt. 1,547m/5,075ft).* Beyond the pass, the road drops into the narrow wooded **Salla Valley** to a tiny village called Salla. Old sawmills and scythe factories that once brought work to the valley are now derelict.

◯ Follow the B 77 for c. 14km/8.7mi past Sallabach and Krenhof to Köflach.

Stift Seckau★

Standing at the foot of the Seckau Alps (Niedere Tauern), this extensive abbey complex, whose corner towers lend it a somewhat military air, was founded in 1140 by Augustinian Canons and served as the seat of the diocese from 1218 until its dissolution by Joseph II in 1782. It was taken over by the Benedictine Order in 1883; the Benedictines have occupied and maintained the abbey ever since.

🛈 **Info:** ✆03514 52 340. www.abtei-seckau.at.

◗ **Location:** 75 km/46mi northwest of Graz, 11km/7mi north of Knittelfeld.

🗺 **Don't Miss:** The altarpiece, the Crucifixion group.

VISIT

🕐 Open year-round daily 7. 30am–noon, 12.30pm–5pm (Fri 7.30am–noon). ⊜Free. ⇝Guided tours May–last Sun in Oct daily 11am and 2pm. ⊜€5. ♿

Exterior

The courtyard monastery is surrounded by arcades. Two 12C stone lions guard the church porch. The south wall is decorated with early 14C frescoes, depicting the Crucifixion and St. Christopher. The north wall depicts the Three Scourges of God (the plague, locusts and Turkish invaders).

Interior

The columns and pillars of the nave (mid-12C) are crowned with huge capitals. Note the first pillar on the left, decorated with six mysterious figures. The interior harmony was disturbed in the late 15C by the addition of lavish net vaulting that was added in the 15C. The main visual focus, however, is the simple but moving **Crucifixion★★** (1260) above the main altar. The figures of Mary and Joseph probably date from earlier, c.1200. The transept and the choir were remodelled in the late 19C.

On the lower left side *(looking from the entrance)* are three chapels of different eras and styles. The first, the chapel of the **Engelkapelle** (Holy Angels), features a large-scale Apocalypse of St. John (1960) by Herbert Boeckl. In the adjacent **Gnadenkapelle** (Chapel of Grace) the 12C Virgin and Child alabaster, of Venetian origin is the oldest Marian image venerated in Austria and the abbey's most valuable treasure.

The **altarpiece★★** (1489), from a workshop in South Tyrol, around the time of Michael Pacher, celebrates the Coronation of the Virgin. Set in a circular frame, the artist has depicted the three members of the Holy Trinity with the same features, observing the Orthodox definition of "one God in three equal and distinct persons".

Karl II Mausoleum★

The chapel to the left of the high altar contains the **Mausoleum of Archduke Karl II**, designed by the Italian artist Alessandro de Verde in 1612. The chapel itself blends Late Renaissance and Baroque-style elements and the same elements can also be seen in, the mausoleum of Ferdinand II in Graz. The chapel features 50 statues, 150 reliefs and some 60 busts in stucco and marble.

ADDRESSES

🏠STAY AND 🍴EAT

⊜ **Gasthof zur Post** – Marktstrasse 42, 8732 Seckau. ✆03514 52 47. www.dorfwirt-zurpost.at. ⌨. 6 rooms. Bright, updated rooms in a period building.

⊜⊜ **Privatzimmer Peinhaupt** – Seckau 9, 8732 Seckau. ✆03514 52 56. ⌨. 4 rooms. Small rooms rented out by the owner.

⊜⊜⊜⊜ **Hofwirt** – Seckau 3 (opposite the Abbey entrance). ✆03514 54 290. www.projekt-spielberg.com/hotel-hofwirt. ⌨. 7 suites. A stately Baroque house with large, bright, modern suites, a formal wood-panelled restaurant and a less formal Jagdstübe for dining. Homemade cakes are served in the afternoon.

Bruck an der Mur★

Bruck an der Mur is dominated by the romantically ruined fortress of Landskron. It's a busy, industrial town whose main sights orbit Koloman-Wallisch-Platz, the main square. The town flourished during the 14C and 15C due to its trade with Venice. Bruck an der Mur became famous for the wrought-ironwork of its blacksmiths especially local master craftsman Hans Prasser, and this can still be seen around the centre. Each summer the town is taken over by mimes, performers and musicians when Bruck an der Mur hosts the Muren, a popular street theatre festival.

▶ **Population:** 15, 900.

Info: Koloman-Wallisch-Platz 1, A-8600. ℘03862 890 1210. www.tourismus-bruckmur.at.

Location: Bruck an der Mur lies at the confluence of the Mur and Mürz rivers in northern Styria, about 50km/31mi north of Graz. Alt. 481m/1,578ft.

Parking: Alongside the Mürz on Wienerstraße.

Don't Miss: Eiserner Brunnen.

SIGHTS
Eiserner Brunnen★★ (Wrought-Iron Well)
The ornate fountain (1626) by local artisan Hans Prasser is a superb example of Styrian wrought-ironwork.

▶ Cross the central square (Koloman-Wallisch-Platz). On the right, the Mariensäule is a column erected in 1710 to thank God for sparing the city from plague, fires and floods.

Old Houses
Bruck still has several 15C and 16C houses with arcaded courtyards, most notably the **Rathaus** (Town Hall) and the **Flößmeisterhaus** (no. 5).
The finest historic building is the **Kornmesserhaus★**, named after its builder, a wealthy merchant called Pankraz Kornmesser.

▶ Head back towards the Rathaus.

Pfarrkirche (Parish Church)
The Gothic parish church counts among its highlights a wrought-iron **sacristy door★**, believed to come from the Kornmesserhaus, and a fine late 18C **altar of the Holy Cross**.

▶ Continue along Herzog-Ernst-Gasse and take the steps leading to the castle. Alternatively, follow Primbsschweg from the end of Hoher Markt, or Schillerstraße to reach the castle.

Landskron Uhrturm
The clock tower is a symbol of Bruck. It was once part of the Landskron fortress that was destroyed by fire in 1792.

▶ Go back down and continue on Dr Theodor Körner-Straße before crossing the river. Turn right on Leobner Straße, then left into Sankt-Ruprecht-Straße, before turning left to reach Heubergstraße church (around 30min).

St. Ruprechts-Kirche
Leobenstraße, St. Ruprecht district, on the other side of the river.
This Gothic church is worth seeking out for its very well preserved early 15C **Last Judgement fresco★**. The ossuary situated near the church, originally a Romanesque rotunda, has memorials to the town's soldiers.

🚗 DRIVING TOUR

AFLENZERSEEBERGSTRASSE★
22km/13mi.

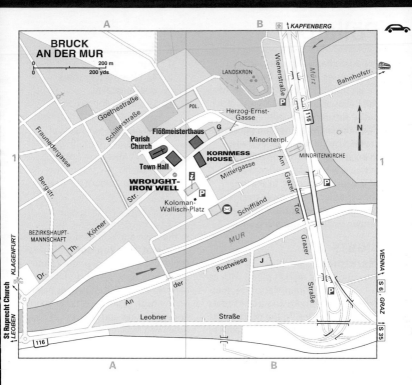

KAPFENBERG

KLAGENFURT

ST RUPRECHT CHURCH / LEOBEN

VIENNA S 6 / GRAZ S 35

Leave Bruck an der Mur on the B 116 and at Kapfenberg take the B 20 towards Mariazell. The road meanders through the narrow Thörlbach Valley to Thörl.

Thörl

This little settlement, lying in a rocky cleft, began as a fortification barring the entrance to the Aflenz basin. Directly in line with the valley, the ruins of the stronghold of Schachenstein stand on a steep-sided spur. The castle was built in 1464 and was the summer residence of the Abbot of St. Lambrecht. Beside the road, to the south, an oratory shelters a Calvary dating from 1530.

On the mountainside there is an 18C building through which the road once passed, a semicircular tower and a chapel dedicated to St. Barbara.

The village is a good starting point for hikes in the Hochschwab massif.

Aflenz-Kurort

Aflenz is a popular, mid-altitude health resort in a quiet location. In winter the chairlift to the Bürgeralm delivers skiers to the sunny Schönleiten plateau, while in summer it serves mountaineers aiming for the Hochschwab massif.

Its Late Gothic **church**, squat and rustic, boasts a fortified tower and a remarkable south door that has a design of little columns and string-courses superimposed on the archwork.

Inside, the most striking features of the pillar-free interior are the rib vaulting and statues of the 12 Apostles. The altars date from the second half of the 18C, while the wooden cross to the left of the choir is Romanesque (1175).

From Aflenz to Au the **road★** runs along the last foothills of the Hochschwab, passing many houses with wooden galleries that are typical of the area.

The final climb begins at **Seewiesen**, whose 14C church is on a small hill.

To the west, the Seetal is enclosed by much of the Hochschwab massif, including the Aflenzer Staritzen and Mitteralm ranges.

Pöllau★

Pöllau, a charming town with red-tiled houses, lies away from the major tourist routes in the heart of the Pöllauer Tal (Pöllau Valley). Much of the surrounding countryside has been turned into a natural park criss-crossed by 100km/62mi of trails. In an area of limited agricultural activity, wine is a significant part of the local economy. In season, the best places to sample the local product are the traditional taverns, known as *Buschenschenken*.

▶ **Population:** 2, 100.
▪ **Info:** Schloss 1. ✆03 335 42 10. www.naturpark-poellauertal.at.
◐ **Location:** Pöllau is in southeastern Austria, about 62km/39mi northeast of Graz. Alt 427m/1,401ft.
⟲ **Don't Miss:** The Abbey Church.
◷ **Timing:** Allow a full day.

SIGHTS
Marktplatz
This traditional market place, with its column to the Virgin Mary, is reminiscent of southern Austria thanks to its many old façades. To the north of the square, one such ancient door leads to the Schloss, a former Augustinian abbey with origins as a moated 12C castle.

Stift (Abbey)
Founded in 1504, the fledgling abbey had a troubled time during the 16C, when Styria was racked by religious disputes and Turkish raids. Despite such adversity, it grew prosperous by the late 17C and was rebuilt in the Baroque style. During secularisation under Emperor Joseph II it was closed in 1785 and turned into a private residence. It now belongs to the town.

Abbey church★
The imposing Baroque church was designed by **Joachim Carlone**, a member of the celebrated family of Graz architects, and has impressive dimensions. The nave and chancel measure 62m/203ft long, the transept is 37m/121ft wide and the cupola 42m/138ft high, creating an unusually generous space for such a small community. It is because of its size that the church is sometimes called the Styrian Peters Dom.
The remarkable **décor** is a delightful blend of paintings, gold, stuccowork and opulent sculptures. The frescoes in the nave and cupola are by Styrian artist, **Matthias von Görz**, and clearly show off his hallmark bright colours, a passion for light, and considerable skill at *trompe-l'œil*. The enormous painting on the **high altar** depicts the martyrdom of St. Vitus and is a work of Joseph Adam von Mölk.
The 24-stop **organ**, built in 1739, stands on an arcaded gallery, beneath a ceiling fresco of David playing the harp.

EXCURSIONS
Pöllauberg★
6km/3.7mi northeast of Pöllau.
Pöllauberg is a tiny village that grew up around its celebrated 14C **pilgrimage church** crowning the top of a steep hill, visible for miles around. Its unusual design features twin naves of equal size, separated by three pillars and with intersecting ribbed vaults. The large and sumptuously decorated 18C high altar centres on a statue of the Virgin Mary that is the main object of worship. The lavishly gilded pulpit dates from 1730.

Pöllauertal Natural Park
Pöllauer Valley is a diverse and hilly patchwork of forests, meadows, fields and orchards. Traditional farming methods have been kept alive and the Hirschbirne Pear, found only in Styria, is carefully cultivated here. The park is home to diverse flora and fauna.

Stift Vorau★
16km/10mi north of Pöllau. Take the scenic route via Schloffereck. ◷*Open*

Library, Stift Vorau

© Austrian National Tourist Office/ Wiesenhofer

Apr–31 Oct by guided tour only Mon–Fri 10am, 2pm and 4pm, Sat 10am (afternoon tours by request), Sun 11am, 2pm and 4pm; Nov–mid-Apr Tue–Fri 10am and 2pm, Sat 10am. ⊛€7. &
℘03 337 23 51. www.stift-vorau.at.
This isolated hilltop monastery, founded in 1163 by Augustinian monks, still serves surrounding parishes today.

Conventional buildings – As you enter the courtyard, the remarkable order of the abbey buildings is apparent.

Abbey church – Completely rebuilt between 1660 and 1662 by the master Swiss builder Domenico Sciassia, the church was decorated (1700–05) with lavish use of gilding and stucco so that only the original façade has been preserved. Indeed it's hard to believe that (according to the records) only 2.5kg/5.5lb of gold leaf were used to achieve such sumptuous decoration. Note the high altar painting (*Assumption of the Virgin*), based on a work by Matthias Steinl.

Sacristy★ – In 1715–16, the artist Johann Cyriak Hackhofer decorated the ceiling with the *Glorification of Christ at the Last Judgement*. The edges of the painting have an altogether darker atmosphere, and end against the western wall of the sacristy in a fanciful representation of the descent into hell, including the sins, vices and monstrous creatures that populate the realm of eternal damnation.

Library – Note the perfectly preserved stucco decoration and frescoes (which represent philosophy, theology and science) dating from 1731. The filigree decoration was added in 1767.

♟♟ Freilichtmuseum

◷*Open Jul–Aug daily 9am–5pm, Apr–Oct daily 10am–5pm.* ⊛€5. &
℘03 337 34 66.
www.freilichtmuseum.vorau.at.
Next to the abbey, this open-air museum features several original buildings (a smokehouse, a mill, a sawmill, a smithy). They were moved from elsewhere in the region to save them. The museum provides a glimpse of bygone rural life.

ADDRESSES

🏨 STAY

⊜⊜ **Gasthof-Restaurant Hubmann** – *Herrengasse 21, 8225 Pöllau. ℘03 335 22 67.* ⌧. *7 rooms.* This cosy inn has been operating here since the 16C. Regional dishes served in the restaurant (⊜⊜).

⊜⊜⊜ **Berggasthof König** – *Oberneuberg 5, Pöllauberg. 6km/4mi S of Pöllau. ℘03 335 23 11. www.berggasthof-koenig.at.* ⌧. *7 rooms. Restaurant closed Mon–Tue* (⊜⊜). Opened as a tavern in 1628, this traditional inn, next to the pilgrimage church, has many of the original features in the reception areas and the rooms.

Mariazell★★

Mariazell is the most important place of pilgrimage in Austria. It is also a popular year-round resort, occupying a picturesque site★ on the gentle, forested slopes at the very eastern end of the Alps. For a bird's-eye view of the region, take the cable-car to the top of the Bürgeralpe, the local mountain.

▶ **Population:** 1, 463.

Info: Hauptplatz 13, A-8630. 03 882 23 66. www.mariazell.at and www.basilika-mariazell.at.

Location: Mariazell is 150km/94mi north of Graz and 130km/80mi southwest of Vienna in central Austria. Alt. 868m/2,848ft.

A BIT OF HISTORY

Soon after the Benedictines from St. Lambrecht Abbey founded a priory here in 1157, pilgrims began flocking to Mariazell to worship a small wooden statuette of the Madonna believed to be responsible for several miracles. Veneration of the statue increased after King Ludwig of Hungary attributed his 1370 victory over the Turks to it and had the Gnadenkapelle (Grace Chapel) built in thanksgiving for the victory.

VISIT
Basilica★★

Open May–Oct daily 7.45am–8pm; Nov–Apr daily 7.45am–7.15pm. 03 882 25 95. www.basilika-mariazell.at.

In the 17C the growing number of pilgrims made it necessary to enlarge the 14C Gothic building. Architect **Domenico Sciassia** lengthened and widened the nave and topped the eastern end with a dome. He also added two much squatter onion-capped towers on either side of the central 90m/295ft-high Gothic spire, resulting in a slightly awkward design that has nonetheless become an emblem of Mariazell.

The object of veneration is enshrined in the **Gnadenkapelle (Chapel of Grace).** The seated Madonna is placed beneath a priceless silver baldaquin resting on 12 columns (designed by Johann Emmanuel Fischer von Erlach the Younger.

To fully appreciate the Baroque decoration of the **nave**, walk along the galleries. In the east nave a monumental piece of Baroque architecture forms a second, inner nave, beyond a false transept. The first bay is lit by an oval lantern-dome, while the second square bay contains a majestic high altar by Johann Bernhard Fischer von Erlach, which shows the Crucifixion, and was completed in 1704.

Schatzkammer (Treasury)

Open May–Oct Tue–Sat 10am–3pm, Sun and hols 11am–3pm. €4. 03 882 25 95.

A staircase in the southwest tower leads up to the treasury, which is filled with six centuries of (often sentimental) votive offerings left here by pilgrims. A highlight is the church's second-most important object of veneration, a 14C painting of the Virgin (also donated by Ludwig of Hungary), by Siennese artist Andrea Vanni.

EXCURSIONS
Bürgeralpe

Alt. 1,266m/4,153ft. Cable-car station, Wiener Straße. 03882 25 55. www.buergeralpe.at.

Open May–mid-Jun Tues–Sun 9.40am–5pm; mid-Jun–mid-Oct daily; second half Oct Sat–Sun and hols. €18.80, including entry to belvedere and Holzknechtland; children €17.

Enjoy the all-encompassing view of Mariazell from the Archduke Johann lookout point; then discover how important forestry is locally in the outdoor park's child-friendly Holzknechtland.

Annaberg

24km/15mi north of Mariazell on road 20. Annaberg's beautifully situated church is a popular stop for pilgrims en route to Mariazell. The first building, a timber chapel, was erected here in 1217, though the present church is 14C–15C. It is dedicated to St. Anne, hence the Madonna and Child with St. Anne (15C) on the high altar. There are Baroque frescoes and stuccowork in the south chapel and profuse gilding and carving on the pulpit and the organ-loft.

During the hairpin bend descent, the Ötscher stands out clearly to the west. Josefsberg is the start of a pleasant downhill run among firs, with fine vistas towards the Gemeindealpe on the right. The road also skirts the Erlaufstausee

reservoir. Continuing the descent, you pass Mitterbach am Erlaufstausee. If you turn right you pass beside a second lake, the (naturally-formed) Erlaufsee.

Erlaufsee
10km/6.2mi northwest of Mariazell.
Erlaufsee is located at the foot of Gemeindealpe (1,626m/5,331ft). It's a popular spot for watersports (boat hire, a diving school, beach) in summer, and in winter, for ice-skating. Skaters can go right out to the centre of the lake.

Salzatal★★

The Salza River, a tributary of the upper Enns, has carved out a 70km/43.5mi-long remote and romantic valley. Except for the villages of Wildalpen and Greith it is almost completely uninhabited, and offers nature lovers plenty of opportunities for expeditions through the forest. The river's lively rapids and churning pools draw scores of white-water enthusiasts.

🛈 **Info:** Hauptplatz 13, Mariazell A-8630. ☏03 832 23 66. www.mariazell.at.

▷ **Location:** The valley is in central Austria, about 100km/62mi northwest of Graz.

🕓 **Timing:** Allow half a day.

🚗 DRIVING TOUR

SALZATAL TOUR
80km/50mi.

▷ Leave Hieflau on the B 115 north along the River Enns.

Between Hieflau and Grossreifling the route follows the Enns, which is dammed in several places. Between Grossreifling and Palfau the road follows a winding, uphill course to Wildalpen.

Wildalpen
Tiny Wildalpen has an attractive setting and is a starting point for white-water sports on the Salza. The **Museum "HochQuellenWasser"★** (🕓open May– 26 Oct Mon–Fri 10am–noon, 1pm–3pm, Sun 10am–noon;⚅€3; ☏03 636 45 13 18 71) gives an interesting visual account of

the building of the aqueduct that supplies Vienna with its drinking water. The **Pfarrkirche St. Barbara,** with its scalloped tower roof, boasts fine frescoes and furnishings.

▷ Turn right Immediately after the Postbus stop (at kilometre stone 31.6).

Brunn
From the Brunn wayside shrine, only a short distance from the road, there is a **view★** down into the bottom of the Brunntal, in the heart of the Hochschwab. There is also a splendid **view★★** along the north slope of the massif. The road winds its way through **Prescenyklause** with its old-fashioned logging dam, then on to **Weichselboden,** before climbing steadily as far as Greith. Beyond, the landscape becomes gradually less mountainous and the road begins its descent to **Gusswerk** and then on to Mariazell (🕓see MARIAZELL).

Eisenerz

Eisenerz ("iron ore" in English) is an old mining town at the foot of the mighty step-pyramid-shaped Erzberg. Since 712, more than 230 million tonnes of iron ore have been extracted from this mountain, at what has become the largest opencast ore mine in central Europe. The outline of the town against the mountain is distinctive, especially in late afternoon light. Despite its mining backdrop, Eisenerz is not without charm and is noted for its many historic and dignified buildings, especially around Bergmannplatz.

▶ **Population:** 4,300.

Info: Dr.-Theodor-Körner-Platz 1. 8790 Eisenerz. ✆ 03 848 25 11 81. www.eisenerz.at.

Location: Northern Styria, about 25km/15.5mi north of Leoben.

Don't Miss: The dynamite tour at Erzberg

SIGHTS

Erzberg★★

Guided 90min tour of exhibition mine May–Oct daily 10am–3pm. Trip on the Hauly truck (1hr) €17. Thu, blasting tour (reservation required). €21. Mine tour €17. Joint ticket for mine and truck €30. ✆ 03 848 32 00. www.abenteuer-erzberg.at.

Although underground mining ceased here in 1986, the Erzberg offers a rare opportunity to don miners' gear and explore a mining atmosphere and working conditions as they were for decades prior.

Visitors can opt to make the descent aboard the "Katl" train, which transported miners beneath the surface. An 800m/2,624ft section of this subterranean labyrinth is now a **Schaubergwerk** (exhibition mine), where you learn all about how the ore was extracted and experience an audiovisual simulation of a blasting.

Another fun way to visit the mine is the trip on the **Hauly**, an 860hp quarry truck with a viewing platform that takes you above ground through many of the 42 slopes.

Above ground, take in a great **view★** of the town, the landscape, and the blue lake that has formed at the foot of the mountain. On Thursdays, visitors can take a "blasting tour" to witness a live open-pit mining blast.

St. Oswald★

By prior arrangement. Closed Advent–Easter. ✆ 03 848 22 670.

The largest fortified house of worship in Styria got its fortress-like ramparts in 1532 to keep marauding Turkish troops

Erzberg

© Austrian National Tourist Office/Wiesenhofer

at bay. From the town centre, hike up the "church stairs," which offer a close-up look at iron ore bands along the way. The tympanum above the north porch has an Expulsion from the Garden of Eden showing Adam as a miner. Also see the old organ loft.

Stadtmuseum

Kammerhof, Schulstraße 1. ○*May–Oct Tue–Sun 10am–4pm.* ⊚€5.50. ℘*03 848 25 11 67.*

The museum vividly presents the art and culture of mining and ore processing.

Schichturm

This Renaissance style "shift tower" was built in 1582. The bell called the miners to work; it was later used as a fire watch. Today it is privately owned. Although the tower is not open to the public, the walk up to it is worth it for the fine views.

Eisenerzer Alpen★

The Eisenerz Alps are best known for their industrial heritage on which the power of the Austrian Empire was built. Today the region's alpine beauty makes it a popular skiing, climbing and hiking destination. The Eisenerzers join up in the northwest with the limestone Ennstal Alps, whose impressive walls line the Gesäuse Gorge, now a national park.

- **ℹ Info:** Hauptplatz 3, A-8700. Leoben. ℘03842 48 148. www.tourismus-leoben.at.
- ▷ **Location:** This mountain range is in upper Styria between the Ennstal and Murtal valleys, which are linked by the Präbichl pass.
- ⊘ **Don't Miss:** The view from Polster, and Gesäuse Gorge.
- ○ **Timing:** Allow half a day for each driving tour.
- ⚲ **Kids:** The Erzbergbahn from Vordenberg.

⇌DRIVING TOURS

① GESÄUSE GORGE TOURA

44km/27.3mi.

Liezen★ *♨See LIENZ.*

The 16km/10mi-long **Gesäuse Gorge★★** takes its name from the noise made by the waters of the Enns rushing over their rocky bed. Between Liezen and Admont the road winds along the Enns Valley.

▷ From the touring route, follow the signposts on the left for Frauenberg.

Frauenberg

This pilgrimage church, in Italianate Baroque style, has lavish stucco decoration to match richly gilded altars and pulpit. The terrace offers a fine **view★** of Admont and various mountains.

Admont Monastery★

Alt. 641m/2,103ft. ℹ *Admont 1, 8911 Admont.* ○*Open mid-Mar–Oct daily 10am–5pm, Dec–Feb Fri 10am–noon and Sat–Sun 10am–2pm.* ⊚€10. ℘*03613 23 12 601.* www.stiftadmont.at.

Admont is in northern Styria, at the western entrance of the Gesäuse Valley. The Benedictine Abbey of Admont was founded in the 11C by St. Hemma of Gurk (*♨see GURK*) and Archbishop Gebhard of Salzburg. The abbey buildings were completely rebuilt after a fire in 1865 that fortunately spared the magnificent library and its precious collection of manuscripts and books. The striking abbey church was rebuilt in the neo-Gothic style. The library and museums are definitely worth a visit.

River Enns and a view of Hochtor, Gesäuse National Park

© Austrian National Tourist Office/ Diejun

Stiftsbibliothek (Abbey Library)★★
🕑Guided tours (40min) mid-Mar–Oct daily 10.30am and 2pm; off-season by request.

The exuberant Late Baroque library, completed in 1776, stretches for 70m/229.6ft and is the world's largest abbey library. Selections from its collection of more than 200,000 volumes are shown on a rotating basis.

The seven **ceiling frescoes** by Bartolomeo Altomonte (1702–83) depict allegorical scenes of theology and the arts and sciences. Bookcases contain medieval illuminated manuscripts and early books.

Museum of Fine Arts
🕑mid-Mar–Oct daily 10am–5pm, Dec–Feb Fri 10am–noon and Sat–Sun 10am–2pm.

The monastery's art museum displays a fine selection of paintings, sculptures, textiles and other objects from the Middle Ages to the Baroque period, including a portable altar dating from 1375. Particularly remarkable are the ceremonial vestments and paraments, all products of the Admont School of Embroidery that flourished in the 17C. Upstairs are works by contemporary Austrian artists, part of a continuously growing collection.

Natural History Museum
🕑Open mid-Mar–Oct daily 10am–5pm, Dec–Feb Fri 10am–noon and Sat–Sun 10am–2pm.

This museum in the monastery is famous for its huge insect collection of more than 252,000 specimens.

The best **view★★ of the Gesäuse** comes after Admont (B 146 at kilometre 93.2, by the bus stop and the turn-off for the village of Weng), when the magnificent rock faces of the Hochtor unfold before you. There's another fabulous **view★** of this mountain from the Haindl-karbrücke, a bridge over a small tributary of the Enns.

Gstatterboden
This popular gateway to the Gesäuse is the starting point for climbing tours.

Hieflau
The village has a wooded setting where the valley widens.

2 THE STYRIAN IRON ROAD TOUR
50km/31mi.

Hieflau
From Hieflau to Eisenerz the Erzbach Valley has beautiful, winding gorges and offers fine panoramas of the Tamisch-

bachturm (tower). When reaching the basin of Eisenerz, where there is a view of the **Erzberg★★**, make a small detour to the Leopoldsteiner See.

Leopoldsteiner See★★

This small lake with its deep green waters lies in one of the finest settings in Styria, below the rock cliffs of the Seemauer in the Hochschwab range.

Eisenerz

See EISENERZ.

Past Eisenerz, the road crosses the **Präbichl Pass** *(alt. 1,232m/4,042ft)*. To the northwest the rocky summit of the Pfaffenstein dominates.

▷ Continue on the 115.

Vordernberg

Tourismus Vordernberg. t03849 206. www.vordernberg.at.
This market town has **monuments** and **museums of technical interest** associated with iron-working. The **Erzbergbahn★★** ▲▲ *(see website for timetable; €16 round-trip; 0664 73 49 19 94; www.erzbergbah.at)*, a railway running from Vordernberg over the Präbichl to Eisenerz, goes both around and through the Erzberg. The steepest standard gauge railway in Austria, it was originally built as a cog railway in 1891 and operated with steam hauled trains. In 1988 the line was closed and it is now operated privately by volunteers and enthusiasts.

▷ Continue on the 115.

Leoben

Leoben is about 20km/12.4mi west of Bruck an der Mur, on the River Mur.
Leoben has been the centre of the Styrian metalworking industry since the Middle Ages, thanks to its proximity to the Erzberg with its vast iron ore deposits. The city's industrial suburbs form a striking contrast to its medieval centre and the Alpine surroundings. The **Hauptplatz** is lined with gracious façades, such as the red 17C **Hacklhaus** with its sculpted decoration.

West of here, the **Stadtpfarrkirche St. Xavera** *(open daily 8am–7pm; 03842 43 236; www.stadtpfarre-leoben.at)* is an Early Baroque church once part of a Jesuit College. The interior preserves the original **furnishings★** of 1670, including the richly gilded main altar with its twisted columns framing a painting of St. Francis Xavier by Heinrich Schönfeld.

Museumscenter & Kunsthalle★

Kirchgasse 6, 8700 Leoben. Open Tue –Sat 10am–5pm. €5. 03842 40 62 408. www.museumscenter-leoben.at.
In 2004 Leoben's local history museum collections were dusted off, rearranged and presented in a modern, appealing fashion using clever lighting techniques and multimedia technology. Seven themed sections spotlight its industrial heritage as well as major historical milestones such as the signing of the peace treaty between Napoleon and Emperor Franz II in 1797. It's all housed in a former Jesuit monastery. A modern glass-and-steel annexe, the **Kunsthalle Leoben**, often presents large-scale, high-calibre temporary exhibitions, usually with an ethnological focus.

Stiftskirche Göss

Church open daily 8am–7pm. Free. Chapel and crypt by guided tour only reserved in advance. By donation. Brewery tours by arrangement. €10.50 (brewery museum), €13 (museum and brewery tour). Church 038422 21 48. Brewery tours 03842 20 90 58 02; www.goesser.at.
In the southern suburb of Göss, this **church★** counts an early Romanesque **crypt**, unusual twisted pillars resting on star-shaped bases and a richly carved **south porch★** among its outstanding features. It is surrounded by a former Benedictine convent whose buildings now house the **Gösser brewery**, which is open for tours and also contains a small **museum** *(museum tours Apr–Oct Sat–Sun 11am and 3pm)*.

Steirisches Thermenland

The Styrian spa region comprises the five spa towns of Bad Waltersdorf, Blumau, Loipersdorf, Bad Gleichenberg and Bad Radkersburg in the southeast corner of Styria. It is one of Austria's most fertile belts of land, as illustrated by the numerous vineyards, orchards and fields of pumpkins and cereal crops.

SIGHTS
Bad Blumau
About 7km/4.3mi north of Fürstenfeld.
Blumau would be just a run-of-the-mill health resort were it not for the **Rogner Bad Blumau**, the avant-garde spa and hotel complex designed by the late Viennese architect, **Friedensreich Hundertwasser**. It is a brightly pigmented fairytale composition where people, architecture and nature are intended to harmonise with each other. Whimsical touches include roofs covered with lawns and buildings shaped like eyes. The hotel uses no fossil fuels but uses the heat from three in-house thermal springs to keep the hotel heated in winter. Access is open to hotel or day-spa guests or those on a **guided tour** *(year-round by appointment; free; 03383 51 000; www.badblumau.com).*

Info: Radersdorf 75, 8263 Grosswilfersdorf. 03385 66 040. www.thermenland.at.

Location: The spa region is east of Graz in the far southeastern corner of Austria, close to the border with Hungary.

Don't Miss: A walk around pretty Bad Gleichenberg.

Timing: Simply driving through the region takes less than a day, but for a more thorough look and perhaps a spa treatment, allow two days.

Kids: Riegersburg (but young ones should avoid the Witch Museum), Styrassic Park.

Schloss Riegersburg★
On the B 66, 10km/6.2mi north of Feldbach. Open May–Sept daily 9am–6pm; Apr and Oct daily 10am–6pm (last admission 5pm). Lift €12.50, €6 round-trip, children €7.50, €4 round-trip. 03153 82 131. www.veste-riegersburg.at. If you

Rogner Bad Blumau Spa and Hotel

© Austrian National Tourist Office/ Rogner Bad Blumau

have a sensitive disposition or are easily frightened and/or have young children, you should avoid the Hexenmuseum.

The 12C Riegersburg castle is one of the most imposing strongholds to have guarded Austria's eastern frontiers. Protected by 3km/1.8mi of ramparts and 11 bastions, it successfully withstood the onslaught of both the Hungarians and the Turks. Its site alone, on the remains of a 482m/1,581ft high volcano above the village that shares its name, is impressive.

Since 1822, the castle has belonged to the royal family of Liechtenstein and now houses a Hexenmuseum *(Witch Museum)* in the cellars detailing the horrors of medieval times when women and sometimes men were tortured and burned at the stake. Other exhibit areas include the Weapons Museum and the Castle Museum.

Architectural highlights include the **Knight's Hall,** with its intricately inlaid wooden doors and coffered ceiling and the Early Baroque **White Hall,** with its delicate stuccowork.

There are wonderful **views★** of the Eastern Styria countryside from the imposing promotory.

♣♣ Seebad Riegersburg

This lakeside resort near the base of Riegersburg Castle boasts 18,000sq m/193,750sq ft of water surface, including watershutes and spa pools.

Bad Gleichenberg⚜

On the B 66, 11km/7mi south of Feldbach. www.bad-gleichenberg.at.
After Graz and Mariazell, the spa town of Bad Gleichenberg is the most popular vacation destination in Styria. Sitting near the Hungarian and Slovenian borders, it is famous for its medicinal springs and mild climate. The oldest of the Styrian thermal resorts, it was a favourite with Austrian aristocracy in the 19C. The town still boasts some **Biedermeier-style villas and hotels** and is set amid countryside reminiscent of a landscaped garden.

♣♣ Styrassic Park

Take the B 66 and follow the signposts.
🕐*Open mid-Mar–Oct daily 9am–5pm (Oct 4pm).* ∞€12, children €8.
🗣*Guided tours.* 📞03159 28 750.
www.styrassicpark.at.
Dinosaurs on the loose in Austria? Well, almost. This sprawling forest park is inhabited by more than 75 life-size model dinosaurs made of steel and concrete. On your tour you will encounter the entire cast of usual characters, from the long-necked Brachiosaurus to vicious Velociraptors to the terrifying Tyrannosaurus rex. Display panels give brief explanations on the chronology, fossil discoveries and dimensions of each species. A dino-cinema, a huge children's playground with the largest slide in the country, and a petting zoo further add to the fun.

Bad Radkersburg★

On the B 69, 26km/16mi south of Bad Gleichenberg, right before the Slovenian border.
www.badradkersburg.at.
Radkersburg is an increasingly popular spa town whose bicarbonate- and carbon-rich springs are thought to be helpful in easing discomfort. Since its foundation in 1182, it has been one of the leading trading centres in Styria and was also an important bastion during the wars against the Turks. The partly preserved **fortifications**, with moats, six bastions and towers, still attest to this period.

A walk around town will inevitably lead to the **Hauptplatz**, the main square, whose many merchant mansions with beautiful stone doorways and courtyards give an indication of the town's former wealth. In the centre is a Virgin Mary Column erected in 1680 by the townspeople in thanks for their deliverance from the plague.

The onion-domed octagonal **town hall tower** has become Radkersburg's emblem.

Kärnten (Carinthia) feels a long way from Vienna, both geographically and culturally. With a suspicion of the capital, Carinthians have often defined themselves in terms of their independence from Vienna. The climate here also feels considerably more southern, with lots of sunshine throughout the year. Carinthia shares a border with Slovenia and has long had a significant, albeit decreasing, Slovene minority. Tensions between the German-speaking majority and the Slovene population have been exploited by xenophobic, nationalist politicians for almost a century, and this less savoury aspect of the province is reflected in local political affiliations. Rugged beauty, medieval heritage and summer festivals are highlights of this under-explored region.

Highlights

1 The region's lakes, such as **Ossiacher See** (p316)

2 Hiking or skiing in the **Reisseck Massiv** (p319)

3 A drive along the **Malta-Hochalmstraße** (p323)

4 Ancient buildings and cutting-edge art in **Friesach** (p328)

5 The Kunsthotel Fuchspalast in **St. Veit an der Glan** (p332)

A Bit of History

Klagenfurt, the capital of Carinthia, is a beautiful city with many fine 16C and 17C buildings, including the exceptional Landhaus. One of the city's main attractions is its location at the eastern end of the Wörther See, a popular destination for holidaymakers who come to swim in its exceptionally warm waters. Aside from the obvious attractions of the lake's watersports, its banks are the location for some charming villages as well as the important pilgrimage church of Maria Wörth. The Wörther See is not the only beautiful lake in the province: there are many others including the Ossiacher See and Millstättersee.

Carinthia is also, like much of Austria, a land of mountains, in particular the Karawanken range that runs across the southern edge of the province. Though not quite as high as the Alps farther west, these are still impressive rocky peaks.

In addition to delightful scenery, this southern part of Austria features a wealth of historic towns. Carinthia's second-largest is Villach, a pleasant place to wander among interesting architecture; there's also a natural spa nearby. Among other towns to include on any itinerary are Gmünd and Gurk

Friesach

© Rhombur/iStockphoto.com

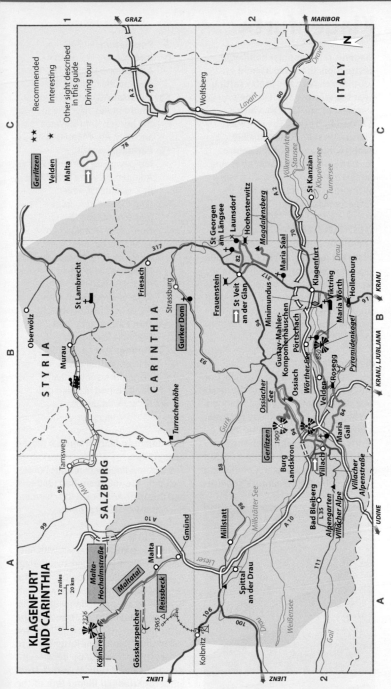

KLAGENFURT AND CARINTHIA

Legend:

★★ Recommended
★ Interesting
○ Other sight described in this guide
Driving tour

Gerlitzen
Velden
Malta

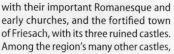

with their important Romanesque and early churches, and the fortified town of Friesach, with its three ruined castles. Among the region's many other castles,

perhaps none is as romantically sited as 9C Burg Hochosterwitz, with its enviable position atop a spectacular rock formation.

Klagenfurt★

Klagenfurt is a popular holiday destination, thanks to its mild southern climate and pretty setting near the Wörther See, Europe's warmest Alpine lake, to which it is linked by a canal. The city was founded in the 12C and quickly evolved into an important centre for trade, although it didn't become capital of the province until it was elevated to that status in 1518 by Emperor Maximilian.

OLD TOWN★★

The idyllic old town, which is at its busiest in summer, reflects almost 800 years of local history. In the 16C and 17C architects from Italy masterminded its distinctive grid pattern of streets and squares as well as over 50 picturesque arcaded courtyards, many of them open to the public.

Neuer Platz

This large square sits at the heart of the Old Town. Its focal point, the **Lind-wurmbrunnen★**, or Dragon Fountain, has become the city emblem. The great monster was created around 1590 by Ulrich Vogelsang, although the basin and Hercules figure weren't added until a few decades later. Completing the ensemble is the country's first-ever

▶ **Population:** 94,796.
▮ **Info:** Neuer Platz/Rathaus, A-9020. ☏0463 537 22 23. www.visitklagenfurt.at.
◖ **Location:** Klagenfurt is in southern Austria, close to the borders with Slovenia and Italy. Alt. 446m/1,463ft.
▯ **Parking:** Long-stay fee-paying car parks: City Arkaden *(St. Veiter Ring 60)*; BKS-Garage *(St. Veiter Ring 43);* Theatergarage *(Purtscherstrasse 1)*; Domgarage *(Paulitschgasse 13);* Apcoa garages on Neuer Platz 13 and Heiligengeist *(Villacher Ring)*; WK-Garage (Gabelsberger Straße); and AK-Garage (Bahnhofsplatz).
☺ **Don't Miss:** Lindwurm-brunnen, Landhaus.
◷ **Timing:** Plan on spending at least one full day in Klagenfurt, another half day if visiting Minimundus.
👥 **Kids:** Minimundus.

monument to Maria Theresia, placed here in 1764.
The square is lined with historic houses, including the 16C **town hall** (Rathaus) and the Adler-Apotheke with charming Rococo stucco decoration.

Alter Platz★

Kramergasse links Neuer Platz with Alter Platz, a lively street-square that derives a certain grandeur from its beautiful 16C mansions. There are many elegant Baroque façades and charming Renaissance arcaded courtyards, such as the **Altes Rathaus★** (Old Town Hall), now called the Palais Orsini-Rosenberg. To the west, the Haus zur Goldenen Gans (Golden Goose House), a gift from Emperor Friedrich III and one of the town's oldest houses, closes off the square. On the southwest corner stands the **Palais Göss** with a Late Baroque pilastered façade.

Alter Platz

© Austrian National Tourist Office/ Volker Preusser

TOURIST INFORMATION

See the **tourist office** website for a searchable **calendar of events**. *www.klagenfurt-tourismus.at.*
Kärnten Card (Carinthia Card)
Available in "denominations" of 1, 2 or 5 weeks, the Carinthia Card is valid mid-Apr–mid-Oct and covers admission to around 100 sights and activities (museums, cable-cars, boat trips, leisure parks and swimming pools) in Klagenfurt and the surrounding areas. It also entitles the bearer to free travel by local rail and bus. Purchase the card at tourism and sales offices throughout the region; the price for a one-week card is €37, children €17. *℘04242 90 525. www.kaerntencard.at.*
CITY TOURS: Check with the tourist office for details about free tours of the city centre Fridays and Saturdays at 10am.

PUBLIC TRANSPORT

Buy a ticket before boarding the bus to avoid paying extra. The **60-Minuten-Karte** is good for unlimited trips within 1hr within Klagenfurt. The **24-Stunden-Karte** (24hr ticket) and the **7-Tage-Karte** (weekly ticket) are transferable. Tickets and information are available from the ticket sales office on the Heiligengeistplatz *(Mon–Fri 6.30am–2.30pm; ℘0463 52 15 42; www.stw.at)* or from Trafiken (tobacconists) or by SMS to a mobile phone. Call *℘0463 52 15 34 (5am–midnight)* for timetable information.

POST OFFICES

Hauptpostamt (main post office): *Dr. Hermann-Gasse 4*; Mon–Fri 8am–6pm, Sat 9am–noon.
Post am Bahnhof: *Südbahngürtel 7a*; Mon–Fri 8am–7pm, Sat 9am–12am.

The Dreifaltigkeitssäule (Trinity Column) was erected in 1680 in gratitude for the town's deliverance from plague; the crescent and cross were added after the 1683 victory over the Turks.

Stadthauptpfarrkirche St. Egid

This 17C church is richly decorated with galleries, sumptuous fittings and fine ceiling paintings by Joseph Molck (nave) and Joseph Fromiller (chancel). There

Grosser Wappensaal, Landhaus

© Austrian National Tourist Office/Trumler

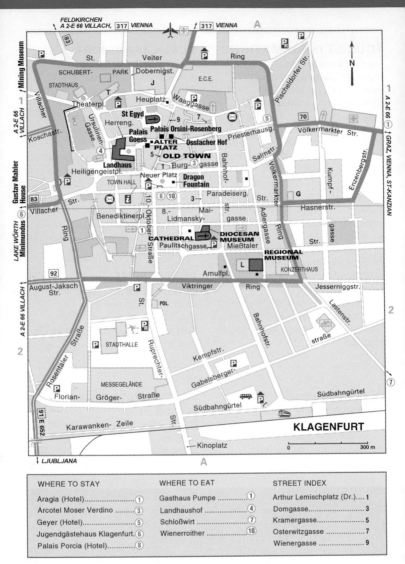

FELDKIRCHEN
A 2-E 66 VILLACH, 317 VIENNA / 317 VIENNA

KLAGENFURT

0   300 m

↓ LJUBLJANA   A

WHERE TO STAY	WHERE TO EAT	STREET INDEX
Aragia (Hotel)......................①	Gasthaus Pumpe ....①	Arthur Lemischplatz (Dr.)....1
Arcotel Moser Verdino ....③	Landhaushof ....④	Domgasse...........................3
Geyer (Hotel).......................⑤	Schloßwirt ....⑦	Kramergasse.......................5
Jugendgästehaus Klagenfurt.⑥	Wienerroither ....⑩	Osterwitzgasse 7
Palais Porcia (Hotel)...........⑧		Wienergasse 9

are tombstones spanning four centuries. A more recent addition is that of French-American author Julien Green (1900–98), whose final wish was to be buried in Klagenfurt.

Landhaus

This imposing building has a well-proportioned **Renaissance courtyard★** with a two-storey arcaded gallery that was built in 1590 as the town's armoury. The building is now the seat of the Carinthian Parliament. The Heraldic Hall, the

Grosser Wappensaal★ (🕐open Apr–Oct Mon–Fri 9am–4pm; Sat and public hols 9am–2pm; ⊛€4; ☏0463 57 75 72 15) was decorated by one of Carinthia's most important Baroque painters, **Joseph Fromiller** (1693–1760). His masterpiece is the magnificent ceiling fresco, framed by trompe-l'œil galleries and depicting a scene showing members of the States of Carinthia paying homage to Emperor Karl VI. Fromiller painted most of the 665 coats of arms of noblemen on the walls.

Dom★ (Cathedral)

The cathedral was built in 1578 as a Protestant house of worship, but fell under the control of the Jesuits in 1604 during the Counter-Reformation. They made numerous alterations, resulting in the Baroque look you still see today. The **high altar**, framed by columns, is the work of Daniel Gran, while the magnificent **pulpit** (1726) is attributed to Carinthian artist Christoph Rudolph. Opposite, the *Apotheosis of St. John of Nepomuk* by Joseph Fromiller counterbalances the pulpit beautifully.

The **side altars★** are a symphony of coloured marble. Of special note is the altar in the **Ignatius-von-Loyola Chapel** in the south aisle, which boasts an altar painting by the great Paul Troger.

MUSEUMS
Landesmuseum Rudolfinum★ (Regional Museum)

🕐*Closed for restoration until 2018–19.* 𝄢*050 536 30 599.* *www.landesmuseum.ktn.gv.at.*

This vast museum offers a comprehensive window on Carinthia's intriguing history and culture. A recently added highlight is the **Glocknerama★**, a multimedia installation that takes you on a virtual climb of the great Grossglockner mountain. Other exhibits are more traditional and drawn from such themes as geology, early- and prehistory, Roman archaeology and folk art.

There are plenty of fascinating items, including the famous "**dragon skull**," a fossilised rhinoceros skull found in 1335 in a gravel pit near Klagenfurt. It is said to have inspired the designer of the famous Lindwurmbrunnen (*see p306*). Also worth seeking out is a large Dionysius **mosaic floor★** from the ancient Roman provincial capital of Virunum in today's Zollfeld plain near Maria Saal (*see MARIA SAAL*).

The 15C and 16C are represented by numerous works of religious art, including the imposing St. Veit altarpiece. Note also Paola Gonzaga's **bridal chests★** decorated with colourful reliefs based on designs by Andrea Mantegna.

EXCURSIONS
👫 Europapark & Minimundus

3km/1.8mi west of Klagenfurt via Villacher Straße. 🕐*Open Jan–Apr, Oct–Dec daily 9am–6pm; May, Jun, Sept daily 9am–7pm; Jul–Aug daily 9am–8pm.* ♿ 🎟€18, children €10. 𝄢*0463 21 19 40. www.minimundus.at.*

The Europapark is a large, leafy recreational area encompassing a mini-golf course, a reptile zoo, an old-fashioned *Strandbad* (lakeside pool) and Minimundus. This child-friendly theme park centres on 150 scale models (1:25) of world monuments made of authentic materials, from Big Ben to the Statue of Liberty, and the Eiffel Tower to St. Mark's in Venice, all displayed in a park-like setting, enhanced by audio-guides that provide background information.

Gustav-Mahler-Komponierhäuschen (Gustav Mahler House)

From Minimundus follow the southern shore of the Wörthersee and park opposite Maiernigg beach; walk 15min to the site. 🕐*Open Jun–Oct Thu–Sun 10am–1pm.* 🎟€3. 𝄢*0463 537 58 25.*

This unprepossessing wooden house hidden in the forest is the place where composer **Gustav Mahler** created some of his masterpieces between 1900 and 1907, including Symphonies *Four* to *Eight* and the Rückert Lieder.

Pörtschach★

10km/6.2mi W of Klagenfurt on the B 83. Much of the charm of this resort community lies in its lovely site on a small peninsular jutting into the Wörthersee. A flower-lined lakeside promenade goes around the spit passing grand hotels and villas hidden among lush greenery. The resort's most popular walk *(30 min, many steps)* is from Castle Leonstein, sited on a cliff in the northwest of the town, up to the viewpoint known as the Gloriette. From there you can admire the lake and the Karawanken mountains.

👫 St. Kanzian Lakes

20km/12.5mi east of Klagenfurt on the B 70, via Völkermarkter Straße.

Wörthersee and Pörtschach

© Austrian National Tourist Office/Popp Hackner

Set among woods, these tranquil lakes are ideal for swimming or windsurfing, or other sports such as tennis and horse riding. Hikers can choose from 150km/93mi of marked trails.

The Klopeinersee has the easiest access and is busy, in contrast with the quieter Turnersee and Kleinsee. A bridge crosses the Völkermarkter Stausee (which is actually a reservoir on the Drava), where swimming is prohibited.

ADDRESSES

STAY

Jugendgästehaus Klagenfurt – *Neckheimgasse 6. ℘0463 23 00 20. www. oejhv.at. 150 beds.* ☐. This smart, modern youth hostel is situated near the bank of the Wörther See.

Hotel Aragia – *Völkermarkter Straße 100. ℘0463 312 22. www.aragia.at. 40 rooms.* ☐. This family-run hotel offers simple functional rooms, a restaurant, café-bar and terrace.

Hotel Geyer – *Priesterhausgasse 5. ℘0463 578 86. www.hotelgeyer.com. 25 rooms.* ☐. This smart modern city-centre hotel has simple but attractive bedrooms and spa area complete with steam bath and sauna.

Arcotel Hotel Moser Verdino – *Domgasse 2. ℘0463 57 87 80. www. arcotel.at. 71 rooms.* ☐. An outpost of the Arcotel chain, the stately pink-and-white hostelry sits on a busy corner; within, updated rooms are designed with modern flair.

Palais Porcia – *Neuer Platz 13. ℘0463 511 59 00. www.palais-porcia.at. 35 rooms.* ☐. Occupying a palatial old city residence, this opulent hotel offers rooms decorated in Baroque, Rococo and Biedermeierthemes.

¶/EAT

Hofbräu zum Lindwurm – *Neuer Platz 10. ℘0463 564 26. www.hofbraeu-zum-lindwurm.at.* Traditional pub serving Bavarian fare.

Gasthaus Pumpe – *Lidmanskygasse 2. ℘0463 571 96. Closed Sat evening & Sun.* This typical Carinthian inn dates from 1882.

Gasthaus im Landhaushof – *Landhaushof 1. ℘0463 50 23 63. www.gut-essen-trinken.at.* Come to this gasthaus for tasty Austrian specialities.

AROUND KLAGENFURT

Schloßwirt – *5km/3mi SE of Klagenfurt, St. Veiter Straße 247. ℘0463 41 621. www.schlosswirt-klagenfurt.at. Closed Sat evening and Sun.* This fine inn is a little way out of Klagenfurt, but its excellent cuisine, served in the garden justifies the detour.

Wörther See★

The Wörther See, a lake stretching for some 17km/10.5mi between Velden and Klagenfurt, receives only a little of its total water from mountain streams and is therefore pleasantly warm (24–28°C/75–82°F in summer). Velden and Pörtschach are among the clutch of popular resort towns along the lake shore. A screen of low hills sometimes hides the Karawanken, but a short stroll is generally enough to bring back into view the magnificent splendour of this mountain barrier extending from Austria into Slovenia and Italy.

🚗 **DRIVING TOUR**

SOUTH SHORE TOUR★
76km/47mi.

The route begins by traversing the Drava River Valley, within sight of the Karawanken. In Velden, follow the road along the south shore of the lake. Note the site of the Maria Wörth promontory and the panorama from the Pyramidenkogel.

▷ Begin at Villach (*see p314*) and take road 84 as far as the east bank of the Gail.

Kirche Maria Gail
The core of this pilgrimage church is Romanesque, although it was remodelled in the Gothic style around 1450 and only a few frescoes remain from the late Romanesque period. The focal point is a valuable Late Gothic **altarpiece★★** (north wall) carved in the early 16C in a Villach workshop. Its central panel depicts the Coronation of the Virgin. Outside, on the south wall, are some interesting stone sculptures depicting what resembles a Last Judgement scene; it is believed to date back to around 1300.

▷ Continue on road 84 to Faaker See.

🛈 **Info:** Villacher Straße 19, 9220 Velden. ℘04274 38 288. www.woerthersee.com.
▷ **Location:** This lake is in the far south of Austria, close to the Slovenian border, about 14km/8.7mi southeast of Klagenfurt.
⊚ **Don't Miss:** Velden, Maria Wörth.
🕐 **Timing:** Plan a full day to cover this route at leisure.
👥 **Kids:** Wildpark Rosegg.

The road continues to climb, offering a wide general view of the Villach basin, where the Gail and the Drava converge before embracing the beautiful **Faaker See** and the solitary Mittagskogel (*alt. 2,143m/7,031ft*).

▷ Just before Egg am Faaker See, turn left. The road descends to the Drava Valley where it follows the river bank.

👥 Tierpark Rosegg
🕐*Open mid-Mar–Oct daily 9am–6pm.* ⊛*€8.50 park, €7 museum, €4.50 labyrinth, €16.50 combination ticket. ℘04274 52 357. www.rosegg.at.*
This wildlife park was laid out almost 200 years ago when the old castle at Rosegg was demolished, and is now home to lynx, monkeys, wolves, deer, mouflon sheep, bison, boar, eagles and many more birds and animals.
Next to the wildlife park is the (newer) **Schloss Rosegg** (🕐*open May–Sept Tue–Sun 10am–6pm; Jul–Aug daily 10am–6pm; ℘04274 52 357; www.rosegg.at*), home to a small museum of historical wax figures, including Empress Elisabeth ("Sisi") and Napoleon. Visitors can also hone their escape skills in the **Labyrinth**, a 2400sq m hedge maze that lies between the park and the castle site.

▷ Take the road N from Rosegg.

Velden by Wörther See

© Austrian National Tourist Office/ Diejun

Velden★

This elegant, long-established spa resort, at the west end of the Wörther See, is easy to spot from afar, heralded by its yellow riverside **castle**. Now operating as a hotel, the castle was completed as a summer residence by the local ruler Bartholomäus Khevenhüller in 1603. Reconstruction after a fire in 1893 retained the 17C plan. The main doorway is surmounted with obelisks and bears, on the pediment, the Khevenhüller family coat of arms. A promenade, casino and grand villas characterise the chic lakeside resort.

◖ Take the Wörthersee Süduferstraße, which follows the southern lake shore.

Maria Wörth★

The towers of the pilgrimage churches of Maria Wörth, in an idyllic setting on a promontory in the Wörther See, together with the round tower of the charnel house form a much-photographed scene. Construction of the Gothic parish church went on from 1399 to 1540, although parts of the original Romanesque building were reused. The high altar of 1685 incorporates a

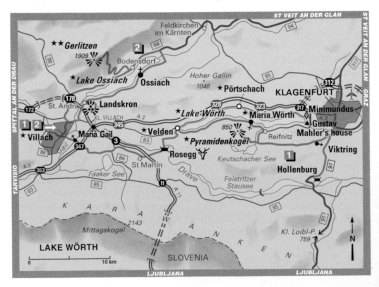

Virgin Mary and Child Enthroned from the late 15C. The imposing Altar of the Holy Cross with its early 16C crucifix and the pulpit of 1761 complete the interior décor. The picture of the Madonna on the north wall of the chancel is a copy of the original gracing the church of Santa Maria del Popolo in Rome. The crypt is decorated with brightly painted floral motifs (17C).

The small chapel **"Winterkirche"** has **Romanesque murals★** in its chancel from the late 11C, the oldest in Carinthia and done in a style echoing Ottonian Romanesque.

▶ Turn right in Reifnitz, and drive 8km/5mi to the Pyramidenkogel.

Pyramidenkogel★

Open May–Sept daily from 9am; Oct–Apr daily from 10am; closing hrs vary. €11; ℘04273 24 43; www.pyramidenkogel.info.
This 100m/328-ft high **viewing tower** crowns the summit *(alt. 850m/2,789ft).* A fine **panorama★★** embraces the great central valley of Carinthia, the Karawanken mountain barrier and far to the west, the jagged Julian Alps. To the northeast lies the Ulrichsberg, looking like a sphinx emerging from the mass of hills. During the Celtic period this was one of the sacred mountains of Carinthia. In the foreground, the peninsula of Maria Wörth juts out into the waters of the lake.

Viktring

The abbey entrance is at the end of the village's main north-south street.
Viktring Abbey, founded by Cistercian monks in 1142, is laid out around two vast courtyards with superimposed galleries. Its church was the only example east of the Rhine to be modelled on the abbey of Fontenay in Burgundy. The 14C saw the addition of Gothic ribbed vaulting and beautiful **stained-glass windows**, which are now partially obscured by the Early Baroque high altar of 1622. Don't miss gazing upward to see the remarkable 15C **ceiling frescoes★**.

▶ Take road 91 towards the Loibl pass. As it descends, turn left for the castle. Park before the covered bridge.

Schloss Hollenburg

The massive Hollenburg fortress, built during the 14C and 15C, overlooks the Drava Valley, here known as the Rosental. Although the castle exterior is relatively austere, the **interior courtyard★** with its Renaissance arcades and outside staircase exudes an almost Italianate exuberance. There is a good **view★** of the Karawanken from the balcony.

▶ Return to road no. 91 to enter Klagenfurt from the S.

ADDRESSES

⌂ STAY

Hotel Garni Lovely In – *Rosentaler Straße 50, 9220 Velden. ℘04274 25 74. www.lovely-in.at. 12 rooms.* ☲. Beautiful, chic, boutique-style family-run guesthouse with delightful garden, terrace and pool

Hotel Krumpendorferhof – *Hauptstraße 164, 9201 Krumpendorf. ℘04229 23 01. www.krumpendorferhof. co.at. Closed 3 weeks Feb, and 23-25 Dec. Restaurant closed Wed. 19 rooms.* ☲. This family-run hotel-restaurant has a lovely lakeside terrace where avant-garde Mediterranean dishes are served.

Hotel Strandhotel Habich – *Walterskirchenweg 10, 9201 Krumpendorf. ℘04229 26 07. www.strandhotelhabich.at. 38 rooms.* ☲. Fantastic lake views and private beach. Prices include half-board.

♈/ EAT

Caramé – *Am Corso 10, 9220 Velden. ℘04274 30 00. www.restaurant-carame.at. Closed Mon.* This modern gourmet restaurant serves classic Austrian cuisine. Tasting menus too.

Linde – *Lindenplatz 3, 9082 Maria Wörth. ℘04273 22 78. www.hotel linde.at.* This luxury hotel-restaurant enjoys a wonderful lakeside setting and serves international and local cuisine.

Villach★

Frequently referred to as the "secret capital" of Carinthia, Villach is the province's second-largest town and a regional economic and cultural hub. Settled since Celtic times, it has an attractive location on the Drava (Drau) River and is considered a gateway to both Italy and Slovenia. In 1007, Emperor Heinrich II donated Villach to his newly founded bishopric at Bamberg, some 540km/335.5mi north, in Bavaria. This arrangement shaped Villach's fortunes until Maria Theresia bought the town back in 1759. Today, part of its appeal lies in its thermal mineral springs and proximity to the Faaker and Ossiach lakes.

▶ **Population:** 61,200.
  Michelin Map: Local map see Wörther See.
  Info: Bahnhofstr. 3 ℗04242 205 2900. www.villach.at.
▶ **Location:** Villach is on the far southern edge of the country, close to the Slovenian border, about 40km/25mi west of Klagenfurt. Alt. 501m/1,644ft.
🅿 **Parking:** There are plenty of pay lots and garages in central Villach as well as a large free parking lot by the train station, about a 15min walk away.
  Don't Miss: Villacher Alpenstraße.
  Kids: Burg Landskron, Affenberg, Terra Mystica and Terra Montana.

⌘ WALKING TOUR

OLD TOWN★

The old town is hemmed in to the north and east by the Drava.
The **Hauptplatz**, an elongated square, is flanked by several interesting houses, including the Paracelsushof (no. 18), named after the great physician who spent his youth in Villach; and the Khevenhüllers' house (now the Romantik Hotel Post), where Emperor Karl V stayed for seven weeks in 1552.

▶ After exploring the Hauptplatz and the little streets off it, make your way to the square housing the parish church with its impressive steeple.

Hauptstadtpfarrkirche St. Jakob

Behind the parish church's simple exterior awaits a lovely hall-church with star vaulting and ribbed vaulting, a high altar with magnificent sculptures, and a canopied stone pulpit (1555). There are also several 15C–18C **tombs★** on the south wall. In summer it is possible to climb up the free-standing church tower for sweeping views (⏰open mid-May–Oct Mon–Sat 10am–4.30pm, Jul–Aug til 6pm; ❧€2.50; ℗4242 205 3540).

▶ Turn right on to Widmanngasse.

Museum der Stadt Villach★

Widmanngasse 38. ⏰*Open May–Oct Tue–Sun 10am–4.30pm.* ❧€4. ℗*04242 205 35 00.* *www.villach.at/museum.*
This Renaissance-style building with its arcaded courtyard forms a fine backdrop to the local historical collections. Exceptional items include the two Gothic panel paintings by **Master Thomas of Villach**, the 1557 gravestone of local governor Christoph Khevenhüller, and large iron chests from the 16C–19C that were used as fire-proof storage places for valuables.

▶ Return to the Hauptplatz. Take 10-Oktober-Straße and then go left onto Peraustraße.

Relief von Kärntern

Schillerpark, Peraustraße. ⏰*Open May–Oct Mon–Sat 10am–4.30pm.* ❧€2.50. ℗*04242 205 35 50. www.villach.at.*
This immense relief model of Carinthia has been made on a scale of 1:10,000

horizontally, and 1:5,000 vertically, allowing you to familiarise yourself with the countryside of the region.

▶ Follow Peraustraße to where it crosses over Ossiacher Zeile.

Wallfahrtskirche Heiligenkreuz

Follow Peraustraße as far as the junction with Ossiacher Zeile.
This Late Gothic pilgrimage church, with its striking twin-towered façade stands on the south bank of the Drava. The richly decorated high altar with the Crucifixion scene, the Lamentation altarpiece in the north transept and the extremely rare depiction of the Thief on Christ's Right in the south transept all contribute to the overall harmony of the church's interior.

Villacher Fahrzeugmuseum

F. Wedenig Straße 9, Villach-Zauchen.
�Open daily 10am–6pm. €9.60.
℘04252 33 031.
www.oldtimermuseum.at.
This small vehicle museum is devoted to means of transport made between 1927 and 1977; its endearing old Fiats and Puch motorcycles are worth the detour alone.

Warmbad-Villach

About 3km/1.8mi south of town.
℘04242 30 01 10. www.warmbad.com.
Every day, 24 million l/6,340 million US gal of therapeutic spring water bubbles up from the six springs (29°C/84°F) in the suburb of Warmbad-Villach.
When Villach was part of the French Illyrian Provinces between 1809 and 1813, Napoleon nursed plans to develop it into a world-renowned spa resort, and although these never materialised, today's modern spa has all the facilities one has come to expect.

EXCURSIONS
Villacher Alpenstraße★

16.5km/10.2mi. €16.50. ℘0662 873
67 30. www.villacher-alpenstrasse.at.
This modern mountain toll road runs from Villach-Möltschach (*alt. 550m/*

1,804ft) up the Dobratsch as far as 1,732m/5,682ft. Many viewpoints have been constructed for views of Villach, the Julian Alps and Dobratsch itself.

Alpengarten Villacher Alpe★

ⓦOpen Jun–Aug daily 9am–6pm.
€3. ℘0664 914 29 53.
www.alpengarten-villach.at.
One of the most beautiful alpine gardens in Europe, this collection is devoted to the flora of the southern Alps. It covers an area of 10,000sq m/11,960sq yd and is home to 900 types alpine plant, complete with explanatory panels.

Dobratsch★★

From the end of the road, a trail leads to the peak of the **Dobratsch** (*alt. 2,167m/ 7,107ft*) in about 2hr. As a reward for your effort, you get to enjoy a famous **panorama** taking in the Karawanken range, the Carinthian lakes, the Julian Alps and the Tauern.

Bad Bleiberg

15km/9.3mi west of Villach.
Bleiberg was a lead-mining settlement until in 1993 when the mine closed due to falling lead prices and exhaustion of the ore deposits making mining uneconomic. Discovery of thermal waters in the mines led to the development of a **spa** and the town received the title **Bad** (spa) in 1978.

♣♟ Terra Mystica and Terra Montana★★★

Bleiberg-Notsch 91. ⚶Guided tours
(2hr) only: ⓦGuided tours May–Jun
and Sept–Oct 11am and 1pm; Jul–Aug
9.30am–3pm; Nov–Apr Sat 3pm.
€18.50. ℘04244 22 55.
www.terra-mystica.at.
Together these make up Austria's most imaginative show mines. **Terra Mystica** was first to be developed and makes use of the old mining galleries. A highlight of the tour is a descent down a 68m/223ft wooden slide to the deeper levels where there is a spectacular sound and light show on mining, the cult of St. Barbara (the patron saint of miners) and mythical subterranean creatures.

Visiting **Terra Montana** involves descending 250m/820ft in a miners' cage at the rate of 4m/s (13ft/s) to the mine. Here a train takes you on a 3km/1.8mi tour to 14 stations where you can learn and experience life in the mine. *This tour is not suitable for those suffering from claustrophobia.*

🚗 DRIVING TOUR

TOUR OF OSSIACHER SEE★

66km/41mi. The Ossiacher See is in southern Austria, about 40km/25mi west of Klagenfurt. ⓘ10-Oktober-Str. 1, Bodensdorf. 𝒫04243 83 83 23. www. ossiachersee.info. 🅿 Several car parks are dotted around the lake.

Ossiach Lake lies a little set back from the Villach basin, tucked amid the wooded slopes of the Gerlitzen, the Hexenberg and the Ossiacher Tauern. It is Carinthia's third-largest lake, measuring 11km/6.8mi long by 1.5km/1mi wide and reaching a depth of 46m/151ft. This is claimed to be Austria's sunniest spot and its inviting shores are perfect for swimming and relaxing. From spring to autumn, boats provide a regular service to all the lakeside resorts.

◐ Leave Villach to the N and take the B 94.

From Villach, the B 94 skirts the ruins of Landskron fortress and follows the north shore overlooked by the steep slopes of the Gerlitzen.

🧗 Gerlitzen★★

The Gerlitzen summit *(alt. 1,909m/ 6,263ft)* dominates central Carinthia, its foothills cascading down to the Ossiach Lake. In winter, its numerous hotels, the cable-car from Annenheim up to the Kanzel, the ski-lifts and sunny slopes attract an international crowd of skiers. In summer, it is the starting point for a number of scenic hiking trails.
From Bodensdorf on the north shore head to Tschöran for the mountain road to Gerlitzen (12km/7.4mi; ⊜toll).

After winding through woods and pastures, the road ends at 1,764m/5,787ft at a complex with restaurants and lodging. Finish the climb on foot or if necessary, by **chairlift** (ⓞ*operates Jun–mid-Oct daily 9am–5pm; Dec–Apr daily 8.15am–5pm, depending on snow levels; ⊜€20.50 round-trip; 𝒫04248 27 22; www.gerlitzen.com).* From Gerlitzen summit, the **panorama★★** embraces the Ossiach, Wörth and Faak lakes and beyond the Drava Valley, the long barrier of the Karawanken. The permanently snow-covered slopes of the Hochalm and Ankogel glaciers rise to the northwest.

◐ Return to the lake. Take the road carries on E to Steindorf. Turn right off the main road and follow the road parallelling the south shore.

Ossiach

The Benedictine **abbey** of Ossiach was founded in the 11C. In the 16C and 17C the abbey went through periods of splendour, even receiving Emperor Charles V in 1552. In 1783 it was dissolved on the orders of Emperor Joseph II. The complex served various roles in the 19C-20C, becoming a stud farm, a military base and a convalescence home, all of which took their toll on the buildings. Today it is available as an event venue and is known internationally as a venue for the Carinthian Summer Festival.

Ossiach Basilica★

ⓞ*Open year-round daily 9am–6pm.*
♿ 𝒫*04243 22 80.*
www.pfarre-ossiach.at.
Ossiach's triple-nave pillared basilica was originally of Romanesque design but it was completely transformed into the Baroque style between 1741 and 1745. The basilica features delicately coloured, lace-like **stuccowork** by master craftsmen of the Wessobrunn School.

🏰 Burg Landskron

5km/3mi north of Villach.
A Habsburg stronghold in the Middle Ages, this castle passed to the Khevenhüller family in the 16C, who refitted it in

View of Villach and Ossiacher See

© Austrian National Tourist Office/ Popp Hackner

sumptuous style but later lost it as punishment for supporting the Reformation. It is now occupied by a hotel-restaurant with a fabulous terrace **view★** of the Villach basin, the Karawanken and Ossiacher See.

Don't miss the birds of prey **flight shows★** (Jul–Aug daily 11am, 2.30pm, 5.30pm; Apr–Jun and Sept Mon–Sat 11am, 2.30pm, also Sun 4.30pm; Oct daily 11am, 2.30pm; €12; 04242 42 888; www.adlerarena.com) staged at the castle, starring kites, falcons and eagles.

En route to Landskron, you pass the **Abenteur Affenberg** (open late Mar–Oct daily 9.30am–6pm; €12, children €6; 04242 43 03 75; www.affenberg.com), where you can walk freely among a colony of Japanese Macaque monkeys in the open countryside.

ADDRESSES

STAY

Hotel Kramer – *Italiener Straße 14. 04242 24 953. www.hotel-kramer.at. 42 rooms.* This fine hotel has been open for over a century but today's rooms have every mod con. There is a Wellness area and a restaurant serving regional food.

Romantik Hotel Post – *Hauptplatz 26. 04242 26 101. www.hotel-villach.com. 70 rooms.* A former 16C palace is now home to a comfortable and modern hotel whose bedrooms enjoy garden views. There is a Wellness area and a delightful garden restaurant.

EAT

Kaufmann & Kaufmann – *Dietrichsteingasse 5. 04242 25 871. www.kauf-mann.at. Closed Sun, Mon. Reservations advisable.* This restaurant in the city centre offers Carinthian, Austrian and Mediterranean dishes.

Urbani-Weinstuben – *Meerbothstr. 22. 0699 11 88 54 54. www.urbaniweinstuben.at. Closed Sat, Sun, one week in Mar and one week in Jul.* This striking and trendy restaurant and wine bar serves both modern cuisine and traditional dishes.

Wirt in Judendorf – *Judendorfer Straße 24, 9504 Villach-Judendorf. 3km/1.8mi from town on the Ossiacher Zeile. 04242 56 525. www.wirt-in-judendorf.at. Closed Mon, Jan and early Apr.* This charming inn serves regional dishes in its pretty garden.

Spittal an der Drau

Charming Spittal lies at the confluence of the Lieser and the Drava (Drau) at the foot of the Goldeck peak and close to the Millstättersee (lake). Thanks to its strategic position on a major trade route between Germany and Venice it flourished over the centuries as an economic and cultural centre. Nowadays, it is still an important hub in Upper Carinthia.

SIGHTS

Schloss Porcia★

This Italian Renaissance palazzo was built for Gabriel Salamanca, a Spanish aristocrat who served as general treasurer to Archduke Ferdinand until 1526. From 1662 to 1918 the palace was the residence of the princes of Porcia, a noble family from northeastern Italy. The park and the three-story **arcaded courtyard★** are open to the public at any time. The latter features antique medallions, balustraded pillars, door frames, and other ornamentation typi-

▶ **Population:** 15,500.

Info: Burgplatz 1, A-9800. ℰ04762 56 50 226. www.lmr-spittal.at.

Location: Spittal is in southern Austria, 37km/23mi west of Villach. Alt. 554m/1,818ft.

Parking: Central options include the City Center garage and the Hauptplatz.

Don't Miss: the Museum für Volkskultur.

Kids: Erlebniswelt Eisenbahn, the Museum für Volkskultur.

cal of the Renaissance style. Also note the splendid 16C wrought-iron **gates★**. Theater performances are held in the courtyard in summer.

Occupying the upper floors of the castle is the **Museum für Volkskultur★★**

Courtyard of Schloss Porcia

© Martin Siepmann/imageBROKER/age fotostock

(○open mid-Apr-Oct daily 9am-6pm; Nov-mid-Apr Mon-Thu 1pm-4pm; ⊸€8, children €4; ♿ ℘04762 28 90. www. museum-spittal.com) which chronicles local history, culture and folklore in 47 attractively presented themed displays (education, farming, mining, etc.). The highlight for many visitors is the 180-degree **3-D film★** that lets you (virtually) soar like a bird above the Hohe Tauern National Park.

👥 Erlebniswelt Eisenbahn★

Gerngross City Center shopping mall, Neuer Platz. ○*Open mid-Apr-late Oct Mon-Sat 9am-6pm (Sat til 5pm).* ⊸€7, *children €3.* ♿ ℘04762 28 90. *www.museum-spittal.com.*

Austria's largest model railway (affiliated to the Museum für Volkskultur) features some 600m/1,968ft of track, 85 locomotives and 350 cars.

Goldeckbahn

○*Open Jun-Sept daily 9am-5pm, mid-Dec-Mar 8.30am-4.45pm.* ⊸€19.50. ℘04762 28 64. *www.sportberg-goldeck.at.*

This scenic 4km/2.5mi cable-car ride climbs, in two stages, to a height of 2,050m/6,726ft, an increase in altitude of 1,500m/4,921ft. From the upper station there is a fine **view★** of Spittal, the surrounding mountains and the Millstättersee lake.

HIKES
🥾 Reisseck-Massiv★★

19km/12mi northwest of Spittal on the B106 towards Kolbnitz. 🏠 *Unterkolbnitz 50, Kolbnitz.* ℘04783 20 50. *www.reisseck.at.*

The Reisseck massif, which towers over the Möll Valley, is one of the most unspoiled places in Carinthia. The mountain wilderness was opened to active tourism after the construction of a funicular and a railway line to serve the power station at Kolbnitz.

Its beautiful location and good snow conditions attract skiers in winter, while summer draws well-informed hikers, who trek around its many lakes and many glorious viewpoints.

Reisseckbahn★

From Kolbnitz. 25min each way by funicular plus 10min on the train. ○*Out of service until further notice.*

The ascent to the top of the Reisseck mountain is awe-inspiring. The funicular follows a very steep – up to 82 degrees – gradient for 3.5km/2mi to the Schokerboden station *(alt. 2,237m/7,339ft),* from which there is a beautiful **view★** of the valley and the rocky foothills of the Reisseck massif. From here the Höhenbahn train travels underground for 3.2km/1.9mi, eventually arriving at a pleasant hotel. From here, take a bracing hike, or the easier "Reisseck Rundwanderung"1hr circuit walk.

🥾 Wanderweg Mühldorfer See★

From the Höhenbahn mountain station, an easy 20min walk leads to the Grosser Mühldorfer See, a reservoir from which there is a **view★** to the east over the Hohe Leier. Beyond here, the trail is quite stony, so sturdy shoes are essential *(follow the red and white markings).* After 10min the path emerges above the Kleiner Mühldorfer See dam.

There is a beautiful **open view★** over both lakes, which lie in an unspoiled rocky landscape. Keen hikers can continue for another hour to the **Riekentörl pass** *(alt. 2,525m/8,284ft),* for a magnificent **panorama★★** over the entire Reisseck massif. The hike climbs along a rocky trail, but presents no technical difficulties.

Grosser Mühldorfer See

© VERBUND

EXCURSION

Teurnia Ausgrabungen (excavations)★

4km/2.5mi west of Spittal at St. Peter in Holz. Turn left off the road to Lienz.

The area around St. Peter im Holz has been settled since the 12C BC, first by Celts, then as the Roman city of Teurnia around AD 50. Excavations have uncovered the remains of this latter settlement, including the forum, a bath house and a temple. In the 5C and 6C, Teurnia was a fortified provincial town and episcopal seat. The remains of the diocesian church are now protected by a modern shelter.

Nearby, the **Römermuseum Teurnia★** (*open May–Oct Tue–Sun 9am–5pm; €6; ♿; ℘04762 33 807; www.landesmuseum.ktn.gv.at*) presents artefacts unearthed by the excavations, including reliefs, daily objects and coins.

Outside the city walls, within the cemetery, the chapel of the early Christian Friedhofskirche is home to a 5C **mosaic floor★** with animal motifs.

ADDRESSES

STAY

Gasthof Edlingerwirt – *Villacherstrasse 88. ℘04762 51 50. www.edlingerwirt.at. 20 rooms.* . This hostelry at the edge of town has welcomed guests for three generations to its spotless accommodations and excellent cuisine. Several rooms offer 3- and 4 beds for families, and half-board is available.

Koller's Hotel am See – *Seepromenade 2-4, 9871 Seeboden. 5km/3mi NE of Spittal on the 98. ℘04762 82 000. www.kollers.at. Closed mid-Mar–early Apr and Nov–mid-Dec. 61 rooms, 4 suites. . Price includes half board.* This luxury hotel has an idyllic setting on Lake Millstatt. Guests are pampered with state-of-the-art spa facilities, including an open-air swimming pool and a lakeside garden. Most bedrooms have balconies overlooking the mountains or the lake. The garden gives direct access to Lake Millstatt.

EAT

Mettnitzer – *Neuer Platz 17. ℘04762 35 899. Closed Mon–Tue, 2 weeks in Jun and 2 weeks in Nov. Reservations advisable.* This stylish *Weinstube* has been serving fine regional and international dishes for over a century.

FESTIVALS

Salamancafest – *Late Jun.* Biennial town fair.

Chowettbewerb – *Early Jul. www.chorbewerb-spittal.at.* A dozen choirs from around the world come to Spittal an der Drau to compete before expert judges and the public.

Millstatt★

Millstatt lies on the north shore of the Millstätter See, a lake boasting water temperatures of up to 26°C/82°F. Owing to its lakeside beach and its favourable climate, Millstatt has become a popular summer resort. Known as the cultural capital of Upper Carinthia, the town is home to the annual Internationale Musikwochen, a series of classical music concerts held between May and October.

- ▶ **Population:** 3,400.
- **Info:** Marktplatz 8, A-9872. ℘04766 20 23. www.millstatt.at.
- ▷ **Location:** Millstatt is in southern Austria, about 10km/6.2mi east of Spittal an der Drau and 83km/52mi northwest of Klagenfurt. Alt. 604m/1,982ft.

VISIT
Stift★

One of the loveliest Romanesque buildings in Austria today, the abbey began in the 11C as a Benedictine monastery, then became the seat of the Knights of St. George in 1469. in 1598 the abbey became the purview of the Jesuits.

A small **museum** (&.○open May–mid-Oct daily 10am–4pm; ∞€3.90; ℘0676 36 00 692; www.stiftsmuseum.at) provides an insight into the abbey's history and its works of art, both religious and secular.

Stiftshof★

The elegant abbey courtyard, framed by two-tiers of arcades, attests to the wealth of the Order of St. George, which was founded by Emperor Friedrich III to defend Christianity against the Turks. Note the 1,000-year-old **Gerichtslinde**, a lime tree which the court used to convene around in the Middle Ages.

Kreuzgang★

Enter from the east side of the courtyard.
○Open year-round daily 24hrs. &.
The peaceful 12C cloister is a superb example of Romanesque architecture despite the addition of Gothic vaulting in the 15C. Its arches are held aloft by slender pillars whose capitals are decorated with animals, plants, gargoyles and faces.

Stiftskirche

The abbey church retains elements from the Romanesque period including the magnificent **door★★** in the west porch and its tympanum showing Abbot Heinrich II (1166–77) paying homage to Christ. The **high altar★** (1648) features gilded columns and larger-than-life-size statues of St. Domitian *(left)* and Margrave Leopold III *(right)*. Though faded, the most noteworthy **fresco** adorning the church is Urban Görtschacher's *Last Judgement* (1515) on the south wall *(at the far end of the aisle)*. Two side chapels contain the red-marble tombs of various grand masters.

EXCURSION
Turracherhöhe

40km/25mi northeast of Millstatt.
Located on the border between Styria and Carinthia, this small mountain resort surrounds the Turracher See lake; it offers watersports in summer and in winter a ski area ranging from 1,400m to 2,240 m (4,594ft to 7,350ft).

Between Predlitz and Turracherhöhe, the road threads forests and pastures. It runs through Turrach, once an important mining and metallurgy centre. In 1863 the first Bessemer converter (for transforming iron into steel) installed in Western Europe began operation here. Fierce International competition meant the village industry was only to last another 46 years, and the final furnace was extinguished in 1909.

More prosperous times are reflected in the handsome administration building near the church.

Gmünd★

(Carinthia)

A 30km/18.6mi stretch of road leads through this magnificent valley, one of the most beautiful destinations in Carinthia. The area became famous in the 1970s after the construction of the Kölnbrein dam and reservoir, but its main appeal lies in its diverse landscape. Until the village of Malta, the valley is wide and characterised by alternating meadows and forested patches. Beyond here it narrows, then opens up again to reveal the glacial panorama of the Ankogel massif and the Hochalmspitze peak. The area is also a good launch pad for medium- and high-altitude Alpine hikes.

🔲 **Info:** Malta 13, 9854 Gmünd. ℘04733 220 15. www.stadtgmuend.at, http://maltatal.com.

▷ **Location:** The valley extends from Gmünd to the foothills of the Hohe Tauern National Park in southern Austria.

👁 **Don't Miss:** Driving the Malta-Hochalmstraße.

🕐 **Timing:** Allow at least two days to include excursions.

🚗 DRIVING TOUR

MALTATAL★★
30km/18.5mi. From Gmünd to the damn at Kölnbrein.

Gmünd in Kärnten
Set in the Maltatal Valley, Gmünd was founded in the 11C by the archbishops of Salzburg to control commercial traffic through the Lieser Valley, a stretch along the busy Nuremberg-Venice trade route. The compact town centre preserves much of its medieval character and is still encircled by fortified walls★ entered via two imposing gateways. These days Gmünd is home to a thriving artists' community; you'll find its cobbled streets lined with numerous galleries and studios; artistic events are frequently held around the town.

An earthquake in 1690 and a fire in 1886 reduced Gmünd's fortress, the **Alte Burg** to a remnant of its medieval self, but recent efforts have restored it into a dynamic cultural centre hosting art exhibits, seminars, concerts and theatre performances (🕐 *open Jul–Aug daily; Apr–Jun, Sept–Oct Tue–Sun from 11.30am, Jul–Aug daily, Nov–Dec Fri–Sun only; ℘04732 36 39; www.alteburg.at).* There are also an excellent café

and restaurant and good views from the keep. Gmünd's handsome **Hauptplatz** (main square) is bookended by fortified gateways and lined by elegant townhouses painted in pastel shades. Near the upper gateway, the 17C **Lodron'sche Schloss**, now a school and public library, opens onto a pretty garden, its entrance flanked by the statues of two massive lions that originally graced the Mirabellgarten in Salzburg. Off the square's northern end, the old prison *(Kirchgasse 48)* contains the **Eva Faschauner Heimatmuseum** (℘*04732 28 80 ; www.malta.gv.at),* a curious exhibit about a local woman accused of poisoning her farmer husband with arsenic just a week after their wedding in 1770. After three years of imprisonment and horrific torture, she finally confessed and was executed shortly thereafter (she was the last person from Gmünd to be sent to the gallows).

The Late Gothic church **Pfarrkirche Maria Himmelfahrt** was consecrated in 1339 and enlarged and redecorated in Baroque style in the 18C. Life-size figures of the Apostles flank the fine altar, and there are numerous interesting tombstones as well.

Porsche-Automuseum Helmut Pfeifhofer
🕐*Open 15 May–15 Oct daily 9am–6pm; 16 Oct–14 May daily 10am–4pm.* ✎€8. ℘*04732 24 71. www.auto-museum.at.*

From 1944 through 1950 Gmünd was the sphere of activity of world-famous engineer **Ferdinand Porsche** (1875–1998). The very first Porsche, the legendary 356, was manufactured here in the late 1940s. Several of the cars are on display at this, Europe's only private Porsche museum, alongside prototypes of military and sports vehicles, actual-size wooden models of the first Porsche car bodies and more than 400 model cars.

▶ Drive N on the road next to the Malta river. for 7km/4.5mi.

Malta

The village at 840m/2,755ft above sea-level is an entrancing holiday spot. The **church of Maria Hilf**, which dates from the 15C, houses some fine frescoes from the same period, including a rare image of Mary in labour *(south wall)*. The Baroque décor is beautifully uniform. The high altar and pulpit date from 1730.

Malta-Hochalmstraße★★

Toll charged May–late Oct. €18.50 *per car past Malta.*

This splendid alpine byway meanders over nine bridges and through seven tunnels, including a memorable hairpin bend tunnel. Along the way the route passes luxuriant vegetation (spruce, larch, alder and birch) and no fewer than 30 waterfalls, roaring down into the valley. The Fallbach, the Melnikfall and the Hinterer Maralmfall are particularly impressive.

Kölnbreinsperre★

In high season (May–Oct), there are guided tours of the dam daily 10am–5pm on the hr (€6).

The road ends at the dam at an altitude of 1,900m/6,233ft above sea-level. It is the largest dam in Austria measuring 200m/656ft high, 41m/134ft thick at its base and 626m/2,054ft wide. Apart from the phenomenal technical prowess of its design, the aesthetic of this concrete colossus with its flowing, parabolic shape, is just as impressive.

Inside the look-out tower, an **information centre** (*open May–Oct daily 9am–5pm; free; 04733 296; www.nationalpark-hohetauern.at*) has short films about the Hohe Tauern National Park and a multimedia display on the dam's construction. Also here is the **Tauernschatzkammer★**, a treasure trove of local rock crystals and other minerals.

The dam is the point of departure for some rewarding walks. Even the easy hike around the lake provides fine views over the surrounding **alpine landscape★★**. However, if you can muster up the time and stamina, you really should tackle the following Arlscharte hike.

Waterfall in Maltatal, Nationalpark Hohe Tauern

© Austrian National Tourist Office/ Jezierzanski

Kölnbreinsperre

© Austrian National Tourist Office/ Homberger

EXCURSIONS
🚶 Hike to the Arlscharte and the Arlhöhe★

3hr45min round trip from the dam. Head towards the Osnabrücker Hütte mountain lodge.

The trail skirts the northern lakeshore and soon accesses a magnificent view over the Ankogel glaciers. After walking for 45min, you will reach a memorial to a tragic accident that occurred during the building of the dam. Turn right and continue along a relatively steep Alpine flower trail. After 10min, when the trail forks, head left for the steep 45min climb to the peak *(🔎 look for the red and white markings)*. At the top, your efforts will be rewarded with magnificent views over lakes, valleys, a small glacier and the towering Hochalmspitze peak.

For another set of impressive views, continue to the Arlhöhe *(alt. 2,326m/ 7,631ft)*. Walk a few steps towards Pfringersee, then turn left and pick up a kind of ridge trail *(marked with a red cross on a white background)* taking you to your destination in about 20min. An orientation map helps identify mountains and other natural landmarks.

Retrace your steps and return along the same trail.

🚶 Gösskarspeicher★

1hr drive and 45min walk. Halfway between Malta and the toll point, turn left towards the Giessener Hütte mountain lodge.

This narrow, 12km/7.4mi mountain road is quite steep and follows the course of the Gössbach, even fording the river bed at one point *(⚠ dangerous, especially during bad weather; watch out for flood warnings)*. The countryside is rugged and unspoiled.

Park your car and continue on foot to the Gösskar reservoir *(15min ascent)*. This is a beautiful **wooded area★**, dominated by the Grosser Gössspitze and the Dösnerspitze peaks.

Walk along the left shore of the lake for fantastic **views★** over the Hochalmspitze peak and its glacier, from which waterfalls thunder down. Return to the reservoir, continue to its end and then to the right along the meadow (through a fence) until you reach a wide, moderately steep trail for a **view★** over the rocky peaks of the Riekenkopf and the Pfaffenberger Nocken. Return to the car park or, if you're feeling ambitious, climb up to the Giessen Hütte mountain lodge *(1hr30min)*, the starting point for the climb to the Hochalm peak.

Nockalmstraße

From Gmünd take the 99 N for around 10km/6.2mi to Kremsbrücke then the minor road right (E) for another 10km/6.2mi, via Krems to Innerkrems. ⏱*Open May–Oct.* ⊜⊛€*17.50 per car (includes admission to all parking, facilities and attractions).* ✆*04736 265.* *www.nockalmstrasse.at.*

This glorious alpine road (35km/21.7mi) leads from Innerkrems south to Ebene Reichenau, crossing over the Nochberg mountains and tracing long stretches of unspoiled mountain scenery. While there are no communities en route, the route leads past several isolated mountain inns offering food and amenities. There are also several small museums and visitor attractions concentrating on subjects such as mining, forestry, alpine farming, and even marmots.

Nationalpark Nockberge

The Nockalmstraße was completed as part of a plan to develop the surrounding region as a ski resort area. However, protests from the citizens of Carinthia forced a referendum in which 94 per cent rejected the planned proposals. On 1 January 1987 the area was given National Park status. The park encompasses the gently rounded "nocken" mountains, unusual in the Alps, and a rare geological entity.

Nationalpark Nockberge

© Austrian National Tourist Office/ Popp Hackner

🚶 The area is popular with hikers, and several hikes depart from inns and rest stops along the Nockalmstraße. For the energetic, there is an organised 3hr circuit hike, the **Grünleitennock Circuit** 👥, from Parkplatz Pfandlalm to Grünleitennock to Friesenhalssee to Zechneralm to Pfandlalm. *See www.nockalmstrasse.at for more information.* Older children will enjoy the circuit for the numerous marmots at the Realm of the Marmot exhibition along the way, though 3hr may be a bit too challenging for them.

ADDRESSES

🛏 STAY AND 🍴 EAT

⊜🍽 **Gasthof Hochalmspitze** – *Malta 57, 9854 Malta.* ✆*0473 32 11.* *www.gasthofhochalmspitze.com. 22 rooms.* ⌷. This English-owned, family-run hotel in a traditional old house boasts beautiful views. Enjoy Austrian specialities on the terrace. Half-board plan available.

⊜⊜🍽 **Berghotel Malta** –*Brandstatt 36, 9854 Malta (Kölnbrein-Staumauer).* ✆*50313 39 130 . www.berghotelmalta.at. Closed Nov–Apr. 39 rooms.* ⌷. High in the mountains at 1,900m/6,233ft, this smart, contemporary hotel has comfortable rooms with superb views over the Kölnbreinspeicher Reservoir.

⊜⊜🍽 **Hotel Malteinerhof** – *Malta 39, 9854 Malta.* ✆*04733 206.* *www.malteinerhof.at. 22 rooms.* ⌷. This 50-year-old hotel offers bright modern-traditional rooms (some with balconies) and dining on a sunny terrace in summer. Excellent restaurant and full programme of outdoor activities.

GALLERIES

Galerie Gmünd – *Hintere Gasse 34, 9853 Gmünd. Daily May–Sept.* Showcases the work of young Austrian artists.

Galerie Miklautz – *Hintere Gasse 32, 9853 Gmünd.* ✆*0664 201 12 55. www.miklautz.at.* Set in an ancient house this gallery specialises in antiques and works of art going back three centuries. Special exhibitions staged.

Murau

Murau is a delightful town on the
Mur River, set deep into the upper
Mur Valley amid forested hillsides
and Alpine meadows. Its historic
centre has an altogether southern
charm, with its warren of narrow
streets lined by handsome merchant
houses painted in a rainbow of
pastel colours.

SIGHTS
Stadtpfarrkirche
St. Matthäus★

The Gothic character of the parish
church, with its majestic nave and splendid decorations, was not destroyed by
17C Baroque alterations. There are beautiful **frescoes** from the 14C to the 16C,
including one showing St. Anthony and
his pig, an *Entombment of Christ* and an
Annunciation. The north transept was
decorated in the late 16C with numerous
small paintings representing epitaphs
of members of the local Liechtenstein
ruling family. The magnificent **Baroque
high altar★** was wrought by local artists and centres on a Gothic Crucifixion
(1500); the sky-blue tabernacle is com-
plemented by wood and gilt work.

▶ **Population:** 3,700.

Info: Liechtensteinstraße 3-5.
📞03532 27 20.
www.murau-kreischberg.at.

◐ **Location:** Murau is in
southwestern Styria,
about 80km/50mi north
of Klagenfurt. Alt. 829m/
2,720ft.

🅿 **Parking:** Look for car parks
along Friesacherstraße,
Bahnhofstraße and the B 97.

⊘ **Don't Miss:** Stadtpfarrkirche
St. Matthäus.

◕ **Timing:** The castle and
church will take around
two hours, the train trip
will take five hours.

♣♦ **Kids:** Murtalbahn
steam train.

Schloss Murau
*Access via the wooden stairway north
of the church.* Guided tours (1hr)
Jun–Sept Wed, Fri 2pm. €6.
📞03532 23 02 58.
All that remains of the original castle,
commissioned in 1232 by Ulrich von

Murau

© Austrian National Tourist Office/Wiesenhofer

Liechtenstein in a commanding spot above the Mur River, are the cellars and a well, 48m/157ft deep.

The present 17C Renaissance-era palace was built by Count Georg-Ludwig von Schwarzenberg. Tours start in the inner courtyard and take in the chapel. The Knight's Hall and other rooms.

EXCURSIONS
🚶👥 Murtalbahn

74km/46mi round trip – about 5hr.
🕐*Mid-Jun–mid-Sept Tue and Thu; call or see website for times.* ⊗*€19.30 round trip.* ✆*03532 22 33, www.stlb.at.*

This privately-run steam train chugs through attractive scenery between Murau and Tamsweg. The stations in both villages rent bicycles, which may be taken on the train free of charge.

St. Lambrecht Monastery

Hauptstraße 1, St. Lambrecht.
15km/9.3mi southeast of Murau.
🗨*Guided tour 1hr 30min (short tour: Peterskirche and Vogelmuseum only, 45min) mid-May–mid-Oct Mon–Sat 10.45am, 2.30pm; Sun after service and 2.30pm; rest of the year Tue & Sat 10:45am.* ⊗*€8, short tour €6.* ✆*03585 23 05 29. www.stift-stlambrecht.at.*

The history of the Benedictine abbey of St. Lambrecht dates back to the 11C, although little remains of the original Romanesque abbey church, which was replaced by the current High Gothic triple-nave hall church in the 14C. The main buildings seen today were built in 1640, based on plans by Domenico Sciassia. Dissolved by Joseph II in 1786, the abbey was re-established by Franz II in 1802.

As you enter the abbey courtyard, the impressive west façade extends for 135m/443ft on your right, while on your left is a bastion adorned with statues by Johann Matthias Leitner in 1746. An open staircase leads up to the Gothic **Peterskirche**, which features a winged altar with a Crucifixion scene and works by the Master of Lambrecht.

Stiftskirche – An elaborate marble doorway opens into the narthex, which houses a 14C Lettner crucifix in a Baroque framework. Medieval frescoes embellish the vaulted ceiling above the chancel and the walls of the nave. The star of the show, though, is the enormous 1632 **high altar**★ by Valentin Khautt, which centres on a painting of the *Assumption*. The decoration of the altar to St. Emmeram in front on the right, the statues of the church Elders on the organ gallery, and the Madonna in the narthex are all works of the famous sculptor Michael Hönell.

The **Stiftsmuseum** gives an overview of the 900-year history of the abbey and an insight into the cloistered life of the Benedictines during that same period. Of special interest is the 250-figure Baroque crib which is set up in the abbey church from 21 Dec–2 Feb. There is also an ancillary **Vogelmuseum** with a collection of over 600 birds.

Oberwölz

27km/16.5mi northeast of Murau.
Take the B96 to Niederwölz, then head towards Oberwölz.

Crowned by the 12C castle of Schloss Rothenfels, and already inhabited at the time of the Hallstatt civilisation, Oberwölz achieved city status in 1300. It owed its early wealth to the salt trade and banking. Parts of its original city wall include three towers and the city gates. Housed in a 14C building, the **Österreichische Blasmusik-Museum** (🕐*open May–Oct daily 10am–noon, 2pm–5pm;* ⊗*€4.50;* ✆*03581 73 66; www.blasmusikmuseum.istsuper.com*) features a collection of wind instruments.

The chapel of **Spitalkirche zum Heiligen Sigismund**★ was founded in the 14C century to serve the old hospital. Beneath is an enormous vaulted hall once used by patients.

Friesach★

Carinthia's oldest town retains the look and feel of a medieval city, thanks to its three ruined castles, six churches and well-preserved fortifications. It belonged to the archbishopric of Salzburg from 960 to 1803 and was a key staging point along the Vienna-Venice trade route.

SIGHTS

Town fortifications

The 820m/896.7yd-long fortifications, protected by the only water-filled city-moat in the German-speaking world, encircle Friesach centre. Three of the original 11 towers remain intact.

Stadtbrunnen★

This Renaissance fountain stands at the heart of the Hauptplatz, surrounded by beautiful old houses. Reliefs with scenes from ancient Greek mythology adorn the basin, which is crowned by a small bronze group depicting Poseidon.

Dominikanerkloster & Kirche

Friesach monastery, dating from 1217, was the first foundation of the Dominican Order in a German-speaking country. Its three-nave church is the largest in Carinthia and quite simple in keeping with the rules of the Mendicant order. There is a splendid winged altar and two precious Early Gothic treasures: a sandstone Madonna and a huge wooden crucifix.

Deutschordenkirche St. Blasius

Established since 1203 at Friesach, the Teutonic Order built this shrine to St. Blasius on the foundations of the original 12C building, from which the frescoes decorating the west bay of the choir date. Note also its wooden sculptures and the magnificent high altar of 1515, The aisle is laid with the tombstones of Knights of the Order, many of these being from Bad Mergentheim, seat of the Teutonic Order until 1809. In the summer, for one week, Friesach

▶ **Population:** 5,010.
Info: Fürstenhofplatz 1, 9360. ℘04268 22 13 40. www.friesach.at.
◖ **Location:** Friesach is some 40km/25mi north of Klagenfurt near the border with Styria on the Metnitz River. Alt. 637m/2,090ft.
Don't Miss: The town fortifications, Erlebnis Burgbau.
◔ **Timing:** Budget two or three hours.
Kids: Spectaculum im Friesach.

turns the clock back to medieval times during the **Spectaculum im Friesach**, an open-air theatre festival. The church cloister is one of the venues, as is the Petersberg Burg courtyard (below).

Petersberg Burg

This small hilltop **church** in the northern part of the old town (10min walk from the Hauptplatz) offers the best town view. Nearby, the 12C keep is all that remains of Petersberg castle, the former residence of the Salzburg archbishops. A climb of 127 steps leads up to the **Stadtmuseum** (◔open mid-May–Sept Wed–Sun 11am–5pm; ⊜€3.50; ℘04268 22 13 40), which relates the history of Friesach.

Erlebnis Burgbau

Visit by guided tour only early Apr–Oct daily 9.30am, 11am, 1.30pm, 3pm, 4.30pm (Oct Mon–Fri 11am and 3pm only); in English by appointment. ⊜€11, children 6-14 years €4.50, 5 and under free. ℘04268 22 13 18. www.burgbau.at.

On a 6.5ha construction site minutes from the town centre, blacksmiths, carpenters, stonemasons and basket weavers, among others, are erecting a medieval castle using period tools, materials and methods. Guided tours visit the keep, the residential quarters, the bailey and the walls as well as other areas of the noble fortification.

Gurker Dom★★

Gurk is a small village that would be fairly unremarkable were it not for its famous cathedral, which ranks as Austria's most important Romanesque building. A convent was founded here in 1043 by Countess Hemma of Friesach-Zeltschach. However, it was dissolved less than three decades later by Archbishop Gebhard of Salzburg, who instead established a new diocese in an effort to consolidate his power in the region. The Augustinian Canons remained in this secluded valley until 1787, when the diocese was transferred to the more prominent city of Klagenfurt. Since 1932, the convent has been run by Salvatorians.

VISIT
Cathedral (Dom)

◔Open Mar–Oct daily 10am–5pm; Nov–Feb daily 10am–4pm. ☞Guided tours (45min) of cathedral and crypt 10am–4pm. ☞€5. ☎04266 82 36 12. www.dom-zu-gurk.at.

This High Romanesque cathedral was built between 1140 and 1200 under Prince-Bishop Roman I, councillor to Frederick Barbarossa. Baroque twin-bay windows and onion domes were added to both towers in 1680.

The exterior wall of the front **porch** dates from the Gothic period, but inside there is some stained glass from 1340 along with **frescoes**★ depicting scenes from the Old Testament *(on the left)* and from the New Testament *(on the right)*. A Romanesque **door**★★ (c. 1200) with richly decorated pillars, arches and capitals leads into the main nave.

Interior

It is immediately evident upon entering that many styles have contributed to this building: the Romanesque triple-nave pillared basilica is surmounted by Gothic net vaulting, the frescoes are from the Gothic and Renaissance periods, while the furnishings are predominantly Baroque.

Info: Dom: ☎04266 82 36 12. www.dom-zu-gurk.at. Tourist office: Dr.-Schnerich-Straβe 12, A-9342. ☎04266 81 25 27. www.gurk.at

Location: Gurk is about 42km/26mi north of Klagenfurt in southern Austria.

Don't Miss: The Cathedral's rare Fastentuch (Lenten veil).

Timing: Allow 1hr for the main tour, a further half hour for the Bishop's Chapel.

(**1**) Jewel-encrusted Hemma reliquary in the form of a tree containing a ring and a pendant thought to have belonged to the saint (1955).

(**2**) Samson doorway: The **tympanum**★ shows Samson slaying the lion (1200).

(**3**) and *(8)*: **Carved panels**★ (16C) vividly depicting scenes from the life of St. Hemma, commissioned before 1508.

(**4**) A gigantic **mural of St. Christopher** (1250). The doorway to the left with its richly decorated ogee arch was built in 1445.

(**5**) **High Altar**★★, a gilded masterpiece by Michael Hönel filling the entire apse. Covered in gold, it features full-size, strikingly realistic figures (72 statues,

Gurker Dom

© F. Waldhäusl/age fotostock

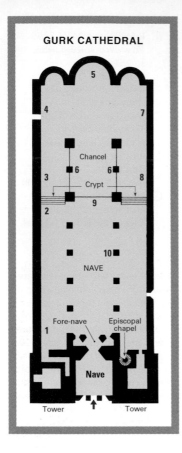

GURK CATHEDRAL

Chancel

Crypt

NAVE

Fore-nave

Episcopal chapel

Nave

Tower

Tower

(7) Gothic murals: uncovered at the beginning of the 20C, these illustrate the conversion of St. Paul, and Christ enthroned as Judge of the World, surrounded by the Twenty Four Elders of the Apocalypse as narrated by St. John the Divine. The donors can be seen at the foot of Christ's throne with their nine children (c. 1390).

(8) ♿See (3).

(9) Altar of the Holy Cross (1741), with a **Pietà★** cast in lead by Georg Raphael Donner, his last work.

(10) Baroque pulpit★ (1740), an accomplished work by Viennese set designers Giuseppe and Antonio Galli Bibiena. The iconography is fully in keeping with the ideas of the Counter Reformation, taking as its subject the triumph of the Church.

Bathed in sombre light, the masterful Romanesque **crypt★★** (1174) is supported by a "forest" of 100 marble pillars. Since 1174 it has sheltered the stone sarcophagus of Hemma, patron saint of Carinthia, who founded a convent in Gurk and was canonised in 1938. The present tomb is a red-marble extravaganza from the 1720s. It rests on three Romanesque support pillars with marble heads.

Bishop's Chapel

🕐*Open daily 9am–dusk.* 👣*Visit by guided tour (20min) only daily 11:50am and 3:20pm;* ✆*€3.70.*
📞*04266 82 36 12.*

The upstairs chapel has some exceptionally well-preserved Romanesque **murals★★** (c. 1260), whose vivid colours have not been touched up. They depict numerous Biblical scenes and characters, including Paradise, Heavenly Jerusalem, the Virgin Mary on King Solomon's throne and the Evangelists. The stained-glass window on the west wall is contemporary with the frescoes and depicts the Descent from the Cross. This is Austria's earliest stained glass in the angular style.

82 angels' heads) and the four Evangelists at pedestal level with the Church Fathers above them. Created between 1626 and 1632, its central theme is the Assumption of the Virgin.

During Lent the altar is shrouded by a **Fastentuch★** (Lenten veil, 1458), a custom that was abolished almost everywhere in the late Middle Ages. The exquisite veil is 9sq m/96.8sq ft in area and is painted with 99 Biblical scenes. (👣*The Lenten veil can be seen as part of a 20min guided tour: enquire about exact times;* ✆*€2.90, free during Lent;* 📞*04266 82 36 12).*

(6) Choir stalls: These richly and decoratively carved stalls are the work of local craftsmen. Each seat is decorated with charming painted floral motifs (1680).

St. Veit an der Glan

St. Veit was the seat of the dukes of Carinthia until 1518 when the role of regional capital passed to Klagenfurt. The well-preserved town wall, the picturesque narrow streets, the two town squares with their handsome houses and arcaded courtyards all contribute to the town's charm.

SIGHTS
Hauptplatz★

Most places of interest in St. Veit are on or near the central square, which is at the heart of a mostly pedestrianised web of lanes. The **Schüsselbrunnen** is a fountain surmounted by a bronze figure in a 16C miner's costume that has become the town mascot. The square's other fountain honours Walther von der Vogelweide, the most famous of the German troubadours who once worked at the court of St. Veit. Take a look inside the **Stadtpfarrkirche**, notable for its Late Baroque high altar and chancel, both by local master woodcarver Johann Pacher.

Rathaus★

The elegant town hall was built during the Late Gothic period but did not get its grand pillastered **stucco façade★** until 1754, the work of Joseph Pittner. On the pediment is the double-headed eagle of the Holy Roman Empire, embossed with the statue of the city's namesake Saint Veit. A vaulted Gothic passageway leads to the sgraffito-decorated **Renaissance courtyard★**, one of the finest in Carinthia. The great hall on the first floor, the **Rathaussaal★** (☉*visits on request; Mon–Fri 8am–noon, 1pm–4pm;* ⅃; ✆*04212 45 608)* is decorated with lacy stuccowork.

👪 Verkehrsmuseum

Hauptplatz 29. ☉*Open Jul–Aug daily 9am–6pm; Apr–Oct Thu–Mon 9am–noon and 2pm–6pm.* ☞*€7, children €3.50.* ✆*04212c55 55 64. www.museum-stveit.at.*

Transport and communication are the main themes of this small but modern museum where you can admire a huge model railway with 200m/219yd of tracks or fancy yourself as a railway engineer thanks to a clever simulator. The century-old post office re-creation provides a window on the past.

Kunsthotel Fuchspalast

Professor-Ernst-Fuchs-Platz 1. ✆*04212 466 00. www.hotel-fuchspalast.at.*

If you only remember one thing about St. Veit it will be this one-of-a-kind art hotel, a whimsical composition by painter Ernst Fuchs. With its patterned red, white and blue façade and fantastical interior, themed around the Zodiac, it blithely defies conventions.

EXCURSIONS
Burg Frauenstein★

5km/3mi northeast then a 30min walk there and back. Leave St. Veit on the Obermühlbach road; around 1,500m/1,640yd after this village, take the second road on the right.

This 16C castle is a picture-postcard scene with its massive towers, turrets and roofs, all at different heights. Inside the walls is an arcaded courtyard.

- ▶ **Population:** 12,500.
- **Info:** Hauptplatz 23, 9300. ✆04212 45 608. www.sv.or.at.
- ▶ **Location:** St. Veit is in southern Austria, about 19km/12mi north of Klagenfurt. Alt. 476m/ 1,562ft.
- **Don't Miss:** The Fuchs Palast hotel.
- ⊙ **Timing:** The town warrants about a half-day visit.
- 👪 **Kids:** Transport Museum.

🚗 DRIVING TOUR

ST. VEIT
38km/23.5mi.

▶ Head southeast out of St. Veit on the old Klagenfurt road. After St-Michael am Zoldeld, bear left around the base of Magdalensberg. After 7km/4.3mi, turn left uphill onto the flank of the Magdalensberg.

Magdalensberg★
🕐*Open May–Oct Tue–Sun 9am–5pm.* ✆*€6.* ♿ ✆*0664 62 02 662.* *www.landesmuseum.ktn.gov.at.*

The road ends at the **Archaeological Park Magdalensberg**, an open-air museum of the excavated traces of an early Roman town, built on the remains of an older Celtic settlement.

Walk *(45min round trip)* to the top of the mountain *(alt. 1,058m/3,470ft)* for a **panorama★** and to visit the Gothic pilgrims' chapel dedicated to St. Helen and St. Mary Magdalene. It houses a panelled 15C altarpiece from the wood-carving workshops at St. Veit.

▶ Make a U-turn and at St. Donat, turn right onto Hochosterwitz Straße which leads to the castle. Park below it.

Burg Hochosterwitz★
🕐*Open late Mar–Oct daily 9am–6pm; Mar–Apr and mid-Sept–Oct daily 10am–5pm.* ✆*€12.* ♿ ✆*04213 34 597. www.burg-hochosterwitz.com.*

This medieval stronghold and castle occupy a dramatic **site★★** on a rounded limestone rock rising 150m/492ft above the countryside. Its towers and turrets can easily be spotted from several miles away.

First documented in 860, the castle remained in the hands of the lords of Osterwitz until

Burg Hochosterwitz

© Austrian National Tourist Office/Diejun

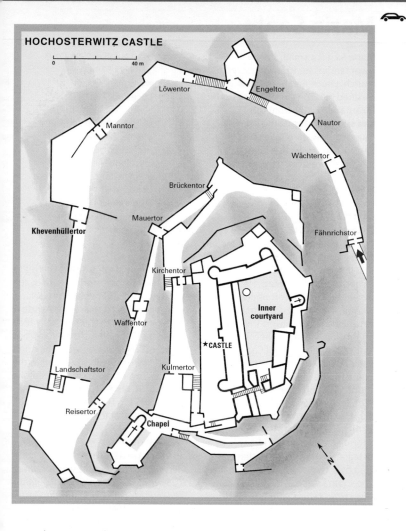

HOCHOSTERWITZ CASTLE

0 40 m

Löwentor
Engeltor
Nautor
Manntor
Wächtertor
Brückentor
Mauertor
Fähnrichstor
Khevenhüllertor
Kirchentor
Inner courtyard
Waffentor
★CASTLE
Landschaftstor
Kulmertor
Reisertor
Chapel
N

1475, then reverted to the emperor and in 1571 was bought by Georg von Khevenhüller, an imperial counsellor and chief stablemaster. He greatly expanded and fortified the castle to defend it against Turkish invasion, adding the 14 gateways and an arsenal. His descendants still own it today.

From the car park, a ramp passing through all 14 gates leads up to the castle (30min), with lovely views along the way. A faster but less scenic way to reach the castle is via a lift (€6 round-trip) carved straight through the rock. The grandest of the gates is the seventh, known as the **Khevenhüllertor**

(1582), surmounted by a lion's head, the family coat of arms, and a bust of Georg Khevenhüller dressed as a military leader. The ramp passes the **Burg-kapelle** (castle chapel) and accesses the **Innere Burghof** (inner courtyard) with a restaurant. Some rooms in the castle have historical exhibits about the Khevenhüller family, family portraits and a fine collection of arms and armour.

◗ On the way back to St. Veit, stop at Launsdorf to see the Gothic choir in the church, and the ancient Benedictine abbey at St. Georgen am Längsee.

333

Maria Saal★

Maria Saal is a small, sleepy town famous for its monastery church, which perches atop a fortified hill. The current Late Gothic incarnation dates from the 15C and stands on top of the original, founded by Bishop Modestus of Salzburg in the 8C as a launch pad for the re-Christianisation of Carinthia following the Barbarian invasions.

SIGHTS
Dom★★

The first church on this site was erected by the monk, Modestus, who was sent as a missionary to pagan Carinthia by Bishop Virgil of Salzburg. He chose as his base the hillock around which the village Maria Saal soon grew. From here he began to convert the local Slav population; Maria Saal became known as the Christian Cradle of Carinthia, and subsequently an important place of pilgrimage. The present church replaced the original and dates from 1460.

With its twin towers of volcanic stone and its vast stone roof, the church makes a striking impression. It is protected by a fortified enclosure and fronted by an octagonal **charnel house** that is encircled by a two-storey arcaded gallery. The south façade incorporates numerous stone reliefs and **tombstones**, including several salvaged from the nearby ruined Roman settlement of Virunum.

Highlights include a relief showing Achilles dragging the corpse of Hector, and another depicting what is thought to be a **Roman post coach★**, a symbol for the journey of a dead soul into the afterlife. The magnificent **Keutschacher Epitaph★** (c. 1510), a red marble tombstone, depicts the Coronation of the Virgin. In the porch another interesting Roman gravestone features a she-wolf feeding Romulus and Remus.

The triple-nave **interior** is typical Late Gothic. The bays of the ribbed vaulting above the nave are decorated with frescoes depicting the Life of Christ.

▶ **Population:** 3,832.

Info: Am Platzl 7, A-9063. ☏04223 51 145. www.mariasaal.at.

▶ **Location:** Maria Saal is about 7km/4.3mi north of Klagenfurt in southern Austria. Alt. 504m/1,654ft.

P Parking: Look for public lots along Hauptstraße and Arnsdorfer Straße near the open-air museum.

Don't Miss: The Dom.

Timing: Allow two or three hours.

The Baroque **high altar** is the place of honour for the stone figure of the Madonna (1425) venerated by pilgrims. Other altars of note are the **Arndorf Altar★** in the north chancel, which shows the Coronation of the Virgin Mary, and the Altar of St. George in the south chancel, which depicts the saint as the Dragon-Slayer. In the Saxon chapel is the **tomb of St. Modestus★** (left side aisle); a **fresco** of the Three Magi is found on the north wall of the chancel.

⚥ Kärntner Freilichtmuseum★

300m/328yd north of the village centre. *⏱Open May–Oct Sun–Fri 10am–4pm (Jul–Aug til 6pm, also Sat til 4pm); last admission 1hr before closing.* ☞€7, *children €3.* ☏04223 28 12. *www.freilichtmuseum-mariasaal.at.*

Some 33 historic farmhouses, stables, barns and other outbuildings offer insight into rural life in 16C and 17C Carinthia. All were taken down and reassembled at this open-air museum, set in a pleasant, hilly wooded setting. Most are log cabins and either thatched with straw or roofed with shingles. The living quarters have a smoking room with an oven and an open hearth.

A reconstructed covered wooden bridge leads to a mill area where mills illustrate both the difficult working conditions endured by the millers and the ingenuity of early mechanisation.

The heart of Austria's mountains is in the exceptionally beautiful region of Tirol (Tyrol). Surrounded by high peaks on all sides, the region's capital is the city of Innsbruck. A centre for both winter and summer mountain sports, it is understandably popular and now sprawls beyond its wonderful late medieval centre. While there is a great deal to see, the two highlights are undoubtedly Herzog Friedrichstraße, where you can find the loggia of the famous Goldenes Dachl (Golden Roof), and the Hofkirche, which houses the monument to Emperor Maximilian I, perhaps the most important Austrian work of Renaissance art.

A Bit of History

Outside Innsbruck, the eastern part of Tyrol is dominated by the mountains of the Karwendel, Kaisergebirge and Kitzbühel. In between the high, glaciated peaks are some wonderful Alpine valleys and beautiful mountain towns. To the north of Innsbruck is the salt-water spa at Hall in Tirol, and close by, the factory of the famous crystal manufacturers Swarovski. To the south of the province's capital is the large Schloss Ambras, in Wilten.

Kitzbühel is now a very popular ski resort with an important Gothic church, just like St. Johann in Tyrol close to the Kaisergebirge. One of the most scenic valleys in the Tyrol is the Zillertal. Mayerhofen in the upper Zillertal is a major centre for walkers and climbers, while from Zell am Ziller a road leads up to the high Gerlos Pass.

Beyond the Gerlos Pass where the Tyrol borders the neighbouring province of

Highlights

1 Hiking or skiing in the **Stubaital valley** (p345)

2 **Rattenberg**'s exquisite Renaissance town centre (p363)

3 Panoramic views on the **Gerlos Alpenstraße** driving tour (p377)

4 Dramatic cable-car and chairlift rides while hiking the **Kalser Tauernpass** (p380)

5 Taking the cure at **Bad Gastein** (p391)

Salzburg, three huge cascades form the Krimml Falls. To the north of the valley is the important Kaprun winter sports area. At the far end of the valley, the Gasteinertal leads to the spa towns of Bad Hofstein and Bad Gastein, whose visitors come to bathe in hot springs.

Schlegeis-Stausee, Zillertal

© Austrian National Tourist Office/ Mallaun

INNSBRUCK AND THE TYROL

The most spectacular sight, in between Krimml and Gastein, is the Großglockner Hochalpenstraße. This extraordinary mountain road winds up to a height of 2,577m/8,454ft from which there are wonderful views of Austria's highest mountain, Großglockner. South of the final pass is East Tirol, a separate part of

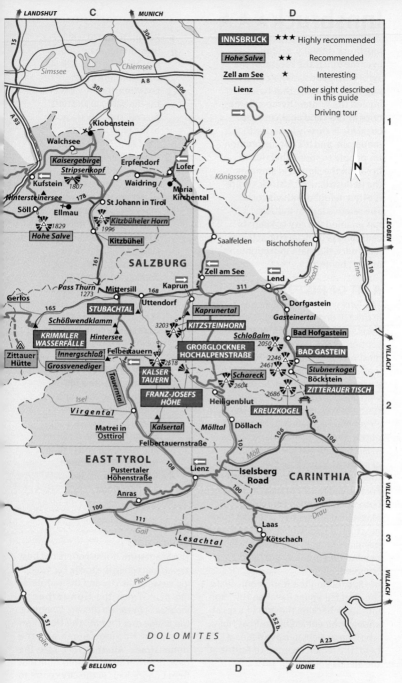

INNSBRUCK	★★★	Highly recommended
Hohe Salve	★★	Recommended
<u>Zell am See</u>	★	Interesting
Lienz		Other sight described in this guide
⇨ ⬭		Driving tour

N

Chiemsee

Simssee

Klobenstein

Walchsee

Kaisergebirge Stripsenkopf

Erpfendorf

⇦ Lofer

Königssee

Kufstein

1807

Waidring

Maria Kirchental

Hintersteinersee

Söll

Ellmau

St Johann in Tirol

1829

Kitzbüheler Horn

1996

Hohe Salve

Kitzbühel

Saalfelden

Bischofshofen

SALZBURG

⇨ Zell am See

⇦ Lend

Pass Thurn 1273

Mittersill

Kaprun

311

Dorfgastein

Gerlos

165

Uttendorf

168

Gasteinertal

STUBACHTAL

Kaprunertal

Schößwendklamm

3203

KITZSTEINHORN

Bad Hofgastein

KRIMMLER WASSERFÄLLE

Hintersee

Schloßalm

2050

BAD GASTEIN

Zittauer Hütte

Innergschlöß

Felbertauern

2246

2461

Grossvenediger

2618

Stubnerkogel

Böckstein

KALSER TAUERN

Schareck

2604

2686

ZITTERAUER TISCH

FRANZ-JOSEFS HÖHE

GROßGLOCKNER HOCHALPENSTRAßE

Virgental

Heiligenblut

KREUZKOGEL

Isel

Matrei in Osttirol

Kalsertal

Mölltal

Döllach

105

EAST TYROL

Felbertauernstraße

Iselsberg Road

CARINTHIA

Pustertaler Höhenstraße

⇦ Lienz

Anras

100

Drau

111

Laas

Gail

Lesachtal

Kötschach

110

Piave

DOLOMITES

A 23

the province of Tyrol. Its administrative centre is Lienz, which has been settled since the Bronze Age. Today, Lienz's well-preserved medieval buildings are the backdrop to a Christmas market during advent, while cafés spill out on to the pavements in summer.

Innsbruck★★★

Innsbruck (literally, Bridge over the Inn) is the capital of the Tyrol (Tirol) and a major cultural and tourism centre that twice hosted the Winter Olympic Games, once in 1964 and again in 1976. Local life is closely linked with the mountain, and it's not uncommon for people to spend their lunch break on the slopes. In summer, the pedestrianised historic centre is often deluged with visitors. The relative lack of industry has enabled the city to keep its charming provincial character, at least once the main thoroughfares are left behind.

A BIT OF HISTORY

The Tyrol came into existence as a state in the 12C under the jurisdiction of the counts of Tirol but passed into Habsburg control in 1363. Duke Friedrich IV made Innsbruck his residence in 1420, ushering in a long heyday that reached its pinnacle under **Maximilian I** (1459–1519), who positioned the city as a European centre of culture and politics. Through clever marriages, first to Maria of Burgundy, then to Bianca Maria Sforza of Milan, he managed to extend his sphere of influence to territories encompassing today's Belgium, Netherlands, northern France, and northern Italy. In 1508, he became Holy Roman Emperor.

Maximilian always had a special fondness for the Tyrol, whose silver and copper mines brought him wealth, while its rich hunting grounds provided entertainment.

In 1806, during the Napoleonic Wars, the Tirol fell under Bavarian rule, and Innsbruck became the hub of a resistance movement led by Andreas Hofer, who is now celebrated as a national folk hero. The region reverted to Austria at the Vienna Congress in 1815.

▶ **Population:** 130,900.

Info: Burggraben 3, 6021 Innsbruck. ☏ 0512 598 50. www.innsbruck.info.

Location: Innsbruck is in the Inn Valley in western Austria, about 30km north of the Brennerpass to Italy. Alt. 574m/1,883ft.

Ⓟ **Parking:** Inner city parking garages and car parks include: Congress Garage, Herrengasse/Rennweg *(daily 24hr)*; Europahaus, Bruneckerstraße *(daily 24hr)*; Landhausplatz Garage, Wilhelm-Greil-Straße *(daily 6am–1am)*; Sparkassen/Hörtnagl Garage, Sparkassenplatz *(daily 24hr)*; Altstadtgarage, Innrain *(daily 24hr)*; City Garage, Kaiserjägerstraße *(daily 24hr)*.

Don't Miss: Dom zu St. Jakob, Hofburg, Hofkirche.

Timing: Devote a full day to seeing the sights of Old Innsbruck, then spend half a day on a trip up the Hafelekar. Add another day if you plan to tour the Mittelgebirge.

Kids: Alpenzoo, Swarovski Kristallwelten.

SIGHTS
Viewpoints

The **Stadtturm** (tower) offers the best views from within the town. For sweeping views of the city and the surrounding peaks, visit the **Hungerburg★** *(accessible by car via the Alte Innbrücke, Old Bridge over the Inn)*, the Höttinger Gasse, the Hötting Church and the Höhenstraße. Alternatively, take the new, futuristically designed funicular from Congreshaus in the city centre to the Hungerburg. Travellers coming from the Brenner via the B 182 get another remarkable **view★★** of the city.

TOURIST INFORMATION

Innsbruck-Tourismus *Burggraben 3. 6021 Innsbruck.* ✆*0512 538 50. www.innsbruck.info.* Open daily 9am–6pm. Also sales and bookings office for tickets, Innsbruck Cards, room reservations, city tours, etc.

Tirol-Werbung: *Maria-Theresien-Str. 55, 6020 Innsbruck.* ✆*0512 532 00.* Open Mon–Fri 8am–6pm, Sat 9am–noon. A monthly events calendar is available from Innsbruck-Tourismus and Innsbruck-Information.

INNSBRUCK CARD: These special visitors' tickets are available from Innsbruck-Information for 24hr (€39), 48hr (€48) or 72hr (€55) and cover free travel on public transport, including round-trip cable-car rides on the Hungerburg-, Nordketten-, Oberfuss- and Patscherkofelbahn (a free guided city tour on foot) and free or discounted entry to numerous museums and sights. Call ✆*0512 53 56.*

CITY TOURS: Daily tours led by **Per Pedes Tirol** *(www.perpedes-tirol.at)* in English and German. Choose from the Imperial Tour, Classic Tour or a variety of special tours. ♿**Tours for wheelchair-users**. 👥 **Tours for children** available.

PUBLIC TRANSPORT

Buy tickets before boarding the bus; drivers sell only single tickets and charge extra. The 24hr pass allows unlimited trips within the city limits. 5-journey, weekly, and monthly tickets are also available.

Tickets are available from **Innsbruck-Information** *(Burggraben 3, ✆0512 53 560)* and Trafiken *(tobacconists)* with the appropriate sign. Further information can be found at www.ivb.at.

POST OFFICES

MAIN POST OFFICE: **Hauptpostamt**, *Innrain 15,* Mon–Fri 8am–6.30pm, Sat 9am–1pm.

STATION POST OFFICE: *Südtiroler Platz 10-12,* Mon–Fri 8am–6pm.

Innsbruck with Dom zu St. Jakob

© Austrian National Tourist Office/Popp Hackner

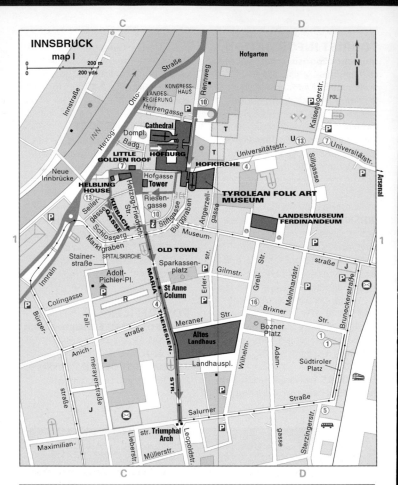

INNSBRUCK
map I

●●WALKING TOUR

Dom zu St. Jakob★ (Cathedral)

🕐 *Open May–Oct Mon–Sat 10.15am–7.30pm, Sun 12.30pm–7.30pm; Nov–Apr Mon–Sat 10.15am–6.30pm, Sun 12.30pm–6.30pm.* ♿ ℘*0512 58 39 02.*
There has been a church on this spot since 1180, but successive buildings were destroyed by fire or earthquake, and the cathedral did not receive its characteristically curving, two-towered façade and great dome until the early 18C.

The Baroque **interior★** was decorated in 1722 by the famous Asam brothers from Munich, Cosmas Damian (painter) and Egid Quirin (stucco artist). Their compositions, with their clever effects of perspective, glorify the Trinity and the intercessions of St. James.

The painting of *Our Lady of Succour* (Mariahilf), by Lucas Cranach the Elder, graces the **high altar★**. In the north transept is the canopied tomb of Archduke Maximilian III, a grand master of the Teutonic Order, who died in 1618. The **Friedensglockenspiel** (peace carillon) sounds daily *(12.15pm)* from the north tower.

◐ Walk along the left side of the cathedral. A covered alley on the left leads to Rennweg.

Hofgarten

This public park, with free-roaming parrots, was laid out in the 16C under Archduke Ferdinand II, and was one of the most ambitious gardens north of the Alps at the time. Given a Baroque character under Maria Theresia, it was landscaped as a less formal park in the early 19C.

◐ Return to the Rennweg and enter the Hofkirche (enter through the Tiroler Volkskunstmuseum to the left).

Hofkirche★★★

◔*Open Mon–Sat 9am–5pm, Sun and hols 12.30pm–5pm.* ◔*Closed public hols.* ▣€7. ♿. ☏0512 59 48 95 16. *www.hofkirche.at.*

This three-nave hall church is still largely Gothic, although the Renaissance style is already in evidence at the tower and the entrance porch, and there are Baroque embellishments as well. It was commissioned by Ferdinand I in the 1560s to house the mausoleum of his grandfather, Maximilian I, even though the emperor was actually buried in the castle chapel at Wiener Neustadt, his birthplace.

Grabmal Kaiser Maximilians I★★★ (Maximilian's Mausoleum)

Personally designed by the Emperor Maximilian I, this tomb is a premier example of German Renaissance sculpture. The lavish design centres on a cenotaph of the kneeling emperor atop a sarcophagus adorned with 24 alabaster reliefs showing scenes from his life, carved by Flemish sculptor, Alexandre Colin. Colin also created the four cardinal virtues positioned at the corners of the sarcophagus, which is surrounded by a splendid wrought-iron grille. Standing guard between the red marble pillars are 28 larger-than-life-size bronze statues (40 were planned) representing ancestors. Some were designed by such famous artists as Albrecht Dürer and Peter Vischer.

The Hofkirche also contains the tomb and memorial of **Andreas Hofer** (1767–1810), hero of the Tyrolean uprising against Napoleon. Look for it in the northern aisle.

The famous **Renaissance organ** in the choir is a work of Jörg Ebert of Ravensburg; it has been largely preserved in its original state.

Silberne Kapelle★★ (Silver Chapel)

This separate chapel, built by Archduke Ferdinand II so that he might rest beside Philippine Welser, his commoner wife, was finished in 1587. It owes its name to a large embossed silver Madonna. The first bay on the left contains the tomb of the duke's wife; it is one of the most accomplished works of Alexandre Colin, who also sculpted the funeral statue of Ferdinand, showing him in full armour. His actual armour is displayed separately on a console, in a kneeling position, facing the altar. A small 16C cedarwood organ, of Italian origin, completes the collection of works of art housed here.

Tiroler Volkskunstmuseum★★ (Folk Art Museum)

◔*Open year-round daily 10am–5pm.* ◔*Closed public hols.* ▣€11 (combined ticket with Hofkirche). ☏0512 59 48 95 16. *www.tiroler-volkskunstmuseum.at.*

Sharing the same address and sitting next to the Hofkirche, this museum comprehensively covers folk art from the entire Tirol, including South Tyrol in today's Italy. The ground floor has special exhibits and a fine collection of Nativity scenes.

Upstairs, displays include models of farmhouses, Gothic rooms and carnival

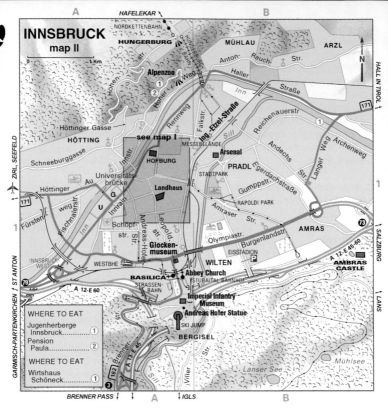

INNSBRUCK
map II

WHERE TO EAT
Jugenherberge
Innsbruck............... (1)
Pension
Paula...................... (2)

WHERE TO EAT
Wirtshaus
Schöneck............... (1)

masks and costumes. The top floor features Renaissance and Baroque period rooms, folkloric festival garments, and a valuable collection of religious folk art.

Riesensaal, Hofburg

© Austrian National Tourist Office/ Trumler

▷ Return to Hofgasse.

Hofburg★

🕒*Open year-round daily 9am–5pm (last entry 4.30pm).* ⌚€9. ♿ ☎*0512 58 71 86 19. www.hofburg-innsbruck.at.*
It's hard to imagine, but this glorious palace has its origins as a humble medieval castle, now well concealed due partly to Maximilian I but, more importantly, to Maria Theresia, who had the complex completely redesigned in the style of the Viennese Rococo in the late 18C.
The state rooms are devoted to the glories of the Tyrol and of the Habsburg monarchy, especially the **Riesensaal★★** (Giants' Hall), which is some 31.5m/103ft long and lined with stucco panels with a porcelain finish. The main theme of the ceiling fresco, by Franz-Anton Maulpertsch, is the triumph of the House of Habsburg-Lorraine. On the walls are full-length portraits of Maria Theresia's children following the Imperial couple in procession.

Stadtturm (Tower)

○ *Open Jun–Sept daily 10am–8pm; Oct–May daily 10am–5pm.* ◈€3. ℘ *0512 58 71 13.*

Rising along **Herzog-Friedrich-Straße**, this 51m/167ft-high Gothic tower was originally part of the old town hall of 1358. It's worth climbing the 148 steps to a platform for a **panorama★** and one of the best views of the Goldenes Dachl (Little Golden Roof).

Goldenes Dachl★
(Little Golden Roof)

The Golden Roof is Innsbruck's most famous symbol. Consisting of 2,738 gilded copper shingles, it tops a Late Gothic balconied oriel added to an existing building in 1500.

Commissioned by Maximlian I to mark his wedding to Bianca Maria Sforza, it was intended to show off his wealth and end rumours about financial woes. From the balcony, the imperial entourage observed festivals, tournaments, and other events taking place on the square below. The oriel itself is lavishly decorated.

The balustrade *(first floor)* is adorned with delicately carved coats of arms. Above, a band of reliefs includes images of the emperor *(middle)* and his two wives. All decorations are replicas, but the originals are in the Tiroler Landesmuseum Ferdinandeum (◖*see p344*).

Maximilianeum/
Museum Goldenes Dachl

○ *Open May–Sept daily 10am–5pm. Oct and Dec–Apr Tue–Sun 10am–5pm.* ◈€4.80. ℘ *0512 53 60 14 41. www.innsbruck.gv.at.*

You can stand in the spot from which the imperial couple used to observe the square's goings-on by visiting this small Maximilian memorial exhibit in the building behind the Goldenes Dachl. The 20min video about the emperor's life and times is worth watching, and an audio-guided tour *(in English)* provides additional insights.

Helblinghaus

M. Hertlein/MICHELIN

Helblinghaus★

Located opposite the Goldenes Dachl, the Helbling House has Gothic origins but acquired its ornate Rococo façade in the 18C.

▷ Turn left into Kiebachgasse.

Kiebachgasse★

This street is lined with ancient noble houses. The corner with Seilergasse used to be called *Vier Viecher Eck* (Four Beast Corner), referring to the four animal signs hanging from each corner of the building and referring to inns that once stood here.

▷ At the end of Kiebachgasse, turn left through the gate and right onto Maria-Theresien-Straße.

Maria-Theresien-Straße★

This lively square has an imposing **vista★★** of the Nordkette (2,334m/7,657ft). Situated along here are several attractive old houses with beautiful façades, most notably Palais Lodron at no. 7, Palais Trapp at no. 38, Palais Troyer at no. 39, and Palais Sarnthein at no. 57.

Maria-Theresien-Straße

© Austrian National Tourist Office/ Popp Hackner

Annasäule (St. Anne Column)

This monumental column (1706) commemorates the defeat of Bavaria on the Feast of St. Anne Day: 26 July 1703. The Virgin Mary perches atop the slender column, with St. Anne appearing only on the base beside St. George and the dragon.

Altes Landhaus

This palace at no. 43 is an excellent example of secular Baroque architecture. It was designed by Georg-Anton Gumpp, completed in 1728 and is now the seat of the provincial government.

Triumphpforte (Triumphal Arch)

This landmark triumphal arch was built to commemorate the marriage of Archduke Leopold to the Infanta of Spain, Maria Ludovica, in 1765. Since the wedding was overshadowed by the death of the duke's father, Emperor Franz I, the arch became a memorial to both the joys and the sorrows that year brought for the imperial court.

Among the features gracing the north side are medallions of Franz I and Maria Theresia, while imagery on the other side honours the newlyweds.

ADDITIONAL SIGHTS

Landesmuseum Ferdinandeum★★

⏱*Open year-round Tue–Sun 9am–5pm.* ⏱*Closed 1 Jan, 2 Oct, 25 Dec.* ⊛€11. ♿ ✆*0512 59 4891 00.* *www.tiroler-landesmuseum.at.*

Although it possesses considerable prehistory and early history collections★, displayed in the basement, this museum is devoted essentially to the development of the fine arts in the Tyrol from the Romanesque through to the present. Highlights include masterworks from the **Gothic age★★** (Multscher, Pacher) and the Baroque (Troger). There is also a good collection of Dutch masters as well as historical musical instruments on the second floor and **modern art★** on the third.

Zeughaus (Arsenal)

⏱*See Landesmuseum Ferdinandeum.* ✆*0512 59 48 91 00.* *www.tiroler-landesmuseen.at.*

The former armoury, commissioned by Maximilian I in 1503 and completed in 1506, now houses the Tyrolean cultural history collection of the Tiroler Landesmuseum. The eight themed rooms take visitors on a journey through the ages, covering such subjects as the importance of silver and salt mining to the region's development, the story of resistance leader and local hero Andreas Hofer, and post-World War II Tyrol.

EXCURSIONS
Stubaital★

This valley lies southwest of Innsbruck in western Austria. 🏛 Stubaitalhaus, Dorf 3, Neustift im Stubaital. ✆0501 88 10. www.stubai.at.

The Stubai Valley is a popular day trip for people based in the Innsbruck area. In summer, it is an ideal launchpad for hiking expeditions, and also provides access to one of the largest all-year ski areas in Europe.

On entering the valley, you will soon face the enormous glacial massif of the **Zuckerhütl** *(alt. 3,511m/11,520ft)*. The well-built road runs past the valley's five resorts. First up are **Schönberg**, **Mieders** and **Telfes** on a sunny terrace opposite. Then comes **Fulpmes**, which specialises in the manufacture of mountaineering equipment and tools. Lastly, **Neustift** is dominated by the striking silhouette of its 18C parish church by Franz de Paula Penz.

Over the last 7km/4.3mi of the journey, the gradient becomes ever steeper and the landscape more rugged. The road finally leaves the forest and arrives at the Mutterbergalm *(alt. 1,728m/5,669ft)* at the foot of a rocky cirque.

Stubaier Gletscher 🎿 (Stubai Glacier)

This popular ski area offers downhill enthusiasts slopes of varying degrees of difficulty covering a total of 53km/33mi

between altitudes of 2,300m/7,546ft and 3,200m/10,498ft. The area's appeal lies in its outstanding snow cover and excellent transportation infrastructure. The ski season generally runs from October to the beginning of July. Good skiers will appreciate the 10km/6.2mi long **Wilde Gruben** descent to Mutterberg through splendid, unspoiled **countryside★★**.

There is also a 4.5km/23mi-long crosscountry course at an altitude of 2,600m/8,530ft (starting from the Gamsgarten cable-car).

The most important viewpoints, which can be reached by lift or on foot, are indicated next (*🕤take warm clothing, sunglasses and thick-soled, waterproof footwear*).

Eisgrat★★

Alt. 2,900m/9,514ft.

A cable-car in two stages leads to the glacial cirque and the foot of the Stubaier Wildspitze peak *(alt. 3,340m/ 10,958ft)* and Schaufelspitze peak *(alt. 3,333m/10,935ft)*. Walk round the restaurant to see the lower part of the valley.

Jochdohle★★

Excursion starting from the Eisgrat.

🚶 Walkers should take the waymarked path on the Schaufel glacier as far as the ski piste *(allow around 1hr)*. Do not venture beyond the markings; mountain walking equipment can be

Neustift, Stubaital area

© Austrian National Tourist Office/ Mallaun

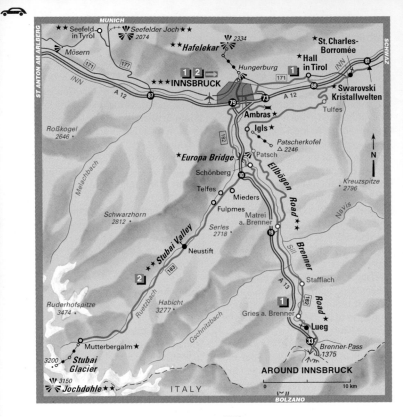

hired in the sports shop in Eisgrat). Skiers should head downhill at the Gamsgarten restaurant and take the Eisjoch chairlift, which, at 3,170m/10,400ft reaches a pass from which you can enjoy a **view★** of the Ötztal Alps. To access the summit of the Jochdohle, transfer to the smaller Windachferner ski lift and you can enjoy refreshments in the highest restaurant in Austria (3,150m/10,335ft). From here a magnificent 360-degree **view★★** unfolds, including the Swiss Alps, the Arlberg, the Ötztal Alps, the Massif de Ortler (in Italy) and the glaciers of the Zillertal to the east.

Daunferner★★

Skiers can reach the glacier (alt. 3,160m/10,367ft) by the Daunfern ski tow, the Wildspitz double chairlift and the Rotadl chairlift. Enjoy impressive **views★★** over the rocky cliffs framing the glacier.

Wilten★

Dominating the southeastern suburb of Wilten is the twin-towered **Basilica★** (🕙open year-round daily when no mass in progress; ☎0512 58 33 85).

Completely restored in the 1750s, this former parish church was raised to basilica status in 1957. Its sumptuous Rococo **interior** was decorated by a team led by stucco artist Franz-Xaver Feichtmayr of the Wessobrunn School, and Matthäus Günther from Augsburg. The latter's ceiling paintings depict the Virgin Mary as an intercessor (chancel) and Esther and Judith (nave). The statue of the Virgin Mary, which is the main object of veneration with pilgrims, is enthroned in glory at the high altar, under a baldaquin (fabric canopy) supported on marble columns.

Nearby is the **Stiftskirche** (Abbey Church; ☎0512 58 30 48; www.stift-wilten.at), a Baroque church with a distinctive yellow-red façade.

Spanischer Saal, Schloss Ambras

© Austrian National Tourist Office/Trumler

According to legend, the abbey was founded by the giant Haymon in atonement for slaying fellow giant Thyrsus. You can see them in stone, guarding the main portal.

The town's **Glockenmuseum** 👤👥 *(Leopoldstraße 53;* 🕐 *open Mon–Fri 9am–5pm, Sat May–Sept only 9am–5pm;* 🕐 *closed public hols;* 💰€8; 📞*0512 594 16; www.grassmayr.at)* is based in one of the oldest bell foundries still operating in the world today. Since 1559, it has been in the hands of the Grassmayr family.

Visitors are welcome to enter the workshop where they can learn about bell manufacturing processes. A small museum details the history of bells with some fine examples throughout the ages and from different countries. Finally, in the last room, visitors can test the acoustics.

Bergisel

Reached by car via the Brennerstraße, the Bergiselweg and the park avenue.

The Bergisel hill was the setting of the bloody battle between Franco-Bavarian troops and the victorious Tyrolean insurgents led by Andreas Hofer. The event is commemorated by a statue of Hofer and the **Kaiserjägermuseum (Museum of the Imperial Light Infantry)** (🕐 *open year-round Wed–Mon 9am–5pm;* 📞*0512 59 48 96 10;* 💰€11; www.

tiroler-landesmuseen.at). The hill itself is now a popular spot for strolling. Also here is the Bergisel ski jump, by Zaha Hadid, who designed the Hungerburgbahn funicular. The third of the famous four-part Vierschanzentournee ski jumping competition is held here annually on 4 January *(www.vierschanzentournee.com).*

Schloss Ambras★ (Ambras Castle)

Take Olympiastraße east; turn right at the skating rink; after passing under the autobahn, turn left onto Aldranser Straße; after 500m/546.8yd turn left to Schloss Ambras. 🕐*Open year-round daily 10am–5pm.* 🕐*Closed 25 Dec.* 💰€10 Apr–Oct, €7 rest of the year. 📞*01525 24 48 02. www.schlossambras-innsbruck.at.*

This fanciful Renaissance palace served as the residence of Archduke Ferdinand II (1529–95) and his beloved commoner wife, Philippine Welser. An avid collector, the prince had the **Unterschloss** (lower palace) built to house his own private museum. Present-day displays include his famous **Kunst-und Wunderkammer**, a cabinet of curiosities, and the arms and armour of the **Rüstkammern★**.

The former residental quarters in the **Hochschloss** (upper palace) now house the **portrait gallery★** (🕐 *open*

Apr–Oct only), with works by Cranach, Titian, Velásquez and other famous artists. Late Medieval art is shown on the ground floor, where the **Georgsaltar**★ is a star exhibit. The inner courtyard sports remarkable frescoes.

South of the Hochschloss is the magnificent **Spanischer Saal**★ (Spanish Hall), built by the archduke for entertaining on a grand scale and now a concert venue.

Hungerburgbahn

Completed in December 2007, the Hungerburgbahn is a funicular running below ground from the Congresshaus to the Löwenhaus, where it crosses an elegant bridge designed by London-based architect Zaha Hadid before entering a tunnel. It re-emerges at the Alpenzoo and ends at the Hungerburg mountain station, which was also completely redesigned by Hadid.

From here you can continue up the mountain aboard a new two-stage cable-car to the **Nordpark-Seegrube** ski area and the Hafelekar peak, at an altitude of 2,334m/7,657ft. From here, you'll have a fabulous **view**★★ over the Inn Valley, the Stubai Alps and the rugged Karwendel cliffs.

♣♦ Alpenzoo

◷*Open daily 9am–6pm (Nov–Mar til 5pm).* ◈€10, children under 15 €5. ℘*0512 29 23 23. www.alpenzoo.at* Halfway up the Hungerburgbahn, Innsbruck's zoo is the highest in Europe. It is home to 2,000 animals from 150 species, most of them found in the Alpine region. Rare indigenous species of fish swim around the cold-water aquarium.

🚗 DRIVING TOURS

① TOUR OF THE MITTELGEBIRGE★★

105km/65mi, including final ascent to the Brenner pass.

⟲ *The route follows a narrow corniche road with hairpin bends and a steep*

gradient which is not suitable for motorhomes or cars towing caravans.

▷ Leave Innsbruck by the Hall in Tirol road (171).

Hall in Tirol★

⟲*See HALL IN TIROL*

▷ The road to Tulfes crosses the Inn and as it climbs, gives attractive views of the town of Hall.

Church of St. Charles Borromeo at Volders★

◷*Open year-round daily 7am–7pm.* The church's unusual 17C main building has a clover-leaf ground plan, six cupolas and an onion dome with three corner turrets at its base. Inside, the most masterful features are the ceiling frescoes illustrating the life of Milan cardinal Charles Borromeo and the painting above the high altar, both by Troger's pupil, **Martin Knoller**.

▷ Continue towards Wattens and follow the signposts to Kristallwelten.

♣♦ Swarovski Kristallwelten in Wattens★

◷*Open year-round daily 8.30am–7.30pm.* ◈€19. ℘*05224 510 80. http://kristallwelten. swarovski.com.* Although essentially a publicity vehicle for the Swarovski crystal company, this underground exhibition is nonetheless a satisfying experience. An overgrown fountain shaped like a giant head guards the entrance to this sparkling world of crystal, designed by Vienna artist André Heller. The blue entrance foyer displays the world's largest crystal as well as crystal art by Keith Haring, Andy Warhol, Salvador Dalí and other internationally famous artists. Thirteen chambers follow, containing fantastic, mystical and meditative installations combining sound, light, objects and natural crystals in every shape and hue. The displays are changed regularly, showcasing works by new artists and designers.

▷ Retrace the route to St. Francis Borgia Church, and turn left to Rinn and Tulfes.

Igls

🕐 *Cable-car operates late May–mid-Oct daily 9am–noon, 12.45pm–4.30pm; late Nov–mid-Apr daily 9am–4pm.* ⊶*€20 round-trip (summer); €36 day pass (winter).* ✆*0512 37 72 34. www.patscherkofelbahnen.at.*

Igls hosted the Winter Olympic Games in 1964 and 1976, and consequently boasts a substantial tourist infrastructure. The **Patscherkofel** (2,247m/7,372ft), served by **cable-car**, offers excellent walking tours in summer and skiing until well into the spring. Other attractions include a vast stone pine forest and the highest botanical gardens in Austria (🕐*open all hours Jun–Sept, by the upper cable-car station at 1,964m/6,444ft).*

▷ Carry on towards Patsch/Matrei.

Ellbögener Straße★★

This mountain road, which was once used for carting salt, leads through several tiny villages and hamlets, giving fine views of the Sill Valley.

The approach to Patsch offers a splendid **view**★ along the length of the Stubaital and the Europa bridge. After Gedeir, the road drops down into the valley, ending at Mühlbach. It then crosses the Sill and joins the Brenner road (B 182) in Matrei am Brenner. At this point, you can either take a detour left as far as the Brenner pass and Italian border (*32km/19.8mi round trip*), or turn immediately right towards Innsbruck.

Brennerstraße★

The Brenner Pass (*alt. 1,375m/4,511ft*) is the lowest Alpine crossing and the only one negotiated by a main railway line in the open air (since 1867). The first Brenner road was built in 1772. The Brenner toll Autobahn (A 13) was opened in 1969 to speed up through-traffic. A slower but more scenic alternative route is the B 182.

From Matrei am Brenner to the Brenner Pass

After leaving pretty Matrei, the road reveals a view of the **Navistal** (valley), with the tiny white churches of St. Kathrein *(left)* and Tiezens *(right)*, before running along the idyllic Sill valley.

As you leave Gries, the **chapel of St. Christopher and St. Sigmund** at Lueg is worth a stop. The road then continues its climb to the pass and the Italian border.

▷ Retrace your route back to Matrei.

From Matrei am Brenner to Innsbruck

On leaving Matrei the road runs above the River Sill, then drops down towards Innsbruck in a seemingly never-ending series of hairpin bends. After crossing the **Europa bridge**★ (785m/858.5yd long, 190m/623.4ft high), it arrives at a parking area with a panoramic viewpoint. The road then leads to the city centre via Wilten.

② FROM INNSBRUCK TO MUTTERBERGALM★
44km/27mi.

▷ Leave Innsbruck by the B 182 heading towards Brenner. After passing under the Europa bridge, turn right. You can also exit the motorway at the Brenner pass (N 10).

At the entrance of the Stubaital, the Zuckerhütl glacier *(alt. 3,511m/11,500ft)* is seen. The road passes the villages of Schönberg, Mieders and Neustift, the latter dominated by its monumental church built in the 18C by Franz de Paula Penz. After around 37km/23mi the road gets steeper, and the surrounding landscape becomes much wilder, entering a section of forest. It finally reaches the Mutterbergalm *(alt. 1,728 m/5,700ft),* a sports centre at the foot of a glacial cirque enclosing the valley.

ADDRESSES

🏠 STAY

For more information on where to stay in Innsbruck, visit www.innsbruck.info.

⌕ Jugendherberge Innsbruck – *Reichenauerstraße 147.* ✆*0512 34 61 79. www.youth-hostel-innsbruck.at.* 🛏. At this hostel located close to the city centre, rooms and dormitories range in price from €22.50 (sharing with 5 others) to €37 (individual room). Satellite TV, Internet access and some sports facilities are on offer. 10pm silence.

⌕ Pension Paula – *Weiherburggasse 15.* ✆*0512 29 22 62. www.pensionpaula.at. 8 rooms.* 🛏. 🚗. This small, welcoming, family-run pension is only a 15min walk from the town centre and offers a spectacular view of the Old Town.

⌕⌕ Hotel Ibis – *Sterzinger Str. 1.* ✆*0512 570 30 00. www.ibis.com. 75 rooms.* 🛏 €12. This member of a modern chain hotel sits beside the railway station in a building that is in the shape of a large black cube. Rooms are functional.

⌕⌕ Weisses Kreuz – *Herzog-Friedrich-Straße 31.* ✆*0512 59 47 90. www.weisses kreuz.at. 40 rooms.* 🚗. Mozart once stayed at this 500-year-old inn.

⌕⌕ Weisses Rössl – *Kiebachgasse 8.* ✆*0512 58 30 570. www.roessl.at. 13 rooms.* 🚗. A traditional old town inn in the pedestrianised centre of the Old Town boasting smart, attractive, modern bedrooms and a restaurant.

⌕⌕🍽 Gasthof Zach – *Wilhelm-Greil-Straße 11.* ✆*0512 58 96 67. www.hotel-zach.at. 24 rooms.* 🚗. This centrally located, family-run hotel is a 5min walk from the Old Town. Bright, attractive modern bedrooms. Free Internet access.

⌕⌕🍽🍽 Hotel Grauer Bär – *Universitätstraße 5-7.* ✆*0512 59 24. www.grauer-baer.at. 196 rooms.* 🚗. This central, modern hotel has renovated rooms, and a half-board plan is available. The spa area on the 5th floor (offering a panoramic view of the Alps) includes a swimming pool, sauna, solarium and fitness room.

⌕⌕🍽🍽 Grand Hotel Europa – *Südtiroler Platz 2.* ✆*0512 59 31. www.grandhoteleuropa.com. 110 rooms, 7 suites.* 🚗€20. Queen Elizabeth II has stayed here. Its magnificent Baroque room is unforgettable. The hotel is equipped with all modern amenities including a spa.

⌕⌕🍽🍽 Schwarzer Adler – *Kaiserjägerstraße 2.* ✆*0512 58 71 09. www.deradler.com. 40 rooms.* 🚗. Situated in the heart of the Old Town, the historic Black Eagles hotel is one of the city's most charming accommodations. Ask for a room with a balcony to enjoy a wonderful view of the mountains. The acclaimed restaurant (⌕⌕🍽🍽) serves traditional Austrian food on the hotel's roof terrace.

🍽 EAT

In the **Ing.-Etzel-Straße** (level with the junction with Dreiheiligen-Straße) in the arches beneath the railway line there is an eatery to suit every taste, from pizza outlets to music bars and trendy wine bars.

⌕🍽 Ottoburg – *Herzog-Friedrich-Straße 1.* ✆*0512 58 43 38. www.ottoburg.at. Daily noon–3pm, 6pm–midnight.* Top-quality restaurant in one of Innsbruck's oldest buildings. Reservation recommended.

⌕🍽 Solo vino – *Universitätsstraße 15b.* ✆*0512 58 72 06. www.solo-vino.at. Mon–Sat 5pm–midnight.* Solovino is refined, matching a fine wine list to fish and antipasti dishes.

⌕🍽🍽 Lichtblick – *Maria-Theresien-Straße 18 (Rathauspassage, take the lift to the 7th floor).* ✆*0512 56 65 50. www. restaurant-lichtblick.at. Open Mon–Sat 10am–1pm, kitchen noon–2pm and 6.30pm–10pm.* This sophisticated restaurant, with full-length glass windows, offers breathtaking views over Innsbruck and serves modern, seasonal Austrian dishes.

⌕🍽🍽 Wirtshaus Schöneck – *Weiherburggasse 6.* ✆*0512 27 27 28. www.wirtshaus-schoeneck.com. Open Wed–Sat noon–midnight, kitchen noon–2pm, 6pm–9.30pm.* Traditional Austrian and Tyrolean cuisine is served in this beautiful 1899 wooden building.

⌕⌕🍽🍽 Pavillon – *Rennweg 4 (1st floor).* ✆*0512 25 70 00. Cafe daily 9am–midnight. Restaurant daily 11.30–2pm, 6.30pm–9.30pm.* On the first floor of a modern glass building with superb views of the Hofgarten, Pavillon is a top gastronomic address for fine cuisine.

🍺🍺🍺🍺 **Europa-Stüberl** – *Südtiroler Platz 2. ☎0512 59 31. www.grandhoteleuropa.at. Mon–Fri 11.30am–2pm, daily 6.30pm–10pm.* The main restaurant of the city's most famous hotel, the Grand Hotel Europa, is famous for international dishes.

CAFÉS AND BARS

Café Central – *Gilmstraße 5. ☎0512 59 20 65. www.central.co.at. Daily 6.30am–9pm.* Viennese coffeehouse-style décor.

Konditorei-Café Munding – *Kiesbachgasse 16. ☎0512 584 118. www.munding.at. Daily 8am–8pm.* This reputed oldest cake shop in the Tyrol has a pleasant summer terrace.

Theresienbräu – *Maria-Theresien-Straße 51-53. ☎0512 587 580. www.theresienbraeu.com. Mon–Wed 11am–11pm, Thu til midnight, Fri–Sat til 2am, Sun til 9pm.* Bar aimed at a younger clientele. Beer brewed on the premises.

Elferhaus – *Herzog-Friedrich-Straße 11. ☎0512 58 28 75. www.innsbruckplus.at. Daily 10am–2am.* Wide selection of beers from all over the world and a limited food menu.

Hofgarten-Café – *Rennweg 6a. ☎0512 58 88 71. www.tagnacht.at. Tue–Sat 6pm–4am.* Very popular summer meeting place with a large terrace in the Hofgarten.

SHOPPING

The main shopping streets are **Maria-Theresien-Straße**, the pedestrian zone in the old town centre around **Herzog-Friedrich-Straße** and **Museumstraße**.

MARKETS
Franziskanerplatz: flea market every Sat 8am–5pm.

Sparkassenplatz: farm produce every Fri 8.30am–2.30pm.

Christmas markets *(Christkindlmärkte)* are held in the Old Town and on Landhausplatz from late Nov to just before Christmas.

SOUVENIRS
Crafts and *Trachten* (traditional costume) *Tiroler Heimatwerk, Meraner Str. 2.*

ENTERTAINMENT

Tiroler Landestheater, *Rennweg 2. ☎0512 52 07 44. www.landestheater.at.*

Christmas market in the Old Town

© Flavio Vallenari/iStockphoto.com

Kellertheater, *Adolf-Pichler-Platz 8. ☎0512 58 07 43. www.kellertheater.at.*

Theater InnStanz, *Richard Berger Straße 5. ☎0512 36 29 29. www.innstanz.at.*

Treibhaus, *Angerzellgasse 8. ☎0512 57 20 00. www.treibhaus.at.* Cabaret, jazz and world music.

Casino Innsbruck, *at the Hilton Hotel, Landhausplatz/Salurner Straße 15. ☎0512 58 70 40. www.casinos.at.*

CINEMAS
Cineplexx, *Tschamlerstraße 7. ☎0512 58 14 57. www.cineplexx.at.*

Metropol Multiplex, *Innstraße 5. ☎0512 28 33 10. www.metropol-kino.at.*

Original-version films are shown at **Cinematograph** *(Museumstraße 31; ☎0512 56 04 70 50; www.leokino.at).*

FESTIVALS

Tanzsommer: *Jun–Jul. www.tanzsommer.at.* High quality dance performances by international artists.

Innsbruck Festival of Early Music/ Ambraser Schlosskonzerte: *Jul–Aug. www.altemusik.at.*

Stams Monastery★★

The Cistercian abbey of Stams was founded in 1273 by Count Meinhard II of Görz-Tirol as the burial place for his dynasty. The majestic architectural ensemble is purely Baroque in style, the result of a thorough make-over between 1650 and 1750 that also added the distinctive twin onion-domed towers.

Info: ✆05263 62 42 5. www.stiftstams.at.

Location: Stams is about 35km/21.7mi west of Innsbruck.

Parking: Park at the foot of the 14C village church.

VISIT

Guided tours (30min) Jun–Sept Mon–Sat 9am–11am, 1pm–5pm, Sun 1pm–5pm only; Oct–May Thu at 4pm or by request. €5.50.

Stiftskirche★★

The church was elevated to basilica minor by Pope John Paul II in 1984. Inside on your right, the famous **Rose Grille★** screen is a masterpiece in ironwork dating from 1716. It closes the passage leading to the Heilig-blutkapelle (Chapel of the Holy Blood). A balustrade in the nave surrounds the open crypt with 12 gilded wood statues representing the princes of the Tyrol who are buried here. The showpiece is the **high altar★** (1613), whose altarpiece represents the Tree of Life in the form of interlacing boughs supporting 84 carved figures of saints surrounding the Virgin Mary.

Bernardisaal★

The Bernardi Hall is reached from the porter's lodge by a **grand staircase** with a fine wrought-iron balustrade. The hall's ceiling is decorated with paintings (1722) recalling outstanding episodes in the life of St. Bernard.

Also visit the **museum**, which displays changing art exhibits.

High altar, Stams Monastery

© Austrian National Tourist Office/Wiesenhofer

Seefeld in Tirol ❄❄

Seefeld lies on a sunny, broad mountain plateau surrounded by thick forest and offering good views of the rocky ridges of the Hohe Munde, Wettersteingebirge and Karwendel range. It is a popular cross-country ski resort, which hosted the Nordic skiing events during the 1964 and 1976 Olympic Games as well as the World Skiing Championship in 1985. Off the pistes, you will find a sophisticated resort with numerous leisure facilities, including ice rinks, riding centres, tennis courts, golf courses, and a modern swimming pool complex with water slides and saunas. Paragliding, rafting and mountain biking are other diversions. Seefeld is also great hiking territory, even in winter when 143km/90mi of trails are kept snow-free.

- ▶ **Population:** 3,300.
- **Michelin Map:** Local Map, see Seefelder Sattel.
- **Info:** Klosterstraße 43. ℘050 88 00. www.seefeld.com.
- **Location:** Seefeld is in western Austria, close to the German border and about 22km/14mi west of Innsbruck. Alt. 1,180m/3,871ft.
- **Don't Miss:** Excursion to Seefelder Joch.
- **Timing:** Allow a day or two to take in the sights and hikes. You will need longer if skiing the slopes to fully explore the area.

SIGHTS

Ski Slopes

Seefeld boasts one of the largest **cross-country ski areas** in the Alps, with 266km/164mi of tracks and good snow cover from Christmas to March. During the 1964 and 1976 Winter Olympics, the resort was the venue for all the Nordic skiing events

For downhill skiers, the resort has 36 ski-lifts leading to slopes that are ideal for beginners or those who prefer gentle skiing. The most interesting runs are on the **Seefelder Joch** and the **Härmelekopf**.

Pfarrkirche St. Oswald

This lovely 15C Gothic church was built on the orders of Archduke Leopold V to perpetuate the worship of a miraculous host, which had been an object of pilgrimage since 1384 and was kept here until 1949. Note the tympanum above the south door that represents, on the right, the martyrdom of St. Oswald of England, the patron saint of the church, and, on the left, the miracle of the host. The same themes are picked up by the frescoes decorating the chancel and in a picture (1502) to the right of the chancel.

Seekirchl

South of the village, this church is noteworthy mostly for its postcard-pretty setting against a mountainous backdrop.

The Miraculous Host

The **Golden Chronicle of Hohenschwangau** records the following miraculous event: one day after Mass, the knight Oswald Milser and his cohorts confronted the priest, insisting that his rank gave him the right to eat the same special wafer as the priest. When the man of God offered it to Milser, the ground opened up beneath the sacrilegious knight. Terrified, he grabbed the altar to save himself, where his fingers left their mark as if in wax. The priest retrieved the wafer and the ground closed again, though shortly afterwards the wafer turned blood-red.

Seefeld in Tirol

© Austrian National Tourist Office/Ascher

EXCURSIONS
Wildsee
1km/0.6mi south of the centre.
This small lake is surrounded by reed beds and a beach. The lake is a popular place for strolling and watching the many wildfowl that make the lake their home.

Seefelder Joch★★
Alt. 2,074m/6,804ft. Funicular to Rosshütte mountain lodge, then Seefelderjochbahn. ○*Operates Jun–Oct daily 9.15am–4.45pm; Dec–Mar daily 9am–4.15pm.* ◎*€18.50 round-trip; winter, €43.50 day pass.* ℘*05212 24 160. www.seefeld-sports.at.*
A short walk from the mountain station leads to the summit; here, a **panorama★★** takes in the Karwendel mountains, the Wetterstein range with the Zugspitze plateau and other peaks. Wear sturdy shoes so you can walk back down into the valley, even in winter.

Reither Spitze★★
🚶 *Alt. 2,374m/7,788ft. For experienced walkers only. Allow 3hr.*
From Seefelder Joch, follow the path up the ridge as far as Seefelder Spitze (*Alt. 2,221m/7,287ft*), then descend on the Scharte Reither path. At the Reither Spitze, an extensive **panorama★★** takes in the Zillertal Alps and the Stubai Alps. Descend to the Nördlinger Hütte and take the cable-car to Hämelekopf. Either walk from here or take the cable- car to Reither Alm.

ADDRESSES

🏠STAY

⊜⊜ **Hotel Christina** – *Reitherspitzstraße 415.* ℘*05212 25 53. www.hotel-in-seefeld.at. Closed Apr–early May, Oct–mid-Dec. 14 rooms.* ⌨. This traditional, welcoming family-run inn has a pretty garden and attractive modern rooms and apartments, some with balconies.

⊜⊜⊜ **Hotel Karwendelhof** – *Bahnhofstr. 124.* ℘*05212 26 55. www.karwendelhof.at. Closed Nov. 48 rooms.* This typical traditional Tyrolean hotel, set in the heart of Seefeld, occupies the former home of renowned local artist Fritz Willberger, whose atmospheric paintings adorn the public areas, alongside antique furnishings. Less traditionally, the hotel is also home to a casino.

♀/EAT

⊜⊜ **Südtiroler Stube** – *Reitherspitzstraße 17.* ℘*05212 50 446. www.suedtirolerstube.com. Daily 10.30am–2.30pm, 6pm–10pm.* This charming rustic wooden chalet restaurant serves typical regional cooking and specialises in grilled dishes.

⊜⊜⊜ **Seespitz** – *Innsbruckerstr. 1.* ℘*052 2 22 17. www.seespitz.at. Daily 11.30am–2pm, 7pm–8.30pm.* This elegant, modern hotel, occupying a rural setting, serves *cuisine créative* in its dining room.

Seefelder Sattel★★

The Seefelder Sattel (Seefeld Saddle), high above the Inn Valley and the Scharnitz ravine, is a mountain pass that cuts a broad breach in the Northern Limestone Alps along the Munich–Innsbruck route.

🚗 DRIVING TOURS

① ZIRLERBERG TOUR★
38km/24mi from Innsbruck (see INNSBRUCK) to Mittenwald in Germany. Leave Innsbruck on the B 171.

Between Innsbruck and Zirl, the road runs along the floor of the Inn Valley beneath the steep slopes of the **Martinswand**, which provided the setting for an episode dear to the heart of the Tyrolean Emperor Maximilian. He is said to have fallen down the cliff in the excitement of the hunt and been saved from a perilous plight by an angel, appearing in the guise of a peasant.

▶ Rather than driving into Zirl, turn right towards Seefeld.

The road passes the Baroque Kalvarienbergkirche (1803–05) and the ruined fortress of Fragenstein, outlined above Zirl. The notoriously steep **Zirlerberg★** road connects Zirl and Reith bei Seefeld. From the **viewpoint★** at the hairpin bend, you can enjoy a great view of the saw-tooth ridges of the Kalkkögel to the south of Zirl.

👥 Reith bei Seefeld★
Goethe described this small village at an altitude of 1,300m/4,265ft as "indescribably beautiful." The local church stands in a charming **setting★** facing the small Roskogel range and the jagged crests of the Kalkkögel. There is a short **Bee Nature Trail,** which provides an insight into the life of the bee. It ends at a bee hotel, where you can see the bees in their hives through glass panels.

ℹ Info: Klosterstraße 43. ☎050 88 00. www.seefeld.com.

▶ Location: This area abuts the German border in western Austria.

⊚ Don't Miss: Mösern.

⊕ Timing: Allow a day, or more if stopping at every sight.

👥 Kids: The Bee Nature Trail in Reith bei Seefeld.

▶ Drive 5km/3mi N to Seefeld in Tirol (see p353). From here take the Bundesstr. 177 (signposted towards Scharnitz, Garmisch).

Mittenwald★
Described by Goethe as a "living picture-book," this violin-making town on the old Augsburg-Verona trade route is a popular tourist destination. It is the starting point for numerous hikes into the mountains. Lined with fine painted **houses★★**, its high street leads to the church fronted by a memorial to Matthias Klotz, the man who brought the art of violin-making to Mittenwald in 1684. Learn more about him at the local **Geigenbaumuseum** (*Ballenhaugasse 3; open Feb–mid-Mar, mid-May–mid-Oct, mid-Dec–early Jan Tue–Sun 10am–5pm; rest of the year Tue–Sun 11am–4pm. €4.50. ☎+49(0)8 823 25 11; www.geigenbaumuseum-mittenwald.de*).

② LEUTASCH VALLEY TOUR★
32km/19.8mi.

This route runs through the Leutasch Valley and visits Mösern, an attractive viewpoint in the upper Inn Valley. Begin in **Mittenwald★** (see above), taking the road south towards Leutasch. South of Mittenwald the road leaves the Isar Valley and immediately climbs above the **Leutaschklamm** (Leutasch Gorge) within view of the Karwendel range. After

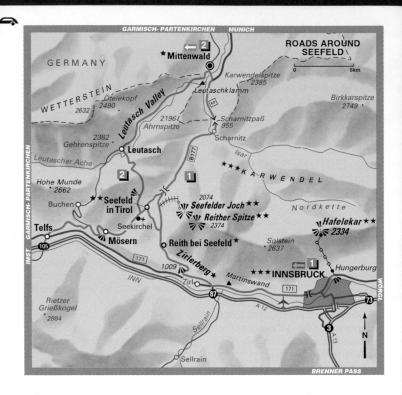

crossing the Leutascher Ache, it runs into the grassy combe of Unterleutasch, majestically bounded by the Ahrnspitze and the Wettersteinwand. A few roofed crosses and farmhouses dot this lonely valley, preserving its primitive air.

Leutaschklamm– Three trails of varying length access the gorge and a 23m/75.5ft waterfall. Part of the longest trail is along a daring man-made section.

Leutasch – This community consists of 24 village segments, strung out along the valley. The road passes through some, then forks left in Gasse towards Seefeld. At the junction, there is a splendid view of the majestic Hohe Munde, to the right.

❯ Proceed to Seefeld in Tirol (ⓒ see p353), then take the road SW road out of town to Seekirchl.

The **Seekirchl** church marks the beginning of a short valley that climbs up *(5km/3mi)* to Mösern, located 600m/1,968ft above the Inn Valley.

Mösern

Known as the swallow's nest of Tyrol, this superbly situated village is a perfect place for a picnic, with particularly fine **views★★** that were immortalised by Albrecht Dürer in his self portrait.

The Inn winds along the floor of the Telfs furrow before slipping into a tangle of crests. Farther to the right, the green terrace of Mieming Plateau snuggles up against the Mieming range culminating in the great dome of the Hohe Munde. South of the valley rise the Sellrain mountains and in the middle distance, the jagged crests of the Kalkkögel.

After Mösern, the road drops down into the Inn Valley in a series of hairpin bends.

Telfs

This bustling market town was a former centre of the textile industry. Today, it is home to the interesting Fasnacht- und Heimatmuseum, a local museum displaying costumes and masks used during the **Telfser Schleicherlaufen**, a carnival celebration held every five years.

Fernpassstraße★

The picturesque road across the Fernpass has been an important Alpine crossing since Roman times, when it was part of the Via Claudia Augusta. A vital trade route connecting Augsburg and Venice in the Middle Ages, it is now primarily a tourist link between the resorts of the Bavarian Alps and Innsbruck.

🚗 **DRIVING TOUR**

TELFS TO REUTTE
64km/39.7mi.

From **Telfs** (*see SEEFELDER SATTEL*) to Holzleiten the road traverses the gentle slopes of the Mieming plateau, from which the well-defined crests of the Miemingergebirge rise up. Near Obermieming, views of the Inn Valley open out to the left against the snow-capped peaks of the Samnaungruppe, which is shared by Austria and Switzerland.
Driving down towards **Nassereith** from the **Holzleitner Sattel** *(alt 1,126m/ 3,694ft)* reveals a series of delightful **views★** of countryside dotted with villages against a mountain backdrop. Several tunnels later, the road reaches Fernstein with Schloss Fernsteinsee hotel on the left.
To the right of the road, below the 🅿 car park, lies the idyllic **Fernsteinsee★**.

Fernpass
Alt. 1,209m/3,967ft.
The pass breaches a crest between Fernstein and Biberwier. The road corkscrews up the south slope through rugged, isolated gorges and cirques. About 1km/0.6mi beyond the pass itself, stop at the "Zugspitzblick" restaurant to take in the stunning **panorama★** of the Zugspitze, the distinctive Sonnenspitze peak and other striking summits. Below lies the **Blindsee★**, a long picturesque lake. It is an ideal spot for a swim or lakeside walk. *Access on the way down from the Fernpass, from the left of the road (before the information point).*

ℹ **Info:** Untermarkt 1, 6410 Telfs. ✆05262 62 245. www.sonnenplateau.net.
▶ **Location:** Links Oberes Lechtal with Inntal in western Austria.
🅿 **Parking:** Several places along the route including at the pass itself.
⊛ **Don't Miss:** Zugspitze Summit.
🕐 **Timing:** Allow a whole day if ascending the Zugspitze.

▶ Follow the road along the north slope of the Fernpass towards Biberwier.

At the Biberwier junction, look for **Weissensee** lake on the right. The road from Biberwier to Lermoos, skirting the Lermoos-Ehrwald basin, offers fine **views★★** of the Wetterstein and the Mieminger range.

Ehrwald★
Despite the numerous lovely hikes, most people come here for the **Tiroler Zugspitzbahn** cable-car ride to the top of Germany's highest mountain.

Ascent to the Zugspitze★★★
Allow about 2hr, including 10min for the cable-car ride. 🕐*Operates mid-May –Oct and mid-Dec–late Apr daily 8.40am–4.40pm every 20min. Journey time: 10min.* 🎫*€42 round-trip.* ✆*05673 23 09. www.zugspitze.at.*
A 4.5km/2.8mi-long road runs from Ehrwald to Obermoos and the valley station of the Tiroler Zugspitzbahn cable-car.

Zugspitze summit★★★ 🚠
The cable-car drops riders off on the western peak of the Zugspitze summit *(alt. 2,964m/9,724ft)*, affording a breathtaking **panorama★★★** taking in four countries and countless peaks, many soaring above 3,000m/10,000ft.
Information boards help you identify the craggy summits of the Hohe Tauern, the

Tyrolean High Alps, the Dachstein and many others. Also here is the multimedia exhibit called **Faszination Zugspitze**★ (*admission included with cable-car ticket*) that traces the history of the mountain from its first ascent in 1820 to the present. Sadly, the glacier is melting away, though covered by special tarpaulins to protect it from the sun. A 3D film lets you experience a virtual flight over the peaks.

In winter there is access to numerous first-class **ski runs**, including the great *Gattlerabfahrt* of nearly 23km/14.8mi back to Ehrwald (*guide recommended*).

Lermoos★

Lermoos is the best place to admire the Northern Limestone Alps, dominated by the Zug-spitze and the Sonnenspitze summit.

▷ To cross from the Loisach basin into that of the Lech, follow the valley named Zwischentoren (between gates).

Ehrenberger Klause

From the 16C to the 18C, Ehrenberg Fortress was key in defending the Tyrol. Before reaching Reutte, it is worth taking a short detour to the Plansee (*20km/12.4mi round trip*).

Plansee★

The road runs through a forest, then skirts the lake shore for a 6km/3.7mi stretch. At the northeast tip, the view stretches southwest through the small strait separating the Plansee from the Heiterwanger See, as far as the Thaneller peak (2,341m/7,680ft). Walks or a scheduled boat trip allow for a relaxing time in great natural surroundings.

▷ From here you can continue to Linderhof and Oberammergau in Germany via the Ammersattel pass.

Reutte

See OBERES LECHTAL.

Karwendel-Gebirge★★★

The impressive limestone massif of the Karwendel, with the Birkkarpitze as its highest point (2,749m/9,019ft), can also be seen from Mittenwald (in Germany). Only an excursion into the Rissbach Valley, with a possible detour through Bavaria, brings you near the greyish, pitted cliffs (the *Kar*) that give these mountains their character. If time is short, it is still worth driving as far as the Achensee, the largest lake in the Tirol.

Info: Münchnerstraße 11, 6130 Schwaz. ☎05242 63 240. www.silberregion-karwendel.at

▷ **Location:** This range is north of Innsbruck in western Austria.

Don't Miss: Achensee.

Timing: This region can be explored on a leisurely day trip.

🚗 DRIVING TOUR

THE INN VALLEY TO GROSSER AHORNBOEN
76km/47mi.

Beginning at the Inn Valley (*take the autobahn exit Wiesing-Achensee*), the panoramic road climbs up to Eben.

Kanzelkehre★★

From this terraced **viewpoint★★**, look down on the Inn Valley and the lower Ziller Valley, dotted with steeples. The scale of these valleys makes a fascinating contrast to the surrounding mountains. The Rofangebirge mountains tower to the north.

Eben

The church of this village contains the chalice of St. Notburga, who is much revered in Bavaria and the Tyrol as the patron saint of workers.

🚶🚶 Maurach

The villages along the shore of **Achensee★★** include Maurach and Achenkirch. The lake is also served by the **Achenseebahn★** (🚃€29.50 round trip; www.achensee-bahn.at), the oldest steam-powered cog railway in Europe that chugs from Jenbach as far as Seespitz (45min, late May–early Oct).

Erfurter Hütte

Alt. 1,834m/6,033ft. 🚠*Rofanbahn cable-car operates every 15min May–Oct daily 8.30am–5pm, mid-Jun–mid-Sept 8am–5.30pm.* 🚃*€20 round-trip.* 📞*05243 52 92. www.rofanseilbahn.at.* The departure point for climbing expeditions into the Rofangebirge massif, this hut enjoys a magnificent panoramic location above the Achensee and the Karwendel.

🚶🚶 Achensee★★

Austria's emperors were the first to discover Achensee as a holiday destination. This fjord-like, 10km/6.2mi-long lake wedged between the Karwendel and the Rofan range is the largest in the Tyrol and a popular and family-friendly destination for watersports and other outdoor recreation.

In the hills above Achensee, oil-laden shale is mined. It is processed (by being heated to 450°C/842°F) into a sulphurous oil called *Steinöl* (literally, stone oil) that is said to have therapeutic qualities. Available in many hotels, local pharmacies and gift shops, it is used in the treatment of rheumatism, arthritis, tennis elbow and other similar ailments. The oil-bearing shale was discovered in 1902 by Martin Albrecht and is still mined there today; Albrecht's family continues the business.

◗ To drive along the edge of the lake, turn round at the village of Achensee and use the old road *(one-way: north-south),* crossing the Austro-German border just after Achenwald. Turn right and cross the Achen pass to reach the Tegernsee in Bavaria *(about 18km/11mi from the border).* Turn left onto B 307 to the Sylvenstein dam.

Sylvenstein-Staudamm

This dam regulates the floodwaters of the Isar. Water is conducted from the vast reservoir into an underground power station to generate electricity.

◗ Continue towards Vorderriß then follow the signs towards Eng, then cross the border back into Austria.

Hinterriss

The hunting lodge, built in the 19C for the Duke of Coburg-Gotha, is a favourite resort of the Belgian royal family. Some 5,000 chamois still live on this massif.

Eng

The road ends here, in the **Großer Ahornboden★**, a grassland where some 2,200 maple trees blaze with colour in autumn, brightening an otherwise severe landscape. The walls of the Spritzkarspitze *(alt. 2,605m/8,547ft)* and the Grubenkarspitze *(alt. 2,661m/8,727ft)* form a natural amphitheatre marking the end of the valley, which forms part of the Alpenpark Karwendel.

🚶 *Hiking trails start from here.*

Hall in Tirol★

Hall on the River Inn was the salt town of the Inn Valley. During the Middle Ages, it played a key role in the economic life of the country and ranked among Austria's wealthiest cities, receiving town rights in 1303. In 1477, the local rulers moved the Tyrolean mint from Meran to Hall. The most famous coin produced here was the Haller Silbertaler, which was accepted all over Europe until the early 19C and became the namesake of the US dollar. Modern Hall is still wrapped in the charm of the Middle Ages, yet keeps firmly in touch with the present as a highly active cultural and economic centre.

▶ **Population:** 13,700.

⚫ **Info:** *Unterer Stadtplatz 19,* A-6060. ℘05223 45 54 40. www.hall-wattens.at.

▷ **Location:** Hall is about 10km/6.2mi east of Innsbruck. Alt. 574m/1,880ft.

🅿 **Parking:** Look for parking on Fassergasse near Stadtgraben and on the corner of Bruckergasse and Stadtgraben.

⊛ **Don't Miss:** A walk around the medieval Old Town.

🕓 **Timing:** Allow at least half a day.

👥 **Kids:** Münze Hall.

●▪WALKING TOUR

UPPER TOWN★ (OBERE STADT)
⊛ No traffic is allowed in the Upper Town on Saturday mornings.

▷ From Unterer Stadtplatz ,take the Langer Graben up to Oberer Stadtplatz.

Oberer Stadtplatz
Hemmed in by attractive medieval buildings, Hall's main square is the heart of the Old Town. Here you'll find the **Stadtpfarrkirche★**, the late 13C parish church that was repeatedly enlarged, resulting in a generously proportioned but asymmetrical three-nave hall church. The decoration is now largely Baroque. Note the ceiling frescoes by Joseph Adam von Molck and a high altar adorned with a painting by Quellini, a pupil of Rubens. The **Waldaufkapelle** (late 15C) to the left of the high altar houses a Late Gothic figure of the Virgin Mary from the circle of Michael Pacher alongside sumptuously decorated reliquaries. On the west side of the square is the **Rathaus** (Town Hall), which was originally the residence of Heinrich, King of Bohemia, and donated to the town by Duke Leopold IV in 1406.

▷ Follow Agramgasse, Quarinongasse and Schulgasse to the Stiftsplatz.

Stiftsplatz
This square is bounded in the east by the austere façade of the Jesuitenkirche (Jesuit church), now a concert hall, and in the south by the Baroque façades of the **Damenstift**, a former convent for noble ladies founded by Archduchess Magdalena, the sister of Archduke Ferdinand II in 1579. The **west front** with its four full-length fluted pilasters is a fine example of the transition from the Renaissance to the Baroque style.

▷ Return to Unterer Stadtplatz via Eugenstraße (3) and the Schweigerhofstiege steps (17) to the left. Follow Münzergasse to Burg Hasegg.

👥 Burg Hasegg (Hasegg Castle)
🕓*Open Apr–Oct Tue–Sun 10am–5pm; Nov–Mar Tue–Sat 10am–5pm.* 🕓*Closed 1 Jan, 1 Nov, 2426 and 31 Dec.* ⬡€8, *children €5.50.* ℘05223 58 55 520. *www.muenze-hall.at.*
Dominated by its landmark tower, Hall's castle originated in the 13C to protect

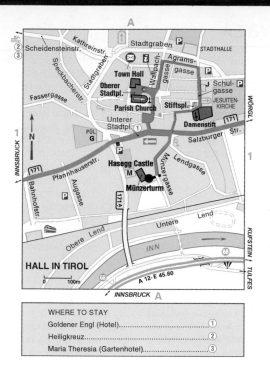

the city, the salt mines and the river traffic. Its historical importance soared in 1567, when the Tyrolean rulers transferred their mint here. Closed in 1809, it reopened in 1975 and still produces commemorative coins on a regular basis.

The city's minting history is chronicled at the **Münze Hall★** 👥 inside the castle. You'll see a cylindrical stamping press and interactive coin displays. Visitors can even mint their own coin. Admission includes audio-guides (also in English). Climb the architecturally distinguished **Münzerturm** (admission €5.50 or €11.50 in combination with museum) with its spiral staircase for splendid views of the town and the impressive mountain range to the north. The castle also houses the **Museum Stadtarchäologie** (Museum of Urban Archeology; www.stadtarchaeologie-hall.at), which uses modern forensics to shed new light on the archaeological history of Hall in Tyrol.

ADDRESSES

🏨 STAY AND 🍴 EAT

Goldener Engl – *Unterer Stadtplatz 5, 6060.* ☎*05223 54 621. www.goldener-engl.at. 18 rooms.* ☕. This ancient building, dating back to around 1300, is home to a charming hotel with comfortable, bright modern rooms. Dine in rustic wood-panelled surroundings in *stuben* (booths).

Heiligkreuz– *Reimmichlstraße 18, 6060.* ☎*05223 57 114. www.heiligkreuz.at. Early Jan–late Oct. 38 rooms.* ☕. *Restaurant Mon–Sat 6.30pm–9.30pm.* Although this inn is 500 years old, its bedrooms are modern and attractive. Skylights of certain rooms open to the night sky's crystal-clear constellation for which this area is famous. The restaurant serves several Austrian specialities

Gartenhotel Maria Theresia – *Reimmichlstraße 25, 6060.* ☎*05223 56 313. www.gartenhotel.at. 27 rooms.* ☕. This traditional-style building is attractive. Its large, grassy garden, complete with café, has a magnificent view of the mountain. The restaurant serves Austrian cuisine in rustic wood-panelled rooms.

Schwaz★

From the 15C to the 16C when its silver and copper mines were in full production, Schwaz was the largest town in the Tirol, after Innsbruck. Its one-time prosperity is attested to today by the unusual size and the decoration of many of its buildings, all erected between 1450 and 1520.

SIGHTS
Pfarrkirche★

Consecrated in 1502, Schwaz's parish church on Franz-Josef-Straße is the largest Gothic four-aisle hall church in the Tyrol; its impressive roof is covered with 15,000 copper tiles. Half the church was originally reserved for the burghers, the other half for the miners.

The finest piece of religious sculpture is the **altar of St. Anne** in the south side aisle. Its Baroque altarpiece (1733), honouring the patron saints of Austria, St. George and St. Florian, frames a fine early 16C group of the Holy Family.

♣♣ Silberbergwerk★ (Silver mine)

Alte Landstraße 3a. ⊕*Bring a warm top as the temperature is about 13°C/55°F.* ☛☛*Guided tours (1hr30min) May–Sept daily 9am–5pm; Oct–Apr daily 10am–4pm.* ○*Closed mid-Nov–late Dec.* ☞*€17, children €10.* ✆*05242 723 72. www.silberbergwerk.at.*

A little train whisks visitors 800m/0.5mi into the Sigmund gallery, created about 500 years ago when Schwaz was a vast silver-mining centre employing 11,000 miners. Steps give access to a labyrinth of galleries where the techniques of mining and excavation of shafts are graphically explained.

Schloss Freundsberg

○*Open Apr–Oct Tue–Sun 10am–5pm; Mar and Nov–Dec Tue–Sun 11.30am–5pm.* ☞*€3.50.* ✆*05242 65 129. www.freundsberg.com.*

The square keep gives this castle a defiant appearance as it sits on its knoll,

- ▸ **Population:** 12,660.
- ℹ **Info:** Münchnerstraße 11, A-6130. ✆05242 63 240. www.silberregion-karwendel.at.
- ◖ **Location:** In western Austria, 30km/18.6mi northeast of Innsbruck. Alt 538m/1,765ft.
- 🅿 **Parking:** Parking is free for the first two hours in the Stadtgarage.
- ○ **Timing:** Budget half a day to a day.
- ♣♣ **Kids:** Silberbergwerk, Schloss Tratzberg.

commanding **views★** of the Inn Valley and the town. The castle is the 12C ancestral seat of the knights of Freundsberg, who sold it to a local duke in 1467. The Late Renaissance palace kitchen is a jewel, while the keep houses the town **museum**.

EXCURSION
♣♣ Schloss Tratzberg★

5km/3mi. Leave Schwaz on the road to Stans. 20min walk from the car park. ☛☛*Guided tours (1hr) mid-Mar–early Nov daily 10am–4pm (Jul–Aug til 5pm).* ☞*€13.50; children €8.* ✆*05242 635 66. www.schloss-tratzberg.at.*

This castle served as a hunting lodge for Emperor Maximilian and the Fuggers, the merchant dynasty from Augsburg, who had interests in Schwaz's silver mine. Tours, including special fairytale-themed ones for children, take in rooms with original furniture, pictures and weapons. The coffered ceiling of the royal chamber (Königinzimmer) of 1569 is magnificent and held together without a single nail. The Habsburg Room features a 46m/151ft-long wall painting depicting 148 of Emperor Maximilian's ancestors in the form of a family tree.

Rattenberg★

This tiny frontier hamlet built its prosperity on silver-mining, but came to a shuddering halt when the mines ran dry in the 17C. As a result, its Old Town is an almost perfectly preserved example of Renaissance urban design. Rattenberg is also famous for its engraved and finely modelled glassware, available in numerous shops along its main street, Südtiroler-Straße.

▶ **Population:** 440.

ℹ **Info:** Südtiroler-Straße 34a, 6240. ℘05337 21 200 50. www.alpbachtal.at.

▶ **Location:** Rattenberg is in western Austria, about 48km/30mi northeast of Innsbruck. Alt 514m/1,686ft.

🅿 **Parking:** There are two large car parks north and south of the train station.

👁 **Don't Miss:** Pfarrkirche St. Virgil.

🕐 **Timing:** Allow half a day for the sights and another half for the excursions.

SIGHTS

Augustinermuseum★

Klostergasse 95. 🕐*Open May–Sept daily 10am–5pm.* ₪€4. ℘05337 648 31. www.augustinermuseum.at.
The Augustinian monastery was founded in 1384. It is now a museum displaying Tirolean art treasures, including exquisite Gothic sculpture in the cloisters and fine examples of local goldsmithing. Processional items are exhibited up in the church gallery; highlights include a *Seated Madonna* and the *Mocking Group*.

Pfarrkirche St. Virgil★★

The twin naves of this Gothic church, separated by four graceful columns, are a harmonious pink and white confection. In former times, the larger nave was reserved for the burghers, while the smaller one was set aside for the miners. Abundant statuary, delicate stuccowork, and elegant frescoes make up the scintillating Baroque decorative scheme.
The masterly **Last Supper** is the work of the Bavarian artist Matthäus Günther, while the *Transfiguration* in the chancel is by Simon Benedikt Faistenberger.
The statues around the **altar** in the miners' chancel were sculpted by Meinrad Guggenbichler, the famous sculptor from Mondsee.

Rattenberg

© Austrian National Tourist Office/ Niederstrasser

Schlossberg

30min round-trip walk.

From this vantage point there is a good **general view** of the town, hemmed in between the Inn River and the mountain, with the belfry of the Servitenkirche (13C–18C) rising above the roof ridges. Downstream, the Kaisergebirge comes into view.

EXCURSION
Freilichtmuseum Tiroler Bauernhöfe★

7km/4.3mi away in Kramsach.
The car park is shortly after the hamlet of Mosen. ○*Open week before Easter–Oct daily 9am–5pm; May–Sept til 6pm (last admission 30min before closing).* ⊜€8. ℘05337 626 36. *www.museum-tb.at.*

More than a dozen farmhouses and their outbuildings, including a sawmill and a school, gathered from throughout the Tyrol have been reassembled here in a quiet Alpine setting.

Alpbach★

12km/7.4mi southeast of Rattenberg.

Idyllic and postcard-pretty Alpbach has been settled since AD 1,000. It wraps around its church, the **Pfarrkirche St. Oswald,** whose pointed spire stands out against the mountainous backdrop. The plain exterior does not hint at its rich interior with fine frescoes and superb altars. The High Altar bears the figures of St. Oswald, St. Martin and St. Catherine. Two side altars are framed in Rococo carvings: the left-hand one with its depiction of *Our Lady of the Victory* has attracted pilgrims for centuries.

Since 1945, the town has hosted the Alpbach European Forum, an annual gathering of academics, politicians, economists and artists of all nationalities to discuss contemporary issues facing the world.

Kufstein

Kufstein, the last Austrian town in the Inn Valley, lies at the foot of a rocky outcrop crowned by a mighty fortress. The town has become a lively and popular tourist resort thanks, in part, to the proximity of the Kaisergebirge range, easily reached by the Wilder Kaiser chairlift.

VISIT
FESTUNG (FORTRESS)

○*Open mid-Apr–Oct daily 9am–6pm; Nov–Mar daily 10am–5pm (last entry 1hr before closing).* ⊜€11.50 summer, €10 winter. ♿ ℘05372 665 25. *www.festung.kufstein.at.*

Kufstein owes much of its character to the citadel that dominates the town. Starting from the Unterer Stadtplatz, an archway above the church leads to the Festungshof *(left)* with the auditorium for the Heldenorgel. Here you can catch the funicular *(included in admission*

▸ **Population:** 18,700.
🛈 **Info:** Unterer Stadtplatz 8, Kufstein. ℘05372 622 07. www.kufstein.com.
◖ **Location:** Kufstein is on the Inn River, just 5km/3mi from the border with Germany. Alt. 499m/1,637ft.
⊛ **Don't Miss:** The Fortress.
○ **Timing:** Spend a couple of hours visiting the castle.

tickets) or continue via a covered stairway. A gateway takes you to the Tiefer Brunnen, a 60m/197ft-deep well. From here, a tunnel carved through the rock leads to the **Pfauenschweif** (Peacock tail) gateway, and then left to the Wallachen and Caroli bastions, where you'll enjoy good **views★** over the Inn River. In summer, tickets also include admission to the **Heimatmuseum**, which presents an array of objects collected by the Kufstein local history society. Of

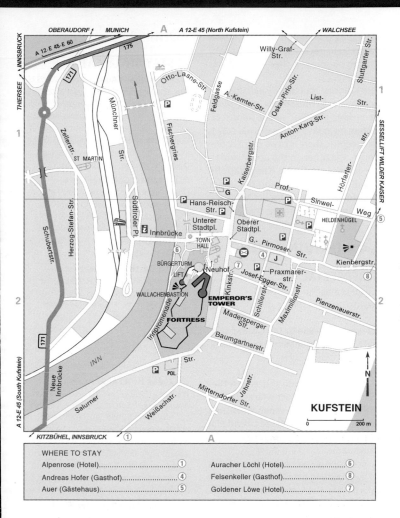

WHERE TO STAY

Alpenrose (Hotel)	①	Auracher Löchl (Hotel)	⑥
Andreas Hofer (Gasthof)	④	Felsenkeller (Gasthof)	⑧
Auer (Gästehaus)	⑤	Goldener Löwe (Hotel)	⑦

particular interest are the rooms illustrating the fortress through the ages.

Kaiserturm★
(Emperor's Tower)

This colossal 16C tower, with walls up to 4.5m/15ft thick, rears up on the highest point of the rocky bluff. The cells on the third floor are reminders of the tower's use as a state prison in the 19C.

Heldenorgel

🕐 *Organ recitals daily noon (10–15min); Jul–Aug also 6pm.*

This giant instrument, known as the Heroes' Organ, was first played in 1931 to commemorate the fallen of World War I. It is located on the top floor of the Bürgerturm, one of the fortress towers, and boasts 4,307 pipes and 46 registers. The organist's keyboard and the gallery for the audience are at the foot of the rock. The recitals can be heard throughout the town, or you can buy a ticket to sit in the auditorium. Since the organ is exposed to the air, it has to be retuned constantly.

EXCURSION
Schloss Mariastein

12km/7.4mi southwest of Kufstein. Park in the valley and climb up to the castle.
In the 14C, a fortified tower was built on a huge rocky outcrop in a small peace-

ful valley paralleling the Inn. It was called Stein (rock) and became a site of Marian pilgrimage after a chapel was built here.

The Knights' Hall (Rittersaal) upstairs houses the **Schlossmuseum** (⏰*daily 9am–5pm; ☎0533 25 64 85)*, whose collection includes a Tyrolean royal crown and sceptre. There are two chapels: one above, the other on the upper stories; the lower Late Gothic **Kreuzkapelle** (Chapel of the Cross) and the upper **Gnadenkapelle** (Chapel of Miracles), decorated in the Baroque style.

🚗 DRIVING TOUR

THIERSEETAL
25km/15.5mi, from Kufstein to Bayrischzell in Germany. Allow 45min.

▶ Leave Kufstein by the NW and take the road to Thierseetal.

Thierseetal
The green valley, with scattered settlements, stretches almost as far as the German border. Thiersee, venue of a Passion play every six years (👁*see Calendar of Events*), lies on a small round lake of the same name.

A succession of combes and gorges leads to the Ursprung pass *(alt. 849m/2,785ft)*, which marks the Austro-German border. After the pass, the road runs through the thickly forested **Ursprungtal** in Germany, a valley that bears hardly any traces of human settlement, except an inn or two. In Bayrischzell, at the foot of the impressive Wendelstein, the road joins the **Deutsche Alpenstraße** (German Alpine Road), which runs 450km/280mi between Lindau at Lake Constance and Berchtesgaden.

ADDRESSES

🛏️STAY AND 🍽️EAT

😐🍽️ **Gästehaus Auer** – *Breiten 47, 6335 Thiersee. 8km/5mi E of Kufstein.* ☎05376 54 12. www.gaestehaus-auer.com. 6 rooms, 1 apartment. 🚋. This charming, family-run guesthouse is in a traditional chalet building in an immaculately kept village close to the ski slopes. Lovely bedrooms, beautiful garden, wonderful views.

😐🍽️ **Hotel Goldener Löwe** – *Oberer Stadtplatz 14.* ☎05372 621 8 10. www.goldener-loewe.at. 40 rooms. 🚋. This small hotel is set in the heart of Kufstein. Rooms are comfortable and modern and there is a rustic dining room (😐🍽️–😐🍽️🍽️).

😐🍽️🍽️ **Gasthof Felsenkeller** – *Kienbergstr. 35.* ☎05372 627 84. www. felsenkeller.at. 23 rooms. 🚋. Situated at the foot of the Kaisergebirge, with splendid views, this sylish Tyrolean hotel is famous for its *Felsenkeller* (rock cellar) cave where guests can rejuvenate themselves. The speciality of the restaurant (😐🍽️) is local trout.

😐🍽️🍽️🍽️ **Hotel Alpenrose** – *Weißachstraße 47.* ☎05372 621 22. www. alpenrose-kufstein.at. 22 rooms. 🚋. This country-style hotel is a 15-min walk from Kufstein centre. Rooms are comfortable with all modern amenities. A sauna and solarium are on-site. The restaurant (😐🍽️–😐🍽️🍽️), renowned for its wine list, serves regional and seasonal specials as well as international cuisine.

😐🍽️🍽️🍽️ **Hotel Auracher Löchl** – *Römerhofgasse 4.* ☎05372 621 38. www. auracher-loechl.at. 32 rooms. 🚋. This picturebook hotel is set on the banks of the Inn, connected by an enclosed bridge over an alley in the Old Town to the tavern part of the hotel, which dates from 1409. Bedrooms are modern but in Tyrolean style, with views over the old city or over the river. The hotel restaurant (😐🍽️🍽️) is picturesque.

😐🍽️🍽️🍽️ **Gasthof Andreas Hofer** – *Pirmoserstraße 8.* ☎05372 69 80. www. andreas-hofer.com. 47 rooms. 🚋. This smart, family-run modern hotel is situated in the centre of town. The rustic-style restaurant (😐🍽️🍽️), decorated with dark oak furniture and painted wooden panels, serves regional cuisine and seasonal specialities.

Kaisergebirge★★

The limestone massif of the Kaisergebirge is perennially popular with hikers and mountaineers. It actually consists of two ranges, separated by the Kaisertal valley: the Wilder Kaiser, a higher and more rugged chain to the south and the lower Zahmer Kaiser characterised by gentler, pasture-covered slopes.

🚗 DRIVING TOURS

1️⃣ WILDER KAISER TOUR
68km/42mi tour from Lofer to Kufstein.

🧍 Lofer★

The village of Lofer, backed by the delicately chiselled, snow-flecked cliffs of the Loferer Steinberge, makes a delightful scene★★. Imposing houses adorned with deep overhanging balconies and ornate façades decorated with flowers and paintings line its narrow lanes, in which traffic is restricted.

The town is a hiker's paradise, with favourite destinations including the Auerwiesen, the Loferer Alm and the **Maria Kirchental pilgrimage church** (👁️see p90).

▷ Leave Lofer on B 312 towards St. Johann.

Beyond Lofer, the valley narrows into a ravine known as the Pass Strub, where there is a memorial to the 1809 resistance fighters led by Andreas Hofer. Those with time should make a brief detour to **Strub**, by turning left about 3km/1.8mi after the memorial.

The stretch of road between Strub and Waidring skirts many splendid traditional Tirolean farmhouses whose living quarters, stables, and granary are all under the same roof.

▷ Return to B 312 and carry on towards St. Johann.

📋 **Info:** Poststraße. 2, St. Johann in Tirol. ☎05352 63 33 50. www.kitzbueheler-alpen.com.

▷ **Location:** Western Austria, on the border with Germany, not far from Kitzbühel.

👁️ **Don't Miss:** the Hohe Salve panorama.

Erpfendorf
Turn left off the road towards the town centre.

The church, finished in 1957, is the work of Clemens Holzmeister, who also designed the new building for the Salzburg Festival (👁️see SALZBURG). Inside is a monumental Crucifixion group, integrated into the roof beam construction above the nave.

St. Johann in Tirol❄️
St. Johann (population 8,600; alt. 670m/2,198ft). 11km/6.8mi north of Kitzbühel.

This market town boasts a number of Baroque houses with façades charmingly decorated with painted, sometimes *trompe-l'œil*, scenes typical of the Tyrolean region. Its location at the intersection of several valleys makes St. Johann a lively tourist resort, especially in winter. The wide, sun-drenched bowl of the valley is enclosed by the Wilder Kaiser and Kitzbüheler Horn peaks.

Ski slopes 🎿🏃

Downhill ski slopes are concentrated on the north face of the Kitzbüheler Horn. All in all there are 60km/37mi of pistes, 28km/17mi of which can be supplemented with snow machines in case nature fails to deliver.

Cross-country skiers have 74km/46mi of tracks, including two of 16km/10mi in length classified as difficult. If you factor in tracks in neighbouring Oberndorf, Going-Ellmau, Kirchdorf-Erpfendorf and Waidring, the distance goes up to almost 200km/124mi.

Pfarrkirche

This Baroque building, designed by Abraham Millauer, has remarkable ceiling paintings by **Simon Benedikt Faistenberger**, a student of Rottmayr. The altar paintings are by Jacob Zanusi, court painter at Salzburg.

▶ Shortly after leaving St. Johann, turn right towards Rettenbach/Weitau. After about 1km/0.6mi the road re-enters St. Johann (signpost). The church is just beyond here on the right, surrounded by the Weitau agricultural college.

Spitalskirche zum hl. Nikolaus in der Weitau★

The church was founded in 1262 as a home for the poor and converted into the Gothic style c. 1460 and the Baroque style in the 18C. In 1744 Simon Benedikt Faistenberger from Kitzbühel painted the ceiling frescoes (showing St. Nicholas as patron of the poor, the Fourteen Auxiliary Saints and St. John of Nepomuk). In 1745 Josef Adam Molk from Vienna created the murals. Behind the altar is the oldest preserved stained-glass window in the Tyrol (c. 1480). The church also houses the province's oldest bell (1262).

Ellmau

Ellmau's trademark feature is the hilltop **Maria-Heimsuchungs-Kapelle** (1719), where you'll have a fine view of the town against the backdrop of the Kaisergebirge mountains.

▶ About 4km/2.5mi after Ellmau, turn right towards Scheffau/Hintersteinersee. The road reaches the lake after a steep, winding stretch of about 5km/3mi.

Hintersteinersee

The crystal clear waters of this mountain lake reflect the rocky crags of the

Wilder Kaiser. It's a nice spot for swimming or a lakeside walk.

▶ Return to B 312 and carry on towards Wörgl.

Söll

This charming little town is grouped around the richly decorated Baroque church of Sts Peter and Paul. To the south lies the Hohe Salve with its rounded summit.

Hohe Salve★★

Alt. 1,829m/6,000ft. Cable-car or chairlift to the summit. Lower station is about 1km/0.6mi southwest of Söll.
Operates mid-May–mid-Oct daily 9am–5.30pm; mid-Dec–Jan daily 8am–4.30pm, Feb–Mar til 4pm.
€19.50 summer; €42.50 winter.
05333 400. www.skiwelt.at.
From the summit with its tiny church and a restaurant, a **panorama★★** extends to the Kitzbüheler Alps, the Hohe Tauern and the Zillertaler Alps.

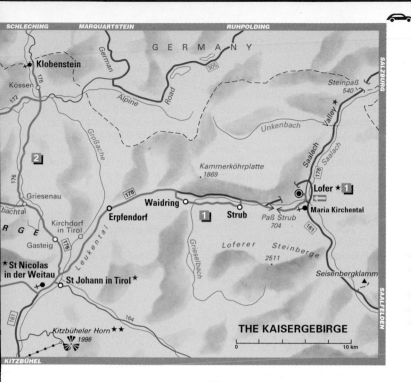

THE KAISERGEBIRGE

To the north, the jagged peaks of the Wilder Kaiser dominate.

A path to the left of the lower station leads after 500m/550yd to the **Stampfanger pilgrimage chapel**, idyllically situated above a little creek and reached via a covered bridge.

Skiwelt Wilder Kaiser-Brixental

Austria's largest contiguous ski region encompasses nine winter-sports resorts in the Wilder Kaiser (Going, Ellmau, Scheffau, Söll, Itter) and the Brixen Valley (Brixen, Westendorf, Kelchsau, Hopfgarten) with 250km/155mi of ski runs and 90 ski-lifts. It is ideal for skiers preferring a gentler and relaxed style of skiing. Access to the ski area is easiest from Scheffau, Söll and Brixen. Cross-country skiers have 170km/68mi of ski runs to enjoy.

▷ Take B 312 back NE and after 2km/1.2mi turn right towards Kufstein.

② ZAHMER KAISER TOUR

61km/38mi from Kufstein to St. Johann in Tirol.

The road continues first along the slopes of the Zahmer Kaiser and then through a harsher landscape towards the imposing Wilder Kaiser rockface.

Kufstein

See KUFSTEIN.

▷ Take B 172 E towards Kössen. Between Durchholzen and the Walchsee it opens out into an attractive valley overlooked by a few peaks of the Zahmer Kaiser.

Walchsee

The road parallels the north shore of Walchsee lake, which is used for watersports and has attracted a healthy level of tourism to the village.

▷ A side road leads for about 8km/5mi up the Klobenstein pass. In Kössen, turn onto B 176 towards

Schleching. After about 3km/1.8mi, follow the signpost to Wallfahrtskirche Maria Klobenstein.

The Ache, which surges down from the Kitzbüheler Alps, forces itself through a narrow gap just behind **Kössen**, forming a natural border between the Tyrol and Bavaria.

The pilgrimage chapel of **Maria Klobenstein** unusually features two church interiors, one inside the other (1707 and 1733). Beneath the chapel a large rock split into two can be seen, the namesake *Klobenstein* (cleft rock).

▷ Take B 176 back southwards until Griesenau and the Kaiserbach Valley. A toll is charged beyond the junction. After 5km/3mi, park by the Griesener Alm.

⚉ Ascent of the Stripsenkopf★
4hr round-trip hike. Nearly 800m/ 2,623ft elevation gain.
From Griesener Alm *(alt. 1,024m/3,360ft)* the trail *(90min)* leads to the Stripsenjoch mountain refuge at 1,605m/5,266ft in about. Beyond here, follow the red-white Stripsenkopf markings to reach the summit *(1,807m/5,928ft) (another 30min)*. ⚆ *Steep, rocky path.* At the top, enjoy excellent close-up **views★** of the imposing north face of the Wilder Kaiser.

▷ Return to B 176 and go S. The road ends after Gasteig, descending through the meadows above the Leukental and St. Johann in Tirol.

Kitzbühel ✳✳

Kitzbühel is one of the oldest and most exclusive resort towns in the Austrian Alps, with a stellar reputation as a winter-sports destination. The village developed thanks to silver- and copper-mining and its position along a trade route from Venice to Munich. Kitzbühel retains some of the atmosphere of the fortified medieval village it once was. The nucleus of the town is formed by two pedestrian streets, the Vorderstadt and the Hinterstadt, which are lined with elegant gabled Tyrolean houses hosting smart boutiques and cafés.

A BIT OF HISTORY

Kitzbühel's winter-sports history was kickstarted in the 1890s by one man: skiing pioneer Franz Reisch. Inspired by Fridtjof Nansen's *The First Crossing of Greenland*, Reisch ordered a pair of skis from Norway and started exploring the mountains.

Other villagers soon followed in his tracks, and it wasn't long before the first small races were staged. However,

▶ **Population:** 8,330.
🛈 **Info:** Hinterstadt 18, A-6370. ☎05356 666 60. www.kitzbuehel.com.
▷ **Location:** Kitzbühel is in the eastern Tyrol, wedged between the Kitzbühel Alps and the Wilder Kaiser range. Alt. 762m/2,500ft.
🅿 **Parking:** Hahnenkamm, Hornbahn and Pfarrau are all car parks within a 5min walk of the town centre.
⊛ **Don't Miss:** Skiing or hiking from the Kitzbüheler Horn.
🕓 **Timing:** In summer or winter, you will need several days to fully explore the Kitzsteinhorn area.

several decades would pass before Kitzbühel's inaugural **Hahnenkamm downhill race** in 1931, which has since become the World Cup classic, taking place every January.

The downhill and the Super-G races are held on the **Streif**, the Hahnenkamm's

Kitzbühel and Hahnenkamm

© Austrian National Tourist Office/ Niederstraßer

most famous slope. Besides skiing, winter activities in Kitzbühel include ice skating, curling and swimming (indoor pool with a health centre). There's also a casino here.

SPORTS IN KITZBÜHEL

Kitzbühel is also a popular summer destination. It has made quite a name for itself as the hub of Austria's tennis circuit (the clay court Austrian Open is held here in July) and also ranks among the country's leading golf venues with two nine-hole and two 18-hole courses. There are even a hang- and paragliding school and several horse riding centres. However, the main summer activity here is hiking, with 200km/124mi of waymarked trails, mostly running along the ski slopes. They're great for those in search of an untaxing hike, picturesque scenery and spectacular views *(lifts give access to some of the best viewpoints)*.

GEOGRAPHY
Kitzbühel Alps

Between the Wörgl-Saalfelden gap and the upper valley of the Salzach, the smoothly rounded Kitzbühel Alps reach an altitude of 2,362m/7,749ft at the Großer Rettenstein. Known locally as Grasberge (grass mountains), they form a charming and tranquil pastoral landscape. The contrasting shapes and colours of the surrounding massifs – the Wilder Kaiser in the north and the Hohe Tauern in the south – make the Kitzbühel Alps much sought after for the quality of their views.

SKIING
Ski slopes

Slopes spread over four separate areas, all served by ski buses: **Hahnenkamm-Steinbergkogel-Pengelstein** *(alt. 750–1,970m/2,450–6,450ft)*, **Kitzbüheler Horn** *(alt. 750 –2,000m/2,450–6,550ft)*, **Stuckkogel** *(alt. 900–1,580m/2,950–5,180ft)* and **Pass Thorn** *(alt. 930–1,980m/3,050–6,500ft)*. Some 56 ski-lifts lead to 55 ski runs covering a total distance of 168km/104.3mi. Although international competitions are held here, the slopes are principally suited to gentler skiing, with long, pleasant runs through pine forests. Only about 12km/7.4mi cover steeper terrain, mainly in the area of the Steinbergkogel peak.

As a result of the resort's relatively low altitude, snow starts disappearing as early as March.

To avoid the long lines at the Hahnenkamm massif, day trippers would be better off travelling to the neighbouring **Kirchberg** peak, where the Fleckalm cable-car takes you to the heart of the mountain range in 15min.

Good snow conditions on the flank of the Kitzbüheler Horn opposite make it possible to ski right down into the valley.

SIGHTS
Pfarrkirche (Parish Church)
Like the neighbouring Liebfrauenkirche, the church is set off by its raised site. The nave showcases the talents of a local artist family, the **Faistenbergers**, who were all well-known artists in the 17C and 18C. Benedikt Faistenberg created the painting in the high altar, while the ceiling painting of the Chapel of St. Rosa of Lima was done by his grandson, Simon-Benedikt.

Liebfrauenkirche (Church of Our Lady)
This two-storey church is distinguished by a massive square tower that seems to dwarf the nave. The Baroque interior of the upper church includes a ceiling fresco of the Coronation of the Virgin by Simon-Benedikt Faistenberger (1739) and a Rococo grille (1778). In the high altar is a 17C painting of Our Lady of Succour (Mariahilf) by Cranach the Elder.

Kitzbühel Museum
Open Tue–Fri 10am–1pm, Sat 10am–5pm. €6.50. 05356 672 74. www.museum-kitzbuehel.at. Check the website for latest opening hours, as they change often.

This local museum is housed in the oldest building in the town– a former grain store. Exhibits highlight the town's mining era, ski history and folklore.

EXCURSIONS
Kitzbüheler Horn★★
Alt. 1,996m/6,549ft. Allow 1hr30min. Cable-car, in two stages, operates mid-May–mid-Oct adaily 8.45am–4.30pm, mid-Dec–Jan 8.30am –4pm, Feb–Apr 8.15am–4.30pm. €23.50 round-trip (summer), €45–53 day pass (winter). 05356 695 10. www.bergbahn-kitzbuehel.at.

From here there is a fabulous **panorama★★** of the jagged peaks of the Kaisergebirge, the Kitzbühel ski slopes and the Hohe Tauern range. In summer, the Kitzbüheler Horn is a departure point for an interesting **hike to the Bichlalm** *(alt. 1,670m/5,479ft – allow 3hr and wear sturdy shoes)*. From here, take the chairlift back down into the valley, and then the bus back to town *(check the timetable with the tourist office)*.

Ehrenbachhütte (Hahnenkamm-Massiv)★
Alt. 1,802m/5,912ft. Cable-car from Klausen (near Kirchberg), 45min round-trip.

There is a good **view★** of the Wilder Kaiser, the Hohe Salve, the Kitzbüheler Horn and the Großer Rettenstein peaks. In winter, it is possible to ski to the **Steinbergkogel** summit *(alt. 1,975m/6,480ft)* for more great **views★★** of the Hohe Tauern and the Leoganger Steinberge. In summer, the hike from the upper cable-car station to the Jufenkamm ridge is popular. From here, you can follow the ridge trail south to the Pengelstein mountain refuge and on to the **Schwarzkogel★★** summit.

🏊 Schwarzsee

5km/3mi on the Kirchberg road and the lake road to the right (level crossing). A lovely walk also leads to the lake via the Liebfrauenkirche and the Lebenberg road.

This little lake, regarded as one of the warmest in the Alps, and measuring only 8m/26.4ft deep, offers swimming opportunities with stunning views of the Kaisergebirge.

Pass Thurn

Alt. 1 273m/4,175ft. 20km/12.5mi south. Leave Kitzbühel on the Mittersill road. The best place to appreciate this high mountain pass is at its **belvédère★** on the slopes of the Oberpinzgau. The Imbiß Tauernblick serves snacks with a view of the Hollersbachtal valley.

ADDRESSES

🏨 STAY

🛏🛏 **Pension Johanna** – *Hammerschmiedstraße 10. ☎0660 29 01 071. www.kitzbuehel-johanna.com. 10 rooms, 2 apartments. ☂.* This is a quiet but convivial pension run by a friendly Danish-Austrian couple just a 3min walk from the Old Town. Lovely bedrooms with wood panelling and balcony. Free Wi-Fi and use of laptop.

🛏🛏🛏 **Gasthof Eggerwirt** – *Untere Gänsbachgasse 12. ☎05356 624 55. www.eggerwirt-kitzbuehel.at. Closed mid-Apr–mid-May and Nov–early Dec. 19 rooms. ☂.* Set in the heart of Kitzbühel in a traditional 300-year-old building with fresh, bright, modern bedrooms this guesthouse boasts a lovely winter garden conservatory restaurant and a cosy main dining room.

Schwarzsee
© Austrian National Tourist Office/Ascher

🛏🛏🛏 – 🛏🛏🛏🛏 **Tiefenbrunner** – *Vorderstadt 3. ☎05356 666 80. www.hotel-tiefenbrunner.at. Closed Apr–May, Oct–Nov. 76 rooms. ☂.* The Tiefenbrunner has been in the same family since 1810. Rooms are luxurious, some decorated with antiques. There is a Wellness area with a panoramic indoor pool and three types of sauna. Fantastic mountain views can be enjoyed from a special relaxing area. The beautiful traditional restaurant serves high-quality typical regional cuisine.

🍴 EAT

🍽🍽 **Gasthaus Bärenbichl** – *Bärenbichlweg 35, 6373 Jochberg (10km/ 6.2mi S on the 161 road). ☎05355 53 47. www.baerenbichl.at. Dec–Mar Mon, Wed–Sat; and Jun–Sept Mon–Wed & Sat.* This cosy, traditional, family-run mountain restaurant serves typical Tyrolean cuisine. Its terrace has beautiful views.

🍽🍽🍽 **Lois Stern** – *Josef-Pirchl-Straße 3. ☎05356 748 82. www.loisstern.com. Tue–Sat.* This smart, trendy, bistro-style restaurant successfully combines European dishes with Asiatic influences.

🍽🍽🍽 **Neuwirt** – *Florianigasse 15. ☎05356 69 11 58. www.restaurant-neuwirt.at. Dec–mid-Apr daily from 6pm; mid-May–Oct Wed–Sat from 6pm.* Three cosy wooden dining rooms, complete with tiled stoves, make up this traditional gourmet restaurant that has been delighting locals and visitors with its regional cuisine since 1884. There's a superb wine list and equally superb sommelier service.

Zillertal★★

The Zillertal is among the most densely populated valleys and most important holiday destinations in the Tyrol. It covers a distance of about 60km/37mi from north to south, stretching from the Inn Valley to the Italian border. The upper, wide part of the valley lies in easily accessible low mountain countryside. After Mayrhofen, the most important resort in the region, it branches into four narrow valleys (Tuxertal, Zemmtal, Stilluppgrund and Zillergrund), which are hemmed in by the Zillertal Alps. This mountain chain, with mighty glaciers extending over almost 40km/25mi, is dominated by the Hochfeller (alt. 3,510m/11,516ft) and the Grosser Möseler (alt. 3,479m/11,414ft).

SIGHTS
Ski Area
The Zillertal Alps are primarily suitable for a more relaxed style of downhill skiing. There is no single integrated ski area; instead almost a dozen, rather scattered, massifs of modest size have been fitted with ski-lifts. The more interesting sections include the **Tux glacier**, **Mayrhofen-Finkenberg**, **Gerlos** and **Zell am Ziller**. A single ski pass is valid for all areas, which are linked by buses. Good snow cover is not always guaranteed.

Zell am Ziller
Alt. 575m/1,886ft.
Zell am Ziller clusters round its **church★**, which was built in 1782 on an octagonal ground plan. The enormous, lantern-crowned dome was painted by Franz Anton Zeiller (1716–93) from Reutte with characters from the Old and New Testaments grouped around the Trinity. In May, valley folks gather in Zell for the traditional Gauderfest, a festival which is celebrated with a procession, wrestling matches and the liberal consumption of the 20 percent proof *Gauderbier*, specially brewed for the occasion.

▶ **Population:** 7,872.
Info: Bundesstr. 27d, Schlitters, A-6262. ℘05288 871 87. www.zillertal.at.
◑ **Location:** The valley is in western Austria, about 67km/42mi east of Innsbruck.
☺ **Don't Miss:** Gefrorene Wand, or a hike to the Berliner Hütte.
◷ **Timing:** All three tours can be done in one (very busy) day if you don't do any of the hikes.

The town gives access to the family-friendly Zillertal Arena ski area with 115km/71mi of pistes and 47 ski-lifts. It is also a popular summer destination as the starting point for walking tours.

Mayrhofen★
Alt. 630m/2,067ft.
Mayrhofen lies 7km/4.3mi up the valley from Zell am Ziller and is the region's main tourist centre with extensive lodging options, shopping opportunities and excellent sports facilities (including a swimming pool and ice rink). For over 100 years it has been highly reputed as a centre for hikers and mountaineers. Skiing takes place mainly on the **Penken massif**, which soars as high as 2,250m/7,382ft (76km/47mi of pistes), and on the Ahorn massif, which is particularly suited to beginners.

🚗 DRIVING TOURS

TUXERTAL TOUR★★★
19km/11.8mi.

After Mayrhofen, the valley narrows noticeably and becomes increasingly steeper. The road passes through Finkenberg and Lanersbach, both with excellent uncrowded ski areas, at the foot of the Rastkogel massif. Beyond here the valley broadens out again level

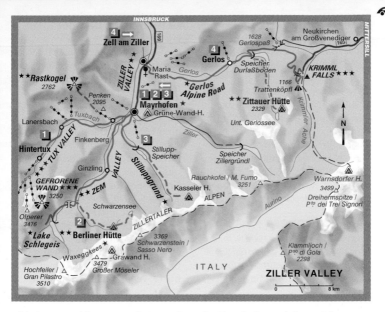

with Juns, providing an unobstructed view of the Tux glacier. The road ends in the small resort of **Hintertux** ⚡ *(alt. 1,500m/4,921ft).*

Ski slopes on the Tux glacier★ ⚡

By virtue of its good snow cover and large differences in altitude, this area is the most interesting for skiing in the entire Ziller Valley. Nineteen ski-lifts lead to 86km/53mi of pistes at altitudes between 1,500m/4,921ft and 3,250m/10,663ft. In winter, superb snow cover is found above only the first section *(alt. 2,100m/6,890ft)* and in summer, only in the fourth section *(alt. 3,050–3,250m/10,000–10,663ft).* The pistes at the Kaserer lifts are suitable for moderately good skiers, while the bumpy slopes on either side of the Lärmstange chairlifts provide good opportunities for experienced skiers.

Gefrorene Wand★★★

Alt. 3,250m/10,663ft. 3hr round-trip. Ascent by two cable-cars and two chairlifts. ☺ *Have thick-soled, water- and snowproof footwear, warm clothing and sunglasses, even in summer.*
From the second section onwards, the eye roves over the vast ice formations of

the Tux glacier and the rock face connecting Kleiner Kaserer and Armstange. From the mountain station of the last chairlift, the view is dominated by the pyramids of the **Olperer** *(alt. 3,476m/11,404ft),* which towers above the gigantic Tux glacier.
If visibility is good, it is possible to see, to the north, the Kitzbühel Alps, the Karwendel mountains and the Zugspitzplatt. Walk 200m/220yd along the ski piste to a rocky peak in the shape of a bird's head.
There is a grand **panorama★★★** over the Schlegeis-Stausee (a reservoir), which is dominated by the glacial cirque of the same name and flanked by the Hochfeiler and Grosser Möseler. Farther to the left, you can see the glaciers of Waxeggkees and Hornkees at the foot of the Tuxerkamm ridge, and also the Schwarzenstein. In the background it is possible to make out the Dolomites *(to the south)* and also the Stubai and Ötztal Alps *(to the west).*
From the chairlift, it is possible to climb up to the Gefrorene Wandspitze peak, where there is a beautiful all-round view. Anyone wishing to go hiking on a glacier can walk down to the third section *(about 20min).*

🚶 Hike up the Rastkogel★★

5hr round-trip, difference in altitude of about 700m/2,296.5ft.

Travel up from Finkenberg *(alt. 840m/ 2,756ft)* by cable-car, and then chair-lift to the **Penken** *(alt. 2,095m/6,873ft; ♿buy a return ticket)*. From the mountain station, a track leads up to the Wanglalm. The route continues to the Wanglspitze peak and past the mountain station of the chairlift from Vorderlanersbach to the Rastkogel. From the summit, a sweeping **panorama★★** takes in the Zillertal Alps.

ZEMMTAL TOUR★★

23km/14.3mi – toll after 15km/9.3mi. Road open May–Oct. Allow a full day if hiking to the Berliner Hütte. The journey can be made by bus from Mayrhofen.

▷ Drive up the valley from Mayrhofen towards Ginzling.

This drive cuts through a stretch of narrow, scenic **gorges★**. If you are travelling in anything larger than a passenger car or prefer to avoid this rather difficult section, you should go to the left through a long tunnel, although this robs the tour of a large part of its charm. After 8km/5mi you will reach **Ginzling**, a peaceful village at the fork of the Floitengrundtal and Gunggltal valleys. The journey continues to the Breitlahn car park, which is the start of the famous hike to the **Berliner Hütte** (mountain lodge).

On the far side, the route continues on a single track **toll road**, on which traffic alternates through two long tunnels, as far as the Schlegeisspeicher (reservoir), which lies in a splendid **setting★** at the foot of the Hochsteller massif and the Schlegeis glacial cirque.

From the final bends in the road, there is a good **view★** of the 131m/430ft-high dam and of the Hochfeiler *(alt. 3,509m/11,512ft)*.

The artificial lake beyond the barrage, the **Schlegeisspeicher★** 👥, is the biggest in the region.

🚶 Hike to the Berliner Hütte★★

Park at the Breitlahn car park. Allow 5hr 15min round-trip with a difference in altitude of 800m/2,624.6ft. The hike doesn't present technical difficulties but does require good stamina.

Large sections of the route are covered on a beautiful trail running alongside a mountain stream and leading through woods and over Alpine pastures. An hour's walk brings you to the **Grawandhütte** (mountain lodge) *(alt. 1,636m/5,367ft)*, where you can enjoy a **view★** of the impressive rock walls of the Grosser Greiner and of the Schönbichl Horn with its small glacier, from which high waterfalls thunder.

On the climb up to the **Alpenrosenhütte**, vegetation thins out, and the stream becomes more tempestuous. Immediately after the lodge, the Waxegg glacial cirque, or **Waxeggkees★**, suddenly comes into view. After another 30min you will finally arrive, up a steep path, at the Hütte, an imposing mountain hut (1898) amid **Alpine scenery★★**. Hikers with a particularly high level of stamina may like to carry on towards the lake of **Schwarzensee**. After 30min, there is a beautiful **view★** of the Schwarzenstein glacier, the Grosser Mörchner and the Zsigmondy peak.

STILLUPPGRUND TOUR★

9km/5.6mi on a toll road. Journey by bus possible.

▷ From Mayrhofen's Hauptstraße, turn left after a small bridge onto Ahornbahnstraße.

The steeply rising road snakes its way uphill, passing through dense forest, small gorges and narrow Alpine pastures between walls of rock. It leads to the far left end of the **Stilluppdamm** *(alt. 1,130m/3,707ft)*, for a fine **view** across the lake, which lies in a rugged, unspoiled **natural landscape★** framed by a waterfall. The road continues through a tunnel to an inn, beyond which it is closed to traffic.

Gerlos Alpenstraße★

The Alpine road zigzagging over the Gerlos Pass connects the Tyrol with Salzburg and offers panoramic views of the Salzach Valley and the Zillertal Alps. It also skirts the spectacular Krimmler Wasserfälle, the highest waterfalls in Europe.

🚗 DRIVING TOUR

ZELL AM ZILLER TO KRIMML
38km/23.6mi.

◖ The road is steep and narrow in places. Between the Gerlos Pass and Krimml, a toll is charged.

Zell am Ziller *◖See ZILLERTAL.*

On leaving Zell am Ziller the road climbs quickly in hairpin bends up the Hainzenberg slope. Soon the pilgrimage chapel of **Maria Rast** (1748), with its distinctive red onion domes, comes into view. After Hainzenberg the road enters the Gerlos Valley.

🏔 Gerlos★ 🎿 🚡

At an altitude of 1,250m/4,101ft, this village offers excellent downhill and cross-country skiing in winter and hiking and climbing in summer. Watersports enthusiasts head to the attractive **Durlassbodensee**.

After the toll point the road reaches the rugged moorland landscape of the Gerlos plateau. There are several car parks here for enjoying superb **views★★** of the Krimml Falls. The walk to the falls starts in the car park farther downhill, just before the toll booths to the Gerlach Pass road.

🏔 Zittauer Hütte Hike★★

Alt. 2 329 m/7,640ft. Regulations are applied mid-Jun–mid-Oct. Allow at least 6hr round-trip for this strenuous walk that climbs a total of 900m/2,953ft. There are snowy areas to cross, even in summer, so hiking boots are recommended.

Info: ✆06564 72 61. www.gerlosstrasse.at.

Location: The road links the Zillertal valley with the Oberpinzgau basin.

Parking: At viewpoints along the route and at Krimml Wasserfälle.

Don't Miss: Views along the Gerlos Alpenstraße.

Timing: Allow plenty of time to negotiate this curvy mountain road. The hike up and down the Krimml falls takes at least 3hr.

Kids: WasserWunderWelt at Krimml Falls.

Shortly before Maut, turn left, then take the first right. Continue for 5 km/3mi to the end of the road, where you can enjoy beautiful views of the lake and the snowy peaks of the Wildgerlostal. There is parking *(charge)* near the hostel Finkau *(alt. 1419 m/4,655ft)*.

The well-marked path climbs into the forest, then through beautiful meadows along the Wilde Gerlos stream. Around a third of the way into the walk, you will come to the Leitenkammer Gorge, reached via a relatively steep rocky path. From here, follow the directions Zur Trissl-Alm *(right)* to join the well-maintained stone path to the Zittau refuge. Follow the red marks to the summit via the steep steps.

The hut is located in a beautiful mountain **setting★★** on the Lower Gerlossee lake.

Continue through Maut to reach the Gerlos plateau. There is parking and a belevedere near the Filzsteinalpe *(alt. 1,628m/5,341ft)*. A little farther on, to the left of the road (near the turnoff to Krimml), a fine **view★** of the Krimml Falls is obtained. Continue on the same road to enjoy two more panoramas of the Trattenköpfl, and a beautiful view of the lower falls.

Continue down this mountain road, and at the end (back at Maut) turn to left of the car park to visit the Krimmler Falls. Follow the same path to return to your car at the Hostel Finkau.

🚶🚶 Krimmler Wasserfälle★★★

The waterfalls can be visited mid-Apr– Oct or at your own risk in winter. ⊛€3 (plus €9 toll/car on the Gerlos Alpine Road, www.gerlosstrasse.at), children (6–15 yrs) €1. ℘06564 72 12. www.wasserfaelle-krimml.at.

The Krimmler Ache river, which flows from the glacier of that name at more than 3,000m/9842.5ft above sea level, cascades in three stages down the forested cliff sides of the Salzachtalkessel. The falls, the highest in Europe, drop 380m/1,246.7ft in total and are a magnificent sight, especially in the midday sun when the spray glitters in every colour of the rainbow.

Before climbing the 4km/2.5mi path up the falls, be sure to take in the viewpoint at the foot of the lowest fall where the water thunders onto a rocky barrier. The broad path zigzags beneath a canopy of trees to the Schettkanzel at the top of the falls at 1,465m/4,806.4ft. Just above the middle falls, pause and refuel at the Schönangerl mountain inn before the final, steep climb.

At the entrance to the falls is the theme park **WasserWunderWelt★** 🚶🚶 *(Water Wonderlands;* 🕐*open May–Oct daily 9am–5pm;* ℘*06564 72 61; www. gerlosstrasse.at)*, with a 3D exhibit, a cinema and other multimedia exhibits. From the top floor of the Aqua Haus you can observe the Krimml Waterfalls through a special Swarowski telescope. Outside, the Aquapark area features playful, large-scale hydraulic toys such as a water-powered swing that pumps riders high into the air, and the Aqua Jojo water jet where you can have fun juggling a ball.

Felbertauernstraße★

The Felbertauern Road has made a considerable difference to the lives of residents in the eastern Alps. Its core is a 5.3km/3.3mi-long tunnel that has connected eastern Tyrol with Innsbruck in northern Tyrol since opening in 1967. The panoramic road carves through the peaceful Alpine countryside of the Hohe Tauern National Park (www.hohetauern.at).

🚗 **DRIVING TOUR**

FROM MITTERSILL TO LIENZ
57km/35mi.

▶ At Mittersil, take the B 108 towards Lienz. 7km/4.3mi farther on, go left towards Hintersee, and after 500m/1,640ft, park on the right to visit the gorges of Schösswendklamm.

🛈 **Info:** Stadtplatz 1. 5730 Mittersill. ℘06562 4292. www.mittersill-tourismus.at.

▶ **Location:** This scenic road runs from Lienz to Mittersill in the Pinzgau.

🅿 **Parking:** Numerous stops along the route with parking and picnic facilities.

⊚ **Don't Miss:** Walk to Innergeschlöss.

🕐 **Timing:** You could easily spend several days hiking in this region.

Schösswendklamm★
15min round-trip walk.
Cross the road to the path leading down to the Felberbach and across the river.

Following the river bank, the trail offers good **views**★ of the sculptured rock faces carved by the crystal-clear water and beautiful waterfalls.

◯ Drive on 3km/1.8mi to the end of the road.

Hintersee★

This mountain lake surrounded by spruce forest lies in the upper Felber Valley below a magnificent high mountain range, from which a number of waterfalls tumble from great heights. To the south lies the Tauernkogel Massif *(alt 2,989m/9,806ft)*. Several information panels explain the geology of the area. It is possible to walk around the lake.

The road now continues through the **Tauern Valley**★★, passing through the Prosschegg Gorge to reach an open valley overlooked by the hanging glacier of the Kristallkopf.

It is possible at this point to continue north directly via the Felbertauern tunnel or to make a detour to explore the Grossvenediger Massif (◔*see below*). Combining the Großglockner Hochalpenstraße *(summer only)* and the Felbertauernstraße into a circular tour gives magnificent views of the Grossvenediger snow fields. The Grossvenediger summit was first conquered in September 1841.

Matrei in Osttirol★

◔*See MATREI IN OSTTIROL.*

Past Matrei is Schloss Weissenstein, a former outpost of the Salzburg archbishops.

Lienz

◔*See LIENZ.*

⚘ EXCURSIONS
Grossvenediger Massif★★

Take a small mountain road to the left of the road leading to the Felbertauerntunnel (toll), and follow it along the valley floor to the Matreier Tauernhaus (alt. 1,512m/4,961ft), a mountain hotel.

Allow at least 2hr there and back for a brief visit, or a whole day to include some sightseeing on foot.

🥾 Walk to Innergschlöss★★

4hr round-trip hike or head up in a horse-drawn carriage or on a little train. It takes 45min to get to Aussergschlöss *(alt. 1,695m/5,561ft)*. The romantic scenery surrounding the chalet almost pales beside the sight of the majestic Großvenediger *(alt. 3,674m/12,054ft)* with its cowl of glaciers. The fairly easy trail continues to Innergschlöss.

🥾 Drei-Seen-Tour★★

From Matreier Tauernhaus, walk along the road towards Venedigerhaus, then climb a steep, grassy slope from the former valley station of the Venedigerblick chairlift to the former mountain station at 1,982m/6,503ft. From here, follow the Panoramaweg to the Tauernbach Creek and then the creek itself across a meadow to St. Pöltner Hütte mountain lodge at 2,481m/8,140ft, then along gravelly and rocky trail sections. From the lodge continue along a narrow, rocky path to the St.Pöltner Ostweg past the Grauer See (Grey Lake), Schwarzer See (Black Lake) and Grüner See (Green Lake), then along the Messeling Creek across meadows and back to the mountain station of the chairlift and down the slope to the valley station.

If you're fit enough, continue on to the Messelingkogel *(alt. 2,694m/8,839ft – 45min round trip),* where you can enjoy a unique **panorama**★★★ over the three lakes, the Großglockner *(in the distance),* the Tauerntal Valley and the huge glaciers of the Großvenediger.

🥾 Hike to the Zirbelkreuz★

1hr 45min, 600m/1,969ft difference in altitude down the mountain.
From the former mountain station of the Venedigerbahn chairlift, the trail leads along the mountain and finally climbs up to a bridge and then to the cross.

◯ After exploring the Großvenediger Massif, drive back to the main road.

Stubachtal★★

About 20km/12.4mi long, the Stubachtal is among the most beautiful Alpine valleys in Austria. A well-built scenic road leads from Uttendorf (alt. 804m/2,638ft) to Enzingerboden (alt. 1,480m/4,856ft). From here, the Weissee Gletscherbahn cable-car transports skiers in winter and hikers in summer to mountain lakes and the magnificent glacial massif of the Hohe Tauern National Park.

Info: 5723 Dorfbachstraße 1, 5723 Uttendorf. ✆06563 827 90. www.uttendorf.com.

Location: The valley is in western Austria, about 34km/21mi southeast of Kitzbühel.

Parking: Park at the valley station of the Weissee Gletscherbahn in Enzingerboden.

Don't Miss: Kaiser Tauern.

Timing: Allow a full day for the drive and the trip to the Kaiser Tauern.

Pasterze glacier and Johannisberg

© senorcampesino/iStockphoto.com

VISIT
From Uttendorf to Enzingerboden★★

17.5km/11mi. The walk begins at Uttendorf, on the B 168, 6km/3.7mi east of Mittersill.

This drive offers views of the Steinkarlhöhe massif before descending into a forest of spruce. The parking area is past the reservoir (at the foot of the gondola), where the mountain pass begins.

Kalser Tauernpass★★★

🥾 *2hr30min round trip (1hr on foot).*

The first section of the 25min cable-car ride is dominated by lush rhodo-

dendrons. Points of interest include the Grüner See lake at the foot of the Kitzkarkogel and *(on the left)* the 3,000m/9,850ft Totenkopf peak on the Glockner range, and the lower Riffel glacier. At the arrival platform *(alt. 2315m/7,595ft)*, the Rudolfshütte shelter enjoys a beautiful **view★★** of the Weißsee lake and the Sonnblick Glacier *(alt. 3,088m/10,130ft)*.

Walk 10min downhill to get to the Medelzkopf chairlift *(alt. 2,564m/8,400ft)*. The 15min ride takes you through the heart of a majestic mountain cirque with splendid **views★★★** constantly appearing. After around 7min, look for the lake behind the Tauernmoos dam, which is dominated by the Kleiner Eiser peak.

At the terminus is the Johannisberg *(alt. 3,453m/11,328ft)*, enthroned at the centre of the cirque. To the right you can see most of the Eiskögele, standing out boldly from the crevasses of the Odenwinkl glacier.

Kalser Tauernpass walk – *45min round trip.* Sturdy walking shoes recommended. This walk offers a beautiful **view★** from the neck of the lake across to the Dorfer valley. It is also of great geological interest with its different coloured red- and white-striped rocks.

Kaprun

This peaceful town at the foot of the Grossglockner Alpine Road offers year-round skiing, thanks to the linking of the Schmieding glacier with the Kitzsteinhorn. Together with **Zell am See★**, 7km/4.3mi away, Kaprun has evolved into a huge recreational zone under the name of Europa-Sportregion. In summer you can ski in the morning and swim in the lake in the afternoon.

🚗 DRIVING TOUR

KAPRUNER VALLEY
9km/5mi.

During the summer, the Kapruner Valley, famed for its magnificent mountain setting, is laced with numerous interesting trails. The **Alexander-Einziger-Weg** from the Alpincenter (upper section of the Kitzsteinhorn) to the summit of the Maiskogel is well worth a detour.

Kaprunertal★★
Allow at least 2hr30min for the Kitzsteinhorn and at least 4hr for the reservoirs, which are only accessible between late May and mid-October.
🅿 *Park at the Kitzsteinhorn cable-car station.*
The Kapruner Valley lies between the ice-capped summits of the Hohe Tauern

- **Population:** 3,150.
- **Info:** Salzburger Platz 6, Kaprun. ✆06547 80 80. www.zellamsee-kaprun.com.
- **Location:** Kaprun is in the Hohe Tauern National Park in western Austria. Alt. 786m/2,579ft.
- **Parking:** Plenty of spaces available at the Kitzsteinhorn cable-car station.
- **Don't Miss:** Kitzsteinhorn.
- **Timing:** Allow a full day to explore the Kapruner Valley.

and the green, shimmering waters of the **reservoirs★★** serving the Glockner-Kaprun power station. Beyond is the Limberg dam.

▶ Park at the foot of the Kitzsteinhorn lifts.

Kitzsteinhorn★★★
🕐*Cable-cars operate daily 8.10am–4.30pm.* ✎€41–50. ✆06547 87 00. www.kitzsteinhorn.at.
☹ *Avoid the underground funicular as you'll miss out on the scenic views.*
The **trip★★** between two particularly sheer rock faces is most impressive.

Reservoirs, Kaprunertal

© Austrian National Tourist Office/ Markowitsch

At the Langwied station *(alt. 2,000m/ 6,562ft)*, switch to the Langwiedbahn, which drops you at the **Alpincenter** station *(alt. 2,452m/8,045ft, restaurant)*. There is a **view** of the Kitzsteinhorn massif and the summer ski slopes.

From Alpincenter, another cable-car climbs to 3,029m/9,938ft, reaching a snow-covered mountain ridge just below the summit *(alt. 3,203m/10,503ft, accessible only to mountaineers)*. From the upper station climb to the second level of the viewing terrace. Straight ahead, the Grossvenediger dominates the **panorama**★★★. On a clear day the view stretches as far as the Zugspitze, Germany's highest mountain, on the other side of the Karwendel range. For another dose of impressive Grossglockner **views**★★, head down to the terrace of the Glocknerkranzl.

▶ Descend 3 floors, then take in the view★★ from the Glocknerkanzl terrace.

Kitzsteinhorn ski slopes

Open year-round, the area is relatively modest in size (18 ski-lifts and 40km/25mi of ski runs), but it offers fantastic snow conditions in a spectacular setting between 2,000m/6,562ft and 3,000m/9,842.5ft above sea level. The facilities are among the most modern and comfortable anywhere in Austria. The ski runs are suitable for all levels of ability, with a slight preponderance of easier runs.

▶ Return to your car and follow signs to the Alpenhaus-Kesselfall car park.

Hydroelectric dams★★

🕐*Open Jun–mid Oct daily 8.10am– 4.45pm.* ⊕€19.50. ♿ ✆*050 31 32 32 01. www.verbund.com.*

Beyond the cable-car station, a road runs to the Wasserfallboden and Mooserboden reservoirs, but it is only open to private vehicles as far as the Kesselfall Alpenhaus, about 2km/1.2mi past the station. Here you must leave your car in a large 🅿 car park and board a bus

to take you to the Lärchwald funicular. During the ascent there is a good view of the valley and Kaprun.

Limbergsperre

At the upper station of the Lärchwald funicular, the Limberg dam *(alt. 1,672m/ 5,486ft)* comes into view.

The power station at the foot of the dam wall receives water from the Mooserbodenspeicher reservoir opposite and expels it into the Wasserfallboden reservoir behind the dam.

From the funicular station, another bus travels through a number of tunnels to the Mooser dam, offering scenic glimpses of the **Wasserfallboden reservoir**★.

Mooser-und Drosensperre★
Alt. 2,036m/6,680ft.

Both valley exits of the Mooserboden are blocked by arch gravity dams to the east and west of the so-called Höhenburg. The **Mooserboden reservoir**★★, amid spectacular Alpine scenery at the foot of the ice-draped Hohe Tauern, is especially scenic.

Crossing the first dam permits a wonderful **view**★★ down onto the green waters of the Wasserfallboden.

EXCURSIONS
Saalbach Hinterglemm★★
The resort is in western Austria, about 29km/18mi northwest of Zell am See.
🛈*Glemmtaler Landesstraße 550, Saalbach.* ✆*06541 68 00 68. www.saalbach.at.*

Together with neighbouring Hinterglemm, Saalbach *(population 2,900; alt. 1,003m/3,291ft)* is one of the largest winter-sports resorts in Austria. Its main attraction lies in its wooded rural setting and the harmonious contours of its broad, gently falling slopes. In winter, its tougher runs attract world championship-level downhill races. Summers are relaxing here and great for hikers, who have more than 400km/248mi of trail to choose from, including the Pinzgau path and the hike to the Tristkogel and Torsee Lake.

Saalbach Hinterglemm

© Austrian National Tourist Office/Weinhaeupl W.

Ski slopes

Saalbach's ski slopes extend between 900m/2,950ft and 2,100m/6,890ft and offer good snow conditions from Christmas to April. Some 55 ski-lifts open up 200km/124mi of pistes for skiers of all levels. Experienced skiers will enjoy the slopes of the Zwölferkogel and the northern downhill section of the Schattberg-Ost. A relaxing 8km/5mi run links the latter with Vorderglemm. The second run on the Bernkogel is recommended for beginners. Some pistes are reserved for snowboarders.

Cross-country skiers will find only 18km/11mi of track between Vorderglemm and Saalbach and above Hinterglemm.

Schattberg-Ost★★

Alt. 2,020m/6,627ft. Cable-car from Saalbach. ◔*Cable car operates mid-Jun–late Sept daily 9am–4.15pm; early Dec–mid-Apr daily 8.30am–4pm.* ⊜*€19.50 round-trip (summer), €44 one-day area ski pass.* ✆*06541 68 00 68.* From the top you'll have an **overall view** of the Glemmtal Valley and its ski area with the Loferer and Leoganger Steinberge and the Hohe Tauern in the distance.

Zell am See★

Zell am See is in western Austria, about 82km/51mi south of Salzburg.
🄸 *Brucker Bundesstraße 1a.* ✆*06542 770. www.zellamsee-kaprun.com.*
🅿 *Parking in town is difficult, but parking is available on the edge of town and around the lake.*

Zell am See *(population 7,960; alt. 757m/2,484ft)* enjoys a postcard-pretty location on the western shore of its namesake lake and close to the Großglocknerstraße mountain road and the Kapruner and Glemm valleys. The glacier-sheathed peaks of the Hohe Tauern, the rugged rocks of the Steinernes Meer and the soft Grasberge mountains define the landscape. The lively town has a well-laid-out pedestrian core and plenty of leisure facilities, including a swimming pool, ice-rink, golf course and riding centre. In summer, Zell am See is the ideal starting point for hiking trips and excursions.

Ski area

In winter, the Schmittenhöhe massif provides a pleasant ski area with fairly gentle slopes at an altitude of between 760m/2,493ft and 2,000m/6,561.6ft. The upper sections can generally guarantee good snow cover from Christmas to April. Together with **Kaprun** *(◔see*

Pinzgauer Spaziergang★★

Allow 6–7hr. ⏱ *Check with local tourist offices about the schedule for the return bus from Saalbach.* 🕐*Mid-May–mid-Oct Thu; meet 8.15am at ticket office located at the Schmittenhöhebahn terminus.* 🎫*€22.50 round-trip lift ride. www.schmitten. at* ⏱ *Sturdy shoes or boots are required, along with plenty of food and drink.*

🚶 The Pinzgau walk is among the most famous hikes in Austria. It starts from the Schmittenhöhebahn mountain station and runs at least 1,000m/3,281ft above the valley floor, crossing almost a dozen passes and often providing breathtaking **views★★** of the surrounding mountains. Although it is not difficult, the trek is long, requiring some stamina. The return is via the Schattberg X-press cable-car down to Saalbach and from there by bus to Zell am See.

KAPRUN), Zell am See forms the **Europa-Sportregion**, which opens up a total of 150km/93mi of pistes on a combined ski pass.

Stadtpfarrkirche

Zell's 11C parish church has a beautiful façade in the Romanesque style. The interior bears the imprint of a number of periods, with a Romanesque nave, a narthex and aisles in the Gothic style, and Baroque ornamental elements. The 16C frescoes to the right of the altar are worth a closer look.

Schmittenhöhe★★

Alt. 1,965m/6,447ft.
Schmittenhöhebahn cable-car 🕐*operates mid-May–early June, mid-Sept–mid-Oct 9am–4.30pm; June–mid-Sept, mid-Dec–mid-Apr daily 8.30am–4.30pm (til 5pm Jun–mid-*

Sept). 🎫*€26 round-trip.* 📞*06542 78 90. www.schmitten.at.*

Enjoy a splendid all-round view of the bold limestone massifs (Wilder Kaiser, Loferer and Leoganger Steinberge, Dachstein) and the sparkling glacial peaks of the Hohe Tauern (Grossvenediger, Sonnblick, Kitzsteinhorn, Großglockner, Wiesbachhorn).

Zwölferkogel★

Alt. 1,984m/6,509ft. Cable-car from Hinterglemm 🕐*operates Jul–late Sept daily 9am–4.15pm; Dec–mid-Apr daily 8.30am–4.15pm.* 🎫*€19.50 round- trip (summer),* 🎫*€36.50–52 one-day area ski pass.* 📞*06541 68 00 68. www.saalbach.at.*

Views from here stretch over the area around Hinterglemm and are dominated by the Hohe Penhab and the Schattberg-West.

Beach volleyball, Zell am See

© Austrian National Tourist Office/Niederstrasser

Großglockner Hochalpen-straße★★★

The most famous of all Austrian mountain roads, the Großglockner Alpine Road leads to the celebrated Großglockner, the highest peak in the Austrian Alps (alt. 3,797m/12,457ft). This road has exerted its magic on more than 50 million people since opening in 1935. The region is an integral part of the Hohe Tauern National Park, designated particularly to protect the Alpine flora and fauna.

🚗 DRIVING TOUR

Promoting tourism loomed large in the concept of this great highway, notably in the construction of two spurs. One leads to the summit of the Edelweissspitze, the other to the Franz-Josefs-Höhe.

😊 *Note that the road is usually blocked by snow from November to early May. The Edelweissspitze and Franz-Josefs-Höhe may be closed even longer.*

GROSSGLOCKNER HOCHALPENSTRASSE TOUR
75km/46.6mi.

Zell am See★
👣*See ZELL AM SEE.*

South of Zell am See, the road to the Großglockner begins at Bruck. It plunges into the **Fuschertal**, a dark and sparsely populated valley. Between Fusch and Ferleiten, the route gets hillier and passes above the **Bärenschlucht**, a little wooded gorge. Beyond here, you can spot the jagged **Sonnenwelleck** group and the rounded Fuscherkarkopf. From **Ferleiten** *(toll point)* to the Fuscher Törl, the route begins its twisting climb. Above the Piffkar ravine *(alt. 1,620m/5,315ft)* the **views**★★ are magnificent, especially from the Hochmais 🅿 car park *(alt. 1,850m/6,070ft).*

🔢 Info: Rainerstraße 2, A-5020, Salzburg. 📞0662 873 67 30. www.grossglockner.com. Heilgenblut office: Hof 4. 📞04824 27 00 20. www.heiligenblut.at.

▶ Location: The road runs north-south through western Austria, essentially linking Bavaria (Germany) with Italy.

🅿 Parking: An early start is recommended if you want parking places at the Franz-Josefs-Höhe. There is a shuttle from overflow car parks.

😊 Don't Miss: Franz-Josefs-Höhe, Edelweissspitze.

🕐 Timing: Allow a full day to negotiate this steep road and to enjoy its breathtaking vistas.

👪 Kids: There's a children's playground at Fuscher Lacke.

The last larches disappear and the road continues as a corniche as far as the Nassfeld bridges. From here it passes through a rocky wasteland known as Hexenküche (Witches' Kitchen) and climbs across the basins of the Nassfeld. About 2km/1.2mi before the pass it reaches a nature museum.

Haus Alpine Naturschau★
🕐*Open May–Oct daily 9am–5pm.* 🎟*Admission free.* 📞06546 650.
This little museum is devoted to alpine ecology above the tree-line and provides a clear demonstration of the complex interrelations between flora and fauna. For an introduction, don't miss the multimedia presentation in the cinema. Outside, a nature trail offers more interesting tidbits about local plant life and geology.

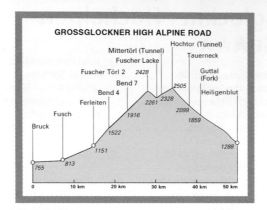

GROSSGLOCKNER HIGH ALPINE ROAD

Edelweissspitze★★

Alt. 2,577m/8,455ft. No access for coaches. ☺ *Very steep road.*

At the highest point of the road, you'll be rewarded with a **panorama** taking in more than 30 mountains above 3,000m/9,842ft high. The peak of the Grossglockner can be seen just behind the Sonnenwelleck.

Fuscher Törl★

Alt. 2,428m/7,966ft.
🅿 *Park at Fuscher Törl 2.*

The road builders used this Törlein (little gate) to form a panoramic bend. **Views★★** of the Glockglockner and surrounding peaks from the platform are among the best along the road. There's also a memorial to the construction workers who died in the building of this road.

♣♦ Fuscher Lacke

Alt. 2,262m/7,421ft.

An information centre here contains displays on the construction of this grand Alpine road. A path leads round the lake for those wishing to stretch their legs. There's also an imaginative **adventure playground,** where little ones can pretend that they are mountain road builders.

Hochtor

The main passage road reaches its highest point *(alt. 2,505m/8,218ft)* at the north end of the tunnel, which marks the boundary between Salzburg and

Carinthia. If you'd like a bit of exercise, follow the 30min educational trail starting at either end of the tunnel, where information panels illustrate the story of this 4,000-year-old trade route once used by Celts and Romans.

The winding descent from the Hochtor passes through Alpine pastures within view of the Schober massif, which forms a crown round the Gössnitz Valley.

From the **Guttal ravine**, turn right onto the Gletscherstraße (Glacier Road) leading to Franz-Josefs-Höhe.

During the holiday season and fine weather there can be delays on the trip up to Franz-Josefs-Höhe, as car parks fill to capacity. 🅿 In this case, visitors will be directed to overflow car parks from which a shuttle service operates to Franz-Josefs-Höhe.

Schöneck

Alt. 1,958m/6,424ft.

Between the inn at Schöneck and the Glocknerhaus lie lush Alpine meadows with a wonderful variety of unique plant life. The **Wunderwelt Glocknerwiesen** nature display and botanical trail at Schöneck give an overview of the Alpine flora and insects in this area.

🔼 Franz-Josefs-Höhe★★★

The Glacier Road ends at a long panoramic terrace, where you'll have the full-on view of the Großglockner as well as the longest glacier in the eastern Alps, the 10km/6.2mi-long **Pasterze**, which is served by the Gletscherbahn funicular

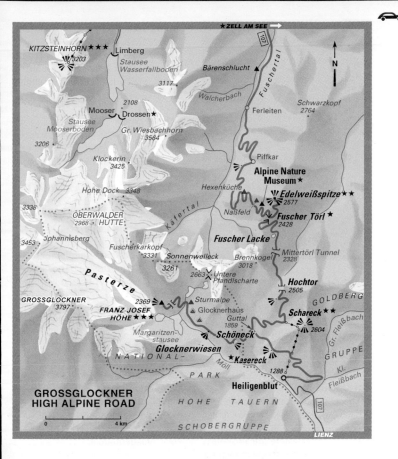

★ ZELL AM SEE ➡

KITZSTEINHORN ★★★ Limberg
✦3203
Stausee
Wasserfallboden
3117
Walcherbach
Bärenschlucht ▲
Schwarzkopf
2764
2108
Mooser
Drossen★
Ferleiten
Stausee
Mooserboden
Gr. Wiesbachhorn
3564
3206
Piffkar
Klockerin
3425
Alpine Nature
Museum ★
Hohe Dock 3348
Hexenküche
✦Edelweißspitze ★★
2577
3338
Na£feld
OBERWALDER
HUTTE
2968
Fuscher Törl ★
2428
3453
Johannisberg
Fuscher Lacke
Fuscherkarkopf
Sonnenwelleck
3331
Mittertörl Tunnel
2328
3261
Brennkogel
3018
Pasterze
2663 ✕ Untere
Pfandlscharte
Hochtor
2505
GROSSGLOCKNER
3797
2369 ▲ Sturmalpe
GOLDBERG
FRANZ-JOSEF
HÖHE ★★★
▲ Glocknerhaus
Schareck ★★
Guttal
1859
2604
Margaritzen-
stausee
Schöneck
Glocknerwiesen
GRUPPE
NATIONAL-
★ Kasereck
Gr. Fleißbach
Moll
Kl.
PARK
1288
Fleißbach
GROSSGLOCKNER
HIGH ALPINE ROAD
Heiligenblut
HOHE   TAUERN
0   4 km
SCHOBERGRUPPE
LIENZ

(🕐 operates mid-Jun–mid-Sept daily 10am
–4pm; ✆€10.50 round-trip; ☎04824 26
40; www.gross-glockner.at).
Views are best from the last platform,
the Freiwandeck. From here the Panoramaweg Kaiserstein, laid out as a
botanical trail, leads to the **Swarovski
observation point**.
The glass-and-wood tower is equipped
with free telescopes for close-ups of the
surrounding mountain scenery. The visitors' centre has four floors of exhibits,
including a "rock and ice path" sensory
experience and a presentation about
the frosty world of glaciers. In summer,
the area is the starting point for hikes
and climbing tours in the Grossglockner
massif.

▶ Retrace the route to the Guttal fork
and turn right towards Heiligenblut.

Kasereck★
Alt. 1,913m/6,276ft.
With more great views of the Großglockner and the Heiligenblut basin, this spot
also has a cheesemaking establishment
(Käserei) open to the public, as well as
a restaurant.
Driving down to Heiligenblut, note the
unusual wooden grain dryers in the
form of grilles (known locally as harps).
A little farther on, there is a famous
view of the church of Heiligenblut, a
slender stone spire standing out against
the background of the far-off Grossglockner.

Heiligenblut❊
*Heligenblut lies at the foot of the
Großglockner in southern Austria,
about 38km/24.6mi north of Lienz.*
🅿 *Small parking area in the centre.*

Heiligenblut

© Austrian National Tourist Office / Herzberger

Charming, pretty Heiligenblut *(population 1,100; alt. 1,288m/4,226ft)* is a gateway to the Hohe Tauern National Park and the Großglockner Hochalpenstraße; it is often deluged with visitors. Its slender-spired church stands photogenically in silhouette against the Großglockner.

Ski slopes

Heligenblut's slopes stretch between the Schareck, Gjaidtroghöhe and Viehbühel peaks *(altitudes 1,300m/4,265ft to 2,912m/9,554ft).* There are 14 ski-lifts and 55km/34mi of pistes with a variety of descents, well laid out through the rugged, treeless mountain landscape. In spite of the high altitude, snow conditions can deteriorate as early as March.

Pfarrkirche (Wallfahrtskirche St. Vinzenz)★

Open daily from 9am.
www.heiligenblut.at.
Heiligenblut's parish church was built in the 15C by the monks of Admont to shelter a tiny vial of blood said to be Christ's, thereby giving the village its name. The twin-aisled crypt contains the tomb of Briccius, an officer of the Imperial Court of Byzantium, who allegedly brought the vial north in the 10C.
Works of outstanding artistic merit include the **altarpiece★** on the high altar (1520), attributed to the school of Michael Pacher, and the Gothic canopy

(1496), ornately carved in pale sandstone.
Opposite the church is the **Hohe Tauern National Park Information Centre,** with a small but interesting exhibition on the Großglockner.

Schareck★★

Alt. 2,604m/8,543ft. Cable-car ascent (Großglockner Bergbahn) in two stages, then 10min walk to the summit.
Operates mid-Jun–early Sept daily 9.30am–4pm (2nd half Jun, 1st half Sept Tue, Fri and Sun only; Dec–mid-Apr daily 9am–4pm. €20 round-trip (summer), €43 day pass (winter). 04824 22 88. www.gross-glockner.at.
From the top of this mountain *(alt. 2,600m/ 8,530ft)*, an impressive **panorama★★** encompasses 40 peaks towering to 3,000m/9,842ft, including the pyramidal Schildberg and the Grossglockner range to the west and the Gjaidtrog to the east.

Nature Trails

Take a guided hiking tour through the Hohe Tauern National Park, in which the village of Heiligenblut nestles comfortably. Find out more about the tours offered by experienced leaders from www.heiligenblut.at.

ADDRESSES

STAY AND EAT

Gasthof Tauernalm – *Untertauern 30, 9844. 4km/2.5mi west of Heiligenblut. 04824 20 59. www.tauernalm.at. 6 rooms.* . This family-run, cosy, traditional wooden Alpine lodge is set high in the mountains at 1,700m/5,577ft. Good local cooking. Half-board option is available.

Chalet Hotel **Senger** – *Hof 23, Heiligenblut. 04824 22 15. www. romantic.at. Closed Easter–mid-Jun and Oct–25 Dec. 16 rooms.* This inviting family-run hotel occupies a picture-postcard wooden chalet. It has a lovely garden and fabulous views. Rooms are very comfortable, well equipped and decorated with antiques. Regional food is served.

Gasteinertal ❄❄❄

The Gasteinertal, a long, wide river valley, is one of the most attractive vacation destinations in Austria. It encompasses three main resorts: Dorfgastein (alt. 830m/2,723ft), Bad Hofgastein (alt. 860m/2,822ft) and Bad Gastein (alt. 1,000m/3,281ft). The latter developed into a leading spa resort as early as the 15C. With its exceptional setting amid medium- and high-altitude mountains, the valley has much to offer both skiers in winter and hikers in summer.

Info: Tauernplatz 1, 5630 Bad Hofgastein. ℘06432 33 930. www.gastein.com.

Location: A 40km/24.8mi-long valley in the Hohe Tauern National Park.

Parking: Plenty of places along the route.

Don't Miss: Climbing the Stubnerkogel peak in summer and skiing the Kreuzkogel in winter.

Timing: Allow at least a couple of days to appreciate the scenery.

A SKIING PARADISE

Much younger than spa tourism in Gasteinertal, but just as attractive, are the valley's winter-sports facilities. Skiers and snowboarders can enjoy four ski areas that are suitable for beginners as well as experts: Stubnerkogel-Angertal-Schlossalm, Dorfgastein-Großarl, Sportgastein and Graukogel. These winter-sports meccas offer some 200km/124mi pistes from late November until the end of April. If snow conditions are not perfect, extensive snow-making makes up for the lack. And, of course, the après-ski scene is very vibrant as well.

Cross-country skiers have 90km/56mi of track at their disposal, covering the whole valley floor from Dorfgastein as far as Sportgastein.

THERMAL CURES

In the 19C Bad Gastein evolved into one of the ritziest spa towns of the age, visited by emperors and politicians, famous artists and writers alike. It is now a thoroughly modern health resort and home of a balnaeological research institute. The thermal water forms from rain water seeping into the Graukogel and Hüttenkogel massifs, which heats up underground and then emerges from 17 thermal springs with a daily output of 5 million litres (1.32 million US gal) and an average temperature of 44ºC/112ºF. The healing effect of Gastein's thermal water is not so much due to its temperature, however, but to its radon content. This radioactive noble gas can be administered through bathing or inhalation. While in the body, radon gives off helium nuclei that energise the body and regenerate damaged cells. In conjunction with the mild mountain climate, the naturally enriched water helps prevent or soothe rheumatism, respiratory diseases, circulatory problems and other ailments.

Visitors can take the cure at numerous hotels, health centres or public pools. Alternatively, spend a session in the *Heilstollen (www.gasteiner-heilstollen. com)*, a tunnel in which the temperature is 37.5–41.5C/99.5–106.7F.

🚗 DRIVING TOUR

FROM LEND TO THE TAUERNTUNNEL
41km/25.5mi including excursion to Sportgastein.

After leaving Lend at the northern entrance to Gasteinertal, the road makes its way over Klamm Pass. Take the tunnel to avoid the often steep old road along the floor of the gorge. Beyond the tunnel, the Gasteinertal soon widens out.

Dorfgastein 🚡
Alt. 830m/2,723ft.
This pretty village on the valley floor, fringed by lush forests, perkily shows off

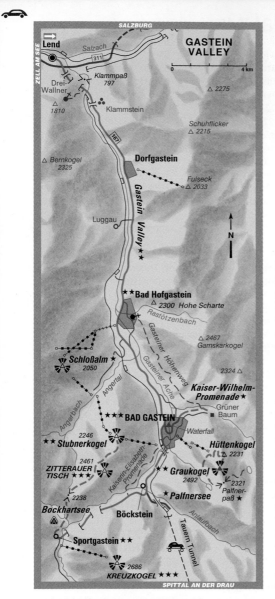

GASTEIN VALLEY

SALZBURG

ZELL AM SEE

Lend

Salzach

311

Klammpaß
797

Drei-
Wallner

△ 1810

Klammstein

△ 2275

Schuhflicker
△ 2215

△ Bernkogel
2325

Dorfgastein

Fulseck
△ 2033

Luggau

Gastein Valley ★★

N

★★ Bad Hofgastein
△ 2300 Hohe Scharte

Rastötzenbach

Gasteiner Höhenweg

△ 2467
Gamskarkogel

Schloßalm ★
2050

2324 △

Kaiser-Wilhelm-
Promenade ★

Angertal

Gasteiner Ache

Grüner
■ Baum

★★★ BAD GASTEIN

Waterfall

2246
★★ Stubnerkogel

Angerbach

Hüttenkogel
△ 2231

2461
ZITTERAUER
TISCH ★★★

Kaiserin-Elisabeth-Promenade

★★ Graukogel
2492

2321
Palfner-
paß ★

2238

★ Palfnersee

Bockhartsee

Böckstein

Anlaufbach

Sportgastein ★★

Tauern Tunnel

2686
KREUZKOGEL ★★★

SPITTAL AN DER DRAU

its idyllic setting below sun-drenched Alpine meadows. In winter, there are extensive ski slopes nearby, with a connection to the Großarl ski slopes, overlooked by the Fulseck summit (55km/34.2mi of slopes). The drop in altitude is more than 1,100m/3,609ft, and there are good opportunities for off-piste skiing as well.

◗ On B 167 Gasteiner Bundesstraße, Bad Hofgastein will be reached within 15min. The B 167 connects all villages in Gasteinertal, except Sportgastein, and ends at the Tauerntunnel.

Bad Hofgastein ♨♨

Alt. 860m/2,821.5ft. Bad Hofgastein Spa & Tourist Office, ℰ *06432 33 930.* *www.gastein.com.*
Bad Hofgastein lies in the broadest, sunniest stretch of the valley. This smart and lively health resort has numerous hotels offering the same spa facilities as Bad Gastein. Furthermore, the resort boasts modern, beautifully laid out spa gardens and the **Alpen-therme** thermal pool and sauna complex. Winter brings excellent cross-country skiing in the valley and downhill in the Schlossalm massif. Slopes are linked with those on the Stubnerkogel above Bad Gastein via the Anger Valley.

Pfarrkirche

The parish church is testimony to Bad Hofgastein's heyday as regional capital when this was the mother church of the valley. The imposing Late Gothic nave has handsome stellar and ribbed vaulting. The church exterior and the niches flanking the main doorway are adorned with elaborate epitaphs of wealthy local gold- and silver-mine owners.

Schlossalm★

Alt. 2,050m/6,726ft. Cable-car, followed by chairlift. ⓒOperates Jun–mid-Oct and Dec–Apr daily 8am–4.40pm (ⓒclosed noon–1pm in summer). ⬚€24 round-trip (summer), €50.50 day pass (winter). ℘06432 64 55. www.skigastein.com.

Come here for a good **panorama★** of the ski slopes and the summits of the Stubnerkogel, Ankogel range, Graukogel and Gamskarkogel. From the second terrace of the restaurant, the view stretches as far as the Dachstein.

Bad Gastein♨♨♨

Alt. 1,013m/3,323ft. ⒤ Bad Gastein, Kaiser-Franz-Josef-Straße 27, A-5640 ℘06432 33 93 560.

Bad Gastein ranks among the most glitteringly beautiful spas and winter-sports resorts in Austria. It is located amid spectacular mountain **scenery★**, flanked by the Stubnerkogel and the Graukogel, and boasts palatial hotels and elegant boutiques. The roaring Gasteiner Ache creates a waterfall right in town.

The east bank of the river is paralleled by the **Kaiser-Wilhelm-Promenade★**, which affords lovely views★ of the town and surroundings.

Bad Gastein has numerous top-notch leisure facilities, including a skating rink, fitness centres, a nine-hole and an 18-hole golf course, tennis courts, and a casino. The **Felsentherme Gastein** is a thermal swimming pool built against the actual rock face.

Local ski slopes include fine runs down the Stubnerkogel and the Graukogel.

Stubnerkogel★★

Alt. 2,246m/7,369ft. Allow 1hr round-trip. Ascent is in a chairlift in two stages. ⓒOperates mid-May–mid-Oct and late Nov–mid-Apr daily 8.30am–4pm (Jul–mid-Sept til 4.30pm; no service

summer noon–1pm). ⬚€24 round-trip, €50.50 day pass (winter). ℘06432 64 55. www.skigastein.com.

The **panorama★★** encompasses the Graukogel, the Ankogel glacier massif, the Kreuzkogel and the Anger Valley with the glaciers of the Hohe Tauern in the background, as well as the lower reaches of the Gasteinertal.

Tauerntunnel

Regular train service between Mallnitz and Böckstein. Journey time: 12min hourly. Mallnitz: 5.50am–10.50pm. Böckstein 6.20am–11.20pm. Phone or see website to check times and prices. ℘05 1717. www.oebb.at.

The 8.37km/5.2mi double-track railway tunnel runs through the Tauern ridge between Böckstein in Salzburg and Mallnitz in Kärnten. Until the opening of the Felbertauern road tunnel, this was the only way through the eastern Alps into the Tauern region. Even now, some motorists prefer loading their vehicle onto the train as opposed to driving through the road tunnel.

EXCURSIONS
SPORTGASTEIN★★ 🎿🏂

Toll road, free to ski pass holders.

From Bad Gastein, the road reaches Sportgastein, a broad high-altitude plateau set against a majestic backdrop of rocky peaks and glaciers after 6km/3.7mi. There's little here except for a large car park and a guesthouse.

The altitude guarantees excellent snow cover, much to the delight of cross-country (7km/4.3mi of tracks) and downhill skiers alike. A modern cable-car leads up to the Kreuzkogel summit, where some exhilarating downhill runs drop more than 1,100m/3,609ft.

Kreuzkogel★★★

Ascent by cable-car in two stages. Wear mountain boots as snow can be deep.

Views★ are impressive from the mountain station, but it's well worth taking the 15min walk up to the summit, marked by a cross, to fully take in the spectacular **panorama★★★**.

▶ Travel back down to Böckstein. It is possible to carry on into Carinthia through the Tauerntunnel.

🚶 EXPLORING ON FOOT

With its varied terrain suited to walkers of all abilities, the Gasteinertal is perfect for hiking. Walks are especially pretty along the **Kaiserin-Elisabeth-Promenade**, from Bad Gastein to Böckstein, and along the **Gasteiner Hohenweg**, which follows the mountain slope from Bad Gastein to Bad Hofgastein.

Zitterauer Tisch und Bockhartsee★★★

Allow a full day, including 4hr30min walking time. Enquire at the tourist office about bus timetables between Sportgastein and Bad Gastein for your afternoon return.

Take the cable-car up to the top of the Stubnerkogel. Turn right at the mountain station and follow the route marked with red and white flashes and red arrows. In just under 1hr the mountain path reaches the Zitterauer Tisch *(alt. 2,461m/8,074ft)*. There is a great **view★★★** of the entire Gasteinertal, especially the upper reaches of the valley and northeast, as far as the Dachstein.

The path plunges down to pastures, before weaving through a bleak and craggy landscape. After another hour, you'll reach the Miesbichlscharte *(alt. 2,238m/7,342.5ft)*.

On the way down to the Unterer Bockhartsee, there are good views★★ of the glaciers and waterfalls of the Schareck massif, as well as of the Hocharn and the Ankogel. From the lakeshore, climb up to the hut and then down to Sportgastein. Take the bus back to Bad Gastein.

🚶 Graukogel★★

2hr30min round trip, recommended for experienced walkers only. Difference in altitude of about 500m/1,640ft.
🚠*Chairlift operates daily Jun–Sept (closed Mon in Jun) and late Dec–late Mar daily 9am–4.15pm on the hour (Jun–mid-Sept til 4.40pm).* 🚫*Closed in poor weather.* 🚠*€24 round-trip, €36*

day pass (winter). 🕾*06432 64 55. www.skigastein.com.*

Take the two chairlifts up to Tonis Almgasthof *(alt. 1,982m/6,502.6ft)*. A path leads from behind the guesthouse up to the Hüttenkogel summit *(alt. 2,231m/7,320ft)*, from which you'll have an incredible **panorama★★** of the Hohe Tauern range, and the spectacular Reedsee lake. Next, follow the path along the ridge *(extra care is needed in some of the steeper places)* to the **Graukogel** summit for an even broader **view★★** as far as the Dachstein. The Palfnersee can be seen glistening directly below.

🚶 Walk to the Palfnersee★

1hr45min round trip.

This is an easy walk through beautiful countryside. Take the two chairlifts up the Graukogel, walk past the hut and continue. The mountain trail gives you a good **view★** of Schareck, Hoher Sonnblick and Hocharn before climbing up to the Palfnersee *(alt. 2,100m/6,890ft)*. From here, you could carry on to the **Palfner Pass★** *(alt. 2,321m/7,615ft)* for even better views *(allow an extra hour round trip)*.

ADDRESSES

🏠 STAY AND 🍴EAT

🛏🍴🛏 **Schiefe Alm** – *Bellevue-Alm-Weg 9, Bad Gastein.* 🕾*06434 38 81. www. schiefe-alm.at. 8 apartments.* 🍽*€12.* Open year-round, these comfortable accommodations are almost next door to the well-known Bad Gastein inn, the Bellevue Alm. They are somewhat out of the way of the main spa area, but nonetheless are charming. There's a pleasant terrace off the Bellevue Alm's restaurant, as well as a swimming pool.

🛏🍴 **Bertahof** – *Vorderschneeberg 15, Bad Hofgastein.* 🕾*06432 76 08. www. bertahof.at. Thu–Tue 11.30am–11pm (daily during high season). Reservations advisable.* This 350-year-old classic alpine chalet uses only the freshest regional produce in its international and regional dishes. Outdoor as well as indoor seating is available.

Lienz

Lying in the shadow of the deeply wrinkled rocky slopes of the Dolomites, Lienz is the southern terminus of the transalpine Grossglockner and Felbertauern roads. Early settlers included the Romans, and a hint of Italy, only 40km/25mi away, still pervades the town today.

WALKING TOUR

LIENZ

Bruck Castle and the Regionalmuseum Osttirol

◷ *Open mid-May–late Oct Tue–Sun 10am–6pm (Sept–Oct til 4pm; open daily Jul–Aug).* ⊚€8.50. ℘04852 625 80. *www.museum-schlossbruck.at.*

The former seat of the counts of Görz, this 13C hilltop schloss dominates Lienz' silhouette and offers wonderful views of the town. It now houses a regional museum, which displays local antiquities, folklore, crafts and Roman stone fragments.

The large **Albin-Egger-Lienz Gallery** provides a comprehensive survey of the work of this painter (1868–1926), who was often inspired by the Tyrol and the

- ▶ **Population:** 12,100.
- 🛈 **Info:** *Mühlgasse 11,* A-9900, ℘050 212 212. www.osttirol.com.
- ◖ **Location:** Lienz is at the confluence of the Drau (Drava) and Isel Rivers in East Tirol. Alt 678m/2,224ft.
- 🅿 **Parking:** Central parking options are at the railway station and the Hauptplatz
- 👁 **Don't Miss:** Driving along the quiet Pustertal Höhenstraße.
- ◷ **Timing:** You can see the best of Lienz and its surroundings in one busy day.
- 👪 **Kids:** Schloss Bruck.

suffering of its people. In 2006, Egger-Lienz's famous *Totentanz 1806* (Dance of Death 1806), which had been seized by the Nazis, was restored to its rightful owner in the USA. It fetched €912,000 at a Vienna auction, then a record for a work by this painter.

The museum also exhibits paintings and sculpture by contemporary artists.

The two-storey, late 13C **chapel** has fanciful cross-ribbed vaulting and 15C

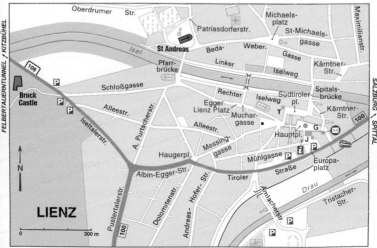

frescoes by Nikolaus Kentner and Simon von Talsten, a pupil of Friedrich Pacher.

▷ Head back to the Hauptplatz in the town centre.

Hauptplatz

In summer, Hauptplatz, with its palm trees, flowers and pavement cafés, evokes an almost Mediterranean atmosphere. The town hall, which occupies the Liebburg castle, built by the Counts von Wolkenstein in the early 17C, is distinguished by its two round towers. At the east end of the square the Church devoted to St. Anthony is a lovely Baroque building from 1660, that now serves as the meeting place for an Orthodox religious community established in Lienz.

▷ Continue towards the Johannesplatz, turn right onto Muchargasse to see the church and the convent of the Franciscans. On your right is the Schulstr. Isel with its tower and its medieval ramparts. Continue on the Rechter Iselweg. Down this street, the Dominican convent is one of the oldest buildings in the city. Cross the Isel and turn into Pfarrgasse.

Stadtpfarrkirche St. Andrä (St. Andreas Church)

If the church is not open, obtain the chapel keys from Pfarrgasse 13.

The church of St. Andrew combines a Late Gothic nave with an 18C choir. During renovations in 1968, wall paintings from the 14C, 15C and 17C were discovered.

The church organ, made in 1618 by the master of Passau Andreas Putz, is one of the oldest in Austria. Its Renaissance-era decoration executed in a studio in Brixen (South Tyrol) is almost completely preserved.

Beneath the gallery are some beautiful **Grabmälern★★** (marble funerary slabs) from the 16C, commemorating Earl Leonard of Salzburg, the last of the line of Görz Tirol, and Michael von Wolkenstein (shown with his wife, Barbara von Thun, 1510), who succeeded him as owner of the castle.

Inside the cemetery (which was once fortified) stands the chapel built by Clemens Holzmeister in 1924-5 to commemorate the veterans of the Great War. Albin Egger-Lienz, who is buried here, contributed a very controversial painting in four panels, which graphically represent the horrors of modern war. It was initially thought so shocking that the chapel was actually closed for a period to prevent people from seeing it.

🚗 DRIVING TOURS

1 THE LIENZ DOLOMITES

112km/70mi. Allow 3 hrs.

Pustertaler Höhenstraße★

Around 35km/22mi. Leave Lienz on the B 100. At the Leisach exit, bear right towards Bannberg, then follow the sign Pustertaler Höhenstraße.

To really enjoy this region away from the traffic, the Pustertal Höhenstraße is the ideal road. Winding far above the valley, it offers several fine views of the Lienzer Dolomites and its small hamlets, with their farms and churches and roofscapes standing out against the verdant landscape. After Kosten where the road turns northwest, you will get a glimpse of the peaks of the Deferegger Alps.

Anras★

Situated on a sunny slope Anras has been inhabited for more than 2,000 years. For many centuries it was the religious and economic centre of Pustertal. In 1236 Emperor Frederick II, Bishop of Brixen (South Tyrol), granted Anras temporal power and thus the jurisdiction of the entire diocese, hence the **Pfleggerichtshaus Schloss Anras (Anras Castle court of justice)** (🕒closed indefinitely for renovation; see website for latest updates: www.schloss-anras.com). The castle served for many years as the summer residence of the bishops of Brixen.

The parish church of St. Stephen's was built between 1753 and 1756 by architect Franz de Paula Penz. It holds some remarkable frescoes by Martin Knoller, a student of Paul Troger.

▶ Continue towards Alfaltersbach and then Strassem. Turn left onto the B 1101.

Lesachtal★

The road follows this charming valley along the Gail, climbing from 900m/2,953ft to 1,200m/3,937ft. Off the beaten track, it has remained largely unspoiled. To the left are the Carnic Alps, to the right the Alps in the valley of the Gail, and on the horizon the Lienzer Dolomites of Lienz. Well away from the mainstream crowds and the resorts, the Lesachtal remains a perfectly unspoiled valley of handsome farms.

Kötschach

Set between the Gailtaler and Karnische Alps, the small market community of **Kötschach-Mauthen** is a popular medium-altitude *(710m/2,329ft)*, mountain-air health resort.

Also known as the cathedral of the Gailtal, **Pfarrkirche Unsere Liebe Frau** was consecrated in 1485 and completely rebuilt by Bartlmä Firtaler in the early 16C. It embodies the final, exuberantly decorative stage of the Gothic style and has **traceried rib vaulting★** that is stunning. The fresco on the north chancel wall depicts the Death and Assumption of the Virgin Mary. The "miraculous" statue enclosed in the high altar is a black Madonna.

▶ Next, take the B 110.

Laas

The Late Gothic **Filialkirche St. Andreas** sports doorways and windows framed in local red sandstone and delicate rib **vaulting★★**. It is a masterpiece by Bartimä Firtaler.

▶ Return to Lienz.

② OBERES MÖLLTAL
38km/23.5mi. Allow 3hr.

A road tracing the twisting Möll Valley, links the Dolomites to Lienz and past an area of the Hohe Tauern National Park (the Alps' largest nature reserve) to the lakes of Carinthia.

▶ Leave Lienz on the B 1070 and then the B 107a.

Iselsberg Road

The Iselsberg Road *(alt. 1,204m/3,950ft)* leads gradually, through heavily forested slopes, into the valley of the Möll. With their views of the Dolomites whose deep grey fissures seem almost to have been carved by hand, the first two bends are an inviting place to stop. At Winklern a vast **panorama★★** of the Möll Valley unfolds.

Döllach

Just before Döllach, note on the left the wooden frames, known as *Harpfen*, which were once used to dry hay and grain and were ubiquitous across the region.

The history of this quaint village, once an important gold- and silver-mining centre is well presented in a small museum housed in the Schloss Großkirchheim, an imposing edifice built in 1561 by Melchior Putz.

Mölltal

The cool, tranquil Möll Valley retains its traditional darkwood houses, redolent of the mountains. In the foreground, note the traditional grain dryers

Heiligenblut
See Grossglockner.

Matrei in Osttirol ❄

The popular holiday resort of Matrei in East Tyrol lies in beautiful and diverse surroundings and boasts an exceptionally pleasant climate. The market town occupies a restful, low-mountain area at the foot of the Grossvenediger and Grossglockner, the highest and most impressive peaks in Austria. Thanks to its extraordinary setting, Mattrei has become a well-known gateway for hikes into the Eastern Alps.

SIGHTS
Ski Slopes
In winter, the **ski area**★ offers satisfactory conditions for skiers. Three chairlifts and three T-bar lifts lead to 30km/18.6mi of pistes of between 1,000m/3,300ft and 2,400m/7,900ft in length, some with artificial snow. With 24km/15mi of long pistes and vast off-piste areas, it is a particularly attractive resort for lovers of long-distance skiing and ski tours.

St. Nikolauskirche
Approach by car.
From the main square in Matrei, cross the bridge to Lienzer Straße, then turn left onto the Bichler Straße. The road leaves the village, leading over another bridge and then right past a wooden well. Turn right at the next two intersections. The road is now unpaved but is quite drivable. Turning right onto the next small road leads you straight to the church.
In a meadow above Matrei, St. Nikolaus is a 12C church with Romanesque and Gothic elements. An outstanding architectural feature is the unusual two-storey Romanesque choir decorated with **frescoes**★. The lower level represents scenes from Genesis, while the upper storey – reached via a double staircase – shows the four elements carrying the 12 Apostles and the Evangelists.

▶ **Population:** 4,700.

🛈 **Info:** Rauterplatz 1, A-9971. ☎050 212 500. www.matreiosttirol.com.

▶ **Location:** Matrei lies at the junction of the Tauerntal, Virgental and Iseltal, about 30km/19mi north of Lienz. Alt. 1,000m/3,300ft.

👁 **Don't Miss:** The frescoes of St. Nikolaukirche.

👨‍👧 **Kids:** The Blauspitzbahn playground.

EXCURSIONS
👨‍👧 Europa-Panoramaweg★★
Budget about 4hr for the entire trip, including about 2hr walking time.
This is a family-friendly hiking excursion, during which you'll be treated to panoramic **views**★ taking in 60 peaks over 3,000m/9,842.5ft, including the **Grossglockner**.
From Matrei, catch the Goldriedbahn cable-car to the mountain station at 2,150m/7,054ft, then embark on the easy walk to the **Kals-Matrei-Törlhaus**★★ along a wildflower-lined path. Stop here for refreshments or continue to the mountain station of the **Blauspitzbahn**, where there is another restaurant as well as a high-altitude **children's playground** 👨‍👧.
Take the Blauspitzbahn down into Kals, where you can hike out to Blauspitze and Kalsertal, or take buses back to Matrei *(information at the tourist office)*.

Virgental★
18km/11mi drive from Matrei to Ströden.
This scenic valley to the south of the Grossvenediger glacier is a delightful summer excursion. The dense forests in the lower part and the Alpine mountain scenery in the upper part are impressive. Prägraten is the most beautiful holiday resort in the valley. The Umbal Falls at the end of the road are well worth a visit.

VORARLBERG AND WEST TYROL

The far west of Austria can seem like a different country compared to the area around Vienna. It is, after all, almost 1,000km/625mi away. Aside from the spectacular high Alpine scenery, even the language is different, with a very strong local dialect, which German-speakers from elsewhere can find difficult to understand. Austria's westernmost province is Vorarlberg, whose capital, Bregenz, lies on the banks of the Bodensee (Lake Constance), a centre for watersports surrounded by vineyards and pretty villages. The town is at its liveliest during the summer when the Bregenz Festival, with its floating *Seebühne* (stage), is in full swing.

A Bit of History

The region around Bregenz, from low-lying pastures to high mountains, is known as the Bregenzerwald. It is an area of splendid views and small, rather sleepy villages. The closest major resort is Lech in the pretty Lechtal, a high-end sports centre (along with neighbouring Zürs and St. Anton) during the winter and a rather low-key, though still pleasant, place to while away the summer. Across the nearby Allgäu mountains lies the Kleinwalsertal, open more to Germany than Austria due to its geography, while to the east rise the mountains of the Arlberg. As well as being a major skiing area, the Arlberggebiet serves as the gateway to the Arlberg Pass, which leads over into neighbouring Tyrol. The whole region is full of delightful small villages and narrow mountain valleys to explore. In the far south of Vorarlberg, the Sil-vretta region is crammed with breath-taking mountains, glaciers, important skiing areas and the frontier with Italy.

Highlights

1 Following the cheese road in **Bregenzerwald** (p404)

2 Resting after a day's hiking in a **mountain hut** (p414)

3 A ride on the **Lünerseebahn cable-car** to the lake shore (p415)

4 Superb winter sports opportunities in the **Arlberg** ski region (p420)

5 Driving tour along one of Europe's highest roads in the **Kaunertal** (p424)

Mountain huts, Brandner Valley

© Austrian National Tourist Office/Popp Hackner

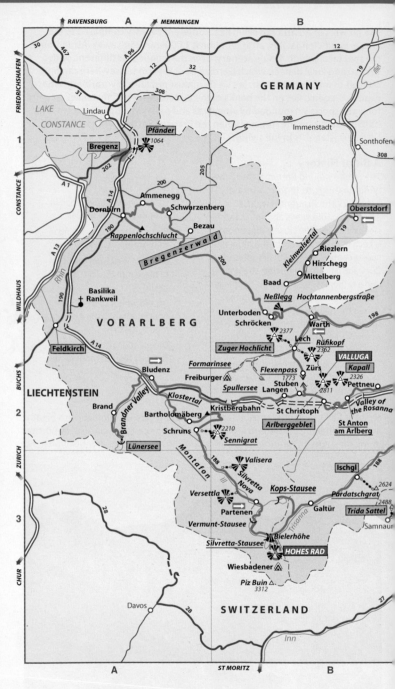

RAVENSBURG · MEMMINGEN

FRIEDRICHSHAFEN

CONSTANCE

WILDHAUS

BUCHS

ZURICH

CHUR

LAKE CONSTANCE

Lindau

Bregenz

Pfänder ▲ 1064

Immenstadt

Sonthofen

GERMANY

Oberstdorf

Ammenegg

Schwarzenberg

Dornbirn

Bezau

Rappenlochschlucht

Riezlern

Hirschegg

Mittelberg

Baad

Kleinwalsertal

Hochtannenbergstraße

Neßlegg

Basilika Rankweil

VORARLBERG

Unterboden

Schröcken

Warth

Rüfikopf 2362

VALLUGA

Feldkirch

Zuger Hochlicht 2377

Lech

Zürs

Kapall 2326

Pettneu

Bludenz

Formarinsee

Freiburger ⌂

Flexenpass 1773

Stuben 2811

LIECHTENSTEIN

Brand

Spullersee

Langen

St Christoph

Valley of the Rosanna

Bartholomäberg

Kristbergbahn

Arlberggeblet

St Anton am Arlberg

Schruns 2210

Sennigrat

Lünersee

Brandner Valley

Klostertal

Montafon

Valisera

Silvretta Nova

Ischgl

Versettla

Kops-Stausee

Pardatschgrat 2624

Partenen

Galtür

Trida Sattel 2488

Vermunt-Stausee

Samnaun

Bielerhöhe

Silvretta-Stausee

HOHES RAD

Wiesbadener ⌂

Piz Buin △ 3312

Davos

SWITZERLAND

Inn

ST MORITZ

Over in the adjoining region of Tyrol, the Oberes Inntal and the Kaunertal each offer awe-inspiring high mountain scenery. Beyond them to the east rise the impressive peaks of the Stubai. Perhaps the most celebrated valley in western Tyrol, however, is the Ötztal. Extremely beautiful, the valley's low-

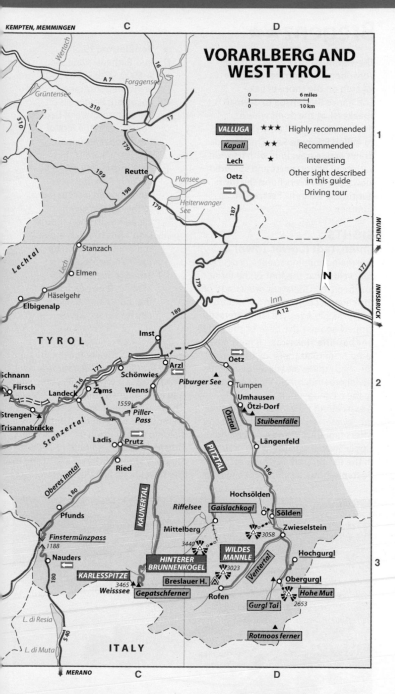

VORARLBERG AND WEST TYROL

0		6 miles
0		10 km

VALLUGA ★★★ Highly recommended

Kapall ★★ Recommended

Lech ★ Interesting

Oetz ⇨ Other sight described in this guide

Driving tour

TYROL

Reutte

Stanzach

Elmen

Häselgehr

Elbigenalp

Lechtal

Schnann

Flirsch

Landeck

Strengen

Trisannabrücke

Stanzertal

Oberes Inntal

Pfunds

Finstermünzpass
1188

Nauders

KARLESSPITZE

Schönwies

Wenns

Zams

Piller-
Pass
1559

Ladis ⇨ Prutz

Ried

KAUNERTAL

Riffelsee

Mittelberg

3440

HINTERER
BRUNNENKOGEL

Weisssee
3465
Gepatschferner

Breslauer H.

Rofen

Imst

Arzl

Piburger See

Oetz ⇨

Tumpen

Umhausen
Ötzi-Dorf

Stuibenfälle

Ötztal

PITZTAL

Längenfeld

Hochsölden

Gaislachkogl

Sölden

3058

Zwieselstein

WILDES
MANNLE

3023

Venertal

Gurgl Tal
2653

Hochgurgl

Obergurgl

Hohe Mut

Rotmoos ferner

ITALY

MERANO

Grüntensee

Forggensee

Plansee

Heiterwanger
See

Inn

MUNICH

INNSBRUCK

N

level bright green pastures lead up to a series of towering mountains, with a string of glaciers along the way. There are myriad opportunities for outdoor enthusiasts to walk, hike and climb in the area, or just to sit quietly and take in the marvellous views.

Bregenz★★

The administrative capital of the Vorarlberg, Bregenz is scenically located on the shore of Lake Constance (Bodensee to German speakers), at the point where the mountains spill down to the so-called Swabian Sea. The lakeside draws active travellers with its wide variety of watersports and splendid views. Music lovers flood the town during the Bregenz Festival in summer.

SIGHTS
Innenstadt (Lower Town)

The main shopping streets (*pedestrian zone*) cluster at the foot of the former fortified city (Oberstadt or Altstadt) of the counts of Bregenz and Montfort.

In the Middle Ages, the lake waters still lapped against the base of the little **Seekapelle** (lakeside chapel). Insulated from road traffic by the railway, the shady quays and flowerbeds of the lake shore stretch from the **Seeanlagen** to the passenger port.

A walk along the landscaped harbour breakwater is particularly pleasant and offers fabulous **views★** extending to Upper Swabia with the island of Lindau in the foreground. Farther west is the **Festspielhaus**, a complex of buildings

▶ **Population:** 29,140.

▯ *Info:* Rathausstraße 35a, A-6900. ℘05574 49 590. www.bregenz.travel.

◖ **Location:** Bregenz is on the eastern shore of Lake Constance at the foot of the Pfänder Mountain. Alt. 398m/1,306ft.

▣ **Parking:** Plenty of public parking. An automated guide system directs you to the nearest garage or car park with open spaces.

☻ **Don't Miss:** A walk around the Oberstadt; a trip up the Pfänder Mountain.

◷ **Timing:** Spend the day in town, then head up the mountain late in the day for sunset views.

designed specifically for the Bregenz Festival (http://bregenzerfestspiele.com), which hosts cultural events year-round and is the prime venue for the festival. The most spectacular performances, though, are held on the **Seebühne**, a floating stage jutting out into the lake outside the festival hall. In 2008 the floating stage featured in a scene in the James Bond film *Quantum of Solace*.

Lake Constance and Bregenz

© McPHOTO/age fotostock

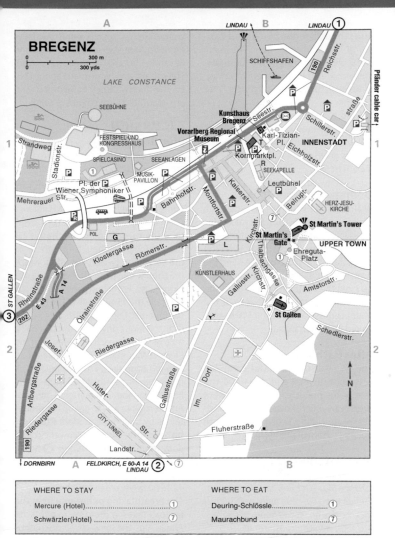

WHERE TO STAY		WHERE TO EAT	
Mercure (Hotel)....................	①	Deuring-Schlössle........................	①
Schwärzler(Hotel)	⑦	Maurachbund	⑦

Vorarlberg Museum★

Kornmarktplatz 1. Open year-round Tue–Sun 10am–6pm (Thu til 8pm). €9. ℘05574 46 050. www.vorarlbergmuseum.at.
Incorporating parts of the old structure, the museum's new building (2013) by Bregenz architects Andreas Cukrowicz and Anton Nachbaur-Sturm is stunningly modern. The façade is dotted with 16,000-plus "flowers" (concrete-cast plastic bottle bottoms).
The collections include prehistory and Roman history, folkloric costumes and musical instruments: a highlight is an

early 16C portable organ. Religious art has been scavenged from the richest churches in the province, including an early 16C crucifix from the former abbey church at Mehrerau west of Bregenz. There are also works of mythological or religious inspiration and portraits *(Duke of Wellington)* by **Angelika Kauffmann** (1741–1807), considered a native of the Vorarlberg because of her connection with the Bregenzerwald. She lived in Italy and England and was a founding member of England's Royal Academy. On nearby Karl-Tizian-Platz and close to the shores of the Bodensee is the 1997

Kunsthaus Bregenz★

(⏰*open year-round Tue–Sun 10am–6pm (Thu 8pm); €9; ☎05574 485 940; www.kunsthaus-bregenz.at)*, an unapologetically modernist structure by Swiss architect Peter Zumthor.

Behind the striking façade of etched glass are changing contemporary art exhibits. An architectural tour *(in German)* is given on the first Sunday of the month (€5).

Oberstadt (Upper Town)★

With its quiet squares and lanes, the charming **Church Quarter** makes for a peaceful contrast to the bustling lake shore. It can be reached by car via the Kirchstraße, the Thalbachgasse and the Amtstorstraße. If you're walking, stroll up from the central intersection of the Leutbühel by the paved ramp of the Maurachgasse as far as the Martinstor, an old fortified gateway.

Altes Rathaus

The 17C, half-timbered Old Town Hall was built in 1662 and remained the seat of the municipal authorities until the 19C. A relief shows the Celtic goddess of agriculture, Epona, on horseback holding a horn of plenty.

Martinsturm (St. Martin's Tower)

⏰*Open May–Oct Tue–Sun 10am–4pm (Thu til 9pm), Jul–Aug daily. €3.50 (ticket office on second floor). ☎05574 410 1561. www.martinsturm.at.*

A Bregenz landmark, this 13C tower got its huge onion dome (one of the largest in Austria) only around 1600. The chapel in the tower base contains a massive Late Gothic altar canopy and fairly well preserved 14C frescoes. Upstairs is a small military museum through whose windows you can enjoy **glimpses★** of the remains of the wall, the Old Town, the lake and belfries of Lindau and, in the distance, the Appenzell Alps.

St. Gallen Parish Church

This streamside single-nave Baroque church is decorated in the restrained ecclesiastical style typical of the Vorarlberg churches, which contrasts with the more opulent style of the Tyrolean and Bavarian churches of the same period. The walnut stalls were made about 1740 for the nearby abbey of Mehrerau and are decorated with effigies of saints.

EXCURSION
Pfänder★★

Summer mists make it advisable to take this excursion either in the early morning or in the evening before sunset. Leave Bregenz on 1 (⏱ see map, top right); take the lakeside road to Lindau.

To drive up the Pfänder, turn right towards the village of **Lochau**. Past the church in Lochau, turn right onto the steep and twisting by-road, which reaches a car park *(fee)* after about 6km/3.7mi. From here, you can get out and take the 15min walk to the Pfänder summit *(alt. 1,064m/3,491ft)*.

If you continue driving for another half a mile or so, you reach a plateau with the Pfänder Mountain refuge (🅿*fee-based parking available)*. From opposite the mountain hut, a small trail leads to the Pfänder summit in a matter of minutes. An alternative way to get up the mountain is by taking the modern **Pfänderbahn cable-car** (⏰*open year-round daily 8am–7pm every 30min;* ⏱*closed mid-Nov, mid-Feb–Mar;* €12.50 round-trip (summer), €36.50 (winter); ☎05 574 42 16 00; www.pfaenderbahn.at).*

The breathtaking **panorama** from the plateau takes in *(from left to right)* the Allgäu Alps, the snow-covered Schesaplana, the great furrow of the Rhine and the Altmann, and the Säntis on the Swiss side. Paragliders usually contribute to the scenery as well.

North of the plateau is the **Alpenwildpark** (Alpine Wildlife Park) game reserve (⏰*open daily, freely open, no set hours;* ☎5574 42 184; www.pfaender.at)*, where a 30min circuit introduces you to Alpine fauna such as mouflons, ibex, marmots and red deer, housed in generous enclosures. There are also children's favourites: dwarf goats, pot-bellied pigs, and rabbits.

ADDRESSES

⌂ STAY

Hotel Mercure – *Platz der Wiener Symphoniker 2.* ✆*05574 46 10 00. www. mercure.at. 94 rooms.* ⌸*€15.* Located near the lake, this reliable chain hotel has good quality rooms and includes Internet access. International dishes are served in a restaurant (⊖⊜) with a terrace.

Hotel Schwärzler – *Landstr. 9.* ✆*0557 44 990. http://schwaerzler.s-hotels. com. 83 rooms.* ⌸. Situated near the meadows of Bregenzerach, a 20min walk from the pedestrian zone, this modern, elegant hotel features a pleasant restaurant (⊖⊜⊜) where patrons can dine by candlelight, accompanied by piano music.

⌁ EAT

Maurachbund – *Maurachgasse 11.* ✆*05574 45 029. www.maurachbund.com. Daily 11am–11pm.* This attractive traditional restaurant in the Old Town specialises in regional dishes using locally produced ingredients.

SHOPPING

Wolford Boutique– *Wolfordstraße 1. Open Mon–Fri 9am–7.30pm, Sat 9am–5pm. www.wolford.com.* Wolford is famous for its fashionable and high-quality legwear and lingerie. Restaurant in store.

Bregenzerwald★★

Its German name implies that the Bregenzerwald is a dense forest ("wald" meaning "forest"). However, it is in fact a wonderfully diverse natural playground with landscapes ranging from softly rolling hills to majestic Alpine peaks. The unspoiled countryside, traditional wooden houses and villages, and a local population that still cherishes their ancient customs make the Bregenzerwald a popular destination.

🛈 **Info:** Gerbe 1135, A-6863 Egg. ✆05512 23 65. www.bregenzerwald.at.
▶ **Location:**
The Bregenzerwald is located between Bregenz on Lake Constance and the Arlberg range.
☺ **Don't Miss:**
Rappenlochschlucht.
👥 **Kids:** Inatura in Dornbirn.

🚗 DRIVING TOUR

HOCHTANNENBERGSTRASSE★
65km/40.4mi.

▶ The road between Warth and Schröcken may be closed for days at a time Nov and Mar due to avalanches.

This route crosses the **Hochtannberg pass** *(alt. 1,675m/5,495ft)*, which is closed occasionally, and follows the twisting Bregenzerach River. The crossing of the Bödele Pass lends a mountainous character to the final leg of the trip and provides magnificent views of the Rhine Valley. Between Warth and Nesslegg the road runs through the Hochtannberg pastureland.

Nesslegg★
From the viewpoint by the Hotel Widderstein, you'll have a fine **overview★** of the cirque closing the upper valley of the Bregenzerach. From left to right you can see the Mohnenfluh, the Braunarlspitz and its snowfields, the Hochberg, the Schadonapass gap and the Hochkünzelspitze.
From Nesslegg, the road plunges down through forest, offering occasional glimpses of the village of **Schröcken**.

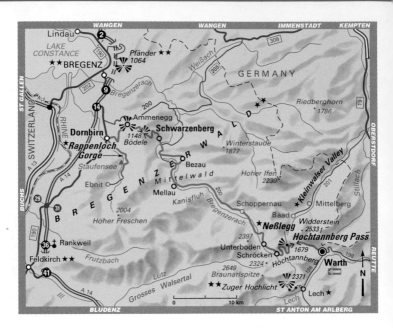

Downstream from the well-engineered Hochtannberg bridge appears the hamlet of **Unterboden**, a typical Valaisian settlement.

Between Schoppernau and the resort of **Mellau**, the varied form of the Kanisfluh is revealed; its north face is formed of particularly steep cliffs.

The road continues through a succession of idyllic landscapes. Farther on, wide valleys with their fruit-growing enterprises are graced by the villages of **Bezau** and Schwarzenberg.

Schwarzenberg

This sleepy village is centred on a pretty **square★** flanked by flower-festooned houses (e.g. Gasthof Hirschen). The parish church features several works by the famous artist **Angelika Kauffmann** (1741–1807), including the medallions representing the Apostles and Jesus' disciples, and the picture on the high altar. Look for the artist's bust on the north wall of the nave. More of her works can be seen in the Vorarlberg Museum

KäseStraße Bregenzerwald

Strictly speaking, the *KäseStraße* (Cheese Road) in Bregenzerwald is not a set route from one sight to another, rather it is an association of farms producers, dairies, guesthouses, inns and restaurants that either produce, sell, or serve local cheeses. What you visit is your choice depending on your interests. Hikers, cyclists and motorists can each choose their own routes on this 70km/43.5mi itinerary. There are mountain huts where cheese is made in the traditional way that are accessible only on foot.

Old sawmills are included, as they provided the wood used to produce the cheese-making tools and the moulds. Numerous restaurants serve typical cheese dishes, including fried cheese and cheese dumplings.

All members of the association are signposted with and display the letter "K" (denoting *KäseStraße*). To find out more, contact ☏05513 428 70 41 or visit www.kaesestrasse.at.

Bregenzerwald

© Austrian National Tourist Office/ Popp Hackner

in Bregenz and the Heimatmuseum in Schwarzenberg.

Crossing the Bödele ridge gives clear **views★** to the east of the open basin of the Bregenzerwald and the Allgäu Alps, marking the German border. On the Rhine slope, after a long run through forest, the **panorama★** opens out near **Ammenegg** extending, in clear weather, to Lake Constance and the Appenzell Alps.

Dornbirn

The largest town in Vorarlberg, Dornbirn has few tourist-worthy sights. An exception is the child-friendly **Inatura** 👫 *(Jahngasse 9;* ◷ *open daily 10am–6pm;* ⊚€11, children 6–15 years €5.50; ℰ05572 23 235; www.inatura.at)*, an educational journey into the natural history of the Vorarlberg. Experiences include a visit to an underwater cinema and a virtual trip back into prehistoric times.

◗ Leave Dornbirn on the road towards Ebnit/Gütle. After about 3.5km/2.2mi you reach the car park for the Rappenlochschlucht 🅿.

Rolls-Royce-Museum

Gütle 11a. ◷*Open Feb–Nov Tue–Sun 10am–6pm (Jul–Aug daily).* ⊚€9. ℰ0557 25 26 52. *www.rolls-royce-museum.at.*

A 19C textile factory houses the world's largest collection of Rolls Royces. The more than 1,000 vehicles include those once used by the Queen Mother, King George V, and General Franco. A reconstruction of F. H. Royce's garage gives an insight into his work over 100 years ago.

🚶 Rappenlochschlucht★

Allow 1hr30min for the walk as far as the road to Ebnit. ◷*Open late Apr–late Oct.* ℰ0557 22 21 88. 👣*Free guided walks Jul–Aug Thu 10.30am: meet at the sequoia in Gütle* 🅿. *www.rappenloch.at.*

A 20min walk along wooden walkways above the turbulent waters of the Dornbirner Ache brings you to the mighty cliffs of the 72m/236ft Rappenloch Gorge. Beyond here, a path along the Staufensee reservoir leads to the impressive Alploch Gorge and waterfall. It takes about 20min as far as the Ebnit road. From here, retrace your steps to the car park.

Lech ❄❄

Lech is indisputably the prettiest holiday destination in the Austrian Alps, and one of the few resorts in the northern Alps to have made a name for itself as an international winter-sports venue. Upscale and imbued with an air of exclusivity, it is a favourite haunt of royalty, celebrities and the wealthy.

SIGHTS

Lech has won its reputation thanks in part to its merging with the neighbouring resorts of **Zürs** 🎿 and **St. Anton** 🎿 (*see separate entries*) to create a ski area capable of meeting the most demanding standards, but most of all because of its insistence on quality above quantity. Here, biggest is not allowed to be best, and tourist facilities have been built very much with the welfare of the natural environment in mind. For this reason, guest capacity is only about 7,000, or three to six times smaller than the demand in the other major European winter-sports resorts. Accommodation consists mainly of hotels and family guesthouses in the luxury category with an après-ski scene to match.

Expect plenty of exclusive boutiques, elegant cafés, gourmet restaurants and upscale cultural activities.

▶ **Population:** 1,500.

🛈 **Info:** *Dorf 2,* A-6764. 𝒫 05583 21 610. www.lech-zuers.at.

◐ **Location:** Lech is in the far western reaches of Austria, close to the borders with Germany, Lichtenstein and Switzerland. Alt. 1,447m/4,747ft.

🅿 **Parking:** In the Anger underground parking garage. Free in summer.

⊛ **Don't Miss:** Zuger Hochlicht.

🕑 **Timing:** Allow two or three days to fully enjoy the mountains.

Lech also has a lot to offer in the summer months, when life takes on a much calmer pace. Although there are no particularly breathtaking panoramas, the soft green meadows of the surrounding countryside are most restorative.

Recreational Sights

The area is great for hiking and mountain bike tours, most popularly in the Formarin, Ferwall and Moos valleys. One of Lech's major attractions is the large, open-air swimming pool in a pretty woodland setting. Anglers can

Lech am Arlberg

© Austrian National Tourist Office/Felder

Cross-country skiing, Lech am Arlberg

© Austrian National Tourist Office/Mallaun

choose among lakes such as the Forma-rinsee, Spullsee, Zürssee or Zugweiher (☞enquire about fishing permits at the Lech tourist office)

The Town★

The town of Lech lies on a mountain pla-teau *(alt. 1,444–1,717m/4,738–5,633ft)*. Limestone peaks (the Mohnenfluh and Braunarlspitze to the north, Rote Wand to the west, Schafberg and Ome-shorn to the south and Rüfispitze to the east) tower above the lush Alpine pastures and forests that grow at up to 1,800m/5,900ft above sea-level. Although difficult access roads and the sheer cliff faces of Omeshorn and Rüfikopf lend the area an undeniably mountainous aspect, the mountains around Lech are not in fact that tall. None of the surrounding peaks is higher than 2,700m/8,850ft, and there is not a single glacier in sight.

The town of Lech is spread along the banks of its namesake river. It retains little physical evidence of its past, although the Gothic **church**, a few farmhouses from the days of the Valais (e.g. Haus Anger at no. 19) and the court in the Weisses Haus (16C) opposite the Hotel Krone, are noteworthy exceptions. Farther uphill, the resort of **Oberlech** *(alt. 1,700m/5,577ft)* hugs a slope of the Kriegerhorn and is blessed with plenty of sunshine, excellent snow conditions and a sweeping view. In winter, Oberlech is car free and accessible only by cable-car. If you're seeking respite from the hub-bub of the ski slopes and fellow skiers, the hamlets of Zug to the west and Stubenbach to the east offer calmer alternatives.

Ski Slopes
Arlberg ski slopes 🎿

These slopes, which encompass *(from north to south)* the resorts of Lech, Zürs, Stuben, and St. Anton, are the largest and most varied in Austria. They include more than 260km/162mi of maintained and 180km/112mi of open slopes, to which 84 ski-lifts give access. It is pos-sible to ski from Lech to Zürs and back, and likewise from Stuben and St. Anton. To get from Zürs to Stuben or St. Anton, however, you need to take the bus.

The **ski area** 🎿 attached to Lech extends over two mountains. Most of the ski runs are on the Kriegerhorn and the Zuger Hochlicht *(alt. 1,450–2,377m/4,757–7,799ft)*. The guaranteed snow cover and the gentle slopes make skiing here an enjoyable and relaxing experience. The Mohnenmähderpiste (very easy) and the Steinmähderpiste (intermediate) are definitely worth a try. Experienced skiers will prefer the Rüfikopf *(alt. 1,450–2,362m/4,757–*

7,749ft). This is the departure point for two off-piste runs (the Langerzug and the Tannegg), which can be tackled with a ski instructor.

EXCURSIONS
Zuger Hochlicht★★

Alt. 2,377m/7,799ft.
In winter accessible to skiers only, allowing 1hr30min round-trip.
Take the Schlegelkopf and then the Kriegerhorn chairlifts, followed by the Mohnenfluh cable-car. In summer, it is possible to take the **Petersboden chairlift** *from Oberlech, and then do the tour of the Zuger Hochlicht round via the Mohnenfluhsattel gap and on to Butzensee Lake (2hr15min round-trip walk).* ⏰*Operates late Jun–Sept daily 8.30am–5pm.* ⊜*€7 round trip.* ℘*05583 21 610. www.lechzuers.com.*

From the Kriegerhorn *(alt.2,173m/7,129ft)* there is a broad view of the Zuger Valley against a backdrop of the Rote Wand cliffs, to the west, and of the Zuger Hochlicht ski slopes, to the north. To the south lies **Zürs**, at the foot of the majestic Rüfispitze and the precipitous Roggspitze.

The Zuger Hochlicht reveals a beautiful **panorama★★** of the Arlberg region, the Lechtal Alps and the Rätikon. There is an all-round panorama from the peak itself, reached in a few minutes from the far left end of the cable-car station. The Hochtannberg pass road can be seen farther below.

Rüfikopf★

Alt. 2,362m/7,749ft. ⏰*Cable-car operates late Jun–Sept daily 8.30am–5.30pm.* ⊜*€17.50 round trip.* ℘*05583 21 61. www.lechzuers.com.*
There is a beautiful overall view from this summit of the resort town and the Lech ski slopes against the rocky Mohnenfluh and Braunarlspitze peaks. The Rüfikopf is a good departure point for a ski trip to Zürs.

🚶 HIKING

The Lechtal Alps offer numerous possibilities for walking and hiking tours, with 200km/124mi of marked trails.

🚶 Spullersee★

The toll road to the lake is closed to cars from 9am to 3pm, but buses make the trip in 30min from the Lech post office (the tourist office has timetables).
🅿 *You can park in the Anger underground garage (free during summer) opposite the post office.*

This scenic **drive★** leads through bucolic countryside. Level with the toll booth, there is a municipal swimming pool set in the woods. Then the road passes through the pretty village of Zug, with Alpine pastures, through which the Spullerbach creek winds a course in between clumps of fir and larch.

Finally, after a very steep climb, the road reaches the **Spullersee★**, which lies in a spectacular natural amphitheatre 1,827m/5,994ft above sea-level. The major summits are the Plattnitzer Spitze and Rohnspitze to the south, the Wildgrubenspitze to the east and the Spuller Schafberg *(alt. 2,679m/8,789ft)* and Pfaffeneck to the north.

🚶 Formarinsee★

Take the bus to the lake. The first half of the trip is identical to that described above. Allow 30min for the bus ride and then 10min walk downhill on a well-maintained trail.
The Formarinsee *(alt. 1,789m/5,869ft)* lies at the foot of the Rote Wand *(Red Wall, after the colour of the limestone; alt. 2,704m/8,871ft).*

🚶 Walk from the Formarinsee to the Spullersee★★

Allow 4hr for this quite taxing walk, parts of which should be tackled with care. Difference in altitude is about 600m/2,000ft. Walking boots are essential. ⚠ *This walk is dangerous in mist or fog, or if the ground is damp.*
Take the bus to the Formarinsee, but instead of walking down to the lake, take the trail that climbs gently up to the left *(waymarked in yellow).* The path, dotted with Alpine roses, leads right along the edge of the cliff, offering lovely views of the Formarinsee below before reaching the **Freiburger Hütte** (mountain refuge).

From here take path no. 601 towards the Ravensburger Hütte *(waymarked in red)*. After 30min of easy climb towards the Formaletsch range, the path crosses a picturesque limestone plateau, a real sea of rocks, known aptly enough as **Steinernes Meer** (Stony Sea).

⊘ *Do not leave the waymarked path!* Beyond here, the trail again becomes more clearly defined, climbing steeply up to the **Gehrengrat**, where chamois and ibex may be spotted. There is a good view of the Verwall range, the Kloster Valley and the Rätikon. A very steep path leads from the summit down to the Spullersee *(allow 1hr30min; follow signs to Ravensburger Hütte, or RH)*. On reaching the lake, turn left. After about 5min, the trail comes to the bus stop for the return trip to Lech.

🚗 DRIVING TOUR

OBERES LECHTAL
61km/37mi from Warth to Reutte. The Upper Lech Valley is in the far western reaches of Austria.
🛈 *Untergiblen 23, 6652 Elbigenalp.*
📞05634 53 15. www.lechtal.at.
⊘ *Avalanches may temporarily close the road between Warth and Steeg.*

Upstream from Reutte, the Upper Lech Valley hollows out a deep 60km/37mi-long furrow between the Allgäu and Lechtal Alps. It's a sparsely inhabited area due, in large part, to poor agricultural soil, forcing many locals to leave the valley to seek employment elsewhere. However, having made their fortune, many return to their home villages for retirement, which accounts for the grand houses, often sporting beautifully painted façades.

Between **Warth** and **Steeg** the road travels through a series of gorges, before entering a harsh landscape of forest and rocks.

Elbigenalp
The Tyrolean tradition of woodcarving is still very much alive in this village. In 1768 the painter **Joseph Anton Koch**, known for his heroic landscapes, was born in the suburb of Untergiblen.

The sharp pointed spire of the **Pfarrkirche St. Nikolaus** has made it one of the most distinctive images of the upper Lech Valley. The exuberant Baroque interior, with a riot of almost luminous fresco decoration is the work of Johann Jakob Zeiller.

◗ Drive 34km/21mi NE on the B 198.

Reutte
Reutte is the economic capital of the Ausserfern district and a good starting point for walks in summer and skiing in winter. Reutte is the home town of the Zeiller family of painters, whose Baroque frescoes adorn many a church interior in the Tyrol and south Germany.

The collection of the **Heimatmuseum** *(*🕐*open May–Oct Tue–Sat 1pm–5pm;* 👝 *€3;* 📞*05672 723 04; www.museum-reutte.at)* focuses mainly on works by the Zeiller family and their pupils, as well as the history and customs of the local district.

ADDRESSES

🏨 STAY AND 🍴EAT

◗◉🛏🛏 **Haus Wöster** – *Strass 176.* 📞*05583 29 97. www.ferienwohnung-in-lech.at. 5 rooms.* 🍽. Small, typical, family-run pension. Bright spacious rooms.

◗◉🛏🛏 **Hotel Alpenrose** – *Lech 237.* 📞*05583 22 92. www.alpenrose-lech.com. Closed late Apr–late Jun and early Oct–Nov. 19 rooms.* 🍽. Beautiful, traditional Alpine lodge.

◗◉🛏🛏 **Hotel Fernsicht** – *Anger 233.* 📞*05583 24 32. www.fernsicht-lech.at. Closed late Apr–mid Jul and early Sept–Nov. 18 rooms.* 🍽. Charming and welcoming hotel with individually decorated rooms.

◗◉🛏🛏 **Post Lech** – *Lech 11.* 📞*05583 22 060. www.postlech.com. Closed mid Apr–mid-Jun, late Sept–Nov. 46 rooms.* 🍽. This Relais & Chateaux establishment features a gourmet restaurant, a spa and beautifully appointed, traditional guest rooms.

Kleinwalsertal★

The Kleinwalsertal is a small region isolated from the rest of Austria by the Allgäu Alps and is thus exclusively oriented towards Germany – whether it be economically or through tourism. It shares a ski area with Oberstdorf across the border and is a departure point for scenic mountain hikes during the warmer seasons.

▶ **Population:** 5 300.

Info: Walserstraße 264, A-6992. ℘05517 511 40. www.kleinwalsertal.com; Oberstdorf, Prinzregenten-Platz 1, D-87561. ℘08 322 70 00. www.oberstdorf.de.

Location: In the north of Bregenzerwald; access is through Germany. Alt of resorts: 1,086m/3,563ft to 1,244m/4,081ft.

Don't Miss: Oberstdorf.

Timing: Allow a day to explore this valley at a leisurely pace.

🚗 DRIVING TOUR

OBERSTDORF (GERMANY) TO BAAD
14km/8.6mi from the border.

Oberstdorf★★
This is a charming mountain spa resort and winter-sports centre at the foot of the majestic Nebelhorn. *Traffic is barred from the town centre.*

▶ From Oberstdorf head S on B 19, reaching the Austrian border after 5km/3mi.

The road through the Kleinwalsertal (*B 201*) serves **Riezlern**, **Hirschegg**, **Mittelberg** and its offshoot **Baad**. The highest mountain at the end of the valley is the imposing Grosser Widderstein (*alt. 2,533m/8,311ft*).

Walsermuseum
Riezlern tourist office. ⏰*Closed for renovation until mid-2017.* ℘05517 5315 286. www.kleinwalertal.com.
Here you will find an exhibition on the history and way of life (including traditional costume) of the valley and its inhabitants. The second floor has reconstructions of a typical Valaisian chalet and an Alpine dairy hut.

▶ Follow the B 201 for 1.7km/1mi SW to Hirschegg.

👥 Skimuseum
In the Walserhaus in Hirschegg. ⏰*Open year-round Mon–Fri 9am–7pm, Sun 8am–1pm, 3pm–7pm.* 🎫*Free.* ℘05517 511 40. www.walserhaus.at.
The evolution of various winter sports from the late 19C to around World War II is retraced here with the help of numerous exhibits on the first and second floors of the Walserhaus.

Bergschau 1122
In the Walserhaus in Hirschegg. ⏰*Open year-round Mon–Fri 9am–7pm, Sun 8am–1pm.* 🎫*Free.* ℘05517 511 40. www.bergschau.com.
This small but engaging exhibit focuses on life in the Allgäu Alps from prehistoric times onwards. Discoveries include the magic world of crystals seen through a video microscope and an interactive relief model of the valley.

▶ Follow the B 201 3km/1.8mi S to Mittelberg, then fork left towards Baad. After around 1.7km/1mi you will see the Walserhaus.

Walserhaus
Bödmerstraße 82, Mittelberg. ⏰*Not open to the public.*
This small, typical Valaisian house has an original one-piece, stone-slab covered roof dating from 1552.

Arlberggebiet★★

Wedged between the Upper Rhine and the Inn corridor, the mountainous region of the Arlberg was for a long time a formidable obstacle to communications. Nowadays, the road to the Arlberg Pass, a 10km/6.2mi-long railway tunnel and the 14km/8.7mi-long Arlberg road tunnel link the Vorarlberg and the Tyrol.

Info: Dorfstraße 8. ℘05446 226 90. www.stantonam arlberg.com.

Location: West of Innsbruck.

Parking: Parking is plentiful and, outside the resorts, free.

Timing: Allow one day for each of the tours described.

A BIT OF HISTORY
Cradle of Alpine skiing

The Arlberg region is one of the prime skiing destinations in the Austrian Alps with a pedigree going back to 1901, when the country's first ski club was formed here. Twenty years later, local boy **Hannes Schneider** (1890–1955), who some consider the father of modern skiing, founded Austria's first ski school in St. Anton. Together with British skiing pioneer **Sir Arnold Lunn** (1888–1974), Schneider organised the first **Arlberg-Kandahar Cup** in 1928 famous downhill and slalom races that continue to this day.

SIGHT
Biosphären Park Großes Walsertal

Rathausgasse 12, A-6700 Bludenz. ℘05554 51 50. www.grosseswalsertal.at.
The six village communities in this Alpine valley are included in the biosphere reserve, which received UNESCO recognition in November 2000. Hiking the 250km/155.3mi of mountain paths takes you to summer alps, where cheese is still made in the traditional way. Traditional farming and forestry management ensure that the great diversity of plant and animal life are not threatened. Follow the educational trails or take a guided walk to learn more of "the way of life in the valley".

🚗 DRIVING TOURS

1 ARLBERG PASS TOUR★
68km/42.3mi.

Bludenz
This town, at the meeting point of five valleys (Walgau, Brandnertal, Montafon, Klostertal, and Großwalsertal), centres

---

Why Kandahar?

The first downhill race on skis was organised at Montana in Switzerland on 6 January 1911 by Sir Arnold Lunn, who promoted competitive Alpine skiing.

The race was sponsored by Lord Roberts of Kandahar (1832–1914), a British Field Marshal who took his title from the name of a town in Afghanistan, which was captured by the Indian army during a military campaign. His name was then adopted for the Kandahar skiing club, founded by Lunn (*see above*) in 1924. The Arlberg-Kandahar Ski Cup, an international skiing event held at Arlberg since 1928 and still contested today, takes its exotic name from this club.

Skiers who are named five times among the first three in the downhill, slalom or combined event, are awarded the Kandahar diamond. Karl Schranz of Austria has gained this honour twice in his career.

The Brotherhood of St. Christoph

Crossing the Arlberg Pass used to be a major hurdle for travellers. Many risked, or even lost, their lives due to storms, severe cold or the hazards of the route. For this reason, Heinrich the Foundling from Kempten had an emergency shelter and chapel built just below the Pass in 1386. Heinrich founded the Brotherhood for the upkeep of the hospice, its charitable works to be funded by donations. Even royalty joined the association, and its patrons came from as far afield as Prague, Magdeburg and Strasbourg. The Reformation heralded the decline of the Brotherhood and it was finally disbanded under Emperor Joseph II. However, it was reinstated by the Tyrolean bishopric in 1961 and now has more than 11,000 members globally, whose donations go towards helping those in need all over the world.

on a handsome Old Town and is an ideal base for local excursions.

▶ An alternative to the Arlberg tunnel road is the old road via Innerbraz, Dalaas, Wald and Klösterle. It takes longer and is quieter but will treat you to plenty of delightful mountain views.

On leaving Bludenz, the craggy outcrop of the Roggelskopf *(alt. 2,284m/7,494ft)* comes into view. After Dalaas, a nice fresh panorama opens out with the steep wooded slopes of the Batzigg *(alt. 1,833m/6,014ft)* backed by the Rohnspitze peak *(alt. 2,455m/8,055ft)*.
At **Langen** is the monumental entrance to the **Arlberg tunnel road**, which ends at St. Anton 14km/8.7mi later.

Stuben ≈

From this tiny, peaceful village, skiers can travel directly to the St. Anton ski slopes. Three chairlifts give access to the **Albonagrat★** ridge. There's excellent off-piste skiing as well.

St. Christoph am Arlberg

The Brotherhood of St. Christoph has maintained a hospice here since 1386. Travellers can still find shelter in a hospice-hotel and visit the Brotherhood Chapel nearby.

St. Anton am Arlberg ≈ ≈

See ST. ANTON AM ARLBERG.

Stanzertal

After St. Anton, the road traverses the bucolic **Stanzertal**, also known as the Valley of the Rosanna, carving its way between the Lechtal Alps to the north and the Hoher Riffler range to the south. After passing through such

attractive resorts as **St. Jakob**, **Pettneu**, **Schnann** and **Flirsch**, the road runs between forested slopes as the valley narrows. Shortly after **Strengen**, the last resort in the Stanzertal, the amazing **Trisannabrücke**, a steel-construction railway bridge across the River Trisanna, comes into view. A masterpiece of engineering, it was completed in 1884 and measures 86m/282ft high and 120m/393.7ft long.

Landeck

Landeck, where the Arlberg road meets the Inn Valley, lies at the foot of an imposing **castle** (13C–18C), now a local history museum.

The nearby **Liebfrauenkirche** is the only Late Gothic church in the northern Tyrol: it has an impressive winged altarpiece representing the Adoration of the Magi.

Stanzertal

© Austrian National Tourist Office/Mallaun

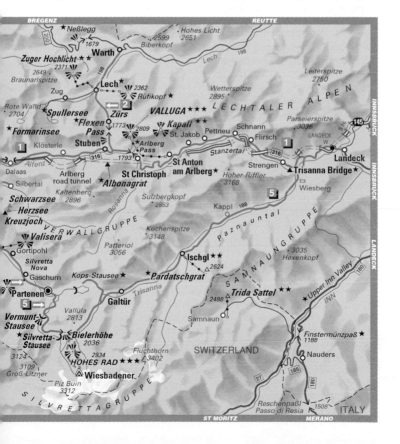

② FLEXENPASS TOUR★

17km/10.5mi.

The road is open year-round from the turn-off as far as Lech. The stretch farther north, between Lech and Warth, is often closed by snow in winter.

The scenic and winding Flexenpass Road branches off the Arlberg Rass road east of Stuben and runs over the Flexenpass *(alt. 1,773m/5,816ft)* into the Lech Valley and to the ski resorts of Zürs and Lech.

Zürs

See ZÜRS.

After two tunnels, just before Lech the valley narrows into a breathtaking, rocky ravine only a few metres wide.

Lech★

See LECH.

After Lech, the road runs halfway up the valley through a less rugged landscape. Softly undulating Alpine meadows alternate with steep rocky cliffs, dotted with majestic spruce trees. At the entrance to Warth, the imposing Biberkopf peak *(alt. 2,599m/8,527ft)* comes into view.

Warth

This small resort is less frenetic than Lech and Zürs, and offers great hiking in summer and the full range of snow sports in winter.

From Warth you can choose between either continuing to Lake Constance through the Bregenzerwald region (*see BREGENZERWALD*) or crossing the Upper Lech Valley (*see OBERES LECHTAL*) towards Reutte and the border with Germany.

③ BRANDNER VALLEY TOUR★★

15km/9.3mi along narrow roads plus a 2hr round-trip walk.

On leaving Bludenz, the well-built road towards Brand offers an overview of the town before climbing through a forest. Past Bürserberg the view opens out along the Brandner Valley towards the Schesaplana summit *(alt. 2,965m/9,728ft)*. Beyond here, the valley gets increasingly narrow.

Through a gorge to the left there is a **view★** of the Zimba peak *(alt. 2,643m/8,671ft)*, the mini-Matterhorn of the Arlberg region. The route down

---

Hut-to-Hut

In summer the mountains are popular with hikers enjoying the hut-to-hut experience. The term hut (or *Hütte*) is a bit of a misnomer, as they are more akin to mountain inns. They are spread across the high Alpine pastures, passes and slopes of the mountain regions. Refreshments are served at these mountain huts, and many of them also offer hostel-style accommodation. Many hikers plan their route around the huts, stopping for a drink, a snack or lunch and maybe dinner and a bed for the night.

In all of Austria there are 528 huts, many of which are operated by the **Österreichischer Alpenverein** *(Wilhelm-Greil-Str. 15; A-6010 Innsbruck; ☎0512 59 54 77; www.alpenverein.at)*. There are also numerous independent, family-run huts. Generally the food is good-but-basic, and because of the difficulty in supplying the huts, the choice is usually limited. Dairy products generally feature in huts where the owner has a few cows or goats pastured during the summer.

Maps of the huts' location can be picked up in most local tourist offices and are also marked on the hiking maps. If planning to stay overnight, booking is recommended. Members of any Alpine club affiliated with Österreichischer Alpenverein get a discount on the overnight rates.

Lünersee

© Austrian National Tourist Office/Ender

into the Brand basin reveals the resort's picturesque **setting**★ to full advantage.

Brand

This village, founded by immigrants from the Valais region, is a popular year-round resort. The road out of the village climbs to the foot of the **cirque**★★, a great natural amphitheatre closing off the valley. The road ends after the Schattenlagant refuge.

▷ Leave the car at the lower cable-car station.

Lünersee★★

2hr round-trip, including 10min by cable-car. ⊙*Operates late May–mid- Oct daily 8am–12.20pm, 1.10pm–4.55pm every half hour.* ⊛€*11.80 round-trip.* ℘*05556 701 80 420. www.luenersee.at.*

The **Lünerseebahn cable-car** delivers riders to the lakeshore next to the Douglasshütte chalet. Set in a ring of jagged rocky crests, the Lünersee *(alt. 1,970m/6,463ft)*, in its original state, was the largest natural mountain lake of the eastern Alps. In 1958 the water level was raised 27m/88.6ft by a dam, creating a vast reservoir feeding the Lünersee and Rodund power stations more than 1,000m/3,281ft below.

④ MONTAFON VALLEY TOUR★

40km/25mi drive from Bludenz to Partenen.

The valley is 39km/24mi long and near the far western edge of Austria, close to Switzerland. ℘*0555 672 25 30. www.montafon.at.*

Montafon★ is a charming, densely populated valley surrounded by three major massifs: the Rätikon in the northwest, the Silvretta in the south and the Verrwall in the northeast. It is a relaxing region dotted with pretty villages and offering good hiking, skiing and mountain biking, as well as access to one of Austria's most scenic Alpine roads, the **Silvretta-Hochalpenstraße**★★ (&*see p417*).

▷ Leave Bludenz on the 188. Turn left in St. Anton im Montafon towards Bartholomäberg.

Bartholomäberg

This settlement is scattered along a sunny terrace. From the parish church there is an impressive **panorama**★ of the villages of Vandans, Schruns and Tschagguns backed by impressive mountains such as the spiky Zimba peak and the Drei Türme massif. The church's **Baroque interior**★ boasts numerous fine art treasures. Stand-outs are the high altar and pulpit, both by Georg Senn, and the triptych dedicated to St. Anne on the right-hand side of the nave. The organ (1792) is one of the finest examples in Austria.

▶ Continue towards Innerberg, turn right towards Silbertal, then left on the main road at the bottom of the valley to the Kristbergbahn railway.

🚶 Kristbergbahn★

🕐 *Open mid-May–Oct and mid-Dec–mid-Apr daily 7.45am–6pm.* ⚙️*€13.40 round-trip (summer), €13.90 (winter).* 📞*05556 74 119. www.kristbergbahn.at.*
The Kristberg inn *(alt. 1,430m/4,691ft)*, with a chapel nearby, can be reached in 5min from the cable-car mountain station. It affords an especially beautiful **all-round view★** over the Montafon. Hikers can climb up to the Kristbergsattel and then follow the ridge path to the **Ganzaleita** viewpoint *(alt. 1,610m/5,282ft)* for views of the Lechtaler Alps and the Rote Wand.

▶ Continue towards Schruns.

🚶 Schruns 🎿🏂

Alt. 690m/2,264ft.
This resort and capital of the Montafon is located in a broad section of the valley; there are plenty of lodging and leisure facilities. In summer it is an ideal departure point for **hikes** in the medium-altitude mountains. In winter, the **ski area** *(40km/25mi of pistes)* is especially suitable for beginners and for relaxed skiing. More experienced skiers can explore the off-piste section at Sennihang.
Thanks to the area's considerable differences in height *(alt. 700–2,400m/2,300–7,100ft)*, skiing is done through a rather varied landscape. Snow machines make it possible to ski all the way down into the village. Ski passes are valid for the entire Montafon Valley, with its 62 ski-lifts and 222km/138mi of pistes. Free buses link the various areas in the villages of Tschagguns-Vandans, Schruns, Kristberg, Gargellen, St. Gallenkirch and Gaschurn.
Cross-country skiers are restricted to 13km/8mi of easy tracks around Schruns. For more demanding exploits, head to Kristberg (11km/6.8mi), Tschagguns (6km/3.7mi), Vandans (8km/5mi) or the extensive cross-country ski area in the Hochmontafon.

Sennigrat★

Allow 1hr. 🕐*Hochjochbahn cable-car operates daily mid-Jun–mid-Oct 8.30am–5pm; late Dec–mid-Apr 8.15am–4.30pm.* ⚙️*€17.90 round-trip.* 📞*05556 721 26. www.silvretta-montafon.at.*
From Schruns, take the Hochjochbahn or Zamangbahn cable-car to the **Kapell** *(alt. 1,850m/6,069ft)*. Enjoy the view down into the valley and the many scattered chalets of Schruns.
In summer only, another chairlift goes up to the **Sennigrat** *(alt. 2,210m/7,250ft)*, where the **panorama★** takes in the Kreuzjoch area, the Madrisa massif and the Rätikon.

🚶 Hike to the Kreuzjoch and the Zamangspitze★★

4hr round-trip. To shorten the route to 2hr, go as far as the mountain lodge and follow the lake path. Walking boots are recommended.
From Sennigrat, the Wormser Hütte mountain lodge *(alt. 2,305m/7,562ft)* can be reached in 20min. From the lodge, follow a ridge path to the Kreuzjoch and then on to the Zamangspitze peak *(alt. 2,386m/7,828ft)*, where a wonderful **panorama★★** opens up over the Silvretta massif and the Hochmontafon. Backtrack to the lodge and take the lake trail past **Herzsee** and **Schwarzsee** lakes back to the Kapell, returning to Schruns in the cable-car.

▶ Follow the road into the Hochmontafon.

Silvretta Nova ski area 🎿🏂

The villages of St. Gallenkirch and Gaschurn have joined together to create an extensive, varied ski area with 114km/71mi of pistes between 900m/2,952.7ft and 2,300m/7,546ft.
Good skiers use the black Buckelpiste and the 14km/8mi ski run into the valley from the Schwarzköpfle and, on powdered snow, the Ziglamstrecke run for remarkable **views★★** over the Silvretta group. Beyond here, **Gargellen,** the highest village in the Montafon *(alt. 1,423m/4,668ft)*, also offers good pistes.

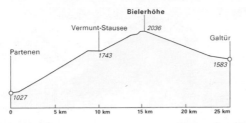

For **cross-country skiers** there are connected ski runs along the valley floor between St. Gallenkirch and Partenen. In addition, a 15km/9.3mi cross-country track around the Silvretta reservoir can be reached by funicular and bus.

Valisera-Seilbahn★★

45min round-trip. Alt 2,100m/6,900ft. ⏱*Cable-car operates mid-Dec–mid-Apr 8.15am–4.30pm.* ☁€14.80 round-trip. *℘05557 63 00.* *www.silvretta-montafon.at.*

The first section of this ascent by cable-car is steep and wooded, looking over the villages of St. Gallenkirch and Schruns. The eye is drawn ever upwards by the craggy Reutehorn, which dominates Gargellental. The second section provides a good overview of the ski area. From the terminal platform, explore the mountain face and the Heimspitze Valiseraspitze, southeast and north of the Silvretta group, including Zamangspitze and Verwallgruppe. The Bella Nova restaurant *(open in winter)*, with sweeping views over the beautiful valley of Gargellen, is just a few steps away.

Versettla-Seilbahn★

45min round-trip. Alt. 2,100m /6,900ft. Cable-car operates mid-Jun–mid-Oct and mid-Dec–mid-Apr 8.45am–5pm. ☁€17.90 round trip. *℘05557 63 00.* *www.silvretta-montafon.at.*

At the entrance, the restaurant offers a **view★** of the Silvretta massif (Piz Buin, Großer Litzner, Großes Seehorn) and the whole of the Silvretta Nova ski area. As you head towards the summits of the Burg and Versettia, a broad panorama unfolds. *(Take the ski-tow to the Burg in winter, to the Versettla in summer).*

5 SILVRETTA ALPINE ROAD TOUR★★
73km/45mi.

This scenic route is right on the Swiss border, about 130km/84mi southeast of Innsbruck. 🛈 *Silvrettastraße 8, Partenen.* *℘050 66 86 410. www.gaschurn-*

Silvretta Alpine Road

© Alexander Studentschnig/Dreamstime.com

Piz Buin

© Austrian National Tourist Office/ Jezierzanski

partenen.com or www.silvretta-bielerhoehe.at. 🅿 *Several car parks available along the route.*

The Silvretta Hochalpenstraße links the Ill Valley (**Montafon★** 🔄*see entry*) with the Trisanna Valley (Paznaun Valley) via the Bielerhöhe Pass *(alt. 2,036m/6,680ft)*. The rugged character of this high-lying pass contrasts with the shimmering green-blue waters of the reservoirs. The road is usually blocked by snow November to May and may be closed to trailers and caravans at any time. There are 30 narrow bends to negotiate on the western slope.

The road climbs from **Partenen** *(alt. 1,051m/3,448ft)* over the Bielerhöhe *(alt. 2,031m/6,664ft)* into Paznaun and the Tirol. Along the way it corkscrews past some of the Vorarlberg's highest peaks (including Piz Buin, alt. 3,312m/10,867ft) and deep blue Alpine reservoirs.

▶ Take the road S from Partenen.

Vermunt-Stausee

This lake forms a reservoir between Partenen and the Silvretta Valley, at an altitude of 1,743m/5,718ft. The **view★** stretches as far as the ridges of the Grosser Litzner and the Grosser Seehorn. As the road winds up to the mountain pass, polished smooth by glaciers, the Silvretta dam and mountain summit come gradually into view.

Bielerhöhe

The **Silvretta-Stausee★** reservoir blends beautifully into the Alpine landscape and makes a pleasant stopping point. Motor boat trips are available on the lake. A walk along the dam (432m/1,417ft long and 80m/262ft high) gives a remarkable **view★** of the surrounding mountains.

Even better, take the easy *(1hr45min)* walk around the **lake★★**, which passes several waterfalls, Alpine rose bushes and offers splendid views★★ of the surrounding peaks.

🧗 Ascent to the Hohes Rad★★★

Allow 5hr30min round trip.

🅿*Park in the lot at the east end of the lake. This is a great hike for experienced walkers. Waterproof walking boots and warm socks are essential. Those with less stamina should steer towards the Wiesbadener Hütte mountain lodge (about 4hr15min round trip).*

It takes about 45min to walk the length of the entire reservoir, where a trail leads uphill along the gushing waters of the Jil, fed by numerous waterfalls and brooks. Gradually, several peaks come into view, with the most eye-catching sight being the glacial cirque that closes off the valley.

From the **Wiesbadener Hütte** mountain lodge *(alt. 2,443m/8,015ft)*, there is a wonderful **view★★** of the highest peak in the Silvretta group, the **Piz Buin** *(alt. 3,312m/10,866ft)*, flanked by glaciers. Next comes a 1hr30min climb to the Radsattel. Turn left past the mountain lodge and follow the **Edmund-Lorenz-Weg** trail, which climbs steeply then levels out. It leads down to a small lake *(alt. 2,532m/8,307ft)*, shimmering in a kaleidoscope of colour from orange to green and lying in a splendid setting below the Rauherkopf glacier. It is uphill from here as far as the **Radsattel** *(alt. 2,652m/8,701ft)*. There is a superb **panorama★★** of the Grosser Litzner and surrounding glaciers. To the east lies the Bieltal valley, with a glacier towering above it.

The trails climbs slightly towards the rocky foothills of the Hohes Rad, then crosses numerous glacial snowfields before arriving, after 45min, at the **Radschulter★★** *(alt. 2,697m/8,843ft)*. Shortly before the pass, the Radsee, its frigid waters tinged a dark green, comes into sight beneath the Madlener Spitze peak. From the pass, there is a great **view★★** of the Bieltal and Rauerkopf glaciers. Experienced hikers not prone to vertigo may like to continue along a rocky trail for at least another 45min up to the **Hohes Rad★★★** summit *(alt. 2,934m/9,626ft)*. The walk down from the Radschulter takes 1hr30min. The very steep **route★★** is usually covered by snow well into August. For the last part of the walk, the trail is flanked by splendid Alpine roses and yellow gentians, and provides a number of magnificent **views★★** of the Silvretta reservoir, with the Hochmaderer in the background.

▶ About 2km/1.2mi before Wirl, take the road left over a bridge and continue for 5km/3mi to Kops-Stausee.

After 5km/3mi, the road reaches the **Kops-Stausee★** *(alt. 1,809m/5,935ft)*, flanked by the Ballunspitze *(south)*, the Versalspitze *(west)* and the Fluhspitzen *(north)*. Return to the main road and drive on to Galtür.

▶ Return to the road no. 188 via Wirl.

Galtür 🎿

This pretty village *(alt. 1,548m/5,197ft)* on the slopes of the Ballunspitze provides access to a small but interesting ski area above the Kops reservoir. A total of 11 ski-lifts lead to 40km/25mi of pistes covering all degrees of difficulty. There are also 45km/28mi of cross-country tracks and good snow cover.

Ischgl 🚡

🚲 *See ISCHGL.*

The Trisanna Valley now narrows further and becomes increasingly picturesque and rugged, with villages clinging to mountain plateaux. The road parallels a rushing creek through fairly dense forest. After a long drive, the appearance of the Burg Wiesberg heralds the famous **Trisanna bridge★**.

Landeck

🚲 *See LANDECK.*

ADDRESSES

🏨STAY AND 🍴EAT

🛏🛏 **Hotel Taleu** – Boden 21, A-6707 *Bürserberg. ☏ 05552 632 57. www.taleu. at. 30 rooms. 🍴. Alpine-style Natur-hotel near Bludenz. Private apartments also available.*

🛏🛏🛏 **Gasthof Rössle** – *Arlbergstraße 61. 6751 Braz. 8km/5mi east of Bludenz. ☏05552 28 10 50. www.roesslebraz.at. 10 rooms. 🍴. Restaurant Mon, Thu–Fri from 4pm, Sat–Sun from 10am; closed Tue–Wed. Reservations recommended.* Set in a traditional house, built in 1776, rooms are modern and attractive. Both regional and international cuisine are served in the restaurant (🍴🍴), which boasts a lovely terrace.

🛏🛏🛏 **Hotel-Restaurant Schrofenstein** – *Malserstr. 31. Landeck ☏05442 623 95. www.schrofenstein.at. Closed Nov. 50 rooms. 🍴.* This long-established hotel right in the town centre has been fully modernised with striking contemporary rooms. The restaurant (🍴🍴🍴) serves traditional Austrian cuisine.

St. Anton am Arlberg ❄❄

St. Anton, draped into a deeply incised valley, is something of a shrine for winter-sports aficionados. It was here in 1921 that ski pioneer Hannes Schneider, who is considered the father of modern skiing, founded Austria's first ski school. From then on, the sport took St. Anton by storm, and today it is one of the largest resorts in the Northern Alps with a youthful, sporty atmosphere and a lively après-ski scene. Summer brings a degree of calm, although the scenic Arlbergstraße does draw its share of tourist traffic. Attractions include an enormous leisure park and 90km/56mi of hiking trails.

- ▶ **Population:** 2,350.
- ⚫ **Michelin Map:** Local map, see Arlberggebiet.
- ℹ **Info:** Dorfstraße 8, A-6580. ☏ 05446 226 90. www.stantonamarlberg.com.
- ◑ **Location:** St. Anton is in western Austria, about 100km/62mi southwest of Innsbruck. Alt. 1,304m/4,278ft.
- 🅿 **Parking:** Look for parking along the main Arlbergstraße.
- 🚫 **Don't Miss:** Skiing, trip up to the Valluga viewpoint.
- 🕐 **Timing:** Half a day for the town; several days for hiking or skiing the mountains.

SIGHTS
SKI SLOPES
Arlberg ski area 🎿🏂

St. Anton is part of the Arlberg ski region that also includes **Lech**, (⚫*see LECH*), **Zürs** (⚫*see ZÜRS, served by bus*) and **Stuben** (⚫*see ARLBERG-GEBIET*).

A single ski pass is good for the entire area, which lies at an altitude of 1,300–2,650m/4,250–8,700ft and has 260km/162mi of marked and 180km/112mi of unmarked pistes, accessed by a total of 80 ski-lifts.

St. Anton is most suitable for experienced skiers, offering steep, undulating pistes from the Schindler Spitze, Kapall and Pfannenkopf peaks. Less proficient skiers will find suitable runs on the Galzig, Gampen and Gampberg slopes.

EXCURSIONS
Valluga★★★

Alt. 2,811m/9,222ft. About 2hr30min round-trip. 🕐*Cable-car operates Dec–mid-Apr Wed–Sun 8.30am–4pm, Jul–Aug 8.15am–4.25pm.* ⚙€25.50 *round-trip (summer), €49.50 day pass (winter).* ☏05446 235 20. *www2.skiarlberg.at, www.abbag.com.* This excursion starts with a ride aboard the **Galzigbahn**, a gondola with Ferris wheel-style boarding housed within

a spectacular glass shelter designed by Tirolean architect Georg Driendl. From the mountain station *(alt. 2,185m/7,169ft)*, there is a lovely **view★★** over the ski slopes.

Next, take the Valluga I gondola to the Valluga ridge *(alt. 2,650m/8,695ft)* for more impressive **views★★**, although for the truly breathtaking **panorama★★★,** catch the short Valluga II gondola to the peak itself.

Kapall★★

Alt. 2,330m/7,644ft. About 1hr round-trip aboard the Nassereinbahn cable-car or the Gampenbahn chairlift, followed by the Kapall chairlift. 🕐*Operates daily Dec–mid-Apr 8.30am–4pm and Jul–Sept Fri–Tue 8.15am–4.25pm.* ⚙€25.50 *round-trip (summer), €49.50 day pass (winter).* ☏05446 235 20. *www2.skiarlberg.at., www.abbag.com.* This trip drops you at the at the foot of the rocky Weissschrofenspitze peak *(alt. 2,752m/9,028ft)* and treats you to an outstandingly beautiful **panorama★★** over the entire St. Anton Valley and across to the Swiss Alps, the Rätikon and the Verwall range.

Zürs

Zürs is a major winter-sports resort that, along with Lech, Stuben and St. Anton, forms part of the Arlberg ski region. The first ski competitions here were held in 1906, the pioneers of modern skiing met here in the 1920s and Austria's first ski-lifts were operating by 1937. Zürs has remained a rather small, upscale resort with excellent leisure facilties, restaurants and nightclubs.

SIGHTS
Ski Slopes 🎿
Though the ski area at Zürs is not vast, it is of outstanding quality. The Rüfikopf, Family run and Muggengrat-Zürsersee pistes are suitable for beginners, while moderately skilled skiers might prefer the Palmen, Steinmännle and Madloch-Zürsersee pistes. More proficient skiers will be drawn to the magnificent **Muggengrat-Täli** piste and the unique run down from the Madlochjoch to Lech, with magnificent **views★★** over the Lechtal Alps. There are also wonderful opportunities for off-piste skiing alongside the Madloch and Muggengrat chairlifts.

Zürs' location makes it the ideal starting point for excursions into the Arlberg area. The Lech snowfields are a perfect training ground for moderately good skiers, while experts prefer the steep pistes of the Valluga at St. Christoph or St. Anton *(bus service)*. The only drawbacks of the Arlberg district are the lack of high-altitude peaks and of skiable links between the areas.

Madlochjoch★
Alt. 2,438m/7,999ft. (Skiers only via the Seekopf and Madlochjoch chairlifts.)
Madloch views of the Schafberg from the mountain station, while **Muggengrat★** *(alt. 2,450m/8,038ft)* presents a scenic **Alpine landscape★**, from which the crags of Hasenfluh and Flexenspitze stand out in particular. The view stretches as far as the Verwall range to the south, and Lech and Oberlech at the foot of the Widderstein to the north.

- ▶ **Population:** 130.
- ⚑ **Michelin Map:** Local map, see Arlberggebiet.
- 🅸 **Info:** ✆05583 22 45. www.lech-zuers.at.
- ◖ **Location:** Zürs is in far western Austria about 112km/69.6mi west of Innsbruck and only 5km/3mi from Lech. Alt. 1,716m/5,630ft.
- 🅿 **Parking:** Free parking by the Trittkopfbahn cable-car.

Muggengrat★
Alt. 2,450m/8,000ft. Access for skiers only via chairlifts to Seekopf and Muggengrat. There is an outstanding **view★** of the mountains, including the Hasenfluh and Flexenspitze. To the south is the Verwall Massif and Lech; to the north is Oberlech at the foot of the Widderstein.

ADDRESSES

🛏STAY

⊖⊜⊜⊜ **Hotel Arlberghaus** – *Haus 126, 6763. ✆05583 22 58 55. www.arlberghaus.com. Closed mid April–early Dec. 54 rooms. ⊡. Rates include half board.* Modern and more traditional rooms. Restaurant (⊖⊜) with a terrace.

⊖⊜⊜⊜ **Hotel Erzberg** – *Haus 383, 6763. ✆05583 264 40. www.hotel-erzberg.at. Closed May–Nov. 25 rooms.* Luxurious modern-traditional rooms, some with balcony. Gourmet dining (⊖⊜⊜⊜) and an extensive wine list.

🍴EAT

⊖⊜ **Flexenhäusl** – *Flexen Pass, Zürs 79. ✆05583 4143. Tue–Sun 11am–6pm.* Open both winter and summer, this dining spot is a great place for local specialities and excellent fondue.

⊖⊜⊜⊜ **Die Ente von Zürs** – *Hotel Albona Nova. ✆05583 2341. www.albonanova.at. Daily 7pm–10pm.* This rather special restaurant offers a molecular-gastronomy take on local dishes and ingredients. Reservations are essential.

Ischgl✲✲✲

Situated on the Silvretta Hochalpenstraße, Ischgl undoubtedly ranks among the most beautiful of Austria's winter-sports resorts. It's a modern village that is well developed for the tourist trade, offering the gamut of lodging options, a lively après-ski scene and off-piste fun in the Silvretta and Freizeit centres with their indoor pools, saunas, tennis courts, billiards room and bowling alley. In summer, Ischgl changes into a peaceful holiday resort.

SIGHTS
Ski slopes ✆✇

The ski slopes at Ischgl and the neighbouring Swiss resort of **Samnaun** (alt. 1,840m/6,037ft) belong to the Silvretta Arena (alt. 1,400–2,900m/4,600–9,500ft; www.samnaun.ch), which has 40 lifts and 230km/143mi of pistes suitable for all skill levels. Almost the entire terrain lies over 2,000m/6,550ft and snow cover remains excellent from late November until early May. **Cross-country skiers** will appreciate the ski tracks towards Galtür (❖see p419), from which are more possibilities.

Ischgl

© Austrian National Tourist Office/ Mallaun

▶ **Population:** 1,580.

🏢 **Info:** Ischgl 320, A-6561, Dorfstr. 43. ℘0509 90 100 . www.ischgl.com.

◗ **Location:** Ischgl is in the Paznauntal, a valley in the far southwestern corner of Austria, right on the border with Switzerland. Alt. 1,377m/4,518ft.

⦿ **Don't Miss:** Trida Sattel for the panoramic views.

Pardatschgrat★ ✇
Alt. 2,624m/8,609ft. ◔Pardatschgrat-bahn cable-car daily 8am–5pm. Daily pass (winter) €49.50. www.ischgl.com. In summer and winter the Silvrettabahn gives access as far as the Idalp, alt. 2,320m/7,612ft. ℘05444 606. www.ischgl.com.

From the mountain station there is a good view of the ski slopes surrounded by the Vesulspitze, Bürkelkopf, Flimspitze and Piz Rots summits. Directly to the south lies the Fimbatal, a valley dwarfed by the Fluchthorn Massif.

Trida Sattel★★ ✇
Alt 2,488m/8,163ft. Cable-car up from Samnaun or follow the ski tracks from Ischgl.

From the terrace of the mountain restaurant, the **view★★** extends southwards over the sheer Stammerspitze, Muttler and Piz Mundin peaks, and to the southeast over the Ötztaler Alps. A more far-ranging **panorama ★★** can be enjoyed from the Visnitzbahn and Mullerbahn chairlifts.

ADDRESSES

🏠STAY AND 🍴EAT

⊜⊜ **Hotel Garni Valülla** – Eggerweg 19, 6561. ℘05544 52 54. www.valuella.at. Closed May–Jun, mid-Sept–Nov. 21 rooms. ⌐. A little out of the town centre but not far from the cable-car. Spacious and well-appointed rooms.

Oberes Inntal★

The Inn Valley has become the backbone of the Tyrol. For 185km/ 115mi, from the Finstermünz ravine to the Kufstein gap, the scenery is typical of the longitudinal furrows of the Alps shaped by the last phases of the Ice Age.

🚗 DRIVING TOUR

NAUDERS TO IMST
61km/38mi.

Nauders 🎿
Nauders is a popular winter-sports resort dominated by Schloss Naudersberg. The cross-country Skiparadies Reschenpass offers 111km/69mi of tracks. In summer, mountain biking is the main sport here, with 600km/372.8mi of tracks covering the sprawling terrain. Past Nauders the road plunges into the Finstermünz Gorge.

Finstermünzpass★
This grim gorge forms the natural frontier between the Tirolean Inn Valley and the Lower Engadine and Alto Adige. Downstream from the Hochfinstermünz hotel, the road clings precariously to the cliffs of the right bank, reaching a viewing terrace after three rock-vaulted tunnel passages. Farther on, it drops down to the valley floor at the Kajetanbrücke (St. Gaëtano) bridge.

▶ After the bridge, head for the Lower Engadine Valley (signposted St. Moritz).

After crossing the Inn, the road runs past **Pfunds**. Between **Ried** and **Prutz** look for the ruins of Laudeck to the left, flanked by the little white church tower of **Ladis**.

▶ In Prutz the road forks off to the right into the **Kaunertal**★★★ (*see p424*).

Info: Johannesplatz 4. Imst. *℘*05412 691 00. www.imst.at. Dr. Tschiggfreystr. 66, Nauders. *℘*050 225 400. www.nauders.com.

▶ **Location:** This valley runs south from the Inn Valley in western Tirol.

😊 **Don't Miss:** The Kaunertal.

🕐 **Timing:** Allow a full day to take in everything and to admire the views.

Landeck
See p413. In Landeck, the ruins of **Schrofenstein** can be seen halfway up a mountain slope, all the way to Zams. Past Zams look for **Kronburg** fortress perched atop a forested mountain peak. After **Schönwies**, the road climbs again and has several pull-outs where you can stop to enjoy the views. At last it reaches the wide Imst basin in sight of the jagged crests of the Stubaier Alps *(east)*.

Imst
The delightful Oberstadt (Upper Town), with its numerous pretty fountains, is punctuated by the imposing 15C **parish church** with a neo-Gothic interior and original 16C murals on the west and south façades. At 84.5m/277ft the tower is the tallest in the Tyrol.

Behind the church is the trailhead for the trail through the 1.5km/1mi-long **Rosengartenschlucht★** *(allow 90min for the round-trip; wear sturdy shoes)*, which passes roaring waterfalls and steep, rugged cliffs, and offers fine views of the mountains.

The well-known **Imst Carnival**, with its procession of ghosts *(Schemenlaufen)*, takes place every four years *(next one, Feb 2016)*, and the **Fasnachtsmuseum** has a permanent display of masks and costumes used on the occasion.

The world's first SOS-Children's Village was founded in Imst in 1949 by the world's largest orphan and abandoned children's charity.

Kaunertal★★★

This long valley, traversed by one of Europe's highest roads, the Kaunertaler Gletscher-Panoramastraße (Kaunertal Glacier Panoramic Road; highest point: 2,750m/9,022ft), makes for an ideal day trip, thanks to magnificent mountain scenery and a large reservoir. Skiing is possible from September to June on the Kaunertal glacier.

- 🔢 **Info:** Feichten 141, Kaunertal. ℘050 225 220. www.kaunertal.com.
- ◖ **Location:** The Kaunertal is in western Austria, not far from the Swiss border.
- ◈ **Don't Miss:** Kaunertal Glacier.
- ◷ **Timing:** The tour is an easy half-day trip.

🚗 DRIVING TOURS

PRUTZ TO THE KAUNERTAL GLACIER★★
40km/25mi.

In Prutz, turn left off the B 315 towards Switzerland and Italy. The road parallels the Faggenbach River through a deeply incised, green valley below the Köpfle and Peischlkopf peaks.
A toll is charged beyond Feichten, which is reached after 12km/7.4mi. Here the valley widens, allowing glimpses of the glacier in the distance. After 10km/6.2mi of steep climbing through a beautiful forest, the road arrives at the Gepatsch reservoir, the largest in western Austria, where you'll get a pretty **view★** of the lake and the Weisseespitze *(alt. 3,535m/11,665ft)*.
The road skirts the left bank for 6km/3.7mi, sprayed by numerous **waterfalls★**. The best view of the pine-fringed lake is just past the Faggenbach bridge. As the vegetation thins, the landscape becomes even rockier.
There is a **view★** to the right of the picturesque Krummgampen Valley, with its reddish cliffs. Shortly after, the Weisssee comes into sight.
The road ends after a final, steep stretch on the edge of the **Kaunertal glacier** *(alt. 2,750m/9,022ft)*, where **skiing** 🎿 is possible from September to June. Another attraction here is a 40m/120ft -long icy walk through a glacier crevasse *(◈ not for the claustrophobic)*.

PILLER-PASS DRIVING TOUR
20km/12.5mi tour from Pritz to Wenns

The valley tour is completed by taking the narrow winding Piller roads. The route passes through the resorts of Kaunas, then Kaunerberg, offering beautiful views down into the valley of the Kaunertal.

◖ Continue on towards the Piller Pass (turn left 500m after the entrance to Kaunerberg).

Go through the hamlet of Puschlin to reach the pass *(alt. 1,559m/5,114ft)*. The road winds through a vast forest , runs through the village of Piller and into the valley floor of the **Pitztal★★★** *(◖see PITZTAL)* at Wenns.

EXCURSION TO KARLESSPITZE★★★
Karlesjochbahn Skilift★★★
Alt. 3,108m/10,000ft. 45min round-trip by ski-lift, which operates daily 10am–4pm. 🎟€17.50. ℘05475 55 66. *www.gletscherpark.com.*
En route to the summit a splendid **view★★★** of the surrounding mountain is afforded. In addition to the summits mentioned above are the Ölgruben-spitzen and Bliggspitze.

Klettersteig Panoramablick★★
🧗 *Alt. 3,160m/10,200ft. 1h30min hike from the top gondola station. Hiking boots, sunglasses and warm clothing are required for this steep and tiring (but*

Kaunertaler Gletscher-Panoramastraße

© Holger Schultz/Fotolia.com

not technically difficult) *walk through the snowfield.*

This hike is a rare opportunity to walk along a large area of safe ice. It reaches a saddle at the foot of the Karlesspitze with a fine **view★** south to the Italian Alps and southwest to the Swiss Alps.

▶ Return to your vehicle and go back down to the bridge across the Faggenbach stream, where there is parking.

Gepatschferner★★

🚶 *1hr15min round-trip from the bridge.* The trail follows the river *(to the right).* After 100m/328ft a spectacular waterfall is seen. The trail rises steeply, passing reddish rocks and rhododendrons. The Gepatsch glacier is the largest in Austria and the wonderful **view★★** includes a mountain cirque (bowl-shaped valley) enclosed by the Rauhekopf and the Schwarze Wand.

ADDRESSES

🛏️ STAY AND 🍽️ EAT

🛏️ **Ferienhaus Waldner** – *6524 Feichten im Kaunertal 106. ☏05475 225. www.ferienhaus-waldner.com. 🚭. 🚱. 6 rooms, 2 apartments.* This traditional family-owned chalet-style house with a sauna and a garden sits very close to cross-country skiing trails.

🛏️ **Gepatschhaus** – *6524 Feichten im Kaunertal 147. 16km/10mi S of Feichten. ☏0664 431 9634. www.gepatschhaus.at. Open Apr–Sept. 6 rooms and dormitory. 🚱€8.* At an altitude of 1,928m/6,325ft, this typical, attractive mountain refuge is the oldest of its kind in the Austrian Alps.

🛏️🛏️🛏️ **Gasthof Falkeis** – *Dorfstrasse 54, 6526 Kauns. ☏05472 6225. www.gasthof-falkeis.at. Closed mid-Nov–mid-Dec. 9 rooms. 🚱.* This attractive, family-owned guesthouse successfully combines modern and traditional furnishings and décor with stylish bedrooms. The restaurant (🛏️🛏️🛏️*closed Mon*) serves *nouvelle* regional cuisine. Reservations recommended.

Pitztal★★★

The long Pitz Valley, which runs north-south, is flanked in the west by the Kaunertal Valley and in the east by the Ötztal Valley. It is famous for the extraordinary Alpine scenery in its upper reaches. It is enclosed by a massive glacier basin over which towers the 3,774m/12,382ft high Wildspitze peak, the highest point in the Tyrol.

- **Info:** Unterdorf 18, Wenns. ✆05414 86 999. www.pitztal.com.
- **Location:** The Pitztal is in western Austria, about 58km/36mi west of Innsbruck.
- **Don't Miss:** Hinterer Brunnenkogel.
- **Timing:** Allow 45min for the drive to Mittelberg and 2hr for the trip up the Hinterer Brunnenkogel.

🚗 DRIVING TOUR

ROAD FROM ARZL TO MITTELBERG★

The 39km/24mi-long road offers views of the glaciers and passes through villages and forest, running past little waterfalls and along the Pitzbach creek to Mittelberg, where lifts reach the glaciers. Allow 4hrs to include the excursions.

EXCURSIONS
Hinterer Brunnenkogel★★★
Alt. 3,440m/11,286ft. Allow 2 hrs round-trip. Gletschnerexpress and Wildspitzbahn cable-car funicular mid-Jul–mid-May daily 8.30am–4.20pm. €38 (combined ticket) round-trip. ✆05413 862 88. www.gletscherpark.com.
The Gletschnerexpress funicular travels underground for 3.7km/2.3mi to the foot

of the Pitztal glacier at 2,860m/9,383ft. Continue on the Wildspitzbahn, the highest cable-car in Austria.
The peak, which offers a fantastic **Alpine panorama★★★**, is only a short hike away from the upper mountain station. The Wildspitze towers majestically over this grandiose landscape. Be sure to have sunglasses, shoes suitable for snow, and warm clothing.

Pitztal Glacier
Open mid-Sept–early May daily 8.30am–4.30pm. €38 ski day pass, also includes Rifflsee area. ✆0541 38 62 88. www.gletscherpark.com.
Seven lifts lead up to 25km/15.5mi of pistes that are usually well covered in snow from autumn to May. The ski area is suitable for skiers of all levels, although easy runs predominate.

Rifflsee
Park in the Mandarfen. Cable-car (Rifflsee-Kabinenbahn) Operates late Sept–early May and mid-Jun–early Oct 8.30am–4.30pm. €18. ✆0541 38 62 88. www.gletscherpark.com.
The cable-car ride offers fine views of the valley and south to the Karlesspitze glacier. At the upper terminus *(alt. 2,300m/7,545ft)*, there is a beautiful view of the Rifflsee. Walkers might like to go round the lake, while a more strenuous trail, the Fuldaer Höhenweg, leads south up to the Taschachhütte refuge *(alt. 2,432m/8,000ft)*, located at the foot of the glaciers.

Pitztal Glacier ski area

© Josef Beck/imagebroker/age fotostock

Ötztal★★

Famous for its series of shining glaciers, the Ötztal is one of three deep river valleys running north from the Ötztaler Alps into the Inn. This section of the Alps encompasses the highest point in the northern Tyrol, the Wildspitze (alt. 3,774m/12,382ft), and the highest parish in Austria (Obergurgl at 1,927m/6,321ft). Until World War I, the valley communities were more closely connected with the Alto Adige to the south, from which their people originally came, than with the Inn Valley. Only in 1969, when the Timmelsjoch road was completed, did the isolation of the Ötztal come to an end, at least in summer.

🚗 DRIVING TOUR

INN VALLEY TO SÖLDEN

88km/28mi. On the Austrian side, the road is generally open all year round, at least to Hochgurgl. On the Italian side, however, it is generally open only snow-free days mid-Jun–mid-Oct. The route demands care and has an irregular surface, especially in tunnels. ⊘Trailers, caravans, buses and trucks not allowed.

The B 186, turning off the busy Inntal road, runs through pleasant pine woods among debris brought down from the Ötztaler Ache, which has been deeply furrowed by the torrent. The river flows beneath the picturesque covered bridge at Ebene to enter the Ötz basin, dominated by the rocky tooth of the Acherkogel. Chestnuts, and fields of maize, and peach and apricot orchards show that the Ötztal corridor, running due south, attracts the warm air of the Föhn.

Oetz

This village, on a sunny slope, sports several traditional buildings with flower-bedecked oriels and painted façades. A popular walk leads to the romantic **Piburgersee** lake.

ℹ️ Info: Gemeindestr. 4, Sölden. ℘0572 00. www.oetztal.com.

Location: The Ötztal runs north-south through western Austria, about 55km/34mi west of Innsbruck.

Don't Miss: Sölden, Stuibenfälle.

Timing: Allow at least a day, although there is enough for two days if you choose to follow some of the hiking trails.

▷ Drive through Trumpen to Umhausen, gateway to the Stuiben Falls.

👥 Ötzi-Dorf

🕐Open May–Oct 9.30am–5.30pm (Oct til 5pm). ⊛€7.50. ℘05255 500 22. www.oetzi-dorf.at.
This archaeological theme park and neolithic village has been developed by the University of Innsbruck Institute of Prehistory and Early History. It shows the agricultural lifestyle and domestic animals of the time.

Stuibenfälle★★

🚶 *About 1hr30min round-trip walk beginning at the Umhausen tourist office.* The path to this large and powerful waterfall leads first to a restaurant-chalet, crosses the torrent and continues up the left bank to the 150m/492ft-high **waterfall**. A second wooded ravine lies downhill, near the swiftly flowing Ötztaler Ache.

▷ After Umhausen, the road descends along the valley in a wild gorge. It widens to form the Längenfeld basin.

🧗 Längenfeld

Together with nearby **Huben**, Längenfeld offers 150km/93mi of hiking trails, several climbing training courses and two actual climbs, as well as a

50km/31mi network of mountain bike tracks. Beyond Huben, a long ravine begins, narrowing after the bridge at Aschbach to a larch-covered **gorge★**. Below the road, the Wildbach churns over massive rocks.

Ötztaler Heimat- und Freilichtmuseum★

Oberried-Lehn. 5km/3mi round-trip from Längenfeld (signposted). ◷*Open Jun–Sept Mon–Fri 10am–noon, 2pm–5pm, Sun 2pm–4pm.* ⊜€5. *www.oetztal-museum.at.*

This outdoor museum illustrates the daily lives of local peasants in the first half of the 20C. It includes several original buildings (farmhouse, barn, mill) many of whose facilities (classroom, a smoking room, lockers for clothes) look as if they are still in use.

▶ Beyond Huben the road runs into a long gorge.

Sölden※※

Sölden is in the Ötztal valley in western Austria, about 84km/53mi southwest of Innsbruck. 🛈 *A-6450.* ☎*057200 200. www.soelden.com.* 🅿 *There is parking at each of the lower cable-car stations.*

Geographically speaking, Sölden (*population 3,200; alt 1,377m/4,518ft*) is the largest municipality in Austria, stretching across 468sq km/181sq mi. Yet only a tiny portion (1sq km/0.4sq mi) of the area is inhabited.

Surrounded by some 90 peaks soaring above 3,000m/9,842.5ft, this classic Tirolean village has developed into an important year-round holiday resort and hub of the **Ötz Valley★★** (*⤳see Ötztal*). It is well known for its après-ski entertainment and sports facilities as well as its many lively bars, cafés and clubs. The little village of Hochsölden (*alt. 2,090m/6,857ft*) occupies a beautiful plateau and offers excellent snow cover and extensive views.

Ski slopes 🎿🎿
(1,377–3,260m/4,518–10,696ft)

Sölden is the main town of the Ötztal Arena, which has 35 ski-lifts, 30 artificial snow machines and 150km/93mi of pistes (53km/33mi blue, 63km/39mi red and 28km/17.4mi black). Ski conditions are good from mid-December to early May.

The long descents from the Gaislachkogl to the Stabele chairlift valley station and the one linking the Hainbachjoch with Sölden are recommended. Less experienced skiers should use the pistes above Hochsölden and the broad trail through the woods from the Gaislachalm.

The **Ötztaler Gletscherstraße★★** climbs to 2,822m/9,258.5ft, making it one of the highest roads in the eastern Alps. It gives access to another ski area (29km/18mi of piste and 10 ski-lifts) in a beautiful Alpine landscape on the Rettenbachfern and Tiefenbachfern glaciers. Cross-country skiers have 8km/5mi of tracks available to them in Sölden, 8km/5mi in Zwieselstein and 3km/1.8mi in Vent.

Gaislachkogl★★

Alt. 3,058m/10,033ft. 1hr round-trip. Gaislachoglbahn cable-car operates ◷*Jul–late Sept, late Dec–Apr 9am–4pm.* ⊜€18 round-trip, ☎*0525 4 23 61. www.soelden.com.*

The ascent is in two stages. From the top mountain station, the summit can be reached on foot in a few minutes (⚠*wear sturdy shoes*) to take in a splendid **panorama★★** of the peaks and glaciers of the Ötztal Alps.

Giggijochbahn

◷*Open mid-Jun–late Sept and mid-Dec–late Apr daily 9am–4pm.* ⊜€13.50 round trip. ☎*05254 2 361. www.soelden.com.*

From the terrace of the mountain station there are beautiful **views** of the Sölden ski slopes extending from the Gaislachkogl to the Hainbachjoch. To the east lie the Söldenkogel, the Rotkogel and the Gurgler Valley.

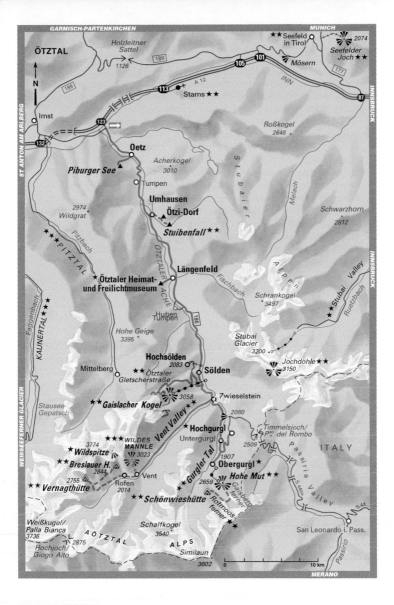

EXCURSIONS
ROAD FROM ZWIESELSTEIN TO ROFEN★
16km/10mi.

🏔 Ventertal★★

This glacier-framed valley is a hiker's paradise. The road first travels through a wooded area, passing the hamlet of Heiligenkreuz with its onion-domed chapel. It soon reaches **Vent** (*alt. 1,900m/6,234ft*), an unpretentious winter-sports resort distinguished by good snow cover and steep slopes. It has 15km/9.6mi of pistes at altitudes of between 1,900m/6,234ft and 2,680m/8,793ft, and four ski-lifts. Most visitors, though, arrive in summer to take

"Ötzi"

In 1991, a pair of climbers discovered a mummified body in the Similaun range in the Ötztaler Alps. They reported their find thinking it was the body of some unfortunate climber. However, the discovery soon became an archaeological sensation, as the body turned out to be about 6,000 years old! The mummy, fondly nicknamed "Ötzi," had been particularly well preserved due to the environmental conditions in the glacier. Even the organs were still intact, so that it was possible to draw conclusions about his diet and the circumstances of his death. Apparently, Ötzi froze to death in a snow storm despite his good thick clothing of furs and a grass cloak. However, recent evidence has questioned the possibility of his being shot in the back with an arrow. Along with the body, a number of significant Stone Age artefacts were retrieved, including a well-made pair of shoes with separate soles and uppers. Austrians adopted the Ice Man, despite the fact that it was common knowledge that the body had been found 10m/32.8ft inside Italy.

After negotiations with the Italians, it was agreed that Ötzi would stay in Austria until Innsbruck University completed their analysis of the body. However, the final resting place of the mummy would be in Italy. Ötzi is now on display in the South Tyrol Museum of Archaeology in Bolzano (Bozen), Italy: www.iceman.it.

advantage of a seemingly inexhaustible range of trips into the high mountains. After Vent, the valley splits into two parts on either side of the imposing Talleitspitze peak *(alt 3,406m/11,174ft)*. The **Rofental** valley, on the right, runs alongside the **Wildspitze** and the **Hochvernagtspitze** peaks before being blocked by the **Weisskugel**. The **Niedertal** valley on the left of the Talleitspitze peak runs along the Ramolkogel and the Schalfkogel, ending in the glacial basin of the **Similaun**. All of these peaks have been the goal of legendary mountain expeditions.

⬆ Wildspitze-Sesselbahn★

Park at the chairlift in Vent. ⏰*Operates mid-Jun–late Sept daily 8am–noon, 1pm–5.30pm; mid-Dec–early Apr daily 9.30am–4pm.* ⬅€12 round-trip. *www.vent.at.*

At 3,774m/12,382ft, the Wildspitze is the highest peak in the Tirol. From the mountain station *(alt. 2,356m/7,730ft)* a splendid **view★** of the ski area and various peaks and glaciers unfolds. This is the starting point of numerous hikes, a couple of which are detailed below.

⬆ Wildes Mannle★★★

This hike covers 670m/2,198ft difference in altitude and requires a fair level of fitness and experience as well as sturdy footwear. Allow at least 3hr round-trip, or 4hr if continuing on to the Breslauer Hütte mountain lodge.

From the chairlift mountain station, start hiking towards the Breslauer Hütte. After a 30min walk, veer to the right *(waymarker)* onto a narrower trail. As the view becomes ever more breathtaking, look out for the markers and "WM" indications. The path gets steep and rocky, but does not present any real difficulties.

From the peak *(alt. 3,023m/9,918ft)*, which is marked with a cross, there is a awesome **panorama★★★** of about 15 glaciers belonging to the Ötztal Alps, the most impressive and closest of which is the Rofenkar glacier. Chamois can often be spotted in this region.

To the west, notice the Breslauer Hütte lodge at the foot of a rocky, reddish natural amphitheatre. A detour to this mountain lodge is a pleasant extension of this hike. ☺ Those with a poor head for heights should first follow the same trail as on the way there, and then turn off towards the right *(waymarked on the rocks)*. Experienced hikers can take a walk of about 15min across the ridge of the Wildes Mannle as far as a metal sign *(towards Breslauer Hütte via Rofenkarsteig)*. Be sure to pay attention to the markers *(stone cairns)*. At the sign, turn off onto a steep, narrow trail that leads down to the foot of the Rofenkar glacier *(ropes available)*.

The path then traverses a narrow ridge to provide lovely **views**★★ of the glacial cirque. Very soon afterwards, turn off to the right *(waymarked BH on a rock)* and reach the Rofenbach brook, which is crossed in two stages, the last on wooden planks. Then follow the brook for about 10m/32.8ft without attempting to climb the slippery rock walls, before regaining the path, which leads up to the Breslauer Hütte mountain lodge. From here, a fine **panorama**★★ is revealed. The descent *(1hr)* to the chairlift back to Vent is easy.

◢ Breslauer Hütte★★

Alt. 2,844m/9,331ft. Easy hike with a difference in altitude of 500m/1,640ft. Allow 2hr30min round-trip starting from the mountain station.

From the hut, there is a stunning **panorama**★★ across the Wildspitze and the ridges of the Wildes Mannle to the north, the glaciers above the Niedertal valley to the east and the Kreuzspitze peak and its glaciers to the south.

◢ Vernagt★★

This circular tour is recommended only for very fit walkers. Take the Wildspitze chairlift (one way) up to the refuge at Breslau. Then allow about 5hrs of walking downhill to return. No climbing is required but the change in altitude is about 1,000m/3,280ft.

From the Breslau refuge, follow the path for 30min, after which you'll see the Mitterbach Falls, which originate from Wildspitze glacier.

Later you'll come to Platteikar, to the right of which is a small lake, and beyond to the northeast, a superb **view**★★ of Vernagt, 250m/820ft above the valley floor. The next interesting feature of

the landscape is the Großer Vernagtferner glacier, dominated by Hochvernagtspitze mountain, with the peaks of Guslarferner and Fluchtkogel rising to the left. Continue your descent to Vent, passing the Plattei, Mitterbach and Rofen waterfalls. At Rofen, cross the suspension bridge to the left bank and take the path that leads to Vent.

Gurgler Tal★★

Gurgler Valley lies in southwestern Austria, close to the border with Italy.
🏠 *Gurglerstraße 118, Obergurgl-Hochgurgl.* ☎*0527 00 100. www.obergurgl.com.*

The Gurgler Valley, which branches off the **upper valley of the Ötz**, ranks among the finest holiday destinations in the Austrian Tyrol. Its exceptional **setting** makes it a favourite for hikers and skiers. Action is concentrated in **Obergurgl**★ *(alt. 1,793–1,930m/5,883–6,332ft)*, a former rural mountain village, which has great **views**★ of the 20 surrounding mountains above 3,000m/9,842ft; and in **Hochgurgl**★ *(alt. 2,150m/7,054ft)*, Austria's highest village and a popular winter sports resort offering six modern hotels.

Ski slopes ◢◢

The slopes offer 110km/68.3mi of pistes of varying degrees of difficulty at altitudes ranging from 1,800m/5,906ft to 3,082m/10,112ft. The pistes are equipped with 22 ski-lifts. The high altitude guarantees snow cover from November to May. There are 12km/7.4mi of cross-country ski runs.

Hohe Mut★★

Alt. 2,653m/8,704ft. Allow 1hr for a round-trip. Take the chairlift up in two stages. ⏱*Lifts operate mid-Jun–mid-Sept and mid-Nov–end Apr daily 9am–4pm.* ☜ *€18 round-trip.* ☎*05256 64 66. www.obergurgl.com.*

A splendid **panorama**★★ is obtained of the Rotmoosferner and Gaisbergferner glaciers to the southeast, and of the Manigenbach to the west.

😊 *The easy walks listed below can be combined for a day's outing.*

🥾 Hohe Mut to Schönwieshütte★★
400m/1,321ft altitude drop. Those in a hurry can reach the Schönwies refuge in about 1hr from the Hohe Mut chairlift station. It is preferable, however, to follow the trail below the cliff to the foot of the **Rotmoosferner glacier★★** and then carry on along the valley floor, following the Gebirgsbach creek. The path leads through a majestic and captivating Alpine setting.

The refuge can also be reached in about 1hr via a wide trail from Obergurgl.

🚶 Around Schönwieshütte★
Allow 1hr30min for a round-trip.
Two easy detours begin from the refuge. Go towards the Langtalereckhütte as far as the so-called **Gurgler Alm** *(alt. 2,252m/7,388ft)* for a **view★** of the three glaciers higher up with the Schalfkogel *(alt. 3,540m/11,614ft)* at the centre. Backtrack and turn left shortly before the refuge towards the Schönwieskopf *(alt. 2,324m/7,625ft).* From the summit a **panorama★** sweeps across the valley.

🥾 Schönwieshütte to Obergurgl via Zirbelwald★
1hr15min, 330m/1,082ft altitude drop.
From the refuge, take the trail towards Obergurgl, soon turning left and heading a steep path downhill past the impressive **Rotmoos waterfall★**.
Take the left fork into the woods and along the valley floor.

Feldkirch★★

Feldkirch is the gateway to Austria for travellers coming from the west. Lying on the busy road to the Arlberg Pass, the little fortified town nestles at the foot of Schattenburg Castle and has preserved the symmetry of its medieval layout and the Old-World charm of arcaded squares.

SIGHTS
Marktplatz
The heart of Feldkirch's **old town★**, this long, arcaded square has retained the charm and tranquillity of a bygone age. Wherever you look, an inn with a colourful façade, an onion-domed corner tower, or a Gothic oriel window catch the eye. To the south the view is bounded by the plain belfry and façade of the Johanniskirche, the former church of the monastery of the Hospitallers of St. John of Jerusalem, who were entrusted with the protection of the **Arlberg Pass** (🡒*see p411*).

▶ **Population:** 32,500.

🛈 **Info:** Montforthaus Feldkirch, Montfortplatz 1. 📞05522 734 67. www.feldkirch.travel.

🔾 **Location:** Feldkirch is on the Liechtenstein/Switzerland border. Alt. 459m/1,506ft.

🅿 **Parking:** Several car parks and garages are near the Old Town. An automated parking guide system directs you to the nearest one with available spaces.

😊 **Don't Miss:** Basilika Rankweil and the Old Rampart Walk.

🕐 **Timing:** Allow half a day.

St. Nikolaus' Cathedral
🕐*Open year-round daily 8am–7pm.*
📞*05522 72 23 20.*
The twin-nave, Late Gothic Domkirche was first mentioned in documents in

1287, but had to be rebuilt after a fire. It sports delicate net vaulting and modern stained-glass windows (1959–1961) by local artist Martin Häusle, depicting some of the saints. Included, high above the altar, is a red-robed St. Nicholas, patron saint of the church. Over the right side altar is a **Descent from the Cross★**, painted in 1521 by Wolf Huber, a native of Feldkirch and a leading artist of the Danube School. The pulpit boasts a splendid wrought-iron canopy that was originally a Gothic tabernacle.

WHERE TO STAY	WHERE TO EAT
Jugendherberge Feldkirch ... ①	Rössle Park (Braugaststätte)..①
Montfort das Hotel .... ④	Schloßwirtschaft
Zimmer in Zentrum .... ⑧	Schattenburg ....③

Schattenburg

🕐 *Open Apr–Oct Mon–Fri 9am––5pm, Sat–Sun 10am–5pm; Nov–Mar Tue–Fri 1.30pm–4pm, Sat–Sun 11am–4pm.* €7. ☏ 05522 719 82. *www.schattenburg.at. Arrive by car via a new access road, on foot via the Schlosssteig stairs.*

The Schattenburg dates back to 1200 and is one of the best preserved castles in Austria, offering wonderful views over the town and surrounds. Originally the seat of the counts of Monfort, it has walls up to 4m/13ft thick and lovely frescoes in the chapel. Some of the Gothic wood-panelled rooms contain the **Heimatmuseum**, displaying local religious art, Gothic furnishings, arms, armour, coins and other medieval bits and pieces.

ADDRESSES

🛏 STAY

☻ **Jugendherberge Feldkirch** – *Reichsstraße 111 (B 190), 6805 Feldkirch Levis.* ☏ 05522 731 81. *www.jungehotels.at.* 🛏. *85 beds.* Located In a half-timbered mid-14C house, this is one of the best youth hostels in the country.

☻☻ **Motel Z** – *Alberweg 12, 6800.* ☏ 05522 35 83. *www.motel-z.at. 8 rooms.* This boxy but attractive modern hotel

has well-equipped rooms with Internet access. It's 5min by car *(free hotel parking)*, 20min on foot from the centre.

☻☻☻ **Montfort das Hotel** – *Galuragasse 7, 6800.* ☏ 055 22 72189. *www.montfort-dashotel.at. 53 rooms.* 🛏. This modern hotel, set in tranquil countryside, is a 15min walk from the town centre. Rooms are bright and well equipped, including Internet access.

🍴 EAT

☻☻ **Braugaststätte Rössle Park** – *Rössle Park 1.* ☏ 05522 765 43. *www.roesslepark.at. Mon–Sat 9am–1am, Sun 11.30am–midnight.* This welcoming and modern lively family-friendly restaurant-brasserie brews its own beer.

☻☻☻ **Schloßwirtschaft Schattenburg** – *Burggasse 1.* ☏ 05522 72 444. *www.schattenburg.cc. Tue–Thu 11am–2pm and 5pm–10pm; Fri–Sun 11am–2pm and 3pm–10pm (Sun til 9pm). Also Jul–Aug Mon 11am–2pm and 3pm–10pm and Sun til 9pm. Closed Nov.* This atmospheric 14C building (its name translates as the Schattenburg castle pub) enjoys a wonderful, romantic view overlooking the rooftops of old Feldkirch. Dine here on traditional dishes such as *Tafelspitz* (Viennese beef broth) and *apfelstrudel.*

INDEX

E

F

INDEX

INDEX

INDEX

INDEX

🏨 STAY

INDEX

♀/EAT

MAPS AND PLANS

MAP LEGEND

	Sight	Seaside Resort	Winter Sports Resort	Spa
Highly recommended	★★★	☆☆☆	✳✳✳	‡‡‡
Recommended	★★	☆☆	✳✳	‡‡
Interesting	★	☆	✳	‡

Tourism

◉ ⟹	Sightseeing route with departure point indicated	AZ B	Map co-ordinates locating sights
� ⸸ â ⸸	Ecclesiastical building	🛈	Tourist information
⊠ ⛊	Synagogue – Mosque	⤙ ⁙	Historic house, castle – Ruins
⌂	Building (with main entrance)	∪ ☼	Dam – Factory or power station
▪	Statue, small building	☆ ⌒	Fort – Cave
⸸	Wayside cross	⚲	Prehistoric site
◎	Fountain	▾ ᴟ	Viewing table – View
━●━▪►	Fortified walls – Tower – Gate	▲	Miscellaneous sight

Recreation

🏇	Racecourse	🏃	Waymarked footpath
⛸	Skating rink	◆	Outdoor leisure park/centre
≈ ▦	Outdoor, indoor swimming pool	🎢	Theme/Amusement park
⚓	Marina, moorings	⩊	Wildlife/Safari park, zoo
⛺	Mountain refuge hut	⊛	Gardens, park, arboretum
▫┅┅▫	Overhead cable-car	◈	Aviary, bird sanctuary
🚂	Tourist or steam railway		

Additional symbols

═ ═	Motorway (unclassified)	⊗ ⊙	Post office – Telephone centre
❶ ❶	Junction: complete, limited	⊠	Covered market
⟺ ═	Pedestrian street	⋅✕⋅	Barracks
⌇═══╪	Unsuitable for traffic, street subject to restrictions	△	Swing bridge
▥ ┄┄	Steps – Footpath	∪ ✕	Quarry – Mine
🚃 🚐	Railway – Coach station	Ⓑ Ⓕ	Ferry (river and lake crossings)
▫┼┼┼┼┼▫	Funicular – Rack-railway	⛴	Ferry services: Passengers and cars
━─ ⓐ	Tram – Metro, underground	⛵	Foot passengers only
Bert (R.)...	Main shopping street	③	Access route number common to MICHELIN maps and town plans

Abbreviations and special symbols

Ⓒ	Capital of a "Canton" (Kantonshauptort)	**P**	Offices of cantonal authorities (Kantonale Verwaltung)
G	Local police station (Kantonspolizei)	**POL.**	Police (Stadtpolizei)
H	Town hall (Rathaus)	**T**	Theatre (Theater)
J	Law courts (Justizpalast)	**U**	University (Universität)
M	Museum (Museum)	🅿	Park and Ride

COMPANION PUBLICATIONS

MAPS OF AUSTRIA

Michelin map 730 Austria
A road map with tourist information, at a scale of 1:400 000, with an index of place names and maps of the Salzburg and Vienna conurbations.

... and for getting to Austria:

Michelin map 719 Germany, Austria, Benelux, Czech Republic
A road map with tourist information, at a scale of 1: 1 000 000.

Michelin map 970 Europe
A road map with tourist information, at a scale of 1: 3 000 000, with an index of place names.

Michelin Road Atlas Europe
Spiral-bound, with an index of place names, more than 40 states, 73 city and conurbation maps, including Salzburg and Vienna.

INTERNET
Michelin is pleased to offer a route-planning service on the Internet:
www.travelguide.michelin.com
www.viamichelin.com
Choose the shortest route, a route without tolls, or the Michelin recommended route to your destination.

OTHER TITLES

France
- Alsace Lorraine Champagne
- Auvergne Rhone Valley
- Battlefields of the Somme: Amiens, Péronne, Albert
- Bordeaux, Aquitaine & the Basque Country
- Brittany
- Burgundy Jura
- Châteaux of the Loire
- Dordogne Berry Limousin
- France
- French Alps
- French Riviera
- Languedoc Roussillon Tarn Gorges
- Languedoc Tarn Gorges
- Normandy
- Northern France and the Paris Region
- Paris
- Poitou-Charentes, La Rochelle & Cognac
- Provence
- Pyrenees Roussillon
- Wine Regions of France

British Isles
- Great Britain
- Ireland
- London
- Scotland

Asia
- Chennai and Tamil Nadu
- Delhi, Agra & Jaipur
- Japan
- South Korea

Rest of Europe
- Andalucia
- Austria
- Germany
- Greece
- Italy
- Portugal Madeira The Azores
- Rome
- Sicily
- Spain
- Switzerland
- Tuscany
- Venice and the Veneto
- Wine Trails of Italy

North America
- California
- Canada
- Chicago
- Montreal & Quebec City
- New England
- New York City
- San Francisco
- USA East
- USA West
- Washington, DC

South America
- Argentina

Visit your preferred bookseller for Michelin's comprehensive range of maps and famous red-cover Hotel and Restaurant guides.

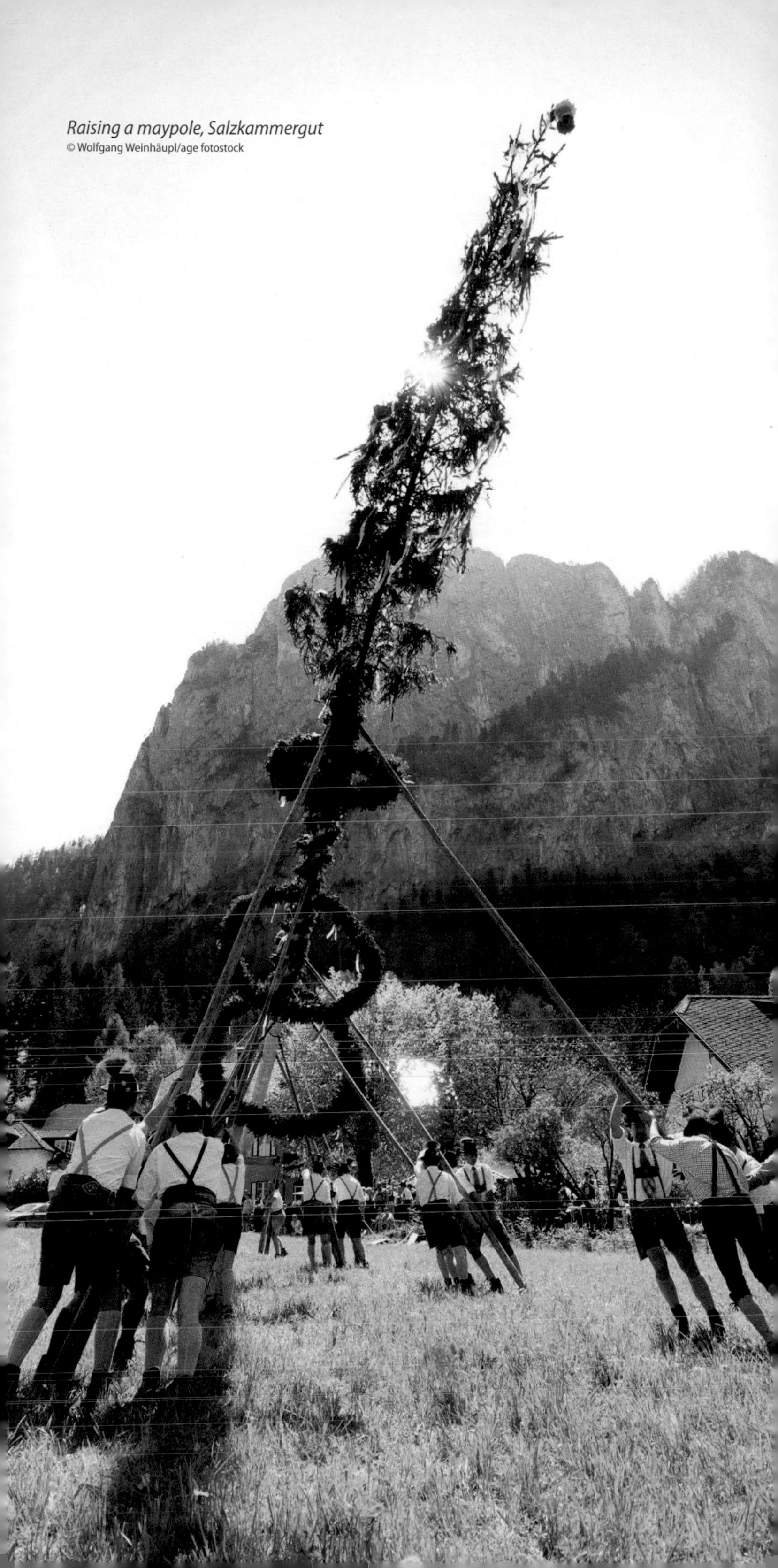

Raising a maypole, Salzkammergut

MICHELIN
IS CONTINUALLY
INNOVATING
FOR SAFER, CLEANER,
MORE ECONOMICAL,
MORE CONNECTED...
BETTER ALL-ROUND
MOBILITY.

HOW TO USE THIS GUIDE

PLANNING YOUR TRIP

The blue-tabbed PLANNING YOUR TRIP section at the front of the guide gives you **ideas for your trip** and **practical information** to help you organise it. You'll find tours, practical information, a host of outdoor activities, a calendar of events, information on shopping, sightseeing, kids' activities and more.

INTRODUCTION

The orange-tabbed INTRODUCTION section explores Austria's **Nature** and geology. The **History** section spans the Habsburg empire to European Union membership. The **Art and Culture** section highlights architecture, art and music, while **Austria Today** delves into the present modern country.

DISCOVERING

The green-tabbed DISCOVERING section features Principal Sights by region, featuring the most interesting local **Sights**, **Walking Tours**, nearby **Excursions**, and detailed **Driving Tours**. Admission prices shown are normally for a single adult.

ADDRESSES

We've selected the best hotels, restaurants, cafés, shops, nightlife and entertainment to fit all budgets. See the Legend on the cover flap for an explanation of the price categories. See the back of the guide for an index of where to find hotels and restaurants.

Sidebars

Throughout the guide you will find blue, peach and green-colored text boxes with lively anecdotes, detailed history and background information.

😊 A Bit of Advice 😊

Green advice boxes found in this guide contain practical tips and handy information relevant to your visit or to a sight in the Discovering section.

STAR RATINGS★★★

Michelin has given star ratings for more than 100 years. If you're pressed for time, we recommend you visit the ★★★, or ★★ sights first:

★★★ **Highly recommended**
★★ **Recommended**
★ **Interesting**

MAPS

- 🗺 Principal Sights map.
- 🗺 Regional maps.
- 🗺 Maps for major cities and villages.
- 🗺 Local tour maps.

All maps in this guide are oriented north, unless otherwise indicated by a directional arrow. The term "Local Map" refers to a map within the chapter or Tourism Region. A complete list of the maps found in the guide appears at the back of this book.

© Austrian National Tourist Office/ Popp Hackner

PLANNING
YOUR TRIP

INTRODUCTION
TO AUSTRIA

DISCOVERING
AUSTRIA

CONTENTS

Welcome to Austria

Sitting at the very heart of Europe, Austria is a spectacularly beautiful land of mountains, forests and lakes. Among its wonderful scenery are some beautiful old towns and villages, as well as cities with exceptional cultural heritage, in the visual arts, architecture and music. The capital, Vienna, is justly celebrated, but the rest of the country is equally as fascinating and offers a huge selection of attractions for visitors of all types and ages.

SALZBURG AND THE SALZKAMMERGUT (pp72–119)

The city of Salzburg, with its famous festival, is dominated by a historic fortress that looms over its atmospheric Old Town. Just to the east is Austria's lake district, the Salzkammergut, a breathtakingly beautiful region of high mountains reflected in long mountain lakes.

LINZ AND THE DANUBE VALLEY (pp120–147)

The industrial city of Linz belies this description, given its attractive old centre and lively cultural life. Elsewhere in Oberösterreich, some important religious centres include St. Florian, Lambach and Kremsmünster, all with exquisite decoration and full of ecclesiastical treasures. To the north extends the wild, forested region of the Mühlviertel and of course, running through the region is the beautiful valley of the Danube River.

NIBELUNGENGAU, WACHAU AND WALDVIERTEL (pp148–179)

From Linz the Danube flows south into Niederösterreich, the region around the capital, Vienna. Wonderfully romantic, the impressive river valley is a land of myth and history, with ruined castles perched on rocky promontories above the Danube. The most famous of these is Dürnstein, where Richard I of England was imprisoned. The attractions continue with a string of vineyards, some of the best around the delightful old town

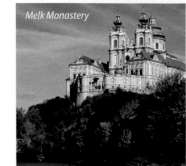

Melk Monastery

© Austrian National Tourist Office/ Volker Preusser

of Krems, more thick forest reaching up to the Czech border, and the abbey at Melk, a masterpiece of Baroque architecture.

VIENNA (pp180–234)

Austria's capital, Vienna, is one of the world's great cities. Founded some 2,000 years ago by the Romans, it grew into the capital of the Habsburg Empire, which stretched across huge swathes of Central and Eastern Europe. This imperial legacy has bequeathed the city grand monuments and architecture, but it is for culture above all else that Vienna is so famed. Its art galleries contain one of the richest collections in the world, and its musical culture is second to none. Composers such as Mozart, Beethoven and Brahms all made Vienna their home, and the Viennese guard their musical heritage with pride. Vienna is also a city of immense charm, embodied in its coffeehouses, wine taverns and boutiques.

EASTERN AUSTRIA *(pp236–263)*

To the south and east of Vienna is the Pannonian Plain, the vast area of flat land that extends right through neighbouring Hungary. Here the climate is quite hot in the summer and fiercely cold in the winter, lending itself to the cultivation of vines. In Burgenland's small villages, you will find some of Austria's finest wines grown close to the shallow Neusiedlersee. To the west, the hills of the Vienna Woods rise up to become the Wiener Alpen, Vienna's local Alps.

GRAZ AND STYRIA
(pp264–303)

Graz is one of Austria's most beloved cities, not only for its well-preserved architecture but also for its vibrant cultural scene that now has its home in a spectacular arts centre. Styria, the region of which it is capital, is known as the "green heart" of the country. It is a land of high, forested mountains and rolling green meadows, where the horses for the famous riding school in Vienna are reared. Nestled in the countryside are some lovely towns, including the important pilgrimage site of Mariazell and the Baroque abbey at Admont.

KLAGENFURT AND CARINTHIA *(pp304–334)*

Independent and proud, the Carinthians are nonetheless extremely welcoming to visitors to their beautiful province. The capital, Klagenfurt, lies at one end of Austria's warmest Alpine lake, a perfect place for a summer swim. Elsewhere rise the mountains, perhaps not as high as the central Alps but just as majestic and spectacular in their own way. There is also a wealth of small towns to explore, many with important churches.

INNSBRUCK AND THE TYROL *(pp335–396)*

Innsbruck can safely lay claim to the title of "capital" of the Austrian Alps. The city has a coveted position surrounded by high mountains, while the old centre still retains many of its late-medieval buildings. Beyond the city are castles, mountain villages, and the mountains of the Karwendel and Kitzbühel ranges, snow-capped and inviting to skiers and climbers. Over the Gerlos Pass is one of Austria's great sights, Krimml Falls, and farther on yet another, the Hochalpenstraße with magnificent views of the country's highest mountain, the Grossglockner.

VORARLBERG AND WEST TYROL *(pp397–433)*

Bregenz, on the shores of the Bodensee, is much closer to Switzerland than Vienna, and Vorarlberg, of which it is capital, is very different from the east of the country. Aside from the famous lakeside music festival, there are awe-inspiring high mountains to explore, with some of the finest skiing areas in the country, especially those of the Lechtal. The Silvretta Pass leads over into Italy, while the Arlberg takes you to Tyrol. Herein lies some of the best mountain scenery in all of Austria, viewed from a series of splendid Alpine valleys, especially the Ötztal.

Vorarlberg

© ARCO/Lenz, G/age fotostock

Tyres wear more quickly on short urban journeys.

TRUE!

You tend to accelerate and brake more often when driving around town so your tyres work harder!
If you are stuck in traffic, keep calm and drive slowly.

Tyre pressure only affects your car's safety.

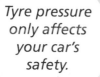

FALSE!

Driving with underinflated tyres (0.5 bar below recommended pressure) doesn't just impact handling and fuel consumption, it will shave 8,000 km off tyre lifespan.
Make sure you check tyre pressure about once a month and before you go on holiday or a long journey.

If you only encounter **winter weather from time to time** - sudden showers, snowfall or black ice - **one type of tyre** will do the job.
?
TRUE!
The revolutionary **MICHELIN CrossClimate** - the very first summer tyre with winter certification - is a practical solution to keep you on the road whatever the weather.

Fitting **2 winter tyres** on my car guarantees maximum safety.

?

FALSE!

In the winter, especially when temperatures drop below 7°C, to ensure better road holding, all four tyres should be identical and fitted at the same time.

2 WINTER TYRES ONLY = risk of compromised road holding.

4 WINTER TYRES = safer handling when cornering, driving downhill and braking.

If you regularly encounter rain, snow or black ice, choose a **MICHELIN Alpin tyre**. This range offers you sharp handling plus a comfortable ride to safely face the challenge of winter driving.

MICHELIN

MICHELIN
IS COMMITTED

▶ MICHELIN IS **GLOBAL LEADER IN FUEL-EFFICIENT TYRES** FOR LIGHT VEHICLES.

▶ **EDUCATING OF YOUNGSTERS IN ROAD SAFETY,**
NOT FORGETTING TWO-WHEELER
LOCAL ROAD SAFETY CAMPAIGNS
WERE RUN IN **16 COUNTRIES**
IN 2015.

QUIZ

1 TYRES ARE BLACK SO WHY IS THE MICHELIN MAN WHITE?

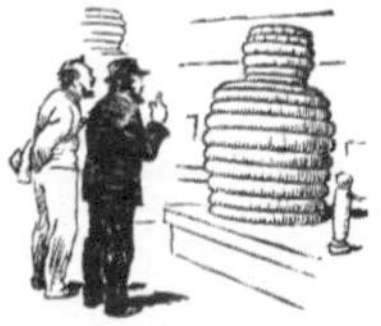

Back in 1898 when the Michelin Man was first created from a stack of tyres, they were made of natural rubber, cotton and sulphur and were therefore light-coloured. The composition of tyres did not change until after the First World War when carbon black was introduced. But the Michelin Man kept his colour!

2 FOR HOW LONG HAS MICHELIN BEEN GUIDING TRAVELLERS?

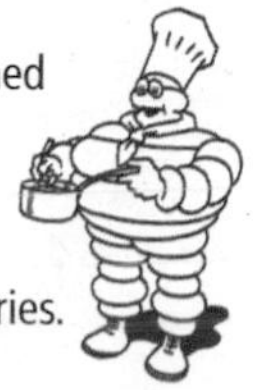

Since 1900. When the MICHELIN guide was published at the turn of the century, it was claimed that it would last for a hundred years. It's still around today and remains a reference with new editions and online restaurant listings in a number of countries.

3 WHEN WAS THE "BIB GOURMAND" INTRODUCED IN THE MICHELIN GUIDE?

The symbol was created in 1997 but as early as 1954 the MICHELIN guide was recommending "exceptional good food at moderate prices". Today, it features on the MICHELIN Restaurants website and app.

If you want to enjoy a fun day out and find out more about Michelin, why not visit the l'Aventure Michelin museum and shop in Clermont-Ferrand, France:

www.laventuremichelin.com

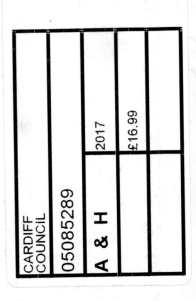

5405078

CARDIFF COUNCIL
05085289
A & H
2017
£16.99

Michelin Travel Partner

Société par actions simplifiées au capital de 11 288 880 EUR
27 cours de l'Ile Seguin - 92100 Boulogne Billancourt (France)
R.C.S. Nanterre 433 677 721

© Michelin Travel Partner
ISBN 978-2-067220-51-5
Printed: October 2016
Printed and bound in France : Imprimerie CHIRAT, 42540 Saint-Just-la-Pendue - N° 201610.0362